READINGS ON
THE DEVELOPMENT
OF CHILDREN

READINGS ON THE DEVELOPMENT OF CHILDREN

Fifth Edition

Edited by

Mary Gauvain
University of California, Riverside

Michael Cole
University of California, San Diego

WORTH PUBLISHERS

Senior Publisher: Catherine Woods
Executive Editor: Jessica Bayne
Developmental Editor: Marna Miller
Project Editor: Leigh Renhard
Executive Marketing Manager: Katherine Nurre
Art Director: Babs Reingold
Cover Design: Kevin Kall
Interior Design: Kevin Kall and Paul Lacy
Photo Editor: Ted Szczepanski
Production Manager: Barbara Anne Seixas
Composition: Matrix Publishing
Printing and Binding: Quebecor-Dubuque

Cover Art: *Two Girls Reading*, Pablo Picasso, 1934. © 2008 Estate of Pablo Picasso / University of Michigan Museum of Art / Artists Rights Society (ARS), New York.

Library of Congress Control Number: 2008936432

ISBN-13: 978-1-4292-1649-4
ISBN-10: 1-4292-1649-2
© 2009 by Worth Publishers

Printed in the United States of America

First printing

Worth Publishers
41 Madison Avenue
New York, NY 10010
www.worthpublishers.com

Contents

Preface ix

INTRODUCTION 1

1. The Adaptive Nature of Cognitive Immaturity 3
   DAVID F. BJORKLUND AND BRANDI L. GREEN

2. Ecological Models of Human Development 14
   URIE BRONFENBRENNER

3. Parent, Child, and Reciprocal Influences 20
   RICHARD Q. BELL

4. Children of the Garden Island 26
   EMMY E. WERNER

5. Development and Learning 33
   JEAN PIAGET

6. Interaction Between Learning and Development 42
   LEV S. VYGOTSKY

PART I: IN THE BEGINNING 51

7. Of Human Bonding: Newborns Prefer Their Mothers' Voices 53
   ANTHONY DECASPER AND WILLIAM P. FIFER

8. The Interplay Between Genotypes and Family Relationships:
   Reframing Concepts of Development and Prevention 58
   DAVID REISS

9. Recall in Infancy: A Neurodevelopmental Account 64
   PATRICIA J. BAUER

10. Culture and Early Infancy Among Central African Foragers and
    Farmers 70
    BARRY S. HEWLETT, MICHAEL E. LAMB, DONALD SHANNON, BIRGIT LEYENDECKER,
    AND AXEL SCHÖLMERICH

11. Temperament and the Reactions to Unfamiliarity 82
    JEROME KAGAN

12. Specificity and Heterogeneity in Children's Responses to Profound
    Institutional Privation 88
    MICHAEL L. RUTTER, JANA M. KREPPNER, AND THOMAS G. O'CONNOR

PART II: INFANCY 97

13. Humans Have Evolved Specialized Skills of Social Cognition: The
    Cultural Intelligence Hypothesis 99
    ESTHER HERMANN, JOSEP CALL, MARÍA VICTORIA HERNÁNDEZ-LLOREDA, BRIAN
    HARE, MICHAEL TOMASELLO

14. Development of Object Concepts in Infancy: Evidence for Early Learning in an Eye-Tracking Paradigm 111
    SCOTT P. JOHNSON, DIMA AMSO, AND JONATHAN A. SLEMMER

15. Becoming a Native Listener 120
    JANET F. WERKER

16. Event Categorization in Infancy 128
    RENÉE BAILLARGEON AND SU-HUA WANG

17. Rethinking Maternal Sensitivity: Mothers' Comments on Infants' Mental Processes Predict Security of Attachment at 12 Months 139
    ELIZABETH MEINS, CHARLES FERNYHOUGH, EMMA FRADLEY, AND MICHELLE TUCKEY

18. Early Experience and Emotional Development: The Emergence of Wariness of Heights 155
    JOSEPH J. CAMPOS, BENNETT I. BERTENTHAL, AND ROSANNE KERMOIAN

PART III: EARLY CHILDHOOD 161

19. The Credible Shrinking Room: Very Young Children's Performance with Symbolic and Nonsymbolic Relations 163
    JUDY S. DELOACHE, KEVIN F. MILLER, AND KARL S. ROSENGREN

20. Understanding Minds and Evidence for Belief: A Study of Mofu Children in Cameroon 171
    PENELOPE G. VINDEN

21. Transmission of Aggression Through Imitation of Aggressive Models 182
    ALBERT BANDURA, DOROTHEA ROSS, AND SHEILA A. ROSS

22. Cultural Differences in American and Mexican Mother-Child Pretend Play 191
    JOANN FARVER AND CAROLLEE HOWES

23. Gender and Group Process: A Developmental Perspective 200
    ELEANOR E. MACCOBY

24. Personal Storytelling as a Medium of Socialization in Chinese and American Families 205
    PEGGY J. MILLER, ANGELA R. WILEY, HEIDI FUNG, AND CHUNG-HUI LIANG

PART IV: MIDDLE CHILDHOOD 217

25. Children's Perception of Gap Affordances: Bicycling Across Traffic-Filled Intersections in an Immersive Virtual Environment 219
    JODIE M. PLUMERT, JOSEPH K. KEARNEY, AND JAMES F. CREMER

26. The Role of Age versus Expertise in Peer Collaboration during Joint Planning 230
    RUTH T. DURAN AND MARY GAUVAIN

27. Electronic Bullying Among Middle School Students 240
    ROBIN M. KOWALSKI AND SUSAN P. LIMBER

28. Cultural Teaching: The Development of Teaching Skills in Maya Sibling Interactions 251
    ASHLEY E. MAYNARD

29. Ethnic Diversity and Perceptions of Safety in Urban Middle Schools 266
    JAANA JUVONEN, ADRIENNE NISHINA, AND SANDRA GRAHAM

30. How Asian Teachers Polish Each Lesson to Perfection 275
    JAMES W. STIGLER AND HAROLD W. STEVENSON

PART V: ADOLESCENCE 289

31. Risk Taking in Adolescence: New Perspectives from Brain and
    Behavioral Science 291
    LAURENCE STEINBERG

32. Toward a New Understanding of Early Menarche: The Role of
    Environmental Stress in Pubertal Timing 297
    MICHELLE WIERSON, PATRICIA J. LONG, AND REX L. FOREHAND

33. Development of Logical Reasoning and the School Performance of
    African American Adolescents in Relation to Socioeconomic Status,
    Ethnic Identity, and Self-Esteem 304
    MARK S. CHAPELL AND WILLIS F. OVERTON

34. Authority, Autonomy, and Family Relationships Among Adolescents in
    Urban and Rural China 318
    WENXIN ZHANG AND ANDREW J. FULIGNI

35. Antisocial Boys and Their Friends in Early Adolescence: Relationship
    Characteristics, Quality, and Interactional Process 325
    THOMAS J. DISHION, DAVID W. ANDREWS, AND LYNN CROSBY

36. Late Adolescents' Self-Defining Memories About Relationships 337
    KATE C. McLEAN AND AVRIL THORNE

Preface

Human development is a process of change that occurs over the entire life span. It involves the interaction of biological, social, and cultural factors that together define the course of human growth. Developmental psychologists strive to explain this process of change by observing children, conducting experiments, and devising theories.

Students approach the subject of human development with rich backgrounds based on their own experiences growing up as well as on their observations of people of all ages. This background is a valuable resource for students attempting to understand the scientific approaches to the study of human development that they encounter in textbooks. However, it has been our experience as instructors that textbooks alone, despite their great value as organized overviews of the field, often leave students puzzled about the process by which developmental psychologists construct their theories, collect their data, and draw conclusions. Textbooks, by their very nature, cannot devote sufficient space to the in-depth discussion of concepts or studies that form the basis of developmental theory.

The articles included in this book of readings have been selected with this issue in mind. Our intention has been to provide students with primary source material that introduces them to a broad range of scientific thinking about human development in all its diversity. We do not shy away from exposing students to classical contributions to the field simply because they do not carry an up-to-the-minute publication date; after all, physicists do not hesitate to teach about Newton's laws of motion although they were formulated several hundred years ago. Of course, the scientific study of human development is a rapidly growing discipline, so most of our selections—especially research reports—were first published in the past few years.

The theoretical articles provide students with direct access to important and provocative statements by acknowledged leaders in the field. For example, selections by Jean Piaget and Lev Vygotsky are included. Each theoretical article was chosen for its power in capturing the essence of the theorist's ideas in a brief, but compelling, way. The articles focusing on research were selected to stimulate thought and discussion about how researchers collect evidence on the process of development and how they interpret and draw conclusions from this evidence. We have taken special care to include articles about the development of children from many cultures to avoid the misrepresentation of middle-class European Americans as the criterion against which the development of all children is measured.

We have changed this reader significantly for this, its fifth edition. The selection includes 36 articles, of which 14 articles, or 39%, are new to this edition. This new collection provides students with an updated look at the field in several ways. First, recent empirical articles in some of the most rapidly changing areas in the field, such as developmental neuroscience, evolutionary developmental psychology, early concept formation, social cognition, socioemotional development, and adolescent relationships, have been added. Second, we have added several articles that focus on developmental processes and experiences that may put children and adolescents at risk of unhealthy development. Finally, we have retained articles that we believe represent classic and central issues in the field. We hope that you agree that this reader is a comprehensive and up-to-date presentation of the major topics and concerns in developmental psychology today.

All the articles were selected with the undergraduate reader in mind. Because most of them were originally written for a professional audience, they contain some concepts that at first may be difficult to grasp. To orient the reader to the article's main points, we have provided an introductory headnote for each article. To help students understand the important issues raised in the selections, we pose a series of six questions after each article. These questions are designed to help students identify the key points of the article, as well as to provoke them to think critically about what they have read.

Over the years, this book has changed as the field has changed. Our efforts to select and update the readings have been aided by valuable comments from colleagues, students, and the following reviewers: Catherine Caldwell-Harris, *Boston University*; Marianella Casasola, *Cornell University*; Nancy Darling, *Oberlin College*; Gary Feng, *Duke University*; Marla Reese-Weber, *Illinois State University*; Catherine Sandhofer, *University of California at Los Angeles*.

M.G.
M.C.

READINGS ON
THE DEVELOPMENT
OF CHILDREN

Introduction

Most developmental theory and research today emphasizes the coordination of the biological, social, and cultural aspects of the human experience. This research is predicated upon the assumption that human beings are complex social, cognitive, and emotional organisms that strive to create meaning and understanding in their daily lives. These efforts to know and understand are supported and constrained by the type of biological organism we are and by the complex and highly structured social and cultural system in which we live.

The articles in this section describe, in various ways, how human development occurs. Each places a somewhat different emphasis on biological, social, and cultural contributions to growth. The lead article by David F. Bjorklund and Brandi L. Green introduces a view of development based on principles of evolutionary psychology. The authors raise provocative questions about the contributions made by human immaturity both to individual development and to human evolution itself. The subsequent article, by Urie Bronfenbrenner, describes an ecological approach to development that includes the complex set of social and contextual factors that contribute to human psychological growth. While the social and cultural context plays a huge role in psychological development, context in and of itself does not define development. Research has shown quite clearly that even when children are raised in similar contexts, they have different experiences, and those experiences affect their development in different ways. This point is taken up in the next article, by Richard Q. Bell, which discusses the ways in which parents and children contribute to the child's development. In this classic paper, the author identifies children as active agents in their own development. Emmy E. Werner also establishes a dynamic relationship between child and environment, examining the results of her highly regarded longitudinal research to find that early experiences, even problematic experiences, do not have a predetermined outcome. The final two articles in this section focus on the relation between learning and development. Their authors, Jean Piaget and Lev S. Vygotsky, proposed different theories about cognitive development, and their views are debated and used to guide research to this day.

These articles introduce several of the main theoretical issues that guide much contemporary research on psychological development: What is the human context, and how does it contribute to psychological growth? What is the significance of early social experience for later development? And how do the processes of learning and development work together to support intellectual change over the course of childhood?

1

The Adaptive Nature of Cognitive Immaturity

David F. Bjorklund • Brandi L. Green

Many psychologists today are interested in how human psychological characteristics may have contributed to the evolution and survival of the species. The relatively new field of evolutionary psychology addresses this question directly by examining how human behavior has been shaped over time by the process of natural selection. This perspective has focused largely on cognitive processes that may have provided our human ancestors with an adaptive advantage, including the capability to engage in complex and creative reasoning. Evolutionary psychologists assert that over the course of human evolution, the process of natural selection favored prehominids, or ancestral humans, that were intellectually capable of solving the types of problems that were present in the dangerous and competitive environments in which they lived. Chief among these capabilities was the ability to band together in groups to solve problems critical to survival.

Although evolutionary psychology has concentrated on mature adaptations–that is, how the behaviors of contemporary human adults may reflect aspects of species evolution–developmental psychologists have directed attention to characteristics of human development that may have influenced human evolution. These characteristics include the long period of dependence by the young on more mature species members, the vast learning capability of human infants and children, the relatively slow pace of cognitive development compared to other primates, and the gradual specialization of human intelligence to local circumstances.

The following article by David F. Bjorklund and Brandi L. Green discusses how these characteristics of human development may have contributed in unique and vital ways to the evolution of the species. Their analysis led these researchers to ask a novel and provocative question about human development: Is cognitive immaturity adaptive? In other words, does human psychological immaturity provide unique and important benefits not only for the development of the individual child but also for the evolution of the human species itself?

The prolonged cognitive immaturity characteristic of human youth is described as adaptive in and of itself. The adaptive nature of cognitive immaturity is examined in developmental research in the areas of metacognition, egocentricity, plasticity and the speed of information processing, and language acquisition.

Some of the consequences of viewing children's immature cognition as adaptive for cognitive development and education are discussed.

Humans are the intelligent species in that we, more than any other species, adapt ourselves and modify

---

Copyright 1992 by the American Psychological Association. Reprinted by permission of the authors and the American Psychological Association from *American Psychologist, Vol. 47, No. 1,* pp. 46–54.

Bernadette Gray-Little served as action editor for this article.

Portions of the article were written while David F. Bjorklund was supported by a grant from The Spencer Foundation. We would like to thank the following people for their helpful comments on earlier drafts of this article: Barbara Bjorklund, Katherine Kipp Harnishfeger, Jean-Louis Gariépy, Ingrid Johanson, Thomas Monson, Jacqueline Muir-Broaddus, and Robin Vallacher. We would also like to thank Robert Cairns, Gilbert Gottlieb, Robert McCall, and an anonymous reviewer for their constructive suggestions.

the environment to suit our needs. Our intelligence has permitted us to alter the typical course of evolution, making cultural changes more rapid and significant than biological changes. This intelligence, however, requires a long apprenticeship. Human development is noted for its extended period of youth (see Gould, 1977; Montagu, 1989), with delayed physical and sexual maturity being associated with delayed cognitive maturity, making the human child's dependency on adults all the greater.

But why must the cognitive abilities of humans stay immature as long as physical abilities? It would seem that if the human child has much to learn, it would be to the species's advantage to have the prolonged physical childhood be accompanied by a relatively mature cognitive system. Surely an intellectually mature organism can learn more and better than an intellectually immature one. This would result in a physically dependent being who is more capable of learning the complexities of the world. Yet, this is not the way nature has chosen to work.

One problem with this line of thinking is the tendency to equate *immaturity* with *inefficiency*—a poorly functioning system that must develop further if true advancement is to occur. An alternative perspective is that the prolonged cognitive immaturity of humans has a specific role in development. From this point of view, there may be many aspects of children's immature cognition that have adaptive functions and are more than mere deficits. For example, what contemporary or future benefits might be afforded children by slow information processing, egocentric thinking, or overly optimistic opinions about their mental abilities?

One of the most popular explanations for the adaptive function of prolonged immaturity is the extended period of time available for practicing adult roles and socialization (Bruner, 1972; Poirier & Smith, 1974; Washburn & Hamburg, 1965). Much of this practice and socialization is realized through play. Like the extended period of youth, and, in fact, correlated with it, play is most frequently found in species that are behaviorally flexible (Beckoff, 1972; Poirier & Smith, 1974; Vandenberg, 1981). Many writers believe that it is primarily through play that children's cognition develops (e.g., Dansky, 1980; Piaget, 1962). Although play itself cannot be regarded as immature cognition, it can be viewed as a vehicle through which an extended childhood affects cognitive development.

In this article we take a different perspective, arguing that aspects of children's immature thinking are adaptive in their own right. We propose, as have others (e.g., Lenneberg, 1967; Oppenheim, 1981), that some aspects of the young child's cognitive system are qualitatively different from those of the older child or adult and are well suited to attain important cognitive–social milestones such as attachment and language. In a similar vein, Oppenheim discussed the presence of neu-

robehavioral characteristics of immature animals that have a specific role in survival during infancy or youth but disappear when they are no longer necessary. These *ontogenetic adaptations* are not simply incomplete versions of adult characteristics but serve specific adaptive functions for the developing animal. Oppenheim went as far as to suggest that "even the absence of adult capabilities may be developmentally adaptive . . . [and] should be considered in any comprehensive theory of ontogeny" (p. 92). Similar arguments have been put forward by Turkewitz and Kenny (1982), who suggested that the limitations (or immaturity) of sensory and motor systems may play adaptive roles in ontogeny. The limited motor capacities of juvenile animals serve to prevent their wandering from the mother, which thereby enhances their chances of survival. In an elegant review, these authors suggested that the sensory limitations of many newborn and juvenile animals are adaptive features that may help reduce the amount of information infants have to deal with and thus aid in constructing a simplified, comprehensive world. Like Oppenheim, Turkewitz and Kenny suggested that the lack of adult characteristics may be an adaptive feature of ontogenetic development.

Other aspects of young children's cognition, we propose, are qualitatively similar to those found in the adult but function poorly. Such low levels of functioning may provide some advantages for young children and do not represent imperfect stages that must be overcome. We propose that the advantages of immature cognition are found in many areas, four broad examples of which are metacognition, egocentricity, speed of cognitive processing, and language acquisition, each of which are discussed below. The belief that cognitive immaturity has a significant role in ontogeny has important implications for how we view cognitive development and education, and these are discussed briefly in a final section.

Adaptive Value of Cognitive Immaturity

Metacognition

Metacognition refers to a person's knowledge about his or her own cognitions and the factors that influence thinking. For every form of cognition, it is possible to think of a corresponding metacognition, and metacognition has been studied with respect to memory, communication, reading, and attention, among others (e.g., Flavell & Wellman, 1977; Garner, 1990; Miller, 1985; Whitehurst & Sonnenschein, 1985). A general finding of developmental metacognitive research is that there is a concomitant age-related improvement in cognitive and metacognitive abilities (see Bjorklund, 1989).

Studies of children's *metamemory* (see, e.g., Flavell, Friedrichs, & Hoyt, 1970; Yussen & Levy, 1975) have shown that young children are prone to overestimate their recall abilities, with the frequency and degree of overestimation declining with age (for reviews, see Cavanaugh & Perlmutter, 1982; Flavell & Wellman, 1977; Schneider, 1985; Schneider & Pressley, 1989). Yussen and Levy noted that preschool children's predictions of their memory abilities were minimally influenced by their previous performance. In their study, Yussen and Levy found that many four-year-old children continued to make unrealistically high predictions, even after being shown that they could not recall the number of items they had predicted. The authors noted that these children appeared to realize that they had failed, but persisted in believing that they could do it the next time.

Unrealistic optimism in performance expectations has also been reported frequently in the achievement motivation literature (see Stipek, 1984; Stipek & Mac Iver, 1989). A series of experiments by Stipek and her colleagues (Stipek, 1981; Stipek & Hoffman, 1980; Stipek, Roberts, & Sanborn, 1984), among others, has shown that young children generally overestimate their skills on a wide variety of academic tasks and have more optimistic (and less realistic) expectations for their own future performance relative to that of other children. Similar results have been reported by Schneider (1988, 1991) for predictions of performance on a memory-span task. Although young children do not ignore past failures altogether, they do not use this information as efficiently as do older children when making predictions about their own future performances (Stipek, 1984).

Again, poor metacognition is usually viewed as a handicap, and in older children and adults it would certainly seem to be a handicap. But children who are out of touch with their own intellectual and motoric abilities may, in some situations, have an advantage. One benefit of poor metacognition, we believe, is motivational. Children's beliefs in their good track record foster feelings of self-efficacy. According to social cognitive theory (Bandura, 1982, 1989a, 1989b), judgments of self-efficacy are based on several sources of information, the most important of which is *perceived enactive mastery*. Children's self-perceptions of their efficacy, whether they are accurate or fanciful, serve to mediate action. Children's perceived self-efficacy influences which environments and activities they select, as well as the amount of time and effort they expend on those activities. When self-efficacy is poor,

people tend to behave ineffectually regardless of their actual abilities (Bandura, 1989a, 1989b).

Unrealistic optimism about their own abilities and an equally unrealistic evaluation of their behaviors give young children the opportunity to practice skills in situations in which accurate metacognition might discourage them from doing so (Bjorklund, Gaultney, & Green, in press). As pointed out by Stipek (1984), learned helplessness, the belief that one has no control over a situation, is relatively rare among young children, who generally expect success in achievement situations and evaluate their competencies favorably. This optimistic attitude may encourage children to attempt behaviors they would not otherwise try if they had more realistic conceptions of their abilities. Ignorance of their limitations allows children to try more diverse and complex behaviors that may be out of their grasp at the present time. This allows them to practice skills to a greater degree and may foster long-term cognitive behaviors.

Some recent research from our laboratory illustrates the potential usefulness of immaturity in perfecting the mechanisms by which imitation operates. In a series of studies, we investigated the development of *meta-imitation,* the knowledge of one's own imitative abilities, in children between three and five years of age (Bjorklund et al., in press). Our findings revealed that very young children consistently overestimated their imitative abilities and therefore attempted to imitate behaviors that were often well beyond their current grasp. Moreover, after attempting to mimic a modeled behavior (e.g., juggling one, two, or three balls or tossing a ball into a basket from one and one half, three, or seven feet away), young children were equally inept at evaluating how successful they had been. Both prediction (how well they thought they could imitate a modeled behavior) and *postdiction* (how well they thought they actually had imitated the behavior) were overestimated by preschool children, with the degree of overestimation being highest among three-year-olds and lowest among five-year-olds.[1]

Bjorklund et al. (in press) proposed that poorly developed meta-imitation encourages young children to attempt to imitate a diverse range of models and behaviors; this in turn permits them to practice and improve these behaviors. In support of this, Bjorklund et al. reported that there was a relationship between degree of overestimation of one's imitative abilities on the tossing and juggling tasks and intelligence, as judged by the vocabulary subscale of the Wechsler

---

1. Three-, four-, and five-year olds overestimated their performance comparably for both prediction and postdiction in an experiment in which children watched a model, stated how well they thought they could imitate the model, performed the task, and then evaluated their own performance (Bjorklund et al., in press, Study 3). Postdiction was more accurate than prediction, however, in a diary study (Study 1) in which parents observed and interviewed their children about their imitative attempts. In the diary study, children between the ages of 3 and 5 years still overestimated their performance approximately 40% of the time. Underestimation was rare in all studies reported by Bjorklund et al.

Preschool and Primary Scale of Intelligence (WPPSI), and that this relationship varied with age. In this study, a negative correlation between WPPSI and accuracy scores is an indication that children with better metacognition (i.e., more accurate estimations) have higher verbal intelligence. This pattern was found for the oldest preschool children in our sample (five-year-olds), a finding consistent with those of other researchers studying the relationship between metacognition and intelligence in school-age children (e.g., Schneider, Körkel, & Weinert, 1987). In contrast, for the three- and four-year-olds tested, positive (albeit low to moderate) correlations were found, reflecting that brighter children overestimated slightly more than less bright children. Correlations were significant only for the postdiction scores for the four-year-olds ($r = +0.46$) and the five-year-olds ($r = -0.39$), but differences in the magnitude of the correlations between the oldest and the younger groups of children were significant or approached significance in three out of four contrasts.

We do not mean to imply that young children with good metacognition will grow up to be older children with poor cognitive abilities, or vice versa. The correlations between WPPSI and meta-imitation scores for the three-year-olds were low and nonsignificant in our study ($rs = 0.19$ and 0.15 for prediction and postdiction, respectively). What is of significance is that the canonical relationship between metacognition and intelligence was not obtained on these tasks until the age of five. Young children, in general, overestimated their imitative abilities, with accurate children having no intellectual edge over inaccurate children, at least through the age of four. Whether the older children would show a similar positive relationship between overestimation and intelligence for more demanding tasks is speculative, although such a finding would be consistent with the data of Stipek and her colleagues (see Stipek, 1984; Stipek & Mac Iver, 1989).

The findings of the meta-imitation study and the hypothesis that poor metacognition is adaptive for young children mirrors the opinions of Oppenheim (1981) and Turkewitz and Kenny (1982) with regard to the adaptive benefits of the absence of adult capacities in early development. Rather than being an imperfect attempt at adult abilities, these limitations may serve the needs of the developing organism at its particular stage of ontogeny.

Egocentricity

Piaget (1955; Piaget & Inhelder, 1967) described preschool children as being *egocentric,* in that they cannot easily take a perspective other than their own. Piaget proposed that young children's cognition is centered around themselves, and they have a difficult time perceiving the world as someone else does. According to Piaget, this egocentricity permeates all areas of children's cognitive lives, influencing their perceptions, their language, and their social interactions. Research over the past two decades has indicated that young children are not as egocentric as Piaget had initially proposed (e.g., Borke, 1975; Gzesh & Surber, 1985; Flavell, Everett, Croft, & Flavell, 1981); yet their abilities to take the perspective of another certainly improve with age, *egocentric* accurately describing many of the cognitions of preschool children.

Although young children's egocentrism has generally been viewed as a cognitive liability, their tendencies to interpret events from their own perspective may have some unforeseen benefits. For example, in memory research with both children and adults, higher levels of recall are achieved when subjects relate the target information to themselves during either encoding or retrieval (see Kail & Levine, 1976; Lord, 1980; Nadelman, 1974; Pratkanis & Greenwald, 1985). If, during the presentation of stimuli, subjects are asked whether each item applies to them, subsequent recall is higher than under control conditions (Pratkanis & Greenwald, 1985). For example, in research by Lord (1980), adult subjects were asked to determine whether each adjective on a list was like themselves, their fathers, or Walter Cronkite. The subjects remembered items identified as related to themselves significantly more often than the other words. Lord concluded that when it comes to semantic processing, remembering is facilitated by self-reference more than other frames of reference.

The results of the self-referencing experiments suggest that young children's egocentric attitude may result in enhanced levels of cognitive performance in some situations, and thus may be adaptive. We do not mean to imply that young children's self-concepts are as well integrated as those of adults. However, because young children's initial bias is to interpret events in terms of their own perspectives, they may retain or comprehend some events better than if they were less self-centered. This was illustrated in a study by Mood (1979) of egocentrism in children's sentence comprehension. Mood reported that sentence content describing the children and their personal experiences facilitated their comprehension. In other words, following Piaget's terminology, enhancing the opportunity for children to bring their own perspectives to bear on the solution of a cognitive task increased their ability to assimilate the requirements of the task to their existing cognitive structures. This egocentric benefit allows the children to practice and refine comprehension skills that they would not have had the opportunity to do otherwise. Egocentrism, then, is not a cognitive deficit; rather, it provides some information-processing benefits to young children. As Mood stated,"Focusing on the nonadaptive aspects of preoperational egocentrism results in an incomplete picture of children's development in that the potential adaptive function of egocentrism is minimized or overlooked" (p. 247).

Another aspect of young children's egocentrism is found in their play. Preschool children often engage in *parallel play;* this involves two (or more) children playing near one another, and possibly being involved in similar activities (e.g., building castles in a sandbox), but not truly being involved in mutual or cooperative play (Rubin, Watson, & Jambor, 1978). During parallel play, children may engage in *collective monologues,* in which they talk with one another, but not really to one another (Piaget, 1955). The children would not be so vocal if they were not playing beside one another, so the social situation influences their behavior. The situation can best be described as semisocial.

Some researchers have suggested that this semisocial parallel play may lead children into more cooperative and social play. For example, Bakeman and Brownlee (1980) showed that preschoolers often move from parallel play to group play during the course of a play session. They suggested that children may play beside one another as an unconscious strategy that leads them into group play. Thus, young children's egocentricity serves as a technique that gives them access to more socially oriented activities. Socially immature children who did not talk to themselves in group settings might be less apt to later find themselves in cooperative play situations.

Although highly speculative, the egocentricity that Inhelder and Piaget (1958) and others (e.g., Elkind, 1967; Elkind & Bowen, 1979; Gray & Hudson, 1984) observed in adolescents may also have some adaptive qualities. During adolescence, egocentricity is expressed in part by teenagers' belief that they are invincible and that bad things happen only to other people. Elkind (1967) has referred to this adolescent viewpoint as the *personal fable.* It is likely that such an attitude facilitates children taking risks and separating themselves from their parents. Such risk-taking behavior clearly can have negative consequences, but it also ensures that adolescents experiment with new ideas and new tasks and generally behave more independently. Many of these experiences will be adaptive for adult life and for making the transition to adulthood. Consistent with this argument and equally speculative is the proposal that hunting skills developed first in humans as a result of the risk-taking and exploratory dispositions of young male hominids (see Crook, 1980).

Plasticity and Speed of Cognitive Processing

A general truism of development is that plasticity is reduced with time (Jacobson, 1969; Lerner, 1984; McCall, 1981; Scott, 1968). Children have shown impressive reversibility of the effects of an intellectually deleterious early environment when conditions in their lives change for the better during their second and third years (e.g., E. A. Clark & Hanisee, 1982; Kagan & Klein, 1973; Skeels, 1966).

A major reason for this plasticity, we believe, is that children's cognitive systems are immature, particularly their ability to process information quickly and efficiently. One well-established fact in the cognitive developmental literature is that there are regular age-related changes throughout childhood in speed of processing (Case, 1985; Dempster, 1985; Hale, 1989; Kail, 1986, 1991). Speed of processing (e.g., in identifying pictures or words) is related to level of cognitive performance (Case, 1985; Case, Kurland, & Goldberg, 1982; Chi, 1977), with older (and quicker) children typically performing at higher levels on cognitive tasks than younger (and slower) children.

Processing speed has been hypothesized to be related to age differences in *myelinization* of associative areas of the brain and to experience (Bjorklund & Harnishfeger, 1990; Case, 1985; Dempster, 1985; Konner, 1991). According to Bjorklund and Harnishfeger, "the slower processing of poorly myelinated nerves affords younger children less time to process information" (p. 61). When one considers that processing resources are limited (Bjorklund, 1987; Case, 1985; Hasher & Zacks, 1979), more of a young child's "limited mental resources must be allocated to the activation of nerve bundles than for older children, who have more completely myelinated nerve bundles" (Bjorklund & Harnishfeger, 1990, p. 61). The overall slower speed of mental processing for younger children means that more of their processing is effortful in nature, in that it consumes substantial portions of their limited mental resources (Hasher & Zacks, 1979). In contrast, more of older children's and adults' cognitive processing is automatic, in that it can be done without conscious awareness and requires little or none of one's limited capacity.

Although processing speed varies with age (presumably as a function of myelinization; see Konner, 1991), it is also affected by experience, so that young children who are especially expert at a particular subject process information from that domain rapidly and perform well on tests related to their area of expertise (Roth, 1983). However, this rapid processing and high level of performance does not generalize, with expert children behaving in an age-appropriate manner when dealing with domains for which they have no special expertise (e.g., Chi, 1978; Opwis, Gold, Gruber, & Schneider, 1990).

Slow and inefficient processing through infancy and early childhood may be the factor most responsible for the intellectual plasticity observed in humans. Because mental operations are slow, less information is activated and processed automatically. This reduced automaticity makes processing more laborious and ineffective for the young child, but at the same time protects the child from acquiring cognitive patterns early in life that may not be advantageous later on. Because little in the way of cognitive processing can be automatized early, presumably because of children's incomplete myelinization, children are better prepared to adapt cognitively to later environments. If experiences early in life yielded automization, the child would lose the flexibility necessary for adult life. Processes automatized in response to the demands of early childhood may be useless and even detrimental for coping with the very different cognitive demands faced by adults. Cognitive flexibility in the species is maintained by an immature nervous system that gradually permits the automization of more mental operations, increasing the likelihood that lessons learned as a young child will not interfere with the qualitatively different tasks required of the adult.[2]

Language Acquisition

In each of the three topics discussed above, immature cognition was defined as cognition characterizing the young children that was less proficient than that characterizing the adult. Thus, adults have superior metacognitive abilities, are less egocentric, and process information faster than children. Despite these disadvantages, some benefits are associated with children's less-skilled cognition. The picture is different for language acquisition. Children are better at acquiring both first and second languages than are adults. The cognitive system of the child is seemingly not less efficient than the adults' when it comes to language learning; rather, it is well suited to the demands, making the immaturity of early cognition highly adaptive for the important human phenomenon of language acquisition. The arguments for a critical period of language acquisition are well known, and we will not belabor them here. We will only restate briefly some of those arguments in terms of our thesis and review some recent findings supportive of them.

Lenneberg (1967) is most associated with the critical period hypothesis for language acquisition. He proposed that language learning occurred exclusively or primarily in childhood. The nervous system loses its plasticity with age, so that by puberty the organization of the brain is fixed for all practical purposes,

making language learning difficult. There has been much evidence consistent with this position, including differences between adults and children in recovery from aphasia (see Witelson, 1987), and behavioral studies examining language acquisition in older children who were severely deprived early in life (e.g., Curtiss, 1977).

More recent research by Johnson and Newport (1989) has examined second language learning as a function of age. They reported that proficiency in a person's second language was related to the age at which language training began, so that people who learned their second language early in childhood showed greater proficiency as adults than did people who learned their second language later. Similar results have recently been reported for deaf people learning American Sign Language (Newport, 1990) as their first language. These data require a modified interpretation of the critical period hypothesis for language development, indicating that there is a gradual decline in a person's ability to acquire a second language through childhood, rather than a discontinuity at puberty.

It is clear that the cognitive system of the young child is especially suited for learning both a first and a second language. This ability is gradually lost over childhood, and although adults are able to acquire a second language, they rarely attain the same proficiency that is achieved when language is acquired in childhood. Slow neurological development affords children the cognitive flexibility to acquire a language. Johnson and Newport (1989) suggested an alternative and complementary hypothesis to describe their data on age of learning a second language. They proposed that "an increase in certain cognitive abilities may, paradoxically, make language learning more difficult" (p. 97). Newport (1990) speculated that young children's limitations in encoding complex stimuli may actually make some aspects of language learning easier. According to Newport, "If children perceive and store only component parts of the complex linguistic stimuli to which they are exposed, while adults more readily perceive and remember the whole complex stimulus, children may be in a better position to locate the components" (p. 24). Specifically, children should be aided in acquiring structures that require some type of componential analysis, such as

---

2. Our colleague Ingrid Johanson suggested to us that the well-known phenomenon of infantile amnesia may be similarly explained. Few people can recall events from early childhood, and those events that are recalled are frequently reconstructions of events that occurred years later. Freud (1905/1953) proposed that the experiences of infancy are traumatic because of their sexual nature and that infantile memories are actively repressed. A more plausible interpretation is that events encoded in infancy cannot be retrieved by the qualitatively different cognitive system that resides in the mind of the older child or adult (e.g., Bjorklund, 1989). Although not wishing to give credence to Freud's repression hypothesis, the general inability of humans to recall details from childhood and infancy is probably adaptive. Many of the experiences of infancy and childhood are relevant only to that time in development. Having vivid memories of early experiences, although not necessarily resulting in traumatization, may interfere with and contradict the knowledge that is needed to function in later environments.

morphology, whereas adults should have an advantage in acquiring aspects of language that require integration of complex wholes, such as whole word learning. Other researchers have suggested that the advent of formal operations in early adolescence interferes with implicit learning strategies, making language acquisition more difficult (Krashen, 1982; Rosansky, 1975).

These interpretations, as well as the critical period explanation for language learning, are consistent with our view that children's immature cognition is adaptive and plays an important role in cognitive development.

Our discussion of language acquisition to this point has dealt with *syntactic* development. There is some evidence that young children's cognitive immaturity may facilitate certain aspects of *semantic* development as well. For example, during the early stages of language acquisition, children tend to overextend the meaning of words. They use one word, such as "doggie," as a label not only for its proper referent but also for related objects, such as mammals in general (de Villiers & de Villiers, 1979). Yet, when given a selection of pictures from which to choose, children who overextend the meaning of words can usually select the proper picture, indicating that they know the correct meaning of the word (Thompson & Chapman, 1977). In most language cultures, such overextensions frequently result in parents correcting children (e.g., "That's not a doggie, that's a kitty"), which provides the children with information they might not have received had they remained silent. Children's overextensions, despite their knowledge of what a word actually refers to, suggests that they have a very low threshold for determining whether an object corresponds to a previously acquired label (cf. Siegler, 1988, 1990). This tendency not to inhibit erroneous responses is a youthful one (see Bjorklund & Harnishfeger, 1990; Dempster, in press; Harnishfeger & Bjorklund, in press) that, in this situation, results in children receiving more important information than they would receive were they to use a more conservative (and mature) criterion. Given the state of young children's knowledge, the use of error-producing thresholds serves them well.

Conclusions and Implications for Education

In viewing the role of prolonged immaturity as simply providing more time for learning and socialization, researchers and educators often assume that acceleration of this learning would be beneficial and would provide more time to do even more learning. However, a closer look at the mechanisms of learning in youth suggests that immaturity, along with its limitations and imperfections, serves an adaptive purpose.

This view of the adaptive nature of cognitive immaturity has important implications for cognitive development and for education. For example, textbooks of developmental psychology have traditionally presented Piaget's account of preoperations by emphasizing what young children cannot do relative to concrete-operational children. Some authors and instructors have tried to rectify this by pointing out some of the cognitive skills that young children possess, stressing that young children are more accomplished than Piaget (and others) had given them credit for (e.g., Lefrancois, 1989; Shaffer, 1989). However, if immature cognition is seen as playing an adaptive role in children's development, the "deficiencies" of the preschool child need not be apologized for, but can be regarded as important and necessary components of a fully developed cognitive system.

Similarly, educators' attempts to enhance young children's intelligence through intense instruction, sometimes beginning in infancy (e.g., Doman, 1984; Eastman & Barr, 1985; Engelmann & Engelmann, 1981), must be seriously rethought. It has become clear over the years that infants and young children are capable of greater intellectual feats than had previously been believed, and some educators have argued that formal instruction should begin in the crib. Perhaps the most vocal proponent of this position is Glenn Doman (1984), who claimed that "It is easier to teach a one-year-old *any* set of *facts* than it is to teach a seven-year-old," and "You can teach a baby anything that you can present in an *honest* and *factual* way." (p. 59). This seems to be taking to the extreme Jerome Bruner's (1960) statement that "any subject can be taught effectively in some intellectually honest form to any child at any stage of development" (p. 33).

Others have argued with equal ardor that academically oriented instruction for low-risk infants and preschoolers has no educational merit (e.g., Ames & Chase, 1981; Elkind, 1987a, 1987b; Gallagher & Coche, 1987; Sigel, 1987; Winn, 1983; Zigler, 1987). David Elkind labeled the academic pressure placed on young children as miseducation. He argued that exposing young children to formal education puts them unnecessarily at both short-term and long-term risk. Short-term risks are associated with the stress formal education places on young children and are expressed as fatigue, loss of appetite, decreased efficiency, and eventual psychosomatic ailments. Long-term risks associated with early formal education include reduced motivation for learning, interference with self-directed learning and reflective abstraction (i.e., reflecting on the outcomes of one's own cognitions), and the potentially deleterious effects of social comparisons of intelligence.

Despite the claims by such educators as Doman (1984) and the counterclaims by such educators as Elkind (1987a, 1987b), there has been surprisingly little research assessing the long-term costs and benefits of infant and toddler instruction. A recent study by Hyson, Hirsh-Pasek, and Rescorla (1989) is a notable exception. In their study, four-year-old children attending academic or nonacademic prekindergarten programs were assessed. The children were given tests of academic skills, creativity, social competence, and emotional well-being at the end of their prekindergarten program and again after kindergarten. Parents were also interviewed about their attitudes about education and their expectations for their children's academic achievement.

Hyson et al. (1989) reported some initial intellectual advantages for children in the academic programs. When tested at the conclusion of the prekindergarten program, children who attended academically oriented schools performed better on tests of academic skills (e.g., knowledge of letters, numbers, and shapes) than did children who did not. However, there was no difference between the groups on more general measures of intelligence, and even the advantage in the specific academic skills was not maintained by the end of kindergarten. Hyson et al. reported that there was no difference in social competence between children who attended the academic and nonacademic schools. Moreover, children in the academic programs showed greater signs of test anxiety and had a more negative attitude toward school at the end of kindergarten than did children from the nonacademic schools. Children who attended the academic preschools were also judged to be less creative. Hyson et al. suggested that creativity during the preschool years may be enhanced by environments that encourage playfulness and minimize adult control. For preschool children from middle- and upper-middle-class homes who receive an average amount of intellectual stimulation, Hyson et al.'s study indicates "that the effort spent on formal, teacher-directed academic learning in preschool may not be the best use of children's time at this point in their development" (p. 15).

It has long been recognized by some scholars that certain aspects of learning must await requisite levels of maturation (e.g., Gesell et al., 1940; Uphoff, Gilmore, & Huber, 1986). We concur with this position. However, we propose that the time spent developing this maturity is not merely a waiting period, but instead encompasses a diverse array of adaptive limitations that function ontogenetically to increase a child's learning potential throughout development. A consideration of the adaptive aspects of slow maturation cautions us to provide children with intellectual experiences tailored to their capabilities, rather than trying to endow them with skills ill suited for their biologically determined cognitive systems. What were once viewed as youthful liabilities (e.g., poor metacognition and egocentrism) may instead be exactly what are needed at a particular period of cognitive development. With this perspective in mind, we should rethink our efforts to hurry children through a childhood that has uses in and of itself.[3]

REFERENCES

Ames, L. B., & Chase, J. A. (1981). *Don't push your preschooler.* New York: Harper & Row.

Bakeman, R., & Brownlee, J. R. (1980). The strategic use of parallel play: A sequential analysis. *Child Development, 51,* 873–878.

Bandura, A. (1982). Self-efficacy mechanism in human agency. *American Psychologist, 37,* 122–147.

Bandura, A. (1989a). Human agency in social cognitive theory. *American Psychologist, 44,* 1175–1184.

Bandura, A. (1989b). Regulation of cognitive processes through perceived self-efficacy. *Developmental Psychology, 25,* 729–735.

Beckoff, M. (1972). The development of social interaction, play, and metacommunication in mammals: An ethological perspective. *Quarterly Review of Biology, 47,* 412–434.

Bjorklund, D. F. (1987). How age changes in knowledge base contribute to the development of children's memory: An interpretive review. *Developmental Review, 7,* 93–130.

Bjorklund, D. F. (1989). *Children's thinking: Developmental function and individual differences.* Pacific Grove, CA: Brooks/Cole.

Bjorklund, D. F., Gaultney, J. F., & Green, B. L. (in press). "I watch, therefore I can do:" The development of meta-imitation over the preschool years and the advantage of optimism in one's imitative skills. In M. L. Howe & R. Pasnak (Eds.), *Emerging themes in cognitive development* (Vol. 2). New York: Springer-Verlag.

Bjorklund, D. F., & Harnishfeger, K. K. (1990). The resources construct in cognitive development: Diverse sources of evidence and a theory of inefficient inhibition. *Developmental Review, 10,* 48–71.

Borke, H. (1975). Piaget's mountains revisited: Changes in the egocentric landscape. *Developmental Psychology, 11,* 240–243.

Bruner, J. S. (1960). *The process of education.* Cambridge, MA: Harvard University Press.

Bruner, J. S. (1972). The nature and uses of immaturity. *American Psychologist, 27,* 687–708.

---

3. It is worth mentioning that the most eminent scholar of this century, Albert Einstein, speculated about the advantages that immature cognition may have on adult thinking. Although we cannot claim Einstein's views as data for our arguments, it is interesting to note that he attributed some of his success to his slower-than-average intellectual development: "I sometimes ask myself how it came about that I was the one to develop the theory of relativity. The reason, I think, is that a normal adult never stops to think about problems of space and time. These are things which he has thought of as a child. But my intellectual development was retarded, as a result of which I began to wonder about space and time only when I had already grown up. Naturally, I could go deeper into the problem than a child with normal abilities" (cited in R. W. Clark, 1971, p. 10).

Case, R. (1985). *Intellectual development: Birth to adulthood.* San Diego, CA: Academic Press.

Case, R., Kurland, M., & Goldberg, J. (1982). Operational efficiency and the growth of short-term memory span. *Journal of Experimental Child Psychology, 33,* 386–404.

Cavanaugh, J. C., & Perlmutter, M. (1982). Metamemory: A critical examination. *Child Development, 53,* 11–28.

Chi, M. T. H. (1977). Age differences in memory span. *Journal of Experimental Child Psychology, 23,* 266–281.

Chi, M. T. H. (1978). Knowledge structures and memory development. In R. S. Siegler (Ed.), *Children's thinking: What develops?* (pp. 73–96). Hillsdale, NJ: Erlbaum.

Clark, E. A., & Hanisee, J. (1982). Intellectual and adaptive performance of Asian children in adoptive American settings. *Developmental Psychology, 18,* 595–599.

Clark, R. W. (1971). *Einstein: The life and times.* New York: The World Publishing Co.

Crook, J. H. (1980). *The evolution of human consciousness.* Oxford, England: Clarendon Press.

Curtiss, S. (1977). *Genie: A psycholinguistic study of a modern day "wild child."* San Diego, CA: Academic Press.

Dansky, J. L. (1980). Make-believe: A mediator of the relationship between play and associative fluency. *Child Development, 51,* 576–579.

Dempster, F. N. (1985). Short-term memory development in childhood and adolescence. In C. J. Brainerd & M. Pressley (Eds.), *Basic processes in memory development: Progress in cognitive development research* (pp. 209–248). New York: Springer.

Dempster, F. N. (in press). Resistance to interference: Developmental changes in a basic information processing mechanism. In R. Pasnak & M. L. Howe (Eds.), *Emerging themes in cognitive development* (Vol. 1). New York: Springer-Verlag.

de Villiers, P. A., & de Villiers, J. G. (1979). *Early language.* Cambridge, MA: Harvard University Press.

Doman, G. (1984). *How to multiply your baby's intelligence.* Garden City, NY: Doubleday.

Eastman, O., & Barr, J. L. (1985). *Your child is smarter than you think.* New York: Morrow.

Elkind, D. (1967). Egocentrism in adolescence. *Child Development, 38,* 1025–1034.

Elkind, D. (1987a). Early childhood education on its own terms. In S. L. Kagan & E. F. Zigler (Eds.), *Early schooling: The national debate.* New Haven, CT: Yale University Press.

Elkind, D. (1987b). *The miseducation of children: Superkids at risk.* New York: Knopf.

Elkind, D., & Bowen, R. (1979). Imaginary audience behavior in children and adolescents. *Developmental Psychology, 15,* 38–44.

Engelmann, S., & Engelmann, T. (1981). *Give your child a superior mind.* New York: Cornerstone.

Flavell, J. H., Everett, B. A., Croft, K., & Flavell, E. (1981). Young children's knowledge about visual perception: Further evidence for level 1–level 2 distinction. *Developmental Psychology, 17,* 99–107.

Flavell, J., Friedrichs, A., & Hoyt, J. (1970). Developmental changes in memorization processes. *Cognitive Psychology, 1,* 324–340.

Flavell, J., & Wellman, H. (1977). Metamemory. In R. V. Kail, Jr. & J. W. Hagen (Eds.), *Perspectives on the development of memory and cognition* (pp. 3–33). Hillsdale, NJ: Erlbaum.

Freud, S. (1953). Three essays on the theory of sexuality. In J. Strachey (Ed. and Trans.), *The standard edition of the complete psychological works of Sigmund Freud* (Vol. 7, pp. 125–145). London: Hogarth Press. (Original work published 1905)

Gallagher, J. M., & Coche, J. (1987). Hothousing: The clinical and educational concerns over pressuring young children. *Early Childhood Research Quarterly, 2,* 203–210.

Garner, R. (1990). Children's use of strategies in reading. In D. F. Bjorklund (Ed.), *Children's strategies: Contemporary views of cognitive development* (pp. 245–268). Hillsdale, NJ: Erlbaum.

Gesell, A., Halverson, H. M., Thomspon, H., Ilg, F. L., Castner, B. M., Ames, L. B., & Amatruda (1940). *The first five years of life: A guide to the study of the preschool child.* New York: Harper.

Gould, S. J. (1977). *Ontogeny and phylogeny.* Cambridge, MA: Harvard University Press.

Gray, W. M., & Hudson, L. M. (1984). Formal operations and the imaginary audience. *Developmental Psychology, 20,* 619–627.

Gzesh, S. M., & Surber, C. F. (1985). Visual perspective-taking skills in children. *Child Development, 56,* 1204–1213.

Hale, S. (1989, April). *A global trend in the development of information processing speed.* Paper presented at the meeting of the Society for Research in Child Development, Kansas City, MO.

Harnishfeger, K. K., & Bjorklund, D. F. (in press). The ontogeny of inhibition mechanisms: A renewed approach to cognitive development. In R. Pasnak & M. L. Howe (Eds.), *Emerging themes in cognitive development* (Vol. 1). New York: Springer-Verlag.

Hasher, L., & Zacks, R. T. (1979). Automatic and effortful processes in memory. *Journal of Experimental Psychology: General, 108,* 356–388.

Hyson, M. C., Hirsh-Pasek, K., & Rescorla, L. (1989). *Academic environments in early childhood: Challenge or pressure?* Summary report to The Spencer Foundation, Chicago, IL.

Inhelder, B., & Piaget, J. (1958). *The growth of logical thinking from childhood to adolescence.* New York: Basic Books.

Jacobson, M. (1969). Development of specific neuronal connections. *Science, 163,* 543–547.

Johnson, J. S., & Newport, E. L. (1989). Critical period effects in second language learning: The influence of instructional state on the acquisition of English as a second language. *Cognitive Psychology, 21,* 60–99.

Kagan, J., & Klein, R. E. (1973). Cross-cultural perspectives on early development. *American Psychologist, 28,* 947–961.

Kail, R. (1986). Sources of age differences in speed of processing. *Child Development, 57,* 969–987.

Kail, R. (1991). Processing time declines exponentially during childhood and adolescence. *Developmental Psychology, 27,* 259–266.

Kail, R. V., & Levine, L. E. (1976). Encoding processes and sex-role preferences. *Journal of Experimental Child Psychology, 21,* 256–263.

Konner, M. (1991). Universals of behavioral development in relation to brain myelinization. In K. R. Gibson & A. C. Petersen (Eds.), *Brain maturation and cognitive development: Comparative and cross-cultural perspectives* (pp. 181–223). New York: Aldine de Gruyter.

Krashen, S. (1982). Accounting for child–adult differences in second language rate and attainment. In S. Krashen, R. Scracella, & M. Long (Eds.), *Child–adult differences in second language acquisition* (202–226). Rowley, MA: Newbury House.

Lefrancois, G. R. (1989). *Of children: An introduction to child development*. Belmont, CA: Wadsworth.

Lenneberg, E. H. (1967). *Biological foundations of language*. New York: Wiley.

Lerner, R. M. (1984). *On the nature of human plasticity*. New York: Cambridge University Press.

Lord, C. G. (1980). Schemas and images as memory aids: Two modes of processing social information. *Journal of Personality and Social Psychology, 38,* 257–269.

McCall, R. B. (1981). Nature–nurture and the two realms of development: A proposed integration with respect to mental development. *Child Development, 52,* 1–12.

Miller, P. H. (1985). Metacognition and attention. In D. L. Forrest-Pressley, G. E., MacKinnon, & T. G. Waller (Eds.), *Metacognition, cognition, and human performance* (Vol. 2, pp. 181–221). San Diego, CA: Academic Press.

Montagu, A. (1989). *Growing young* (2nd Ed.). Grandy, MA: Bergin & Garvey.

Mood, D. W. (1979). Sentence comprehension in preschool children: Testing an adaptive egocentrism hypothesis. *Child Development, 50,* 247–250.

Nadelman, L. (1974). Sex identity in American children: Memory, knowledge, and preference tests. *Developmental Psychology, 10,* 413–417.

Newport, E. L. (1990). Maturational constraints on language learning. *Cognitive Science, 14,* 11–28.

Oppenheim, R. W. (1981). Ontogenetic adaptations and retrogressive processes in the development of the nervous system and behavior. In K. J. Connolly & H. F. R. Prechtl (Eds.), *Maturation and development: Biological and psychological perspectives* (pp. 73–108). Philadelphia: International Medical Publications.

Opwis, K., Gold, A., Gruber, H., & Schneider, W. (1990). Zum Einfluss von Expertise auf Gedachtnisleistungen und ihre Selsteinschätzung bei Kindern und Erwachsesen [The impact of expertise on memory performance and performance prediction in children and adults]. *Zeitschrift für Entwicklungspsychologie und Pädagogische Psychologie, 21,* 207–224.

Piaget, J. (1955). *The language and thought of the child*. New York: World.

Piaget, J. (1962). *Play, dreams, and imitation in childhood*. New York: Norton.

Piaget, J., & Inhelder, B. (1967). *The child's conception of space*. New York: Norton.

Poirier, F. E., & Smith, E. O. (1974). Socializing functions of primate play. *American Zoologist, 14,* 275–287.

Pratkanis, A. R., & Greenwald, A. B. (1985). How shall the self be conceived? *Journal for the Theory of Social Behavior, 15,* 311–328.

Rosansky, E. (1975). The critical period for the acquisition of language: Some cognitive developmental considerations. *Working Papers on Bilingualism, 6,* 10–23.

Roth, C. (1983). Factors affecting developmental changes in the speed of processing. *Journal of Experimental Child Psychology, 35,* 509–528.

Rubin, K. H., Watson, K. S., & Jambor, T. W. (1978). Free-play behaviors in preschool and kindergarten children. *Child Development, 49,* 534–536.

Schneider, W. (1985). Developmental trends in the metamemory–memory behavior relationship: An integrative review. In D. L. Forrest-Pressley, G. E. MacKinnon, & T. G. Waller (Eds.), *Cognition, metacognition, and human performance* (Vol. 1, pp. 57–109). San Diego, CA: Academic Press.

Schneider, W. (1988, March). *Conceptual and methodological problems in doing self-report research*. Paper presented at the annual meetings of the American Educational Research Association, New Orleans, LA.

Schneider, W. (1991, April). *Performance prediction in young children: Effects of skill, metacognition, and wishful thinking*. Paper presented at meeting of the Society for Research in Child Development, Seattle, WA.

Schneider, W., Körkel, J., & Weinert, F. E. (1987). The effects of intelligence, self-concept, and attributional style on metamemory and memory behaviour. *International Journal of Behavioral Development, 10,* 281–299.

Schneider, W., & Pressley, M. (1989). *Memory development between 2 and 20*. New York: Springer-Verlag.

Scott, J. P. (1968). *Early experience and the organization of behavior*. Monterey, CA: Brooks/Cole.

Shaffer, D. R. (1989). *Developmental psychology: Childhood and adolescence* (2nd ed.). Pacific Grove, CA: Brooks/Cole.

Siegler, R. S. (1988). Individual differences in strategy choices: Good students, not-so-good students, and perfectionists. *Child Development, 59,* 833–851.

Siegler, R. S. (1990). How content knowledge, strategies, and individual differences interact to produce strategy choice. In W. Schneider & F. E. Weinert (Eds.), *Interactions among aptitudes, strategies, and knowledge in cognitive performance* (pp. 74–89). New York: Springer-Verlag.

Sigel, I. E. (1987). Does hothousing rob children of their childhood? *Early Childhood Research Quarterly, 2,* 211–225.

Skeels, H. M. (1966). Adult status of children with contrasting early life experiences. *Monograph of the Society for Research in Child Development, 31* (Serial No. 105).

Stipek, D. (1981). Children's perceptions of their own and their classmates' ability. *Journal of Experimental Child Psychology, 73,* 404–410.

Stipek, D. (1984). Young children's performance expectations: Logical analysis or wishful thinking? In J. G. Nicholls (Ed.), *Advances in motivation and achievement: Vol. 3. The development of achievement motivation* (pp. 33–56). Greenwich, CT: JAI Press.

Stipek, D., & Hoffman, J. (1980). Development of children's performance-related judgments. *Child Development, 51,* 912–914.

Stipek, D., & Mac Iver, D. (1989). Developmental change in children's assessment of intellectual competence. *Child Development, 60,* 521–538.

Stipek, D., Roberts, T., & Sanborn, M. (1984). Preschool-age children's performance expectations for themselves and another child as a function of the incentive value of success and the salience of past performance. *Child Development, 55,* 1983–1989.

Thompson, J. R., & Chapman, R. S. (1977). Who is "Daddy" revisited? The status of two-year-olds' overextended words in use and comprehension. *Journal of Child Language, 4,* 359–375.

Turkewitz, G., & Kenny, P. (1982). Limitations on input as a basis for neural organization and perceptual development: A preliminary theoretical statement. *Developmental Psychobiology, 15,* 357–368.

Uphoff, J., Gilmore, J., & Huber, R. (1986). *Summer children: Ready or not for school.* Middletown, OH: J & J Publishing.

Vandenberg, B. (1981). Play: Dormant issues and new perspectives. *Human Development, 24,* 357–365.

Washburn, S., & Hamburg, D. (1965). The implications of primate research. In I. Devore (Ed.), *Primate behavior: Field studies of monkeys and apes* (pp. 607–623). New York: Holt, Rinehart & Winston.

Whitehurst, G. J., & Sonnenschein, S. (1985). The development of communication: A functional analysis. In G. J. Whitehurst (Ed.), *Annals of child development* (Vol. 2, pp. 1–48). Greenwich, CT: JAI Press.

Winn, M. (1983). *Children without childhood.* New York: Penguin.

Witelson, S. F. (1987). Neurobiological aspects of language in children. *Child Development, 58,* 653–688.

Yussen, S., & Levy, V. (1975). Developmental changes in predicting one's own span of short-term memory. *Journal of Experimental Child Psychology, 19,* 502–508.

Zigler, E. (1987). Formal schooling for 4-year-olds? No. In S. L. Kagan & E. Zigler (Eds.), *Early schooling: The national debate.* New Haven, CT: Yale University Press.

Questions

1. Describe what Bjorklund and his colleagues found when they compared the meta-imitation skills of preschool and early school-age children and the relation of these skills to cognitive performance. What do these findings suggest about the role of cognitive immaturity in early development?

2. How do Bjorklund and Green interpret the evidence that young children and adolescents tend to reason in egocentric ways? Does their interpretation change your view of a behavior that Piaget and others see as a limitation in children's thinking?

3. Bjorklund and Green proposed slower processing in young children relative to older children in many areas of cognitive development. However, they modify this view in their discussion of language learning. Why might language acquisition be on a somewhat different course in early learning?

4. As the authors point out, education is often aimed at accelerating learning and development. From an evolutionary perspective, does this aim make sense, especially in the early years of childhood? Why or why not?

5. New products appear regularly that are designed to teach young children, even very young infants, about the world. In advertisements for these products, parents are told how these products will benefit their children's cognitive development. Based on this article, how would you advise a friend or family member who plans to invest in these products for their newborn?

6. Bjorklund and Green point out that long-term studies have rarely been conducted to determine whether early efforts to teach children actually accelerate children's thinking. How would you design such a study and, given the arguments presented in this article, what would be one of your main questions in this study?

2 Ecological Models of Human Development

Urie Bronfenbrenner

Human development occurs in the midst of a vibrant, complex environment. This environment includes social and cultural practices and institutions that provide most of the experiences that people have. Developmental psychologists, examining this environment, are presented with an interesting question: How does development emerge from the interaction of the child's biological capabilities and their sociocultural experiences? It is not easy to understand the contributions that society and culture make to psychological development and how these contributions coordinate with children's developing capabilities. An initial step in gaining this understanding is to describe the social and cultural context of psychological development.

Throughout much of the twentieth century, psychological research, including research on child development, was conducted largely in laboratory settings. As a result, this research provided few insights into the social and cultural aspects of psychological development. However, in the late 1970s, the psychologist Urie Bronfenbrenner extended this understanding when he introduced the ecological systems approach. This approach, which Bronfenbrenner discusses in the following article, is based on ecology, the branch of biology concerned with the connections between organisms and their environments.

Bronfenbrenner's framework concentrates on the subsystems, or components, of the human ecological niche as well as the ways that these subsystems interact with each other. Bronfenbrenner describes these subsystems as a series of layers, similar to the layers of an onion or to *matryoshka,* the nested dolls from Russia (Bronfenbrenner's native country). The subsystems range from the immediate, or proximal, processes of development (the microsystem), such as the family or school, to patterns of culture, such as the economy, customs, and bodies of knowledge (the macrosystem). The historical context of development is described in the chronosystem.

Bronfenbrenner's framework provided developmental psychologists with a new way of thinking about the social and cultural components of human development. This framework does not provide a simple story about psychological development; nor does it offer ready answers about specific issues or challenges that confront children as they grow. Rather, its contribution is in the types of questions, hypotheses, and designs for research that it inspires. This potential is illustrated in this article's description of research on the developmental challenges that confront low-birthweight babies and on the effect that growing up during the Great Depression had on later development.

Ecological models encompass an evolving body of theory and research concerned with the processes and conditions that govern the lifelong course of human development in the actual environments in which human beings live. Although most of the systematic theory-building in this domain has been done by [Urie] Bronfenbrenner, his work is based on an analysis and integration of results from empirical investigations conducted over many decades by researchers from diverse disciplines, beginning with a study carried out in Berlin in 1870 on the effects of neighborhood on the development of children's concepts (Schwabe and Bartholomai 1870). This entry consists of an exposition of Bronfenbrenner's theoretical system, which is also used as a framework for illustrating representative research findings.

Reprinted from the *International Encyclopedia of Education*, Vol. 3, 2nd ed., 1643–1647. Copyright 1994 with permission from Elsevier.

1. The Evolution of Ecological Models

Bronfenbrenner's ecological paradigm, first introduced in the 1970s (Bronfenbrenner 1974, 1976, 1977, 1979), represented a reaction to the restricted scope of most research then being conducted by developmental psychologists. The nature of both the restriction and the reaction is conveyed by this oft-quoted description of the state of developmental science at that time: "It can be said that much of developmental psychology is the science of the strange behavior of children in strange situations with strange adults for the briefest possible periods of time" (Bronfenbrenner 1977, p. 513).

In the same article, Bronfenbrenner presented a conceptual and operational framework (supported by the comparatively small body of relevant research findings then available) that would usefully provide the basis and incentive for moving the field in the desired direction. During the same period, he also published two reports pointing to the challenging implications of an ecological approach for child and family policy (1974) and educational practice (1976).

Within a decade, investigations informed by an ecological perspective were no longer a rarity. By 1986, Bronfenbrenner was able to write:

> Studies of children and adults in real-life settings, with real-life implications, are now commonplace in the research literature on human development, both in the United States and, as this volume testifies, in Europe as well. This scientific development is taking place, I believe, not so much because of my writings, but rather because the notions I have been promulgating are ideas whose time has come. (1986b p. 287).

At the same time, Bronfenbrenner continued his work on the development of a theoretical paradigm. What follows is a synopsis of the general ecological model as delineated in its most recent reformulations (Bronfenbrenner 1989, 1990, Bronfenbrenner and Ceci 1993).

2. The General Ecological Model

Two propositions specifying the defining properties of the model are followed by research examples illustrating both.

Proposition 1 states that, especially in its early phases, and to a great extent throughout the life course, human development takes place through processes of progressively more complex reciprocal interaction between an active, evolving biopsychological human organism and the persons, objects, and symbols in its immediate environment. To be effective, the interaction must occur on a fairly regular basis over extended periods of time. Such enduring forms of interaction in the immediate environment are referred to as *proximal processes*. Examples of enduring patterns of proximal process are found in parent-child and child-child activities, group or solitary play, reading, learning new skills, studying, athletic activities, and performing complex tasks.

A second defining property identifies the threefold source of these dynamic forces. Proposition 2 states that the form, power, content, and direction of the proximal processes effecting development vary systematically as a joint function of the characteristics of the developing person; of the environment—both immediate and more remote—in which the processes are taking place; and the nature of the developmental outcomes under consideration.

Propositions 1 and 2 are theoretically interdependent and subject to empirical test. A research design that permits their simultaneous investigation is referred to as a process-person-context model. A first example illustrating the model is shown in Figure 1. The data are drawn from a classic longitudinal study by Drillien (1963) of factors affecting the development of children of low birth weight compared to those of normal weight. The figure depicts the impact of the quality of mother-infant interaction at age 4 on the number of observed problems at age 4 as a joint function of birth weight and social class. As can be seen, a proximal process, in this instance mother-infant interaction across time, emerges as the most powerful predictor of developmental outcome. In all instances, good maternal treatment appears to reduce substantially the degree of behavioral disturbance exhibited by the child. Furthermore, as stipulated in Proposition 2, the power of the process varies systematically as a function of the environmental context (in this instance, social class)

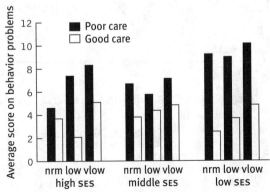

nrm = normal birth rate: low = between normal and 5.5 lbs: vlow = 5.5 lbs or less

figure 1
Problem behavior at age 4 (by birth weight, mother's care, and social class).

and of the characteristics of the person (in this case, weight at birth). Note also that the proximal process has the general effect of reducing or buffering against environmental differences in developmental outcome; specifically, under high levels of mother-child interaction, social class differences in problem behavior become much smaller.

Unfortunately, from the perspective of an ecological model the greater developmental impact of proximal processes in poorer environments is to be expected only for indices of developmental dysfunction, primarily during childhood. For outcomes reflecting developmental competence (e.g., mental ability, academic achievement, social skills) proximal processes are posited as having greater impact in more advantaged and stable environments throughout the life course. An example of this contrasting pattern is shown in Figure 2, which depicts the differential effects of parental monitoring on school achievement for high school students living in the three most common family structures found in the total sample of over 4,000 cases. The sample is further stratified by two levels of mother's education, with completion of high school as the dividing point. Parental monitoring refers to the effort by parents to keep informed about, and set limits on, their children's activities outside the home. In the present analysis, it was assessed by a series of items in a questionnaire administered to adolescents in their school classes.

Once again, the results reveal that the effects of proximal processes are more powerful than those of the environmental contexts in which they occur. In this instance, however, the impact of the proximal process is greatest in what emerges as the most advantaged ecological niche, that is, families with two biological parents in which the mother has had some education beyond high school. The typically declining slope of the curve reflects the fact that higher levels of outcome are more difficult to achieve so that at each successive step, the same degree of active effort yields a somewhat smaller result.

3. Environments as Contexts of Development

The foregoing example provides an appropriate introduction to another distinctive feature of the ecological model, its highly differentiated reconceptualization of the environment from the perspective of the developing person. Based on Lewin's theory of psychological fields (Bronfenbrenner 1977; Lewin 1917, 1931, 1935), the ecological environment is conceived as a set of nested structures, each inside the other like a set of Russian dolls. Moving from the innermost level to the outside, these structures are defined as described below.

3.1 Microsystems

A microsystem is a pattern of activities, social roles, and interpersonal relations experienced by the developing person in a given face-to-face setting with particular physical, social, and symbolic features that invite, permit, or inhibit engagement in sustained, progressively more complex interaction with, and activity in, the immediate environment. Examples include such settings as family, school, peer group, and workplace.

It is within the immediate environment of the microsystem that proximal processes operate to produce and sustain development, but as the above definition indicates, their power to do so depends on the content and structure of the microsystem. Specific hypotheses regarding the nature of this content and structure, and the as yet limited research evidence on which they are based are documented in the work of Bronfenbrenner (1986a, 1986b, 1988, 1989, 1993). Most of the relevant studies of proximal processes have focused on the family, with all too few dealing with other key developmental settings, such as classrooms and schools. A notable exception in this regard is the work of Stevenson and his colleagues (Stevenson and Stigler 1992, see also Ceci 1990).

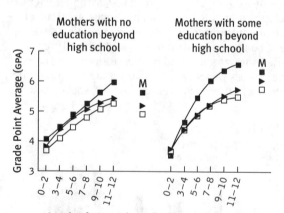

Levels of parental monitoring range from 0–12.

"M" = Mean GPA for each group

- ■ Living with two biological parents
- ▶ Living with own mother and stepfather
- □ Living with mother only

GPA Scale: 2 = mostly D's or less. 3 = $\frac{1}{2}$C's, $\frac{1}{2}$D's. 4 = mostly C's. 5 = $\frac{1}{2}$B's, $\frac{1}{2}$C's. 6 = mostly B's. 7 = $\frac{1}{2}$A's, $\frac{1}{2}$B's. 8 = mostly A's.

figure 2

Effect of parental monitoring on grades in high school by family structure and mother's level of education.

3.2 Mesosystems

The mesosystem comprises the linkages and processes taking place between two or more settings containing the developing person (e.g., the relations between home and school, school and workplace, etc.). In other words, a mesosystem is a system of microsystems.

An example in this domain is the work of Epstein (1983a, 1983b) on the developmental impact of two-way communication and participation in decision-making by parents and teachers. Elementary school pupils from classrooms in which such joint involvement was high not only exhibited greater initiative and independence after entering high school, but also received higher grades. The effects of family and school processes were greater than those attributable to socioeconomic status or race.

3.3 Exosystems

The exosystem comprises the linkages and processes taking place between two or more settings, at least one of which does not contain the developing person, but in which events occur that indirectly influence processes within the immediate setting in which the developing person lives (e.g., for a child, the relation between the home and the parent's workplace; for a parent, the relation between the school and the neighborhood peer group).

Especially since the early 1980s, research has focused on three exosystems that are especially likely to affect the development of children and youth indirectly through their influence on the family, the school, and the peer group. These are the parents' workplace (e.g., Eckenrode and Gore 1990), family social networks (e.g., Cochran et al. 1990), and neighborhood-community contexts (e.g., Pence 1988).

3.4 Macrosystems

The macrosystem consists of the overarching pattern of micro-, meso-, and exosystems characteristic of a given culture or subculture, with particular reference to the belief systems, bodies of knowledge, material resources, customs, life-styles, opportunity structures, hazards, and life course options that are embedded in each of these broader systems. The macrosystem may be thought of as a societal blueprint for a particular culture or subculture.

This formulation points to the necessity of going beyond the simple labels of class and culture to identify more specific social and psychological features at the macrosystem level that ultimately affect the particular conditions and processes occurring in the microsystem (see Bronfenbrenner 1986a, 1986b, 1988, 1989, 1993).

3.5 Chronosystems

A final systems parameter extends the environment into a third dimension. Traditionally in the study of human development, the passage of time was treated as synonymous with chronological age. Since the early 1970s, however, an increasing number of investigators have employed research designs in which time appears not merely as an attribute of the growing human being, but also as a property of the surrounding environment not only over the life course, but across historical time (Baltes and Schaie 1973, Clausen 1986, Elder 1974, Elder et al. 1993).

A chronosystem encompasses change or consistency over time not only in the characteristics of the person but also of the environment in which that person lives (e.g., changes over the life course in family structure, socioeconomic status, employment, place of residence, or the degree of hecticness and ability in everyday life).

An excellent example of a chronosystem design is found in Elder's classic study *Children of the Great Depression* (1974). The investigation involved a comparison of two otherwise comparable groups of families differentiated on the basis of whether the loss of income as a result of the Great Depression of the 1930s exceeded or fell short of 35 percent. The availability of longitudinal data made it possible to assess developmental outcomes through childhood, adolescence, and adulthood. Also, the fact that children in one sample were born eight years earlier than those in the other permitted a comparison of the effects of the Depression on youngsters who were adolescents when their families became economically deprived with the effects of those who were still young children at the time.

The results for the two groups presented a dramatic contrast. Paradoxically, for youngsters who were teenagers during the Depression years, the families' economic deprivation appeared to have a salutary effect on their subsequent development, especially in the middle class. As compared with the nondeprived who were matched on pre-Depression socioeconomic status, deprived boys displayed a greater desire to achieve and a firmer sense of career goals. Boys and girls from deprived homes attained greater satisfaction in life, both by their own and by societal standards. Though more pronounced for adolescents from middle-class backgrounds, these favorable outcomes were evident among their lower-class counterparts as well. Analysis of interview and observation protocols enabled Elder to identify what he regarded as a critical factor in investigating this favorable developmental trajectory: the loss of economic security forced the family to mobilize its own human resources, including its teenagers, who had to take on new roles and responsibilities both within and outside the home and to work together toward the common goal of getting and keeping the family on its feet. This experience provided effective training in initiative, responsibility, and cooperation.

4. Genetic Inheritance in Ecological Perspective

The most recent extension of the ecological paradigm involves a reconceptualization of the role of genetics in human development (Bronfenbrenner and Ceci 1993). The new formulation calls into question and replaces some of the key assumptions underlying the established "percentage-of-variance" model employed in behavior genetics. Specifically, in addition to incorporating explicit measures of the environment conceptualized in systems terms, and allowing for nonadditive, synergistic effects in genetics-environment interaction, the proposed "bioecological" model posits proximal processes as the empirically assessable mechanisms through which genotypes are transformed into phenotypes. It is further argued, both on theoretical and empirical grounds, that heritability, defined by behavioral geneticists as "the proportion of the total phenotypic variance that is due to additive genetic variation" (Cavalli-Storza and Bodmer 1971 p. 536), is in fact highly influenced by events and conditions in the environment. Specifically, it is proposed that heritability can be shown to vary substantially as a direct function of the magnitude of proximal processes and the quality of the environments in which they occur, potentially yielding values of heritability that, at their extremes, are both appreciably higher and lower than those hitherto reported in the research literature.

If this bioecological model sustains empirical testing, this would imply that many human beings may possess genetic potentials for development significantly beyond those that they are presently manifesting, and that such unrealized potentials might be actualized through social policies and programs that enhance exposure to proximal processes in environmental settings providing the stability and resources that enable such processes to be maximally effective.

Certainly, thus far it has by no means been demonstrated that this latest extension of the ecological paradigm has any validity. Nor is the validation of hypotheses the principal goal that ecological models are designed to achieve. Indeed, their purpose may be better served if the hypotheses that they generate are found wanting, for the primary scientific aim of the ecological approach is not to claim answers, but to provide a theoretical framework that, through its application, will lead to further progress in discovering the processes and conditions that shape the course of human development.

However, beyond this scientific aim lies a broader human hope. That hope was expressed in the first systematic exposition of the ecological paradigm:

> Species *Homo sapiens* appears to be unique in its capacity to adapt to, tolerate, and especially to create the ecologies in which it lives and grows. Seen in different contexts, human nature, which I had once thought of as a singular noun, turns out to be plural and pluralistic; for different environments produce discernible differences, not only across but within societies, in talent, temperament, human relations, and particularly in the ways in which each culture and subculture brings up the next generation. The process and product of making human beings human clearly varies by place and time. Viewed in historical as well as cross-cultural perspective, this diversity suggests the possibility of ecologies as yet untried that hold a potential for human natures yet unseen, perhaps possessed of a wiser blend of power and compassion than has thus far been manifested. (Bronfenbrenner 1979 p. xiii)

REFERENCES

Baltes, P. B., Schaie, W. 1973. *Life-span Developmental Psychology: Personality and Socialization*. Academic Press, New York.

Bronfenbrenner, U. 1974. Developmental research, public policy, and the ecology of childhood. *Child Dev.* 45(1): 1–5.

Bronfenbrenner, U. 1976. The experimental ecology of education. *Teach. Coll. Rec.* 78(2): 157–204.

Bronfenbrenner, U. 1977. Toward an experimental ecology of human development. *Am. Psychol.* 32: 515–31.

Bronfenbrenner, U. 1979. *The Ecology of Human Development: Experiments by Nature and Design*. Harvard University Press, Cambridge, Massachusetts.

Bronfenbrenner, U. 1986a. Ecology of the family as a context for human development: Research perspectives. *Dev. Psychol.* 22(6): 723–42.

Bronfenbrenner, U. 1986b. Recent advances in the ecology of human development. In: Silbereisen, R. K., Eyferth, K., Rudinger, G. (eds.) 1986. *Development as Action in Context: Problem Behavior and Normal Youth Development*. Springer-Verlag, Berlin.

Bronfenbrenner, U. 1988. Interacting systems in human development: Research paradigms, present and future. In: Bolger, N., Caspi, A., Downey, G., Moorehouse, M. (eds.) 1988. *Persons in Context: Developmental Processes*. Cambridge University Press, Cambridge.

Bronfenbrenner, U. 1989. Ecological systems theory. In: Vasta, R. (ed.) 1989. *Six Theories of Child Development: Revised Formulations and Current Issues*. Vol. 6. JAI Press, Greenwich, Connecticut.

Bronfenbrenner, U. 1990. The ecology of cognitive development. *Zeitschrift für Sozialisationsforschung und Erziehungssoziologie (ZSE)*. 10(2): 101–14.

Bronfenbrenner, U. 1993. The ecology of cognitive development: Research models and fugitive findings. In: Wozniak, R. H., Fischer, K. (eds.) 1993 *Thinking in Context*. Erlbaum, Hillsdale, New Jersey.

Bronfenbrenner, U., Ceci, S. J. 1993. Heredity, environment, and the question "how?": A new theoretical perspective for the 1990s. In: Plomin, R., McClearn, G. E. (eds.) 1993 *Nature, Nurture, and Psychology*. APA Books, Washington, DC.

Cavalli-Storza, L. L., Bodmer, W. F. 1971. *The Genetics of Human Populations*. W. H. Freeman, San Francisco, California.

Ceci, S. J. 1990. *On Intelligence . . . More or Less: A Bioecological Treatise on Intellectual Development*. Prentice-Hall, Englewood Cliffs, New Jersey.

Clausen, J. A. 1986. *The Life Course: A Sociological Perspective*. Prentice-Hall, Englewood Cliffs, New Jersey.

Cochran, M., Larner, M., Riley, D., Gunnarsson, L., Henderson, C. R., Jr. 1990. *Extending Families: The Social Networks of Parents and their Children*. Cambridge University Press, New York.

Drillien, C. M. 1963. *The Growth and Development of the Prematurely Born Infant*. E. and S. Livingston Ltd., Edinburgh.

Eckenrode, J., Gore, S. (eds.) 1990. *Stress between Work and Family*. Plenum Press, New York.

Elder, G. H., Jr. 1974. *Children of the Great Depression: Social Change in the Life Experience*. University of Chicago Press, Chicago, Illinois.

Elder, G. H., Jr., Modell, J., Parke, R. D. 1993. *Children in Time and Place: Individual, Historical and Developmental Insights*. Cambridge University Press, New York.

Epstein, J. L. 1983a. *Effects on Parents of Teacher Practices of Parent Involvement*. Center for the Social Organization of Schools, Johns Hopkins University, Baltimore, Maryland.

Epstein, J. L. 1983b. Longitudinal effects of family-school-person interactions on student outcomes. *Research in Sociology of Education and Socialization* 4: 101–27.

Lewin, K. 1917. Kriegslandschaft. *Zeitschrift für Angewandte Psychologie* 12: 440–47.

Lewin, K. 1931. Environmental forces in child behavior and development. In: Murchison, C. (ed.) 1931 *A Handbook of Child Psychology*. Clark University Press, Worcester, Massachusetts.

Lewin, K. 1935. *A Dynamic Theory of Personality*. McGraw-Hill, New York.

Pence, A. R. (ed.) 1988. *Ecological Research with Children and Families: From Concepts to Methodology*. Teachers College, Columbia University, New York.

Schwabe, H., Bartholomai, F. 1870. Der Vorstellungskreis der Berliner Kinder beim Eintritt in die Schule. In: *Berlin und seine Entwicklung: Städtisches Jahrbuch für Volkswirthschaft und Statistik Vierter Jahrgang*. Guttentag, Berlin.

Stevenson, H. W., Stigler, J. W. 1992. *The Learning Gap: Why Our Schools are Failing and What We Can Learn from Japanese and Chinese Education*. Summit Books, New York.

Questions

1. What are the subsystems of the ecological approach? Think of a particular process of development, such as peer relations or language development, and describe it in relation to each of these subsystems.
2. Why was Bronfenbrenner interested in the role that genetic inheritance may play in the ecology of psychological development?
3. What types of interventions could be provided for parents from disadvantaged backgrounds that would increase the likelihood that their children will have fewer behavior problems in childhood and succeed in high school?
4. How might the ecological systems framework contribute to research and social policy related to children's nutrition and the problem of child obesity?
5. What do you think will be the psychological consequences for a child if his or her experiences in two different microsystems are in conflict with one another—if, for example, the family emphasizes cooperation but the school rewards competition?
6. One implication of the ecological systems approach is that a change made in one element or subsystem will have little effect if the other subsystems remain the same. Does this mean that only large-scale interventions are worthwhile? In other words, can small changes in a child's life ever make a difference?

3 Parent, Child, and Reciprocal Influences

Richard Q. Bell

Children spend a huge portion of their time in the company of their family, especially their parents, and this experience has profound consequences for development. Parents contribute to child development in many ways: through the behaviors they encourage in their children, through the experiences and resources they provide, and through the actions they model for their children. Psychologists describe these influences in theories or models of socialization. Socialization is the process by which parents and others ensure that a child's standards of behavior, attitudes, skills, and motives conform closely to those deemed appropriate to his or her role in society. Although models of socialization have emphasized the contributions that parents make to child development, it would be a mistake to assume that this process operates solely in unidirectional fashion. A unidirectional view casts the child as a passive recipient of parents' socialization efforts. This view of development, as this article by Richard Q. Bell makes clear, could not be further from the truth. Like their parents, children play active roles in the socialization process. In fact, it is through the active contributions of both parents and children, as they strive to understand and influence one another, that child socialization occurs.

Characteristics of the parent and of the child are important parts of this process. Parental characteristics that contribute to socialization include personality, beliefs, emotional responsiveness, control, and expectations about child behavior. Contributions of children include temperament and emotionality, cognitive and social skills, and the child's age and unique, individual experiences. Some of the characteristics that parents and children bring to these joint socialization efforts are interrelated. Parents and children are biologically related and, as a result, they may share certain characteristics, such as emotional intensity or particular social or intellectual tendencies. Parents and children also share an interactional history, which may influence how they approach new situations. For example, if an animal, let's say a dog, frightened the child on a prior occasion, both parent and child will approach a new dog with this knowledge in mind.

The following article discusses the view that parent-child interaction is a mutual, reciprocal process and that, together, parents and children create children's socialization experiences. This understanding, now central to developmental research, raises important questions about how parents and children work together to support development in ways that respect the interests and needs of both parents and children.

Progress in science often yields a simplification of what previously seemed to be a complex and confusing phenomenon. It may yet do this in the area of parent–child interaction, but at the present time progress is making the phenomenon look more intricate, and the foreseeable future portends still further complication. Investigators of socialization in the 1940s recognized the fact that reciprocal influences were involved—child to parent and parent to child—but lacking any obvious way of identifying or controlling for the child's effects, they proceeded with research on parent influences to see what could be learned from this source alone. Others, coming on the scene later, assumed that the study of parent–child interaction was unnecessary. To them it was only necessary to set goals for development, since principles of learning theory could then be applied and the goals readily reached. Still others brought the evolutionary adaptive approach that had been so successful in analyzing the interaction of parents and their young in animal species, identifying specific components, then ascertaining how they controlled interaction.

Several factors confronted these investigators with a more complex reality. Research that focused exclusively on parent influences yielded few consistent relations, and these of low order. The few findings that appeared with some consistency were based in the main on correlational studies from which the direction of effects could not be determined. These findings could be explained very plausibly as due to the effects of children on parents. In the 1960s a wealth of new information accumulated on the sensorimotor, perceptual, information-seeking, and information-processing skills of infants, as well as on their individual differences, making it quite unreasonable to treat them as homogeneous tabulae rasae, passive recipients of parental teaching. It became difficult to ignore the cognitive capabilities of infants or the way they actively shaped and synthesized their worlds. All of this has been reviewed in more detail in my book with Lawrence Harper (Bell & Harper, 1977) and in an article by Parke (1978).

The active infant and child have now been put back into the picture with a thinking parent. This parent is far more than a coequal in a push–pull, stimulus–response billiard game. A recent interest in ecology has placed the reciprocal system in the context of overlapping circles of family, neighborhood, ethnic, and larger groups. New research approaches in socialization have been identified that can isolate parent and child effects (chap. 5).[1]

These changes hold many implications for the well-being of children. It is expected that a mere recognition of child effects alone, let alone reciprocal influences, should act to weaken the influence of certain pervasive but unrealistic positions on child rearing that have made parents unnecessarily wary and indecisive. This article elaborates on these implications and their bases, after first discussing ways of putting the thinking parent back in the picture at the level of research operations and after providing illustrative findings on reciprocal influences that give an indication of where research will be likely to lead us in the next decade.

The Thinking Parent

In a series of sound-spectrographic studies, it was demonstrated that infants' hunger and pain cries differ physically and can be distinguished by caregivers (p. 173). However, it was then found that a mother's response to an infant cry is not a simple response to its auditory qualities. Mothers report that their reaction depends on such factors as the time since the last feeding, whether the feeding was satisfactory, or whether they know that the infant has been having other difficulties that might be producing pain (pp. 130–131). In other words, the mother is using her head rather than responding mechanically as would a moth to a light. It is for reasons such as this that Parke (1978) called for more attention to the impact of parental cognitions, attitudes, and knowledge on the socialization process. At first glance this might appear to be a return to such unproductive efforts as the attempt to find correlations between parental attitudes and child behavior (Becker & Krug, 1965), but Kelman (1974) subsequently analyzed the many factors, including the nature of the situation (child behavior to which the parent is reacting, for example), that determine whether an attitude contributes to a behavior. Most of these factors were not indexed in the unsuccessful studies.

One other very important problem in these earlier unidirectional studies is that they confused the process by which a child acquires new behaviors with the end result. Techniques used by a parent to guide a child's behavior toward a goal may or may not be present in their interactions when the child has reached the goal. A mother may act as though her feelings are hurt, and express sympathy for a child who was the target of her child's transgressions, but may later use simple verbal approval when her now compliant child imitates her behavior on seeing the transgressions of others (see Roger Burton's example of the development of other behavior, p. 78). Most of the earlier studies of parental attitudes selected children who differed on certain behaviors (school achievement and social adjustment, for example) and then tested the differences between their parents' attitudes. Such research confused the process with the product. We cannot find out how parental attitudes affect a parent's socialization techniques unless we study the attitudes in the sequence of child behaviors and parent responses that lead to behavioral change.

Since parental cognitions, attitude, and knowledge are so important, the problem becomes how to include these factors so that we can detect their likely influence. The solution lies in the construction of theoretical models that accommodate the thinking parent and of research approaches that are dictated by the models rather than by expediency. One such model is available, an application of control theory involving feedback systems with homeostatic functions (pp. 65–67). The model is based on the position that parents do not have fixed child-rearing techniques that are used repetitively without regard to the child's

---

1. To simplify, in the remainder of the article, material that can be read in more detail in the book (Bell & Harper, 1977) is cited only by chapter or page numbers.

behavior. The model assumes that both parents and children have repertoires of hierarchically organized behaviors that are shown in predictable sequence, depending on the output of the other participant.

> Each participant in a parent–child interaction has upper and lower limits relative to the intensity, frequency, or situational appropriateness of behavior shown by the other. When the upper limit for one participant is reached, the reaction of the other is to redirect or reduce the excessive, inappropriate behavior (upper-limit control reaction). When the lower limit is reached, the reaction is to stimulate, prime, or in a variety of other ways to increase the insufficient or nonexistent behavior of the other (lower-limit control reaction). From the standpoint of the parent, upper-limit control behavior reduces and redirects child behavior that exceeds parental standards. Lower-limit control behavior primes and stimulates child behavior that is below parental standards. In other words, one very general principle about the activating power of children is that they contribute too much or too little or that they show some behaviors too early or too late in terms of parents' expectations. In a sense, then, the function of parent control behavior is to maintain child behavior within an optimal range. (p. 65)

The statement above uses intensity for illustration. Frequency, situational appropriateness, and other parameters could replace or work in combination with intensity. Attitudes and knowledge contribute to expectations and standards. Information processing is involved in receiving and classifying the behavior of the other participant, in comparing child behavior with standards or expectations, and in the selection of an appropriate response from the parental repertoire.

Research has yet to map parental and child repertoires in each major area of socialization, to measure knowledge and attitudes, to identify the connecting links between these, and to determine the manner in which behaviors are selected from those available. Again, Kelman (1974) provided a guide. Pretty complex? Of course. However, if we wish to capture the richness of reciprocal influences in ongoing behavior, our research must be able to encompass this degree of complexity.

Reciprocal Influences

The basic principle underlying reciprocal influences in development arising from parent–offspring interaction is that of a moving bidirectional system in which the responses of each participant serve not only as the stimuli for the other but also change as a result of the same stimulus exchanges, leading to the possibility of altered response on the part of the other.

A fascinating example from the comparative literature illustrates reciprocal influences as well as the reason why a major impetus for a changed perspective relative to the importance of child effects came from parallels between man and other mammals (chap. 3, pp. 7–11). Leon (1977) reported his own research and that of others concerned with an odorant released by female rats. These studies showed that pups induce a hormonal change that causes female rats to emit a chemical signal called a *pheromone*. Its release occurs at about the onset of locomotion in the pups and orients them to the mother's location. The release of the pheromone is then terminated by pup-induced hormonal changes at the time of weaning and the emergence of other behavioral indicators of the pup's increasing autonomy. The unraveling of this instructive series of events was based on several prior studies in which separate pup and parent effects were carefully isolated by different investigators before the overall sequence of reciprocal effects could be identified.

If we keep in mind that it is principles of exchange between parents and their young in which we are interested, not pheromones, and that it is going to be more difficult to establish the existence of such exchanges at the human level, it appears that we must do more than simply shift perspectives in order to identify reciprocal influences. We cannot climb by clichés. Nor does it seem likely that we can often achieve a complete synthesis in a single study, though complex multivariate studies may be able to gather most of the effective variables together after earlier, more limited studies have isolated causal effects. Demonstrated child effects are especially needed to complement and put into perspective findings from the preponderance of studies devoted for over 40 years to identifying parent effects. Far from producing an imbalance in the opposite direction, a concern expressed by Parke (1978), studies of child effects have not accumulated sufficiently in the last 10 years to supply the data needed as a base for understanding reciprocal influences. Without an adequate empirical base, advocacy of immediate commitment to studies of reciprocal influences (Parke, 1978) may be building castles in the air.

Implications for the Well-Being of Children

READING CUES FROM CHILDREN

Although attainment of any appreciable body of precise information on reciprocal influences is unlikely at present, there are many implications for the well-being of children that seem reasonable from the standpoint of the considerable literature that provided a base for the child-effects perspective. I have already referred to the research in the 1960s that documented the previously unrecognized skills of very young infants. At the outset, the repertoire appears to be remarkably well matched to that of the mother. Darwin's concept of the correlation of organisms appears to apply at the human level as well, though the human lock-and-key relationship is not as mechanical and inflexible as it seems to be in other species. For example, the young infant is specifically responsive to qualities of the human voice. In this and other areas of the infant's behavioral repertoire, however, wide individual differences exist, one particularly interesting area being the clarity of the infant's cue to its state. Some infants are more readable than others (chap. 6). Herein lies one very basic implication of the child-effects perspective. Parents will be more effective and the caregiving system will function more smoothly if close attention is paid to the signals that babies emit and to the variations on these shown by a particular infant. The same principle should apply to children and to the handicapped. Parents of blind children gain confidence and feel more effective after learning to interpret their children's hand movements (p. 194).

We associate the concept of the tabular rasa with John Locke but forget that he only intended it to mean that the infant does not start life with preformed ideas, such as that of original sin. He enjoined parents to pay close attention to congenital differences in order to adjust handling to their particular infant.

Reading cues in short-term sequences involving caregiving is only part of what Hunt (1966) has described as the "problem of the match," relative to training for cognitive development. Each action of a parent or other child trainer has the capability of changing not only the momentary behavior of the child but also its status, or "platform," from which further construction of cognitive structures will develop.

Thus, the child-effects perspective implies the need for parents to attend to the infant's or child's individual characteristics, its signals of momentary needs or readiness to respond, and its long-term changes that dictate general changes in parent functioning, as well as opportunities to stimulate growth to the next level. Enhancement of parent effectiveness by this kind of fine tuning could be expected, quite reasonably, to promote the well-being of the child.

So Small But So Powerful

One aspect of the infant's capabilities that has unique psychological impact on parents is the discrepancy between its size and its power. The power lies in the baby's ability to compel action by its eye-to-eye gaze, smiling, crying, appearing helpless, or thrashing. Few can resist the appeal to play residing in its positive

stimuli or the call for help when it is distressed. There are many indications that caregiving in the first two months is largely guided by signals from the infant (pp. 123–126). It has been remarked that a newborn is more competent than its mother, if this is her first baby.

The infant's characteristics are only an extreme form of similarly compelling features of childhood. One of the most surprising indications of the psychological power of infants and children comes from studies of child abuse (pp. 56–57). Parents who abused their child saw the child as the cause of the problem, mentioning annoying, persistent crying, unusual cry sounds, or other abrasive behaviors not shown by other children in the family. Putting together the fact that the pediatric records of abused children show more instances of low birth weight than would be expected statistically and that in some instances battered children have been further battered in successive foster homes, it appears that some deviant characteristics of the infant or young child have exaggerated the normal potency of the stimuli they emit. These stimuli constitute only one link in a chain of events involving stress on the family and personality characteristics of the abuser, but the fact that a small infant or child can induce an assault by a much larger individual, against all the sanctions of society, tells us something about the power of the young in normal child rearing, including their ability to resist and divert the socialization efforts of their parents.

Parents' commonsense impressions of the power residing in their tiny charges would be more compatible with the view that both they and their child determine the flow of events, that the direction of impetus for action passes back and forth. The parental role will always be complex and difficult, involving day-to-day problem solving yet also demanding progress toward long-term goals. Nonetheless, it could be a more reasonable role, more comfortable on a moment-to-moment basis, if the child-effects perspective begins to be expressed in the mass media.

Current Effects of Ideological Relics

As a parent-effects outlook becomes balanced by a child-effects view and, ultimately, as parents and scientists become accustomed to thinking in terms of reciprocal influences, two very extreme ideological positions on child rearing should lose force in favor of a middle ground. The two positions are highly discrepant with the realities of child rearing experienced by parents, thus yielding perplexity, confusion, and guilt. Better reading of cues and more appreciation of the unique power of children should reduce adherence to these extreme positions, which have shown functional autonomy over centuries (chap. 2).

Strangely enough, one of our major tasks is to counter movements initiated by defenders of children in earlier times.

We have already mentioned the view that parents are exclusively responsible for their children's current behavior and long-term outcome. If this ideological bogeyman appears to be made of straw, the reader should be reminded that the American parent has been exposed for several decades to overzealous extrapolations from both psychoanalytic theory and John B. Watson's radical behaviorism. The Watsonian view in effect picked up where John Locke's concept of the tabular rasa left off, informing parents that application of conditioning principles was faulty if it failed to produce a lawyer or a doctor. The popularized psychoanalytic view was that infantile trauma and socialization that suppressed biological urges (very largely created or transmitted by parents) cast shadows over the entire life span of the child. Currently, on the basis of child intervention research with disadvantaged families, even middle- or upper-middle-class parents are being told that their child's future intellectual development depends on what they do in the first three years of its life (White, 1975). All of these viewpoints make parents wary and unsure of themselves.

The other major ideological force emphasizes parental passivity. This stance derives from at least two sources. The earliest was in the efforts of progressive educators to counter the repressive 19th-century educational institutions that restricted freedom and spontaneity in children. Basing their reasoning on Rousseau's view of the innate goodness of people if unspoiled by corrupting influences, these educators espoused the notion that proper growth and maturation would be natural outcomes of a stimulating, supportive, and permissive environment for the child. In their view the role of the parent or educator was merely to provide such an environment while interfering as little as possible. The child was placed on a pedestal, a most uncomfortable location, as it eventually turned out. In a sense, the Gesellian writings on the inevitability of the maturation process complemented those of the educators. Recognition of the demand characteristics of the child's behavior was missing from both child-oriented positions, as was the recognition of complementary parental functions.

In humans and most other mammals, parents regulate the intensity and extensity of behavior so that adults can enjoy as well as tolerate and benefit from the activity of the young. Wariness or passivity does not support the intensity of commitment needed to engage children in a process of reciprocal interaction in which limits must be set and some lines of activity redirected. Friction and conflict characterize optimal child-rearing situations (Baumrind, 1973). Functions of guidance and control can be performed more readily by a parent who is not wary because of fear of long-

term consequences, or passive because of an uncritical acceptance of permissiveness as a superordinate system of child rearing. It is noteworthy that one of the few productive lines of research on the effects of parents on children has been Baumrind's (1973) demonstration of the importance of parental guidance and control versus permissiveness in relation to child competence.

The need to regulate the activity and intensity of child behavior is tragically represented in the excesses of the youth revolt of the 1960s. King (1969) commented on the basis of counseling college students during this period:

> One of the poignant notes we hear from adolescents today is that they have not had enough control, that parents have not taken a stand at the right times. Often they wish the father would say No; clearly, firmly, and with assurance about the reasons for No. They think parents have often been confused about child rearing and lack direction. (p. 8)

It once seemed most important to sensitize parents to the ways in which their child rearing could traumatize children, to the fact that children could develop quite differently in different environments, and to the growth capabilities within the child, but it may now be more important to offset the undesirable effects of these somewhat heroically exaggerated views and turn our attention to a less dramatic but no less important topic—the leadership and guidance required from parents.

The Contribution of the Young to Society

Up to this point in the article I have suggested some ways in which the well-being of children might result from increased recognition of child effects and reciprocal influences. That society will benefit in turn is obvious, but there is an interesting way in which this may occur, uncovered by Lawrence Harper (chap. 11) while reviewing the comparative literature for examples of effects of the young. In most mammals, the young play a key role in what might be called the adaptive radiation of species, because of their lack of caution and their intense interest in exploring new foods and habitats. Psychologists have long been aware that scientists and artists make some of their most creative and unique contributions to society when relatively young. What has not been appreciated is the generality of this phenomenon or its likely applicability to a much wider age range and to more commonplace behaviors. If we consider the novelty, interest, and excitement that are introduced into a family by a young child's exploration in the home, yard, and neighborhood, we have an example in early human ontogenesis. From the young of the 1960s came changes in hairstyles, dress, and patterns of social interaction that were adopted widely by adults. From the college student population came the impetus for a dramatic change in our foreign policy. If this capability for innovation is carefully nurtured and managed by parents, it becomes a vital force in the family, the larger society and, indeed, an essential national resource. Whether this force results in excesses or becomes destructive and self-defeating, however, may depend on whether parents are wary and passive rather than full participants in the social interaction system to which they must contribute guidance and control.

References

Baumrind, D. The development of instrumental competence through socialization. In A. Pick (Ed.), *Minnesota symposia on child psychology* (Vol. 7). Minneapolis: University of Minnesota Press, 1973.

Becker, W. C., & Krug, R. S. The Parent Attitude Research Instrument—A research review. *Child Development,* 1965, *36,* 329–365.

Bell, R. Q., & Harper, L. V. *The effect of children on parents.* Hillsdale, N.J.: Erlbaum, 1977.

Hunt, J. M. Toward a theory of guided learning in development. In R. H. Ojemann & K. Pritchett (Eds.), *Giving emphasis to guided learning.* Cleveland, Ohio: Educational Research Council, 1966.

Kelman, H. C. Attitudes are alive and well and gainfully employed in the sphere of action. *American Psychologist,* 1974, *29,* 310–324.

King, S. H. Youth in rebellion: An historical perspective. In S. Cohen & D. D. Swenson (Eds.), *Drug dependence.* Washington, D.C.: U.S. Government Printing Office, 1969.

Leon, M. Pheromonal mediation of maternal behavior. In T. Alloway, C. Pliner, & L. Kramer (Eds.), *Advances in the study of communication and affect: Vol. 3. Attachment behavior.* New York: Plenum Press, 1977.

Parke, R. Parent–infant interaction: Progress, paradigms, and problems. In G. Sackett (Ed.), *Observing behavior: Vol. 1. Theory and applications in mental retardation.* Baltimore, Md.: University Park Press, 1978.

White, B. L. *The first three years of life.* Englewood Cliffs, N.J.: Prentice-Hall, 1975.

Questions

1. What did early researchers find when they first studied parental influences on child development? Does this pattern surprise you? Why or why not?
2. What does Bell mean when he states that both parents and children have "repertoires of hierarchically organized behaviors that are shown in predictable sequence, depending on the output of the other participant?" Can you think of what such a repertoire might be like for a parent-child dyad that includes a child who has a very high activity level?
3. Why is it important to examine individual differences in infant and child behavior to understand reciprocal parent-child influences? In other words, what do individual differences reveal about the bi-directional nature of the parent-child relationship?
4. Imagine that there is a new trend in parenting that claims that the human brain is incredibly plastic and responsive to input and, therefore, parents can make their children into anything they want them to be. As a student of child development, would you support or contest this claim?
5. In contrast, imagine a trend that claims that children should be allowed to make and shape their own development and that the best thing parents can do for their children is stay out of their way. What would you say in response to this claim?
6. Parents who abuse their children often state that the child provoked the abuse. Although this article suggests that children play a role in their developmental experiences, it does not suggest that the roles and responsibilities of parents and children in this process are the same. Given what you have learned from this article, what would you say to someone who argues that abused children cause their own abuse?

4 Children of the Garden Island

Emmy E. Werner

Does exposure to problematic and stressful experiences early in life lead to the development of an unhealthy personality? Are some individuals more resilient than others when confronted by developmental difficulties, such as birth complications or poverty? These are difficult but important questions to answer. After all, many children face hardships, and it is valuable to know if such children can be helped to overcome these early challenges and go on to lead happy, meaningful lives. The stories of individuals who have done so may teach us how to help others who confront barriers to healthy development early in life.

The best technique available in developmental psychology for determining how early experiences relate to later development is the longitudinal research design, in which the same individuals are observed over time. A classic longitudinal study of the long-term effects of early developmental difficulties was conducted on the Hawaiian island of Kauai. This study took place over a 30-year period and involved a group of approximately 700 individuals. Researcher Emmy E. Werner found that a number of "high risk" children were resistant to the stresses they had undergone and had developed into healthy adults. Resilient children such as these challenge the traditional assumption that there is a simple and direct link between early experiences and later development. Werner describes this research and its intriguing findings in the following article.

This study is regarded as one of the most important longitudinal studies in the field of developmental psychology. It stands as a model of how to conduct research that truly studies the process of development— that is, changes in the same individual over time. It also provides an explanation of psychological development that emphasizes the important contributions of the child's own behaviors and the social context. Finally, it attests to the adaptability of the human organism to various circumstances of growth.

In 1955, 698 infants on the Hawaiian island of Kauai became participants in a 30-year study that has shown how some individuals triumph over physical disadvantages and deprived childhoods.

Kauai, the Garden Island, lies at the northwest end of the Hawaiian chain, 100 miles and a half-hour flight from Honolulu. Its 555 square miles encompass mountains, cliffs, canyons, rain forests and sandy beaches washed by pounding surf. The first Polynesians who crossed the Pacific to settle there in the eighth century were charmed by its beauty, as were the generations of sojourners who visited there after Captain James Cook "discovered" the island in 1778.

The 45,000 inhabitants of Kauai are for the most part descendants of immigrants from Southeast Asia and Europe who came to the island to work on the sugar plantations with the hope of finding a better life for their children. Thanks to the islanders' unique spirit of cooperation, my colleagues Jessie M. Bierman and Fern E. French of the University of California at Berkeley, Ruth S. Smith, a clinical psychologist on Kauai, and I have been able to carry out a longitudinal study on Kauai that has lasted for more than three decades. The study has had two principal goals: to assess the long-term consequences of prenatal and perinatal stress and to document the effects of adverse early rearing conditions on children's physical, cognitive and psychosocial development.

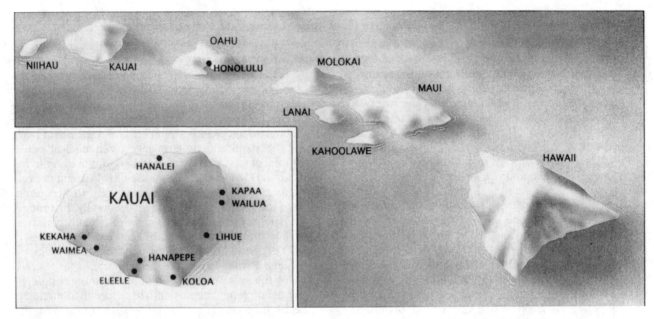

figure 1

Kauai, the Garden Island, lies at the northwest end of the Hawaiian archipelago. The towns that participated in the Kauai Longitudinal Study are shown in the inset. Lihue is the county seat; it is about 100 miles from Honolulu, the capital of Hawaii.

The Kauai Longitudinal Study began at a time when the systematic examination of the development of children exposed to biological and psychosocial risk factors was still a bit of a rarity. Investigators attempted to reconstruct the events that led to physical or psychological problems by studying the history of individuals in whom such problems had already surfaced. This retrospective approach can create the impression that the outcome is inevitable, since it takes into account only the "casualties," not the "survivors." We hoped to avoid that impression by monitoring the development of all the children born in a given period in an entire community.

We began our study in 1954 with an assessment of the reproductive histories of all the women in the community. Altogether 2,203 pregnancies were reported by the women of Kauai in 1954, 1955 and 1956; there were 240 fetal deaths and 1,963 live births. We chose to study the cohort of 698 infants born on Kauai in 1955, and we followed the development of these individuals at one, two, 10, 18 and 31 or 32 years of age. The majority of the individuals in the birth cohort—422 in all—were born without complications, following uneventful pregnancies, and grew up in supportive environments.

But as our study progressed we began to take a special interest in certain "high risk" children who, in spite of exposure to reproductive stress, discordant and impoverished home lives and uneducated, alcoholic or mentally disturbed parents, went on to develop healthy personalities, stable careers and strong interpersonal relations. We decided to try to identify the protective factors that contributed to the resilience of these children.

Finding a community that is willing or able to cooperate in such an effort is not an easy task. We chose Kauai for a number of reasons, not the least of which was the receptivity of the island population to our endeavors. Coverage by medical, public-health, educational and social services on the island was comparable to what one would find in communities of similar size on the U.S. mainland at that time. Furthermore, our study would take into account a variety of cultural influences on childbearing and child rearing, since the population of Kauai includes individuals of Japanese, Philipino, Portuguese, Chinese, Korean and northern European as well as of Hawaiian descent.

We also thought the population's low mobility would make it easier to keep track of the study's participants and their families. The promise of a stable sample proved to be justified. At the time of the two-year follow-up, 96 percent of the living children were still on Kauai and available for study. We were able to find 90 percent of the children who were still alive for the 10-year follow-up, and for the 18-year follow-up we found 88 percent of the cohort.

In order to elicit the cooperation of the island's residents, we needed to get to know them and to introduce our study as well. In doing so we relied on the skills of a number of dedicated professionals from the

University of California's Berkeley and Davis campuses, from the University of Hawaii and from the island of Kauai itself. At the beginning of the study five nurses and one social worker, all residents of Kauai, took a census of all households on the island, listing the occupants of each dwelling and recording demographic information, including a reproductive history of all women 12 years old or older. The interviewers asked the women if they were pregnant; if a woman was not, a card with a postage-free envelope was left with the request that she mail it to the Kauai Department of Health as soon as she thought she was pregnant.

Local physicians were asked to submit a monthly list of the women who were coming to them for prenatal care. Community organizers spoke to women's groups, church gatherings, the county medical society and community leaders. The visits by the census takers were backed up with letters, and milk cartons were delivered with a printed message urging mothers to cooperate. We advertised in newspapers, organized radio talks, gave slide shows and distributed posters.

Public-health nurses interviewed the pregnant women who joined our study in each trimester of pregnancy, noting any exposure to physical or emotional trauma. Physicians monitored any complications during the prenatal period, labor, delivery and the neonatal period. Nurses and social workers interviewed the mothers in the postpartum period and when the children were one and 10 years old; the interactions between parents and offspring in the home were also observed. Pediatricians and psychologists independently examined the children at two and 10 years of age, assessing their physical, intellectual and social development and noting any handicaps or behavior problems. Teachers evaluated the children's academic progress and their behavior in the classroom.

From the outset of the study we recorded information about the material, intellectual and emotional aspects of the family environment, including stressful life events that resulted in discord or disruption of the family unit. With the parents' permission we also were given access to the records of public-health, educational and social-service agencies and to the files of the local police and the family court. My collaborators and I also administered a wide range of aptitude, achievement and personality tests in the elementary grades and in high school. Last but not least, we gained the perspectives of the young people themselves by interviewing them at the age of 18 and then again when they were in their early 30's.

Of the 698 children in the 1955 cohort, 69 were exposed to moderate prenatal or perinatal stress, that is, complications during pregnancy, labor or delivery. About 3 percent of the cohort—23 individuals in all—suffered severe prenatal or perinatal stress; only 14 infants in this group lived to the age of two. Indeed, nine of the 12 children in our study who died before reaching two years of age had suffered severe perinatal complications.

Some of the surviving children became "casualties" of a kind in the next two decades of life. One out of every six children (116 children in all) had physical or intellectual handicaps of perinatal or neonatal origin that were diagnosed between birth and the age of two and that required long-term specialized medical, educational or custodial care. About one out of every five children (142 in all) developed serious learning or behavior problems in the first decade of life that required more than six months of remedial work. By the time the children were 10 years old, twice as many children needed some form of mental-health service or remedial education (usually for problems associated with reading) as were in need of medical care.

By the age of 18, 15 percent of the young people had delinquency records and 10 percent had mental health problems requiring either in- or outpatient care. There was some overlap among these groups. By the time they were 10, all 25 of the children with long-term mental-health problems had learning problems as well. Of the 70 children who had mental health problems at 18, 15 also had a record of repeated delinquencies.

As we followed these children from birth to the age of 18 we noted two trends: the impact of reproductive stress diminished with time, and the developmental outcome of virtually every biological risk condition was dependent on the quality of the rearing environment. We did find some correlation between moderate to severe degrees of perinatal trauma and major physical handicaps of the central nervous system and of the musculo-skeletal and sensory systems; perinatal trauma was also correlated with mental retardation, serious learning disabilities and chronic mental-health problems such as schizophrenia that arose in late adolescence and young adulthood.

But overall rearing conditions were more powerful determinants of outcome than perinatal trauma. The better the quality of the home environment was, the more competence the children displayed. This could already be seen when the children were just two years old: toddlers who had experienced severe perinatal stress but lived in middle-class homes or in stable family settings did nearly as well on developmental tests of sensory-motor and verbal skills as toddlers who had experienced no such stress.

Prenatal and perinatal complications were consistently related to impairment of physical and psychological development at the ages of 10 and 18 only when they were combined with chronic poverty, family discord, parental mental illness or other persistently poor rearing conditions. Children who were raised in middle-class homes, in a stable family envi-

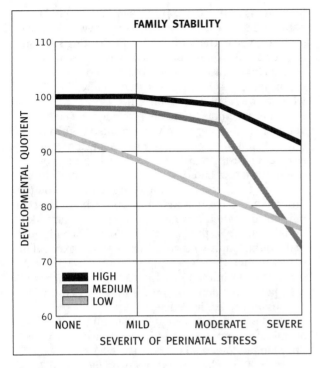

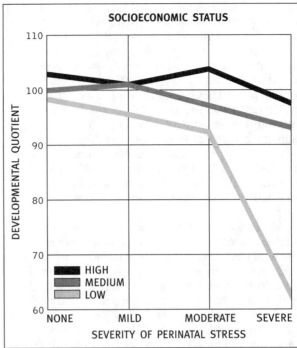

figure 2

Influence of environmental factors such as family stability (left) or socioeconomic status (right) appears in infancy. The "developmental quotients" derived from tests given at 20 months show that the rearing environment can buffer or worsen the stress of perinatal complications. Children who had suffered severe perinatal stress but lived in stable, middle-class families scored as well as or better than children in poor, unstable households who had not experienced such stress.

ronment and by a mother who had finished high school showed few if any lasting effects of reproductive stress later in their lives.

How many children could count on such a favorable environment? A sizable minority could not. We designated 201 individuals—30 percent of the surviving children in this study population—as being high-risk children because they had experienced moderate to severe perinatal stress, grew up in chronic poverty, were reared by parents with no more than eight grades of formal education or lived in a family environment troubled by discord, divorce, parental alcoholism or mental illness. We termed the children "vulnerable" if they encountered four or more such risk factors before their second birthday. And indeed, two-thirds of these children (129 in all) did develop serious learning or behavior problems by the age of 10 or had delinquency records, mental-health problems or pregnancies by the time they were 18.

Yet one out of three of these high-risk children—72 individuals altogether—grew into competent young adults who loved well, worked well and played well. None developed serious learning or behavior problems in childhood or adolescence. As far as we could tell from interviews and from their record in the com-

munity, they succeeded in school, managed home and social life well and set realistic educational and vocational goals and expectations for themselves when they finished high school. By the end of their second decade of life they had developed into competent, confident and caring people who expressed a strong desire to take advantage of whatever opportunity came their way to improve themselves.

They were children such as Michael, a boy for whom the odds on paper did not seem very promising. The son of teen-age parents, Michael was born prematurely, weighing four pounds five ounces. He spent his first three weeks of life in a hospital, separated from his mother. Immediately after his birth his father was sent with the U.S. Army to Southeast Asia, where he remained for two years. By the time Michael was eight years old he had three siblings and his parents were divorced. His mother had deserted the family and had no further contact with her children. His father raised Michael and his siblings with the help of their aging grandparents.

Then there was Mary, born after 20 hours of labor to an overweight mother who had experienced several miscarriages before that pregnancy. Her father was an unskilled farm laborer with four years of formal education. Between Mary's fifth and 10th birthdays her mother was hospitalized several times for repeated bouts of mental illness, after having inflicted both physical and emotional abuse on her daughter.

Surprisingly, by the age of 18 both Michael and Mary were individuals with high self-esteem and sound values who cared about others and were liked by their peers. They were successful in school and looked forward to the future. We looked back at the lives of these two youngsters and the 70 other resilient individuals who had triumphed over their circumstances and compared their behavioral characteristics and the features of their environment with those of the other high-risk youths who developed serious and persistent problems in childhood and adolescence.

We identified a number of protective factors in the families, outside the family circle and within the resilient children themselves that enabled them to resist stress. Some sources of resilience seem to be constitutional: resilient children such as Mary and Michael tend to have characteristics of temperament that elicit positive responses from family members and strangers alike. We noted these same qualities in adulthood. They include a fairly high activity level, a low degree of excitability and distress and a high degree of sociability. Even as infants the resilient individuals were described by their parents as "active," "affectionate," "cuddly," "easygoing" and "even tempered." They had no eating or sleeping habits that were distressing to those who took care of them.

The pediatricians and psychologists who examined the resilient children at 20 months noted their alertness and responsiveness, their vigorous play and their tendency to seek out novel experiences and to ask for help when they needed it. When they entered elementary school, their classroom teachers observed their ability to concentrate on their assignments and noted their problem-solving and reading skills. Although they were not particularly gifted, these children used whatever talents they had effectively. Usually they had a special hobby they could share with a friend. These interests were not narrowly sex-typed; we found that girls and boys alike excelled at such activities as fishing, swimming, horseback riding and hula dancing.

We could also identify environmental factors that contributed to these children's ability to withstand stress. The resilient youngsters tended to come from families having four or fewer children, with a space of two years or more between themselves and the next sibling. In spite of poverty, family discord or parental mental illness, they had the opportunity to establish a close bond with at least one caretaker from whom they received positive attention during the first years of life.

The nurturing might come from substitute parents within the family (such as grandparents, older siblings, aunts or uncles) or from the ranks of regular baby-sitters. As the resilient children grew older they seemed to be particularly adept at recruiting such surrogate parents when a biological parent was unavailable (as in the case of an absent father) or incapacitated (as in the case of a mentally ill mother who was frequently hospitalized).

Maternal employment and the need to take care of younger siblings apparently contributed to the pronounced autonomy and sense of responsibility noted among the resilient girls, particularly in households where the father had died or was permanently absent because of desertion or divorce. Resilient boys, on the other hand, were often first-born sons who did not have to share their parents' attention with many additional children in the household. They also had some male in the family who could serve as a role model (if not the father, then a grandfather or an uncle). Structure and rules in the household and assigned chores were part of the daily routine for these boys during childhood and adolescence.

Resilient children also seemed to find a great deal of emotional support outside their immediate family. They tended to be well liked by their classmates and had at least one close friend, and usually several. They relied on an informal network of neighbors, peers and elders for counsel and support in times of crisis and transition. They seem to have made school a home away from home, a refuge from a disordered household. When we interviewed them at 18, many resilient youths mentioned a favorite teacher who had become a role model, friend and confidant and was particularly supportive at times when their own family was beset by discord or threatened with dissolution.

For others, emotional support came from a church group, a youth leader in the YMCA or YWCA or a favorite minister. Participation in extracurricular activities—such as 4-H, the school band or a cheerleading team which allowed them to be part of a cooperative enterprise—was also an important source of emotional support for those children who succeeded against the odds.

With the help of these support networks, the resilient children developed a sense of meaning in their lives and a belief that they could control their fate. Their experience in effectively coping with and mastering stressful life events built an attitude of hopefulness that contrasted starkly with the feelings of helplessness and futility that were expressed by their troubled peers.

In 1985, 12 years after the 1955 birth cohort had finished high school, we embarked on a search for the members of our study group. We managed to find 545 individuals—80 percent of the cohort—through parents or other relatives, friends, former classmates, local telephone books, city directories and circuit-court, voter-registration and motor-vehicle registration records and marriage certificates filed with the State Department of Health in Honolulu. Most of the young men and women still lived on Kauai, but 10 percent had moved to other islands and 10 percent lived on the mainland; 2 percent had gone abroad.

We found 62 of the 72 young people we had characterized as "resilient" at the age of 18. They had finished high school at the height of the energy crisis and joined the work force during the worst U.S. recession since the Great Depression. Yet these 30-year-old men and women seemed to be handling the demands of adulthood well. Three out of four (46 individuals) had received some college education and were satisfied with their performance in school. All but four worked full time, and three out of four said they were satisfied with their jobs.

Indeed, compared with their low-risk peers from the same cohort, a significantly higher proportion of high-risk resilient individuals described themselves as being happy with their current life circumstances (44 percent versus 10 percent). The resilient men and women did, however, report a significantly higher number of health problems than their peers in low-risk comparison groups (46 percent versus 15 percent). The men's problems seemed to be brought on by stress: back problems, dizziness and fainting spells, weight gain and ulcers. Women's health problems were largely related to pregnancy and childbirth. And although 82 percent of the women were married, only 48 percent of the men were. Those who were married had strong commitments to intimacy and sharing with their partners and children. Personal competence and determination, support from a spouse or mate, and a strong religious faith were the shared qualities that we found characterized resilient children as adults.

We were also pleasantly surprised to find that many high-risk children who had problems in their teens were able to rebound in their twenties and early thirties. We were able to contact 26 (90 percent) of the teen-age mothers, 56 (80 percent) of the individuals with mental-health problems and 74 (75 percent) of the former delinquents who were still alive at the age of 30.

Almost all the teen-age mothers we interviewed were better off in their early thirties than they had been at 18. About 60 percent (16 individuals) had gone on to additional schooling and about 90 percent (24 individuals) were employed. Of the delinquent youths, three-fourths (56 individuals) managed to avoid arrest on reaching adulthood. Only a minority (12 individuals) of the troubled youths were still in need of mental-health services in their early thirties. Among the critical turning points in the lives of these individuals were entry into military service, marriage, parenthood and active participation in a church group. In adulthood, as in their youth, most of these individuals relied on informal rather than formal sources of support: kith and kin rather than mental-health professionals and social-service agencies.

Our findings appear to provide a more hopeful perspective than can be had from reading the extensive literature on "problem" children that come to the attention of therapists, special educators and social-service agencies. Risk factors and stressful environments do not inevitably lead to poor adaptation. It seems clear that, at each stage in an individual's development from birth to maturity, there is a shifting balance between stressful events that heighten vulnerability and protective factors that enhance resilience.

As long as the balance between stressful life events and protective factors is favorable, successful adaptation is possible. When stressful events outweigh the protective factors, however, even the most resilient child can have problems. It may be possible to shift the balance from vulnerability to resilience through intervention, either by decreasing exposure to risk factors or stressful events or by increasing the number of protective factors and sources of support that are available.

It seems clear from our identification of risk and protective factors that some of the most critical determinants of outcome are present when a child is very young. And it is obvious that there are large individual differences among high-risk children in their responses to both negative and positive circumstances in their caregiving environment. The very fact of individual variation among children who live in adverse conditions suggests the need for greater assistance to some than to others.

If early intervention cannot be extended to every child at risk, priorities must be established for choosing who should receive help. Early-intervention programs need to focus on infants and young children who appear most vulnerable because they lack—permanently or temporarily—some of the essential social bonds that appear to buffer stress. Such children may be survivors of neonatal intensive care, hospitalized children who are separated from their families for extended periods of time, the young offspring of addicted or mentally ill parents, infants and toddlers whose mothers work full time and do not have access to stable child care, the babies of single or teen-age parents who have no other adult in the household and migrant and refugee children without permanent roots in a community.

Assessment and diagnosis, the initial steps in any early intervention, need to focus not only on the risk factors in the lives of the children but also on the protective factors. These include competencies and informal sources of support that already exist and that can be utilized to enlarge a young child's communication and problem-solving skills and to enhance his or her self-esteem. Our research on resilient children has shown that other people in a child's life—grandparents, older siblings, day-care providers or teachers—can play a supportive role if a parent is incapacitated or unavailable. In many situations it might make better sense and be less costly as well to strengthen such available informal ties to kin and community than it would to introduce additional layers of bureaucracy into delivery of services.

Finally, in order for any intervention program to be effective, a young child needs enough consistent nurturing to trust in its availability. The resilient children in our study had at least one person in their lives who accepted them unconditionally, regardless of temperamental idiosyncrasies or physical or mental handicaps. All children can be helped to become more resilient if adults in their lives encourage their independence, teach them appropriate communication and self-help skills and model as well as reward acts of helpfulness and caring.

Thanks to the efforts of many people, several community-action and educational programs for high-risk children have been established on Kauai since our study began. Partly as a result of our findings, the legislature of the State of Hawaii has funded special mental-health teams to provide services for troubled children and youths. In addition the State Health Department established the

Kauai Children's Services, a coordinated effort to provide services related to child development, disabilities, mental retardation and rehabilitation in a single facility.

The evaluation of such intervention programs can in turn illuminate the process by which a chain of protective factors is forged that affords vulnerable children an escape from adversity. The life stories of the resilient individuals on the Garden Island have taught us that competence, confidence and caring can flourish even under adverse circumstances if young children encounter people in their lives who provide them with a secure basis for the development of trust, autonomy and initiative.

FURTHER READING

Kauai's Children Come of Age. Emmy E. Werner and Ruth S. Smith. The University of Hawaii Press, 1977.

Vulnerable But Invincible: A Longitudinal Study of Resilient Children and Youth. Emmy E. Werner and Ruth S. Smith. McGraw-Hill Book Company, 1982.

Longitudinal Studies in Child Psychology and Psychiatry: Practical Lessons from Research Experience. Edited by A. R. Nichol. John Wiley & Sons, Inc., 1985.

High Risk Children in Young Adulthood: A Longitudinal Study from Birth to 32 Years. Emmy E. Werner in *American Journal of Orthopsychiatry,* Vol. 59, No. 1, pages 72–81; January, 1989.

Questions

1. Does this article focus too much on the importance of nurture in development? Can the ill effects of early adverse events really be reversed?
2. In this research, did all the high-risk children who had problems in their teens end up with difficulties in adulthood? Why or why not?
3. What gender differences were found in this research, and how can they be explained?
4. What do these findings suggest about the long-term prognosis for children and adolescents who are identified as high risk?
5. Do you think that intervention programs for children or adolescents who are at risk are worthwhile? What ingredients should they have?
6. Could something about the culture on the island of Kauai have contributed to the results of this study, or do you think they would have been the same in any cultural setting?

5

Development and Learning

Jean Piaget

Jean Piaget was one of the twentieth century's most influential thinkers on the topic of child development. Although Piaget was not trained as a psychologist, his life's work was devoted to the study of cognitive development. A number of intellectual influences contributed to Piaget's theory of cognitive development; chief among them were biology and philosophy. From biology, Piaget drew on ideas in evolutionary theory, such as organization and adaptation. From philosophy, Piaget relied mainly on the areas of logic and epistemology, which is concerned with the nature of human knowledge. From these two interests, Piaget carved out a new area of study called genetic epistemology, which focuses on the genesis, or origins, of logical thinking.

Piaget developed a theory of cognitive development in which he held that the child's thinking proceeds through four qualitatively distinct stages, beginning in infancy and concluding when biological maturity is reached in adolescence. For Piaget, cognitive development is the process by which the child's understanding of the world becomes increasingly adapted to the world. Like most psychologists who study cognitive development, Piaget considered learning a critical part of this process. However, for a child to learn, Piaget argued, he or she must be able to understand the information that is presented. In other words, the child needs to be at a stage of development that allows him or her to process this new information. Thus, Piaget believed that the child's current stage of development regulates the learning that can occur in a given situation. This view is described in the following article, which is based on a lecture that Piaget gave in the United States in 1961.

Before you read this article, several things are important to note. First, Piaget did not write like a modern psychologist. Recall that his intellectual influences included philosophy and biology in addition to psychology. Second, Piaget relied on forms of explanation that are rare in contemporary psychology, such as thought demonstrations. Third, Piaget introduced many new concepts, such as *operation* and *equilibration,* both of which are discussed in this article.

In his attempt to explain the development of the human mind, Piaget proposed one of the few grand theories in the field of psychology. Piaget's thinking remains influential in developmental psychology, although many aspects of his theory have been challenged.

In his opening remarks Piaget makes a distinction between development and learning—development being a spontaneous process tied to embryogenesis, learning being provoked by external situations. He proceeds to discuss the concept of an operation as an interiorized action linked to other operations in a structure. Four stages of development are enumerated—sensori-motor, pre-operational, concrete operations, and formal operations. Factors explaining the development of one structure of operations from another are discussed— maturation, experience, social transmission, and equilibration. Equilibration is defended as the most fundamental factor. Commenting on the inadequacy of the stimulus-response approach to understanding learning, Piaget presents evidence negating the effectiveness of external reinforcement in hastening the development of operational structures. These operational structures can be learned only if one bases the learning

This article was reprinted with permission from R. E. Ripple (ed. with V.N. Rockcastle) from *Piaget Rediscovered,* 1964 and 1972, pp. 7–20.

on simpler, more elementary structures—only if there is a natural relationship and development of structures. The learning of these structures is held to follow the same basic laws as does their natural development, i.e., learning is subordinated to development. Piaget concludes that the fundamental relation involved in development and learning is assimilation, not association.

My dear colleagues, I am very concerned about what to say to you, because I don't know if I shall accomplish the end that has been assigned to me. But I've been told that the important thing is not what you say, but the discussion which follows, and the answers to questions you are asked. So this morning I shall simply give a general introduction of a few ideas which seem to me to be important for the subject of this conference.

First I would like to make clear the difference between two problems: the problem of *development* in general, and the problem of *learning.* I think these problems are very different, although some people do not make this distinction.

The development of knowledge is a spontaneous process, tied to the whole process of embryogenesis. Embryogenesis concerns the development of the body, but it concerns as well the development of the nervous system, and the development of mental functions. In the case of the development of knowledge in children, embryogenesis ends only in adulthood. It is a total developmental process which we must resituate in its general biological and psychological context. In other words, development is a process which concerns the totality of the structures of knowledge.

Learning presents the opposite case. In general, learning is provoked by situations—provoked by a psychological experimenter; or by a teacher, with respect to some didactic point; or by an external situation. It is provoked, in general, as opposed to spontaneous. In addition, it is a limited process—limited to a single problem, or to a single structure.

So I think that development explains learning, and this opinion is contrary to the widely held opinion that development is a sum of discrete learning experiences. For some psychologists development is reduced to a series of specific learned items, and development is thus the sum, the cumulation of this series of specific items. I think this is an atomistic view which deforms the real state of things. In reality, development is the essential process and each element of learning occurs as a function of total development, rather than being an element which explains development. I shall begin, then, with a first part dealing with development, and I shall talk about learning in the second part.

To understand the development of knowledge, we must start with an idea which seems central to me— the idea of an *operation.* Knowledge is not a copy of reality. To know an object, to know an event, is not simply to look at it and make a mental copy, or image, of it. To know an object is to act on it. To know is to modify, to transform the object, and to understand the process of this transformation, and as a consequence to understand the way the object is constructed. An operation is thus the essence of knowledge; it is an interiorised action which modifies the object of knowledge. For instance, an operation would consist of joining objects in a class, to construct a classification. Or an operation would consist of ordering, or putting things in a series. Or an operation would consist of counting, or of measuring. In other words, it is a set of actions modifying the object, and enabling the knower to get at the structures of the transformation.

An operation is an interiorised action. But in addition, it is a reversible action; that is, it can take place in both directions, for instance, adding or subtracting, joining or separating. So it is a particular type of action which makes up logical structures.

Above all, an operation is never isolated. It is always linked to other operations, and as a result it is always a part of a total structure. For instance, a logical class does not exist in isolation; what exists is the total structure of classification. An asymmetrical relation does not exist in isolation. Seriation is the natural, basic operational structure. A number does not exist in isolation. What exists is the series of numbers, which constitute a structure, an exceedingly rich structure whose various properties have been revealed by mathematicians.

These operational structures are what seem to me to constitute the basis of knowledge, the natural psychological reality, in terms of which we must understand the development of knowledge. And the central problem of development is to understand the formation, elaboration, organization, and functioning of these structures.

I should like to review the stages of development of these structures, not in any detail, but simply as a reminder. I shall distinguish four main stages. The first is a sensory-motor, pre-verbal stage, lasting approximately the first 18 months of life. During this stage is developed the practical knowledge which constitutes the substructure of later representational knowledge. An example is the construction of the schema of the permanent object. For an infant, during the first months, an object has no permanence. When it disappears from the perceptual field it no longer exists. No attempt is made to find it again. Later, the infant will try to find it, and he will find it by localizing it spatially. Consequently, along with the construction of the permanent object there comes the construction of practical, or sensory-motor, space. There is similarly the construction of temporal succession, and of elementary sensory-motor causality. In other words, there is a series of structures which are indispensable for the structures of later representational thought.

In a second stage, we have pre-operational representation—the beginnings of language, of the symbolic function, and therefore of thought, or representation. But at the level of representational thought, there must now be a reconstruction of all that was developed on the sensory-motor level. That is, the sensory-motor actions are not immediately translated into operations. In fact, during all this second period of pre-operational representations, there are as yet no operations as I defined this term a moment ago. Specifically, there is as yet no conservation which is the psychological criterion of the presence of reversible operations. For example, if we pour liquid from one glass to another of a different shape, the pre-operational child will think there is more in one than in the other. In the absence of operational reversibility, there is no conservation of quantity.

In a third stage the first operations appear, but I call these concrete operations because they operate on objects, and not yet on verbally expressed hypotheses. For example, there are the operations of classification, ordering, the construction of the idea of number, spatial and temporal operations, and all the fundamental operations of elementary logic of classes and relations, of elementary mathematics, of elementary geometry and even of elementary physics.

Finally, in the fourth stage, these operations are surpassed as the child reaches the level of what I call formal or hypothetic-deductive operations; that is, he can now reason on hypotheses, and not only on objects. He constructs new operations, operations of propositional logic, and not simply the operations of classes, relations, and numbers. He attains new structures which are on the one hand combinatorial, corresponding to what mathematicians call lattices; on the other hand, more complicated group structures. At the level of concrete operations, the operations apply within an immediate neighborhood: for instance, classification by successive inclusions. At the level of the combinatorial, however, the groups are much more mobile. These, then, are the four stages which we identify, whose formation we shall now attempt to explain.

What factors can be called upon to explain the development from one set of structures to another? It seems to me that there are four main factors: first of all, *maturation,* in the sense of Gesell, since this development is a continuation of the embryogenesis; second, the role of *experience* of the effects of the physical environment on the structures of intelligence; third, *social transmission* in the broad sense (linguistic transmission, education, etc.); and fourth, a factor which is too often neglected but one which seems to me fundamental and even the principal factor. I shall call this the factor of *equilibration* or if you prefer it, of *self-regulation.*

Let us start with the first factor, maturation. One might think that these stages are simply a reflection of an interior maturation of the nervous system, following the hypotheses of Gesell, for example. Well, maturation certainly does play an indispensable role and must not be ignored. It certainly takes part in every transformation that takes place during a child's development. However, this first factor is insufficient in itself. First of all, we know practically nothing about the maturation of the nervous system beyond the first months of the child's existence. We know a little bit about it during the first two years but we know very little following this time. But above all, maturation doesn't explain everything, because the average ages at which these stages appear (the average chronological ages) vary a great deal from one society to another. The ordering of these stages is constant and has been found in all the societies studied. It has been found in various countries where psychologists in universities have redone the experiments but it has also been found in African peoples for example, in the children of the Bushmen, and in Iran, both in the villages and in the cities. However, although the order of succession is constant, the chronological ages of these stages vary a great deal. For instance, the ages which we have found in Geneva are not necessarily the ages which you would find in the United States. In Iran, furthermore, in the city of Teheran, they found approximately the same ages as we found in Geneva, but there is a systematic delay of two years in the children in the country. Canadian psychologists who redid our experiments, Monique Laurendeau and Father Adrien Pinard, found once again about the same ages in Montreal. But when they redid the experiments in Martinique, they found a delay of four years in all the experiments and this in spite of the fact that the children in Martinique go to a school set up according to the French system and the French curriculum and attain at the end of this elementary school a certificate of higher primary education. There is then a delay of four years, that is, there are the same stages, but systematically delayed. So you see that these age variations show that maturation does not explain everything.

I shall go on now to the role played by experience. Experience of objects, of physical reality, is obviously a basic factor in the development of cognitive structures. But once again this factor does not explain everything. I can give two reasons for this. The first reason is that some of the concepts which appear at the beginning of the stage of concrete operations are such that I cannot see how they could be drawn from experience. As an example, let us take the conservation of the substance in the case of changing the shape of a ball of plasticene. We give this ball of plasticene to a child who changes its shape into a sausage form and we ask him if there is the same amount of matter, that is, the same amount of substance as there was before. We also ask him if it now has the same weight and thirdly if it now has the same volume. The volume is measured by the displacement of water when we put the ball or the sausage into a glass of water. The findings, which have been the same every time this experiment has been done, show us that first of all there is conservation of the amount of substance. At about eight years old a child will say, "There is the same amount of plasticene." Only later does the child assert that the weight is conserved and still later that the volume is conserved. So I would ask you where the idea of the conservation of substance can come from. What is a constant and invariant substance when it doesn't yet have a constant weight or a constant volume? Through perception you can get at the weight of the ball or the volume of the ball but perception cannot give you an idea of the amount of substance. No experiment, no experience, can show the child that there is the same amount of substance. He can weigh the ball and that would lead to the conservation of weight. He can immerse it in water and that would lead to the conservation of volume. But the notion of substance is attained before either weight or volume. This conservation of substance is simply a logical necessity. The child now understands that when there is a transformation something must be conserved because by reversing the transformation you can come back to the point of departure and once again have the ball. He knows that something is conserved but he doesn't know what. It is not yet the weight, it is not yet the volume; it is simply a logical form—a logical necessity. There, it seems to me, is an example of a progress in knowledge, a logical necessity for something to be conserved even though no experience can have led to this notion.

My second objection to the sufficiency of experience as an explanatory factor is that this notion of experience is a very equivocal one. There are, in fact, two kinds of experience which are psychologically very different and this difference is very important from the pedagogical point of view. It is because of the pedagogical that I emphasize this distinction. First of all, there is what I shall call physical experience, and secondly, what I shall call logical-mathematical experience.

Physical experience consists of acting upon objects and drawing some knowledge about the objects by abstraction from the objects. For example, to discover that this pipe is heavier than this watch, the child will weigh them both and find the difference in the objects themselves. This is experience in the usual sense of the term—in the sense used by empiricists. But there is a second type of experience which I shall call logical-mathematical experience where the knowledge is not drawn from the objects, but it is drawn by the actions effected upon the objects. This is

not the same thing. When one acts upon objects, the objects are indeed there, but there is also the set of actions which modify the objects.

I shall give you an example of this type of experience. It is a nice example because we have verified it many times in small children under seven years of age, but it is also an example which one of my mathematician friends has related to me about his own childhood, and he dates his mathematical career from this experience. When he was four or five years old—I don't know exactly how old, but a small child—he was seated on the ground in his garden and he was counting pebbles. Now to count these pebbles he put them in a row and he counted them one, two, three, up to ten. Then he finished counting them and started to count them in the other direction. He began by the end and once again he found ten. He found this marvelous that there were ten in one direction and ten in the other direction. So he put them in a circle and counted them that way and found ten once again. Then he counted them in the other direction and found ten once more. So he put them in some other direction and found ten once more. So he put them in some other arrangement and kept counting them and kept finding ten. There was the discovery that he made.

Now what indeed did he discover? He did not discover a property of pebbles; he discovered a property of the action of ordering. The pebbles had no order. It was his action which introduced a linear order or a cyclical order, or any kind of an order. He discovered that the sum was independent of the order. The order was the action which he introduced among the pebbles. For the sum the same principle applied. The pebbles had no sum; they were simply in a pile. To make a sum, action was necessary—the operation of putting together and counting. He found that the sum was independent of the order, in other words, that the action of putting together is independent of the action of ordering. He discovered a property of actions and not a property of pebbles. You may say that it is in the nature of pebbles to let this be done to them and this is true. But it could have been drops of water, and drops of water would not have let this be done to them because two drops of water and two drops of water do not make four drops of water as you know very well. Drops of water then would not let this be done to them, we agree to that.

So it is not the physical property of pebbles which the experience uncovered. It is the properties of the actions carried out on the pebbles and this is quite another form of experience. It is the point of departure of mathematical deduction. The subsequent deduction will consist of interiorizing these actions and then of combining them without needing any pebbles. The mathematician no longer needs his pebbles. He can combine his operations simply with symbols and the point of departure of this mathematical deduction is logical-mathematical experience and this is not at all experience in the sense of the empiricists. It is the beginning of the coordination of actions, but this coordination of actions before the stage of operations needs to be supported by concrete material. Later, this coordination of actions leads to the logical-mathematical structures. I believe that logic is not a derivative of language. The source of logic is much more profound. It is the total coordination of actions, actions of joining things together, or ordering things, etc. This is what logical-mathematical experience is. It is an experience of the actions of the subject, and not an experience of objects themselves. It is an experience which is necessary before there can be operations. Once the operations have been attained this experience is no longer needed and the coordinations of actions can take place by themselves in the form of deduction and construction for abstract structures.

The third factor is social transmission—linguistic transmission or educational transmission. This factor, once again, is fundamental. I do not deny the role of any one of these factors; they all play a part. But this factor is insufficient because the child can receive valuable information via language or via education directed by an adult only if he is in a state where he can understand this information. That is, to receive the information he must have a structure which enables him to assimilate this information. This is why you cannot teach higher mathematics to a five-year-old. He does not yet have structures which enable him to understand.

I shall take a much simpler example, an example of linguistic transmission. As my very first work in the realm of child psychology, I spent a long time studying the relation between a part and a whole in concrete experience and in language. For example, I used Burt's test employing the sentence, "Some of my flowers are buttercups." The child knows that all buttercups are yellow, so there are three possible conclusions: the whole bouquet is yellow, or part of the bouquet is yellow, or none of the flowers in the bouquet is yellow. I found that up until nine years of age (and this was in Paris, so the children certainly did understand the French language) they replied, "The whole bouquet is yellow or some of my flowers are yellow." Both of those mean the same thing. They did not understand the expression, "some *of* my flowers." They did not understand this *of* as a partitive genitive, as the inclusion of some flowers in my flowers. They understood some of my flowers to be my several flowers as if the several flowers and the flowers were confused as one and the same class. So there you have children who until nine years of age heard every day a linguistic structure which implied the inclusion of a subclass in a class and yet did not understand this structure. It is only when they themselves are in firm possession of this logical structure, when they have

constructed it for themselves according to the developmental laws which we shall discuss, that they succeed in understanding correctly the linguistic expression.

I come now to the fourth factor which is added to the three preceding ones but which seems to me to be the fundamental one. This is what I call the factor of equilibration. Since there are already three factors, they must somehow be equilibrated among themselves. That is one reason for bringing in the factor of equilibration. There is a second reason, however, which seems to me to be fundamental. It is that in the act of knowing, the subject is active, and consequently, faced with an external disturbance, he will react in order to compensate and consequently he will tend towards equilibrium. Equilibrium, defined by active compensation, leads to reversibility. Operational reversibility is a model of an equilibrated system where a transformation in one direction is compensated by a transformation in the other direction. Equilibration, as I understand it, is thus an active process. It's a process of self-regulation. I think that this self-regulation is a fundamental factor in development. I use this term in the sense in which it is used in cybernetics, that is, in the sense of processes with feedback and with feedforward, of processes which regulate themselves by a progressive compensation of systems. This process of equilibration takes the form of a succession of levels of equilibrium, of levels which have a certain probability which I shall call a sequential probability, that is, the probabilities are not established a priori. There is a sequence of levels. It is not possible to reach the second level unless equilibrium has been reached at the first level, and the equilibrium of the third level only becomes possible when the equilibrium of the second level has been reached, and so forth. That is, each level is determined as the most probable given that the preceding level has been reached. It is not the most probable at the beginning, but it is the most probable once the preceding level has been reached.

As an example, let us take the development of the idea of conservation in the transformation of the ball of plasticene into the sausage shape. Here you can discern four levels. The most probable at the beginning is for the child to think of only one dimension. Suppose that there is a probability of 0.8, for instance, that the child will focus on the length, and that the width has a probability of 0.2. This would mean that of ten children, eight will focus on the length alone without paying any attention to the width, and two will focus on the width without paying any attention to the length. They will focus only on one dimension or the other. Since the two dimensions are independent at this stage, focusing on both at once would have a probability of only 0.16. That is less than either one of the two. In other words, the most probable in the beginning is to focus only on one dimension and in fact the child will say, "It's longer, so there's more in the sausage." Once he has reached this first level, if you continue to elongate the sausage, there comes a moment when he will say, "No, now it's too thin, so there's less." Now he is thinking about the width, but he forgets the length, so you have come to a second level which becomes the most probable after the first level, but which is not the most probable at the point of departure. Once he has focused on the width, he will come back sooner or later to focus on the length. Here you will have a third level where he will oscillate between width and length and where he will discover that the two are related. When you elongate you make it more thin, and when you make it shorter, you make it thicker. He discovers that the two are solidly related and in discovering this relationship, he will start to think in terms of the transformation and not only in terms of the final configuration. Now he will say that when it gets longer it gets thinner, so it's the same thing. There is more of it in length but less of it in width. When you make it shorter it gets thicker; there's less in length and more in width, so there is compensation—compensation which defines equilibrium in the sense in which I defined it a moment ago. Consequently, you have operations and conservation. In other words, in the course of these developments you will always find a process of self-regulation which I call equilibration and which seems to me the fundamental factor in the acquisition of logical-mathematical knowledge.

I shall go on now to the second part of my lecture, that is, to deal with the topic of learning. Classically, learning is based on the stimulus-response schema. I think the stimulus-response schema, while I won't say it is false, is in any case entirely incapable of explaining cognitive learning. Why? Because when you think of a stimulus-response schema, you think usually that first of all there is a stimulus and then a response is set off by this stimulus. For my part, I am convinced that the response was there first, if I can express myself in this way. A stimulus is a stimulus only to the extent that it is significant and it becomes significant only to the extent that there is a structure which permits its assimilation, a structure which can integrate this stimulus but which at the same time sets off the response. In other words, I would propose that the stimulus-response schema be written in the circular form—in the form of a schema or of a structure which is not simply one way. I would propose that above all, between the stimulus and the response there is the organism, the organism and its structures. The stimulus is really a stimulus only when it is assimilated into a structure and it is this structure which sets off the response. Consequently, it is not an exaggeration to say that the response is there first, or if you wish at the beginning there is the structure. Of course we would

want to understand how this structure comes to be. I tried to do this earlier by presenting a model of equilibration or self-regulation. Once there is a structure, the stimulus will set off a response, but only by the intermediary of this structure.

I should like to present some facts. We have facts in great number. I shall choose only one or two and I shall choose some facts which our colleague, Smedslund, has gathered. (Smedslund is currently at the Harvard Center for Cognitive Studies.) Smedslund arrived in Geneva a few years ago convinced (he had published this in one of his papers) that the development of the ideas of conservation could be indefinitely accelerated through learning of a stimulus-response type. I invited Smedslund to come to spend a year in Geneva to show us this, to show us that he could accelerate the development of operational conservation. I shall relate only one of his experiments.

During the year that he spent in Geneva he chose to work on the conservation of weight. The conservation of weight is, in fact, easy to study since there is a possible external reinforcement, that is, simply weighing the ball and the sausage on a balance. Then you can study the child's reactions to these external results. Smedslund studied the conservation of weight on the one hand, and on the other hand, he studied the transitivity of weights, that is, the transitivity of equalities if A = B and B = C, then A = C, or the transitivity of the equalities if A is less than B, and B is less than C, then A is less than C.

As far as conservation is concerned, Smedslund succeeded very easily with five- and six-year-old children in getting them to generalize that weight is conserved when the ball is transformed into a different shape. The child sees the ball transformed into a sausage or into little pieces or into a pancake or into any other form, he weighs it, and he sees that it is always the same thing. He will affirm it will be the same thing, no matter what you do to it; it will come out to be the same weight. Thus Smedslund very easily achieved the conservation of weight by this sort of external reinforcement.

In contrast to this, however, the same method did not succeed in teaching transitivity. The children resisted the notion of transitivity. A child would predict correctly in certain cases but he would make his prediction as a possibility or a probability and not as a certainty. There was never this generalized certainty in the case of transitivity.

So there is the first example, which seems to me very instructive, because in this problem in the conservation of weight there are two aspects. There is the physical aspect and there is the logical-mathematical aspect. Note that Smedslund started his study by establishing that there was a correlation between conservation and transitivity. He began by making a statistical study on the relationships between the spontaneous responses to the questions about conservation and the spontaneous responses to the questions about transitivity, and he found a very significant correlation. But in the learning experiment, he obtained a learning of conservation and not of transitivity. Consequently, he was successful in obtaining learning of what I called earlier physical experience (this is not surprising; it is simply a question of noting facts about objects) but he was not successful in obtaining a learning in the construction of the logical structure. This doesn't surprise me either, since the logical structure is not the result of physical experience. It cannot be obtained by external reinforcement. The logical structure is reached only through internal equilibration, by self-regulation, and the external reinforcement of seeing the balance did not suffice to establish this logical structure of transitivity.

I could give many other comparable examples, but it seems to me useless to insist upon these negative examples. Now I should like to show that learning is possible in the case of these logical-mathematical structures, but on one condition—that is, that the structure which you want to teach to the subjects can be supported by simpler, more elementary, logical-mathematical structures. I shall give you an example. It is the example of the conservation of number in the case of one-to-one correspondence. If you give a child seven blue tokens and ask him to put down as many red tokens, there is a pre-operational stage where he will put one red one opposite each blue one. But when you spread out the red ones, making them into a longer row, he will say to you, "Now, there are more red ones than there are blue ones."

Now how can we accelerate, if you want to accelerate, the acquisition of this conservation of number? Well, you can imagine an analogous structure but in a simpler, more elementary, situation. For example, with Mlle. Inhelder, we have been studying recently the notion of one-to-one correspondence by giving the child two glasses of the same shape and a big pile of beads. The child puts a bead into one glass with one hand and at the same time a bead into the other glass with the other hand. Time after time he repeats this action, a bead into one glass with one hand and at the same time a bead into the other glass with the other hand and he sees that there is always the same amount on each side. Then you hide one of the glasses. You cover it up. He no longer sees this glass but he continues to put one bead into it while putting at the same time one bead into the other glass which he can see. Then you ask him whether the equality has been conserved, whether there is still the same amount in one glass as in the other. Now you will find that very small children, about four years old, don't want to make a prediction. They will say, "So far, it has been the same amount, but now I don't know. I can't see anymore, so

I don't know." They do not want to generalize. But the generalization is made from the age of about five and one-half years.

This is in contrast to the case of the red and blue tokens with one row spread out, where it isn't until seven or eight years of age that children will say there are the same number in the two rows. As one example of this generalization, I recall a little boy of five years and nine months who had been adding the beads to the glasses for a little while. Then we asked him whether, if he continued to do this all day and all night and all the next day, there would always be the same amount in the two glasses. The little boy gave this admirable reply, "Once you know, you know for always." In other words, this was recursive reasoning. So here the child does acquire the structure in this specific case. The number is a synthesis of class inclusion and ordering. This synthesis is being favored by the child's own actions. You have set up a situation where there is an iteration of one same action which continues and which is therefore ordered while at the same time being inclusive. You have, so to speak, a localized synthesis of inclusion and ordering which facilitates the construction of the idea of number in this specific case, and there you can find, in effect, an influence of this experience on the other experience. However, this influence is not immediate. We study the generalization from this recursive situation to the other situation where the tokens are laid on the table in rows, and it is not an immediate generalization but it is made possible through intermediaries. In other words, you can find some learning of this structure if you base the learning on simpler structures.

In this same area of the development of numerical structures, the psychologist Joachim Wohlwill, who spent a year at our Institute at Geneva, has also shown that this acquisition can be accelerated through introducing additive operations, which is what we introduced also in the experiment which I just described. Wohlwill introduced them in a different way but he too was able to obtain a certain learning effect. In other words, learning is possible if you base the more complex structure on simpler structures, that is, when there is a natural relationship and development of structures and not simply an external reinforcement.

Now I would like to take a few minutes to conclude what I was saying. My first conclusion is that learning of structures seems to obey the same laws as the natural development of these structures. In other words, learning is subordinated to development and not vice-versa as I said in the introduction. No doubt you will object that some investigators have succeeded in teaching operational structures. But, when I am faced with these facts, I always have three questions which I want to have answered before I am convinced.

The first question is, "Is this learning lasting? What remains two weeks or a month later?" If a structure develops spontaneously, once it has reached a state of equilibrium, it is lasting, it will continue throughout the child's entire life. When you achieve the learning by external reinforcement, is the result lasting or not and what are the conditions necessary for it to be lasting?

The second question is, "How much generalization is possible?" What makes learning interesting is the possibility of transfer of a generalization. When you have brought about some learning, you can always ask whether this is an isolated piece in the midst of the child's mental life, or if it is really a dynamic structure which can lead to generalizations.

Then there is the third question, "In the case of each learning experience what was the operational level of the subject before the experience and what more complex structures has this learning succeeded in achieving?" In other words, we must look at each specific learning experience from the point of view of the spontaneous operations which were present at the outset and the operational level which has been achieved after the learning experience.

My second conclusion is that the fundamental relation involved in all development and all learning is not the relation of association. In the stimulus-response schema, the relation between the response and the stimulus is understood to be one of association. In contrast to this, I think that the fundamental relation is one of assimilation. Assimilation is not the same as association. I shall define assimilation as the integration of any sort of reality into a structure, and it is this assimilation which seems to me fundamental in learning, and which seems to me the fundamental relation from the point of view of pedagogical or didactic applications. All of my remarks today represent the child and the learning subject as active. An operation is an activity. Learning is possible only when there is active assimilation. It is this activity on the part of the subject which seems to me underplayed in the stimulus-response schema. The presentation which I propose puts the emphasis on the idea of self-regulation, on assimilation. All the emphasis is placed on the activity of the subject himself, and I think that without this activity there is no possible didactic or pedagogy which significantly transforms the subject.

Finally, and this will be my last concluding remark, I would like to comment on an excellent publication by the psychologist Berlyne. Berlyne spent a year with us in Geneva during which he intended to translate our results on the development of operations into stimulus-response language, specifically into Hull's learning theory. Berlyne published in our series of studies of genetic epistemology a very good article on this comparison between the results of Geneva and Hull's theory. In the same volume, I published a commentary on Berlyne's results. Now the essence of Berlyne's results is this: our findings can very well be translated into Hullian language, but only on condition that two modifications are introduced. Berlyne himself found these modifications quite considerable, but they seemed to him to concern more the conceptualization than the Hullian theory itself. I'm not so sure about that. The two modifications are these. First of all, Berlyne wants to distinguish two sorts of responses in the S-R schema. First, responses in the ordinary, classical sense, which I shall call "copy responses," and secondly, what Berlyne called "transformation responses." Transformation responses consist of transforming one response of the first type into another response of the first type. These transformation responses are what I call operations, and you can see right away that this is a rather serious modification of Hull's conceptualization because here you are introducing an element of transformation and thus of assimilation and no longer the simple association of stimulus-response theory.

The second modification which Berlyne introduces into the stimulus-response language is the introduction of what he calls internal reinforcements. What are these internal reinforcements? They are what I call equilibration or self-regulation. The internal reinforcements are what enable the subject to eliminate contradictions, incompatibilities, and conflicts. All development is composed of momentary conflicts and incompatibilities which must be overcome to reach a higher level of equilibrium. Berlyne calls this elimination of incompatibilities internal reinforcements.

So you see that it is indeed a stimulus-response theory, if you will, but first you add operations and then you add equilibration. That's all we want!

Editor's note: A brief question and answer period followed Professor Piaget's presentation. The first question related to the fact that the eight-year-old child acquires conservation of substance prior to conservation of weight and volume. The question asked if this didn't contradict the order of emergence of the pre-operational and operational stages. Piaget's response follows:

The conservation of weight and the conservation of volume are not due only to experience. There is also involved a logical framework which is characterized by reversibility and the system of compensations. I am only saying that in the case of weight and volume, weight corresponds to a perception. There is an empirical contact. The same is true of volume. But in the case of substance, I don't see how there can be any perception of substance independent of weight or volume. The strange thing is that this notion of substance comes before the two other notions. Note that in the history of thought, we have the same thing. The first Greek physicists, the pre-Socratic philosophers, discovered conservation of substance independently of any experience. I do not believe this is contradictory with the theory of operations. This conservation of substance is simply the affirmation that something must be conserved. The children don't know specifically what is conserved. They know that since the sausage can become a ball again there must be something which is conserved, and saying "substance" is simply a way of translating this logical necessity for conservation. But this logical necessity results directly from the discovery of operations. I do not think that this is contradictory with the theory of development.

Editor's note: The second question was whether or not the development of stages in children's thinking could be accelerated by practice, training, and exercise in perception and memory. Piaget's response follows:

I am not very sure that exercise of perception and memory would be sufficient. I think that we must distinguish within the cognitive function two very different aspects which I shall call the figurative aspect and the operative aspect. The figurative aspect deals with static configurations. In physical reality there are states, and in addition to these there are transformations which lead from one state to another. In cognitive functioning one has the figurative aspects—for example, perception, imitation, mental imagery, etc.

Secondly, there is the operative aspect, including operations and the actions which lead from one state to another. In children of the higher stages and in adults, the figurative aspects are subordinated to the operative aspects. Any given state is understood to be the result of some transformation and the point of departure for another transformation. But the pre-operational child does not understand transformations. He does not have the operations necessary to understand them so he puts all the emphasis on the static quality of the states. It is because of this, for example, that in the conservation experiments he simply compares the initial state and the final state without being concerned with the transformation.

In exercising perception and memory, I feel that you will reinforce the figurative aspect without touching the operative aspect. Consequently, I'm not sure that this will accelerate the development of cognitive structures. What needs to be reinforced is the operative aspect—not the analysis of states, but the understanding of transformations.

Questions

1. Does a child in the pre-operational stage use logical operations when he or she thinks?
2. Why is Piaget not concerned about age variations in the appearance of his stages across different cultures?
3. Piaget gives an example of how young children respond when he presents them with a conservation or classification problem. In both cases the child's explanation is limited by their logical understanding. How might a teacher who does not agree with Piaget respond to the child?
4. Piaget turns traditional learning theory on its head by stating that the response comes before the stimulus. What does he mean by this statement?
5. Earlier in this section an article by Bell discusses the mutual contributions of adults and children to child development. Does Piaget account for mutual contributions in the process of cognitive development?
6. If you were a consultant to an elementary school that was designing new class lessons to help children learn scientific concepts, what types of experiments might you suggest to help children learn scientific concepts such as weight, volume, and class inclusion?

6

Interaction Between Learning and Development

Lev S. Vygotsky

In the early part of the twentieth century, a new form of psychology developed in Russia. This psychology was different from that in the United States at the time because it emphasized (1) mental processes and (2) the contributions of society and culture to the development of mental processes. One of the main figures in this new theoretical approach was Lev S. Vygotsky, who was interested in the following question: How do social and cultural experiences become part of each individual's thinking?

Vygotsky held the view that intelligence is a social product, and he strove to describe the development of intelligence from this vantage point. He hypothesized that the development of thinking occurs in the everyday experiences that children have, particularly in their interactions with more experienced members of their cultural community. Through social interaction, adults pass on to children the practices, values, and goals of their culture. These interactions direct children's thinking toward the content and processes that are valued in their culture. In other words, social interaction helps organize the developing mind in ways that mesh with the needs and aspirations of the community at large.

The following article is reprinted from one of Vygotsky's books, *Mind in Society,* which was published in the United States posthumously. In it, Vygotsky describes one type of social interaction that he felt was the most likely to promote cognitive development—namely, interactions that occur within the child's zone of proximal (or potential) development. Vygotsky also discusses his views on the relation between learning and development. As you will see, Vygotsky's position on this topic is quite different from Piaget's: He argues that learning precedes development, not vice versa.

Vygotsky's theory and theories related to it, such as sociocultural approaches to development, are influential in research on cognitive development today. This approach is the first systematic attempt in modern psychology to formalize a view of human development that takes into account the cultural and social nature of intellectual growth.

The problems encountered in the psychological analysis of teaching cannot be correctly resolved or even formulated without addressing the relation between learning and development in school-age children. Yet it is the most unclear of all the basic issues on which the application of child development theories to educational processes depends. Needless to say, the lack of theoretical clarity does not mean that the issue is removed altogether from current research efforts into learning; not one study can avoid this central theoretical issue. But the relation between learning and development remains methodologically unclear because concrete research studies have embodied theoretically vague, critically unevaluated, and sometimes internally contradictory postulates, premises, and peculiar solutions to the problem of this fundamental relationship; and these, of course, result in a variety of errors.

Essentially, all current conceptions of the relation between development and learning in children can be reduced to three major theoretical positions.

The first centers on the assumption that processes of child development are independent of learning. Learning is considered a purely external process that is not actively involved in development. It merely utilizes the achievements of development rather than providing an impetus for modifying its course.

In experimental investigations of the development of thinking in school children, it has been assumed that processes such as deduction and understanding, evolution of notions about the world, interpretation of physical causality, and mastery of logical forms of thought and abstract logic all occur by themselves, without any influence from school learning. An example of such a theory is Piaget's extremely complex and interesting theoretical principles, which also shape the experimental methodology he employs. The questions Piaget uses in the course of his "clinical conversations" with children clearly illustrate his approach. When a five-year-old is asked "why doesn't the sun fall?" it is assumed that the child has neither a ready answer for such a question nor the general capabilities for generating one. The point of asking questions that are so far beyond the reach of the child's intellectual skills is to eliminate the influence of previous experience and knowledge. The experimenter seeks to obtain the tendencies of children's thinking in "pure" form entirely independent of learning.[1]

Similarly, the classics of psychological literature, such as the works by Binet and others, assume that development is always a prerequisite for learning and that if a child's mental functions (intellectual operations) have not matured to the extent that he is capable of learning a particular subject, then no instruction will prove useful. They especially feared premature instruction, the teaching of a subject before the child was ready for it. All effort was concentrated on finding the lower threshold of learning ability, the age at which a particular kind of learning first becomes possible.

Because this approach is based on the premise that learning trails behind development, that development always outruns learning, it precludes the notion that learning may play a role in the course of the development or maturation of those functions activated in the course of learning. Development or maturation is viewed as a precondition of learning but never the result of it. To summarize this position: learning forms a superstructure over development, leaving the latter essentially unaltered.

The second major theoretical position is that learning is development. This identity is the essence of a group of theories that are quite diverse in origin.

One such theory is based on the concept of reflex, an essentially old notion that has been extensively revived recently. Whether reading, writing, or arithmetic is being considered, development is viewed as the mastery of conditioned reflexes; that is, the process of learning is completely and inseparably blended with the process of development. This notion was elaborated by James, who reduced the learning process to habit formation and identified the learning process with development.

Reflex theories have at least one thing in common with theories such as Piaget's: in both, development is conceived of as the elaboration and substitution of innate responses. As James expressed it, "Education, in short, cannot be better described than by calling it the organization of acquired habits of conduct and tendencies to behavior."[2] Development itself is reduced primarily to the accumulation of all possible responses. Any acquired response is considered either a more complex form of or a substitute for the innate response.

But despite the similarity between the first and second theoretical positions, there is a major difference in their assumptions about the temporal relationship between learning and developmental processes. Theorists who hold the first view assert that developmental cycles precede learning cycles; maturation precedes learning and instruction must lag behind mental growth. For the second group of theorists, both processes occur simultaneously; learning and development coincide at all points in the same way that two identical geometrical figures coincide when superimposed.

The third theoretical position on the relation between learning and development attempts to overcome the extremes of the other two by simply combining them. A clear example of this approach is Koffka's theory, in which development is based on two inherently different but related processes, each of which influences the other.[3] On the one hand is maturation, which depends directly on the development of the nervous system; on the other hand is learning, which itself is also a developmental process.

Three aspects of this theory are new. First, as we already noted, is the combination of two seemingly opposite viewpoints, each of which has been encountered separately in the history of science. The very fact that these two viewpoints can be combined into one theory indicates that they are not opposing and mutually exclusive but have something essential in common. Also new is the idea that the two processes that make up development are mutually dependent and interactive. Of course, the nature of the interaction is left virtually unexplored in Koffka's work, which is limited solely to very general remarks regarding the relation between these two processes. It is clear that for Koffka the process of maturation prepares and makes possible a specific process of learning. The learning process then stimulates and pushes forward the maturation process. The third and most important new aspect of this theory is the expanded role it ascribes to learning in child development. This emphasis leads us directly to an old pedagogical problem, that of formal discipline and the problem of transfer.

Pedagogical movements that have emphasized formal discipline and urged the teaching of classical languages, ancient civilizations, and mathematics have assumed that regardless of the irrelevance of these particular subjects for daily living, they were of the greatest value for the pupil's mental development. A variety of studies have called into question the soundness of this idea. It has been shown that learning in one area has very little influence on overall development. For example, reflex theorists Woodworth and Thorndike found that adults who, after special exercises, had achieved considerable success in determining the length of short lines, had made virtually no progress in their ability to determine the length of long lines. These same adults were successfully trained to estimate the size of a given two-dimensional figure, but this training did not make them successful in estimating the size of a series of other two-dimensional figures of various sizes and shapes.

According to Thorndike, theoreticians in psychology and education believe that every particular response acquisition directly enhances overall ability in equal measure.[4] Teachers believed and acted on the basis of the theory that the mind is a complex of abilities—powers of observation, attention, memory, thinking, and so forth—and that any improvement in any specific ability results in a general improvement in all abilities. According to this theory, if the student increased the attention he paid to Latin grammar, he would increase his abilities to focus attention on any task. The words "accuracy," "quick-wittedness," "ability to reason," "memory," "power of observation," "attention," "concentration," and so forth are said to denote actual fundamental capabilities that vary in accordance with the material with which they operate; these basic abilities are substantially modified by studying particular subjects, and they retain these modifications when they turn to other areas. Therefore, if someone learns to do any single thing well, he will also be able to do other entirely unrelated things well as a result of some secret connection. It is assumed that mental capabilities function independently of the material with which they operate, and that the development of one ability entails the development of others.

Thorndike himself opposed this point of view. Through a variety of studies he showed that particular forms of activity, such as spelling, are dependent on the mastery of specific skills and material necessary for the performance of that particular task. The development of one particular capability seldom means the development of others. Thorndike argued that specialization of abilities is even greater than superficial observation may indicate. For example, if, out of a hundred individuals we choose ten who display the ability to detect spelling errors or to measure lengths, it is unlikely that these ten will display better abilities regarding, for example, the estimation of the weight of objects. In the same way, speed and accuracy in adding numbers are entirely unrelated to speed and accuracy in being able to think up antonyms.

This research shows that the mind is not a complex network of general capabilities such as observation, attention, memory, judgment, and so forth, but a set of specific capabilities, each of which is, to some extent, independent of the others and is developed independently. Learning is more than the acquisition of the ability to think; it is the acquisition of many specialized abilities for thinking about a variety of things. Learning does not alter our overall ability to focus attention but rather develops various abilities to focus attention on a variety of things. According to this view, special training affects overall development only when its elements, material, and processes are similar across specific domains; habit governs us. This leads to the conclusion that because each activity depends on the material with which it operates, the development of consciousness is the development of a set of particular, independent capabilities or of a set of particular habits. Improvement of one function of consciousness or one aspect of its activity can affect the development of another only to the extent that there are elements common to both functions or activities.

Developmental theorists such as Koffka and the Gestalt School—who hold to the third theoretical position outlined earlier—oppose Thorndike's point of view. They assert that the influence of learning is never specific. From their study of structural principles, they argue that the learning process can never be reduced simply to the formation of skills but embodies an intellectual order that makes it possible to transfer general principles discovered in solving one task to a variety of other tasks. From this point of view, the child, while learning a particular operation, acquires the ability to create structures of a certain type, regardless of the diverse materials with which she is working and regardless of the particular elements involved. Thus, Koffka does not conceive of learning as limited to a process of habit and skill acquisition. The relationship he posits between learning and development is not that of an identity but of a more complex relationship. According to Thorndike, learning and development coincide at all points, but for Koffka, development is always a larger set than learning. Schematically, the relationship between the two processes could be depicted by two concentric circles, the smaller symbolizing the learning process and the larger the developmental process evoked by learning.

Once a child has learned to perform an operation, he thus assimilates some structural principle whose sphere of application is other than just the operations of the type on whose basis the principle was assimilated. Consequently, in making one step in learning, a child makes two steps in development, that is, learning and development do not coincide. This concept is the essential aspect of the third group of theories we have discussed.

Zone of Proximal Development: A New Approach

Although we reject all three theoretical positions discussed above, analyzing them leads us to a more adequate view of the relation between learning and development. The question to be framed in arriving at a solution to this problem is complex. It consists of two separate issues: first, the general relation between learning and development; and second, the specific features of this relationship when children reach school age.

That children's learning begins long before they attend school is the starting point of this discussion. Any learning a child encounters in school always has a previous history. For example, children begin to study arithmetic in school, but long beforehand they have had some experience with quantity—they have had to deal with operations of division, addition, subtraction, and determination of size. Consequently, children have their own preschool arithmetic, which only myopic psychologists could ignore.

It goes without saying that learning as it occurs in the preschool years differs markedly from school learning, which is concerned with the assimilation of the fundamentals of scientific knowledge. But even when, in the period of her first questions, a child assimilates the names of objects in her environment, she is learning. Indeed, can it be doubted that children learn speech from adults; or that, through asking questions and giving answers, children acquire a variety of information; or that, through imitating adults and through being instructed about how to act, children develop an entire repository of skills? Learning and development are interrelated from the child's very first day of life.

Koffka, attempting to clarify the laws of child learning and their relation to mental development, concentrates his attention on the simplest learning processes, those that occur in the preschool years. His error is that, while seeing a similarity between preschool and school learning, he fails to discern the difference—he does not see the specifically new elements that school learning introduces. He and others assume that the difference between preschool and school learning consists of non-systematic learning in one case and systematic learning in the other. But "systematicness" is not the only issue; there is also the fact that school learning introduces something fundamentally new into the child's development. In order to elaborate the dimensions of school learning, we will describe a new and exceptionally important concept without which the issue cannot be resolved: the zone of proximal development.

A well known and empirically established fact is that learning should be matched in some manner with the child's developmental level. For example, it has been established that the teaching of reading, writing, and arithmetic should be initiated at a specific age level. Only recently, however, has attention been directed to the fact that we cannot limit ourselves merely to determining developmental levels if we wish to discover the actual relations of the developmental process to learning capabilities. We must determine at least two developmental levels.

The first level can be called the *actual developmental level*, that is, the level of development of a child's mental functions that has been established as a result of certain already completed developmental cycles. When we determine a child's mental age by using tests, we are almost always dealing with the actual developmental level. In studies of children's mental development it is generally assumed that only those things that children can do on their own are indicative of mental abilities. We give children a battery of tests or a variety of tasks of varying degrees of difficulty, and we judge the extent of their mental development on the basis of how they solve them and at what level of difficulty. On the other hand, if we offer leading questions or show how the problem is to be solved and the child then solves it, or if the teacher initiates the solution and the child completes it or solves it in collaboration with other children—in short, if the child barely misses an independent solution of the problem—the solution is not regarded as indicative of his mental development. This "truth" was familiar and reinforced by common sense. Over a decade even the profoundest thinkers never questioned the assumption; they never entertained the notion that what children can do with the assistance of others might be in some sense even more indicative of their mental development than what they can do alone.

Let us take a simple example. Suppose I investigate two children upon entrance into school, both of whom are ten years old chronologically and eight years old in terms of mental development. Can I say that they are the same age mentally? Of course. What does this mean? It means that they can independently deal with tasks up to the degree of difficulty that has been standardized for the eight-year-old level. If I stop at this point, people would imagine that the subsequent course of mental development and of school learning for these children will be the same, because it depends on their intellect. Of course, there may be other factors, for example, if one child was sick for half a year while the other was never absent from school; but generally speaking, the fate of these children should be the same. Now imagine that I do not terminate my study at this point, but only begin it. These children seem to be capable of handling problems up to an eight-year-old's level, but not beyond that. Suppose that I show them various ways of dealing with the problem. Different experimenters might employ different modes of demonstration in different cases: some might run through an entire demonstration and ask the children to repeat it, others might initiate the solution and ask the child to finish it, or offer leading questions. In short, in some way or another I propose that the children solve the problem with my assistance. Under these circumstances it turns out that the first child can deal with problems up to a twelve-year-old's level, the second up to a nine-year-old's. Now, are these children mentally the same?

When it was first shown that the capability of children with equal levels of mental development to learn under a teacher's guidance varied to a high degree, it became apparent that those children were not mentally the same age and that the subsequent course of their learning would obviously be different. This difference between twelve and eight, or between nine and eight, is what we call *the zone of proximal development. It is the distance between the actual developmental level as determined by independent problem solving and the level of potential development as determined through problem solving under adult guidance or in collaboration with more capable peers.*

If we naively ask what the actual developmental level is, or, to put it more simply, what more independent problem solving reveals, the most common answer would be that a child's actual developmental level defines functions that have already matured, that is, the end products of development. If a child can do such-and-such independently, it means that the functions for such-and-such have matured in her. What, then, is defined by the zone of proximal development, as determined through problems that children cannot solve independently but only with assistance? The zone of proximal development defines those functions that have not yet matured but are in the process of maturation, functions that will mature tomorrow but are currently in an embryonic state. These functions could be termed the "buds" or "flowers" of development rather than the "fruits" of development. The actual developmental level characterizes mental development retrospectively, while the zone of proximal development characterizes mental development prospectively.

The zone of proximal development furnishes psychologists and educators with a tool through which the internal course of development can be understood. By using this method we can take account of not only the cycles and maturation processes that have already been completed but also those processes that are currently in a state of formation, that are just beginning to mature and develop. Thus, the zone of proximal development permits us to delineate the child's immediate future and his dynamic developmental state, allowing not only for what already has been achieved developmentally but also for what is in the course of maturing. The two children in our example displayed the same mental age from the viewpoint of developmental cycles already completed, but the developmental dynamics of the two were entirely different. The state of a child's mental development can be determined only by clarifying its two levels: the actual developmental level and the zone of proximal development.

I will discuss one study of preschool children to demonstrate that what is in the zone of proximal development today will be the actual developmental level tomorrow—that is, what a child can do with assistance today she will be able to do by herself tomorrow.

The American researcher Dorothea McCarthy showed that among children between the ages of three and five there are two groups of functions: those the children already possess, and those they can perform under guidance, in groups, and in collaboration with one another but which they have not mastered independently. McCarthy's study demonstrated that this second group of functions is at the actual developmental level of five-to-seven-year-olds. What her subjects could do only under guidance, in collaboration, and in groups at the age of three-to-five years they could do independently when they reached the age of five-to-seven years.[5] Thus, if we were to determine only mental age—that is, only functions that have matured—we would have but a summary of completed development while if we determine the maturing functions, we can predict what will happen to these children between five and seven, provided the same developmental conditions are maintained. The zone of proximal development can become a powerful concept in developmental research, one that can markedly enhance the effectiveness and utility of the application of diagnostics of mental development to educational problems.

A full understanding of the concept of the zone of proximal development must result in reevaluation of the role of imitation in learning. An unshakable tenet of classical psychology is that only the independent activity of children, not their imitative activity, indicates their level of mental development. This view is expressed in all current testing systems. In evaluating mental development, consideration is given to only those solutions to test problems which the child reaches without the assistance of others, without demonstrations, and without leading questions. Imitation and learning are thought of as purely mechanical processes. But recently psychologists have shown that a person can imitate only that which is within her developmental level. For example, if a child is having difficulty with a problem in arithmetic and the teacher solves it on the blackboard, the child may grasp the solution in an instant. But if the teacher were to solve a problem in higher mathematics, the child would not be able to understand the solution no matter how many times she imitated it.

Animal psychologists, and in particular Köhler, have dealt with this question of imitation quite well.[6] Köhler's experiments sought to determine whether primates are capable of graphic thought. The principal question was whether primates solved problems independently or whether they merely imitated solutions they had seen performed earlier, for example, watching other animals or humans use sticks and other tools and then imitating them. Köhler's special experiments, designed to determine what primates could imitate, reveal that primates can use imitation to solve only those problems that are of the same degree of difficulty as those they can solve alone. However, Köhler failed to take account of an important fact, namely, that primates cannot be taught (in the human sense of the word) through imitation, nor can their intellect be developed, because they have no zone of proximal development. A primate can learn a great deal through training by using its mechanical and mental skills, but it cannot be made more intelligent, that is, it cannot be taught to solve a variety of more advanced problems independently. For this reason animals are incapable of learning in the human sense of the term; *human learning presupposes a specific social nature and a process by which children grow into the intellectual life of those around them.*

Children can imitate a variety of actions that go well beyond the limits of their own capabilities. Using imitation, children are capable of doing much more in collective activity or under the guidance of adults. This fact, which seems to be of little significance in itself, is of fundamental importance in that it demands a radical alteration of the entire doctrine concerning the relation between learning and development in children. One direct consequence is a change in conclusions that may be drawn from diagnostic tests of development.

Formerly, it was believed that by using tests, we determine the mental development level with which education should reckon and whose limits it should not exceed. This procedure oriented learning toward yesterday's development, toward developmental stages already completed. The error of this view was discovered earlier in practice than in theory. It is demonstrated most clearly in the teaching of mentally retarded children. Studies have established that mentally retarded children are not very capable of abstract thinking. From this the pedagogy of the special school drew the seemingly correct conclusion that all teaching of such children should be based on the use of concrete, look-

and-do methods. And yet a considerable amount of experience with this method resulted in profound disillusionment. It turned out that a teaching system based solely on concreteness—one that eliminated from teaching everything associated with abstract thinking—not only failed to help retarded children overcome their innate handicaps but also reinforced their handicaps by accustoming children exclusively to concrete thinking and thus suppressing the rudiments of any abstract thought that such children still have. Precisely because retarded children, when left to themselves, will never achieve well-elaborated forms of abstract thought, the school should make every effort to push them in that direction and to develop in them what is intrinsically lacking in their own development. In the current practices of special schools for retarded children, we can observe a beneficial shift away from this concept of concreteness, one that restores look-and-do methods to their proper role. Concreteness is now seen as necessary and unavoidable only as a stepping stone for developing abstract thinking—as a means, not as an end in itself.

Similarly, in normal children, learning which is oriented toward developmental levels that have already been reached is ineffective from the viewpoint of a child's overall development. It does not aim for a new stage of the developmental process but rather lags behind this process. Thus, the notion of a zone of proximal development enables us to propound a new formula, namely that the only "good learning" is that which is in advance of development.

The acquisition of language can provide a paradigm for the entire problem of the relation between learning and development. Language arises initially as a means of communication between the child and the people in his environment. Only subsequently, upon conversion to internal speech, does it come to organize the child's thought, that is, become an internal mental function. Piaget and others have shown that reasoning occurs in a children's group as an argument intended to prove one's own point of view before it occurs as an internal activity whose distinctive feature is that the child begins to perceive and check the basis of his thoughts. Such observations prompted Piaget to conclude that communication produces the need for checking and confirming thoughts, a process that is characteristic of adult thought.[7] In the same way that internal speech and reflective thought arise from the interactions between the child and persons in her environment, these interactions provide the source of development of a child's voluntary behavior. Piaget has shown that cooperation provides the basis for the development of a child's moral judgment. Earlier research established that a child first becomes able to subordinate her behavior to rules in group play and only later does voluntary self-regulation of behavior arise as an internal function.

These individual examples illustrate a general developmental law for the higher mental functions that we feel can be applied in its entirety to children's learning processes. We propose that an essential feature of learning is that it creates the zone of proximal development; that is, learning awakens a variety of internal developmental processes that are able to operate only when the child is interacting with people in his environment and in cooperation with his peers. Once these processes are internalized, they become part of the child's independent developmental achievement.

From this point of view, learning is not development; however, properly organized learning results in mental development and sets in motion a variety of developmental processes that would be impossible apart from learning. Thus, learning is a necessary and universal aspect of the process of developing culturally organized, specifically human, psychological functions.

To summarize, the most essential feature of our hypothesis is the notion that developmental processes do not coincide with learning processes. Rather, the developmental process lags behind the learning process; this sequence then results in zones of proximal development. Our analysis alters the traditional view that at the moment a child assimilates the meaning of a word, or masters an operation such as addition or written language, her developmental processes are basically completed. In fact, they have only just begun at that moment. The major consequence of analyzing the educational process in this manner is to show that the initial mastery of, for example, the four arithmetic operations provides the basis for the subsequent development of a variety of highly complex internal processes in children's thinking.

Our hypothesis establishes the unity but not the identity of learning processes and internal developmental processes. It presupposes that the one is converted into the other. Therefore, it becomes an important concern of psychological research to show how external knowledge and abilities in children become internalized.

Any investigation explores some sphere of reality. An aim of the psychological analysis of development is to describe the internal relations of the intellectual processes awakened by school learning. In this respect, such analysis will be directed inward and is analogous to the use of x-rays. If successful, it should reveal to the teacher how developmental processes stimulated by the course of school learning are carried through inside the head of each individual child. The revelation of this internal, subterranean developmental network of school subjects is a task of primary importance for psychological and educational analysis.

A second essential feature of our hypothesis is the notion that, although learning is directly related to the course of child development, the two are never accomplished in equal measure or in parallel. Development in children never follows school learning the way a shadow follows the object that casts it. In actuality, there are highly complex dynamic relations between developmental and learning processes that cannot be encompassed by an unchanging hypothetical formulation.

Each school subject has its own specific relation to the course of child development, a relation that varies as the child goes from one stage to another. This leads us directly to a reexamination of the problem of formal discipline, that is, to the significance of each particular subject from the viewpoint of overall mental development. Clearly, the problem cannot be solved by using any one formula; extensive and highly diverse concrete research based on the concept of the zone of proximal development is necessary to resolve the issue.

Notes

1. J. Piaget, *The Language and Thought of the Child* (New York: Meridian Books, 1955).

2. William James, *Talks to Teachers* (New York: Norton, 1958), pp. 36–37.

3. Koffka, *The Growth of the Mind* (London: Routledge and Kegan Paul, 1924).

4. E. L. Thorndike, *The Psychology of Learning* (New York: Teachers College Press, 1914).

5. Dorothea McCarthy, *The Language Development of the Pre-school Child* (Minneapolis: University of Minnesota Press, 1930).

6. W. Köhler, *The Mentality of Apes* (New York: Harcourt, Brace, 1925).

7. Piaget, *Language and Thought.*

Questions

1. Why was Vygotsky dissatisfied with Piaget's view of cognitive development?
2. If you were to design a new IQ test based on Vygotsky's idea of the zone of proximal development, what would it be like? How might a child's score on this test be interpreted?
3. How do social and cultural experiences become part of each individual's way of thinking?
4. Vygotsky worked as a psychologist during the Russian Revolution of the early 1900s, when socialism took hold in that country. Do you think that this circumstance had any influence on his ideas about the development of intellectual functioning?
5. Think of a skill you have today that you learned as a child, and then think about how you learned it. Did other people help you in this learning? Was the way you learned this skill similar to the process described in Vygotsky's discussion of the zone of proximal development? Explain.
6. If Vygotsky's ideas were incorporated into public school curricula, how would current educational practices change?

PART I

In the Beginning

The articles in this section concentrate on early development, with particular attention to biological contributions and the dynamic interplay of biology and experience in this period of growth.

The last few decades have brought dramatic changes in our understanding of biological contributions to psychological development. In a classic article based on auditory research conducted in the 1970s, DeCasper and Fifer establish that infants are born biologically prepared to respond to their environment. Progress in genetics and neuroscience have allowed developmental researchers to further explore the interaction between a child's genetic inheritance and the social environment in which the child is reared, as seen in the article by David Reiss. The subsequent article by Patricia Bauer discusses brain development, concentrating on how advances in neuroscience are redefining scientific views of the process of early cognitive development.

In addition to progress in these biologically based areas of developmental research, there has been significant change in our understanding of the period of infancy. Articles by Hewlett and colleagues on the social and cultural organization of infant experience, by Kagan on temperament and early behavioral development, and by Rutter, Kreppner, and O'Connor on psychological adjustment following institutional deprivation, all describe how, very early in childhood, the rich biological template of the human organism combines with social experiences and other constitutional factors to steer the developmental course.

Together, the articles in this section underscore the importance of taking an interactional view to the study of human development. That is, the contributions of the biological and the social aspects of growth should be considered as mutually defining and inseparable.

7 Of Human Bonding: Newborns Prefer Their Mothers' Voices

Anthony J. DeCasper • William P. Fifer

The last three decades have seen technological innovations that have made possible a huge increase in developmental research describing infant capabilities such as attention, emotional regulation, and social behavior. The following article describes one of these early human capabilities: the ability to discriminate the sounds of particular human voices. Authors Anthony DeCasper and William Fifer devised an ingenious method of study that allowed them to probe the capabilities of babies less than 3 days of age. What is particularly remarkable about their method is that it used the very limited behavioral abilities of neonates as a way of showing what they are able to understand.

The ability to discriminate human voices early in life has immense consequences for human adaptation and attests to the complex biological preparedness of the human infant—a preparedness that helps even newborn babies play an active role in their own development. The research described here, along with many other studies that demonstrate the amazing capabilities of newborns, has redefined our understanding of human development. No longer considered helpless, reactive beings, infants are now seen as active, information-seeking organisms that are ready to learn about and interact with the world. This research also indicates that infants are biased toward, or prefer, information from other people. We do not yet know whether a preference for the mother's voice early in an infant's life is a result of familiarity acquired while the baby was in utero or of some other complex process, such as emotional arousal immediately after birth. But it is certain that a preference for the sound and sight of other human beings helps infants become integrated with their surroundings, especially the social world in which they live. Moreover, this integration sets the stage for further development. After all, caregivers not only protect infants but are also a fount of information about the world and how it works. One cannot imagine a preference that is better suited to helping the developing infant face the many tasks that lie ahead.

By sucking on a nonnutritive nipple in different ways, a newborn human could produce either its mother's voice or the voice of another female. Infants learned how to produce the mother's voice and produced it more often than the other voice. The neonate's preference for the maternal voice suggests that the period shortly after birth may be important for initiating infant bonding to the mother.

Human responsiveness to sound begins in the third trimester of life and by birth reaches sophisticated levels (*1*), especially with respect to speech (*2*). Early auditory competency probably subserves a variety of developmental functions such as language acquisition (*1, 3*) and mother-infant bonding (*4, 5*). Mother-infant bonding would best be served by (and may even require) the ability of a newborn to discriminate its mother's voice from that of other females. However, evidence for differential sensitivity to or discrimination of the maternal voice is available only for older infants for whom the bonding process is well advanced (*6*). Therefore, the role of maternal voice discrimination in formation of the mother-infant bond is unclear. If the newborn's sensitivities to speech subserves bonding, discrimination of and preference for the maternal voice should be evident near birth. We now report that a newborn infant younger than 3 days of age can not only discriminate its mother's voice but also will work to produce her voice in preference to the voice of another female.

The subjects were ten Caucasian neonates (five male and five female) (*7*). Shortly after delivery we

From DeCasper, A. J., & Fifer, W. P. (1980). Of human bonding: Newborns prefer their mothers' voices. *Science,* 208, pp. 1174–1176. Reprinted with permission from AAAS.

tape-recorded the voices of mothers of infants selected for testing as they read Dr. Seuss's *To Think That I Saw It On Mulberry Street.* Recordings were edited to provide 25 minutes of uninterrupted prose, and testing of whether infants would differentially produce their mothers' voices began within 24 hours of recording. Sessions began by coaxing the infant to a state of quiet alertness (*8*). The infant was then placed supine in its basinette, earphones were secured over its ears, and a nonnutritive nipple was placed in its mouth. An assistant held the nipple loosely in place; she was unaware of the experimental condition of the individual infant and could neither hear the tapes nor be seen by the infant. The nipple was connected, by way of a pressure transducer, to the solid-state programming and recording equipment. The infants were then allowed 2 minutes to adjust to the situation. Sucking activity was recorded during the next 5 minutes, but voices were never presented. This baseline period was used to determine the median interburst interval (IBI) or time elapsing between the end of one burst of sucking and the beginning of the next (*9*). A burst was defined as a series of individual sucks separated from one another by less than 2 seconds. Testing with the voices began after the baseline had been established.

For five randomly selected infants, sucking burst terminating IBI's equal to or greater than the baseline median (*t*) produced only his or her mother's voice (IBI $\geq$ *t*), and bursts terminating intervals less than the median produced only the voice of another infant's mother (*10*). Thus, only one of the voices was presented, stereophonically, with the first suck of a burst and remained on until the burst ended, that is, until 2 seconds elapsed without a suck. For the other five infants, the conditions were reversed. Testing lasted 20 minutes.

A preference for the maternal voice was indicated if the infant produced it more often than the nonmaternal voice. However, unequal frequencies not indicative of preference for the maternal voice per se could result either because short (or long) IBI's were easier to produce or because the acoustic qualities of a particular voice, such as pitch or intensity, rendered it a more effective form of feedback. The effects of response requirements and voice characteristics were controlled (i) by requiring half the infants to respond after short IBI's to produce the mother's voice and half to respond after long ones and (ii) by having each maternal voice also serve as the nonmaternal voice for another infant.

Preference for the mother's voice was shown by the increase in the proportion of IBI's capable of producing her voice; the median IBI's shifted from their baseline values in a direction that produced the maternal voice more than half the time. Eight of the ten medians were shifted in a direction of the maternal voice (mean = 1.90 seconds, a 34 percent increase) (sign test, *P* = .02), one shifted in the direction that

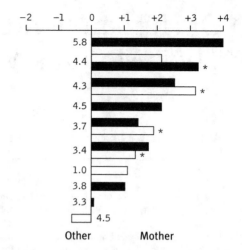

figure 1

For each subject, signed difference scores between the median IBI's without vocal feedback (baseline) and with differential vocal feedback (session1). Differences of the four reversal sessions (*) are based on medians with differential feedback in sessions 1 and 2. Positive values indicate a preference for the maternal voice and negative values a preference for the nonmaternal voice. Filled bars indicate that the mother's voice followed IBI's of less than the baseline median; open bars indicate that her voice followed intervals equal to or greater than the median. Median IBI's of the baseline (in seconds) are shown opposite the bars.

produced the nonmaternal voice more often, and one median did not change from its baseline value (Figure 1).

If these infants were working to gain access to their mother's voice, reversing the response requirements should result in a reversal of their IBI's. Four infants, two from each condition, who produced their mother's voice more often in session 1 were able to complete a second session 24 hours later, in which the response requirements were reversed (*11*). Differential feedback in session 2 began immediately after the 2-minute adjustment period. The criterion time remained equal to the baseline median of the first session. For all four infants, the median IBI's shifted toward the new criterion values and away from those which previously produced the maternal voice. The average magnitude of the difference between the medians of the first and reversal sessions was 1.95 seconds.

Apparently the infant learned to gain access to the mother's voice. Since specific temporal properties of sucking were required to produce the maternal voice, we sought evidence for the acquisition of temporally differentiated responding. Temporal discrimination

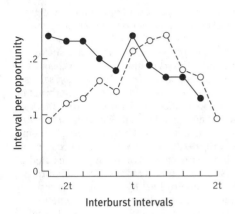

figure 2

Interburst interval per opportunity when the maternal voice followed intervals less than the baseline median (solid line) and intervals equal to or greater than the median (dashed line). The IBI's are represented on the abscissa by the lower bound of interval classes equal to one-fifth the baseline median (t).

table 1   Mean $\bar{X}$ and Standard Deviation (S.D.) of the Relative Frequency of Sucking During a Stimulus Associated with the Maternal Voice Divided by the Relative Frequency of Sucking During a Stimulus Associated with the Nonmaternal Voice

Stimulus associated with maternal voice	First third		Last third	
	$\bar{X}$	S.D.	$\bar{X}$	S.D.
Tone	0.97	.33	1.26	.33
No tone	1.04	.31	1.22	.19
Last: Combined	1.00[a]	.32	1.24	.27

[a]A ratio of 1.0 indicates no preference.

within each condition was ascertained by constructing the function for IBI per opportunity: IBI's were collected into classes equal to one-fifth the baseline median, and the frequency of each class was divided by the total frequency of classes having equal and larger values (*12*). When IBI's less than the baseline median were required, the likelihood of terminating interburst intervals was highest for classes less than the median (Figure 2), whereas when longer intervals were required, the probability of terminating an IBI was maximal for intervals slightly longer than the median. Feedback from the maternal voice effectively differentiated the temporal character of responding that produced it: the probability of terminating IBI's was highest when termination resulted in the maternal voice.

Repeating the experiment with 16 female neonates and a different discrimination procedure confirmed their preference for the maternal voice (*13*). The discriminative stimuli were a 400-Hz tone of 4 seconds duration (tone) and a 4-second period of silence (no tone). Each IBI contained an alternating sequence of tone-no-tone periods, and each stimulus was equally likely to begin a sequence. For eight infants, a sucking burst initiated during a tone period turned off the tone and produced the Dr. Seuss story read by the infant's mother, whereas sucking bursts during a no-tone period produced the nonmaternal voice. The elicited voice remained until the sucking burst ended, at which time the tone-no-tone alternation began anew. The discriminative stimuli were reversed for the other eight neonates. Testing with the voices began

immediately after the 2-minute adjustment period and lasted 20 minutes. Each maternal voice also served as a nonmaternal voice.

During the first third of the testing session, the infants were as likely to suck during a stimulus period correlated with the maternal voice as during one correlated with the nonmaternal voice (Table 1). However, in the last third of the session the infants sucked during stimulus periods associated with their mother's voice approximately 24 percent more often than during those associated with the nonmaternal voice, a significant increase [$F(1, 14) = 8.97$, $P < .01$]. Thus, at the beginning of testing there was no indication of stimulus discrimination or voice preference. By the end of the 20-minute session, feedback from the maternal voice produced clear evidence of an auditory discrimination; the probability of sucking during tone and no-tone periods was greater when sucking produced the maternal voice.

The infants in these studies lived in a group nursery; their general care and night feedings were handled by a number of female nursery personnel. They were fed in their mothers' rooms by their mothers at 9:30 A.M. and at 1:30, 5:00, and 8:30 P.M. At most, they had 12 hours of postnatal contact with their mothers before testing. Similarly reared infants prefer the human voice to other acoustically complex stimuli (*14*). But, as our data show, newborns reared in group nurseries that allow minimal maternal contact can also discriminate between their mothers and other speakers and, moreover, will work to produce their mothers' voices in preference to those of other females. Thus, within the first 3 days of postnatal development, newborns prefer the human voice, discriminate between speakers, and demonstrate a preference for their mothers' voices with only limited maternal exposure.

The neonate's capacity to rapidly acquire a stimulus discrimination that controls behavior (*15*) could provide the means by which limited postnatal experience with the mother results in preference for her voice. The early preference demonstrated here is possible because newborns have auditory competencies adequate for discriminating individual speakers: they are sensitive to rhythmicity (*16*), intonation (*17*), frequency variation (*1, 13*), and phonetic components of speech (*18*). Their general sensory competency may enable other maternal cues, such as her odor (*19*) and the manner in which she handles her infant (*20*), to serve as supporting bases for discrimination and vocal preference. Prenatal (intrauterine) auditory experience may also be a factor. Although the significance and nature of intrauterine auditory experience in humans is not known, perceptual preferences and proximity-seeking responses of some infrahuman infants are profoundly affected by auditory experience before birth (*21*).

REFERENCES AND NOTES

1. R. B. Eisenberg, *Auditory Competence in Early Life: The Roots of Communicative Behavior* (University Park Press, Baltimore, 1976.)
2. P. D. Eimas, in *Infant Perception: From Sensation to Cognition*, L. B. Cohen and P. Salapatek, Eds. (Academic Press, New York, 1975), vol. 2., p. 193.
3. B. Friedlander, *Merrill-Palmer Q., 16*, 7 (1970).
4. R. Bell, in *The Effect of the Infant on Its Caregiver*, M. Lewis and L. A. Rosenblum, Eds. (Wiley, New York, 1974), p. 1; T. B. Brazelton, E. Tronick, L. Abramson, H. Als, S. Wise, *Ciba Found. Symp., 33*, 137 (1975).
5. M. H. Klaus and J. H. Kennel, *Maternal Infant Bonding* (Mosby, St. Louis, 1976); P. DeChateau, *Birth Family J., 41*, 10 (1977).
6. M. Miles and E. Melvish, *Nature (London) 252*, 123 (1974); J. Mehler, J. Bertoncini, M. Baurière, D. Jassik-Gershenfeld, *Perception, 7*, 491 (1978).
7. The infants were randomly selected from those meeting the following criteria: (i) gestation, full term; (ii) delivery, uncomplicated; (iii) birth weight, between 2500 and 3850 grams; and (iv) APGAR score, at least eight at 1 and 5 minutes after birth. If circumsized, males were not observed until at least 12 hours afterward. Informed written consent was obtained from the mother, and she was invited to observe the testing procedure. Testing sessions began between 2.5 and 3.5 hours after the 6 A.M. or 12 P.M. feeding. All infants were bottle-fed.
8. P. H. Wolff, *Psychol. Issues, 5*, 1 (1966). The infants were held in front of the experimenter's face, spoken to, and then presented with the nonnutritive nipple. Infants failing to fixate visually on the experimenter's face or to suck on the nipple were returned to the nursery. Once begun, a session was terminated only if the infant cried or stopped sucking for two consecutive minutes. The initial sessions of two infants were terminated because they cried for 2 minutes. Their data are not reported.

Thus, the results are based on 10 of 12 infants meeting the behavioral criteria for entering and remaining in the study.
9. With quiet and alert newborns, nonnutritive sucking typically occurs as bursts of individual sucks, each separated by a second or so, while the bursts themselves are separated by several seconds or more. Interburst intervals tend to be unimodally distributed with modal values differing among infants. [K. Kaye, in *Studies in Mother-Infant Interaction*, H. R. Schaffer, Ed. (Academic Press, New York, 1977)]. A suck was said to occur when the negative pressure exerted on the nipple reached 20 mm-Hg. This value is almost always exceeded during nonnutritive sucking by healthy infants, but is virtually never produced by nonsucking mouth movement.
10. The tape reels revolved continuously, and one or the other of the voices was electronically switched to the earphones when the response threshold was met. Because the thresholds were detected electronically, voice onset occurred at the moment the negative pressure reached 20 mm-Hg.
11. Two infants were not tested a second time, because we could not gain access to the testing room, which served as an auxiliary nursery and as an isolation room. The sessions of two infants who cried were terminated. Two other infants were tested a second time, but in their first session one had shown no preference and the other had shown only a slight preference for the nonmaternal voice. Their performance may have been affected by inconsistent feedback. Because their peak sucking pressures were near the threshold of the apparatus, very similar sucks would sometimes produce feedback and sometimes not, and sometimes feedback would be terminated in the midst of a sucking burst. Consequently, second session performances of these two infants, which were much like their initial performances, were uninterpretable.
12. D. Anger, *J. Exp. Psychol., 52*, 145 (1956).
13. Three other infants began testing with the voices, but their sessions were terminated because they cried. Their data are not included. This study is part of a doctoral thesis submitted by W.P.F.
14. E. Butterfield and G. Siperstein, in *Oral Sensation and Perception: The Mouth of the Infant*, J. Bosma, Ed. (Thomas, Springfield, Ill., 1972).
15. E. R. Siqueland and L. P. Lipsitt, *J. Exp. Child. Psychol. 3*, 356 (1966); R. E. Kron, in *Recent Advances in Biological Psychiatry*, J. Wortis, Ed. (Plenum, New York, 1967), p. 295.
16. W. S. Condon and L. W. Sander, *Science, 183*, 99 (1974).
17. R. B. Eisenberg, D. B. Cousins, N. Rupp, *J. Aud. Res., 7*, 245 (1966); P. A. Morse, *J. Exp. Child. Psychol., 14*, 477 (1972).
18. E. C. Butterfield and G. F. Cairns, in *Language Perspectives: Acquisition, Retardation and Intervention*, R. L. Schiefelbusch and L. L. Lloyd, Eds. (University Park Press, Baltimore, 1974), p. 75; A. J. DeCasper, E. C. Butterfield, G. F. Cairns, paper presented at the fourth biennial conference on Human Development, Nashville. April 1976.
19. A. MacFarlane, *Ciba Found. Symp., 33*, 103 (1975).

20. P. Burns, L. W. Sander, G. Stechler, H. Julia. *J. Am. Acad. Child Psychiatry, 11*, 427 (1972), E. B. Thoman, A. F. Korner, L. Bearon-Williams, *Child Dev., 48*, 563 (1977).

21. G. Gottlieb, *Development of Species Identification in Birds: An Inquiry into the Prenatal Determinants of Perception* (Univ. of Chicago Press, Chicago, 1971); E. H. Hess. *Imprinting* (Van Nostrand-Reinhold, New York, 1973).

22. Supported by Research Council grant 920. We thank the infants, their mothers, and the staff of Moses Cane Hospital, where this work was performed, and A. Carstens for helping conduct the research.

Questions

1. Briefly describe the method that DeCasper and Fifer used to test an infant's preference for the mother's voice. Are you surprised that infants are capable of doing this task? Why?

2. Why was the study designed so that, to hear the mother's voice, half of the infants needed to increase their sucking rate and the other half needed to decrease their sucking rate?

3. Do you think that prenatal exposure to the mother's voice may play a role in the preferences shown in this study?

4. What function does such early auditory discrimination serve for infants?

5. What types of perceptual information about mothers do you think deaf infants rely on in the early days of life?

6. What do these findings suggest about the nature of human development, especially the role that social experiences play in it?

8 The Interplay Between Genotypes and Family Relationships: Reframing Concepts of Development and Prevention

David Reiss

An explosion of knowledge in the field of genetics has redefined our understanding of human biology. It is now possible to map precisely many heritable traits and conditions. At the same time, it has become increasingly clear that gene expression is enormously complex and has many indeterminate outcomes. Individual genotypes may be fixed, but their expression is responsive to environmental input. In the following article, David Reiss describes how child development arises from the interaction of the child's genetic template and the child's social environment. Whereas some social environments may increase the likelihood that a child will express certain genetically based characteristics, other social environments can decrease this likelihood.

Interactions between the child's genotype and family environment are especially complex. Parents and children share the same social environment *and* they are related biologically, therefore sharing many genetic traits. In other words, the social and psychological character of the family environment is itself influenced by inherited characteristics, leading to huge variation in the ways that the child's genotype and family environment may interact. In this article, David Reiss explains how researchers dissect these interactions, especially by comparing the development of twins and of adopted and nonadopted children in the same family. He also discusses how these studies inform us about nongenetic factors that are important components of parenting.

Reiss concludes by describing the value of this research for helping children who are at risk for forming developmental problems, such as maladaptive behavior and certain types of psychopathology. As you will see, findings from this research suggest innovative approaches for identifying and treating these children and their families, approaches that may help these children lead positive and productive lives.

Children's genotypes and their social relationships are correlated throughout their development. Heritable characteristics of children evoke strong and specific responses from their parents; frequently, these same heritable characteristics also influence the children's adjustment. Moreover, parental heritable traits that influence their parenting are also transmitted to children and influence their children's adjustment. Thus, genetically influenced evocative processes from children and parental-transmission mechanisms influence the co-variances between measures of family relationships and child development. These findings suggest new targets for preventing adverse development: altering parental responses to heritable characteristics of children and influencing the genetically influenced ontogeny of parenting.

Conventional models of psychological development acknowledge that genetic and social factors both play a role. Older models assumed that these two influ-

Reprinted with permission from Reiss, D. (2005). The interplay between genotypes and family relationships. *Current Directions in Psychological Science, 14,* 139–143. © 2005 Blackwell Publishers.

ences were independent from each other and that differences among individuals in personality development, cognitive development and psychological development could be explained by adding their effects together. More recently, it has become clear that, in many cases, the social environment interacts with genetic influences. For example, the genetic risk for schizophrenia seems to be fully expressed only when children at genetic risk grow up in families with high conflict, emotional restriction, and chaotic intergenerational boundaries (Tienari et al., 2004). Such a perspective still allows social and genetic variables to be thought of as relatively distinct: Genetic factors render individuals susceptible to adverse social environments; then, at some point—perhaps in early childhood or much later in development—unfavorable social factors elicit behavioral difficulties.

Recent data suggest that genetic and social influences are even more intertwined, however. From early development through adulthood, genetic and social factors are *correlated*; that is, individuals' genotypes are associated with many specific characteristics of their environment. This association occurs in two ways. First, as can be inferred from twin, sibling, and adoption studies, heritable characteristics of children can evoke highly specific responses from the social environment. For example, certain heritable characteristics of children evoke warmth and involvement from their parents. More importantly, the same genetic factors that evoke parental warmth also contribute to a child's social responsibility, including adherence to community norms and helping and sharing behaviors. In the research of my colleagues and I, almost all of the covariance between maternal warmth and child social responsibility is due to these genetic influences common to both parenting and child development (Reiss, Neiderhiser, Hetherington, & Plomin, 2000).

The second way such associations may occur is that heritable traits that influence a mother's or father's parenting may be genetically transmitted to their children. Those same traits in children may make them vulnerable to psychopathology. For example, a recent twin study suggests that heritable factors influence maternal smoking during pregnancy and, when transmitted to children, increase the childrens' likelihood of having conduct problems. These data raise questions about whether fetal exposure to tobacco products is the main cause of their postnatal conduct problems (Maughan, Taylor, Caspi, & Moffitt, 2004).

In behavioral genetics, associations between individuals' genotypes and their environment are called *genotype–environment correlations*. When a correlation is due to the effects of heritable features stimulating responses from the environment, it is called an *evocative* genotype–environment correlation. When it

is due to genes transmitted by parents to their children, the term is *passive* genotype–environment correlation. Use of the word *genotype* in this type of research signifies the cumulative effect of all genetic influences on a particular trait, as examined in studies that usually use twin, sibling, or adoption designs.

Genotype–Environment Correlations and Mechanisms of Development

Parent–Child Relationships May Amplify Genetic Influences

Rowe (1981) first reported data suggesting evocative genotype–parenting correlations. Monozygotic (i.e. derived from a single egg and genetically identical) twins' reports of how accepted they were by their parents were correlated more than twice as highly as the reports of dizygotic (i.e. from different eggs and 50% genetically related) twins. Figure 1 illustrates how

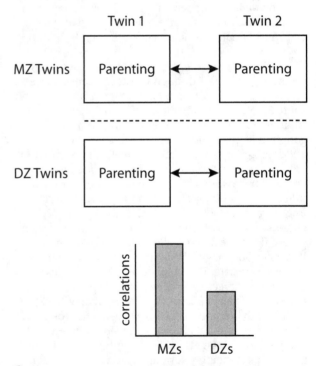

figure 1

Diagram showing how inferences about genetic influences on variation of a measured variable, in this case parenting, may be drawn from twin data. Boxes represent measured variable in a comparison of monozygotic (MZ) and dizygotic (DZ) child twins; the arrows represent correlations. The bar graph at the bottom of the figure represents example findings. The example finding shows MZ child twins correlate much more strongly than DZ child twins, enabling the inference that heritable characteristics of the child influence parenting (Reiss, Neiderhiser, Hetherington, & Plomin, 2000).

monozygotic–dizygotic comparisons are used to make inferences about such correlations. Rowe's finding was subsequently replicated many times using different methods of assessing parent–child relationships: interviews of parents (Goodman & Stevenson, 1991), parental self-reports, and direct observation of parent–child relationships (O'Connor, Hetherington, Reiss, & Plomin, 1995). These findings do not reflect parental bias due to their knowledge of whether their twins were monozygotic or dizygotic, since the findings also hold where monozygotic twins have been misdiagnosed as dizygotic (Goodman & Stevenson, 1991).

Adoption studies have confirmed the importance of evocative genotype–parenting correlations: The behavior of an adoptive parent toward his or her child can be predicted from patterns of behavior in the birth parent. For example, two separate studies predicted adoptive parents' degree of harsh discipline and hostility toward their children from the level of aggressive behavior in the birth parents. These studies suggest that inherited externalizing (including aggressive and delinquent) behavior in the children evoked the response in the adoptive parents (Ge et al., 1996; O'Connor, Deater-Deckard, Fulker, Rutter, & Plomin, 1998).

Heritable evoked parental responses have been reported from age 1 through late adolescence. For example, one study compared nonadoptive siblings, who share 50% of their individual-differences genes, with siblings adopted from different birth parents. Data gathered at age 1 and again at age 2 suggested that children's genotypes greatly influenced how much intellectual stimulation their parents provided to them: Parental behavior correlated much higher toward the nonadoptive siblings than toward the adoptive siblings (Braungart, Plomin, Fulker, & DeFries, 1992). Other studies have reported on genetic influences on parenting at age 3, in middle childhood, and in adolescence. One longitudinal twin study suggested that heritable evocative effects increase across adolescence; this increase across age was particularly marked for fathers (Elkins, McGue, & Iacono, 1997).

To study heritable evocative effects, the Nonshared Environment in Adolescent Development study (NEAD; Reiss et al., 2000) combined a twin design with a stepfamily design. We drew genetic inferences from comparisons among monozygotic twins, dizygotic twins, full siblings, half siblings (e.g., a mother brings a child from a previous marriage and has a child with her new husband) and unrelated siblings (i.e., each parent brings a child from a previous marriage). NEAD showed that heritable evocative effects may be quite specific. For example, genetic factors that evoke maternal warmth are distinct from those that evoke parental warmth.

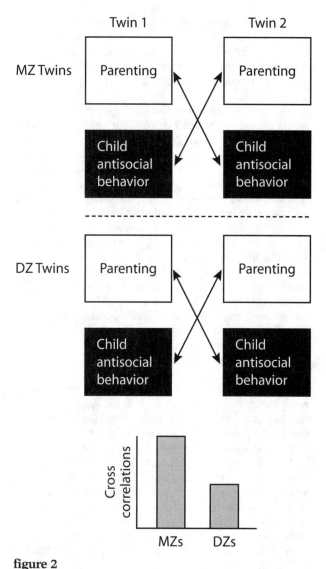

figure 2

Example cross correlation of parenting and child adjustment across sibling types. Parenting in one twin cross correlates with antisocial behavior in the other, more highly for monozygotic (MZ) twins than for dizygotic (DZ) twins. This suggests that the covariation between parenting and child antisocial behavior can be attributed to genetic influences common to both variables (Reiss et al., 2000).

Additional findings reveal that heritable effects go beyond evocative effects on parents. The same genetic factors in a child that evoke particular parenting responses also influence many dimensions of their own adjustment during childhood and adolescence. Inferences about these influences are drawn by comparing *cross correlations* across sibling types (see Fig. 2). For example, a mother's harsh parenting towards sibling A can be correlated with the level of antisocial behavior of sibling B. Genetic influences on covariance are inferred when these cross correlations decline systematically from monozygotic twins at the highest to dizygotic twins and full siblings in the middle to unrelated siblings at the lowest.

NEAD found that over 70% of the covariance between a mother's hostile parenting and her adolescents' antisocial behavior was accounted for by genetic influences common to both. These findings have been confirmed by several subsequent studies (e.g., Burt, Krueger, McGue, & Iacono, 2003). NEAD found sizable genetic contributions to many other covariances including mothers' hostile parenting with impairment in adolescents' cognitive performance, fathers' warmth with adolescents' social responsibility, and fathers' hostility with adolescents' depression. NEAD, using longitudinal data collected from earlier and later adolescence, found that, in many cases, the child's heritable impact on parental response preceded the development of the behavior in question. For example, genetic influence on hostile parenting preceded the evolution of antisocial behavior.

Evocative genotype–parenting correlations may amplify more direct genetic influences on the child's problem behavior. Indeed, it is possible that parental responses to their children's heritable characteristics— responses to which the parents themselves are insensible—are critical for transforming heritable influences on children's temperaments into problems requiring clinical attention. To verify this hypothesis and test its significance for preventive intervention, my colleagues and I are currently conducting a prospective adoption study. We are following birth- and adoptive parents and adopted toddlers from age 9 months. This Early Growth and Development Study (EGADS) will allow us to pinpoint exactly what heritable noxious behaviors in the child evoke adverse parental responses and the consequence of these parental responses for subsequent child development.

The Heritable Development of Parenting

Evidence for passive genotype–parenting correlation requires evidence that (a) the parents' genes influence their parenting and (b) genetic factors that influence parenting are transmitted to their children and influence important dimensions of the children's adjustment. Evidence of this kind provides clues to childhood origins of parenting styles. For example, suppose it is observed that the same genetic factors that influence lack of warmth in mothers also influence depressive symptoms in their children. This would suggest that genetic factors link childhood internalizing with reduced maternal warmth, thereby offering clues about how genetically influenced parenting patterns unfold over the long term. Evidence for these passive effects comes from two sources.

First, studies using twins who are parents have shown genetic influences on dimensions of parenting. Our Twin Mom study investigated a sample of monozygotic and dizygotic twins who were mothers of adolescents. It showed that mothers' reports of their own warmth, hostility, and monitoring of the whereabouts of their children were more highly correlated for monozygotic than for dizygotic twins. A similar pattern of findings was shown using observer ratings for mothers' warmth and for children's ratings of their mothers' monitoring (Neiderhiser et al., 2004).

Second, adoption studies have found evidence for passive genetic links between parenting and the adjustment of children both in early childhood and in later adolescence. The correlation between parenting and child adjustment in birth families reflects evocative genotype–parenting correlations, environmental mechanisms, and passive genotype–parenting correlations. The last type are missing in adoptive families. Thus, by comparing correlations between parenting and child adjustment between the two groups it is possible to estimate—by elimination—the strength of passive genotype–parenting correlations. For example, one adoption study assessed parents' ratings of cohesiveness, lack of conflict, and open expression of feelings in their family during the time their children were 1 to 5 years old. For boys but not for girls, these ratings predicted teacher ratings of child delinquency and aggression at age 7, but only for boys raised by their own birth parents (Braungart-Rieker, Rende, Plomin, & DeFries, 1995). The correlations between parenting and teacher-rated aggression were insignificant in adoptive families. The correlations between adolescent problems and ratings of the quality of family relationships by their mothers were higher in families in which parents reared their own children than in adoptive families (McGue, Sharma, & Benson, 1996).

Taken together, these findings suggest that genotypic differences among parents influence their parenting and that these genotypic differences are transmitted to children, in whom they are manifested by psychiatric symptoms. We are currently investigating whether there are specific genetic links between childhood behavioral characteristics and patterns of parenting. For example, might internalizing problems in childhood be genetically linked to parental withdrawal and lack of support? Might childhood externalizing be genetically linked to aggressive and hostile parenting styles?

Highlighting Relationship Influences

Genetically informed studies highlight two sorts of family relationships that are linked with child psychological development independently of children's genotypes. Parent–child relationships are the first sort of such relationships identified by behavioral genetic data. For example, NEAD found that maternal rapport and affection was linked to adolescent autonomy and sociability. This is the case no matter what the child's genotype. Moreover, siblings within the same family are similar in their autonomy and sociability whether they are dizygotic or monozygotic twins or unrelated siblings. In contrast to parent hostility, the amount of maternal warmth received is also similar across both types of twins and unrelated siblings. Thus, taken together, our data suggest that mothers are relatively consistent in the positive feelings they show to children in their family and that all children benefit, no matter their genotype (Reiss et al., 2000).

Second, behavioral genetic data have highlighted nonparental family relationships that appear to influence children's development independently of their genotype. For example, NEAD showed that hostility and conflict in sibling relationships was strongly associated with adolescent antisocial behavior and depression. Conflict and hostility were highly reciprocal in adolescent siblings and put both siblings at equal risk for psychiatric symptoms independently of their genotypes. Moreover, NEAD showed a strong association between marital conflict and parent–child conflict on the one hand and sibling hostility on the other. More importantly, these links across family subsystems were independent of child genotype. Thus, in adolescence, hostility between siblings may be an indirect route through which family discord increases the vulnerability of children regardless of their genotype (Reiss et al., 2000).

Because it included the partners of the sisters who were the biological parents of the adolescent children, the Twin Mom study was able to yield valuable data on the role of adult genotypes in marital relationships. The study found that although genetic factors had a substantial influence on marital quality, as reported by both the twin siblings and their husbands, genetic factors explained little of the covariance between marital satisfaction and levels of wives' depressive symptoms. Rather, in this association, the dynamics of the marital relationships may play a central role (Spotts et al., 2004). These findings extend nongenetic studies of adult development that appeared to show that good marriages protect against depression and other behavior difficulties. However, nongenetic studies may miss heritable features of individuals that lead to both sustained, high-quality marriages and invulnerability to depression. Yet if the Twin Moms data is replicated, heritable features will seem unlikely to play a significant role in how marriages protect the marital partners.

Implications: New Targets for Prevention

Data on genotypes and family relationships offer three novel opportunities to design preventive interventions to forestall the development of serious problem behaviors and psychopathology.

First, findings suggesting that parent–child relationships amplify maladaptive genetic influences offer some of the most promising leads in preventing the expression of unfavorable genetic influences on many domains of child and adolescent adjustment. EGADS is designed to specify particular targets for intervention: parents' responses to heritable difficulties in their children. Numerous studies show that highly focused interventions can produce sustained changes in how parents respond to challenging children (Bakermans-Kranenburg, van Ijzendoorn, & Juffer, 2003). EGADS is designed to ascertain whether such interventions might suppress the parental amplification process and thus diminish adverse genetic influences.

Second, findings on passive genotype correlations provide a new target for interventions: promoting favorable parenting. The discovery of genetic links between childhood behavior and parenting suggests some childhood and adolescent origins of parenting behavior that should be addressed in efforts to prevent risky parental behavior such as drug abuse during pregnancy or hostile and abusive parenting subsequently. For example, efforts to prevent the early emergence of conduct problems may prevent later serious antisocial behavior as well as abusive parenting.

Finally, studies of genotype–environment correlation suggest new psychosocial targets for preventing psychological and behavioral disorder: siblings and marriages. Techniques already developed for clinical interventions with maladaptive sibling relationships and with marriages might be refashioned for preventing psychological disorders in the siblings or marital partners.

RECOMMENDED READING

Maughan, B., Taylor, A., Caspi, A., & Moffitt, T.E. (2004). (See References)

Reiss, D., Pederson, N.L., Cederblad, M., Lichtenstein, P., Hansson, K., Neiderhiser, J.M., et al. (2001). Genetic probes of three theories of maternal adjustment: I. Recent evidence and a model. *Family Process, 40,* 247–259.

Rutter, M., Pickles, A., Murray, R., & Eaves, L. (2001). Testing hypotheses on specific environmental causal effects on behavior. *Psychological Bulletin, 127,* 291–324.

REFERENCES

Bakermans-Kranenburg, M.J., van Ijzendoorn, M.H., & Juffer, F. (2003). Less is more: Meta-analyses of sensitivity and attachment interventions in early childhood. *Psychological Bulletin, 129,* 195–215.

Braungart, J.M., Plomin, R., Fulker, D.W., & DeFries, J.C. (1992). Genetic mediation of the home environment during infancy: A sibling adoption study of the HOME. *Developmental Psychology, 28,* 1048–1055.

Braungart-Rieker, J., Rende, R.D., Plomin, R., & DeFries, J.C. (1995). Genetic mediation of longitudinal associations between family environment and childhood behavior problems. *Development & Psychopathology, 7,* 233–245.

Burt, S., Krueger, R.F., McGue, M., & Iacono, W. (2003). Parent–child conflict and the comorbidity among childhood externalizing disorders. *Archives of General Psychiatry, 60,* 505–513.

Elkins, I.J., McGue, M., & Iacono, W.G. (1997). Genetic and environmental influences on parent–son relationships: Evidence for increasing genetic influence during adolescence. *Developmental Psychology, 33,* 351–363.

Ge, X., Conger, R.D., Cadoret, R.J., Neiderhiser, J.M., Yates, W., Troughton, E., & Stewart, M.A. (1996). The developmental interface between nature and nurture: A mutual influence model of child antisocial behavior and parent behaviors. *Developmental Psychology, 32,* 574–589.

Goodman, R., & Stevenson, J. (1991). Parental criticism and warmth towards unrecognized monozygotic twins. *Behavior and Brain Sciences, 14,* 394–395.

Maughan, B., Taylor, A., Caspi, A., & Moffitt, T.E. (2004). Prenatal smoking and early childhood conduct problems: Testing genetic and environmental explanations of the association. *Archives of General Psychiatry, 61,* 836–843.

McGue, M., Sharma, A., & Benson, P. (1996). The effect of common rearing on adolescent adjustment: Evidence from a U.S. adoption cohort. *Developmental Psychology, 32,* 604–613.

Neiderhiser, J.M., Reiss, D., Pedersen, N.L., Lichtenstein, P., Spotts, E.L., Hansson, K., Cederblad, M., & Elthammar, O. (2004). Genetic and environmental influences on mothering of adolescents: A comparison of two samples. *Developmental Psychology, 40,* 335–351.

O'Connor, T.G., Deater-Deckard, K., Fulker, D., Rutter, M., & Plomin, R. (1998). Genotype–environment correlations in late childhood and early adolescence: Antisocial behavioral problems and coercive parenting. *Developmental Psychology, 34,* 970–981.

O'Connor, T.G., Hetherington, E.M., Reiss, D., & Plomin, R. (1995). A twin-sibling study of observed parent–adolescent interactions. *Child Development, 66,* 812–829.

Reiss, D., Neiderhiser, J., Hetherington, E.M., & Plomin, R. (2000). *The relationship code: Deciphering genetic and social patterns in adolescent development.* Cambridge, MA: Harvard University Press.

Rowe, D.C. (1981). Environmental and genetic influences on dimensions of perceived parenting: A twin study. *Developmental Psychology, 17,* 203–208.

Spotts, E.L., Neiderhiser, J.M., Ganiban, J., Reiss, D., Lichtenstein, P., Hansson, K., Cederblad, M., & Pedersen, N. (2004). Accounting for depressive symptoms in women: A twin study of associations with interpersonal relationships. *Journal of Affective Disorders, 82,* 101–111.

Tienari, P., Wynne, L.C., Sorri, A., Lahti, I., Laksy, K., Moring, J., Naarala, M., Nieminen, P., & Wahlberg, K. (2004). Genotype–environment interaction in schizophrenia spectrum disorder. *British Journal of Psychiatry, 184,* 216–222.

Questions

1. What does it mean that genetic and social factors are correlated? Can you give an example that shows how parent and child behaviors may be correlated in this way?
2. Name and describe the two types of genotype-environment correlations that researchers have identified. What do these relations add to our understanding of child development, especially regarding the active role that children play in their own development?
3. Why do researchers who study genotype-environment interactions often use twins and adopted children in their studies? Why are siblings also interesting to examine in this type of research?
4. What social and genetic factors have been found to contribute to the development of antisocial behavior in children?
5. Why is it important that treatment interventions for children at risk for unhealthy development focus on both parents and children? Can you provide an example to support your argument?
6. Do genes determine our destiny? Why or why not?

9 Recall in Infancy: A Neurodevelopmental Account

Patricia J. Bauer

Over the course of childhood, the human brain goes through enormous changes that have profound effects on all aspects of psychological development. Using recently established techniques of studying changes in the brain, researchers are now able to examine the relations between these changes and psychological development. In the following article, Patricia J. Bauer traces connections between neural development and memory development in infancy, posing a number of questions: When do the processes of memory develop? How do they operate in the very early years of life? What changes in the brain reflect, and are perhaps responsible for, this developing capability?

Although neurological research with infants is still in its infancy, so to speak, researchers are forming a picture of what develops in the brain in the early years of life, and they are beginning to see how these changes relate to early memory capabilities. In the last decades, research on memory in adults has been aided greatly by advances in neuroimagining techniques, particularly fMRIs and PET scans. However, as Bauer points out, these techniques present problems for research with infants and, therefore, developmental researchers have relied on other ways of studying the brain, such as event-related potentials (ERPs) that measure brain activity. This information allows researchers to make predictions about the type of memory processing infants may rely on before and after certain neural connections are formed. Studies can then be designed to distinguish these processes in infant behavior, and the hypotheses are tested.

This new direction of research is valuable for many reasons. It provides an account of the neural basis of human memory development, and thus an additional window for studying memory development in the very early years of life, a time when knowledge formation and memory processes are difficult to assess. In addition, it provides insight into the relation between neural change and memory development. As Bauer points out, results from brain development research have opened discussion about fundamental aspects of early memory, including one of the most perplexing and intriguing questions of all: why do we remember so little about the early years of our life?

Relations between developments in neural structures and changes in memory in infancy are a relatively recent focus of research. Greater knowledge about brain development, as well as methodological advances such as combined use of behavioral and electrophysiological techniques, have led to the generation and testing of specific hypotheses regarding sources of age-related change. Theory and data converge to suggest that the early-stage processes of encoding and consolidation are a significant source of age-related variability in memory early in life. Additional research is needed to determine how these processes change and interact with myriad other determinants of recall.

Memory is fundamental to cognition. We depend on it to remember the past, to predict the future, and to accrue knowledge of the world. Given the centrality of memory to mental life, it is fortunate that it develops

---

Reprinted with permission from Bauer, P. J., (2007). Recall in infancy: A neurodevelopmental account. *Current Directions in Psychological Science, 16,* 142–146. © 2007 Blackwell Publishers.

Acknowledgments   Much of my work discussed here was supported by the National Institute of Child Health and Human Development (HD-28425, HD-42483). I also thank the many colleagues who have helped to shape my thinking on memory and its development, as well as the infants, children, and families who make this research possible.

early and rapidly. Indeed, by the end of infancy, long-term memory is reliable and robust (Bauer, 2002, 2004). Because no special training is necessary for memory to develop, it might seem that the capacity is a simple one. Yet memory processes are complex, multifaceted, and multiply determined. The purpose of this article is to consider one major factor: the developing brain. Explicating the links between behavior and the brain enhances the description of developmental change and simultaneously advances explanation of it.

Significant progress in the search for the neural bases of memory in adults came from the study of patient H.M. After major portions of his medial-temporal lobes were removed to treat his epilepsy, H.M.'s ability to form new memories of names, dates, places, and events that he later could recall or explicitly recognize was impaired. In contrast, he was able to learn, for example, new motor skills. The case of H.M. and others like him led many researchers to the conclusion that memory is not a single ability but is organized into separate systems or is subserved by different processes. The system or process that is impaired in H.M. is one allowing for conscious recall or recognition of verbally accessible information. The system or process that is intact is one that supports learning that is neither accessible to consciousness nor expressed through language. The link between structures in the medial-temporal lobe—particularly the hippocampus—and the formation of new memories that are accessible to recall or explicit recognition has been verified by animal models (e.g., Squire, 1992) and is further indicated by neuroimaging studies (e.g., functional magnetic resonance imaging, fMRI, and positron emission tomography, PET; e.g., Nyberg & Cabeza, 2000).

Challenges in the Study of the Neural Bases of Recall in Development

In the developmental literature, the search for the neural foundations of memory is just getting underway. Although interest in age-related differences in memory dates to Ebbinghaus (1897), for definitional and methodological reasons the neural bases of memory in development were not a focus of research until the late 20th century. Because different types of memory seemingly depend on different neural structures and networks, it is important to specify the type of memory under study. However, different types of memory are distinguished by features, such as accessibility to consciousness and language, that are difficult to evaluate in infants. Nor has it been easy to investigate links between neural structures and memory functions in infants. Human infants rarely have the types of brain damage that inform researchers of the neural bases of memory in adults; animal models

tend to be of mature systems; and many neuroimaging techniques are not appropriate for infants in particular because they require radioactive substances (PET) or exposure to strong magnetic fields (fMRI).

In the late 20th century, a number of these challenges were met. Perhaps because historically recall was thought to be late to develop (see Bauer, 2006b), a major focus has been on relations between structural change and developments in the ability to form memories and then retrieve them once the event is past or the object is no longer present. To assess recall in infants who can neither speak nor comment on their state of consciousness, researchers frequently use imitation-based tasks in which props are used to produce actions or multi-step sequences that subjects imitate immediately, after a delay, or both. As I have discussed elsewhere (Bauer, 2006b), memories of events learned via imitation sometimes can later be expressed through language; adults with impairments in verbal recall due to medial-temporal damage also are impaired on imitation tasks; and ordered reproduction of multistep sequences requires recall—the order in which the actions should be produced is not apparent in the props themselves. Simultaneous with the advance of a nonverbal means of assessing recall were increases in the understanding of pre- and postnatal brain anatomy and physiology. The study of relations between brain and behavior was furthered by research with special populations (e.g., those with developmental amnesia), an increase in work with animal models of cognition in development, and studies employing noninvasive imaging techniques (e.g., event-related potentials or ERPs—scalp-recorded signals associated with neuronal activity). With the addition of each new piece of the puzzle, the picture has sharpened.

Relations Between Structure and Function in Infancy

Recall depends not only on the hippocampus but also on other medial-temporal and cortical structures (e.g., Zola & Squire, 2000). Experience initially registers in cortical regions across the surface of the brain. For experience to endure as a memory trace, its distributed representation must be integrated and consolidated, processes carried out by medial-temporal structures in concert with the cortex. Retrieval of memories from long-term cortical stores is especially dependent on the prefrontal cortex (at the front of the brain).

As reviewed elsewhere (e.g., Bauer, 2004; Nelson, Thomas, & de Haan, 2006), some aspects of the medial-temporal structures develop relatively early. In contrast, the prefrontal cortex and a portion of the hippocampus known as the dentate gyrus develop later. It is not until 20 to 24 months that these structures become able to subserve their functions (functional maturity). It is only late in the preschool years and adolescence or early adulthood, however, that the dentate gyrus and prefrontal cortex, respectively, reach full maturity, as indexed by the adult number of synapses.

The relatively late development of aspects of the temporal-cortical network has implications for behavior (see Bauer, 2004, 2006a, 2006b). Protracted development of cortical structures likely affects all phases of the life of a memory: encoding, consolidation, storage, and retrieval. Late development of the dentate gyrus is critical because it is the major "route in" to the hippocampus, where new memory traces are consolidated for long-term storage. The immaturity of these temporal-cortical structures and the connections between them is expected to hinder all of the life-phases of a memory. As these structures develop, age-related changes in behavior should be apparent.

At a general level, the time course of changes observed in recall matches what is known about developments in the temporal-cortical network. As noted, the network likely reaches the peak number of synaptic connections late in the first year and over the second year of life. As a result, we should expect improved communication between the medial-temporal cortices and the hippocampus and, thus, between the hippocampus and the neocortex. This in turn should herald increases in the reliability and robustness of recall. This is precisely what is observed. As illustrated in Figure 1, between 9 and 20 months of age, the length of time over which events can apparently be recalled increases from 1 to 12 months. Consistent with the loci of the neural changes taking place between 9 and 20 months, there is evidence that the major contributors to the increase in temporal extent

of recall over the second year are specifically the processes of encoding and consolidation (see Bauer, 2006a).

Encoding

Studies combining behavioral and electrophysiological (Fig. 2a) measures have revealed age-related changes in encoding of events into memory in the first year that relate to variability in recall. In a longitudinal study (Bauer et al., 2006), we exposed infants to event sequences (Fig. 2b) and immediately thereafter used ERPs to test their recognition of the props of the sequences (by showing pictures of props of familiar sequences interspersed with pictures of props from novel sequences; Fig. 2c). Differential responses to props they had seen before and to novel props indicated that the infants recognized them and thus must have encoded the sequences. Infants had more robust ERP responses to sequences encoded when they were 10 months old than they did to sequences encoded when they were 9 months old. These differences in encoding were associated with differential recall between the two ages: Infants had greater recall of sequences encoded at 10 months than of sequences encoded at 9 months; at 10 months, more robust ERP indices of encoding were associated with higher level of recall. Age-related differences in encoding continue throughout the second year, as evidenced by faster learning to a specific criterion (such as perfect reproduction of a sequence) and higher levels of recall immediately after exposure to events by older infants than by younger ones (see Bauer, 2005, 2006a, 2006b for reviews).

Consolidation

Even with encoding controlled (statistically, through matching, or by learning to criterion; Bauer, 2004, 2005), developmental differences still are apparent: Older infants remember longer than their younger counterparts do. This compels examination of the next phase of memory processing—namely, consolidation. We tested the role of post-encoding processes in another study that combined behavior and ERP (Bauer, Wiebe, Carver, Waters, & Nelson, 2003). We administered ERP tests immediately after exposure to events (to measure encoding) and 1 week later (to measure the integrity of the memory trace during the period of consolidation). We then tested recall 1 month later. The immediate ERP indicated that the infants had encoded the sequences; variability in encoding did not predict long-term recall. In contrast, measures of how well the trace had been consolidated accounted for 28% of the variance in recall 1 month later.

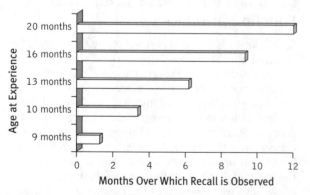

figure 1
Lengths of time (in months) over which infants 9 to 20 months of age at the time of experiencing an event sequence have been shown to recall it. Data on 9- and 10-month-olds are from Carver and Bauer (2001); data on 13-, 16-, and 20-month-olds are from Bauer, Wenner, Dropik, and Wewerka (2000).

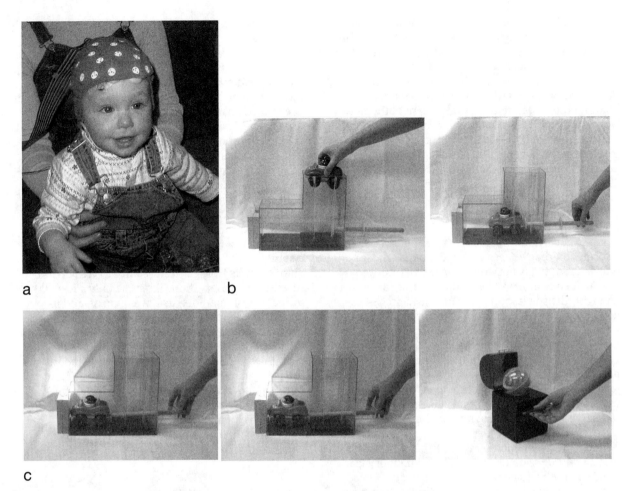

a

b

c

figure 2

Task to measure infants' differential neural processing of familiar and novel stimuli. Infant participants watch a 2-step sequence (panel b)—in this case, putting a car into an L-shaped apparatus and pushing a handle to move the car along the track (causing a light at the end to go on). Some amount of time later, the infants are shown photographs of the props from the previously experienced event (panel c, left) interspersed with props from an event they have not seen before (panel c, right) while wearing a 32-channel electrode cap (panel a) for recording event-related potentials (ERPs). ERPs are scalp-recorded electrical oscillations that indicate brain activity; differences in the latency and amplitude of infants' response to the different classes of stimuli can be interpreted as evidence of differential neural processing. Panel a reprinted from Remembering the Time of Our Lives: Memory in Infancy and Beyond, *by P.J. Bauer, 2007, Mahwah, NJ: Erlbaum, p. 198. Copyright 2007, Lawrence Erlbaum Associates. Reprinted with permission.*

Consolidation processes continue to explain variance in the second year. For 20-month-olds, the amount of information retained over 48 hours explains 25% of the variance in recall after 1 month (see Bauer, 2004). Moreover, variability in consolidation is observed in infants suspected (based on animal models) to have damage to the hippocampus associated with maternal gestational diabetes (DeBoer, Wewerka, Bauer, Georgieff, & Nelson, 2005). Infants born to mothers with and without gestational diabetes did not differ in immediate recall of events. After a 10-minute delay, however, recall by infants of mothers with diabetes was significantly impaired. In DeBoer's longitudinal sample, the deficit was apparent at 12 months and had not resolved at 24 months. Because differences were not observed at immediate testing, consolidation (rather than encoding) processes are implicated.

Neurodevelopmental Analysis Brings New Perspective

Consideration of the biology of memory is important not only for accurate description of age-related changes but also for explaining such changes. It leads to identification of components of the temporal-cortical network as rate-limiting variables in development of recall and to new hypotheses regarding the sources of developmental change.

An implicit assumption is that there are changes in how long children remember because, with age, children become more successful at keeping their memories fresh and robust, whereas the memories of younger children fade with time. However, consideration of the processes whereby new memories are made, and of the timing of development of the network involved, leads to a different conclusion: namely, that age-related differences come into play even as a representation is being transformed from an immediate experience into an enduring trace (Bauer, 2006a). That transformation is especially hard for younger infants because of late developments within the responsible neural network. Early vulnerability of memories is critical because it confers later vulnerability: Information that is not encoded cannot be consolidated; information that escapes consolidation is not stored; information that is not stored cannot be retrieved.

The behavioral profiles outlined earlier are consistent with the suggestion that early-stage processes (encoding and consolidation) account for developmental variance in long-term recall. Another assumption following from this perspective is that the proportion of variance accounted for by early-stage processes declines with age, as more memories survive the initial periods of vulnerability (Bauer, 2006a; the relation may actually be curvilinear, with increases associated with changes in the aging brain). Ultimately, whether these specific suggestions are supported is not the important thing. What is critical is that a neurodevelopmental analysis of memory leads to new hypotheses about the sources of age-related change, tests of which will provide new data that will aid in description as well as explanation of the development of memory.

The Future of Research on Recall of the Past

In a relatively short time, a neurodevelopmental approach to the study of memory has yielded new empirical data and spurred theoretical advances. Although there are many directions for future research, two seem especially compelling. The first I called for in 2002 (Bauer, 2002): We need "more detailed models of how developmental changes in the underlying substrate for memory relate to changes in the reliability and robustness of recall" (p. 140). Progress has been made in understanding how age-related and individual variability in encoding and consolidation relate to long-term recall. Additional research to determine how these processes operate not only in infancy but throughout childhood is needed. With it, we will be able to evaluate hypotheses such as the suggestion of a shift in the locus of developmental differences in forgetting from early-stage to later-stage processes.

The second avenue for research is investigation of how the neural processes and mechanisms interact with myriad other influences on memory development. Ultimately, both description and explanation of age-related change in memory will entail multiple levels of analysis, from proteins and genes to cultural influences on narrative expression. For example, as described in Bauer (2006b), even in some of its early manifestations, memory is influenced by the social world. Maternal support relates to children's performance on imitation-based tasks; it relates to autobiographical-narrative competence both concurrently and over time. Cultural influences are apparent in the preschool years and are implicated as a source of the pattern of later earliest memories among adults from Eastern relative to Western cultures. These observations illustrate only a few of the influences on memory, its development, and its expression. Further progress in understanding the development of memory will require that the multiple determinants of this complex process be studied in concert with one another. A multilevel perspective is necessary to our understanding not only of how developments in the brain impact behavior but of how behavior (and experience more broadly) impacts neural development. The neurodevelopmental window is but one of many that let in the full light of explanation.

RECOMMENDED READING

Eichenbaum, H., & Cohen, N.J. (2001). *From conditioning to conscious recollection: Memory systems of the brain*. New York: Oxford University Press.

Kandel, E.R., & Squire, L.R. (2000). Neuroscience: Breaking down scientific barriers to the study of brain and mind. *Science, 290*, 1113–1120.

Nelson, C.A., & Webb, S.J. (2002). A cognitive neuroscience perspective on early memory development. In M. de Haan & M.H. Johnson (Eds.), *The cognitive neuroscience of development* (pp. 99–125). London, UK: Psychology Press.

REFERENCES

Bauer, P.J. (2002). Long-term recall memory: Behavioral and neurodevelopmental changes in the first 2 years of life. *Current Directions in Psychological Science, 11*, 137–141.

Bauer, P.J. (2004). Getting explicit memory off the ground: Steps toward construction of a neuro-developmental account of changes in the first two years of life. *Developmental Review, 24*, 347–373.

Bauer, P.J. (2005). Developments in declarative memory: Decreasing susceptibility to storage failure over the second year of life. *Psychological Science, 16*, 41–47.

Bauer, P.J. (2006a). Constructing a past in infancy: A neuro-developmental account. *Trends in Cognitive Sciences, 10,* 175–181.

Bauer, P.J. (2006b). Event memory. In W. Damon & R.M. Lerner (Series Eds.) and D. Kuhn & R. Siegler (Vol. Eds.), *Handbook of Child Psychology: Vol. 2. Cognition, Perception, and Language* (6th ed., pp. 373–425). Hoboken, NJ: Wiley.

Bauer, P.J. (2007). *Remembering the times of our lives: Memory in infancy and beyond.* Mahwah, NJ: Erlbaum.

Bauer, P.J., Wenner, J.A., Dropik, P.L., & Wewerka, S.S. (2000). Parameters of remembering and forgetting in the transition from infancy to early childhood. *Monographs of the Society for Research in Child Development, 65*(4, Serial No. 263).

Bauer, P.J., Weibe, S.A., Carver, L.J., Lukowski, A.F., Haight, J.C., Waters, J.M., & Nelson, C.A. (2006). Electrophysiological indices of encoding and behavioral indices of recall: Examining relations and developmental change late in the first year of life. *Developmental Neuropsychology, 29,* 293–320.

Bauer, P.J., Wiebe, S.A., Carver, L.J., Waters, J.M., & Nelson, C.A. (2003). Developments in long-term explicit memory late in the first year of life: Behavioral and electrophysiological indices. *Psychological Science, 14,* 629–635.

Carver. L.J., & Bauer, P.J. (2001). The dawning of a past: The emergence of long-term explicit memory in infancy. *Journal of Experimental Psychology: General, 130,* 726–745.

DeBoer, T., Wewerka, S., Bauer, P.J., Georgieff, M.K., & Nelson, C.A. (2005). Explicit memory performance in infants of diabetic mothers at 1 year of age. *Developmental Medicine and Child Neurology, 47,* 525–531.

Ebbinghaus, H.(1897). Über eine neue Methode zur Prüfung geistiger Fähigkeiten und ihre Anwendung bei Schulkindern [About a new method for testing intellectual abilities and its application with school children]. *Zeitschrift für Psychologie und Physiologie der Sinesorgane, 13,* 401–457.

Nelson, C.A., Thomas, K.M., & de Haan, M. (2006). Neural bases of cognitive development. In W. Damon & R. M. Lerner (Series Eds.) and D. Kuhn & R. Siegler (Vol. Eds.), *Handbook of Child Psychology: Vol. 2. Cognition, Perception, and Language* (6th ed., pp. 3–57). Hoboken, NJ: Wiley.

Nyberg, L., & Cabeza, R. (2000). Brain imaging of memory. In E. Tulving & F.I.M. Craik (Eds.), *The Oxford handbook of memory* (pp. 501–519). New York: Oxford University Press.

Squire, L.R. (1992). Memory and the hippocampus: A synthesis from findings with rats, monkeys, and humans. *Psychological Review, 99,* 195–231.

Zola, S.M., & Squire, L.R. (2000). The medial temporal lobe and the hippocampus. In E. Tulving & F.I.M. Craik (Eds.), *The Oxford handbook of memory* (pp. 485–500). New York: Oxford University Press.

Questions

1. What are some of the reasons that memory is difficult to study in infants?
2. What are ERPs and what can they tell researchers about the brain?
3. How do age-related changes in temporal-cortical structures affect infant behavior from 9 to 20 months of age?
4. What does research on brain development suggest about why it is that young infants forget many of the experiences they have?
5. As Bauer discusses, research has shown that parents can provide social support for infant cognition in several areas of development. Given what you have learned from this article, what do you think parents can do to enhance their infants' memory?
6. If, in the future, there are ways to ask infants questions about what they know and remember, what questions would you want to ask them?

Culture and Early Infancy Among Central African Foragers and Farmers

Barry S. Hewlett • Michael E. Lamb • Donald Shannon
Birgit Leyendecker • Axel Schölmerich

One technique used by psychologists to study the contributions of experience to human development involves comparing the behaviors and abilities of children reared in different cultural settings. Behavioral observations are the main method of data collection in this type of research. To conduct the research described in the following article, a team of developmental psychologists went to two communities in central Africa and studied how adults care for infants. These neighboring communities, the Aka and the Ngandu, were of interest to the researchers because they are both small in scale, have little consumerism, and are socioeconomically similar to each other. However, they differ in some interesting ways, primarily in their subsistence practices—that is, the means by which they obtain the necessities of life. The Aka are hunter-gatherers, or foragers, and the Ngandu are settled, or sedentary, people who farm.

Barry Hewlett and his colleagues observed adults' caregiving of two age groups of infants, 3- to 4-month-olds and 9- to 10-month-olds, as families went about their daily activities. Using an observational technique called time sampling, the researchers observed and recorded adult caregiving behaviors (such as physical affection and vocalizing), the dyadic behaviors of adults and infants (such as holding and face-to-face contact), and the independent behaviors of the infants (such as fussing and smiling). The main differences observed were that Aka infants were more likely to be in close proximity to their care providers, to sleep more, and to fuss less than the Ngandu infants. Did differences in the behaviors of the caregivers correlate in any systematic way with these infant behaviors? As you read the article, you will discover differences in caregiver behavior that may explain why babies behaved differently in these two communities.

This study illustrates the utility of investigating child development as it occurs in different cultural circumstances. Such research can advance understanding of how cultural context, social experience, and individual behavior fit together. Finding different patterns of child rearing and infant behaviors in different communities does not explain why these patterns exist, however. This article concludes with an interesting discussion of some of the possible explanations for the differences that were observed in these two communities. As you will see, potential explanations are many, ranging from differences in subsistence patterns to maternal workloads to environmental hazards to cultural ideologies. Perhaps future research will reveal which of these explanations is the most useful for understanding variations in child-rearing practices and infant development across cultural communities.

Everyday infant experiences among the Aka hunter-gathers and the neighboring Ngandu farmers were observed and compared. Twenty Aka and 21 Ngandu 3- to 4-month-olds and 20 Aka and 20 Ngandu 9- to 10-month-olds were observed for 3 hr on each of 4 days so that all 12 daylight hr were covered. The Aka infants were more likely to be held, fed, and asleep or drowsy, whereas Ngandu infants were more likely to be alone and to fuss or cry, smile, vocalize, or play. The amount of crying, soothing, feeding, and sleeping declined over time in both groups. Distal social interaction increased over time among the Ngandu but not among the Aka. Despite striking cultural differences on many variables, however, functional context systematically affected the relative prominence of the infants' behavior in both cultural groups.

In this article, we examine infant care among two culturally distinct peoples in central Africa—Aka foragers and Ngandu farmers. Both cultures could be described as "traditional," small scale, preindustrial, or non-Western because industrial production and wage labor are minimal and no socioeconomic class structure (beyond age and sex) exists. Infancy in small-scale traditional cultures is frequently contrasted with infancy in European American cultures, which are typically referred to as global scale, industrial, or Western (Dixon, Tronick, Keefer, & Brazelton, 1981; Konner, 1977; LeVine, 1994; Super & Harkness, 1981; Tronick, Morelli, & Winn, 1987). Although comparative studies of these types of cultures have contributed substantially to the understanding of infant development, they often give the impression that infant care practices vary little across traditional non-Western societies or that the variability between Western and small-scale traditional cultures is greater than the variability within either one of these groups. LeVine (1974, 1989, 1994), for instance, described two parenting strategies—the agrarian (or pediatric) and the urban-industrial (or pedagogical)—following his work among the Gusii of East Africa. In his view, agrarian parents focus on the survival, health, and physical development of their infants because infant mortality levels are high, with half of the children not surviving to reproductive maturity. To monitor and respond to indicators of health and survival, agrarian parents hold or keep their infants in close proximity, quickly respond to fusses or cries, and feed their infants on demand. By contrast, urban-industrial parents focus on active engagement, social exchange, stimulation, and proto-conversation with their infants because these parents are concerned with the acquisition of cognitive skills essential to success in an environment in which infant mortality is low, children cost more and contribute less, and a competitive labor market builds on an academically graded occupational hierarchy.

Several researchers have confirmed that European Americans emphasize verbal and distal interaction, whereas mothers in traditional small-scale societies stress proximal interaction (Bakeman, Adamson, Konner, & Barr, 1990; Barr, 1990; Goldberg, 1977; Keller, Schölmerich, & Eibl-Eibesfeldt, 1988; Konner, 1976, 1977; Richman et al., 1988; Richman, Miller, & LeVine, 1992; Super & Harkness, 1981). Unfortunately, these comparative studies tended to sample from only one traditional non-Western group (e.g., Gusii in the Richman studies, Kipsigis in the Super and Harkness study, and !Kung in the Konner and Barr studies) compared with one or more European American groups, implicitly suggesting that traditional small-scale cultures have similar patterns of parenting. Some researchers have compared European Americans with more than one non-Western group (e.g., Bornstein et al., 1992; Roopnarine, Talukder, Jain, Joshi, & Srivastav, 1990), but the non-Western samples in these studies tend to be drawn from urban-industrial cultures (e.g., Japan and China). In this study, we focused on variability in infant care in small-scale or traditional non-Western cultures—cultures with minimal consumerism and social-economic stratification.

Researchers have also relied on brief observations (usually 1–2 hr of observation at each age), and this has precluded examination of the ways in which context might influence parent–infant interactions in different cultures. In addition, the differences between the Western and traditional small-scale cultures sampled have been so pronounced that the focus on these differences precluded analysis of within-group variability. High levels of parent–child proximity in traditional cultures are often attributed to high infant mortality and a resultant concern with survival, for example. In this article, our goal is to explore differences between two small-scale non-Western groups, on the assumption that a focus on both within- and between-culture variability promotes better understanding of the forces that shape infant development.

The comparison between Aka and Ngandu is interesting because these neighboring societies make a living in the same tropical forest, have similar mortality and fertility levels (infant mortality is 15–20%, juvenile [<15 years] mortality is 40–50%, total fertility rate is about six live births per woman); have frequent social, economic, and religious interactions; and are exposed to one another's practices on a regular basis, yet have distinct modes of production, male–female relations, and patterns of child care (see Hewlett, 1991b, for a detailed description of the cultures). The Aka are foragers (also known as hunter-gatherers), move their camps several times a year, have minimal political hierarchy, and have relatively high gender and intergenerational egalitarianism, whereas the Ngandu are sedentary "slash-and-burn" farmers with stronger chiefs and marked gender and intergenerational inequality. As a result, Aka–Ngandu comparisons may provide insights into several issues, including the role of natural selection (i.e., differential reproduction) in shaping infant care.

Noting that in comparison with Western cultures, non-Western foragers and farmers hold their infants extensively, breastfeed frequently, and respond promptly to fusses and cries, developmentalists have described these practices as part of a hazard-prevention strategy that serves to buffer vulnerable infants from health risks in contexts of high infant mortality (Blurton Jones, 1993; Kaplan & Dove, 1987; LeVine, 1994; Tronick, Morelli, & Ivey, 1992). By studying the Aka and Ngandu, we can evaluate this hypothesis because they both experience high infant mortality rates, have lived in association with each other for generations, and observe one another frequently. As a result, holding, responsiveness to fussing or crying, and the frequency of breastfeeding should be similarly high in the two cultures if they enhance infant survival. Moreover, parents in both cultures have had the opportunity both to evaluate the costs and benefits of different infant practices and to modify their own.

Studying these two cultures further allows researchers to explore the impact of different socioeconomic lifestyles on infant care. With the exception of Konner's (1977) research on the !Kung hunter-gatherers and Tronick et al.'s (1987, 1992) research on the Efe hunter-gatherer-traders, most of the traditional non-Western societies studied have comprised agriculturists. Like LeVine (1974, 1989, 1994), the Whitings (Whiting & Edwards, 1988; Whiting & Whiting, 1975) have suggested that parenting practices are determined by the modes of production, which they called *maintenance systems,* because the subsistence demands, especially the workloads of women, lead to different patterns of child care. The Aka–Ngandu comparison may thus elucidate the differential effects of foraging and agricultural lifestyles on infant care.

Several cross-cultural theorists (such as Keller, 1997; Kornadt & Trommsdorff, 1990; Tronick et al., 1987) have hypothesized that differences between Western and traditional small-scale cultures with respect to infant–adult proximity are linked to distinct cultural goals: Western parents engage in frequent verbal and face-to-face interaction to promote independence and autonomy, whereas parents in small-scale and other non-Western cultures use close body contact and affective tuning to promote more social sensitivity and group-oriented tendencies. Structural aspects of a culture may also be significant in this regard. In cultures such as India, Japan, and China that are highly patriarchal, women can exert political and economic power and control primarily through their children (Keller, 1997). For example, Wolf (1972) has hypothesized that Chinese mothers hold, indulge, and limit access to their infants to develop more dependent and loyal children who will give support and status as the mothers grow older. As a result, both patriarchy and a strong cultural emphasis on social unity or conformity should be associated with more infant–adult proximity.

Both of the cultures we studied share more and are in many ways more egalitarian than European American cultures, but Aka sharing and egalitarianism are substantially greater than among the Ngandu. Ngandu households that accumulate more than others and do not share with neighboring families are prime targets of sorcery. This promotes some sharing between households, but there is marked inequality within Ngandu households, with men and elderly individuals receiving more than others. The Aka, by contrast, share with many people in many households on a daily basis, and there is greater gender and age egalitarianism. To foster egalitarianism, Aka also avoid drawing attention to themselves and eschew evaluative rankings, while also respecting individuality and autonomy. By contrast, the Ngandu promote social unity and conformity.

The Ngandu live alongside roads in sedentary communities of about 100 to 400 people. The Ngandu in this study lived in Bagandu, where two or three vehicles pass each day. Bagandu has a Catholic church, local market, health clinic, and several small shops, run mostly by Tchadians. Ngandu men build the 40-ft by 20-ft (12.19 m × 6.10 m), one- to three-roomed mud-and-thatch houses. Polygyny is common among the Ngandu (35% of the men have more than one wife), and each wife has her own room or house. Houses are about 40 ft (12.19 m) from each other, but there are no walls or fences between houses and other villagers frequently walk by. By contrast, the Aka live in camps of 25 to 35 blood or marriage relatives and move camp several times a year for various reasons (e.g., better hunting, death in camp). The dome-shaped Aka houses are made by women and have just enough room for a narrow 4-ft-long (1.22 m) log bed and a fire. Camps consist of four to six houses that are very close to each other (1–2 ft, .30 m–1.22 m) so all camp members live in an area (around 200 ft^2, 18.58 m^2) about the size of a large living and dining room in the United States. Cooperative net hunting involves men, women, and children, who connect their nets to form a circle. The men go to the center of the circle and try to chase game into the net, while the women stay close to the net, tackling the animals once they are trapped.

Whereas Aka men and women contribute equally to subsistence, Ngandu women are the primary providers. Ngandu men clear and burn plantations, whereas women plant, weed, harvest, and prepare all subsistence food items (manioc, corn, peanuts, plantains, etc.). Unlike the Aka, the Ngandu are actively engaged in a local cash economy, and many women are small-scale merchants, selling plantains, peanuts, nuts, mushrooms, and alcohol. Men are completely responsible for coffee production, hunting with trap lines or guns, and searching for gold or diamonds in the local streams. Ngandu women are responsible for home maintenance, laundry, and collecting water and firewood. Ngandu subsistence involves "delayed returns" (Woodburn, 1982, p. 435), in that the Ngandu have to delay the rewards of investment until harvest time. By contrast, the Aka subsistence system involves "immediate returns" (Woodburn, 1982, p. 435) in that the Aka consume everything within a day or two after capture or collection. The Aka may thus share more frequently in part because relatively little has been invested. The workload of Ngandu mothers also appears to be greater than that of the Aka, especially given the extensive sharing and cooperation among the Aka. Meanwhile, Aka infants are socialized in a denser social context than are Ngandu infants. Like the !Kung, Aka infants are carried in slings on the left-hand side of the adults' bodies (Konner, 1976, 1977). This leaves the head, arms, and legs free and allows the infant to nurse on demand. By contrast, Ngandu infants are tied rather snugly on the adults' backs. When the adults are sitting, both Aka and Ngandu care providers place infants on their laps or between their legs facing outwards. When infants are laid down, they are always placed on their backs. Aka infants sleep with their parents and siblings, whereas Ngandu infants often sleep with their mothers (or in separate cots, when husbands come to visit).

The Ngandu have more caregiving devices than Aka; some parents make small chairs, beds or mats for the infants to lie on. Ngandu infants also have more clothes, are often dressed more warmly than adults even in the middle of a hot day, and are washed once or twice a day. By comparison, Aka infants seldom have more than a protective forest cord around their waists and are infrequently given a complete bath. Both Aka and Ngandu caregivers carefully keep insects and debris off their infants.

Method

Participants

Twenty Aka and 21 Ngandu 3- to 4-month-olds and 20 Aka and 20 Ngandu 9- to 10-month-olds were observed for 3 hr on each of 4 different days so that all 12 daylight hours were covered (roughly, 6 a.m. to 6 p.m.). Thirteen of the Aka 3-month-olds, 12 of the Ngandu 3-month-olds, 9 of the Aka 9-month-olds, and 12 of the Ngandu 9-month-olds were boys. Six (3 Aka, 3 Ngandu) of the Aka and Ngandu 3- to 4-month-olds and 14 (6 Aka) of the 9- to 10-month-olds were firstborns, and 20% of the Aka and Ngandu fathers in both age cohorts had more than one wife. None of the Aka had received a formal education nor were they engaged in the cash economy, and all Aka parents engaged in subsistence activities during the observations. Most of the Ngandu men and several of the Ngandu women had received some elementary education. Men and women engaged in subsistence and market activities, but none were employed outside the households.

Procedure

Families were asked to follow their everyday activities and to ignore the observer, although, as always, it is difficult to know precisely how much the caregivers changed their daily activities to accommodate the observations. Ngandu mothers, in particular, seldom left their homes to participate in public activities (e.g., going to the market or standing in line for hours at the health clinic), in part, we believe, because the observer's presence elicited such curiosity. Aka generally do not accommodate others very much, and they pursued a great variety of activities outside their houses or camps. Observations took place in both rainy and dry seasons, but the majority of the 3- to 4-month-old observations took place in the dry season, whereas the majority of the observations of the 9- to 10-month-olds took place in the rainy season. Both Aka and Ngandu are more likely to stay home during the rainy season.

Using a 20-s observe–10-s record time sampling procedure for 45 min, observers noted on a checklist the occurrence of 11 adult and 9 infant behaviors, 5 dyadic behaviors, as well as the location, position, and identity of the adult near, holding, or caring for the infant. Observers then took a 15-min break before starting the next 45 min of observation. The beginning and end of each time sampling unit were signaled through an earphone from a small tape recorder.

The codes, which were also used and defined by Belsky, Gilstrap, and Rovine (1984) and by Fracasso, Lamb, Schölmerich, and Leyendecker (1997), are listed in Table 1. Observers were trained until they were reliable using videotaped interactions, but interobserver reliability was checked during the data gathering by having two different coders independently observe infants at the same time. Interobserver reliability coefficients were computed by correlating the two observers' scores on each variable. Mean reliability of codes was .82 (range = .65–.96), and the interobserver reliability of each code is provided in Table 1. Most (75%) of the observations were conducted by one observer. Interobserver reliability was checked twice—before observations began with each age group. Warm-up observations were used to acclimate Ngandu but not Aka parents and children. Because the observers were living with the Aka, Aka houses are open, and the camp is a public sphere (in contrast to the United States, where houses are considered private spheres), there was no apparent need to acclimate Aka parents and children to the observers. The Aka adults and children appeared unaffected by the observers' activities.

In addition to assessing the number of intervals in which certain behaviors were observed, we also defined five mutually exclusive and exhaustive contexts (feeding, caretaking, object play, social interaction, and no interaction) to describe the overall activity of the dyad as suggested and previously demonstrated by Leyendecker, Lamb, Schölmerich, and Miranda Fricke (1997). As in Leyendecker et al.'s study, the feeding and caretaking contexts were identified as such by the coders, and even when other activities such as so-

table 1   Codes Used for the Observation of Care Provider–Infant Interaction

Behavior	Interobserver reliability
Dyadic behavior	
Face-to-face	.75
Mutual visual	.67
C holds	.96
C proximal (within arm's length)	.82
C grooms, dresses, cleans, etc.	.91
C feeds or nurses	.96
Care provider behavior	
C attention is focused on infant (watches)	.78
C checks on infant (brief glances)	.84
C stimulates or arouses infant	.83
C physical affect towards infant	.79
C nonphysical affect towards infant	.72
C physically soothes infant	.87
C nonphysically soothes infant	.82
C vocalizes to infant	.76
M leisure (no subsistence activity)	.73
M works	.70
C talks to others	.83
Infant behavior	
I fussing	.78
I crying	.95
I sleeps	.87
I drowses	.65
I looks at *C*	.83
I smiles	.73
I vocalizes	.81
I plays alone (distracts self with objects, including own body)	.81
I plays with objects	.86
I responds to care provider stimulation	.77
Other behavior	
Location (lap, bed, arms, sling)	.92
Room (in house, outside house, forest, plantation)	.89

Note. *C* = care provider; *M* = mother; *I* = infant.

cial play and object play occurred in one of these two contexts, the functional context was still labeled as *feeding* or *caretaking,* respectively, because feeding or care-providing were the adults' primary goals at the time. Dyadic *object play* was coded when both infant and adult were involved in object play outside of feeding and caretaking, and *social interaction* was coded when the dyads were engaged in visual-verbal interactions, physical and nonphysical affect, and soothing outside of the other contexts. Whereas feeding, caretaking, object play, and social interaction describe dyadic states, all monadic states were coded as *no interaction* (e.g., infant looks at mother while mother does not look at the infant and vice versa; infant plays with object while mother is at leisure, etc.) as were all other units not included in the other four contexts.

Results

Because preliminary multi- and univariate analyses revealed no reliable effects of gender, the data concerning boys and girls were combined for the purposes of further analysis. A series of 2 (ethnic group: Aka or Ngandu) × 2 (age: 3–4 months or 9–10 months) multivariate analyses of variance (MANOVAs) were first used to assess the effects of ethnic group and age on the three groups of dependent variables—care provider behaviors, infant behaviors, and dyadic behaviors—and are displayed in Table 2. These analyses yielded significant effects for ethnic group on the care provider, $F(10, 68) = 3.56$, $p < .001$; infant, $F(11, 67) = 7.34$, $p < .0001$; and dyadic behaviors, $F(6, 72) = 26.38$, $p < .0001$, and significant effects for age on all three groups of dependent variables as well, $F(10, 68) = 6.76$, $p < .0001$; $F(11, 67) = 18.28$, $p < .0001$; $F(6, 72) = 4.57$, $p < .001$, respectively. Univariate analyses were used to explore these effects further, and the result of these analyses are provided in Table 2, along with the relevant means. Inspection of the table shows that, as expected, older infants slept and drowsed less, fussed or cried less, and consequently received less physical or nonphysical soothing than did the younger infants. The frequency of feeding, face-to-face interaction, and caregiving also declined over time, but the amount of adult leisure increased, presumably because observations of the young infants took place in the dry season, when the workload for Ngandu women is especially high, whereas observations of older infants took place in the rainy season, when maternal workloads are lower. The unavoidable confounds between age and season are unlikely to have accounted for any other effects reported here.

The Aka infants were substantially more likely than Ngandu infants to sleep, drowse, to be held or fed, or to be within proximity of their care providers, whereas

table 2 Age Cohort and Ethnic Group Differences in the Behavior of Adults and Infants

| | 3–4 Months | | | | 9–10 Months | | | | Effect | |
| | Aka | | Ngandu | | Aka | | Ngandu | | | |
Variable	M^a	SD	M^a	SD	M^a	SD	M^a	SD	Ethnic	Age
Dyadic behavior										
Face-to-face	2.57	3.32	2.17	2.37	0.14	0.13	0.99	1.13	0.19	14.85***
Mutual visual	2.35	3.62	1.10	0.82	0.05	0.07	2.72	4.36	1.26	0.29
C holds I	95.91	6.57	54.21	19.99	86.71	10.98	54.46	16.17	132.55**	1.93
C proximal (within arm's length)	97.29	4.03	65.31	16.19	86.57	15.63	63.42	17.06	75.34***	3.94
C grooms, dresses, cleans, etc.	5.03	1.74	6.50	3.32	2.74	1.29	6.10	3.86	15.35***	4.75*
C nurses or feeds	15.23	5.53	12.63	5.02	13.30	4.50	10.13	4.20	7.19**	4.34*
Care provider behavior										
C watches or checks on I	30.14	8.87	23.50	12.62	22.35	6.95	31.72	10.59	0.37	0.01
C stimulates or arouses I	0.63	0.75	1.73	1.52	0.06	0.09	2.57	3.85	14.97***	0.07
C physical affect toward I	4.18	2.18	3.08	2.86	1.38	1.01	1.72	1.26	0.76	22.14***
C nonphysical affect toward I	0.90	1.67	2.14	3.03	1.31	1.37	1.29	1.51	1.88	0.23
C physically soothes I	3.39	2.30	4.22	4.11	0.75	0.60	1.56	1.02	2.25	23.60***
C nonphysically soothes I	2.28	1.93	4.04	4.33	0.86	0.82	1.22	1.03	3.67	14.59***
C vocalizes to I	3.91	3.45	2.84	2.22	2.31	1.59	5.23	5.21	1.52	0.27
Mother leisure: no subsistence activity	67.45	23.63	50.34	22.68	70.71	15.04	65.75	11.58	6.84**	4.89*
Mother works	28.29	20.46	39.13	20.40	28.34	15.15	29.81	11.88	2.53	1.44
C talks to others	40.19	12.66	30.95	13.57	43.13	10.37	41.23	15.16	3.68	5.18*
Infant behaviors										
I fusses or cries	4.67	3.26	12.38	7.03	2.42	1.39	6.81	5.67	81.07**	12.96***
I alone, asleep	0.47	0.94	10.56	9.72	1.09	1.67	9.81	8.63	40.82***	0.00
I alone, awake	0.06	0.19	4.81	7.12	0.43	0.82	6.09	8.42	17.79***	0.45
I sleeps	41.34	14.99	31.40	10.30	19.77	9.13	18.41	9.80	5.11**	47.81***
I drowses	19.30	14.48	11.38	10.30	11.72	7.83	6.90	5.36	8.09**	7.24**
I looks at C	4.16	4.23	2.62	2.03	0.95	1.12	3.64	6.38	0.73	2.65
I smiles	0.51	0.56	1.25	1.57	0.26	0.25	3.56	4.11	9.55**	1.16
I vocalizes	2.37	3.14	9.32	7.85	3.53	3.23	11.88	11.13	22.98***	1.36
I plays alone (distracts self with objects, fingers, etc.)	1.11	1.67	2.79	3.14	1.95	1.39	14.86	22.74	8.2**	6.42**
I plays with objects	1.69	2.93	2.15	2.83	12.41	7.45	28.62	17.11	15.58***	77.65***
I responds to C stimulation	0.16	0.28	0.81	1.05	0.08	0.17	1.78	2.71	13.14***	1.92

Note. C = care provider; I = infant. Watch or check, fuss or cry, infant alone (nobody present in room) and infant alone and awake are combined behaviors from Table 1.

Only significant F values are reported in the two right-hand columns; in each case ($dfs = 1, 77$).

[a]Represents the mean percentage of the total number of intervals (1,080) during which the behavior was observed.

*$p < .05$. **$p < .01$. ***$p < .001$.

Ngandu infants were more likely than Aka infants to be alone, fuss, cry, smile, vocalize to care providers, play alone, or play with objects. Ngandu infants were stimulated and aroused more by their care providers than Aka infants were. There were no differences between ethnic groups in the frequency of care provider soothing, affect, watching or checking the infant, and face-to-face or mutual visual interactions.

Significant multivariate interactions between age and ethnic group were also evident for care provider, $F(10, 68) = 2.62$, $p < .009$; infant, $F(11, 67) = 3.73$, $p < .0001$; and dyadic, $F(6, 72) = 2.44$, $p < .034$, behaviors. Subsequent analyses using Tukey honestly significant difference tests revealed no group differences in adult vocalizations to infants at 3 months, although the Ngandu engaged in more mutual visual interactions at 9 ($p < .02$) but not at 3 months, and en-face interactions increased over time among the Aka ($p < .003$) but not among the Ngandu. The frequency of looking at care providers decreased over time among the Aka ($p < .007$) but did not change among the Ngandu. There were no group differences in the frequencies of object play and playing alone at 3 months, but the Ngandu engaged in significantly more play than the Aka ($p < .0001$ and $p < .003$, respectively) at 9 months. The frequency of watching and checking by the adults did not change over time among the Aka but increased among the Ngandu ($p < .05$).

Although there were striking Aka–Ngandu differences on a number of variables, it is instructive to examine these differences across functional contexts. For illustrative purposes, we focus here only on the observations of the 3- to 4-month-olds; the same

points could be made using the data for the 9- to 10-month-olds. Figures 1 to 4 graphically display variations across context on four variables in which there were significant differences between ethnic groups (fuss, cry, smile, and infant vocalization). In general, the figures indicate that, although ethnic differences were consistent across contexts (i.e., Ngandu infants fussed and cried more than Aka infants in all contexts), context systematically affected the relative prominence of the infants' behavior (i.e., both Aka and Ngandu fussed and cried more in social interaction). One implication is that both similarities and differences between Aka and Ngandu groups can be magnified or minimized unless steps are taken to ensure that observations take place in comparable contexts.

Discussion

Overall, the statistical analyses reported here revealed that Aka infant–adult interactions are more proximal, whereas Ngandu adult–infant interactions are more distal and that these differences become especially pronounced in late infancy. Aka care providers—usually mothers, fathers, or other adults—hold their infants, keep them close, feed them more frequently (2.2 vs. 4.0 times per hour) and longer, and soothe them just as long as Ngandu care providers do, even though Aka infants fuss or cry half as much as Ngandu infants. Aka respond to each fuss or cry, often by soothing, whereas Ngandu care providers are more likely to let the infant fuss or cry (Hewlett, Lamb, Leyendecker,

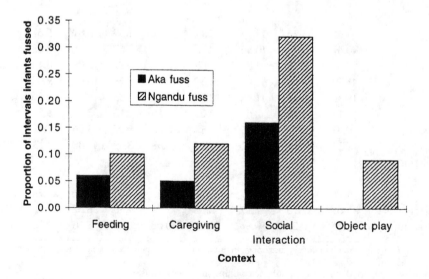

figure 1
Aka and Ngandu infant fussing in various contexts.

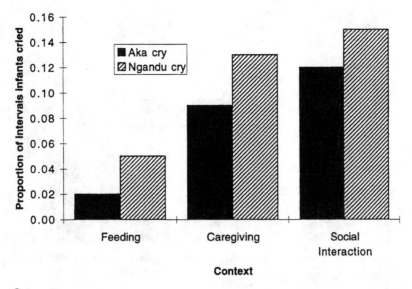

figure 2

Aka and Ngandu infant crying in various contexts (there was no crying during object play).

& Schölmerich, 1998). The differences are especially remarkable in light of the fact that Aka holding is energetically more costly to Aka mothers than to Ngandu mothers because, as pygmies, the Aka are considerably shorter and lighter than Ngandu women, whereas the Aka and Ngandu infants are of comparable weight. On the other hand, Ngandu stimulate their infants more by using distal behaviors; they are more likely to arouse and to vocalize to infants who are, in turn, more likely to respond by smiling and by vocalizing. The differentiation between these two non-Western populations is greater than the differences

between and among those Western groups that have been studied at similar ages with comparable methods (e.g., Fracasso et al., 1997; Leyendecker et al., 1997).

The fact that the Aka infants are held almost all the time may explain why these infants sleep or drowse more than Ngandu infants do and may also increase the potential for nonverbal communication, like that documented by McKenna, Mosko, Dungy, and McAninch (1990). When infants are held, the body movements, heartbeats, sounds, and smells of infants and adults provide the basis for a subtle "dance" that is obviously not captured when gross ob-

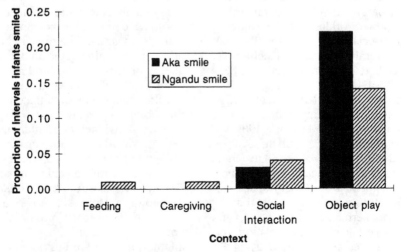

figure 3

Aka and Ngandu infant smiling in various contexts.

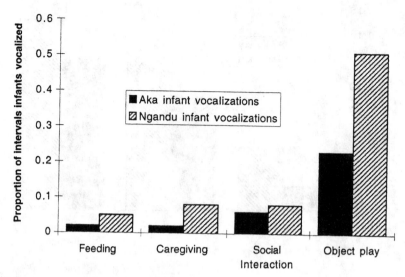

figure 4

Aka and Ngandu infant vocalizations in various contexts.

servational methods are used, so we cannot conclude that Aka adults and infants interact rarely. Meanwhile, because Ngandu infants are held about half as frequently as Aka infants, their interactions tend to depend on more distal forms of communication: Ngandu infants thus fuss, cry, smile, and vocalize to maintain or attract their parents' attention, and Ngandu adults vocalize and stimulate their infants in return.

Although this may explain why distal interaction is more common in Ngandu than in Aka infant–adult dyads, it does not explain why the Aka hold their infants so much or why the Ngandu tend not to do so. Are these differences explained by considerations of infant survival (more hazards in Aka environment), mode of production (lower workload by Aka women), or cultural ideologies (social unity, communalism), as suggested by cross-cultural theorists (Bornstein et al., 1992; Keller, 1997; LeVine, 1994; Tronick et al., 1987; Whiting & Whiting, 1975)?

Infant mortality is similarly high among both Aka and Ngandu, as it is in other contemporary forager and farmer environments (Bailey & Peacock, 1989; Bentley, Goldberg, & Jasienska, 1993; Cohen, 1989; Hewlett, 1991a), so this cannot explain the substantial cultural differences in the frequencies of proximal behaviors, although it might be argued that worries about survival are greater among Aka parents than among Ngandu parents, perhaps because the Aka environment is more dangerous (i.e., exposure to more hazards such as snakes, predators, or falling trees). Kaplan and Dove (1987) have suggested that Aché foragers in Paraguay hold their infants all the time

because the forest is potentially hazardous, and Blurton Jones (1993) has developed a simulation model influenced, in part, by his observation that Hadza and !Kung foragers always hold their infants; the model predicts greater reproductive fitness from constant holding even when hazards are rare. The differential infant mortality hypothesis is also not supported by Barry S. Hewlett's observations during 25 years of fieldwork (1973–1997) that there are as many poisonous snakes, spiders, and scorpions in the Ngandu villages and fields as in the forest and that Ngandu fields attract large and dangerous game animals, including elephants. Nor is it clear how holding an infant as opposed to laying it down nearby would affect survival differentially or why survival-focused Aka mothers would have primary responsibility for tackling trapped animals, a task that requires them to put their infants down and run after game animals. And if holding, frequency of breastfeeding, and responsiveness to crying dramatically affect survival, why would the Ngandu not alter their behavior to match that of the neighbors they observe so frequently?

Nutritional factors or infant morbidity might also explain why Aka are more proximal; Wachs, Sigman, Bishry, and Moussa (1992) have shown that caregiver behaviors are influenced by infant nutritional status. The hypothesis would be that Aka infants, in general, have lower nutritional status than Ngandu infants and are therefore more proximal. Although we did not directly measure the nutritional status of these infants, previous studies of infant and child health among the Aka and Ngandu (Cordes & Hewlett, 1990) indicated that infants and children in both groups were healthier than most infants in the developing world (measures included weight for height, head circumference, and hemoglobin levels). Both Aka and Ngandu are more proximal with ill infants, but sick infants were excluded from the study. Overall, it appears that the observed differences between Aka and Ngandu caregiver–infant interactions cannot be explained by differential health or survival rates.

What about the workloads of Ngandu and Aka mothers? The Whitings' (1975) hypotheses suggest that Ngandu infant–adult dyads might involve more distal-verbal interactions because Ngandu women's workloads are greater or because Ngandu subsistence tasks are incompatible with holding infants. In fact, Ngandu women usually put infants down when they fall asleep rather than switching activities, and none of their subsistence tasks are incompatible with infant care. Meanwhile, Aka parents have plenty of opportunities (in camp and on the hunt) to put their infants down but do not do so. Further, one deficiency of the maternal work hypothesis is the implication that infants are a burden, constraining their mothers' activities; many parents may feel this way in European American cultures, but such complaints are rare among the Aka and Ngandu. In addition, the Ngandu and Aka women we studied devoted equivalent amounts of time to subsistence and household work, although the Aka mothers had slightly more leisure time than the Ngandu mothers, especially when the infants were younger. These differences are likely to be artifacts of seasonal variations, however; the observations of the 3-month-olds were conducted in the dry season, when Ngandu women are unusually busy preparing the fields before the rains, whereas the observations of the 9-month-olds were conducted in the rainy season, when both Ngandu and Aka women have more leisure time. Aka mothers also "work" much more than Ngandu women when child care is included because they hold their infants so often. On the other hand, Aka mothers' other work may be less intense because they are not primary providers and they can count on extensive within-group sharing.

Cultural ideologies, such as the social unity hypothesis, do not explain the differences between the Aka and Ngandu either. Social unity, conformity, and patriarchy are central constructs in Ngandu culture, whereas autonomy in the context of the community and egalitarianism is the cultural script among the Aka. These cultural patterns predicted greater proximal behaviors among the Ngandu than among the Aka (Keller, 1997; Tronick et al., 1987), whereas the reverse was actually observed.

In sum, extant hypotheses, most of which were developed to explain Western versus non-Western differences rather than variation among Western or non-Western cultures (the Whitings' [1975] hypotheses being the exception) do not help explain the observed differences between the Aka and Ngandu.

Several features of the Aka and Ngandu cultures may be of explanatory value, however. First, the Aka move much more frequently than do the Ngandu: The whole camp moves from 4 to 18 times a year, camp composition changes daily as families arrive or leave temporarily to visit relatives and friends, and families travel several kilometers every day through open forest to hunt and gather. The Ngandu, on the other hand, stay in the same house for about 10 years and farm the same fields for 2 to 4 years. Absences are not as frequent or as long because the women have to maintain and protect their fields. As a result, the mobile Aka may perceive more risk than do the sedentary Ngandu because they are less familiar with their "home" and hold their infants more to accommodate potential hazards associated with the changing environment.

Second, differences between the social contexts may be pertinent. Aka camps comprise 25 to 35 people—many related to one another—who live together in an area about the size of a large living and dining room in the United States and engage in frequent cooperative activities like hunting. Ngandu households, by comparison, are much farther apart, and daily cooperation is limited to that between mothers and their children. Among nonhuman primates, interestingly, mothers in group-living pairs nurse and spend more time in contact with their infants than do mothers in isolated pairs (Konner, 1977). Isolated mothers distance themselves from, avoid, and punish their infants more. Similarly, Aka parents may be more willing to hold and nurse infants if their denser social contexts provide substantial alternative stimulation for both mothers and infants. Of course, by European American standards, the Ngandu are not socially isolated but by comparison with the Aka, their social contacts with other adults are fewer and shorter in duration.

Third, cooperative hunting and food sharing practices may ensure that the Aka are less concerned about having adequate supplies of food, and this may make them more willing (or able) to invest in energetically costly infant care.

Fourth, the Aka focus on immediate returns rather than on delayed gratification, and this may make them more willing to accommodate their infants' demands for gratification.

Whatever the reason for the observed differences between the Aka and the Ngandu, the data presented in this article suggest that there may be a forager pattern of infant care. When describing farming (agrarian) and urban-industrial parental goals and infant care patterns, LeVine (1989, p. 6) suggested a decade ago that foraging would generate unique parenting patterns, but he never described the distinguishing features. These data help describe the parenting style and some of the forces that shape it. Specifically, the Aka niche is marked by integration into small, dense groups of related individuals who have intimate relationships dominated by extensive sharing and cooperation in many activities, including hunting and gathering in the forest they inhabit and exploit on foot. Perhaps as a result, their infant care practices are characterized by almost continuous holding, frequent nursing, and prompt responsiveness, especially to signs of distress.

REFERENCES

Bailey, R. C., & Peacock, N. (1989, November). *The demography of foragers and farmers in the Ituri forest.* Paper presented at the meeting of the American Anthropological Association, Washington, DC.

Bakeman, R., Adamson, L. B., Konner, M., & Barr, R. G. (1990). !Kung infancy: The social context of object manipulations. *Child Development, 6,* 794–809.

Barr, R. G. (1990). The early crying paradox. *Human Nature, 1,* 355–389.

Belsky, J., Gilstrap, B., & Rovine, M. (1984). The Pennsylvania Infant and Family Development Project, I: Stability and change in mother–infant and father–infant interactions in a family setting at one, three and nine months. *Child Development, 55,* 692–705.

Bentley, G. R., Goldberg, T., & Jasienska, G. (1993). The fertility of agricultural and non-agricultural traditional societies. *Population Studies, 47,* 269–281.

Blurton Jones, N. (1993). The lives of hunter-gatherer children: Effects of parental behavior and parental reproductive strategy. In M. E. Pereira & L. A. Fairbanks (Eds.), *Juvenile primates* (pp. 309–326). New York: Oxford University Press.

Bornstein, M. H., Tamis-LeMonda, C., Tal, J., Ludemann, P., Toda, S., Rahn, C. W., Pecheux, M. G., Azuma, H., & Vardi, D. (1992). Maternal responsiveness to infants in three societies: The United States, France, and Japan. *Child Development, 63,* 808–821.

Cohen, M. N. (1989). *Health and the rise of civilization.* New Haven, CT: Yale University Press.

Cordes, L., & Hewlett, B. S. (1990, May). *Health and nutrition among Aka pygmies.* Paper presented at the International Conference on Hunting and Gathering Societies, Fairbanks, AK.

Dixon, S. D., Tronick, E. Z., Keefer, C., & Brazelton, T. B. (1981). Mother–infant interaction among the Gusii of Kenya. In T. M. Field, A. M. Sostek, P. Vietze, & P. H. Leiderman (Eds.), *Culture and early interactions* (pp. 149–170). Hillsdale, NJ: Erlbaum.

Fracasso, M. P., Lamb, M. E., Schölmerich, A., & Leyendecker, B. (1997). The ecology of mother–infant interaction in Euro-American and immigrant Central American families living in the United States. *International Journal of Behavioral Development, 20,* 207–217.

Goldberg, S. (1977). Infant development and mother–infant interaction in urban Zambia. In P. H. Leiderman, S. R. Tulkin,

& A. Rosenfeld (Eds.), *Culture and infancy* (pp. 211–243). New York: Academic Press.

Hewlett, B. S. (1991a). Demography and childcare in preindustrial societies. *Journal of Anthropological Research, 47,* 1–37.

Hewlett, B. S. (1991b). *Intimate fathers.* Ann Arbor: University of Michigan Press.

Hewlett, B. S., Lamb, M. E., Leyendecker, B., & Schölmerich, A. (1998). *Internal working models, trust, and sharing among hunter-gatherers.* Unpublished manuscript, Washington State University, Pullman.

Kaplan, H., & Dove, H. (1987). Infant development among the Aché of Eastern Paraguay. *Development Psychology, 23,* 190–198.

Keller, H. (1997). Evolutionary approaches. In J. W. Berry, Y. H. Poortinga, & J. Pandey (Eds.), *Handbook of cross-cultural psychology. Vol. 1: Theory and method* (2nd ed., pp. 215–255). Boston: Allyn & Bacon.

Keller, H., Schölmerich, A., & Eibl-Eibesfeldt, I. (1988). Communication patterns in adult–infant interactions in Western and non-Western cultures. *Journal of Cross-Cultural Psychology, 19,* 427–445.

Konner, M. J. (1976). Maternal care, infant behavior and development among the !Kung. In R. B. Lee & I. DeVore (Eds.), *Kalahari hunter-gatherers* (pp. 218–245). Cambridge, MA: Harvard University Press.

Konner, M. (1977). Infancy among Kalahari Desert San. In P. H. Leiderman, S. T. Tulkin, & A. Rosenfeld (Eds.), *Culture and infancy: Variations in the human experience* (pp. 287–328). New York: Academic Press.

Kornadt, H. J., & Trommsdorff, G. (1990). Naive erziehungstheorien japanischer Mutter-deutsch-japanischer Kulturvergleich [Naive theories of development: A cultural comparison between Japanese and German mother–infant interaction]. *Zeitschrift fur Sozialisations-forschung und Erziehungssoziologie, 2,* 357–376.

LeVine, R. A. (1974). Parental goals: A cross-cultural view. *Teachers College Record, 76,* 226–239.

LeVine, R. A. (1989). Human parental care: Universal goals, cultural strategies, individual behavior. In R. A. LeVine, P. M. Miller, & M. M. West (Eds.), *Parental behavior in diverse societies* (pp. 3–12). San Francisco: Jossey-Bass.

LeVine, R. A. (1994). *Child care and culture: Lessons from Africa.* Cambridge, England: Cambridge University Press.

Leyendecker, B., Lamb, M. E., Schölmerich, A., & Miranda Fricke, D. (1997). Contexts as moderators of observed interaction: A study of Costa Rican mothers and infants from differing socio-economic backgrounds. *International Journal of Behavioral Development, 21,* 15–34.

McKenna, J. J., Mosko, S., Dungy, C., & McAninch, J. (1990). Sleep and arousal patterns of co-sleeping human mother/infant pairs: A preliminary physiological study with implications for the study of Sudden Infant Death Syndrome (SIDS). *American Journal of Physical Anthropology, 83,* 331–347.

Richman, A. L., LeVine, R. A., New, R., Howrigan, G. A., Welles-Nystrom, B., & LeVine, S. E. (1988). Maternal behavior to infants in five cultures. In R. A. LeVine, P. M. Miller, & M. West

(Eds.), *Parental behavior in diverse societies* (pp. 81–98). San Francisco: Jossey-Bass.

Richman, A. L., Miller, P. M., & LeVine, R. A. (1992). Cultural and educational variations in maternal responsiveness. *Developmental Psychology, 28,* 614–621.

Roopnarine, J. L., Talukder, E., Jain, D., Joshi, P., & Srivastav, P. (1990). Characteristics of holding, patterns of play, and social behaviors between parents and infants in New Delhi, India. *Developmental Psychology, 26,* 667–673.

Super, C. M., & Harkness, S. (1981). The infant's niche in rural Kenya and metropolitan America. In L. L. Adler (Ed.), *Cross-cultural research at issue* (pp. 47–55). New York: Academic Press.

Tronick, E., Morelli, G. A., & Ivey, P. K. (1992). The Efe forager infant and toddler's pattern of social relationships: Multiple and simultaneous. *Developmental Psychology, 28,* 568–577.

Tronick, E., Morelli, G. A., & Winn, S. (1987). Multiple caretaking of Efe (Pygmy) infants. *American Anthropologist, 89,* 96–106.

Wachs, T. D., Sigman, M., Bishry, Z., & Moussa, W. (1992). Caregiver–child interaction patterns in two cultures in relation to nutritional intake. *International Journal of Behavioral Development, 15,* 1–18.

Whiting, B. B., & Edwards, C. P. (1988). *Children of different worlds: The formation of social behavior.* Cambridge, MA: Harvard University Press.

Whiting, B. B., & Whiting, J. W. M. (1975). *Children of six cultures.* Cambridge, MA: Harvard University Press.

Wolf, M. (1972). *Women and the family in rural Taiwan.* Stanford, CA: Stanford University Press.

Woodburn, J. (1982). Egalitarian societies. *Man* (New Series), *17,* 431–451.

Questions

1. What were some of the limitations of earlier cross-cultural research on parenting that Hewlett and his colleagues tried to overcome in this study?
2. How do the workloads of mothers differ in these two communities, and how does mothers' workload affect their caregiving behaviors?
3. How are infants carried in these two communities? How might these different ways of carrying babies influence psychological development?
4. Using Figures 1 and 2, what conclusions can you reach about how infants in these two communities behave? Do observations from different contexts, depicted in the figures, support your conclusions? If so, how?
5. Can the different caregiving patterns of the Aka and Ngandu be explained by infant health or survival rates? Use evidence from the article to support your answer.
6. How might these observations of two cultures influence a more general understanding of the correlation between parenting practices and early infant development?

Jerome Kagan

Temperament is defined as the way an individual behaves. It includes stylistic aspects of behavior, such as the emotional vigor, tempo, and regularity of an infant's responsiveness to caregivers. Temperament is of interest to developmental psychologists because it is evident early in life, it relates to behavior across a wide range of situations, and it appears to be relatively stable over time. There is also evidence that some aspects of temperament may be inherited; for example, emotionality, activity, and sociability have been found to be more similar in identical than in fraternal twins. For these reasons, many psychologists consider temperament to be the seed of what becomes an individual's unique personality.

One way in which researchers measure temperament in infancy is by observing babies' reactions to unfamiliar events. Some babies react in a heightened fashion, with much movement and distress, while other babies remain relaxed and calm. In the following article, Jerome Kagan, a leading researcher in the area of infant temperament, discusses longitudinal research that examined how children reacted to unfamiliar events when they were infants, toddlers, and 5-year-olds. The types of reactions included motor activity, fearfulness, and friendliness. The data revealed some stability in these styles of reaction over this time period—and change in some aspects of temperament. In addition to describing behaviors associated with high and low reactivity and how these behaviors looked over time, Kagan discusses the biological bases of these behaviors and the possible connections between these behavioral tendencies and later psychopathology.

This research illustrates several important points about development. First, even when characteristics are developmentally stable, they may assume different forms at different ages. Second, maturation of the organism can sometimes modify even extreme behaviors. Third, the development of temperament involves the coordination of biologically based tendencies with the emotional, cognitive, and social aspects of psychological growth.

The behavioral reactions to unfamiliar events are basic phenomena in all vertebrates. Four-month-old infants who show a low threshold to become distressed and motorically aroused to unfamiliar stimuli are more likely than others to become fearful and subdued during early childhood, whereas infants who show a high arousal threshold are more likely to become bold and sociable. After presenting some developmental correlates and trajectories of these 2 temperamental biases, I consider their implications for psychopathology and the relation between propositions containing psychological and biological concepts.

Introduction

A readiness to react to events that differ from those encountered in the recent or distant past is one of the distinguishing characteristics of all mammalian species. Thus, the events with the greatest power to produce both an initial orienting and sustained attention in infants older than 3 to 4 months are variations on what is familiar, often called discrepant events (Fagan, 1981; Kagan, Kearsley, & Zelazo, 1980). By 8 months of age, discrepant events can produce a vigilant posture of quiet staring and, occasionally, a wary face and a cry of distress if the event cannot be assimi-

Reprinted with permission from Kagan, J. (1997). Temperament and the reactions to unfamiliarity. _Child Development, 68_, 139–143. © 1997 Blackwell Publishers.

Acknowledgments This paper represents portions of the G. Stanley Hall Lecture delivered at the annual meeting of the American Psychological Association, New York City, August 1995. Preparation of this paper was supported, in part, by grants from the John D. and Catherine T. MacArthur Foundation, William T. Grant Foundation, and NIMH grant 47077. The author thanks Nancy Snidman and Doreen Arcus for their collaboration in the research summarized.

lated easily (Bronson, 1970). That is why Hebb (1946) made discrepancy a major basis for fear reactions in animals, why a fear reaction to strangers occurs in the middle of the first year in children growing up in a variety of cultural settings, and, perhaps, why variation in the initial behavioral reaction to novelty exists in almost every vertebrate species studied (Wilson, Coleman, Clark, & Biederman, 1993).

Recent discoveries by neuroscientists enrich these psychological facts. The hippocampus plays an important role in the detection of discrepant events (Squire & Knowlton, 1995). Projections from the hippocampus provoke activity in the amygdala and lead to changes in autonomic function and posture and, in older children, to reflection and anticipation (Shimamura, 1995). Because these neural structures and their projections are influenced by a large number of neurotransmitters and neuromodulators, it is reasonable to expect inherited differences in the neurochemistry of these structures and circuits and, therefore, in their excitability. Variation in the levels of, or receptors for, corticotropin releasing hormone, norepinephrine, cortisol, dopamine, glutamate, GABA, opioids, acetylcholine, and other molecules might be accompanied by differences in the intensity and form of responsivity to unfamiliarity (Cooper, Bloom, & Roth, 1991). This speculation is supported by research with infants and children (Kagan, 1994). This article summarizes what has been learned about two temperamental types of children who react in different ways to unfamiliarity, considers the implications of these two temperamental categories for psychopathology, and comments briefly on the relation between psychological and biological constructs.

Infant Reactivity and Fearful Behavior

About 20% of a large sample of 462 healthy, Caucasian, middle-class, 16-week-old infants became both motorically active and distressed to presentations of brightly colored toys moved back and forth in front of their faces, tape recordings of voices speaking brief sentences, and cotton swabs dipped in dilute butyl alcohol applied to the nose. These infants are called high reactive. By contrast, about 40% of infants with the same family and ethnic background remained motorically relaxed and did not fret or cry to the same set of unfamiliar events. These infants are called low reactive. The differences between high and low reactives can be interpreted as reflecting variation in the excitability of the amygdala and its projections to the ventral striatum, hypothalamus, cingulate, central gray, and medulla (Amaral, Price, Pitkanen, & Carmichael, 1992; Davis, 1992).

When these high and low reactive infants were observed in a variety of unfamiliar laboratory situations at 14 and 21 months, about one-third of the 73 high reactives were highly fearful (4 or more fears), and only 3% showed minimal fear (0 or 1 fear) at both ages. By contrast, one-third of the 147 low reactives were minimally fearful at both ages (0 or 1 fear), and only 4% displayed high levels of fear (Kagan, 1994).

The profiles of high and low fear to unfamiliar events, called inhibited and uninhibited, are heritable, to a modest degree, in 1- to 2-year-old middle-class children (DiLalla, Kagan, & Reznick, 1994; Robinson, Kagan, Reznick, & Corley, 1992). Further, high reactives show greater sympathetic reactivity in the cardiovascular system than low reactives during the first 2 years (Kagan, 1994; Snidman, Kagan, Riordan, & Shannon, 1995).

As children approach the fourth and fifth years, they gain control of crying to and reflex retreat from unfamiliar events and will only show these responses to very dangerous events or to situations that are not easily or ethically created in the laboratory. Hence, it is important to ask how high and low reactive infants might respond to unfamiliar laboratory situations when they are 4–5 years old. Each species has a biologically preferred reaction to novelty. Rabbits freeze, monkeys display a distinct facial grimace, and cats arch their backs. In humans, restraint on speech seems to be an analogue of the immobility that animals display in novel situations (Panksepp, Sacks, Crepeau, & Abbott, 1991), for children often become quiet as an initial reaction to unfamiliar situations (Asendorpf, 1990; Kagan, Reznick, & Gibbons, 1989; Kagan, Reznick, & Snidman, 1988; Murray, 1971). It is also reasonable to expect that the activity in limbic sites provoked by an unfamiliar social situation might interfere with the brain states that mediate the relaxed emotional state that is indexed by smiling and laughter (Adamec, 1991; Amaral et al., 1992).

When the children who had been classified as high and low reactive were interviewed at 4½ years of age by an unfamiliar female examiner who was blind to their prior behavior, the 62 high reactives talked and smiled significantly less often (means of 41 comments and 17 smiles) than did the 94 low reactives (means of 57 comments and 28 smiles) during a 1 hour test battery: $F(1, 152) = 4.51$, $p < .05$ for spontaneous comments; $F(1, 152) = 15.01$, $p < .01$ for spontaneous smiles. Although spontaneous comments and smiles were positively correlated ($r = 0.4$), the low reactives displayed significantly more smiles than would have been predicted from a regression of number of smiles on number of spontaneous comments. The high reactives displayed significantly fewer smiles than expected. Every one of the nine children who smiled more than 50 times had been a low reactive infant.

However, only a modest proportion of children maintained an extreme form of their theoretically expected profile over the period from 4 months to 4½ years, presumably because of the influence of intervening family experiences (Arcus, 1991). Only 19% of the high reactives displayed a high level of fear at both 14 and 21 months (> 4 fears), together with low values (below the mean) for both spontaneous comments and smiles at 4½ years. But not one low reactive infant actualized such a consistently fearful and emotionally subdued profile. By contrast, 18% of low reactive infants showed the opposite profile of low fear (0 or 1 fear) at both 14 and 21 months together with high values for both spontaneous smiles and spontaneous comments at 4½ years. Only one high reactive infant actualized that prototypic, uninhibited profile. Thus, it is uncommon for either temperamental type to develop and to maintain the seminal features of the other type, but quite common for each type to develop a profile that is characteristic of the less extreme child who is neither very timid nor very bold.

The 4½-year-old boys who had been high reactive infants had significantly higher resting heart rates than did low reactives, but the differences between high and low reactive girls at this older age took a different form. The high reactive girls did not show the expected high negative correlation (−0.6 to −0.8) between heart rate and heart rate variability. It is possible that the greater sympathetic reactivity of high reactive girls interfered with the usual, vagally induced inverse relation between heart rate and heart rate variability (Porges, Arnold, & Forbes, 1973; Richards, 1985).

Honest disagreement surrounds the conceptualization of infant reactivity as a continuum of arousal or as two distinct categories. The raw motor activity score at 4 months formed a continuum, but the distribution of distress cries did not. Some infants never fretted or cried; others cried a great deal. A more important defense of the decision to treat high and low reactivity as two distinct categories is the fact that within each of the two categories variation in motor activity and crying was unrelated to later fearfulness or sympathetic reactivity. If reactivity were a continuous trait, then a low reactive infant with extremely low motor and distress scores should be less fearful than one who showed slightly more arousal. But that prediction was not affirmed. Second, infants who showed high motor arousal but no crying or minimal motor arousal with frequent crying showed developmental profiles that were different from those who were categorized as low or high reactive. Finally, high and low reactives differed in physical and physiological features that imply qualitatively different genetic constitutions. For example, high reactives have narrower faces than low reactives in the second year of

life (Arcus & Kagan, 1995). Unpublished data from our laboratory reveal that the prevalence of atopic allergies among both children and their parents is significantly greater among high than low reactive infants. Studies of monozygotic and dizygotic same-sex twin pairs reveal significant heritability for inhibited and uninhibited behavior in the second year of life (Robinson et al., 1992). These facts imply that the two temperamental groups represent qualitatively different types and do not lie on a continuum of arousal or reactivity to stimulation.

The decision to regard individuals with very different values on a construct as members of the discrete categories or as falling on a continuum will depend on the scientists' purpose. Scientists who are interested in the relation, across families and genera, between brain size and body mass treat the two measurements as continuous. However, biologists interested in the maternal behavior of mice and chimpanzees regard these two mammals as members of qualitatively different groups. Similarly, if psychologists are interested in the physiological foundations of high and low reactives, it will be more useful to regard the two groups as categories. But those who are giving advice to mothers who complain about the ease of arousal and irritability of their infants may treat the arousal as a continuum.

Implications

The differences between high reactive–inhibited and low reactive–uninhibited children provoke speculation on many issues; I deal briefly with implications for psychopathology and the relation between psychological and biological propositions.

Anxiety Disorder

The high reactive infants who became very inhibited 4-year-olds—about 20% of all high reactives—have a low threshold for developing a state of fear to unfamiliar events, situations, and people. It is reasonable to expect that these children will be at a higher risk than most for developing one of the anxiety disorders when they become adolescents or adults. The childhood data do not provide a clue as to which particular anxiety profile will be most prevalent. However, an extensive clinical interview with early adolescents (13–14 years old), who had been classified 11 years earlier (at 21 or 31 months) as inhibited or uninhibited (Kagan et al., 1988), revealed that social phobia was more frequent among inhibited than among uninhibited adolescents, whereas specific phobias, separation anxiety, or compulsive symptoms did not differentiate the two groups (Schwartz, personal communication). This intriguing result, which requires replication, has interesting theoretical ramifications.

Research with animals, usually rats, suggests that acquisition of a fear reaction (e.g., freezing or potentiated startle) to a conditioned stimulus (light or tone) that had been paired with electric shock is mediated by a circuitry that is different from the one that mediates the conditioned response to the context in which the conditioning had occurred (LeDoux, 1995).

Davis (personal communication) has found that a potentiated startle reaction in the rat to the context in which light had been paired with shock involves a circuit from the amygdala to the bed nucleus of the stria terminalis and the septum. The potentiated startle reaction to the conditioned stimulus does not require that circuit. A phobia of spiders or bridges resembles an animal's reaction of freezing to a conditioned stimulus, but a quiet, avoidant posture at a party resembles a fearful reaction to a context. That is, the person who is extremely shy at a party of strangers is not afraid of any particular person or of the setting. Rather, the source of the uncertainty is a situation in which the shy person had experienced anxiety with other strangers. Thus, social phobia may rest on a neurophysiology that is different from that of specific phobia.

Conduct Disorder

The correlation between social class and the prevalence of conduct disorder or delinquency is so high it is likely that the vast majority of children with these profiles acquired their risk status as a result of life conditions, without the mediation of a particular temperamental vulnerability. However, a small proportion—probably no more than 10%—who began their delinquent careers before age 10, and who often committed violent crimes as adolescents, might inherit a physiology that raises their threshold for the conscious experience of anticipatory anxiety and/or guilt over violating community standards for civil behavior (Tremblay, Pihl, Vitaro, & Dubkin, 1994). Damasio (1994) and Mountcastle (1995) have suggested that the surface of the ventromedial prefrontal cortex receives sensory information (from the amygdala) that originates in the peripheral targets, like heart, skin, gut, and muscles. Most children and adults who think about committing a crime experience a subtle feeling that accompanies anticipation of the consequences of an antisocial act. That feeling, which might be called anticipatory anxiety, shame, or guilt, provides an effective restraint on the action. However, if a small proportion of children possessed a less excitable amygdala, or a ventromedial surface that was less responsive, they would be deprived of the typical inten-

sity of this feeling and, as a result, might be less restrained than the majority (Kochanska, Murray, Jacques, Koenig, & Vandegeest, 1996; Zahn-Waxler, Cole, Welsh, & Fox, 1995). If these children are reared in homes and play in neighborhoods in which antisocial behavior is socialized, they are unlikely to become delinquents; perhaps they will become group leaders. However, if these children live in families that do not socialize aggression consistently and play in neighborhoods that provide temptations for antisocial behavior, they might be candidates for a delinquent career.

Biology and Psychology

The renewed interest in temperament has brought some psychologists in closer intellectual contact with neuroscientists. Although this interaction will be beneficial to both disciplines, there is a tension between traditional social scientists who describe and explain behavioral and emotional events using only psychological terms and a smaller group who believe that an acknowledgment of biological events is theoretically helpful. The recent, dramatic advances in the neurosciences have led some scholars to go further and to imply that, in the future, robust generalizations about psychological processes might not be possible without study of the underlying biology (LeDoux, 1995).

Although some neuroscientists recognize that the psychological phenomena of thought, planning, and emotion are emergent—as a blizzard is emergent from the physics of air masses—the media suggest, on occasion, that the biological descriptions are sufficient to explain the psychological events. This publicity creates a misperception that the biological and psychological are competing explanations when, of course, they are not. Vernon Mountcastle notes that although "every mental process is a brain process, . . . not every mentalistic sentence is identical to some neurophysiological sentence. Mind and brain are not identical, no more than lung and respiration are identical" (Mountcastle, 1995, p. 294).

Some neuroscientists, sensing correctly the community resistance to a strong form of biological determinism, are emphasizing the malleability of the neuron's genome to environmental events. A few neurobiologists have come close to declaring that the human genome, like Locke's image of the child's mind, is a tabula rasa that is subject to continual change. This position tempts citizens unfamiliar with neuroscience to conclude that there may be a linear cascade that links external events (e.g., loss of a loved one) directly to changes in genes, physiology, and, finally, behavior, with the psychological layer (e.g., a mood of sadness) between brain physiology and apathetic behavior being relatively unimportant. This error is as serious as the one made by the behaviorists

60 years ago when they assumed a direct connection between a stimulus and an overt response and ignored what was happening in the brain. Both corpora of evidence are necessary if we are to understand the emergence of psychological qualities and their inevitable variation. "The phenomena of human existence and experience are always simultaneously biological and social, and an adequate explanation must involve both" (Rose, 1995, p. 380).

REFERENCES

Adamec, R. E. (1991). Anxious personality and the cat. In B. J. Carroll & J. E. Barett (Eds.), *Psychopathology in the brain* (pp. 153–168). New York: Raven.

Amaral, D. J., Price, L., Pitkanen, A., & Carmichael, S. T. (1992). Anatomical organization of the primate amygdaloid complex. In J. P. Aggleton (Ed.), *The amygdala* (pp. 1–66). New York: Wiley.

Arcus, D. M., (1991). *Experiential modification of temperamental bias in inhibited and uninhibited children.* Unpublished doctoral dissertation, Harvard University.

Arcus, D. M., & Kagan, J. (1995). Temperament and craniofacial variation in the first two years. *Child Development, 66,* 1529–1540.

Asendorpf, J. B. (1990). Development of inhibition during childhood. *Developmental Psychology, 26,* 721–730.

Bronson, G. W. (1970). Fear of visual novelty. *Developmental Psychology, 2,* 33–40.

Cooper, J. R., Bloom, F. E., & Roth, R. H. (1991). *Biochemical basis of neuropharmacology.* New York: Oxford University Press.

Damasio, A. (1994). *Descartes' error.* New York: Putnam.

Davis, M. (1992). The role of the amygdala in conditioned fear. In J. P. Aggleton (Ed.), *The amygdala* (pp. 256–305). New York: Wiley.

DiLalla, L. F., Kagan, J., & Reznick, J. S. (1994). Genetic etiology of behavioral inhibition among two year olds. *Infant Behavior and Development, 17,* 401–408.

Fagan, J. F. (1981). Infant intelligence. *Intelligence, 5,* 239–243.

Hebb, D. O. (1946). The nature of fear. *Psychological Review, 53,* 259–276.

Kagan, J. (1994). *Galen's prophecy.* New York: Basic.

Kagan, J., Kearsley, R. B., & Zelazo, P. R. (1980). *Infancy.* Cambridge, MA: Harvard University Press.

Kagan, J., Reznick, J. S., & Gibbons, J. (1989). Inhibited and uninhibited types of children. *Child Development, 60,* 838–845.

Kagan, J., Reznick, J. S., & Snidman, N. (1988). Biological bases of childhood shyness. *Science, 240,* 167–171.

Kochanska, G., Murray, K., Jacques, T. Y., Koenig, A. L., & Vandegeest, K. A. (1996). Inhibitory control in young children and its role in emerging internalization. *Child Development, 67,* 490–507.

LeDoux, J. E. (1995). In search of an emotional system in the brain. In M. S. Gazzinaga (Ed.), *The cognitive neurosciences* (pp. 1049–1062). Cambridge, MA: MIT Press.

Mountcastle, V. (1995). The evolution of ideas concerning the function of the neocortex. *Cerebral Cortex, 5,* 289–295.

Murray, D. C. (1971). Talk, silence, and anxiety. *Psychological Bulletin, 75,* 244–260.

Panksepp, J., Sacks, D. S., Crepeau, L. J., & Abbott, B. B. (1991). The psycho and neurobiology of fear systems in the brain. In M. R. Denny (Ed.), *Fear, avoidance, and phobias* (pp. 17–59). Hillsdale, NJ: Erlbaum.

Porges, S. W., Arnold, W. R., & Forbes, E. J. (1973). Heart rate variability: An index of attention responsivity in human newborns. *Developmental Psychology, 8,* 85–92.

Richards, J. E. (1985). Respiratory sinus arrhythmia predicts heart rate and visual responses during visual attention in 14 to 20 week old infants. *Psychophysiology, 22,* 101–109.

Robinson, J. L., Kagan, J., Reznick, J. S., & Corley, R. (1992). The heritability of inhibited and uninhibited behavior: A twin study. *Developmental Psychology, 28,* 1030–1037.

Rose, R. J. (1995). Genes and human behavior. In J. T. Spence, J. M. Darley, & D. P. Foss (Eds.), *Annual review of psychology* (pp. 625–654). Palo Alto, CA: Annual Reviews.

Shimamura, A. P. (1995). Memory and frontal lobe function. In M. S. Gazzinaga (Ed.), *The cognitive neurosciences* (pp. 803–814). Cambridge, MA: MIT Press.

Snidman, N., Kagan, J., Riordan, L., & Shannon, D. (1995). Cardiac function and behavioral reactivity in infancy. *Psychophysiology, 31,* 199–207.

Squire, L. R., & Knowlton, B. J. (1995). Memory, hippocampus, and brain systems. In M. S. Gazzinaga (Ed.), *The cognitive neurosciences* (pp. 825–838). Cambridge, MA: MIT Press.

Tremblay, R. E., Pihl, R. O., Vitaro, F., & Dubkin, P. L. (1994). Predicting early onset of male antisocial behavior from preschool behavior. *Archives of General Psychiatry, 51,* 732–739.

Wilson, D. S., Coleman, K., Clark, A. B., & Biederman, L. (1993). Shy-bold continuum in pumpkinseed sunfish (*Lepomis gibbosus*): An ecological study of a psychological trait. *Journal of Comparative Psychology, 107,* 250–260.

Zahn-Waxler, C., Cole, P., Welsh, J. D., & Fox, N. A. (1995). Psychophysiological correlates of empathy and prosocial behavior in preschool children with behavioral problems. *Development and Psychopathology, 7,* 27–48.

Questions

1. Why are reactions to unfamiliar events used to assess infant temperament?
2. What do the longitudinal findings indicate about the stability of reactivity over the first 5 years of life?
3. Are boys or girls more likely to be classified as high-reactive? What are some implications of this gender difference for later development?
4. Are high-reactive children more likely than low-reactive children to have anxiety disorders when they grow up? Explain.
5. Does temperamental inhibition play a role in antisocial behavior in adolescence? If so, what proportion of antisocial behavior might it explain and why?
6. What implications might the long-term patterns of temperament described in this article have for parents, teachers, and others who work with young children?

12 Specificity and Heterogeneity in Children's Responses to Profound Institutional Privation

Michael L. Rutter • Jana M. Kreppner • Thomas G. O'Connor

A universal characteristic of the human species is that children have a lengthy period of dependence on adults. During early development, other people, especially primary caregivers, provide children with the social and emotional support that children need for psychological growth. In fact, many theories of social and emotional development, most notably attachment theory, consider a child's early relationships to be fundamental to healthy development. Children reared in institutional settings in which they experience extreme privation, receiving little or no social and emotional support, may be especially vulnerable to long-term psychological dysfunction as a result of their institutionalization.

The following article describes how a team of researchers examined the development of Romanian children who had spent their early years in institutions in which their physical and psychological needs were barely met. These children were adopted by parents in the United Kingdom (UK) before they were 42 months of age. The researchers compared them on a variety of measures at age 4 and age 6 with children who had been born in the UK and adopted before they were 6 months of age. The researchers measured the children's socioemotional functioning (including their difficulties with attachment and peer relationships, attentional needs, and activity levels) and cognitive impairments. The results indicate more dysfunction on several of these measures among children who had been reared in institutions than among children who had not. There were also some areas of functioning in which these two groups of children were similar.

This research tells us that, while extreme early deprivation can interfere with psychological development, these problems are not inevitable and these experiences may not be directly linked with later psychopathology. In addition, the problems that result from severe privation are likely to involve some areas of psychological functioning more than others. These results hold out hope for children who experience extreme privation early in life and offer encouragement to individuals who care for such children.

Background *The sequelae of profound early privation are varied.*

Aims *To delineate the behavioural patterns that are specifically associated with institutional privation.*

Method *A group of 165 children adopted from Romania before the age of 42 months were compared at 4 years and 6 years with 52 non-deprived UK children adopted in infancy. Dysfunction was assessed for seven domains of functioning. The groups were compared on which, and how many, domains were impaired.*

Results *Attachment problems, inattention/overactivity, quasi-autistic features and cognitive impairment were associated with institutional privation, but emotional difficulties, poor peer relationships and conduct problems were not. Nevertheless, one-fifth of children who spent the longest time in institutions showed normal functioning.*

Reproduced with permission from Rutter, M. L., Kreppner, J. M., & O'Connor, T. G. (2001). Specificity and heterogeneity in children's responses to profound institutional privation. *British Journal of Psychiatry, 179,* 97–103. © 2001 The Royal College of Psychiatrists.

The research was supported by funds from the Department of Health, the Medical Research Council and the Helmut Horten Foundation.

Conclusions *Attachment disorder behaviours, inattention/overactivity and quasi-autistic behaviour constitute institutional privation patterns.*

Studies of children suffering profound institutional privation in infancy and early childhood have shown that it results in major developmental impairment, that there is considerable developmental catch-up following adoption into well-functioning families, and that there are clinically significant sequelae in some of the children (Chisholm *et al*, 1995; Ames, 1997; Fisher *et al*, 1997; Chisholm, 1998; Rutter *et al*, 1998, 2001; O'Connor *et al*, 2000). However, the studies also show that, at least in relation to specific outcomes, there is considerable heterogeneity in response. Thus, in our own study, for children who experienced at least 2 years of institutional privation in infancy, the measured IQ scores at 6 years ranged from the severely retarded range to high superior (O'Connor *et al*, 2000). Because the published reports all consider outcomes in relation to specific impairments, it is not known whether the children who fare well on one type of outcome also fare well on others. It is necessary to determine the extent to which impairments tend to be pervasive across domains and to ask what proportion of profoundly deprived children achieves generally normal psychological functioning. Equally, it is not known whether profound institutional privation results in a general increase in all forms of psychopathology or whether there are certain behavioural patterns or syndromes that are particularly strongly associated with early privation. The aim of this investigation was to use findings from a follow-up study (to age 6 years) of institution-reared Romanian children who were adopted into UK families to answer these questions on specificity and heterogeneity in children's responses to profound institutional privation.

Method

Subjects

The sample comprised 165 children adopted from Romania before the age of 42 months, selected at random from within bands stratified according to age of entry to the UK, and a comparison group of 52 non-deprived within-UK adoptees placed before the age of 6 months (for details see Rutter *et al*, 1998). Of these, 156 children from Romania and 50 within-UK adoptees had complete data-sets and were used for analyses where these were required. Four-fifths of the Romanian adoptees had been reared in institutions for most of their life and nearly all had been admitted to institutions in the neonatal period (mean age of admission was 0.34 months). The conditions in the Romanian institutions were generally extremely bad (see Kaler & Freeman, 1994; Castle *et al*, 1999; Johnson, 2001); and the condition of most of the children on arrival in the UK was also very poor. Their mean weight was 2.4 standard deviations below the mean (with over half below the third percentile) and the (retrospectively administered) Denver scale produced a mean quotient of 63, with three-fifths functioning in the severely retarded range. By the time the children reached the age of 4 years substantial catch-up had occurred, with the mean weight and Denver quotient both being near normal for UK children (Rutter *et al*, 1998). Eighty-one per cent of the adoptive parents of Romanian children who were approached to participate in the study agreed to do so.

Measures

The assessments at age 6 years comprised a standardised investigator-based interview that included (among other things) systematic questions on attachment disorder behaviours (O'Conner *et al*, 1999, 2001), completion of parent and teacher versions of the Rutter behavioural scales (Elander & Rutter, 1996; Hogg *et al*, 1997) and individually administered McCarthy Scales of Children's Abilities (McCarthy, 1972). In order to assess possible autistic features, the parents completed the Autism Screening Questionnaire (ASQ; Berument *et al*, 1999). In addition, the Autism Diagnostic Interview–Revised (ADI–R; Le Couteur *et al*, 1989; Lord *et al*, 1994) was given by a researcher experienced in its use (M.L.R.) when parental interview reports suggested the possibility of autistic features (see Rutter *et al*, 1999).

In order to obtain a categorical measure of probable dysfunction in each of seven specific domains of functioning, the data were dealt with as follows.

Attachment problems Three items from the parental interview—definite lack of differentiation between adults; clear indication that the child would readily go off with a stranger; and definite lack of checking back with the parent in anxiety-provoking situations—were scored as 0 for 'no abnormality', 1 for 'probable problem' and 2 for 'definite problem'. These were summated to produce a composite score ranging from 0 to 6, and a cut-off of 4 or more was used to indicate dysfunction.

Inattention/overactivity The Rutter scales completed by mothers and fathers were standardised and then averaged to produce a single parent score (see Kreppner *et al*, 2001). The teachers' scale was similarly standardised. The inattention/overactivity items on the parents' scale were: very restless, has difficulty staying seated for long; squirmy, fidgety child; cannot settle to anything for more than a few moments and inattentive; and easily distracted. The teachers' scale included all the preceding items plus: excessive demands for teacher's attention; and fails to finish things started—short attention span. Using the distribution of scores in the within-UK adoptees sample, three categories were created for the parents' and teachers' scales separately with a score of 0 for a score below the median, 1 for a score between the median and the top 10% cut-off, and 2 for a score in the top 10% of the range. Pervasive inattention/overactivity required a score of 2 on either the parents' or teachers' scale and a score of 1 or 2 on the other scale. Children with a missing score on one scale were not included in the 'pervasive' category.

Emotional difficulties The scores on the Rutter parents' and teachers' scales were standardised in the same way as for hyperactivity. The emotional difficulties items were: has had tears on arrival at school or has refused to go into the building in the past 12 months; gives up easily; often worried, worries about many things; often appears miserable, unhappy, tearful or distressed; cries easily; tends to be fearful or afraid of new things or new situations; stares into space and often complains of aches and pains (see Hogg *et al,* 1997). These were dealt with according to the distribution of scores in the within-UK adoptees sample. Children with scores in the top 5% on either or both of the parents' and teachers' scales were treated as having emotional difficulties.

Autistic features Using the ASQ and the ADI–R, 20 children were diagnosed as showing quasi-autistic features (Rutter *et al,* 1999). As this provided the combination of total screening coverage of both groups and individual diagnoses, this categorisation was used.

Cognitive impairment The general cognitive index (GCI) of the McCarthy Scales was used as the measure. Children who scored at least 2 standard deviations below the UK sample's mean were treated as showing cognitive impairment. The UK sample mean was 117, with a standard deviation of 18. Twice the standard deviation (36) subtracted from 117 equated to a score of 81; accordingly all children with an IQ of 81 or less were included in this domain of dysfunction.

Peer difficulties Peer difficulties were assessed through a combination of the Rutter parents' and teachers' scales, together with nine items from the parental interview. The three items in the parents' scale were 'not much liked by other children', 'tends to be solitary' and 'does not get on well with other children'. The mother and father scales were combined into a parental composite, using the approach described for inattention/overactivity. The three items in the teachers' scale were 'not much liked by other children', 'tends to be on own' and 'cannot work in a small peer group'. The nine parental interview items were: group play; differentiation between children (i.e. clear preferences, with one or more special friends); popularity; age preference of peers; harmony of peer interaction;

teased by other children; teases others; picked on/bullied; and picks on/bullies others. Peer group difficulties were regarded as present if the score on any of the three measures was in the top (most deviant) 5% of the distribution for the UK sample.

Conduct problems The scores on the Rutter parents' and teachers' scales were standardised as for hyperactivity and emotional difficulties. The conduct items were: often destroys own or others' property; frequently fights or is extremely quarrelsome with other children; is often disobedient; often tells lies; has stolen things on one or more occasions in the past 12 months; disturbs other children; bullies other children; blames others for things; is inconsiderate of others; kicks, bites other children (see Hogg *et al,* 1997). Children who scored in the top 5% of scores in the UK sample distribution on either scale were categorised as showing conduct problems.

Statistical Analysis

Between-group differences in the proportion of children showing dysfunction on each of the seven domains were examined using Fisher's two-tailed exact test and one degree of freedom. Within-group differences according to age of entry to the UK were examined for a linear trend on a chi square comparing entry at under 6 months, 6–24 months, and over 24 months ($n = 58$, 59 and 48 respectively). Polychoric correlations were used to examine the association among the binary domains of dysfunction variables.

Cluster analysis was used to examine the ways in which children in the Romanian adoptees sample showed similarities in their patterns of dysfunction. The technique is valuable for grouping individuals according to shared patterns of psychopathology. The seven dichotomous variables were cluster analysed using Ward's method of agglomeration based on

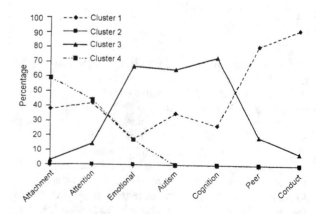

figure 1

Percentage extreme score across seven outcomes according to cluster membership.

squared Euclidean distance (Aldenderfer & Blashfield, 1988). A four-cluster solution was chosen based on co-efficient of linkage, practical considerations (such as sample size) and interpretability. The cluster analyses were then rerun using alternative indices of similarity in order to determine the consistency of the cluster profiles. All approaches gave patterns closely similar to those displayed in Fig. 1. As an additional check, cluster analyses were repeated using continuously distributed dimensions, rather than binary categories, again with similar findings (further details available from the authors upon request).

Results

Of the seven domains of dysfunction when the children were aged 6 years, three (emotional problems, peer difficulties and conduct problems) showed no difference in rate between the adoptees from Romania and the within-UK adoptees (Table 1). For each of these three domains, there was no association, within the Romanian adoptees sample, with the children's age at the time of entry to the UK. In sharp contrast, the other four domains (attachment problems, inattention/overactivity, quasi-autistic problems and cognitive impairment) were all much more common in the Romanian sample and, in each case, there was a significant association with age at entry, the rate of problems being much higher in those who left Romania when they were older. The implication is that the former three domains are not particularly associated with institutional privation, whereas the latter four seem to be.

Table 2 summarises the findings on the number of domains showing dysfunction in the two groups, to-gether with the association with age at entry within the Romanian sample. As would be expected in any general population sample, a substantial minority of the UK adoptees showed dysfunction in at least one domain. Less than four-fifths were free of dysfunction on any domain. Nevertheless, dysfunction was substantially more likely to be present in the Romanian adoptees, and the proportion without dysfunction on at least one domain was significantly lower in those who came to the UK when they were older. Of those leaving Romania after their second birthday, between a fifth and a quarter were free of any measurable dysfunction at 6 years of age. The trend for more dysfunction, and more pervasive dysfunction, in Romanian adoptees and for an association with age at entry was apparent at all levels of frequency of dysfunction. The main difference between the groups, however, was evident in the presence or absence of any dysfunction, rather than in the pervasiveness of dysfunction across domains.

What characterised the Romanian adoptees sample were the particular domains involved in the pervasive dysfunction pattern. Almost always, this involved some admixture of attachment problems, inattention/overactivity and quasi-autistic problems. In contrast, in the UK sample pervasive impairment usually involved either conduct or emotional disturbance plus another problem, but not one of the patterns that was distinctive of the institutional privation children.

Of the 40 children in the Romanian adoptees group who showed impairment on just one domain, 13 did so on attachment problems, 11 on inattention/overactivity, 7 on peer difficulties and 6 on cognitive impairment (with only an additional 3 on other domains). Of the 6 children in the within-UK adoptees group with impairment on just one domain,

Domains	Rate in Romanian Adoptees		Rate in Within-UK Adoptees		Between-Group Differences	Association with Age at Entry to UK	
					Fisher's Exact P (Two-tailed)	χ^2 Trends	P
	%	n	%	n			
Attachment problems	20.7	164	3.8	52	0.003	11.13	0.001
Inattention/overactivity	25.3	162	9.6	52	0.019	9.04	0.003
Emotional difficulties	3.7	162	9.6	52	NS	0.03	NS
Quasi-autistic features	12.1	165	0.0	52	0.005	4.61	0.032
Cognitive impairment	14.0	157	2.0	50	0.018	14.61	0.001
Peer difficulties	18.9	164	9.6	52	NS	0.45	NS
Conduct problems	8.0	162	9.6	52	NS	0.97	NS

table 1   Seven Domains of Dysfunction at 6 Years of Age in Romanian and Within-UK Adopted Children

table 2   Romanian and Within-UK Adopted Children: Percentages of Children with Impairment in 0, 1, 2, or 3 or More Domains

Number of Domains in Which There Is Impairment	Within-UK Adoptees (n=50)	Romanian Adoptees, Age at Entry into UK			χ² Trends	P
		<6 Months (n=56)	6–24 Months (n=35)	24–42 Months (n=45)		
0 (n=112) (%)	78.0	69.6	43.6	23.9	34.81	0.001
1 (n=46) (%)	12.0	17.9	23.6	37.0	19.79	0.002
2 (n=20) (%)	2.0	7.1	12.7	17.4	9.75	0.002
3 or more (n=28) (%)	8.0	5.4	20.0	21.7	6.73	0.009

2 showed it on emotional difficulties, 2 on inattention/overactivity, 1 on conduct problems and 1 on attachment problems.

Table 3 presents the polychoric correlations among domains of dysfunction within the Romanian adoptees sample. The intercorrelations are no more than moderate in most instances but there was a stronger correlation (0.66) between autistic features and cognitive impairment and between autistic features and peer difficulties (0.59). Cognitive impairment showed a near-zero correlation with emotional difficulties and with conduct problems. Attachment problems had their strongest correlation with inattention/overactivity (0.47). There were only 6 children in the Romanian sample with emotional difficulties but 5 of these showed a quasi-autistic pattern, giving rise to a high polychoric correlation.

Figure 1 shows the cluster analysis for Romanian adoptees. The largest cluster (n=74) was cluster 2, in which there was no dysfunction on any of the seven domains (Table 4). Cluster 1 was the one with the greatest pervasiveness of dysfunction, with about half of the children (or more) showing difficulties in attachment, inattention/overactivity, peer relationships and conduct. A few also showed quasi-autistic features or cognitive impairment. Cluster 3 is largely defined by the presence of both quasi-autistic features and cognitive impairment. Cluster 4 comprised children who showed only attachment problems and inattention/overactivity (apart from one child who also showed an emotional difficulty). The mean age at entry was 10.3 months for cluster 2, 18.4 months for cluster 1, 22.3 months for cluster 3 and 20.0 months for cluster 4. The only significant contrast was that between cluster 2 and the other three clusters. The effect of age at entry was similarly shown in the trend across the three age-at-entry groups. Thus, the proportion in the late-placed group (over 2 years) was 15% in cluster 2, compared with 38% in cluster 1, with 52% in cluster 3 and with 39% in cluster 4.

table 3   Polychoric Correlation Among Domains of Dysfunction in Romanian Adoptee Sample

	Attachment Problems	Inattention/ Overactivity	Emotional Difficulties	Autistic Features	Cognitive Impairment	Peer Difficulties
Attachment problems						
Inattention/overactivity	0.47					
Emotional difficulties	0.16	0.29				
Autistic features	0.25	0.24	0.81			
Cognitive impairment	0.20	0.26	0.05	0.66		
Peer difficulties	0.30	0.48	0.39	0.59	0.47	
Conduct problems	0.38	0.49	0.46	0.36	0.03	0.68

Correlations based on dichotomous variables; n = 157.

table 4	Associations Between Clusters and Domains Impaired							
Cluster	Domains							Mean No. of Domains Impaired per Child
	Attachment Problems	Inattention/ Overactivity	Emotional Difficulties	Autistic Features	Cognitive Impairment	Peer Difficulties	Conduct Problems	
2 (*n*=74)	0	0	0	0	0	0	0	0.0
1 (*n*=29)	13	17	1	7	6	25	12	2.79
3 (*n*=23)	1	6	4	13	16	6	1	2.04
4 (*n*=31)	20	18	1	0	0	0	0	1.25

There were no gender differences among the seven domains or among the four clusters.

Discussion

Escape from Dysfunction

In order to determine whether children who experience prolonged early institutional privation could nevertheless show normal psychological function at age 6 years, several years after leaving the depriving environment and after being adopted into generally well-functioning adoptive homes, we assessed dysfunction across seven different domains that were relevant at that age, occurred with a reasonable frequency and could be assessed with reasonable reliability. Normal functioning was defined according to the stringent criterion of no abnormality on any of the seven domains. As would be expected, over a fifth of the children in the non-deprived within-UK adoptee sample failed to show normal functioning on this very strict criterion.

Two findings stand out with respect to the Romanian sample. First, the proportion with normal functioning among those who left Romania before the age of 6 months was nearly as high (70%) as in the within-UK adopted sample. Second, even among the children who were over the age of 2 years when they left Romania, between a fifth and a quarter showed normal functioning on all seven domains. It is sometimes supposed that lasting damage is inevitable after prolonged early institutional privation, but our results run counter to that view. The chances of normal social functioning were substantially less the older the child was at the time of leaving the institution, but some of the children who had the most long-lasting privation appeared to be functioning entirely normally by the age of 6 years. Of course, it would be wrong to suppose that there are no scars and it is possible that there may be sequelae that be-

come evident only at a later age. Nevertheless, the degree of resilience shown was remarkable. Because our sample extended only up to an age of entry of 42 months, we can draw no conclusions on whether or not there is an age at which recovery becomes extremely unlikely. Extrapolation from the linear trends found on all analyses suggests that the chance of normal functioning diminishes progressively the older the child at the time when profound privation comes to an end, but it is not known whether—or when—that chance eventually ceases to exist.

The findings on pervasiveness of dysfunction make the additional point that, of the children showing some form of impairment, nearly half showed impairment on only one domain, and only just over a quarter showed impairment on at least three domains. Even within the group of children who were over the age of 2 years when they arrived in the UK, only just over a fifth showed pervasive dysfunction of that extent.

Specificity of Sequelae of Institutional Privation

Across a large number of studies, the relative nonspecificity of the patterns of psychopathology associated with psychosocial stresses and adversity has been the general finding (Rutter, 2001). Thus, negative life events carrying long-term threat have been associated with a wide range of psychiatric disorders (Brown & Harris, 1989; Goodyer, 1990), and the same applies to the experience of physical and sexual abuse (Kendall-Tackett *et al*, 1993; Trickett & McBridge-Chang, 1995). Accordingly, it might have been expected that prolonged institutional privation would be associated with a general increase in all forms of psychopathology. However, that is not what we found. Strikingly, there was no increase in either emotional or conduct problems, and although the rate of peer difficulties was twice as high in the Romanian adoptees, the difference between groups fell short of statistical significance. The finding that none of these three domains of dysfunction showed any association with the children's age at entry to the UK also indicates that it is unlikely that these particular areas of problem at 6 years of age were consequences of the children's early institutional experiences. The children are too young for any firm conclusions with respect to late sequelae but, at least up to the age of 6 years, these do not seem to be a particular consequence of the depriving institutional upbringing. Accordingly, if such problems occur in young institution-reared children, they may arise for reasons that have little to do with their early adverse upbringing. However, this might change in later childhood and adolescence, when the situations with respect to both emotional disturbance and peer relationships are different.

Although there was no single pattern that characterised children who experienced institutional privation, three main features stood out, occurring both on their own and in varying combinations. First, there were attachment disturbances of various kinds (O'Connor *et al*, 1999, 2001). These were particularly characterised by a relatively undiscriminating social approach, a seeming lack of awareness of social boundaries and a difficulty in picking up social cues on what is socially appropriate or acceptable to other people. This is a pattern also identified in a parallel Canadian study of adoptees from Romania (Chisholm *et al*, 1995; Chisholm, 1998). Second, there was the pattern of inattention/overactivity. Of the 41 children in the Romanian sample who showed this behaviour, nearly half (16) showed it in association with attachment problems, but 11 children showed only inattention/overactivity and 8 showed it in association with quasi-autistic behaviour (in 4 of the 8 cases also with attachment problems). Attention-deficit and hyperkinetic disorders have usually been thought of as psychiatric conditions that are strongly influenced by genetic factors, with psychosocial influences playing only a subsidiary role in aetiology (Taylor, 1994, 1999). It is striking, therefore, that this has emerged as one of the patterns most strongly associated with prolonged institutional privation. It could be, of course, that the key causal influence derived from nutritional privation rather than psychological privation in the institutions. On the other hand, more detailed analyses suggest that nutritional privation was not the key risk factor (further details available from the authors upon request). The finding that inattention/overactivity is also common in children reared in group homes within the UK, where nutritional privation is not an issue, suggests that it may well be the psychological features of the institutional environment that are more important (Roy *et al*, 2000). It remains to be determined whether the clinical picture of inattention/overactivity in these children is the same

as in more 'ordinary' varieties of attention-deficit or hyperkinetic disorders, and a follow-up study that is now in progress should throw light on this point. Meanwhile, the evidence suggests that the problems may lie more in dealing with social group situations than with overactivity as such.

The third pattern particularly associated with a background of institutional privation was that of quasi-autistic features. Again, this appears surprising at first sight because of the evidence that autism as diagnosed in children from more ordinary backgrounds involves a strong genetic influence, with little evidence of psychosocial features playing a part in the causal process (Rutter, 2000). The clinical picture in the sample of Romanian adoptees was, however, somewhat different from that characteristic of 'ordinary' autism with respect to the tendency to improve between the ages of 4 and 6 years and the extent of social approach (Rutter *et al*, 1999).

Institutional privation was quite strongly associated with cognitive impairment (Rutter *et al*, 1998, 2000; O'Connor *et al*, 2000). In 6 of the 22 children showing cognitive impairment, this occurred without dysfunction on any of the other domains. It was, however, much more common for it to be accompanied by either quasi-autistic patterns (present in 10 out of the 20 children and in some cases with dysfunction in other domains as well) or with attachment disturbances (7 children). At the age of 6 years, there was nothing particularly distinctive about the patterns of impairment but distinctive features may be more evident at age 11 years, when the children are to be seen again. With the Romanian adoptee sample, it is also noteworthy that inattention/overactivity was more strongly associated with attachment problems (17/41 cases) than with cognitive impairment (7/41). Moreover, of these 7 children characterised by inattention/overactivity and cognitive impairment, 5 also showed attachment disturbance.

In summary, profound institutional privation was particularly associated with patterns involving attachment disturbance, inattention/overactivity, quasi-autistic features and cognitive impairment in varying combinations, but it was not associated with any marked general increase in other forms of psychopathology. There is a need for more detailed study of these psychopathological patterns; in the meantime, clinicians need to be alert to their occurrence and to the possibility that these patterns derive from early institutional privation. It is important, too, that effective methods of intervention should be developed for these privation-related problems (Rutter *et al*, 2000).

Clinical Implications

- Profound early institutional privation tends to be particularly associated with attachment disorder behaviours, inattention/overactivity (especially when associated with attachment disturbances) and quasi-autistic behaviour.

- Such privation is not followed by a significant increase in conduct problems, emotional disturbance or peer relationship difficulties other than in the context of institutional privation patterns (see first implication), at least by age 6 years.

- Profound institutional privation from infancy to age 3 years is still compatible with normal psychological functioning provided that the child has experienced several years in a good adoptive family.

Limitations

- So far, the children have been followed only up to the age of 6 years.

- Only some of the children have received detailed individual clinical assessments.

- Because the children could not be studied while in the Romanian institutions, it was not possible to determine which aspect of privation was most influential.

REFERENCES

Aldenderfer, M. & Blashfield, R. (1988) *Cluster Analysis*. San Francisco, CA: Jossey-Bass.

Ames, E. W. (1997) *The Development of Romanian Orphanage Children Adopted to Canada*. Final report to Human Resources Development, Canada. Available upon request from the Adoptive Families Association of British Columbia, Ste. #205, 15463–104th Avenue, Surrey, BC, V3R IN0, Canada.

Berument, S. K., Rutter, M., Lord, C., *et al* (1999) Autism screening questionnaire: diagnostic validity. *British Journal of Psychiatry, 175*, 444–451.

Brown, G. W. & Harris, T. O. (1989) *Life Events and Illness*, London: Unwin & Hyman.

Castle, J., Groothues, C., Bredenkamp, D., *et al* (1999) Effects of qualities of early institutional care on cognitive attainment. *American Journal of Orthopsychiatry, 40*, 424–437.

Chisholm, K. (1998) A three year follow-up of attachment and indiscriminate friendliness in children adopted from Romanian orphanages. *Child Development, 69*, 1092–1106.

——, Carter, M. C., Ames, E. W., *et al* (1995) Attachment security and indiscriminately friendly behavior in children adopted from Romanian orphanages. *Development and Psychopathology. 7*, 283–294.

Elander, J. & Rutter, M. (1996) Use and development of the Rutter parents' and teachers' scales. *International Journal of Methods in Psychiatric Research, 6*, 63–78.

Fisher, L., Ames, E. W., Chisholm, K., *et al* (1997) Problems reported by parents of Romanian orphans adopted to British Columbia. *International Journal of Behavioural Development, 20*, 67–82.

Goodyer, I. M. (1990) *Life Experiences, Development and Child Psychopathology*. Chichester: John Wiley & Sons.

Hogg, C., Rutter, M. & Richman, N. (1997) Emotional and behavioural problems in children. In *Child Psychology Portfolio* (ed. I. Sclare), pp. 1–34. Windsor: NFER–Nelson.

Johnson, D. E. (2001) Medical and developmental sequelae of early childhood institutionalization in international adoptees from Romania and the Russian Federation. In *The Effects of Early Adversity on Neurobehavioral Development* (ed. C. Nelson). Mahwah, NJ: Lawrence Erlbaum.

Kaler, S. R. & Freeman, B. J. (1994) Analysis of environmental deprivation: cognitive and social development in Romanian orphans. *Journal of Child Psychology and Psychiatry, 35*, 769–781.

Kendall-Tackett, K. A., Meyer Williams, L. & Finkelhor, D. (1993) Impact of sexual abuse on children: a review and synthesis of recent empirical studies. *Psychological Bulletin, 113*, 164–180.

Kreppner, J. M., O'Connor, T. G., Rutter, M., *et al*. (2001) Can inattention/hyperactivity be an institutional deprivation syndrome? *Journal of Abnormal Child Psychology, 29*, 513–528.

Le Couteur, A., Rutter, M., Lord, C., *et al* (1989) Autism Diagnostic Interview: a standardized investigator-based instrument. *Journal of Autism and Developmental Disorders, 19*, 363–387.

Lord, C., Rutter, M. & Le Couteur, A. (1994) Autism Diagnostic Interview–Revised: a revised version of a diagnostic interview for caregivers of individuals with possible pervasive developmental disorders. *Journal of Autism and Developmental Disorders, 24*, 659–685.

McCarthy, D. (1972) *The McCarthy Scales of Children's Abilities*. New York: Psychological Corporation/Harcourt Brace.

O'Connor, T. G., Bredenkamp, D., Rutter, M., *et al* (1999) Attachment disturbances and disorders in children exposed to early severe deprivation. *Infant Mental Health Journal, 20*, 10–29.

——, Rutter, M., Beckett, C., *et al* (2000) The effects of global severe privation on cognitive competence: extension and longitudinal follow-up. *Child Development, 72*, 376–390.

——, —— & the English and Romanian Adoptees Study Team (2001) Attachment disorder behavior following early severe deprivation: extension and longitudinal follow-up. *Journal of the American Academy of Child and Adolescent Psychiatry, 39*, 703–712.

Roy, P., Rutter, M. & Pickles, A. (2000) Institutional care: risk from family background or pattern of rearing? *Journal of Child Psychology and Psychiatry, 41*, 139–149.

Rutter, M. (2000) Genetic studies of autism: from the 1970s into the millennium. *Journal of Abnormal Child Psychology, 28*, 3–14.

—— (2001) Psychological influences: critiques, findings and research needs. *Development and Psychopathology*, in press.

—— & the English and Romanian Adoptees (ERA) Study Team (1998) Developmental catch-up, and deficit, following adoption after severe early privation. *Journal of Child Psychology and Psychiatry, 39*, 465–476.

——, Andersen-Wood, L., Beckett, C., *et al* (1999) Quasi-autistic patterns following severe early global privation. *Journal of Child Psychology and Psychiatry 40,* 537–549.

——, O'Connor, T. G., Beckett, C., *et al* (2000) Recovery and deficit following profound early deprivation. In *Inter-country Adoption: Developments, Trends and Perspectives* (ed. P. Selman), pp. 107–125. London: BAAF.

Taylor, E. (1994) Syndromes of attention deficit and overactivity. In *Child and Adolescent Psychiatry: Modern Approaches* (3rd edn) (eds M. Rutter, E. Taylor & L. Hersov), pp. 285–307. Oxford: Blackwell.

—— (1999) Developmental neuropsychopathology of attention deficit and impulsiveness. *Development and Psychopathology, II,* 607–629.

Trickett, P. K. & McBridge-Chang, C. (1995) The developmental impact of different forms of child abuse and neglect. *Developmental Review, 15,* 311–337.

Questions

1. Why did Rutter and his colleagues think it was necessary to determine whether the impairments of children who had experienced extreme privation were evident across domains of functioning or were limited to one type of outcome?
2. Which areas of functioning were assessed in this research, and why were these particular areas chosen for study? What other areas of functioning could have been discussed?
3. Did the age at which children from Romania were adopted relate to the severity of the difficulties they showed at age 6? Why do you think age is significant in this process?
4. Do these results make you think that extreme institutional deprivation early in life necessarily has negative lifelong consequences? Why or why not?
5. This study followed the children until they were 6 years of age. What patterns do you predict for these two groups of children when they enter puberty? Are there any specific areas of dysfunction that may present difficulties at this later point in development?
6. Do this study's findings suggest any types of interventions that would help children who experienced extreme privation early in life?

II

Infancy

Infancy is a time of remarkable development. The rapid pace of change in the first two years of life makes infancy the fastest period of growth that human beings experience after birth. Changes during infancy occur across the entire spectrum of human behavior, including physical growth, perceptual and cognitive skills, language, and social and emotional competence. Most research on infants concentrates on development in one of these areas. In part, this is because infant research is difficult to design and conduct. One reason for this difficulty is that infants have only brief periods every day during which their behavioral state is suited to research observation. Another is that infants' social and language skills are just emerging, so many of the usual data-gathering techniques that involve social interaction or conversation cannot be used.

Despite these challenges, two important points stand out in the research described in this section. First, infants are extremely competent in a number of ways. The articles that follow reveal infants' competence in social cognition (Esther Herrmann, Josep Call, María Victoria Hernández-Lloreda, Brian Hare, and Michael Tomasello), object knowledge (Scott P. Johnson, Dima Amso, and Jonathan A. Slemmer), language (Janet F. Werker), concept formation (Renée Baillargeon and Su-hua Wang), and emotion (Joseph J. Campos, Bennett I. Bertenthal, and Rosanne Kermoian). These emerging competencies are situated within the context of rich social relationships that provide infants with physical, emotional, and cognitive support for development (Elizabeth Meins, Charles Fernyhough, Emma Fradley, and Michelle Tuckey). Considered together, these competencies paint a portrait of the infant as an extremely complex organism that is on a rapid, directed, and socially supported course of growth.

Second, the articles in this section demonstrate several creative techniques that researchers have devised for observing infants. These techniques have allowed psychologists to begin to understand infants "on their own terms." That is, researchers can use these procedures to build on the capabilities and interests of infants to determine what is developing early in life.

13 Humans Have Evolved Specialized Skills of Social Cognition: The Cultural Intelligence Hypothesis

Esther Herrmann • Josep Call • María Victoria Hernández-Lloreda •
Brian Hare • Michael Tomasello

What characteristics make us human? Some suggest it is the capability to create and use tools. Others claim it is the use of symbols, especially language. And still others argue it has to do with social life, especially how human beings are able to understand and work with one another to reach their goals.

Despite great interest in this question, it is very difficult to answer. Although the human evolutionary record is rich in many ways, it offers little information about the behavior of our early ancestors. One way developmental researchers have tried to tackle this question is by comparing the behavior of human children with that of other primates. The hope is that these comparisons will allow us to distinguish intellectual capabilities that are uniquely human from the intellectual capabilities that we share with other primates.

The following article by Esther Herrmann and her colleagues describes research that used this approach. Their aim was to discover whether human beings possess unique intellectual skills that enable them to participate in human culture. Comparing the performances of human children with the performances of chimpanzees and orangutans, the authors hypothesized that these three groups would have similar cognitive skills pertaining to the physical world because this information is important to the activities of each of them. However, they expected that human children would possess better social cognitive skills because these skills are instrumental to learning from others, which is particularly critical to human development.

As you will see, these findings raise many provocative questions about the nature and development of human intelligence. By examining different groups of primates on a range of cognitive tasks, the researchers were able to show that it is not general intelligence that distinguishes human beings from other primates. Rather, humans possess a very specific kind of social intelligence; one that allows us to understand and learn from others. These fundamental social cognitive skills give children an appreciation of and access to the thinking of other people and, by extension, the ability to participate in the accumulated skills and practices of their culture.

Humans have many cognitive skills not possessed by their nearest primate relatives. The cultural intelligence hypothesis argues that this is mainly due to a species-specific set of social-cognitive skills, emerging early in ontogeny, for participating and exchanging knowledge in cultural groups. We tested this hypothesis by giving a comprehensive battery of cognitive tests to large numbers of two of humans' closest primate relatives, chimpanzees and orangutans, as well as to 2.5-year-old human children before literacy and schooling. Supporting the cultural intelligence hypothesis and contradicting the hypothesis that humans simply have more "general intelligence," we found that the children and chimpanzees had very similar cognitive skills for dealing with the physical world but that the children had more sophisticated cognitive skills than either of the ape species for dealing with the social world.

Humans have brains roughly three times larger than those of their nearest primate relatives, the great apes (1,2), and of course have many cognitive skills not possessed by other primates as well, from language to symbolic mathematics to scientific reasoning. The questions from an evolutionary point of view—especially given the enormous energetic expense of a large

From Herrmann, E., Call, J., Hernández-Lloreda, M. V., Hare, B., & Tomasello, M. (2007). Humans have evolved specialized skills of social cognition: The cultural intelligence hypothesis. *Science, 317*, 1360–1366. Reprinted with permission from AAAS.

brain (3)—are how and why humans have evolved such powerful and distinctive cognitive abilities requiring so much neural tissue.

One hypothesis is the general intelligence hypothesis. Larger brains enable humans to perform all kinds of cognitive operations more efficiently than other species: greater memory, faster learning, faster perceptual processing, more robust inferences, longer-range planning, and so on. The alternative is the adapted intelligence hypothesis (4). Cognitive abilities evolve in response to relatively specific environmental challenges, and so we may see caching birds with exceptional memory skills, homing pigeons with marked skills of spatial navigation, bees with complex systems of communication, and so forth (5). In the case of primates, some theorists have proposed that the distinctive aspects of primate cognition evolved mainly in response to the especially challenging demands of foraging for seasonal fruits and resources embedded in substrates [the ecological intelligence hypothesis (6,7)], whereas others have proposed that the distinctive aspects of primate cognition evolved mainly in response to the especially challenging demands of a complex social life of constant competition and cooperation with others in the social group [the social intelligence hypothesis (8–11)].

In the case of humans, one reasonable hypothesis involves extending the primate social intelligence hypothesis to reflect the fact that humans are not just social but "ultra-social" (12). That is, whereas primates in general have evolved sophisticated social-cognitive skills for competing and cooperating with conspecifics, humans have also evolved skills that enable them to actually create different cultural groups, each operating with a distinctive set of artifacts, symbols, and social practices and institutions. To function effectively in the cultural world into which they are born, human children simply must learn to use these artifacts and tools and to participate in these practices, which require some special social-cognitive skills of social learning, communication, and "theory of mind" (13). Some other ape species transmit some behaviors socially or culturally (14,15), but their species-typical cognition does not depend on participating in cultural interactions in the same way as it does in humans, who must (i) learn their native language in social interactions with others, (ii) acquire necessary subsistence skills by participating with experts in established cultural practices, and (iii) (in many cultures) acquire skills with written language and mathematical symbols through formal schooling (16). In the end, human adults will have all kinds of cognitive skills not possessed by other primates, but this outcome will be due largely to children's early emerging, specialized skills for absorbing the accumulated skillful practices and knowledge of their social group (so that a child growing up outside of any

human culture would develop few distinctively human cognitive skills). Humans' especially powerful skills of social-cultural cognition early in ontogeny thus serve as a kind of "bootstrap" for the distinctively complex development of human cognition in general. We may call this the cultural intelligence hypothesis.

There have been no direct tests of the cultural intelligence hypothesis, nor any direct comparisons of it with other hypotheses of human cognitive evolution. The social intelligence hypothesis for primates in general is supported by positive correlations between relative brain size (i.e., neocortex size) and social variables such as group size or grooming clique size [as an index of social complexity (11,17–20)]. This evidence provides support for the general social direction of the cultural intelligence hypothesis, but overall correlations do not tell us the basis of the brain size differences in terms of particular cognitive skills, nor do they help us to identify which cognitive skills humans may have that other primates lack. There have also been some experimental studies that directly compared the performance of several primate species on a few cognitive tasks, but in the only meta-analysis of those studies, none of the tasks targeted social cognition and humans were not represented (21). Several other experimental studies have directly compared some individual cognitive skills of humans (mostly children) and nonhuman primates (mostly apes), but each of these studies has been conducted with different individuals, and indeed the ages of the children and the members of the nonhuman primate species are inconsistent across studies (22).

What is needed to test the cultural intelligence hypothesis is a systematic comparison of a representative range of cognitive skills among a single set of human and nonhuman primate individuals, which has so far not been done. In such a comparison, the cultural intelligence hypothesis predicts that there should be an age in early human ontogeny (specifically, an age before children have been seriously influenced by written language, symbolic mathematics, and formal education) at which humans' skills of physical cognition (concerning things such as space, quantities, and causality) are very similar to those of our nearest primate relatives but at which their skills of social-cultural cognition (specifically those most directly involved in cultural creation and learning, such as social learning, communication, and theory of mind) are already distinctively human. This is in stark contrast to the general intelligence hypothesis, which predicts that human cognition should differ from that of other primates uniformly, with no difference between physical and social cognition.

In the current study, therefore, we sought to identify any distinctive features of human cognition that may exist at an early stage of ontogeny and, in this way, to assess and directly compare the cultural intelligence and general intelligence hypotheses of human cognitive evolution. We did this by administering a comprehensive battery of cognitive tests to a large number of chimpanzees (*Pan troglodytes*) (one of humans' two closest living relatives), orangutans (*Pongo pygmaeus*) (a more distantly related great ape), and human children (*Homo sapiens*) at 2.5 years of age. Of crucial importance to our analysis were the following: (i) all subjects from all three species were naïve to the tests from the test battery; (ii) the apes lived in rich, semi-natural environments; and (iii) there was a sufficient number of subjects to properly test, as virtually no previous studies have done, the role of gender, age, and temperament (measured in a separate test) as possible mediators of cognitive performance on the tasks.

Methods: The Test Battery and Its Administration

The Primate Cognition Test Battery (PCTB) was constructed based on the theoretical analysis of primate cognition by Tomasello and Call (22). In this analysis, the primary division is between physical cognition and social cognition. Although primates in their natural habitats regularly use skills of physical and social cognition together [e.g., foraging for food while competing with groupmates (23,24)], in theory the two sets of skills are distinct because physical cognition deals with inanimate objects and their spatial-temporal-causal relations, whereas social cognition deals with other animate beings and their intentional actions, perceptions, and knowledge.

More specifically, in this analysis, primate cognition of the physical world evolved mainly in the context of foraging: To locate food, primates need cognitive skills for dealing with "space"; to choose wisely among multiple food sources, they need cognitive skills for dealing with "quantities"; and for extracting food from difficult places, they need cognitive skills for understanding "causality" (including, for some species, the context of tool use). In this analysis, primate social cognition evolved because of the tension between cooperation and competition among group members: To manipulate the behavior of others, primates need skills of "communication"; to learn things vicariously from observing others, they need skills of "social learning"; and to predict the behavior of others in competition, they need cognitive skills for understanding psychological states such as goals and perceptions ("theory of mind"). The PCTB therefore comprised the two domains of physical cognition and social cognition, each of which comprised three cognitive scales (the six terms enclosed in quotes above), with each scale being constructed with one or more specific tasks composed of several items each. Most of the items were derived from previously published studies of primate cognition (table S2), whereas others were created for the PCTB and validated

before use with the chimpanzees and orangutans at the Wolfgang Köhler Primate Research Center in Leipzig, Germany. Table 1 briefly summarizes the structure of PCTB (25) (movies S1 to S32).

The PCTB was administered to three groups of participants. First were 106 chimpanzees (53 males and 53 females; 3 to 21 years of age; mean age: 10 years) that lived either at the Ngamba Island chimpanzee sanctuary, Lake Victoria, Uganda, or at the Tchimpounga chimpanzee sanctuary, Republic of Congo. Second were 32 orangutans (17 males and 15 females; 3 to 10 years of age; mean age: 6 years) that lived at the Orangutan Care Center and Quarantine in Pasir Panjang, Kalimantan, Indonesia. All of these apes live in the richest social and physical environments available to captive apes and have grown up in close contact with humans who feed and care for them. Third were 105 human children [52 males and 53 females; 2.5 years of age (±2 months)] from a medium-sized city in Germany. All children had been using language for ~1 year (25) (table S1).

Participants were individually tested by a human experimenter, with the same experimenter testing a subject throughout the entire battery. Each participant completed all tasks in the PCTB, which took from 3 to 5 hours altogether, generally in the same order across several days of testing (table S3). The human children were tested on 5 days within a 2-week period, and the apes were tested on consecutive days, averaging a total of 8 days. Chimpanzees and orangutans were tested in a familiar room, and human children were tested in a child laboratory and accompanied by a parent who was told not to influence or help in any way. To measure the comfort level of participants in the test situation (because this could be a mediator of their performance in the PCTB), we also gave subjects (within the first 4 days of testing) a temperament test designed to assess their reaction to novel objects, people, and rewards (25) (tables S6 and S7). All testing was videotaped.

For most of the tasks, a human experimenter (E1) sat behind a table facing the subject through a Plexiglas window (children and some apes) or a mesh panel (apes only). The window had three holes at different positions, through which subjects could insert a finger to indicate their choice when necessary (figs. S1 and S2). On all trials, E1 always waited until the subject was facing her before beginning the trial. For trials requiring a choice, the position of the reward was counterbalanced across either two or three locations (depending on the task) but the reward was never hidden for more than two consecutive trials in the same place. In a few tasks, subjects were tested in other setups, requiring them to do such things as to use a simple tool, follow gaze direction, or gesture to E1 (25).

Subjects' responses were initially coded live by E1 except for gaze-following trials, which E1 coded from videotape after the test. A second observer indepen-

table 1   The PCTB, Including Domains, Scales, and Tasks (25)

Domain	Scale	Task	Description
Physical	Space	Spatial memory (1 item, 3 trials)	Locating a reward.
		Object permanence (3 items, 9 trials)	Tracking of a reward after invisible displacement.
		Rotation (3 items, 9 trials)	Tracking of a reward after a rotation manipulation.
		Transposition (3 items, 9 trials)	Tracking of a reward after location changes.
	Quantities	Relative numbers (1 item, 13 trials)	Discriminating quantity.
		Addition numbers (1 item, 7 trials)	Discriminating quantity with added quantities.
	Causality	Noise (2 items, 6 trials)	Causal understanding of produced noise by hidden rewards.
		Shape (2 items, 6 trials)	Causal understanding of appearance change by hidden rewards.
		Tool use (1 item, 1 trial)	Using a stick in order to retrieve a reward which is out of reach.
		Tool properties (5 items, 15 trials)	Understanding of functional and nonfunctional tool properties.
Social	Social learning	Social learning (3 items, 3 trials)	Solving a simple but not obvious problem by observing a demonstrated solution.
	Communication	Comprehension (3 items, 9 trials)	Understanding communicative cues indicating a reward's hidden location.
		Pointing cups (1 item, 4 trials)	Producing communicative gestures in order to retrieve a hidden reward.
		Attentional state (4 items, 4 trials)	Choosing communicative gestures considering the attentional state of the recipient.
	Theory of mind	Gaze following (3 items, 9 trials)	Following an actor's gaze direction to a target.
		Intentions (2 items, 6 trials)	Understanding what an actor intended to do (unsuccessfully).

dently scored (from videotape) 100% of the trials for human children and chimpanzees and 20% of the trials for orangutans. The inter-observer agreement for all tasks combined was 98% for orangutans, 99% for chimpanzees, and 99% for human children (table S4).

Results

Figure 1 presents the results at the most general level of analysis. Averaging across all of the tasks in the physical domain, humans and chimpanzees were correct on ~68% of the trials, whereas orangutans were correct on ~59% of the trials (the absolute values are not especially meaningful because some tasks had a 50 or 33% chance of success by guessing, and some tasks had no possibility for guessing). Statistically, the humans and chimpanzees did not differ from one another in the physical domain, but they were both more skillful than the orangutans ($P < 0.001$ in both cases). In the social domain, a very different pattern emerged. Averaging across all of the tasks in the social domain, the human children were correct on ~74% of the trials, whereas the two ape species were correct about half as often (33 to 36% of the trials). Statistically, the humans were more skillful than either of the two ape species ($P < 0.001$ in both cases), which did not differ from one another.

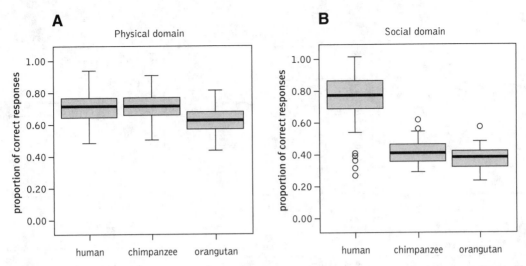

figure 1

Physical domain (A) and social domain (B). The box plots show the full distribution of the proportion of correct responses for physical and social domains of the PCTB for each species: median, quartiles, and extreme values. Boxes represent the interquartile range that contains 50% of values (range from the 25th to the 75th percentile). The line across the box indicates the median. The whiskers represent maximum and minimum values, excluding outliers [indicated by circles, at least 1.5 times the interquartile range (i.e., 1.5 box lengths from the upper or lower edge of the box)] and extremes [indicated by asterisks, at least 3 times the interquartile range (i.e., >3 box lengths from the edge)]. Statistical comparisons on each domain were made by multivariate analysis of variance (MANOVA), followed by analysis of variance (ANOVA) tests for each domain. Post-hoc tests (the Bonferroni correction was used when the equality of variances assumption holds, and the Dunnett t3 correction was used otherwise) followed in case a significant effect was detected. Performance on the PCTB as a whole differed significantly across species (MANOVA with species and gender as between-subject factors and performance in both domains of the PCTB as the dependent variable; Wilk's Lambda: $F_{4,472} = 123.965$, $P < 0.001$, $\eta^2 = 0.51$). No statistically significant differences were detected between genders, but there was an interaction between species and gender (Wilk's Lambda: $F_{4,472} = 2.815$, $P < 0.025$, $\eta^2 = 0.02$). Univariate analyses (ANOVA) showed that the differences across species were significant for both domains: physical ($F_{2,237} = 19.921$, $P < 0.001$, $\eta^2 = 0.14$) and social ($F_{2,237} = 311.224$, $P < 0.001$, $\eta^2 = 0.72$). Univariate analyses for the interaction between species and gender revealed that there was a significant interaction for the physical domain ($F_{2,237} = 5.451$, $P = 0.005$, $\eta^2 = 0.04$) but not for the social domain ($F_{2,237} = 0.224$, $P = 0.799$). Post-hoc tests (Dunnett t3 correction) revealed that humans and chimpanzees performed better than orangutans in the physical domain (for both $P < 0.001$, with no difference between humans and chimpanzees). However, post-hoc tests (Dunnett t3 correction) showed that human children outperformed both chimpanzees and orangutans in the social domain (both $P < 0.001$). Post-hoc tests for the interaction between species and gender in the physical domain showed that female children were better than male children ($P = 0.001$). No other gender differences were found.

Figure 2 (on p. 104) presents the results at the level of the six scales. In the physical domain, there were no differences among species on the quantities scale. On both the space and causality scales, however, humans and chimpanzees did not differ from one another, but both were more skillful than orangutans ($P < 0.001$ in all cases). The difference between chimpanzees and orangutans remained even after controlling for age (25). In the social domain, the pattern was again different from the physical domain and the same for all three of the scales. Human children were more skillful than either of the ape species in each of the three so-

cial scales ($P < 0.001$ in all cases), and the apes did not differ from one another.

Table 2 (on p. 106) lists species' performance on the 16 different tasks within each of the scales (note that social learning is a scale and a task). The overall pattern is that within the physical domain, human children and chimpanzees each were better at some tasks than the other, with orangutans often representing an outlier. Within the four spatial tasks, children were better than chimpanzees at one task (object permanence), whereas the chimpanzees outperformed the children at another task (transposition). In terms

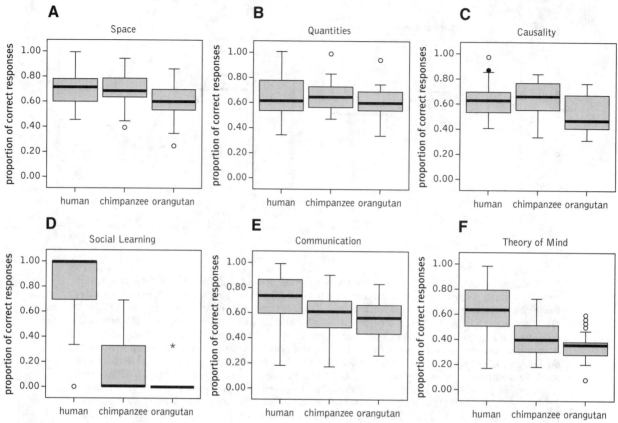

figure 2

*Space (**A**), quantities (**B**), causality (**C**), social learning (**D**), communication (**E**), and theory of mind (**F**). The box plots show the full distribution of the proportion of correct responses on the six scales of the PCTB for each species: median, quartiles, and extreme values. Boxes, lines, whiskers, outliers, and extremes are as described in Fig. 1. Statistical comparisons on each scale were made by MANOVA, followed by ANOVAs for each scale. Post-hoc tests (the Bonferroni correction was used when the equality of variances assumption holds, and the Dunnett t3 correction was used otherwise) followed in case a significant effect was detected. Performance in the physical domain differed significantly across species (MANOVA with species and gender as between-subject factors and performance in the three scales of the physical domain as the dependent variables; Wilk's Lambda: $F_{6,470} = 6.934$, $P < 0.001$, $\eta^2 = 0.08$). No statistically significant differences were detected between genders. However, there was a significant interaction between species and gender (Wilk's Lambda: $F_{6,470} = 2.393$, $P = 0.027$, $\eta^2 = 0.03$). Univariate analyses (ANOVA) showed that the differences across species were significant for the scales space ($F_{2,237} = 11.033$, $P < 0.001$, $\eta^2 = 0.09$) and causality ($F_{2,237} = 8.617$, $P < 0.001$, $\eta^2 = 0.07$). No species difference was found for the scale quantities ($F_{2,237} = 1.970$, $P = 0.142$). Univariate analyses for the interaction between species and gender revealed that there was a significant interaction for the scales space ($F_{2,237} = 4.095$, $P = 0.018$, $\eta^2 = 0.03$) and quantities ($F_{2,237} = 3.147$, $P = 0.045$, $\eta^2 = 0.03$) but not for causality ($F_{2,237} = 0.199$, $P = 0.820$). Post-hoc tests (Bonferroni correction) revealed that humans and chimpanzees performed better than orangutans in the scales of space and causality (for all $P < 0.001$), with no difference between chimpanzees and humans on these scales. Post-hoc tests for the interaction between species and gender for space showed that chimpanzee males outperformed females ($P = 0.047$). Post-hoc tests showed that human females outperformed males on the quantities scale ($P = 0.004$). No other gender differences were found. Performance in the social domain differed significantly across species (MANOVA with gender and species as between-subject factors and performance in the three scales of the social domain as the dependent variables; Wilk's Lambda: $F_{6,470} = 96.846$, $P < 0.001$, $\eta^2 = 0.55$). No statistically significant differences were detected between gender, and no significant gender-species interaction was found. Univariate analyses (ANOVA) showed that the differences across species were significant for the all three scales: social learning ($F_{2,237} = 382.145$, $P < 0.001$, $\eta^2 = 0.76$), communication ($F_{2,237} = 24.717$, $P < 0.001$, $\eta^2 = 0.17$), and theory of mind ($F_{2,237} = 70.646$, $P < 0.001$, $\eta^2 = 0.37$). Post-hoc tests (Dunnett t3 correction) revealed that humans outperformed chimpanzees ($P < 0.001$) and orangutans ($P < 0.001$) in social learning, communication, and theory of mind. The performance of chimpanzees and orangutans in all three scales did not differ.*

of quantities, all three species were similar at judging which of two quantities is larger, but chimpanzees were better than both of the other species at combining quantities in order to make a judgment. Children were better than both ape species at the three causality tasks in which a judgment must be made before manipulation or choice, whereas chimpanzees were better than children and orangutans at the one causality task involving active tool use. Within the social domain, again the pattern was very different. As predicted, the human children were consistently more skillful than both of the ape species (at five out of six tasks), and the two apes did not differ from one another on any task.

To test for possible species differences in individual variability, we computed a coefficient of variation and a 95% two-sided exact confidence interval for both domains for each of the three species (table S5). There were no significant species differences in variability. For two of the three species (humans and chimpanzees), there was more individual variability in the social than in the physical domain (the trend for orangutans was in the same direction but not significantly so), but this may be due to the larger proportion of tasks with the possibility of chance success in the physical domain (90% in the physical domain and 33% in the social domain), which provides a higher baseline for unskillful individuals (25).

There was no effect of gender for any of the species on any of the social scales. On the physical scales, chimpanzee males outperformed chimpanzee females on the scale space, whereas human females outperformed human males on the scale quantities. Human females also outperformed human males at the level of the physical domain as a whole (although this was not so for the two ape species).

In terms of temperament (operationalized as approach behavior to novel objects, people, and rewards), the human children were shyer or less interested in the novel items in the test situation than were the two ape species, which were bolder or more interested ($P < 0.001$ in both cases) [(25) and tables S6 and S7]. Also, children's temperament measures did not correlate with any aspect of their cognitive performance. For the two ape species, there was also no correlation of temperament with any of the social scales, but ape individuals that approached novel situations more quickly (i.e., were bolder and more interested) performed better in the physical domain. In terms of inhibitory control, children showed a greater ability to inhibit than either ape species, and chimpanzees inhibited more readily than orangutans. There was a positive correlation for all three species of inhibitory control and cognitive performance in the physical, but not in the social, domain (25).

Discussion

The current results provide strong support for the cultural intelligence hypothesis that human beings have evolved some specialized social-cognitive skills (beyond those of primates in general) for living and exchanging knowledge in cultural groups: communicating with others, learning from others, and "reading the mind" of others in especially complex ways. Young human children who had been walking and talking for about 1 year, but who were still several years away from literacy and formal schooling, performed at basically an equivalent level to chimpanzees on tasks of physical cognition but far outstripped both chimpanzees and orangutans on tasks of social cognition. This was true at both the most general and the most specific levels of analysis, for individuals never before exposed to these tests, and across the most comprehensive test battery ever given to multiple primate species.

The current results provide no support for the general intelligence hypothesis that human cognition differs from that of apes only in general cognitive processes such as memory, learning, or perceptual processing, which should have led to children differing from apes in both the physical and social domains to an equal degree. However, we should note that because the children were somewhat more skillful than the apes in the causality tasks not involving active tool manipulation, as well as in the tasks of social cognition, it is possible that what is distinctively human is not social-cultural cognition as a specialized domain, as we have hypothesized. Rather, what may be distinctive is the ability to understand unobserved causal forces in general, including (as a special case) the mental states of others as causes of behavior (22,23,26). Even in this case, however, it is a plausible hypothesis that understanding hidden causal forces evolved first to enable humans to understand the mental states of other persons, and this generalized only later to the physical domain (22).

We may thus think of 2-year-old children's cognitive development in the physical domain as still basically equivalent to that of the common ancestor of humans and chimpanzees some 6 million years ago (with perhaps a little more sophisticated understanding of causality outside the context of tool use) but their social cognition as already well down the species-specific path. As one example, the finding that 2.5-year-old children's quantitative skills are basically equivalent to those of apes suggests a great ape "starting point" for human mathematical skills before serious instruction from adults (using written numerals) has begun (27). Also, another recent study found that young human children have preferences for spatial orientation similar to those of great apes, but older children have preferences that align with those of

table 2

Proportion of correct responses on each of the tasks across species. Statistical comparisons on each scale were made by MANOVAs (with species and gender as between-subject factors and performance on the different tasks within each scale as dependent variables), followed by ANOVAs (with species and gender as between-subject factor) for each scale and task. Post-hoc tests (the Bonferroni correction was used when the equality of variances assumption holds, and the Dunnett t3 correction was used otherwise) followed in case a significant effect was detected. In case of important deviations of the model assumptions, a Kruskal-Wallis test with post-hoc Mann-Whitney U tests with the Bonferroni correction was performed. The tool-use task was analyzed separately with a chi-square analysis because it consisted only of one trial with a yes or no response. Space: Performance in the scale space differed significantly across species (MANOVA, Wilk's Lambda: $F_{8,468} = 11.273$, $P < 0.001$, $\eta^2 = 0.16$). No significant differences were detected between genders, and there was no significant interaction between species and gender. Univariate analyses (ANOVA) showed that the differences across species were significant for each spatial task: for spatial memory ($F_{2,237} = 3.329$, $P = 0.038$, $\eta^2 = 0.03$), object permanence ($F_{2,237} = 27.911$, $P < 0.001$, $\eta^2 = 0.19$), rotation ($F_{2,237} = 3.564$, $P < 0.030$, $\eta^2 = 0.03$), and transposition ($F_{2,237} = 14.038$, $P < 0.001$, $\eta^2 = 0.11$). There was a statistically significant effect for spatial memory, but post-hoc tests (Dunnett t3 correction) revealed no significant difference across the three species. Pair-wise comparisons (Bonferroni correction) for object permanence showed that humans performed better than chimpanzees ($P < 0.001$) and orangutans ($P < 0.001$). Chimpanzees performed significantly better than orangutans on the task rotation ($P = 0.028$). Post-hoc tests for transposition revealed that chimpanzees outperformed humans ($P < 0.001$) and orangutans ($P < 0.001$) [see (25) for age effect]. Quantities: Performance in the scale quantities differed significantly across species (MANOVA, Wilk's Lambda: $F_{4,472} = 3.994$, $P = 0.003$, $\eta^2 = 0.03$). No statistically significant difference between genders was detected, and there was no significant interaction between species and gender. Because the model assumptions for an ANOVA were not met for both tasks

	Human	Chimpanzee	Orangutan
Physical	0.68[O]	0.68[O]	0.59
Space	0.71[O]	0.71[O]	0.60
Spatial memory	0.91	0.95	0.85
Object permanence	0.79[C,O]	0.64	0.60
Rotation	0.55	0.56[O]	0.46
Transposition	0.57	0.70[H,O]	0.47
Quantities	0.67	0.68	0.63
Relative numbers	0.71	0.66	0.64
Addition numbers	0.64	0.69[H,O]	0.61
Causality	0.65[O]	0.66[O]	0.55
Noise	0.85[C,O]	0.61	0.56
Shape	0.83[C,O]	0.68	0.64
Tool use	0.23	0.74[H,O]	0.38
Tool properties	0.71[C,O]	0.61	0.63
Social	0.74[C,O]	0.36	0.33
Social learning	0.86[C,O]	0.10	0.07
Communication	0.72[C,O]	0.57	0.55
Comprehension	0.84[C,O]	0.63	0.65
Pointing cups	0.72	0.74	0.73
Attentional state	0.59[C,O]	0.34	0.26
Theory of mind	0.65[C,O]	0.40	0.36
Gaze following	0.45[C,O]	0.22	0.17
Intentions	0.85[C,O]	0.59	0.56

Superscripts indicate that values are significantly higher than human (H), chimpanzee (C), or orangutan (O) values.

within the quantities scale, nonparametric tests were performed. Kruskal-Wallis one-way ANOVA showed that the differences across species were significant for addition numbers ($\chi^2_2 = 9.574$, $P = 0.008$) but not for relative numbers ($\chi^2_2 = 4.149$, $P = 0.126$). Post-hoc tests, with Mann-Whitney U tests for addition numbers, revealed that chimpanzees performed better than humans ($U = 4462.00$, $z = -2.556$, $P = 0.011$) and orangutans ($U = 1192.50$, $z = -2.638$, $P = 0.008$). The species difference in addition numbers between chimpanzees and orangutans remained even after controlling for age by matching the age of chimpanzees and orangutans and comparing the performance of these individuals ($U = 735.50$, $z = -2.540$, $P = 0.011$). Causality: Performance in the scale causality differed significantly across species (MANOVA, Wilk's Lambda: $F_{6,470} = 33.093$, $P < 0.001$, $\eta^2 = 0.30$). No statistically significant differences were detected between genders, and there was no significant interaction between species and gender. Univariate analyses (ANOVA) showed that the differences across species were significant for each causality task: for noise ($F_{2,237} = 74.163$, $P < 0.001$, $\eta^2 = 0.39$), shape ($F_{2,237} = 29.335$, $P < 0.001$, $\eta^2 = 0.20$), and tool properties ($F_{2,237} = 20.211$, $P < 0.001$, $\eta^2 = 0.15$). Post-hoc tests (Bonferroni correction) revealed that humans performed better than chimpanzees ($P < 0.001$) and orangutans ($P < 0.001$) on the noise task. The same difference was found for the shape task (chimpanzees, $P < 0.001$; orangutans, $P < 0.001$) and for tool properties (chimpanzees, $P < 0.001$; orangutans, $P = 0.003$). Performance in tool use was significantly different across species ($\chi^2_2 = 55.815$, $P < 0.001$). Pair-wise comparison revealed that chimpanzees outperformed humans (Fisher's exact test, $P < 0.001$) and orangutans (Fisher's exact test, $P < 0.001$). The species difference in tool use between chimpanzees and orangutans remained even after controlling for age by matching the age of chimpanzees and orangutans and comparing the performance of these individuals (Fisher's exact test, $P = 0.018$).

Social Learning: The social-learning scale was analyzed with a Kruskal-Wallis one-way ANOVA. A significant difference between species was found ($\chi^2_2 = 183.301$, $P < 0.001$). Post-hoc tests, with Mann-Whitney U tests, revealed that humans performed better than chimpanzees ($U = 255.00$, $z = -12.593$, $P < 0.001$) and orangutans ($U = 56.50$, $z = -8.935$, $P < 0.001$), which did not differ from one another. Communication: Performance in the communication scale differed significantly across species (MANOVA, Wilk's Lambda: $F_{6,470} = 24.462$, $P < 0.001$, $\eta^2 = 0.24$). No statistically significant differences were detected between genders, and there was no interaction between species and gender. Univariate analyses (ANOVA) showed that the differences across species were significant for the comprehension ($F_{2,237} = 67.021$, $P < 0.001$, $\eta^2 = 0.36$) and attentional-state tasks ($F_{2,237} = 19.155$, $P < 0.001$, $\eta^2 = 0.14$). However, there were no species differences in the pointing-cups task ($F_{2,237} = 0.087$, $P = 0.916$). Post-hoc tests (Bonferroni correction) revealed that humans performed better than chimpanzees ($P < 0.001$) and orangutans ($P < 0.001$) on the comprehension task. The same difference was found in the attentional-state task (chimpanzees, $P < 0.001$; orangutans, $P < 0.001$). Theory of mind: Performance in the theory-of-mind scale differed significantly across species (MANOVA, Wilks' Lambda: $F_{4,472} = 44.868$, $P < 0.001$, $\eta^2 = 0.28$). No statistically significant differences were detected between genders, and there was no interaction between species and gender. Univariate analyses (ANOVA) showed that the differences across species were significant for both the gaze-following task ($F_{2,237} = 23.096$, $P < 0.001$, $\eta^2 = 0.16$) and the intentions task ($F_{2,237} = 87.129$, $P < 0.001$, $\eta^2 = 0.42$). Post-hoc tests (Bonferroni correction) revealed that humans performed better than chimpanzees ($P < 0.001$) and orangutans ($P < 0.001$) on the gaze-following task. The same difference was found for the intentions task (chimpanzees, $P < 0.001$; orangutans, $P < 0.001$).

their culture, presumably as a result of experiencing their culture's ways of dealing with space, including the use of particular kinds of spatial language (28). This provides one example of the kind of cognitive transformation that may result from children using

their specialized social-cognitive skills to participate in the cultural practices around them.

In terms of human evolution, it is likely that the crucial developments in skills of social-cultural cognition probably had not yet occurred in *H. erectus* 1 to 2 million years ago, because (i) their rapid pattern of brain growth during ontogeny was more similar to that of chimpanzees than to that of modern humans (29) and (ii) there are few signs in this early hominid of elaborate cultural differences between groups (30). The ecological conditions within which post-*erectus* humans' special skills of social-cultural cognition evolved are not known, but one hypothesis is that those skills evolved in support of especially complex forms of collaborative activity, such as hunting or gathering, supported by special skills of communication and social learning (31). These skills presumably grew out of earlier evolved primate skills of social cognition and learning in general, such as those that nonhuman primates display in their everyday interactions with groupmates in the wild, involving an understanding of the intentions, perceptions, and motivations of others (24).

It is certainly an issue that the test battery was both constructed and administered by humans. But in previous studies with these same tasks from the social domain, there is no evidence that the use of human versus conspecific interactants had any significant effect on performance (table S2) (25). And our temperament measures did not correlate with performance on the social domain of the test battery, which is where there were the largest differences among species (and indeed the children were more shy or less interested in general in the temperament task), providing no support for the notion that the apes related less well to the testing situation. In terms of test construction, we of course could have obtained different results with a different test battery. But the PCTB was constructed from a comprehensive theory of primate cognition based on the ecological tasks that primates face most commonly in both their physical and social environments. In general, we suspect that there would be more consensus among experts about the appropriateness of our tasks of physical cognition, whereas there might be more controversy about the social tasks. But a major factor in the choice of the social tasks was our focus on humans and the cultural intelligence hypothesis, and this meant testing those social-cognitive skills relevant to participation in culture by young children and then seeing the degree to which closely related species have these skills as well. It is perhaps relevant, in this regard, that domestic dogs (*Canis familiaris*) (which, in some sense, have been selected to live in human cultures) do not perform as well as chimpanzees on tasks of physical cognition but outperform them on tasks of social cognition (32,33).

The role played by individual variability and gender in our results requires further investigation. The finding that, at a very general level of analysis, there were no species differences in cognitive variability is somewhat unexpected, given that apes are much more genetically variable in general than are humans (34). Gender did not play a large role either. The one

finding for gender with the apes (that male chimpanzees were better than female chimpanzees at space) fits with previous research. But our finding that human females were better than human males at tasks of physical cognition in general (and quantities in particular) does not fit so well with previous research (35), though not so much research has been done with children this young, and so there may be developmental differences involved.

The past few years have seen the sequencing of both the human and the chimpanzee genome (36–38) [the orangutan and bonobo (*P. paniscus*) genomes are currently being sequenced], with a major goal being to identify domains of human genetic distinctiveness. But to do this with specific reference to behavior and cognition, what is needed first are comprehensive and detailed comparisons among humans and closely related primates at the level of the phenotype, in terms of the actual behavioral and cognitive skills that have promoted survival and reproduction (39). A major avenue of future research is thus to use the PCTB to characterize the behavioral-cognitive phenotype of a wide variety of primate species. This could be done through systematic testing of carefully chosen representatives of the more than 50 genera of primates, which should then enable us to map out cladistically the evolution of primates' most important cognitive skills at the level of both the phenotype and, ultimately, the genotype.

REFERENCES AND NOTES

1. H. J. Jerison, *Evolution of the Brain and Intelligence* (Academic Press, New York, 1973).

2. P. Harvey, R. Martin, T. Clutton-Brock, in *Primate Societies,* B. B. Smuts, D. L. Cheney, R. M. Seyfarth, R. W. Wrangham, T. T. Struhsaker, Eds. (Univ. of Chicago Press, Chicago, 1987), pp. 181–196.

3. L. C. Aiello, P. Wheeler, *Curr. Anthropol.* **36,** 199 (1995).

4. J. Tooby, L. Cosmides, in *The Adapted Mind: Evolutionary Psychology and the Generation of Culture,* J. H. Barkow, L. Cosmides, J. Tooby, Eds. (Oxford Univ. Press, New York, 1992), pp. 19–136.

5. S. J. Shettleworth, *Cognition, Evolution, and Behavior* (Oxford Univ. Press, New York, 1998).

6. K. Milton, in *Machiavellian Intelligence: Social Expertise and the Evolution of Intellect in Monkeys, Apes and Humans,* R. W. Byrne, A. Whiten, Eds. (Clarendon Press, Oxford, 1988), pp. 285–306.

7. R. W. Byrne, in *Modelling the Early Human Mind,* P. Mellars, K. Gibson, Eds. (McDonald Institute Research Monographs, Cambridge, 1996), pp. 49–56.

8. N. K. Humphrey, in *Growing Points in Ethology,* P. P. G. Bateson, R. A. Hinde, Eds. (Cambridge Univ. Press, Cambridge, 1976), pp. 303–321.

9. F. B. M. de Waal, *Chimpanzee Politics: Power and Sex Among Apes* (Harper and Row, New York, 1982).

10. R. W. Byrne, A. Whitten, Eds. *Machiavellian Intelligence: Social Expertise and the Evolution of Intellect in Monkeys, Apes and Humans* (Clarendon Press, Oxford, 1988).

11. R. I. M. Dunbar, *Annu. Rev. Anthropol.* **32,** 163 (2003).

12. R. Boyd, P. J. Richerson, *Proc. Br. Acad.* **88,** 77 (1996).

13. L. S. Vygotsky, *Mind in Society: The Development of Higher Psychological Processes* (Harvard Univ. Press, Cambridge, MA, 1978).

14. A. Whitten *et al., Nature* **399,** 682 (1999).

15. C. P. van Schaik *et al., Science* **299,** 102 (2003).

16. M. Tomasello, *The Cultural Origins of Human Cognition* (Harvard Univ. Press, Cambridge, MA, 1999).

17. R. I. M. Dunbar, *J. Hum. Evol.* **22,** 469 (1992).

18. R. I. M. Dunbar, *Behav. Brain Sci.* **16,** 681 (1993).

19. R. I. M. Dunbar, *Evol. Anthropol.* **6,** 178 (1998).

20. H. Kudo, R. I. M. Dunbar, *Anim. Behav.* **62,** 711 (2001).

21. R. O. Deaner, C. P. van Schaik, V. E. Johnson, *Evol. Psychol.* **4,** 149 (2006).

22. M. Tomasello, J. Call, *Primate Cognition* (Oxford Univ. Press, New York, 1997).

23. D. L. Cheney, R. M. Seyfarth, *How Monkeys See the World: Inside the Mind of Another Species* (Univ. of Chicago Press, Chicago, 1990).

24. D. L. Cheney, R. M. Seyfarth, *Baboon Metaphysics: The Evolution of a Social Mind* (Univ. of Chicago Press, Chicago, 2007).

25. See supporting material on *Science* Online.

26. A. Whitten, in *Theories of Theories of Mind,* P. Carruthers, P. K. Smith, Eds. (Cambridge Univ. Press, Cambridge, 1996), pp. 277–292.

27. M. D. Hauser, F. Tsao, P. Garcia, E. S. Spelke, *Proc. R. Soc. London Ser. B* **270,** 1441 (2003).

28. D. B. M. Haun, C. Rapold, J. Call, G. Janzen, S. C. Levinson, *Proc. Natl. Acad. Sci. U.S.A.* **103,** 17568 (2006).

29. H. Coqueugniot, J.-J. Hublin, F. Veillon, F. Houët, T. Jacob, *Nature* **431,** 299 (2004).

30. R. G. Klein, *The Human Career: Human Biological and Cultural Origins* (Univ. of Chicago Press, Chicago, ed. 2, 1999).

31. M. Tomasello, M. Carpenter, J. Call, T. Behen, H. Moll, *Behav. Brain Sci.* **28,** 675 (2005).

32. B. Hare, M. Brown, C. Williamson, M. Tomasello, *Science* **298,** 1634 (2002).

33. J. Bräuer, J. Kaminski, J. Call, M. Tomasello, *J. Comp. Psychol.* **120,** 38 (2006).

34. A. Fischer, J. Pollack, O. Thalmann, B. Nickel, S. Pääbo, *Curr. Biol.* **16,** 1133 (2006).

35. D. Voyer, S. Voyer, M. Bryden, *Psychol. Bull.* **117,** 250 (1995).

36. J. C. Venter *et al., Science* **291,** 1304 (2001).

37. E. S. Lander *et al., Nature* **409,** 860 (2001).

38. The Chimpanzee Sequencing and Analysis Consortium, *Nature* **437,** 69 (2005).

39. M. Hauser, *Nature* **437,** 60 (2005).

ACKNOWLEDGMENT

We thank L. Pharoah, R. Atencia, K. Brown, and the Jane Goodall Institute USA and staff of Tchimpounga Sanctuary, as well as L. Ajarova, D. Cox, R. Ssunna, and the trustees and staff of Ngamba Island Chimpanzee Sanctuary, for their enthusiasm, help, and support. We also thank B. M. Galdikas and the staff of the Orangutan Care Center and Quarantine in Pasir Panjang for their great help and support. In particular, we appreciate the hard work of the animal caregivers from the three sanctuaries: J. Maboto, B. Moumbaka, A. Sitou, M. Makaya, B. Bissafi, C. Ngoma, W. Bouity, J. A. Tchikaya, L. Bibimbou, A. Makosso, C. Boukindi, G. Nzaba, B. Ngoma, P. Kibirege, I. Mujaasi, S. Nyandwi L. Mugisha, M. Musumba, G. Muyingo, P. Melok, P. Usai, and P. Yoyong. We also appreciate the permission from the Ugandan National Council for Science and Technology and the Uganda Wildlife Authority, as well as the Congolese Ministere de la Recherche Scientifique et de l'Innovation Technique, the Indonesian Institute of Sciences (LIPI), and the Indonesian Ministry of Forestry for allowing us to conduct our research in their countries. Special thanks go to A. Loose, M. Schäfer, K. Greve, E. Graf, V. Wobber, J. Cissewski, and S. Hastings for their enormous help with organizing, data collection and coding. In addition, we thank J. Uebel, L. Jorschik, A. Gampe, H. Roethel, K. Haberl, A. P. Melis, J. Riedel, D. Hanus, S. Girlich, P. Jahn, C. Gerisch, S. Rolle, A. Buergermeister, L. Gieselmann, D. Lagner, J. Kramareva, A. Misch, S. Helmig, E. Scholl, and A. Rosati for their various help to make this study successful. Thanks to D. Haun for helpful comments on the manuscript. We also thank the parents and children who participated in the study. The research of B.H. is supported by a Sofja Kovalevskaja award from the Alexander von Humboldt Foundation and the German Federal Ministry for Education and Research. The research of E.H. is supported by a grant from the Studienstiftung des Deutschen Volkes.

Supporting Online Material

www.sciencemag.org/cgi/content/full/317/5843/1360/DC1
Materials and Methods

SOM Text
Figs. S1 and S2
Tables S1 to S7
References
Movies S1 to S32

Questions

1. What is the general intelligence hypothesis and how does it differ from the cultural intelligence hypothesis?

2. According to Herrmann and her colleagues, what type of research is needed to test the cultural intelligence hypothesis, and what would be the main focus of this research?

3. How might young children have learned these social cognitive skills, and what other types of skills might these social cognitive skills depend on?

4. Would it be possible or meaningful to include younger children in this study? What information might such a comparison provide?

5. What do the results presented in Figure 1 tell us about the performances of the different groups of participants on the PCTB? Do the results represented in Figure 2 expand on this overall pattern and, if so, how?

6. Do these results support the cultural intelligence hypothesis? Describe the evidence on which you base your answer.

14 Development of Object Concepts in Infancy: Evidence for Early Learning in an Eye-Tracking Paradigm

Scott P. Johnson • Dima Amso • Jonathan A. Slemmer

Developmental psychologists debate what types of knowledge infants are born with and what types of knowledge infants need to develop early in life. Within this debate, substantial research attention has been paid to knowledge of objects.

Research indicates that infants develop object knowledge rather quickly, perhaps even before they have much opportunity to explore objects manually. Some researchers have used this evidence to support the view that object knowledge, especially regarding fundamental properties of objects, is innate. However, other researchers disagree with this interpretation and argue that knowledge of objects develops over the period of infancy. The latter view does not necessarily claim that innate processes are not involved, however. Certain tendencies or biases inherent to the visual system, for example, may underlie the rapid development of object knowledge.

The fact that infants are very young when they develop basic knowledge of objects presents a significant challenge to researchers in this area. Unique research methods and sensitive measurement techniques are needed to discover through the infants' behaviors whether object knowledge is already present or has been learned. One such technique involves the study of infants' eye movements as they explore and learn about novel objects.

In the following article, Scott P. Johnson, Dima Amso, and Jonathan A. Slemmer describe their observations of 4- and 6-month-old infants viewing images of objects moving in patterns on a computer screen. Johnson and his colleagues recorded the infants' eye movements as these objects moved behind and were obscured by another image. The researchers developed precise ways of assessing how infants followed, or tracked, the objects. They were especially interested in whether the infants anticipated the trajectory of the object's movement by looking where the object would reappear from behind the obscuring image. However, this information alone would not indicate whether the knowledge was innate or learned. To explore this question the researchers needed to try to teach the infants something about objects that they did not appear to know already.

Although the results do support a learning view of object knowledge, the processes by which this knowledge develops remain unknown. Using the differences they observed between the 4- and 6-month-old infants on these tasks, the researchers conclude with an interesting discussion about what some of these processes may be.

Concepts of objects as enduring and complete across space and time have been documented in infants within several months after birth, but little is known about how such concepts arise during development. Current theories that stress innate knowledge may neglect the potential contributions of experience to guide acquisition of object concepts. To examine whether learning plays an important role in early development of object representations, we used an eye-tracking paradigm with 4- and 6-month-old infants who were provided with an initial pe-

Note Abbreviations: POG, point of gaze; RT, response time; NS, not significant.

riod of experience viewing an unoccluded trajectory, or no experience with this particular stimulus. After exposure to the unoccluded trajectory for only 2 min, there was a reliable increase in 4-month-old infants' anticipatory eye movement when the infants subsequently viewed occluded-trajectory displays, relative to 4-month-old infants who did not receive this experience. This effect of training in 4-month-old infants was found to generalize to another category of trajectory orientation. Older infants received no additional benefits from training, most likely because they enter the task capable of forming robust object representations under these conditions. This finding provides compelling evidence that very brief training facilitated formation of object representations, and suggests more generally that infants learn such representations from real-world experience viewing objects undergoing occlusion and disocclusion.

The question of how humans acquire and represent object knowledge is fundamental to cognitive science, and there has been a long standing and relentless debate concerning its developmental origins. These debates have centered on mechanisms of development, which lead infants to view objects as coherent entities that endure across time (i.e., existence constancy), and whose boundaries may extend beyond what is visible directly (i.e., amodal completion; ref. 1). Initial investigations revealed a progression across the first two postnatal years in object-oriented behavior, which was assumed to reflect emergence of object representations from a nascent inability to perceive occlusion (2). On this view, concepts arise from active manual exploration of objects, in particular search for hidden objects, with the advent of reaching and grasping skills at 4–6 months of age. An alternative view emerged from more recent evidence of object representations in infants too young to engage in skilled search, and led to postulates of innate knowledge (3–5). The assumption of this latter view is that, in the absence of evidence to the contrary, functional object representations are rooted in processes that operate independent of experience (6).

A third possibility, which we examine here, is that initial object concepts (i.e., existence constancy) are learned from experience early in postnatal life. We note five lines of evidence that highlight the potential importance of infants' attunement to the visual environment in guiding development of object representations. First, the visual system is organized at birth. Neonates tend to direct visual attention toward areas of high contrast (i.e., edges) and motion, providing suitable conditions for extraction of information specifying segregated surfaces (7). Second, natural scenes are richly structured and characterized by a considerable degree of predictability across space and time (8), and there is evidence that development of response

properties of visual neurons exploits the statistical redundancy in the input (9). Third, infants are prodigious learners, responding readily to classical and operant conditioning regimes (10), and exhibiting statistical learning soon after birth (11,12). Fourth, object concepts arise with the onset of visual experience. Human neonates are not born with the capacity to perceive occlusion, a necessary condition supporting any functional object representation (13,14). Finally, infants receive an abundance of exposure to the visual environment antecedent to occlusion perception, which has been documented first at 2 months (15). Neonates spend 2–3 h per day in a state of quiet alertness (16), engaging in active scanning of the visual field during the bulk of this time (17). Like adults, young infants produce two to three eye movements per sec (18,19). Assuming a doubling of the daily duration of alertness by 2 months (20), this result provides the 2-month-old infant with >200 h of visual experience, having executed some 2,500,000 eye movements. Despite these numerous reasons to suspect a strong role for learning in early object concept development, direct evidence has yet to be reported in support of this hypothesis. Obtaining such support for this hypothesis is the goal of this article.

We presented simple object-trajectory displays (Fig. 1) to 4- and 6-month-old infants as we recorded their eye movements with a corneal reflection eye tracker. We reasoned that a representation of the object and its trajectory under occlusion would be reflected in a consistent pattern of anticipatory eye movements toward the place of reemergence, before the object's appearance. We explored three hypotheses. First, we predicted that the older infants would make more anticipatory eye movements than would the younger infants because 4-month-old infants' object representations under these conditions are fragile, and 6-month-old infants' representations are more robust. In experiments using an habituation paradigm, 4-month-old infants have been found unable to perceive continuity in the occlusion display depicted in Fig. 1. Instead, they responded to visible path segments only, failing to link them into a continuous trajectory. However, 4-month-old infants perceived continuity under less demanding conditions, when occluder size and occlusion time were reduced. Six-month-old infants responded to continuity, even under the more challenging conditions (21). These experiments provide evidence for vital developments in object representations between 4 and 6 months of age, and support the notion that 4 months is a time of transition toward veridical concepts of object continuity. Our second hypothesis concerned the effect of experience on development of continuity perception. We predicted that when provided with initial exposure to an unoccluded trajectory, 4-month-old infants would subsequently produce more frequent anticipations

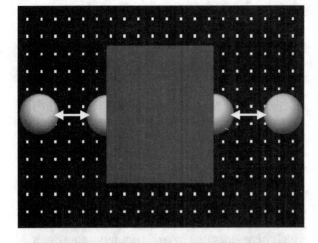

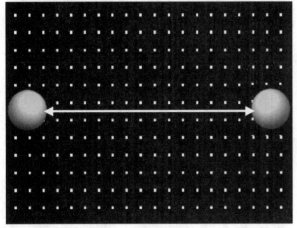

figure 1

(Upper) *The partly occluded trajectory display. A green ball translates repetitively on a linear trajectory, alternately moving behind a blue box and reemerging. (Note: Ball and box shown here were originally green and blue, respectively).* Infants in the baseline condition (experiment 1) viewed this display for eight trials, each consisting of six complete cycles of motion. (Lower) *The fully visible trajectory seen for four trials in the training condition (experiment 2), followed by the partly occluded trajectory display for four trials. Not shown is the fully visible vertical trajectory shown to infants in the training generalization condition (experiment 3), which was identical to the horizontal training condition except for the trajectory orientation.*

than would 4-month-old infants who received no prior training. Six-month-old infants, in contrast, were predicted to receive no benefit, because they enter the task with a more robust facility to form object representations (21). Our third hypothesis centers on the question of training generalization. We predicted that

4-month-old infants would exhibit facilitation of object concepts even when training and test tasks came from different categories of trajectory orientation. These hypotheses were tested in experiments 1, 2, and 3, respectively.

Experiment 1 establishes any baseline difference between 4- and 6-month-old infants in their ability to anticipate the emergence of a moving object from behind an occluder. Experiments 2 and 3 then determine the role that short-term experience plays in the learning of information about object movement during occlusion. The critical issue is not whether older infants are better at oculomotor anticipation, but whether younger infants who receive brief exposure to unoccluded object movement show subsequent facilitation of anticipation during occlusion, and whether such training can be generalized beyond the original context.

Methods

In all experiments, infants sat in a parent's lap 100 cm from the 76-cm computer monitor used to present the stimuli. Stimuli were prepared by using METACREATIONS INFINI-D 4.0 software, and were presented by using custom software on a G4 Macintosh. Each stimulus consisted of a 30-sec animation depicting a 6.7-cm (3.8° visual angle at the infant's viewing distance) green ball translating laterally across 45.4 cm (25.5°) at 18.2 cm/sec (10.4°/sec). The ball changed direction (left-right) every 2.5 sec. The center of the trajectory was occluded by a 21.5 × 17.7 cm (12.3 × 10.1°) blue box (Note: Ball and box shown in Figure 1 were originally green and blue, respectively). Ball and occluder were presented against a textured background (a 20 × 12 grid of white dots on black) measuring 48.8 × 33.0 cm (27.4 × 18.7°). In each of the eight trials, a nonrhythmic sound was played to maximize attention toward the stimulus. Each trial had a different sound, and the order of sounds was randomized for each infant. Infants in the training condition (experiment 2) were first presented with four identical stimuli except for the absence of the occluder. (Stimuli used in the habituation experiments described in ref. 21 were identical, except they were silent.) Infants in the generalization condition (experiment 3) were first presented with four stimuli in which the ball translated vertically, rather than horizontally (at the same rate and extent of motion), against the same textured background, with no occluder. Between stimuli an "attention getter" (a target that loomed and contracted in time with a beeping sound) was presented to maintain the infant's interest across trials and recenter the infant's point of gaze (POG). Eye movements were recorded with an ASL model 504 (Applied Science Laboratories, Waltham, MA) remote optics corneal reflection eye tracker. Data (the POG superimposed on the stimuli) were recorded onto videotape and coded offline. Temporal accuracy was determined by the temporal resolution of the videotape system (30 fps; each frame = 33.3 ms).

Each infant's POG was calibrated with a "quick-calibration" routine. Infants were shown the attention getter at the top left and bottom right corners of an imaginary rectangle corresponding to the corners of the stimulus background (the texture elements) viewed during test. The eye tracker interpolated the positions of the remaining calibration points. Calibration was checked by moving the attention getter to random positions on the screen. If the infant's POG was not directed within .5° of the center of the attention getter at all positions (minimum of six), the calibration routine was repeated until this criterion was reached. We estimate therefore that spatial accuracy was at most 1° error, given estimates of the inherent accuracy of the eye tracker provided by the ASL (i.e., an additional 0.5° of error possible).

In experiment 1, infants viewed eight trials of the occlusion display, each with six complete cycles of the object trajectory (12 left-right or right-left excursions per trial, 96 excursions total), as depicted in Fig. 1. In experiments 2 and 3, infants viewed four trials in which the moving object was presented without an occluder, followed by four trials with the occlusion display (48 excursions total). Eye movements were coded for instances of perceptual contact. In each of the 96 excursions from experiment 1 and 48 excursions from experiments 2 and 3, an eye movement was entered into the data set if the infant's POG was directed toward a region of the display within 1.5° (horizontal) and 3° (vertical) of the moving-object trajectory as it was visible on either side of the occluder, after a starting position of the POG outside this region. (Trials in which the POG did not leave the anticipation region across object excursions were not counted, as when infants remained fixated on one or the other side of the display.) Eye movements leading to perceptual contact that were initiated <150 ms subsequent to object emergence were coded as *anticipations,* and those that were initiated later than 150 ms subsequent to object emergence were coded as *reactions.* The 150-ms criterion was derived from past reports of predictive and reactive eye movements in infants (22) and adults (23).

We tested 48 4-month-old infants (mean age = 122.2 days, SD = 10.7; 22 girls and 26 boys) in experiments 1–3 and 32 6-month-old infants (mean age = 185.4 days, SD = 14.4; 19 girls and 13 boys) in experiments 1 and 2. There were 16 infants in each condition. We found no sex differences in performance in any experiment (i.e., proportion of anticipation); all *t* values <1, not significant (NS). All infants were full term and had no known developmental difficulties.

Experiment 1: Baseline Age Differences in Oculomotor Anticipation

Experiment 1 yielded 2,183 eye movements meeting criteria for an anticipation or a reaction: 1,035 from the 4-month-old infants and 1,148 from the 6-month-old infants, representing 67.4% of trials for 4-month-old infants and 74.7% of trials for 6-month-old infants. (Other trials were characterized by missing data or eye movements that did not meet the criteria.) The histograms in Fig. 2 present eye movement frequencies for each age group, plotted as response times (RTs) relative to the emergence of the ball from behind the occluder (RT = 0, the first video frame when the ball became visible). Eye movement latencies tended to cluster into two distributions for both age groups, which were separated by a discontinuity consistent with the 150-ms criterion for classification as an anticipation or a reaction.

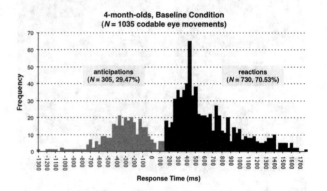

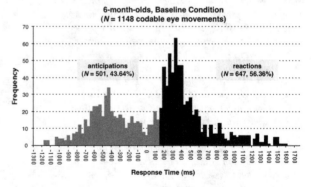

figure 2

Histograms of eye movement response times (RTs) relative to the reemergence of the object from behind the occluder (RT = 0). The object began occlusion at − 1,300 ms, was fully occluded at − 700 ms, was fully visible at 400 ms, and remained visible until 1,800 ms had elapsed. Anticipations are gray, and reactions are black. (Upper) Four-month-old infants in experiment 1. (Lower) Six-month-old infants in experiment 1. The older infants reliably produced more anticipations than did the younger infants.

Our first prediction was supported. Six-month-old infants produced a reliably higher proportion of anticipations than did 4-month-old infants, $\chi^2 = 46.94$, $P < 0.0001$, providing corroborating evidence for age differences in formation of object representations between 4 and 6 months when viewing occluded-trajectory displays (21). Additional evidence for this suggestion comes from a trial-by-trial analysis of response patterns (Table 1). Anticipations declined across trials for both age groups, $F(7,210) = 11.73$, $P < 0.0001$, more precipitously in the younger infants, $F(7,210) = 2.73$, $P < 0.01$, indicating that the infants did not learn to anticipate simply by viewing the repetitive pattern. Past reports of anticipatory eye movements in infancy have found that young infants anticipate repetitive, predictable events on 15–30% of trials, depending on the specific paradigm (22). There are few improvements in anticipation frequency in simple event sequences from 3 to 12 months of age (22), but there are some improvements with age in response to complex sequences (24). In the present baseline condi-

tion, which contains a perfectly predictable object movement, the greater proportion of anticipations in the older infants may be taken as evidence for the influence of functional object representations on eye movements.

To further probe the differences in performance as a function of age group, we examined the temporal characteristics of eye movements (Table 2). Older infants were faster overall, including both anticipations and reactions.

Finally, a comparison of the 4-month-old infants' performance to a second group of 16 4-month-old infants (mean age = 126.5 days, SD = 10.0; nine girls and seven boys) who viewed the object moving on a random, unpredictable trajectory revealed no reliable differences in anticipations between the groups, $F(1,30) = .32$, NS. Infants in the random condition received eight trials with stimuli that were identical to those viewed by infants in the baseline condition except the place of the object's reemergence (left or right) was not predictable from its place of entry behind

table 1   Mean Trial-by-Trial Percentages of Anticipations and Reactions by Each Age Group

	4-month-old infants		6-month-old infants	
Trial	Anticipations, %	Reactions, %	Anticipations, %	Reactions, %
Experiment 1: baseline condition				
1	32.29 (4.55)	51.04 (5.15)	43.23 (4.89)	41.13 (4.33)
2	29.69 (3.22)	53.64 (3.95)	42.71 (5.31)	45.83 (5.22)
3	20.81 (3.40)	51.56 (4.11)	40.62 (4.86)	47.91 (3.77)
4	20.31 (3.48)	56.26 (4.78)	37.51 (4.23)	36.99 (3.95)
5	14.05 (2.61)	55.20 (5.43)	26.57 (4.18)	33.85 (4.47)
6	18.23 (4.38)	46.88 (4.68)	22.91 (4.72)	42.17 (6.65)
7	16.15 (4.05)	34.89 (5.65)	18.75 (2.58)	50.00 (4.75)
8	9.38 (2.62)	41.14 (6.43)	23.44 (3.16)	41.16 (4.90)
Mean	20.11 (2.47)	48.83 (2.98)	31.97 (1.77)	42.38 (2.45)
Experiment 2: training condition				
5	43.75 (5.56)	35.94 (5.58)	34.37 (3.39)	48.44 (5.55)
6	38.00 (4.86)	48.44 (5.06)	30.73 (4.42)	42.19 (5.72)
7	36.99 (3.57)	41.15 (4.47)	23.43 (4.18)	47.39 (3.78)
8	27.09 (4.33)	41.16 (4.89)	18.23 (3.82)	41.15 (3.99)
Mean	36.46 (2.88)	41.67 (3.42)	26.69 (2.53)	44.79 (3.52)
Experiment 3: generalization condition				
5	40.11 (5.03)	35.93 (6.15)		
6	40.62 (5.63)	40.09 (3.89)		
7	39.58 (4.59)	43.34 (5.01)		
8	28.65 (4.30)	31.76 (4.32)		
Mean	37.23 (3.91)	37.78 (3.42)		

Note that these data encompass all trials, not only eye movements that met the criteria for anticipations or reactions, to highlight decreases in response across trials. Numbers do not sum to 100 because on some trials there were no codable eye movements, or eye movements were directed to locations other than the object. Numbers in parentheses are SE.

table 2   Mean RTs (in Milliseconds) of Codable Eye Movements, Relative to Object Emergence

	4-month-old infants	6-month-old infants	Independent samples t test
Experiment 1: baseline condition			
Anticipations	−297.98 (29.66)	−402.60 (29.92)	$t(30) = 2.48, P < .05$
Reactions	675.57 (33.24)	518.00 (22.51)	$t(30) = 3.92, P < .001$
Mean	395.65 (35.16)	114.09 (30.48)	$t(30) = 6.05, P < .001$
Experiment 2: training condition			
Anticipations	−391.21 (34.61)	−417.90 (26.57)	$t(30) = .61$, NS
Reactions	631.76 (35.82)	510.92 (46.36)	$t(30) = 2.06, P < .05$
Mean	158.95 (47.93)	141.39 (34.05)	$t(30) = .30$, NS
Experiment 3: generalization condition			
Anticipations	−395.19 (34.33)		
Reactions	603.83 (24.40)		
Mean	108.26 (51.89)		

Numbers in parentheses are SE. NS, not significant.

the occluder: that is, the ball moved behind the occluder and was as likely to emerge from the same side as from the other side relative to the point of entry. An observer would thus be unable to form a representation of a simple, linear object trajectory in this type of display. Infants in the random condition anticipated on 22.46% of trials (SE = 3.36), which is comparable to anticipation performance of the 4-month-old infants in the baseline condition (see Table 1), $t(30) = 0.56$, NS. These comparisons imply that the 4-month-old infants' eye movements that met our criterion for anticipations were more likely to be spontaneous eye movements rather than "true" predictions of object emergence.

In sum, a variety of age differences in oculomotor behavior provide evidence of stronger object concepts in 6-month-old infants relative to 4-month-old infants. In particular, the older infants produced anticipations that were both more frequent and faster. Frequency of anticipations in the 4-month-old infant baseline group did not differ reliably relative to the random condition, suggesting that they were unable to capitalize on the visible portions of the trajectory to predict the future position of the object. Therefore, there is little indication that the majority of the anticipations they produced resulted from a representation of the hidden object and its trajectory.

Experiment 2: Effects of Training on Oculomotor Anticipation

In experiment 2, we explored the possibility that incipient object concepts might be facilitated by experience.

Four- and 6-month-old infants' eye movements were recorded as they viewed four trials with the occluded-trajectory display used in experiment 1, after first receiving training by viewing four 30-sec trials with an unoccluded trajectory (see Fig. 1). Experiment 2 yielded 1,116 eye movements meeting the criteria described previously; 611 from the 4-month-old infants (79.6% of trials) and 505 from the 6-month-old infants (65.8% of trials; Fig. 3). As in experiment 1, eye movement latencies tended to cluster into two distributions corresponding to anticipations and reactions. In contrast to experiment 1, however, there were age differences in the proportions of the two categories that favored 4-month-old infants, who produced a higher proportion of anticipations, $\chi^2 = 9.78, P < 0.01$. Nevertheless, parametric trial-by-trial analyses revealed no significant age differences in performance as a function of trial or eye movement category, $F(1,30) = 3.46$, NS (Table 1). Comparisons of age differences in temporal characteristics of anticipations and reactions revealed that the 6-month-old infants' reactions were faster, but there were no significant differences in timing of anticipations, or overall RTs (Table 2). These results begin to provide evidence that with training, object representations guided eye movement response patterns in the 4-month-old infants.

This suggestion was investigated further with comparisons of data from the first two experiments. We asked first whether the 4-month-old infants' performance in the training condition was similar to that of the 6-month-old infants in the baseline condition; this age difference was not statistically reliable in

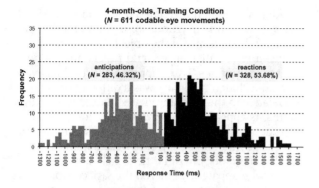

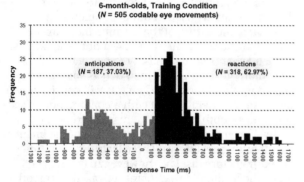

figure 3

Histograms of eye-movement RTs in experiment 2. (Upper) Four-month-old infants. (Lower) Six-month-old infants. Here, 4-month-old infants actually produced a higher proportion of anticipations relative to 6-month-old infants, in contrast to experiment 1 results, implying that functional object representations were facilitated by experience viewing the unoccluded trajectory in the younger infants. Older infants' performance was not improved by experience, implying that they enter the task with the ability to form representations of object continuity under these conditions.

terms of anticipations vs. responses, $\chi^2 = 0.16$, NS. The difference between the two 4-month-old infant groups, however, was reliable. Infants in the training condition produced a higher proportion of anticipations relative to baseline, $\chi^2 = 47.50$, $P < 0.0001$. A second set of analyses compared timing of anticipations and reactions. Six-month-old infants' reactions in the baseline condition were significantly faster than those of 4-month-old infants in the training condition, $t(30) = 2.69$, $P < 0.05$, but there were no reliable differences in timing of anticipations, $t(30) = 0.81$, NS, nor in mean overall RT, $t(30) = 0.79$ NS. We also compared performance of the two groups of 4-month-old infants. Four-month-old infants' reactions in the training condition were not reliably faster than those of 4-month-old infants in the baseline condition, $t(30) = 0.90$ NS, but anticipations were faster in the training

condition, $t(30) = 2.05$, $P < 0.05$, and mean overall RT (which includes both anticipations and reactions) was faster also, $t(30) = 3.98$, $P < 0.001$.

The fact that the 4-month-old infants' anticipatory eye movements occurred more frequently after training suggests that these changes were not simply a matter of the four preexposure trials entraining pursuit eye movements that continued into the four occlusion trials. One possible alternative explanation of this finding stems from the observation that anticipations decrease reliably with repetition. Is the proportion of anticipations higher in the training condition because only *four* training trials are being compared with *eight* baseline trials? An examination of Table 1 reveals that this is not the case. The proportion subsequent to training is greater even if compared with the mean for the first four baseline trials only, $t(30) = 2.70$, $P < 0.05$.

Taken together, these data suggest that object representations directed anticipatory eye movements in the 6-month-old infants and the 4-month-old infants in the training condition, but not the 4-month-old infants in the baseline or random conditions. In particular, comparisons of data sets from the 4-month-old infants in the first two experiments reveal striking differences in performance as a function of training, and support our hypotheses regarding the facilitation of object representations from a short time of experience.

Experiment 3: Effects of Training Generalization on Oculomotor Anticipation

In the final experiment, we asked whether training with a different trajectory event would generalize to improved performance with the test events used in experiments 1 and 2. Four-month-old infants' eye movements were recorded as they viewed four horizontal occlusion trials after seeing four 30-sec trials with an unoccluded vertical trajectory, identical to the training event from experiment 2 (i.e., the same background texture) except for its orientation. Experiment 3 yielded 575 eye movements meeting the criteria described previously (75.0% of trials; Fig. 4). The distribution of anticipations vs. reactions is very similar to that produced by the 4-month-old infants in experiment 2, and indeed, there was no reliable difference in proportions between the two groups, $\chi^2 = 1.39$, NS. Parametric trial-by-trial analyses likewise revealed no significant differences in performance between the two groups, $F(1,30) = 0.17$, NS (Table 1). A comparison to baseline data from the 4-month-old infants in experiment 1, in contrast, revealed a significantly higher proportion of anticipations after experience with the vertical trajectory, $\chi^2 = 65.37$, $P < 0.0001$.

A final set of analyses examined the temporal characteristics of anticipations and reactions across experiments. Anticipation latencies in experiment 3

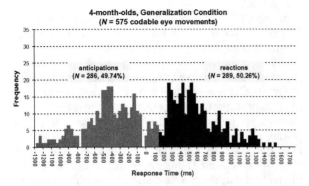

figure 4

Histograms of eye-movement RTs in experiment 3. The distribution of anticipations vs. responses is not reliably different relative to the data from 4-month-old infants in experiment 2, but there are significantly more anticipations relative to baseline, and anticipations are faster overall. This finding suggests that 4-month-old infants generalized training from a different trajectory category.

were significantly faster than those of the 4-month-old infants in experiment 1, $t(30) = 2.14$, $P < 0.05$, although reactions were not reliably different, $t(30) = 1.74$, NS (Table 2). Comparisons with data from the 4-month-old infants in experiment 2, however, revealed no reliable differences, t values < 0.7, NS. Comparisons of latencies from experiment 3 with data from the 6-month-old infants in experiments 1 and 2, likewise, yielded no significant differences in anticipation latency, t values < 0.6, NS.

The findings from experiment 3 confirm and extend the conclusions reached from the first two experiments. Four-month-old infants' oculomotor anticipations to occluded-trajectory stimuli were facilitated after experience with a pre-exposure event whose trajectory differed in orientation, suggesting an ability to generalize object concepts across trajectory category. This finding would appear to obviate an alternative account based on expediting a relatively simple motor "habit," such as facilitation of horizontal eye movements.

Discussion

We found that 4-month-old infants who viewed an object moving on a repetitive, center-occluded trajectory provided little evidence of forming or maintaining a concept of the object as enduring across a short time of occlusion. The infants did not show an increase in anticipations, even after dozens of exposures. Six-month-old infants, in contrast, produced a pattern of eye movements consistent with object representations. We found also that 4-month-old infants' oculomotor behavior was dramatically improved if they were pre-

sented first with an unoccluded object trajectory for 2 min, providing unambiguous information for the spatiotemporal continuity of the object. These infants produced *more* anticipations, and *faster* anticipations, akin to older infants. This improvement resulted even if the unoccluded trajectory was a different orientation relative to the stimulus viewed at test. Six-month-old infants appeared to receive no additional benefit from such training. This finding suggests that training facilitated formation of object representations in 4-month-old infants, but did little to help 6-month-old infants, who apparently entered the task capable of establishing representations of continuity under the occlusion conditions used in our experiments.

What is the nature of the learning mechanisms that led to success at our task in 4-month-old infants? These mechanisms are unlikely to be centered in simple oculomotor improvements, such as smooth pursuit. Four- and 6-month-old infants will consistently track a small moving target with a combination of saccadic and smooth eye movements, the proportion of the two depending on object speed, age of the infant, and attentiveness (25,26). Three features of our unoccluded-trajectory displays, however, may have reduced the likelihood that infants engaged in smooth pursuit to track the ball. First, the velocity of the object (10.4°/sec) was high enough to present a challenge to the developing smooth-pursuit system (27). Second, the object moved against a textured background, which tends to inhibit smooth pursuit (28,29). Third, the object changed direction every 2.5 sec, perhaps making it difficult to predict direction of motion from moment to moment. In fact, we found no instances of smooth pursuit during training. Instead, tracking was entirely saccadic, the infants' POG consistently lagging behind the ball during training. The anticipatory eye movements we observed during the test trials, therefore, were qualitatively different from object tracking during training, the former by definition consisting of eye movements that led, not followed, the object.

We propose instead that the 4-month-old infants in the training condition learned about object continuity with an associative learning mechanism, which provided a representation of the similarity of fully visible and partly occluded object trajectories. This tendency to form associations appears to be robust to category of trajectory orientation. The increase in anticipations that we observed underscores the readiness of this age group to learn object concepts from experience. There are broader implications as well: In addition to highlighting potential contributions of rapid associative learning in 4-month-old infants, our results reveal that representations of object continuity are acquired by 6 months of age in the absence of direct experience with the unoccluded trajectory. Presumably, this occurrence is induced by viewing the many instances of object movement, occlusion, and disocclusion that are part of the natural visual environment. We obtained no evidence that additional experience with such events produces superior performance on our task in 6-month-old infants. By 6 months, then, infants have had sufficient exposure to occlusion over the normal course of development, which provides appropriate experiences to support formation of rudimentary object concepts.

ACKNOWLEDGMENTS

We thank Richard N. Aslin, David H. Rakison, and the reviewers for helpful comments, Leslie B. Cohen for stimulus presentation software, and especially the infant participants and their parents. The parents of all participants provided informed consent. This work was supported by National Science Foundation Grant BCS-0094814 and National Institutes of Health Grant R01-HD40432.

REFERENCES

1. Michotte, A., Thinès, G. & Crabbé, G. (1991) in *Michotte's Experimental Phenomenology of Perception,* eds. Thinès, G., Costall, A. & Butterworth, G. (Erlbaum, Hillsdale, NJ), pp. 140–167.

2. Piaget, J. (1952) *The Origins of Intelligence in Children* (International Univ. Press, New York).

3. Spelke, E. S., Breinlinger, K., Macomber, J. & Jacobson, K. (1992) *Psychol. Rev.* **99,** 605–632.

4. Aguiar, A. & Baillargeon, R. (1999) *Cognit. Psyhol.* **39,** 116–157.

5. Wynn, K. (1992) *Nature* **358,** 749–751.

6. Spelke, E. S. & Newport, E. L. (1998) in *Handbook of Child Psychology: Theoretical Models of Human Development,* Series ed. Damon, W., Vol. ed. Lerner, R. M. (Wiley, New York), 5th. Ed., pp. 275–340.

7. Slater, A. (1995) in *Advances in Infancy Research,* eds. Rovee-Collie, C. & Lipsitt, L. P. (Ablex, Norwood, NJ), Vol. 9, pp. 107–162.

8. Field, D. J. (1994) *Neural Comput.* **6,** 559–601.

9. Olshausen, B. A. & Field, D. J. (1996) *Nature* **381,** 607–609.

10. Bower, T. G. R. (1974) *Development in Infancy* (Freeman, San Francisco).

11. Kirkham, N. Z., Slemmer, J. A. & Johnson, S. P. (2002) *Cognition* **83,** B35–B42.

12. Saffran, J. R., Aslin, R. N. & Newport, E. L. (1996) *Science* **274,** 1926–1928.

13. Slater, A., Morison, V., Somers, M., Mattock, A., Brown, E. & Taylor, D. (1990) *Infant Behav. Dev.* **13,** 33–49.

14. Slater, A., Johnson, S. P., Brown, E. & Badenoch, M. (1996) *Infant Behav. Dev.* **19,** 145–148.

15. Johnson, S. P. & Aslin, R. N. (1995) *Dev. Psychol.* **31,** 739–745.

16. Wolff, P. H. (1966) *Psychol. Issues* **5,** 1–105.

17. Haith, M. M. (1980) *Rules That Babies Look by: The Organization of Newborn Visual Activity* (Erlbaum, Hillsdale, NJ).

18. Bronson, G. W. (1994) *Child Dev.* **65,** 1243–1261.

19. Schiller, P. H. (1998) in *Cognitive Neuroscience of Attention: A Developmental Perspective,* ed. Richards, J. E. (Erlbaum, Hillsdale, NJ), pp. 3–50.

20. Roffwarg, H. P., Muzio, N. J. & Dement, W. C. (1966) *Science* **152,** 608–610.

21. Johnson, S. P., Bremner, J. G., Slater, A., Mason, U., Foster, K. & Cheshire, A. (2003) *Child Dev.* **74,** 94–108.

22. Canfield, R. L., Smith, E. G., Brezsnyak, M. P. & Snow, K. L. (1997) *Monogr. Soc. Res. Child Dev.* **62,** 1–145.

23. Fischer, B. & Weber, H. (1993) *Behav. Brain Sci.* **16,** 553–610.

24. Clohessy, A. B., Posner, M. I. & Rothbart, M. K. (2001) *Acta Psychol. (Amst.)* **106,** 51–68.

25. Aslin, R. N. (1981) in *Eye Movements: Cognition and Visual Perception,* eds. Fisher, D. F., Monty, R. A. & Senders, J. W. (Erlbaum, Hillsdale, NJ), pp. 31–51.

26. Richards, J. E. & Holley, F. B. (1999) *Dev. Psychol.* **35,** 856–867.

27. von Hofsten, C. & Rosander, K. (1997) *Vision Res.* **37,** 1799–1810.

28. Howard, I. P. & Marton, C. (1992) *Exp. Brain Res.* **90,** 625–629.

29. Keller, E. L. & Khan, N. S. (1986) *Vision Res.* **26,** 943–955.

Questions

1. Why is it important for infants to develop object knowledge very early in life?
2. How are infants prepared at birth to learn about objects?
3. Why were anticipatory eye movements used as the main measure of object knowledge? In other words, what do these types of anticipations tell us about what infants know?
4. Why did Johnson, Amso, and Slemmer make different predictions for 4-month-old and 6-month-old infants on their object trajectory task? Does the information presented in figure 2 provide a basis for their predictions? Why or why not?
5. Why did the researchers think that 4-month-olds benefited more than 6-month-olds from the training trials?
6. How do you think this developing ability may help infants form relationships with their caregivers?

15 Becoming a Native Listener

Janet F. Werker

For many researchers, the development of language is humanity's most impressive accomplishment. In fact, some researchers argue that language is the distinguishing characteristic of the human species. But when does language development begin? A quick reply would most likely be "when someone begins to speak." However, this is not so.

Long before children utter their first word at about 12 months of age, much has happened to mark the development of language. One important skill that develops before children produce speech is the ability to distinguish the speech sounds produced by others. Human speech is composed of a vast range of sounds, which are called *phones,* but only a subset of these sounds is used in any single language. Adults are quite adept at recognizing the phones in their own language, and this ability is what enables adults to process language so quickly and effectively. Learning to distinguish phones occurs in childhood, but when?

In the following article, Janet F. Werker describes her research on the development of this ability. The article reports the results of several studies in which Werker tried to home in on the timing and nature of early phonetic sensitivity. Her research focuses on changes in speech perception over the first year of life. Results indicate that children learn to discriminate the sounds of their own language even before they begin to speak. This ability provides a foundation for language learning in that it helps infants attend to the sounds of their own language, the very sounds that they will eventually learn to produce.

This research is important for several reasons. It describes achievements in the first year of life that are critical to later language learning. It also provides interesting information about how maturation, or biological change, and experience influence the perceptual abilities related to early language learning. Finally, it demonstrates the amazing capability of even very young members of our species to develop skills uniquely adapted to the circumstances in which growth occurs.

The syllables, words, and sentences used in all human languages are formed from a set of speech sounds called phones. Only a subset of the phones is used in any particular language. Adults can easily perceive the differences among the phones used to contrast meaning in their own language, but young infants go much farther: they are able to discriminate nearly every phonetic contrast on which they have been tested, including those they have never before heard. Our research has shown that this broad-based sensitivity declines by the time a baby is one year old. This phenomenon provides a way to describe basic abilities in the young infant and explore the effects of experience on human speech perception.

To put infants' abilities in perspective, adult speech perception must be understood. The phones that distinguish meaning in a particular language are called phonemes. There is considerable acoustic variability

Reprinted with permission of Sigma Xi Scientific Research Society from *American Scientist,* 77(1989), pp. 54–59. The research reported here was supported by the Natural Sciences and Engineering Research Council of Canada and the Social Science and Humanities Research Council. In addition, portions of this work were made possible by an NICHD grant to Haskins Laboratories. Address: Department of Psychology, University of British Columbia, Vancouver, British Columbia, V6T 1Y7, Canada.

in the way each individual phoneme is realized in speech. For example, the phoneme /b/ is very different before the vowel /ee/ in "beet" from the way it is before the vowel /oo/ in "boot." How do adults handle this variability? As first demonstrated in a classic study by Liberman and his colleagues (1967), they treat these acoustically distinct instances of a single phoneme as equivalent. This equivalency is demonstrated in the laboratory by presenting listeners with a series of pairs of computer-synthesized speech stimuli that differ by only one acoustic step along a physical continuum and asking them first to label and then to try to discriminate between the stimuli. Adult listeners are able to discriminate reliably only stimuli that they have labeled as different—that is, they cannot easily discriminate between two acoustically different stimuli that they labeled /pa/, but they can discriminate between two similar stimuli if one is from their /ba/ category and one is from their /pa/ category.

The phenomenon by which labeling limits discrimination is referred to as categorical perception. This has obvious advantages for language processing. It allows a listener to segment the words he hears immediately according to the phonemic categories of his language and to ignore unessential variations within a category.

Given that adults perceive speech categorically, when do such perceptual capabilities appear? To find out, Eimas and his colleagues (1971) adapted the so-called high-amplitude sucking procedure for use in a speech discrimination task. This procedure involves teaching infants to suck on a pacifier attached to a pressure transducer in order to receive a visual or auditory stimulus. After repeated presentations of the same sight or sound, the sucking rate declines, indicating that the infants are becoming bored. The infants are then presented with a new stimulus. Presumably, if they can discriminate the new sight or sound from the old, they will increase their sucking rate.

In Eimas's experiment, infants one and four months old heard speech sounds that varied in equal steps from /ba/ to /pa/. Like adults, they discriminated between differences in the vicinity of the /ba/-/pa/ boundary but were unable to discriminate equal acoustic changes from within the /ba/ category. Rather than having to learn about phonemic categories, then, infants seem capable of grouping speech stimuli soon after birth.

Experiments in the 17 years since Eimas's original study have shown that infants can discriminate nearly every phonetic contrast on which they are tested but are generally unable to discriminate differences within a single phonemic category (for a review, see Kuhl 1987). That is, like adults, infants perceive acoustically distinct instances of a single phoneme as equivalent but easily discriminate speech sounds from two different categories that are not more acoustically distinct.

Of special interest are demonstrations that young infants are even able to discriminate phonetic contrasts not used in their native language. In an early study, Streeter (1976) used the high-amplitude sucking procedure to test Kikuyu infants on their ability to discriminate the English /ba/-/pa/ distinction, which is not used in Kikuyu. She found that the infants could discriminate these two syllable types. Similar results have been obtained from a variety of laboratories using other nonnative phonetic contrasts (Lasky et al. 1975; Trehub 1976; Aslin et al. 1981; Eilers et al. 1982). This pattern of results indicates that the ability to discriminate phones from the universal phonetic inventory may be present at birth.

Developmental Changes

Given these broad-based infant abilities, one might expect that adults would also be able to discriminate nearly all phonetic contrasts. However, research suggests that adults often have difficulty discriminating phones that do not contrast meaning in their own language. An English-speaking adult, for example, has difficulty perceiving the difference between the two /p/ phones that are used in Thai (Lisker and Abramson 1970). So too, a Japanese-speaking adult initially cannot distinguish between the English /ra/ and /la/, because Japanese uses a single phoneme intermediate between the two English phonemes (Miyawaki et al. 1975; MacKain et al. 1981). This pattern of extensive infant capabilities and more limited capabilities in the adult led to the suggestion that infants may have a biological predisposition to perceive all possible phonetic contrasts and that there is a decline in this universal phonetic sensitivity by adulthood as a function of acquiring a particular language (Eimas 1975; Trehub 1976).

My work has been designed to explore this intriguing possibility. In particular, I wanted to trace how speech perception changes during development. Are infants actually able to discriminate some pairs of speech sounds better than adults, or have they simply been tested with more sensitive procedures? If infants do have greater discriminative capacities than adults, when does the decline occur and why?

The first problem that my colleagues and I faced was to find a testing procedure which could be used with infants, children of all ages, and adults. We could then begin a program of studies comparing their relative abilities to perceive the differences between phonetic contrasts of both native and nonnative languages.

The testing routine we chose is a variation of the so-called infant head turn procedure (for a complete description, see Kuhl 1987). Subjects are presented with several slightly different versions of the same

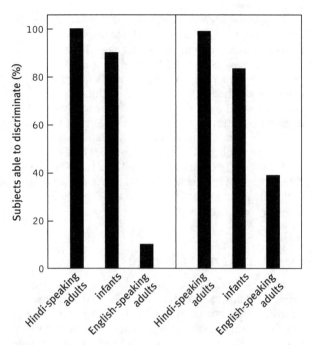

figure 1

When tested on their ability to discriminate two Hindi syllables that are not used in English, six-to-eight-month-old infants from English-speaking families do nearly as well as Hindi-speaking adults. English-speaking adults, however, have great difficulty with this discrimination task, depending on the degree of difference from English sounds. The graph on the left shows a contrast involving two "t" sounds, one dental (i.e., made with the tip of the tongue touching the upper front teeth) and the other retroflex (made with the tongue curled back under the palate). This contrast is rare in the world's languages. The contrast in the graph on the right involves two kinds of voicing, a phenomenon that is less unusual and thus somewhat more recognizable to English-speaking adults. (After Werker et al. 1981.)

In the first series of experiments, we compared English-speaking adults, infants from English-speaking families, and Hindi-speaking adults on their ability to discriminate the /ba/-/da/ distinction, which is used in both Hindi and English, as well as two pairs of syllables that are used in Hindi but not in English (Werker et al. 1981). The two pairs of Hindi syllables were chosen on the basis of their relative difficulty. The first pair contrasts two "t" sounds that are not used in English. In English, we articulate "t" sounds by placing the tongue a bit behind the teeth at the alveolar ridge. In Hindi, there are two different "t" phonemes. One is produced by placing the tongue on the teeth (a dental t—written /t/). The other is produced by curling the tip of the tongue back and placing it against the roof of the mouth (a retroflex t—written /T/). This contrast is not used in English, and is in fact very rare among the world's languages.

The second pair of Hindi syllables involves different categories of voicing—the timing of the release of a consonant and the amount of air released with the consonant. Although these phonemes, called /tʰ/ and /dʰ/, are not used in English, we had reason to believe that they might be easier for English-speaking adults to discriminate than the /t/-/T/ distinction. The timing difference between /tʰ/ and /dʰ/ spans the English /t/-/d/ boundary. Moreover, this contrast is more common among the world's languages.

The results of this study, which are presented in Figure 1, were consistent with the hypothesis of universal phonetic sensitivity in the young infant and a decline by adulthood. As expected, all subjects could discriminate /ba/ from /da/. Of more interest, the infants aged six to eight months performed like the Hindi adults and were able to discriminate both pairs of Hindi speech contrasts. The English-speaking adults, on the other hand, were considerably less able to make the Hindi distinctions, especially the difficult dental-retroflex one.

Timing of Developmental Changes

The next series of experiments was aimed at determining when the decline in nonnative sensitivity occurs. It was originally believed that this decline would coincide with puberty, when, as Lenneberg (1967) claims, language flexibility decreases. However, our work showed that twelve-year-old English-speaking children were no more able to discriminate non-English syllables than were English-speaking adults (Werker and Tees 1983). We then tested eight- and four-year-old English-speaking children, and, to our surprise, even the four-year-olds could not discriminate the Hindi contrasts. Hindi-speaking four-year-olds, of course, showed no trouble with this discrimination.

phoneme (e.g., /ba/) repeated continuously at 2-sec intervals. On a random basis every four to twenty repetitions, a new phoneme is introduced. For example, a subject will hear "ba," "ba," "ba," "ba," "ba," "da," "da." Babies are conditioned to turn their heads toward the source of the sound when they detect the change from one phoneme to another (e.g., from "ba" to "da"). Correct head turns are reinforced with the activation of a little toy animal and with clapping and praise from the experimental assistant. Adults and children are tested the same way, except that they press a button instead of turning their heads when they detect a change in the phoneme, and the reinforcement is age-appropriate.

Before testing children even younger than age four, we felt it was necessary to determine that the phenomenon of developmental loss extended to other languages. To this end, we chose a phonemic contrast from a North American Indian language of the Interior Salish family, called Nthlakapmx by native speakers in British Columbia but also referred to as Thompson.

North American Indian languages include many consonants produced in the back of the vocal tract, behind our English /k/ and /g/. The pair of sounds we chose contrasts a "k" sound produced at the velum with another "k" sound (written /q/) produced by raising the back of the tongue against the uvula. Both are glottalized—that is, there is an ejective portion (similar to a click) at the beginning of the release of the consonants.

Again, we compared English-speaking adults, infants from English-speaking families, and Nthlakapmx-speaking adults in their abilities to discriminate this pair of sounds (Werker and Tees 1984a). As was the case with the Hindi syllables, both the Nthlakapmx-speaking adults and the infants could discriminate the non-English phonemes, but the English-speaking adults could not.

We were now satisfied that there is at least some generality to the notion that young infants can discriminate across the whole phonetic inventory but that there is a developmental decline in this universal sensitivity. Our next series of experiments involved testing children between eight months and four years of age to try to determine just when the decline in sensitivity might start. It quickly became apparent that something important was happening within the first year of life. We accordingly compared three groups of infants aged six to eight, eight to ten, and ten to twelve months. Half of each group were tested with the Hindi (/ta/-Ta/) and half with the Nthlakapmx (/k̉/-/q̉i/) contrast.

As shown in Figure 2, the majority of the six-to-eight-month-old infants from English-speaking families could discriminate the two non-English contrasts, whereas only about one-half of the eight-to-ten-month-olds could do so. Only two out of ten ten-to-twelve-months-olds could discriminate the Hindi contrast, and only one out of ten the Nthlakapmx. This provided strong evidence that the decline in universal phonetic sensitivity was occurring between six and twelve months of age. As a further test to see if this developmental change would be apparent within the same individuals, six infants from English-speaking families were tested at two-month intervals beginning when they were about six to eight months old. All six infants could discriminate both the Hindi and Nthlakapmx contrasts at the first testing, but by the third testing session, when they were ten to

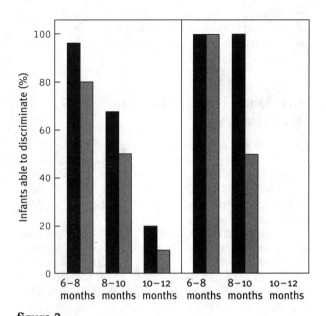

figure 2

Infants show a decline in the universal phonetic sensitivity demonstrated in Figure 1 during the second half of their first year, as shown here in the results of experiments performed with babies from English-speaking families and involving non-English syllables from Hindi (black bars) and Nthlakapmx, a language spoken by some native Indians in British Columbia (gray bars). The graph on the left gives results from experiments with three groups of infants aged six to eight months, eight to ten months, and ten to twelve months. The graph on the right gives results from testing one group of infants three times at the appropriate ages. None of the latter group were able to discriminate either of the non-English contrasts when they were ten to twelve months old. (After Werker and Tees 1984a.)

twelve months old, they were not able to discriminate either contrast.

To verify that the decline in nonnative sensitivity around ten to twelve months was a function of language experience, we tested a few infants from Hindi- and Nthlakapmx-speaking families when they reached eleven to twelve months old. As predicted, these infants were still able to discriminate their native contrasts, showing quite clearly that the decline observed in the infants from English-speaking families was a function of specific language experience. Since doing these studies, we have charted the decline between six and twelve months old using a computer-

generated set of synthetic syllables which model another pair of Hindi sounds not used in English
(Werker and Lalonde 1988).

How Does Experience Affect Development?

A theoretical model for considering the possible effects of experience on perceptual development was
suggested by Gottlieb in 1976. As expanded by both
Gottlieb (1981) and Aslin (1981), the model includes
several roles experience might—or might not—play, as
shown in Figure 3.

Induction refers to cases in which the emergence
and form of a perceptual capability depend entirely
on environmental input. In this case, an infant
would not show categorical perception of speech
sounds without prior experience. Attunement refers
to a situation in which experience influences the
full development of a capability, enhancing the level
of performance; for example, categorical boundaries
between phonetic contrasts might be sharper with
experience than without. In facilitation, experience
affects the rate of development of a capability, but it
does not affect the end point. If this role were valid,
speech perception would improve even without listening experience, but hearing specific sounds
would accelerate the rate of improvement. Mainte-
nance/loss refers to the case in which a perceptual
ability is fully developed prior to the onset of specific experience, which is required to maintain that
capability. Without adequate exposure an initial capability is lost. Finally, maturation refers to the unfolding of a perceptual capability independent of
environmental exposure. According to this hypothetical possibility, the ability to discriminate speech
sounds would mature regardless of amount or timing of exposure.

Our work is often interpreted as an illustration of
maintenance/loss, since it suggests that young infants
can discriminate phonetic contrasts before they have
gained experience listening but that experience hearing the phones used in their own language is necessary to maintain the ability to discriminate at least
some pairs of phones.

Support for this view was provided by another
study in which we tested English-speaking adults who
had been exposed to Hindi during the first couple of
years of life and had learned their first words in Hindi
but had little or no subsequent exposure. These subjects could discriminate the Hindi syllables much
more easily than other English-speaking adults, and
performed virtually as well as native Hindi speakers
on the discrimination task (Tees and Werker 1984).
This is consistent with the view that early experience

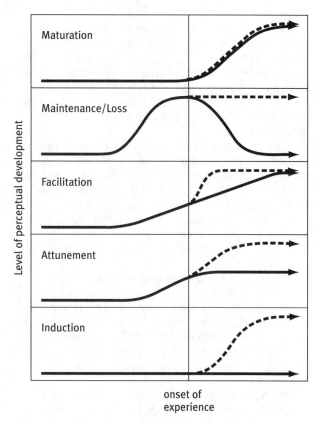

figure 3

*Researchers have suggested several roles that ex-
perience might—or might not—play in the development of particular perceptual capabilities.
These possibilities are shown graphically here:
— — — curves represent development after the onset of experience, and ——— curves represent development in the absence of experience.
Induction refers to cases in which a capability
depends entirely on experience. Attunement
refers to a situation in which experience makes
possible the full development of a capability. In
facilitation, experience affects only the rate of
development of a capability. Maintenance/loss
refers to the case in which a capability is fully
developed before the onset of experience, but experience is necessary to maintain the capability.
Maturation refers to the development of a capability independent of experience. The phenomenon of universal phonetic sensitivity followed by
a narrowing of sensitivity to native language
sounds appears to illustrate maintenance/loss,
since it suggests that young infants can discriminate phonetic contrasts before they have gained
experience listening but that experience with
language is necessary to maintain the full ability. (After Aslin 1981; Gottlieb 1981.)*

functions to maintain perceptual abilities, suggesting that no further experience is necessary to maintain them into adulthood.

Recovery of Sensitivity

Our early work led us to believe that the loss of non-native sensitivity is difficult to reverse in adults. In one study, we tested English-speaking adults who had studied Hindi for various lengths of time. Adults who had studied Hindi for five years or more were able to discriminate the non-English Hindi syllables, but those who had studied Hindi for one year at the university level could not do so. In fact, even several hundred trials were insufficient to teach English-speaking adults to discriminate the more difficult Hindi contrasts (Tees and Werker 1984). This implies that while the ability is recoverable, considerable experience is required. Similar conclusions can be drawn from a study by MacKain and her colleagues (1981), who tested Japanese speakers learning English. Only after one year of intensive English training in the United States could they discriminate /ra/ from /la/.

The question still remained whether recovery of nonnative sensitivity results from new learning in adulthood or from a latent sensitivity. To explore this question, we asked English-speaking adults to discriminate both the full syllables of the difficult Hindi and Nthlakapmx phonemes and shortened portions of the syllables which do not sound like speech at all but contain the critical acoustic information specifying the difference between the phonemes (Werker and Tees 1984b). Subjects were first tested on the shortened stimuli and then on the full syllables. To our surprise, they were able to discriminate the shortened stimuli easily but were still not able to discriminate the full syllables, even immediately after hearing the relevant acoustic information in shortened form. This finding reveals that the auditory capacity for discriminating the acoustic components of these stimuli has not been lost but that it is difficult to apply when processing language-like sounds.

In a further set of experiments, we attempted to make English-speaking adults discriminate the full-syllable nonnative stimuli (Werker and Logan 1985). One task involved presenting adults with pairs of stimuli and asking them to decide simply if the stimuli were the same or different, a test that proved to be much more sensitive than the head turn procedure. In this "same/different" task, listeners have to compare only two stimuli at a time. Moreover, if the interval between the two stimuli is short enough, listeners can hold the first stimulus in auditory memory while comparing it to the second. In the head turn task, on the other hand, listeners have to compare each stimulus

to a whole set of variable stimuli and judge whether it is a member of the same category.

We found that English-speaking adults could discriminate the Hindi syllables when tested in the same/different procedure, particularly after practice. Thus there was evidence that adults can discriminate nonnative contrasts if tested in a more sensitive procedure. Similar results have been reported by other researchers (Pisoni et al. 1982). This suggests that the developmental changes between infancy and adulthood should be considered a language-based reorganization of the categories of communicative sounds rather than an absolute loss of auditory sensitivity. The increasing reliance on language-specific categories accounts for the age-related decline, implying that maintenance has its effect at the level of linguistic categories rather than simple peripheral auditory sensitivity (see Best et al. 1988).

Parallels in Speech Production

It is interesting to compare our findings of developmental changes in speech perception to recent work on speech production. Although it is impossible to survey this substantial literature here, there appear to be systematic regularities in the repertoire of sounds produced at different stages of babbling. These regularities may reflect vocal tract and neuromuscular maturation, with phones appearing as a child develops the ability to articulate them (Locke 1983). In contrast to early work suggesting that the sounds produced during babbling gradually narrow to those that are used in the language-learning environment, recent research shows very little influence from the native language on vocal development during the babbling stage. This conclusion is particularly strong for consonants. However, it is clear that after the acquisition of the first word children's vocal productions start becoming differentiated on the basis of language experience. That is, once a child begins to talk, the sounds produced conform more and more closely to the subset of phones used in his native language. The stage at which these changes occur is consistent with our work showing universal sensitivity in early infancy followed by only language-specific sensitivity beginning around ten to twelve months.

This leads us to believe that just as a reorganization of language production is related to the emergence of the first spoken word, so too may the reorganization of perceptual abilities be related to the emergence of the ability to understand words. By the time he is one year old, a child understands a fair amount of spoken language, even though he may produce only a few words. We are currently conducting experiments to see if the reorganization of speech perception is related to the emerging ability to understand words. This work will add another piece to the solution of the puzzle of how early sensitivity to all language sounds becomes limited to the functional categories that are necessary for communicating in one's own language.

References

Aslin, R. N. 1981. Experiential influences and sensitive periods in perceptual development: A unified model. In *Development of Perception*, ed. R. N. Aslin, J. R. Alberts, and M. R. Petersen, vol. 2, pp. 45–94. Academic Press.

Aslin, R. N., D. B. Pisoni, B. L. Hennessy, and A. J. Perey. 1981. Discrimination of voice onset time by human infants: New findings and implications for the effect of early experience. *Child Devel.* 52:1135–45.

Best, C. T., G. W. McRoberts, and N. N. Sithole. 1988. The phonological basis of perceptual loss for non-native contrasts: Maintenance of discrimination among Zulu clicks by English-speaking adults and infants. *J. Exper. Psychol.: Human Percept. Perform.* 14:345–60.

Eilers, R. E., W. J. Gavin, and D. K. Oller. 1982. Cross-linguistic perception in infancy: Early effects of linguistic experience. *J. Child Lang.* 9:289–302.

Eimas, P. D. 1975. Developmental studies in speech perception. In *Infant Perception: From Sensation to Cognition*, ed. L. B. Cohen and P. Salapatek, vol. 2, pp. 193–231. Academic Press.

Eimas, P. D., E. R. Siqueland, P. W. Jusczyk, and J. Vigorito. 1971. Speech perception in infants. *Science*, 171:303–06.

Gottlieb, G. 1976. The roles of experience in the development of behavior and the nervous system. In *Studies on the Development of Behavior and the Nervous System*, ed. G. Gottlieb, vol. 3, pp. 1–35. Academic Press.

_____ 1981. Roles of early experience in species-specific perceptual development. In *Development of Perception*. ed. R. N. Aslin, J. R. Alberts, and M. R. Petersen, vol. 1, pp. 5–44. Academic Press.

Kuhl, P. K. 1987. Perception of speech and sound in early infancy. In *Handbook of Infant Perception*, ed. P. Salapatek and L. Cohen, vol. 2., pp. 275–382. Academic Press.

Lasky, R. E., A. Syrdal-Lasky, and R. E. Klein. 1975. VOT discrimination by four to six and a half month old infants from Spanish environments. *J. Exper. Child Psychol.* 20:215–25.

Lenneberg, E. H. 1967. *Biological Foundations of Language*. Wiley.

Liberman, A. M., F. S. Cooper, D. P. Shankweiler, and M. Studdert-Kennedy. 1967. Perception of the speech code. *Psychol. Rev.* 74:431–61.

Lisker, L., and A. S. Abramson. 1970. The voicing dimension: Some experiments in comparative phonetics. In *Proceedings of the 6th International Congress of Phonetic Sciences*, pp. 563–67. Prague: Academia.

Locke, J. L. 1983. *Phonological Acquisition and Change.* Academic Press.

MacKain, K. S., C. T. Best, and W. Strange. 1981. Categorical perception of English /r/ and /l/ by Japanese bilinguals. *Appl. Psycholing.* 2:269–90.

Miyawaki, K., et al. 1975. An effect of linguistic experience: The discrimination of [r] and [l] by native speakers of Japanese and English. *Percept. Psychophy.* 18:331–40.

Pisoni, D. B., R. N. Aslin, A. J. Perey, and B. L. Hennessy. 1982. Some effects of laboratory training on identification and discrimination of voicing contrasts in stop consonants. *J. Exper. Psychol.: Human Percept. Perform.* 8:297–314.

Streeter, L. A. 1976. Language perception of two-month old infants shows effects of both innate mechanisms and experience. *Nature* 259:39–41.

Tees, R. C., and J. F. Werker. 1984. Perceptual flexibility: Maintenance or recovery of the ability to discriminate non-native speech sounds. *Can. J. Psychol.* 34:579–90.

Trehub, S. 1976. The discrimination of foreign speech contrasts by infants and adults. *Child Devel.* 47:466–72.

Werker, J. F., J. H. V. Gilbert, K. Humphrey, and R. C. Tees. 1981. Developmental aspects of cross-language speech perception. *Child Devel.* 52:349–53.

Werker, J. F., and C. E. Lalonde. 1988. The development of speech perception: Initial capabilities and the emergence of phonemic categories. *Devel. Psychol.* 24:672–83.

Werker, J. F., and J. S. Logan. 1985. Cross-language evidence for three factors in speech perception. *Percept. Psychophys.* 37:35–44.

Werker, J. F., and R. C. Tees. 1983. Developmental changes across childhood in the perception of non-active speech sounds. *Can. J. Psychol.* 37:278–86.

_____ 1984a. Cross-language speech perception: Evidence for perceptual reorganization during the first year of life. *Infant Behav. Devel.* 7:49–63.

_____ 1984b. Phonemic and phonetic factors in adult cross-language speech perception. *J. Acoustical Soc. Am.* 75:1866–78.

Questions

1. What is categorical perception, and what role does it play in the development of language?
2. What laboratory procedure did Werker use to study infants' perception of phonetic contrasts?
3. To study developmental change in nonnative language sensitivity, Werker studied infants in English-speaking communities. Why do you think she did follow-up research in which she also tested a few infants from Hindi-speaking and Nthlakapmx-speaking families?

4. Of the five types of explanations for the role that experience plays in development, represented in Figure 3, which one best explains the evidence Werker provides about the development of the ability to perceive phonetic contrasts in infancy?

5. Is the ability to discriminate sounds that do not appear in a person's native language completely lost in infancy? Use evidence to support your answer.

6. Werker's results suggest that one important development in the first year is a reorganization of speech-related functions in the brain. How do you think this process develops for children raised in bilingual homes?

16 Event Categorization in Infancy

Renée Baillargeon • Su-hua Wang

Much of the psychological research on cognitive development early in life has concentrated on infants' understanding of physical features of the world. Even Jean Piaget, in describing cognitive development during the sensorimotor stage, focused on the emergence and development of infants' understanding of objects, which he referred to as the object concept. For many years, Piaget and his followers argued that infants' physical knowledge is limited and that it takes the entire first two years of life for children to develop a basic understanding of the physical properties of the world, including objects. Recently, as researchers have devised new methods for studying infant cognition, this view has changed. The consensus now is that infants have a far better understanding of physical properties than Piaget and other researchers once thought.

In the following article, Renée Baillargeon and Su-hua Wang describe their research on early infant cognition. They are particularly interested in the ability of infants to sort physical information into distinct categories, described in this article as events. Event knowledge of the physical world basically includes information about things that can happen to objects; for example, an object can be put inside another object, which is a containment event, or an object can be hidden behind another object, which is an occlusion event. Much of what we know about the physical world consists of such event-based information.

The research described in this article relied primarily on the violation-of-expectation method, which is quite effective at revealing what infants understand about the physical world. The results of several studies using this method are reviewed; in addition, graphic illustrations are provided that will help you follow the behavior of the experimenters and the infants in these studies. Baillargeon and Wang use this research to argue that (1) over the first year of life, infants develop a rather complex set of understandings about physical events; and (2) this body of knowledge allows infants to categorize events and create expectations or predictions about the likely outcomes of these events. In other words, this knowledge helps form the foundation of the comforting realization that the physical world is an ordered and predictable place in which to live.

Recent research suggests that one of the mechanisms that contribute to infants' acquisition of their physical knowledge is the formation of event categories, such as occlusion and containment. Some of this research compared infants' identification of similar variables in different event categories. Marked developmental lags were found, suggesting that infants acquire event-specific rather than event-general expectations. Other research on variable priming, perseveration, and object individuation presented infants with successive events from the same or from different event categories. To understand the world as it unfolds, infants must not only represent each separate event, but also link successive events; this research begins to explore how infants respond to multiple events over time.

Over the past 15 years, a dramatic change has taken place in the field of infant cognition: researchers have come to realize that, contrary to traditional claims [1, 2], infants possess sophisticated expectations

---

Reprinted from Baillargeon, R., & Wang, S-H. (2002). Event categorization in infancy, *Trends in Cognitive Science*, 6, 85–93. Copyright 2002, with permission from Elsevier.

Acknowledgments: The preparation of this article was supported by a grant from the National Institute of Child Health and Human Development (HD-21104) to the first author. We would like to thank Jerry DeJong, Cindy Fisher, and Kris Onishi for helpful comments and discussions, and the Assistant Editor of *TICS* for help in preparing the article for publication.

about physical events [3–12]. Of main concern today is the issue of how infants acquire their physical knowledge. In particular, what specialized mechanisms contribute to this acquisition process [13–17]? In this article, we review evidence that one such mechanism involves the formation of *event categories*: Infants appear to 'sort' physical events into distinct categories, and to learn and reason in terms of these categories.

The article is organized into two main sections. In the first, we summarize experiments that compared infants' knowledge of similar expectations in different event categories. This research has brought to light striking developmental lags (or décalages, to use a Piagetian term [18]) in infants' acquisition of their physical knowledge, with several months separating similar acquisitions across categories. In the second section of the article, we review experiments on variable priming, perseveration, and object individuation, all of which presented infants with successive events from the same or from different event categories. Depending on the task, the change in event category either improved or impaired infants' performance.

Learning About Event Categories

Research conducted during the 1990s revealed a clear overall pattern in the development of infants' physical knowledge (for reviews, see Refs [13,19–21]). When learning about occlusion, support, and other physical events, infants first form an initial concept centered on a primitive, all-or-none distinction. With further experience, infants identify discrete and continuous variables that elaborate this initial concept, resulting in increasingly accurate predictions over time.

One limitation of this research was that it left unclear how general or specific were infants' expectations. Because the events examined—such as occlusion and support—were physically very different, the variables identified for each event were naturally also very different. To ascertain whether infants acquire general or specific expectations about events, it was necessary to compare their knowledge of the same variable in different events. Evidence that infants considered a given variable when reasoning about all relevant events would suggest that their expectations were 'event-general'. On the other hand, evidence that infants took into account a given variable when reasoning about one but not other, equally relevant events, would suggest that their expectations were 'event-specific'.

To date, three series of experiments have compared infants' reasoning about similar variables in different events. All of these experiments used the violation-of-expectation method [21]. In a typical experiment conducted with this method, infants see two test events: one (expected event) is consistent with the expectation being examined in the experiment; the other (unexpected event) violates this expectation. With appropriate controls, evidence that infants look reliably longer at the unexpected than at the expected event indicates that they: (1) possess the expectation under examination; (2) detect the violation in the unexpected event; and (3) are interested or surprised by this violation.

Height in Occlusion and Containment Events

In a recent experiment, Hespos and Baillargeon [22] compared 4.5-month-old infants' ability to reason about the variable height in occlusion and in containment events. The infants watched test events in which an object was lowered either behind an occluder (occlusion condition; Fig. 1a) or inside a container (containment condition; Fig. 1b). The object consisted of a tall cylinder with a knob affixed to its top; in all of the events, the object was lowered until only the knob remained visible. In the expected events, the occluder or container was as tall as the cylindrical portion of the object; in the unexpected events, the occluder or container was only half as tall, so that it should have been impossible for the cylindrical portion of the object to become fully hidden (see Fig. 1). The tall and short occluders were identical to the tall and short containers with their back halves and bottoms removed.

The infants in the occlusion condition looked reliably longer at the unexpected than at the expected event, but those in the containment condition did not. These and control results indicated that, at 4.5 months of age, infants realize that the height of an object relative to that of an occluder determines whether the object can be fully or only partly hidden behind the occluder, but they do not yet realize that the height of an object relative to that of a container determines whether the object can be fully or only partly hidden inside the container.

The positive results obtained in the occlusion condition were confirmed in a second experiment in which the tall object was lowered behind, rather than inside, the tall and short containers. In this experiment, the containers served merely as occluders, and the infants again detected the violation in the unexpected event (see also Refs [23,24]).

In a third experiment, 5.5-, 6.5-, and 7.5-month-old infants were shown the containment condition test events. Only the 7.5-month-old infants looked reliably longer at the unexpected than at the expected event. These and control results indicated that it is not until infants are about 7.5 months of age that they begin to consider height information when predicting the outcomes of containment events.

Together, the results of these experiments suggested three conclusions. First, infants view occlusion

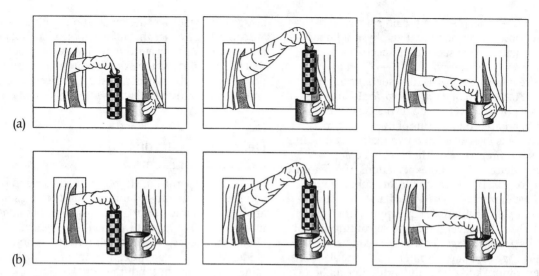

figure 1

Schematic drawing of the unexpected test events in the experiment of Hespos and Baillargeon [22]. (a) Occlusion condition. (b) Containment condition. (See text for discussion.)

and containment as distinct event categories. Second, infants do not generalize the variable height from occlusion to containment, even though it is relevant to both categories and invokes in each case the same general physical principles. Third, several months typically separate infants' acquisition of the variable height in occlusion and in containment events, resulting in a marked décalage in their responses to these events.

Height in Containment and Covering Events

Building on the results of Hespos and Baillargeon [22], Wang *et al.* (unpublished data, reviewed in Ref. [25]) compared 9-month-old infants' ability to reason about the variable height in containment and in covering events. The infants saw either test events in which a tall object was lowered inside a container (containment condition; Fig. 2a), or test events in which a cover was lowered over the same tall object (covering condition; Fig. 2b). In all of the events, the object became fully hidden. In the expected events, the container or cover was slightly taller than the object; in the unexpected events, the container or cover was only half as tall, so that it should have been impossible for the object to become fully hidden (see Fig. 2). The tall and short covers were identical to the containers turned upside-down.

The infants in the containment condition looked reliably longer at the unexpected than at the expected event, but those in the covering condition did not. In a subsequent experiment, 11- and 12-month-old in-

fants were tested with the covering condition events. Only the 12-month-old infants detected the violation in the unexpected event. These results, together with those discussed in the last section, indicated that, although infants recognize at about 7.5 months of age that the height of an object relative to that of a container determines whether the object can be fully or only partly hidden inside the container, it is not until infants are about 12 months of age that they realize that the height of an object relative to that of a cover determines whether the object can be fully or only partly hidden under the cover.

Transparency in Occlusion and Containment Events

All of the experiments described in the preceding sections examined infants' reasoning about height information in various events. A recent series of experiments focused on a different variable, that of transparency. Luo and Baillargeon (unpublished data, reviewed in Ref. [25]) compared 8.5-month-old infants' reasoning about transparency information in occlusion and in containment events.

At the beginning of each test event, the infants saw either a transparent occluder (occlusion condition; Fig. 3a) or a transparent container (containment condition; Fig. 3b); to the right of the occluder or container was a slightly shorter object. First, an opaque screen was raised to hide the occluder or container. Next, the object was lifted above the screen and then lowered behind the transparent occluder or inside the transparent container. Finally, the opaque screen was re-

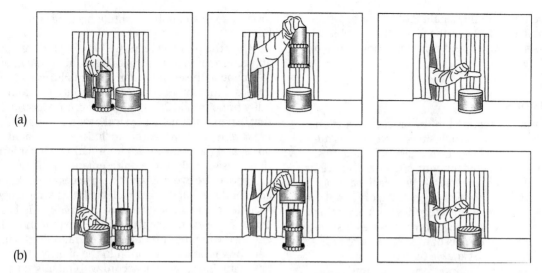

figure 2
Schematic drawing of the unexpected test events in the experiment of Wang et al. (unpublished data).
(a) Containment condition. (b) Covering condition.

moved to reveal the occluder or container once more. In the expected events, the object was visible through the front of the occluder or container. In the unexpected events, the object was absent (Fig. 3). The container was made of Plexiglas, and its edges were outlined with red tape; the occluder was identical to the front of the container.

The infants in the occlusion condition looked reliably longer at the unexpected than at the expected event, but those in the containment condition did

not. In subsequent experiments, it was found that older, 10-month-old infants tested with the containment condition events succeeded in detecting the violation in the unexpected event; and that 7.5-month-old (but not 7-month-old) infants tested with the occlusion condition events were similarly successful. These and control results thus revealed another décalage in infants' reasoning about occlusion and containment events: infants realize at about 7.5 months of age that an object placed behind a trans-

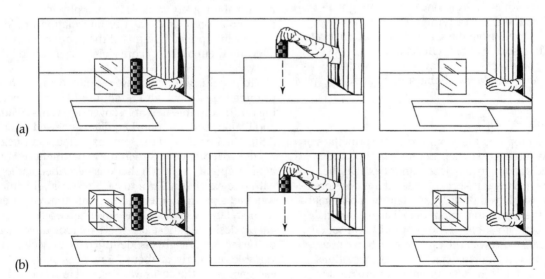

figure 3
Schematic drawing of the unexpected test events in the experiment of Luo and Baillargeon (unpublished data). (a) Occlusion condition. (b) Containment condition.

parent occluder should remain visible, but do not realize until about 10 months of age that an object placed inside a transparent container should also remain visible.

Conclusions

The experiments reported in the preceding sections suggest three general conclusions. First, infants appear to sort physical events into distinct categories, such as occlusion, containment, and covering events. Second, infants learn separately how each category operates. A variable identified in one category is not generalized to other relevant categories; rather, it is kept tied to the individual category where it was first acquired. Third, when weeks or months separate the acquisition of the same variable in two or more categories, striking décalages arise in infants' responses to events from the different categories. Thus, infants are surprised when a tall object becomes hidden behind but not inside a short container; when a tall object becomes hidden inside a short container but not under a short cover; and when an object becomes hidden behind a transparent occluder but not inside a transparent container.

Reasoning Across Event Categories

If infants do form distinct event categories, one might expect them to respond differently, in some situations at least, when exposed to successive events from the same or from different event categories. How infants reason about an event from one category might affect—for better or for worse—their reasoning about a subsequent event from the same or from another category. To date, such category effects have been observed in three areas of infancy research: variable priming, perseveration, and object individuation.

Variable Priming

Spelke has proposed that from birth core principles of continuity (objects exist continuously in time and space) and solidity (two objects cannot exist at the same time in the same space) guide infants' interpretation of physical events [11, 17, 26]. This proposal might be taken to suggest that infants, at all ages, should detect all salient violations of the continuity and solidity principles. As we saw in the previous sections, however, infants often fail to detect such core violations. Recall, for example, that 8.5-month-olds are not surprised when an object is placed inside a transparent container which is then revealed to be empty, and that 11-month-olds are not surprised when a short cover is

lowered over a tall object until it becomes fully hidden.

Over the past few years, we have been developing an account of infants' physical reasoning that attempts to reconcile these and other similar failures with the proposal that infants possess core continuity and solidity principles [6,25,27,28]. This account assumes that, when watching a physical event, infants build a *physical representation* that includes basic spatial, temporal, and mechanical [15] information. This information is used, early in the representation process, to categorize the event. Infants then access their knowledge of the event category selected; this knowledge specifies the variables that have been identified as relevant to the event category and hence that should be encoded when representing the event. Both the basic and the variable information in the physical representation are interpreted in accord with infants' core principles.

To illustrate this account, consider once again the finding that infants aged 11 months and younger are not surprised when a short cover is lowered over a tall object until it becomes fully hidden. Upon seeing the cover being lowered over the object, infants would categorize the event as a covering event and would then access their knowledge of this category. Because this knowledge does not yet include the variable height—which is typically not identified until about 12 months—infants would include no information in their physical representation about the relative heights of the cover and object. As a result, infants would be unable to detect the core violation in the event.

The preceding account makes an intriguing prediction. If infants could be 'primed' to include information about a key variable in their physical representation of an event, this information would then be interpreted in terms of their core principles, allowing them to detect core violations involving this key variable.

To test this prediction, we recently conducted a priming experiment with 8-month-old infants focusing on the variable height in covering events (Wang and Baillargeon, unpublished data, reviewed in Ref. [25]). The infants saw the same expected and unexpected covering events as in the experiment by Wang *et al.* (unpublished data) that was described earlier, with one exception. Prior to each test trial, the infants watched a pre-trial intended to prime them to attend to the relative heights of the cover and object (see Fig. 4a). In designing these pre-trials, we took advantage of the fact that heights is identified as an occlusion variable very early, at about 3.5 months of age [23]. In each pre-trial, the cover was first slid in front of the object, to create an occlusion event; after 5s, the cover was slid back to its original position, and then the trial proceeded as in Wang *et al.*'s experiment,

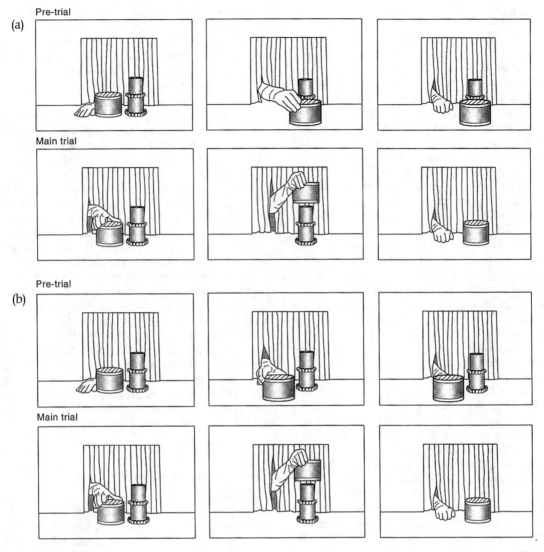

figure 4

Schematic drawing of the unexpected test events in the experiment of Wang and Baillargeon (unpublished data). (a) Occlusion priming condition. (b) Display priming condition.

with the cover being lowered over the object. We reasoned that the infants would categorize the event as an occlusion event and would then access their knowledge of this category; because this knowledge at 8 months includes the variable height, the infants would include information about the relative heights of the cover and object in their physical representation of the event. We speculated that this information might still be available (or might once again be included) when the infants next represented the covering event.

The results supported our prediction: the infants looked reliably longer at the unexpected than at the expected event, suggesting that the occlusion priming pre-trials led them to include the key height information in their representation of the covering event. This conclusion was supported by the results of a control condition with different pre-trials. In this condition, the cover was simply slid forward, next to the object, so that the infants saw a display rather than an occlusion event (Fig. 4b). These infants failed to detect the violation in the unexpected event, suggesting that they did not include information about the heights of the cover and object in their representation of either the display or the covering event.

Perseveration

When watching physical events, do infants always engage in the careful monitoring process described in the last section, attending to all of the variables they have identified as relevant to the events? Recent findings by Aguiar and Baillargeon [29] suggest that the answer to this question is negative. When infants are shown the same event repeatedly for several trials, they determine in a *preliminary analysis* at the start of each trial whether the event before them is similar or different from that on preceding trials. If they judge the event to be similar, infants do not engage in any careful monitoring of the event, but simply retrieve their previous prediction about its likely outcome. If they judge the event to be different, infants monitor it carefully and compute a new prediction about its likely outcome. This response pattern makes for efficient problem solving—as long as infants are accurate in their preliminary analyses. If infants fail to notice a crucial change and as a result mistakenly judge an event to be similar to that on preceding trials, they will retrieve their previous prediction instead of computing a new one, thus committing a perseverative error.

To explore infants' perseverative tendencies in a violation-of-expectation task, Aguiar and Baillargeon [29] conducted experiments focusing on 6.5-month-old infants' reasoning about the variable width in containment events; infants this age were known to be able to reason about this variable [30]. In one condition (same-category condition), the infants watched containment events during both familiarization and test (Fig. 5a). In the familiarization event, a ball attached to the end of a rod was lowered into a wide, shallow container. In the test events, the same ball was lowered into a tall container that was either slightly wider (expected event) or much narrower (unexpected event) than the ball; in either case, only the rod protruded from the rim of the container. In another condition (different-categories condition), the infants saw containment events during the test but not familiarization: the bottom and back of the wide, shallow container were removed to create a rounded occluder (Fig. 5b).

The infants in the different-categories condition looked reliably longer at the unexpected than at the expected event, but those in the same-category condition did not. Aguiar and Baillargeon [29] speculated that the infants in the same-category condition did not notice the change in the width of the container in their preliminary analyses of the test events. As a result, the infants judged the events to be similar to the familiarization event, and they retrieved the prediction they had formed for this event ('the ball will fit into the container'). Because this prediction was correct for the expected but not the unexpected event, the infants failed to detect the violation in the latter event. By contrast, the infants in the different-

categories condition noticed in their preliminary analyses of the test events that these were from a different category than the familiarization event, namely, containment rather than occlusion. The infants thus judged the test events to be novel, computed appropriate predictions for their outcomes, and detected the violation in the unexpected event.

Additional experiments by Aguiar and Scott (unpublished data) confirmed and extended these initial results. First, 5.5-month-old infants tested in the same-category condition also responded perseveratively. Second, 5.5- and 6.5-month-old infants did not perseverate when tested with a novel version of the different categories condition. This new version was similar to the last with one exception: during familiarization, the occluder was removed and the infants saw a simple display event in which the ball was lowered to the apparatus floor. Finally, further evidence of perseveration was obtained in new experiments focusing on the variable height in containment events (recall that this variable is identified at about 7.5 months of age [22]). After watching a tall object being repeatedly hidden in a very tall container, 9-month-old infants were not surprised to see the same object being hidden in a very short container (same-category condition); however, they did show surprise at this event when no container was present during familiarization and the tall object was simply lowered to the apparatus floor (different-categories condition).

Object Individuation

The field of object individuation focuses on infants' ability to determine, when faced with an event, how many distinct objects are involved in the event. Current research suggests that, although infants typically succeed at individuating objects when given spatio-temporal information [27,31–33], the same is not true of featural information.

This last point was first uncovered by Xu and Carey [33]. In one experiment, 12- and 10-month-old infants received expected and unexpected test trials. During the initial phase of each trial, the infants repeatedly watched an occlusion event: an object (e.g., a ball) emerged from behind one edge of a screen and then returned behind it; next, a different object (e.g., a bottle) emerged from behind the other edge of the screen and again returned behind it. During the final phase, the screen was removed to reveal either one (unexpected trials) or both (expected trials) of the objects resting on the apparatus floor. Only the 12-month-old infants showed surprise during the unexpected trials. Xu and Carey concluded that the younger infants did not realize that two distinct objects were involved in the occlusion event. They speculated that 10-month-old infants still lack specific

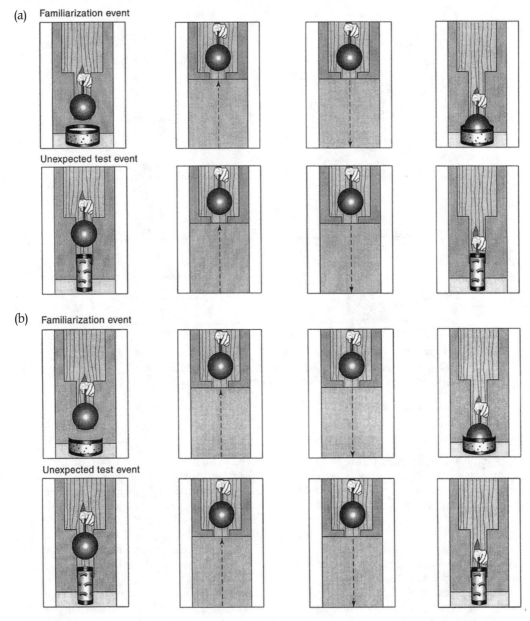

figure 5

Schematic drawing of the familiarization and unexpected test events in the experiment of Aguiar and Baillargeon [29]. (a) Same-category condition. (b) Different-categories condition.

object concepts such as ball and bottle, and that these concepts are not acquired until word learning begins, at the end of the first year.

Although the negative finding Xu and Carey [33] obtained with the 10-month-old infants has been confirmed in additional experiments [32–36], their interpretation of this finding has been questioned. First, rhesus macaques succeed at similar tasks, despite their lack of language [37, 38]. Second, prelinguistic infants also succeed at similar tasks when processing de-

mands are reduced [32, 35, 36, 39–41]. For example, Wilcox and Schweinle [41] found that even 5.5-month-old infants show surprise during unexpected trials when the occlusion event is made very brief (e.g., the first object disappears behind one edge of the screen, the second object emerges from behind the other edge, and the screen is immediately lowered).

Wilox and Baillargeon [32, 40] have proposed a novel intepretation of the negative results obtained by Xu and Carey [33], which rests on the distinction be-

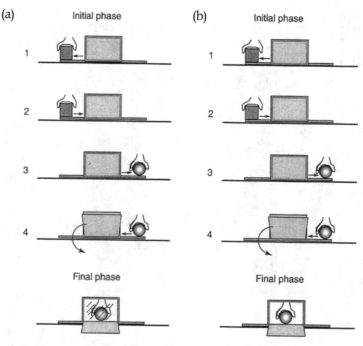

figure 6

Schematic drawing of the unexpected test trials in the experiment of Wilcox and Chapa [35] (a) Event-monitoring condition. (b) Event-mapping condition. (Redrawn with permission from the description in Wilcox et al. [36].)

tween event-mapping and event-monitoring tasks. In an event-mapping task, infants see events from *two* different event categories and judge whether the two events are consistent. In an event-monitoring task, infants see an event from *one* event category and judge whether the successive portions of the event are consistent. According to this scheme, the task devised by Xu and Carey is an event-mapping task: each test trial involves first an occlusion event (during the initial phase, when the objects emerge successively from behind the screen) and then a display event (during the final phase, when one or both objects rest on the apparatus floor). To succeed, infants must (1) retrieve their representation of the occlusion event and (2) map the objects in this representation onto those in the display event. The negative results obtained by Xu and Carey and others suggest that, under some conditions, young infants have difficulty completing this retrieval and mapping process.

The preceding analysis makes a number of interesting predictions, several of which have already been experimentally confirmed (for reviews, see Refs [36, 42]). For example, in one experiment by Wilcox and Chapa, 9.5-month-old-infants were assigned to an event-monitoring or an event-mapping condition, and again received expected or unexpected test trials composed of an initial and a final phase [35] (see Fig. 6). During the initial phase, a ball (expected trials) or a box (unexpected trials) emerged from behind the left edge of a screen and then returned behind it; next, the ball emerged from behind the right edge of the screen and again returned behind it. During the final phase, the central portion of the screen was lowered, leaving a thin rectangular frame; through this frame, the infants could see the ball resting alone on the apparatus floor. For the infants in the event-monitoring condition (Fig. 6a), the frame was filled with a clear plastic, to create a transparent screen; for the infants in the event-mapping condition (Fig. 6b), the frame was empty.

The infants in the event-monitoring condition looked reliably longer during the unexpected than the expected trials, but those in the event-mapping condition did not. According to Wilcox and Chapa [35], the infants tested with the empty frame faced an event-mapping task: they saw first an occlusion and then a display event, as in Xu and Carey's experiment [33], and they experienced the usual difficulty mapping the objects from one event onto the other. By contrast, the infants tested with the filled frame faced an event-monitoring task: they saw a singular, ongoing occlusion event involving first an opaque and then a transparent occluder, and they easily kept track of the objects as the event unfolded.

Conclusions

The research reviewed in this final section suggests several conclusions about infants' representations of physical events. When watching an event, infants first categorize it and then access their knowledge of the category selected; this knowledge specifies the variables that have been identified as relevant to the category and should be included in the event representation. Under special priming conditions, however, infants can be induced to include a novel variable in their representation of an event, leading to more accurate predictions about the event's outcome. When presented with similar events repeatedly, infants judge in a preliminary analysis at the start of each event whether it is familiar (in which case they retrieve their prior prediction) or novel (in which case they compute a new prediction). Events from different event categories are consistently judged to be novel, suggesting that category information is a salient part of the preliminary analysis.

Finally, when presented with an occlusion event followed by a display or other event, infants sometimes have difficulty mapping the objects from the first to the second event. This result suggests that an event representation is maintained until a category change occurs, at which point a new event representation is set up; and that establishing links between successive representations can be challenging for young infants.

REFERENCES

1. Piaget, J. (1952) *The Origins of Intelligence in Children,* International University Press.
2. Piaget, J. (1954) *The Construction of Reality in the Child,* Basic Books.
3. Aguiar, A. and Baillargeon, R. (1999) 2.5-month-old infants' reasoning about when objects should and should not be occluded. *Cogn. Psychol. 39,* 116–157.
4. Baillargeon, R. *et al.* (1985) Object permanence in 5-month-old infants. *Cognition 20,* 191–208.
5. Goubet, N. and Clifton, R. K. (1998) Object and event representation in 6.5-month-old-infants. *Dev. Psychol. 34,* 63–76.
6. Hespos, S. J. and Baillargeon, R. (2001) Knowledge about containment events in very young infants. *Cognition 78,* 204–245.
7. Hood, B. and Willatts, P. (1986) Reaching in the dark to an object's remembered position: evidence of object permanence in 5-month-old infants. *Br. J. Dev. Psychol. 4,* 57–65.
8. Kotovsky, L. and Baillargeon, R. (1998) The development of calibration-based reasoning about collision events in young infants. *Cognition 67,* 311–351.

9. Leslie, A.M. and Keeble, S. (1987) Do six-month-old infants perceive causality? *Cognition 25,* 265–288.
10. Needham, A. and Baillargeon, R. (1993) Intuitions about support in 4.5-month-old infants. *Cognition 47,* 121–148.
11. Spelke, E.S. *et al.* (1992) Origins of knowledge. *Psychol. Rev. 99,* 605–632.
12. Wilcox, T. *et al.* (1996) Location memory in healthy preterm and full-term infants. *Infant Behav. Dev. 19,* 309–323.
13. Baillargeon, R. (1994) How do infants learn about the physical world? *Curr. Dir. Psychol. Sci. 3,* 133–140.
14. Karmiloff-Smith, A. (1992) *Beyond Modularity: A Developmental Perspective on Cognitive Science,* MIT Press.
15. Leslie, A.M. (1995) A theory of agency. In *Causal Cognition: A Multidisciplinary Debate* (Sperber, D. *et al.,* eds), pp. 121–141, Clarendon Press.
16. Mandler, J.M. (1992) How to build a baby: II. Conceptual primitives. *Psychol. Rev. 99,* 587–604.
17. Spelke, E.S. (1994) Initial knowledge: six suggestions. *Cognition 50,* 431–445.
18. Flavell, J.H. (1963) *The Developmental Psychology of Jean Piaget,* Nostrand.
19. Baillargeon, R. (1995) A model of physical reasoning in infancy. In *Advances in Infancy Research* (Rovee-Collier, C. and Lipsitt, L.P., eds), pp. 305–371, Ablex.
20. Baillargeon, R. *et al.* (1995) The acquisition of physical knowledge in infancy. In *Causal Cognition: A Multidisciplinary Debate* (Sperber, D. *et al.,* eds), pp. 79–116, Clarendon Press.
21. Baillargeon, R. (1998) Infants' understanding of the physical world. In *Advances in Psychological Science* (Sabourin, M. *et al.,* eds), pp. 503–529, Psychology Press.
22. Hespos, S.J. and Baillargeon, R. (2001) Infants' knowledge about occlusion and containment events: a surprising discrepancy. *Psychol. Sci. 12,* 140–147.
23. Baillargeon, R. and DeVos, J. (1991) Object permanence in 3.5- and 4.5-month-old infants: further evidence. *Child Dev. 62,* 1227–1246.
24. Baillargeon, R. and Graber, M. (1987) Where's the rabbit? 5.5-month-old infants' representation of the height of a hidden object. *Cogn. Dev. 2,* 375–392.
25. Baillargeon, R. (2002) The acquisition of physical knowledge in infancy: A summary in eight lessons. In *Handbook of Childhood Cognitive Development* (Goswami, U., ed.), pp. 47–83, Blackwell.
26. Spelke, E.S. *et al.* (1995) Infants' knowledge of object motion and human action. In *Causal Cognition: A Multidisciplinary Debate* (Sperber, D. *et al.,* eds), pp. 44–78, Clarendon Press.
27. Aguiar, A. and Baillargeon, R. (2002) Developments in young infants' reasoning about occluded objects. *Cogn. Psychol. 45,* 267–336.
28. Baillargeon, R. Infants' physical knowledge: of acquired expectations and core principles. In *Language, Brain, and Cognitive Development: Essays in Honor of Jacques Mehler* (Dupoux, E., ed.), MIT Press (in press).
29. Aguiar, A. and Baillargeon, R. (2000) Perseveration and problem solving in infancy. In *Advances in Child Development and Behavior* (Reese, H.W., ed.), pp. 135–180, Academic Press.

30. Sitskoorn, S.M. and Smitsman, A.W. (1995) Infants' perception of dynamic relations between objects: passing through or support? *Dev. Psychol. 31,* 437–447.

31. Spelke, E.S. *et al.* (1995) Spatio-temporal continuity, smoothness of motion, and object identity in infancy. *Br. J. Dev. Psychol.* 13, 113–142.

32. Wilcox, T. and Baillargeon, R. (1998) Object individuation in infancy: the use of featural information in reasoning about occlusion events. *Cogn. Psychol.* 17, 97–155.

33. Xu, F. and Carey, S. (1996) Infants' metaphysics: the case of numerical identity. *Cogn. Psychol.* 30, 111–153.

34. Van de Walle, G. *et al.* (2001) Bases for object individuation in infancy: evidence from manual search. *J. Cogn. Dev.* 1, 249–280.

35. Wilcox, T. and Chapa, C. (2002) Infants' reasoning about opaque and transparent occluders in an individuation task. *Cognition 85,* B1–B10.

36. Wilcox T. *et al.* Object individuation in infancy. In *Progress in Infancy Research* (Fagan, F. and Hayne, H., eds), Erlbaum (in press).

37. Santos, L.R. *et al.* (2002) Object individuation using property/kind information in rhesus macaques (macaca mulatta). *Cognition 83,* 241–264.

38. Uller, C. *et al.* (1997) Is language needed for constructing sortal concepts? A study with nonhuman primates. In *Proceedings of the 21st Annual Boston University Conference on Language Development* (Hughes, E., ed.), pp. 665–677, Oxford University Press.

39. Wilcox, T. (1999) Object individuation: infants' use of shape, size, pattern, and color. *Cognition* 72, 125–166.

40. Wilcox, T. and Baillargeon, R. (1998) Object individuation in young infants: further evidence with an event-monitoring task. *Dev. Sci.* 1, 127–142.

41. Wilcox, T. and Schweinle, A. (2002) Object individuation and event mapping: developmental changes in infants' use of featural information. *Dev. Sci. 5,* 132–150.

42. Needham, A. and Baillargeon, R. (2000) Infants' use of featural and experiential information in segregating and individuating objects: a reply to Xu, Carey, and Welch. *Cognition* 74, 255–284.

43. Baldwin, D.A. *et al.* (1993) Infants' ability to draw inferences about non-obvious object properties: evidence from exploratory play. *Child Dev.* 64, 711–728.

44. Mandler, J.M. (2000) Perceptual and conceptual processes in infancy. *J. Cogn. Dev.* 1, 3–36.

45. Needham, A. and Modi, A. (2000) Infants' use of prior experiences with objects in object segregation: Implications for object recognition in early infancy. In *Advances in Child Development and Behavior* (Reese, H.W., ed.), pp. 99–133. Academic Press.

46. Quinn, P.C. and Eimas, P.D. (1996) Perceptual organization and categorization in young infants. In *Advances in Infancy Research* (Rovee-Collier, C. and Lipsitt, L.P., eds), pp. 1–36, Ablex.

Questions

1. In research conducted in the 1990s on infants' physical knowledge, such as occlusion and support, what general conclusion was reached about the development of this understanding?

2. What is the violation-of-expectation method, and why is it useful for studying infants' physical knowledge?

3. What does the infants' behavior on tasks involving occlusion, containment, and covering events suggest about their understanding of the physical world?

4. Do infants act differently when they are shown the same event repeatedly and when they are shown a new event? How?

5. What, according to Baillargeon and Wang, explains the development of event categorization in infants?

6. Try to think of an alternative explanation for the infant behavior observed in one of the studies described in this article. Do you prefer the researchers' interpretation or your own? Explain.

17 Rethinking Maternal Sensitivity: Mothers' Comments on Infants' Mental Processes Predict Security of Attachment at 12 Months

Elizabeth Meins • Charles Fernyhough • Emma Fradley • Michelle Tuckey

Human beings are social animals; we cannot survive without social contact and support. Because of the great importance that sustained social contact has in human development, psychologists have conducted much research on how and when early relationships are formed, what role they play in development, and what happens when they don't work out very well.

In the mid-twentieth century, British psychologist John Bowlby introduced the idea of attachment, defining it as an enduring emotional bond between an infant and another person. Bowlby was especially interested in how attachment provides a feeling of security for human infants. In the 1960s, American psychologist Mary Ainsworth extended Bowlby's ideas to the study of individual differences in attachment. This research has shown that the attachment an infant forms with a caregiver is critical to adjustment in infancy and throughout childhood.

In attachment theory, mother-infant attachment stems from the mother's sensitivity to the infant's needs. Research has shown that when mothers provide high levels of sensitivity to their infants' needs, children are more likely to be securely attached to their mothers. Despite extensive research support for this general view, greater clarity is needed regarding the definition and enaction of sensitive mothering.

In the following article, Elizabeth Meins, Charles Fernyhough, Emma Fradley, and Michelle Tuckey discuss their research on maternal sensitivity. These researchers draw a distinction between maternal sensitivity that responds to the child's physical and emotional needs and maternal sensitivity that recognizes and engages with the mental state that underlies the child's behavior—referred to as maternal mind-mindedness. In this study, the research team observed interactions between mothers and their 6-month-old infants, paying particular attention to maternal mind-mindedness. When the infants were 12 months of age, they once again observed these dyads and assessed the mother-infant security of attachment using the strange-situation procedure developed by Ainsworth.

As they predicted, Meins and colleagues found support for the importance of maternal mind-mindedness in the development of secure attachment between mothers and their infants. These results suggest that in addition to the physical and emotional support that mothers provide for their infants, these early relationships may help set the stage for critical developments in theory of mind.

This study investigated predictors of attachment security in a play context using a sample of 71 mothers and their 6-month-old infants. We sought to rethink the concept of maternal sensitivity by focusing on mothers' ability accurately to read the mental states governing infant behaviour. Five categories were devised to assess this ability, four of which were dependent on maternal responses to infant behaviours, such as object-directed

Reprinted with permission from Meins, E., Fernyhough, C., Fradley, E., & Tuckey, M. "Rethinking Maternal Sensitivity: Mothers' Comments on Infants' Mental Processes Predict Security of Attachment at 12 Months", *Journal of Child Psychology and Psychiatry, 42,* 637–648, © 2001 Blackwell Publishers.

activity. The fifth, mothers' Appropriate mind-related comments, assessed individual differences in mothers' proclivity to comment appropriately on their infants' mental states and processes. Higher scores in this fifth category related to a secure attachment relationship at 12 months. Maternal sensitivity and Appropriate mind-related comments were independent predictors of attachment security at 12 months, respectively accounting for 6.5% and 12.7% of its variance. We suggest that these findings are in line with current theorising on internal working models of attachment, and may help to explain security related differences in mentalising abilities.

Introduction

Since the seminal work of Ainsworth and colleagues (Ainsworth, Bell, & Stayton, 1971, 1974; Ainsworth, Blehar, Waters, & Wall, 1978), there have been a number of attempts to identify the antecedents of infantile security of attachment. Of the many aspects of early infant-mother interaction that have been investigated as possible precursors of the secure attachment relationship, there has been some consensus that a key variable may be sensitive mothering in the first year of life. In their pioneering study, Ainsworth et al. (1971) established four dimensions for assessing maternal behaviour in early infant–mother interactions: sensitivity, acceptance, cooperation, and accessibility. They reported that infants of mothers who demonstrated higher levels of sensitivity were more likely to show secure attachment behaviour in the Strange Situation at 12 months, with mothers who scored highly on sensitivity also showing more acceptance, cooperation, and accessibility in their interactions with their infants.

Subsequent researchers have found broad support for the relation between early maternal sensitivity and the security of the attachment relationship. For example, several studies employing Ainsworth et al.'s sensitivity scale have replicated the original findings, not just in comparable American samples (e.g. Isabella, 1993), but also in German infant–mother dyads (Grossmann, Grossmann, Spangler, Suess, & Unzner, 1985) and in high-risk populations (Egeland & Farber, 1984; Goldberg, Perotta, Minde, & Corter, 1986). The quality of early infant–mother interaction has also been assessed using indices of maternal behaviour such as interactional synchrony (Isabella, Belsky, & Von Eye, 1989) and harmony (Schölmerich, Fracasso, Lamb, & Broberg, 1995), and a measure of the extent to which the mother stimulates the infant (Belsky, Rovine, & Taylor, 1984). Although not directly assessing maternal sensitivity, these latter studies have shown that mothers demonstrating greater attunement to their infants in these areas of measurement were more likely to have securely at-

tached infants, a fact that has been interpreted as further evidence for the link between sensitive mothering and security. At the same time, the conclusion that maternal sensitivity is the key determinant of attachment security has not been left unchallenged. For example, the results of a recent meta-analysis on the parental antecedents of infant attachment (De Wolff & Van IJzendoorn, 1997) raised doubts about whether the relation between sensitivity and security was as strong as Ainsworth's original findings led one to believe. This meta-analysis also highlighted a wide range of parental behaviours that were related to attachment security, leading De Wolff and Van IJzendoorn (1997) to conclude that "[s]ensitivity cannot be considered to be the exclusive and most important factor in the development of attachment" (p. 585).

The resulting picture of maternal sensitivity as a determinant of attachment security is thus a somewhat confused one. We suggest that this confusion may have arisen for a number of reasons: (1) the rather general and coarse-grained nature of Ainsworth et al.'s original maternal sensitivity scale; (2) a lack of consensus among subsequent researchers concerning which behaviours are taken to constitute maternal sensitivity; and (3) the failure of research in this area consistently to consider maternal behaviour in light of its interactional context. As we shall argue, the central criterion of Ainsworth et al.'s original definition of sensitivity is that the mothers' response to the infant is not merely prompt or contingent, but *appropriate* to the infant's behaviour. This feature of maternal behaviour, which in Ainsworth et al.'s theorising is crucial to the establishment of a secure attachment relationship, has been increasingly overlooked by recent research. We suggest that a rethinking of the concept of maternal sensitivity, which goes some way to take into account the appropriateness of maternal responses to their infants, might allow us to clear up some of the confusion surrounding this important concept, and thus make possible an investigation of the antecedents of attachment security that is more in line with Ainsworth et al.'s original insights.

Defining Maternal Sensitivity

Ainsworth et al. (1971) described the mother of a securely attached child as being "capable of perceiving things from [the child's] point of view" and regarding her child "as a separate person; she also respects his activity-in-progress and thus avoids interrupting him" (p. 43). This definition suggests that the distinguishing feature of such mothers is their ability to use information from their children's outward behaviour in making accurate inferences about the mental states governing that behaviour. This feature of maternal cognition would thus appear to go beyond a basic ability merely to recognise and respond to the child's physical states, such as hunger, and emotional states, such as distress. Ainsworth et al. reported that, compared with their secure group counterparts, insecure group mothers appeared less able to "read" their infants' behaviour, leading them to try to "socialize with the baby when he is hungry, play with him when he is tired, and feed him when he is trying to initiate social interaction" (Ainsworth et al., 1974, p. 129). What distinguishes insecure group mothers is thus not a general failure to respond to their children; rather their responses are more likely to be inappropriate because they are less able or willing to evaluate *why* the child is demonstrating a particular behaviour.

Unfortunately, much of the research on maternal behavioural antecedents of attachment in the interim has paid insufficient attention to Ainsworth et al.'s distinction between mothers' responsiveness to infants' emotional cues and the appropriateness of each response. For example, over half of the 68 studies included by De Wolff and Van IJzendoorn (1997) in their meta-analysis focused exclusively on the contiguity or synchrony of responses, or on maternal stimulation or support, without any assessment of whether a mother's responses were appropriate to cues from the child. Indeed, even when researchers have measured sensitivity using Ainsworth et al.'s (1971) scale, a lack of specificity in the original operationalisation of the construct has led inevitably to differing interpretations of the criteria for sensitive mothering. Ainsworth et al.'s scale is a global measure based on the observer's perception of the mother's sensitivity throughout the observation period; each mother receives a score between 1 and 9, with higher scores indicating greater sensitivity. Observers are not given guidelines about the specific behaviours that should be coded, or whether the frequency with which behaviours occur is important; the individual researcher may also choose the length and structure of the observational period. This lack of specificity n the original scale may help to explain the general failure to replicate the very strong relation between sensitivity and attachment security reported by Ainsworth et al. (1978) (see De Wolff & Van IJzendoorn, 1997; Goldsmith & Alansky, 1987).

Observational Contexts

As well as considering the appropriateness of maternal responses to their children, it is also important that researchers pay full attention to the *context* within which such behaviours occur. Ainsworth et al. (1978) concluded that "the most important aspect of maternal behaviour commonly associated with the security–anxiety dimension of infant attachment *is manifested in different specific ways in different situations,* but in each it emerges as sensitive responsiveness to infant signals and communications" (p. 152, emphasis added). For example, if one observes

infant–mother interaction in a situation that is likely to provoke distress, the most appropriate demonstration of sensitivity will be for the mother promptly to offer comfort and reassurance. If one observes feeding routines, then sensitivity will be manifested in the mothers' attunement to the infant's cues of hunger and satiety, and the tempo at which the infant wishes to feed. However, when the child is physically and emotionally satisfied, the most appropriate kind of sensitivity would appear to be the mothers' reading of her infant's focus of attention, readiness to play, and enjoyment of particular kinds of activity. The latter type of sensitivity–that demonstrated when the child is physically and emotionally satisfied–is clearly a manifestation of the mother's sensitivity to her infant's mental state. Indeed, we suggest that this capacity to "[perceive] things from [the child's] point of view" (Ainsworth et al., 1971, p. 43) provides the key to a successful rethinking of the concept of maternal sensitivity.

Rethinking Maternal Sensitivity

In response to the rather confused picture of maternal sensitivity that has emerged since Ainsworth et al.'s (1971) original findings, researchers in this area have begun to call for a re-examination of this important concept. In particular, Fonagy, Steele, Steele, Higgitt, and Target (1994) and Meins (1997) have argued that responsiveness to the child's physical and emotional needs should be clearly distinguished from mothers' capacity or willingness to engage with their infants at a *mental* level. Using new theoretical constructs, Fonagy et al. and Meins have hypothesised that maternal behaviours that betray a sensitivity to infants' mental states, rather than responsivity to their physical and emotional needs, will be more useful than a generalised construct of maternal sensitivity in predicting the security of the attachment relationship.

To this end, Meins (1997) coined the term maternal *mind-mindedness* to describe the mother's proclivity to treat her infant as an individual with a mind, rather than merely as a creature with needs that must be satisfied. The concept of mind-mindedness clearly captures the flavour of Ainsworth et al.'s distinction between sensitive and insensitive mothering. That is, the mind-minded mother is sensitive to the child's "work-in-progress", is willing to change her focus of attention in response to cues from the infant, and so on.

As an alternative to Ainsworth et al.'s original construct of maternal sensitivity, the construct of mind-mindedness allows us to distinguish between a mother's general sensitivity to her child's physical and emotional needs (suggested by Ainsworth et al., 1974, to be a feature of both secure- and insecure-group mothers), and a more specific sensitivity to the child's mental states and ongoing activity. This ability to "read" the mental states underlying a child's behaviour is most likely to be apparent in situations where the child's physical and emotional needs are satisfied. In contexts such as free play, mind-minded mothers will be able to respond to behaviours such as their infants' current level of engagement in joint activities, shifts of attention, etc. in a manner that is unconstrained by the requirements of caregiving. Inasmuch as they capture the essential quality of maternal sensitivity as defined by Ainsworth et al., individual differences in such behaviour will in turn be expected to relate to the subsequent security of the attachment relationship with infants of mothers with higher levels of mind-mindedness being more likely to be classified as securely attached.

Meins and colleagues have already investigated maternal mind-mindedness and its relation to security of attachment within the contexts of mothers' descriptions of their children, and their interpretations of their children's vocabulary items at 20 months. Meins, Fernyhough, Russell, and Clark-Carter (1998) reported a link between security of attachment in infancy and mothers' descriptions of their children at age 3 years. In comparison to their insecure group counterparts, mothers whose infants had been securely attached were more likely to focus on their mental characteristics, rather than their physical appearance or behavioural tendencies, when given an open-ended invitation to describe their children 2 years later. In addition, Meins (1998) found that secure group mothers were more willing or able to attribute meaning to their children's early vocalisations by, for example, maintaining that certain utterances that did not conform to actual English words were nevertheless being used systematically by their children to convey a specific meaning. Such proclivities in the secure group mothers were interpreted as evidence for their greater mind-mindedness. Other researchers (Beeghly, Bretherton, & Mervis, 1986; Dunn, Bretherton, & Munn, 1987) have noted individual differences in the frequency with which mothers use mental state language when interacting with their children during the second and third years of life. Both Beeghly et al. (1986) and Dunn et al. (1987) also reported that, as children get older, their mothers increasingly refer to internal states, such as cognitions, emotions, and obligations. Previous research has not, however, investigated whether such differences in mind-minded psychological discourse exist in mothers' interactions with their very young infants, and thus *predate* the formation of the attachment relationship. Extending the scope of the existing concept of mind-mindedness to evaluate its role as a predictor, rather than a consequence, of attachment security is the focus of this paper.

Our general aim is thus to attempt a rethinking of maternal sensitivity in terms of mothers' specific proclivity to focus on and respond to their infants' mental states, as manifested in their ongoing behaviour. In so doing, we hope to refine the concept of maternal sensitivity in a way that is more in line with Ainsworth et al.'s original insights. Any new concept that results from such a rethinking must, however, be at least as good a determinant of subsequent patterns of attachment as maternal sensitivity. For example, it will be necessary to demonstrate that maternal mind-mindedness can not only distinguish between infants using the dichotomous secure and insecure categories, but also between infants in the avoidant and resistant insecure groups. In terms of sensitivity, mothers of the three original attachment categories, tending to reject their infants' bids for attention and interaction (Ainsworth et al., 1978; Main, 1981). Mothers of insecure-resistant infants have been found to be inconsistent in their patterns of mothering, sometimes demonstrating high levels of sensitivity and at other times being insensitive to their infants' needs (Isabella, 1993). Thus, in order to represent a progression in understanding the antecedents of attachment security, any new construct will similarly need to be able to distinguish between the insecure groups.

The study reported below involved assessing maternal behaviour in an interactional play context on scales of both maternal mind-mindedness and maternal sensitivity, in order to investigate their relative power in predicting subsequent security of attachment. The initial goal was to establish empirical measures for assessing maternal mind-mindedness which were appropriate to the age of the infants studied (6 months) and to the interactional context. This in turn allowed us: (1) to investigate the relation between maternal mind-mindedness and Ainsworth et al.'s construct of maternal sensitivity; (2) to attempt to replicate the previously observed relation between maternal sensitivity and subsequent security of attachment; (3) to test the hypothesis that infants whose mothers show higher levels of mind-mindedness at 6 months will be more likely to be securely attached at 12 months; (4) to determine the relative contribution of maternal sensitivity and mind-mindedness to children's subsequent security of attachment; and (5) to investigate whether differences in maternal mind-mindedness could distinguish between infants in the avoidant and resistant insecure attachment categories.

Method

Participants

Participants were 71 pairs of mothers and infants (36 boys, 35 girls) who were first seen when the infants were 6 months of age ($M = 25$ weeks; range: 23–28 weeks). The average age of the mothers at the beginning of the study was 28 years (range: 19–42 years) and the participating families were predominantly lower-middle class. The sample was recruited via local health centres and baby clinics, and 60% of mothers who were approached agreed to take part[1]. Mothers and infants were followed up at 12 months ($M = 53$ weeks; range: 52–56 weeks).

Maternal Education

Mothers' level of education was included as an independent variable, since it was necessary to control for the possibility that aspects of infant–mother interaction, and particularly mind-mindedness, may relate to the amount of time mothers have spent in the education system. Given the focus of this study, maternal education was therefore deemed to be a more appropriate control variable than a general measure of socio-economic status. Mothers were given a questionnaire in which they were asked to identify their highest educational qualification by choosing one of six categories. Each mother was awarded one of the following scores for educational level[2]: 0: no examinations; 1: CSEs (equivalent to high school up to age 16 for less academic students); 2: GCSEs or O-Levels (high school up to age 16 for more academic students); 3: A-Levels (high school up to age 18); 4: further qualification, not to degree level (e.g. nursing); 5: undergraduate degree; 6: postgraduate qualification. Of the 71 mothers taking part: 7 scored 0; 7 scored 1; 22 scored 2; 3 scored 3; 23 scored 4; 5 scored 5; and 3 scored 6.

Phase One Testing (Age 6 Months)

The testing session at 6 months of age was carried out in the University's developmental research laboratory. Mothers had been sent a letter explaining the time course of the study, and detailing what was required of them at each testing phase. However, participants were not explicitly told that the study was assessing infant–mother attachment and investigating ways in which mothers could demonstrate their mind-mindedness. Mothers and infants were introduced into the testing room, in which there were several easy chairs, three large floor cushions, and a range of age-appropriate toys. Mothers were told that they could move around the room as they wished as the session pro-gressed, but all sessions began with the mother and infant sitting on the floor cushions in the middle of the room. No specific instructions were given, other than an invitation to each mother to play with her baby as she would do if they had a few spare minutes together at home.

The mother and infant were allowed a 5-minute settling-in period before the video recording began. There were two video cameras, mounted on the walls in diagonal corners of the room. The video mixing desk allowed a split-screen representation, so that the faces of both the mother and infant could be clearly seen at all times. The first 20 minutes of videotape from these sessions was used in the analyses.

Phase One Scoring Procedure

The infant–mother interactions at the 6-month testing session were coded for a range of maternal and infant behaviours.

Infant behaviours. Three types of infant behaviour were coded:

(1) Infant vocalisations: any vocal noise made by the infant. A gap of at least 2 seconds between discrete vocalisations was required for them to be counted separately.
(2) Infant changes in direction of gaze, where a "gaze" was defined as any look of 2 or more seconds in duration.
(3) Infant object-directed actions: any action directed toward an object, such as touching, grasping, fingering, pointing.

Infants received a frequency score for each of these categories. The videotaped interactions were coded by a trained researcher, and a randomly chosen fifth of these tapes were coded by a second researcher, both of whom were blind to the measures of maternal sensitivity, security of attachment, and infants' general cognitive ability. Inter-rater agreement was $\kappa = .86$.

Maternal behaviours. Mothers' behaviour was coded for: (1) sensitivity; and (2) mind-mindedness.

(1) *Maternal sensitivity.* The sensitivity of mothers' interactions with their infants was coded using Ainsworth et al.'s (1971) scale. This is a 9-point scale,

---

[1] The percentage of mothers agreeing to participate is somewhat low. We attribute this to the fact that the local inhabitants were unused to being approached by university researchers seeking participants for their projects. Rather than being a university town, the catchment area for the study consisted of a large conurbation of towns in an industrial area of the English Midlands, and this study was the first on infant psychological development to be carried out using this population. Mothers who did not wish to participate were not asked directly to give specific reasons for refusing, but in the vast majority of cases mothers explained that refusal resulted from time constraints and pressures. The information available on mothers who refused gave no reason to suggest that they differed in any significant way from those who agreed to participate.

[2] North American equivalents to the British educational system are shown in parentheses.

with 5 "anchor points" (*highly sensitive, sensitive, inconsistently sensitive, insensitive, highly insensitive*). Rather than coding specific behaviours, this scale gives a global rating of how sensitive the mother is to the infant's cues. The coder was therefore not required to score or assess the minutiae of the interactions, but rather assessed each mother's overall sensitivity during the course of the whole 20-minute session. Higher scores on this scale are indicative of more sensitive mothering. The videotaped sessions were coded by a trained researcher, and a fifth of the tapes chosen at random were coded by a second researcher. Both researchers were blind to all of the other measures. Using the 9-point scale, inter-rater agreement was $\kappa = 75$, with exact agreement for 79% of the observations.

(2) *Mind-mindedness*. In order to devise dimensions for measuring maternal mind-mindedness, the first two authors made detailed observations of the videotaped interactions of six infant–mother pairs who were chosen at random. The development of the coding system involved determining ways in which a mother could demonstrate that she was treating her infant as a mental agent, capable of intentional action. In order for a behaviour to become established as a category of mind-mindedness, all of the six mothers had to demonstrate this behaviour at least once during the 20-minute session. Five measures of mind-mindedness were identified: *Maternal responsiveness to change in infant's direction of gaze; Maternal responsiveness to infant's object-directed action; Imitation; Encouragement of autonomy;* and *Appropriate mind-related comments.* These categories are described in detail below.

The two researchers who coded the *infant behaviours* categories (see above) also coded the videotapes for the maternal mind-mindedness categories. Every vocal comment the mother made was categorised. A maternal vocal comment was defined as a discrete sound or single word, or at the level of a sentence in longer utterances. For example, mothers often made single word comments which served to label some aspect of the environment, and would repeat this word several times, e.g. "Teddy. Teddy". This utterance would be scored as two separate comments. Mothers thus received scores for the total number of vocal interjections made during the 20-minute episode.

Obviously, the mind-mindedness categories were not exhaustive of all types of maternal behaviours observed during the free play sessions. Therefore, in addition to the mind-mindedness categories, there was a miscellaneous *Other* category, and any maternal behaviours the coders deemed not to be mind-minded were placed into this category. The *Other* category included comments giving positive or negative feedback on the infant's behaviour, behaviours which served to direct the infant's attention, and engagement in stan-

dardised game routines, such as "peekaboo". Inter-rater agreement for assignment of maternal behaviours across the five mind-mindedness categories and the *Other* category was $\kappa = .90$.

One way in which mothers appeared to demonstrate their mind-mindedness was in their responses to the three *Infant behaviour* categories described above. The first two categories of mind-mindedness emerged from the ways in which mothers responded to subtle infant behaviours which could be interpreted as cues for engagement in or disengagement from activities. Infants' line of gaze and object-directed action appeared to function as this type of cue, giving the categories *Maternal responsiveness to change in infant's direction of gaze* and *Maternal responsiveness to infant's object-directed action*.

For these two categories, maternal responsiveness included mothers looking at the object on which the infant's attention was focused, touching or picking the object up, or naming or describing the event or object to which the infant was directing behaviour. Scores for both of these categories were proportional. For the first category, each mother received a score for the number of changes in attention she made in response to her infant's line of gaze as a proportion of the total number of gaze changes made by her infant (see *Infant behaviours* above). For the second category, each mother received a score for the number of changes in attention she made to the infant's object-directed actions performed by her infant (see *Infant behaviours* above). These proportional scores, based on the contingency of maternal responses, were used in the analyses. Mothers' responses in such situations were deemed to be indicative of mind-mindedness since they provided an assessment of each mother's capacity to recognise that her infant's agenda was not always the same as her own. Mothers who are sensitive to their infants' mental life will be more likely to use the infant's change of attention as a cue to centre their own behaviour on the infant's new focus of interest. In contrast, a less mind-minded mother might ignore such changes in attention, attempt to focus the infant back on the activity in which she herself is engaged, or simply fail to register that her infant is no longer paying attention. These two categories were dependent on the infant's behaviour and can thus be seen as a measure of maternal responsiveness to the infant's focus of attention and interest. Inter-rater agreement for the contingency of maternal responses in these two categories (*Maternal responsiveness to change in infant's direction of gaze* and *Maternal responsiveness to infant's object-directed action*) was $\kappa = .80$.

Mothers' responses to infants' vocalisations emerged as the third category of mind-mindedness. Some mothers responded to vocalisations by imitating the precise sound that the infant had produced, and a category of *Imitation* was therefore established. Imitation was included as a measure of mind-mindedness since we reasoned that mothers would only imitate their infants if they interpreted their behaviour as having meaning and having been performed intentionally. In order to control for differences in the frequency of infant vocalisations, mothers' *Imitation* scores were expressed as a proportion of the total number of infant vocalisations.

These three categories of mind-mindedness (*Maternal responsiveness to change in infant's direction of gaze; Maternal responsiveness to infant's object-directed action;* and *Imitation*) thus arose from mothers' responses to their infants' behaviour.

The fourth category of mind-mindedness centred on mothers' elicitations of certain types of behaviour. Some mothers encouraged their infants to perform actions by themselves, such as retrieving an object that was out of reach, sitting up, manipulating a toy independently, and so on. *Encouragement of autonomy* was included as a measure of mind-mindedness since only mothers who deemed their infants to be capable of intentional action would encourage them to do things autonomously. In order to control for variations in mothers' verbosity and physical interaction during the session, mothers' *Encouragement of autonomy* scores were computed as a proportion of the total number of maternal behaviours coded.

The final category of mind-mindedness emerged not from assessing maternal responsiveness, or the function of mothers' behaviour, but from analysing the content of maternal speech. Of particular interest for the assessment of maternal mind-mindedness were comments mothers made which appeared to relate to their infants' minds. Mothers' mind-related comments can be subdivided as follows. First, mothers commented on their infants' mental states, such as their knowledge, thoughts, desires, and interests. The following are some examples: "You know what that is, it's a ball"; "Which toy do you prefer?"; "I think that you think it's a drum". Second, mothers commented on their infants' mental *processes,* e.g. "Do you remember seeing a camel?"; "Do you recognise that?"; "Are you thinking?" Third, mothers refered to the infant's level of emotional engagement, including assertions that the infant was bored, worried, self-conscious, solemn, impressed, or excited. Fourth, the most sophisticated psychological states attributed to infants were instances where mothers commented on their infants' attempts to manipulate other people's beliefs, e.g. "You're joking"; "You're just teasing me"; "Are you playing games with me?". Finally, some mind-related comments involved the mother "putting words into her infant's mouth", so that the mother's discourse took on the structure of a dialogue between her infant and herself. Invariably, these comments detailed what the infant would be likely to say if he or she could

speak: "She says, 'I'm not interested in him, I've already got one' "; "He says, 'I think I've got the hang of that now' "; " 'Ah, they look nice', he says, 'them toys, cor they look lovely' "; "She says, 'Mummy, roll me back over' "; "Say, 'Mummy, can I play with something else?' ".

It should be noted that behaviours classified as mind-related comments were independent of the quality of interaction between mother and infant, and appeared to be solely a reflection of the mother's proclivity to use language to frame the interaction in a mentalistic context. This distinction is best illustrated using a real example. An interaction typical of many dyads consisted of the mother showing her infant his or her reflection in a mirror, which was included in the selection of toys. The less mind-minded mother's discourse accompanying this interaction was as follows: "Who's that in there? Is that you?"; whereas the more mind-minded mother framed the interaction thus: "Who do you *think* that is? Who do you *think* it is? Do you *think* that might be you?" Thus, two mothers who may score identically on this interaction in terms of general sensitivity and responsiveness may still demonstrate wide-ranging differences in their proclivity to talk about their infants' minds. What is therefore most interesting is that mothers' mind-related comments were not determined by general maternal sensitivity or responsiveness, nor by the contiguity between infant behaviour and maternal response. However, since this category is not dependent upon the child's behaviour, and involves the mother *inferring* her infant's mental state, it was necessary to obtain an independent assessment of whether mothers' mind-related comments were accurate and appropriate.

Appropriateness of mothers' mind-related comments. Each mind-related comment was coded dichotomously as appropriate or inappropriate. The criteria for a comment being appropriate were as follows: (1) the independent coder agreed with the mother's reading of her infant's psychological state, e.g. if a mother commented that her infant wanted a particular toy, then it would be classified as an appropriate mental state comment if the independent coder concurred that the infant's behaviour was consistent with such a desire; (2) the comment linked current activity with similar events in the past or future, e.g. "Do you remember seeing a camel?" (while playing with a toy camel); (3) the comment served to clarify how to proceed if there was a lull in the interaction, e.g. "Do you want to look at the posters?" (after the infant had been gazing around the room and not focused on any object or activity for 5 seconds). Mind-related comments were classified as inappropriate if: (1) the independent coder believed that the mother was misinterpreting her infant's psychological state, e.g. stating that the infant was bored with a toy when he/she was still actively engaged in playing with it; (2) the comment referred to a past or future event that had no obvious relation to current activity; (3) the mother asked what the infant wanted to do, or commented that the infant wanted or preferred a different object or activity, when the infant was already actively engaged in an activity or was showing a clear preference for a particular object; (4) the referent of the mother's comment was not clear, e.g. saying "You like that" when the object or activity to which the comment referred was not obvious.

A researcher who was blind to all other measures coded the videotapes to assess the appropriateness of mothers' mind-related comments, and a second blind researcher coded a random fifth of the tapes. Inter-rater agreement was $\kappa = .79$.

In order to control for variations in mothers' verbosity during the session, mothers' *Appropriate mind-related comments* were computed as a proportion of the total number of maternal verbal comments coded during the testing session[3].

Phase Two Testing (Age 12 Months)

Mothers were contacted by telephone 6 months after Phase One testing had been carried out and invited to come to the University for the second testing session, which was conducted when the infants were 12 months of age. The session began with the experimenter administering the "mental scale" from the Bayley Scales of Infant Development (Bayley, 1993), which is a standardised scale for assessing infants' general cognitive ability. The mean standardised score on the Bayley mental scale for the whole sample of infants was $M = 91.70$ ($SD = 8.81$).

After a short break, infant–mother security of attachment was assessed using the Strange Situation procedure (Ainsworth & Wittig, 1969). The Bayley mental scale always preceded the Strange Situation procedure to control for possible effects of separation distress on the child's cognitive performance. The mental scale and Strange Situation were performed in different rooms.

Assessment of security of attachment.   Forty-nine infants were classified as securely attached, and 22 as insecurely attached (14 insecure-avoidant, 5 insecure-resistant, and 3 insecure-disorganised). This distribution amongst the secure and insecure categories is

similar to that reported by other researchers working on comparable samples of infants and mothers (e.g. Fish & Stifter, 1995). The Strange Situation tapes were coded by the first author, who has formal training in the Strange Situation coding procedure (Ainsworth et al., 1978), and 16 of the tapes were chosen at random and coded for a second time by an independent trained rater. Both of the raters were blind to all of the other measures. Inter-rater agreement was $\kappa = .87$ using the ABCD categories, and $\kappa = .85$ using a secure versus insecure distinction. The classification of the one child about whom the raters disagreed was resolved by discussion.

Results

The six infant–mother pairs who had been used to establish the mind-mindedness criteria were excluded from the analysis, giving an overall sample size of 65 (33 boys, 32 girls). Of the excluded children, four were subsequently classified as securely attached, with the remaining two being insecure-avoidant.

The Relation between Maternal Sensitivity and Mind-mindedness

Our first aim was to investigate whether maternal sensitivity and mind-mindedness can be distinguished empirically, and how these constructs relate to one another. Table 1 shows the correlation matrix for all of the continuous variables. As Table 1 shows, the correlations between maternal sensitivity and the proportional scores for the mind-mindedness categories were all positive, and all except the relation between *Sensitivity* and *Encouragement of autonomy* were statistically significant. That said, the two mind-mindedness variables most strongly related to maternal sensitivity (*Maternal responsiveness to change in infant's direction of gaze* and *Appropriate mind-related comments*) each accounted for only 16% ($r^2 = .16$) of the variance in sensitivity, suggesting that mind-mindedness and sensitivity are measuring related but distinct aspects of infant–mother interaction.

The proportional scores for the five categories of mind-mindedness were positively correlated with one another, with the majority of these correlations reaching statistical significance. For the most strongly related pair, *Maternal responsiveness to change in*

---

[3] It could be argued that *Appropriate mind-related comments* should be calculated as a proportion of the total number of *mind-related* comments, rather than as a proportion of the overall total of maternal comments. We used this more conservative index in order to present a truer picture of the frequency with which mothers made appropriate mind-related comments throughout the testing session. We reasoned that a proportional score of 1.0 awarded to a mother who made only one (appropriate) mind-related comment might not provide an accurate picture of mind-minded discourse. That said, analyses using this alternative index-produced exactly the same pattern of results as those reported in the Results section.

table 1   Correlation Matrix for the Continuous Variables

	MS	Gaze	Object	Imit	Aut	App	Mat Ed	Bayley
MS	1.00							
Gaze	.32**	1.00						
Object	.40**	.48**	1.00					
Imit	.30*	.26*	.23	1.00				
Aut	.09	.36**	.21	.19	1.00			
App	.40**	.39**	.40**	.18	−.03	1.00		
MatEd	.22	.33**	.07	−.06	−.15	.20	1.00	
Bayley	−.02	.21	−.08	.04	.21	.07	−.05	1.00

MS = maternal sensitivity; Gaze = maternal responsiveness to change in infant's direction of gaze; Object = maternal responsiveness to infant's object-directed action; Imit = mother imitates infant's vocalisation; Aut = mother encourages autonomy; App = mothers' appropriate mind-related comments; MatEd = mothers' highest educational level; Bayley = infants' Bayley Scale scores.
*$P < .025$; **$p < .005$. Probability levels for any correlations using the variables MatEd and Bayley are two-tailed; the levels for all of the other correlations are one-tailed.

infant's direction of gaze accounted for 23% ($r^2 = .23$) of the variance in *Maternal responsiveness to infant's object-directed action,* suggesting that the five categories of mind-mindedness are measuring related but distinct aspects of a mother's proclivity to treat her infant as an individual with a mind.

Relations with Infant- and Mother-centred Variables

Table 1 also shows the correlation coefficients for the relations between the infant–mother interaction variables (maternal sensitivity and maternal mind-mindedness), mothers' educational level, and infants' Bayley Scale scores. Maternal educational level was positively correlated with *Maternal responsiveness to change in infant's direction of gaze,* with more highly educated mothers being more likely to respond to changes in their infants' direction of gaze. Maternal educational level was not significantly correlated with any of the other infant–mother interaction variables or with infants' general cognitive ability scores. Infants' Bayley Scale scores were not related to maternal sensitivity or to any of the mind-mindedness variables.

Table 2 shows the mean scores of the secure and insecure groups with respect to infants' scores on the Bayley mental scale, and the three indices of infant behaviour from the infant–mother interactions at 6 months. As Table 2 shows, security of attachment was not related to any of these variables. Thus, secure and insecure group infants did not differ in their general cognitive ability or in their frequency of vocalisation, change in gaze, and object-directed activity during the 20 minute session. Table 2 shows the mean scores of the secure and insecure group mothers with respect to

highest educational level and total number of comments made during the session. Mothers of securely and insecurely attached children did not differ in the level to which they had been educated or in how frequently they spoke during the testing session. Table 2 also shows the effect sizes for these relations. The effect size was calculated using the formula $d = (M_{higher} - M_{lower})/SD$ (Cohen, 1977); two values are thus given (obtained by dividing by the two SDs), representing the range of effect size. All of the effect sizes in Table 2 are small (Cohen, 1977), showing that the relation between attachment security and these variables is weak.

Security-related Differences in Infant–Mother Interaction at 6 Months

The mean scores for sensitivity and the mean proportional scores for the five maternal mind-mindedness categories of the secure and insecure groups are given in Table 3. As this table shows, mothers who scored more highly on Ainsworth et al.'s (1971) scale of maternal sensitivity were more likely to have securely attached children. With respect to mind-mindedness and security of attachment, the relations between the proportional scores for all of the mind-mindedness categories and security were in the predicted direction, with mothers who scored more highly in these categories being more likely to have securely attached infants. Security of attachment was significantly related to *Maternal responsiveness to infant's object-directed action* and mothers' *Appropriate mind-related comments.* The relations between security of attachment and the categories *Maternal responsiveness to change in infant's direction of gaze, Imitation,* and *Encouragement of autonomy* were not statistically significant.

table 2   **Mean Scores for the Secure and Insecure Groups with Respect to Infant- and Mother-centred Variables**

| | Security of attachment | | | | | |
| | Secure ($N = 45$) | | Insecure ($N = 20$) | | | |
Variable	Mean	SD	Mean	SD	Statistic t values[a]	Effect sizes d
Bayley	92.23	8.77	89.55	9.17	1.14	0.29–0.31
Vocalisation	28.84	19.56	24.25	19.14	0.88	0.23–0.24
Infant gaze	73.24	22.32	71.95	19.00	0.23	0.06–0.12
Infant object	50.56	20.83	53.25	21.85	0.47	0.12–0.13
Education	2.60	1.72	2.90	1.25	0.70	0.17–0.24
Comments	141.71	41.78	130.35	43.74	1.00	0.26–0.27

Bayley = infant score on the Bayley mental scale; Vocalisation = total number of infant vocalisations; Infant gaze = total number of changes in infant direction of gaze; Infant object = total number of infant object-directed actions; Education = mothers' highest educational level; Comments = total number of maternal comments.
[a] The t-tests were two-tailed; none reached statistical significance.

Table 3 also shows the effect sizes for these relations, calculated according to the formula given above. The effect size for the relation between *Maternal sensitivity* and security of attachment at 12 months was medium, that for the relation between *Maternal responsiveness to infant's object-directed action* and security was medium to large, and that between *Appropriate mind-related comments* and security was large (Cohen, 1977). Effect sizes for all of the other relations shown in Table 3 were small (Cohen, 1977).

Mind-mindedness as a Predictor of Security of Attachment

In order to determine the relative predictive strengths of the five mind-mindedness categories and subse-

table 3   **Mean Scores and Effect Sizes for the Relation between Security of Attachment and Maternal Sensitivity, and Mean Proportional Scores and Effect Sizes for Relations between Security of Attachment and the Maternal Mind-mindedness Categories**

| | Security of attachment | | | | | |
| | Secure ($N = 45$) | | Insecure ($N = 20$) | | | |
Variable	Mean	SD	Mean	SD	Statistic t values[a]	Effect sizes d
Sensitivity	5.80	2.02	4.50	2.26	2.31*	0.57–0.64
Gaze	0.49	0.14	0.46	0.21	0.71	0.14–0.21
Object	0.91	0.09	0.84	0.21	1.92*	0.33–0.78
Imitate	0.07	0.05	0.06	0.04	1.14	0.26–0.35
Autonomy	0.06	0.04	0.05	0.04	0.44	0.21–0.24
App Mind	0.11	0.06	0.05	0.04	4.34**	1.00–1.50

Sensitivity = maternal sensitivity; Gaze = maternal responsiveness to change in the infant's line of gaze; Object = maternal responsiveness to infant's object-directed action; Imitate = mother imitates infant's vocalisation; Autonomy = mother encourages an autonomous act; App Mind = mothers' appropriate mind-related comments.
*$p < .025$; **$p < .001$. Levels of significance are for one-tailed tests.

quent security of attachment, a forward logistic regression was carried out. The five categories (*Maternal responsiveness to change in infant's direction of gaze*; *Maternal responsiveness to infant's object-directed action*; *Imitation*; *Encouragement of autonomy*; and *Appropriate mind-related comments*) were the only factors entered into the regression. *Appropriate mind-related comments* was found to be the only predictor of security of attachment, χ^2 ($N = 65$) = 23.56, $p < .001$.

Overall Predictors of Security of Attachment

Our next aim was to investigate the relative predictive strength of maternal sensitivity and mind-mindedness with respect to subsequent security of attachment. Given that mothers' *Appropriate mind-related comments* was the only mind-mindedness category found to be a predictor of attachment security, the other four mind-mindedness categories were omitted from the regression. Four factors were entered into a hierarchical logistic regression in the following order: *Maternal educational level, Bayley Scale score, Maternal sensitivity,* and *Appropriate mind-related comments.* When entered on the first step of the regression, *Maternal educational level* was not a predictor of attachment security, χ^2($N = 65$) = 0.06, n.s.; on the second step, *Bayley Scale score* was not a predictor of attachment security, χ^2($N = 65$) = 2.00, n.s. With mothers' educational level and infants' Bayley Scale scores entered into the prediction equation, *Maternal sensitivity* was found to be a significant predictor of attachment security, χ^2($N = 65$) = 8.30, $p < .005$, accounting for 6.5% of its variance. When *Appropriate mind-related comments* was entered on the final step of the regression, it was found to be a significant predictor of attachment security, χ^2($N = 65$) = 17.62, $p < .001$, accounting for 12.7% of its variance. Thus even when maternal sensitivity had been accounted for, mothers' *Appropriate mind-related comments* was a significant predictor of infant–mother security of attachment.

Exploratory Analyses Using the ABC Attachment Categories

A final aim was to investigate potential differences in early infant–mother interaction between the separate insecure attachment categories. Given the small numbers of children in the insecure categories, only descriptive statistics are reported here. Table 4 shows the mean scores of the four attachment categories for the two maternal variables found to be significant predictors of attachment security (*Maternal sensitivity* and mothers' *Appropriate mind-related comments*). No further analyses were conducted using the insecure-disorganised group since no specific predictions were made regarding this group and it contained only three infants. Effect sizes to compare the scores of the secure, insecure-avoidant, and insecure-resistant categories were calculated as before. The effect size for the difference in *Maternal sensitivity* scores between the secure and insecure-avoidant groups was found to be medium to large ($d = 0.69$–0.81), and that between the insecure avoidant and insecure-resistant groups was large ($d = 0.77$–0.98). However, the secure and insecure-resistant groups could not be distinguished from one another in terms of maternal sensitivity, with the resistant group scoring marginally higher than the secure group, resulting in a small effect size ($d = 0.10$–0.11). All three attachment groups could be distinguished from one another with respect to their scores on mothers' *Appropriate mind-related comments,* with large effect sizes between the secure and insecure-avoidant groups ($d = 1.15$–1.82) and secure and insecure-resistant groups ($d = 0.82$–1.36). The effect size for the difference between the avoidant and resistant groups was medium ($d = 0.53$–0.55).

Discussion

The initial goal of the study reported here was to establish empirical measures of mothers' proclivity to

table 4 Mean Scores for the Four Attachment Categories with Respect to Maternal Sensitivity and Mothers' Appropriate Mind-related Comments

Attachment category	Maternal sensitivity		Appropriate mind-related comments	
	Mean	SD	Mean	SD
Insecure-avoidant ($N = 12$)	4.17	2.37	0.04	0.04
Secure ($N = 45$)	5.80	2.02	0.11	0.06
Insecure-resistant ($N = 5$)	6.00	1.87	0.06	0.04
Insecure-disorganised ($N = 3$)	3.33	1.53	0.05	0.02

treat their 6-month-old infants as individuals with minds (maternal mind-mindedness) within a play context. Five measures of maternal mind-mindedness were devised on the basis of distinct ways in which mothers demonstrated their tendency to attribute intention to their infants. The first three of these measures dealt with mothers' responses to their infants' behaviour. The categories *Maternal responsiveness to change in infant's direction of gaze* and *Maternal responsiveness to infant's object-directed action* arose from maternal responses to infant actions that could be interpreted as cues for engagement in or disengagement from activities. Mothers' responses to their infants' changes in gaze or object-directed activity are indicative of mind-mindedness since they assess the mother's capacity to recognise that her infant's agenda may be different from her own. More mind-minded mothers will respond to their infants' change of attention, resulting in interactions that are contingent and responsive. Mothers also demonstrated their mind-mindedness by imitating their infants' vocalisations. *Imitation* was deemed to be indicative of mind-mindedness since mothers will only imitate their infants' vocalisations if they interpret them as having meaning and as having been performed intentionally. The fourth way in which mothers demonstrated mind-mindedness was by encouraging their infants to perform actions by themselves. *Encouragement of autonomy* was regarded to be a measure of mind-mindedness since only mothers who deem their infants capable of intentional action will encourage them to do things autonomously. The final mind-mindedness category focused on mothers' use of psychological discourse to refer to their infants' mental and emotional states and cognitive processes. In order to be coded as engaging in mind-minded behaviour, mothers did not only have to talk about their infants' minds, but had to make comments on mental states and processes that were deemed by independent raters to be accurate and appropriate. The category *Appropriate mind-related comments* was taken to be a measure of mothers' ability to read their infants' minds.

The first specific aim of the study reported here was to investigate the relation between maternal mind-mindedness and Ainsworth et al.'s (1971) original construct of maternal sensitivity. Our findings suggest that it is possible to differentiate between sensitive (as conceived by Ainsworth et al., 1971) and mind-minded maternal behaviours in interactions between mothers and their 6-month-olds. Although each of the five mind-mindedness categories was positively correlated with maternal sensitivity, the mind-mindedness categories most strongly related to sensitivity (*Maternal responsiveness to change in infant's direction of gaze* and *Appropriate mind-related comments*) each only accounted for 16% of its variance. One can therefore argue that mind-

mindedness and sensitivity are capturing related but distinct aspects of maternal behaviour, and that any relations that obtain between mind-mindedness and subsequent attachment security cannot be explained simply in terms of equivalence between mind-mindedness and sensitivity.

Our second aim was to attempt to replicate the finding that more sensitive mothers are more likely to establish secure attachment relationships subsequently with their infants. This aim was achieved. The medium effect size (Cohen, 1977) for the relation between these variables was in line with previous work, being very similar to the value reported in De Wolff and Van IJzendoorn's (1997) meta-analysis.

The third aim of the study was to test the hypothesis that infants whose mothers showed higher levels of mind-mindedness at 6 months will have formed secure attachment relationships with their infants 6 months later. Only two of the five mind-mindedness categories were significantly related to later security of attachment. Mothers who at 6 months commented appropriately on their infants' psychological states and processes, and who responded to their infants' object-directed activity, were more likely to have securely attached infants. However, an initial regression analysis showed that, of the five mind-mindedness variables, mothers' *Appropriate mind-related comments* was the only significant predictor of attachment security. The hypothesised relation between early maternal mind-mindedness and subsequent security was thus not supported for all of the mind-mindedness categories.

The fourth aim was to investigate the relative strength of maternal sensitivity and maternal mind-mindedness as predictors of attachment security. A hierarchical regression showed that both maternal sensitivity and mothers' *Appropriate mind-related comments* were significant predictors of subsequent security. After maternal sensitivity had been entered into the regression (accounting for 6.5% of the variance), mothers' appropriate mind-related comments accounted for a further 12.7% of the variance in attachment security. This category of maternal mind-mindedness was therefore a better predictor of infant–mother attachment security than maternal sensitivity.

Our final aim was to explore whether differences in maternal mind-mindedness could distinguish between infants across the three major attachment categories. Although the data from the insecure-avoidant and insecure-resistant groups should be treated with caution due to the low numbers of infants in these groups, there appears to be reason to suggest that differences in mothers' appropriate mind-related comments can discriminate between different types of insecurity. The insecure-avoidant group mothers made fewer appropriate mind-related comments than mothers in the insecure-resistant group. Mothers in both of the insecure groups made significantly fewer appropriate mind-related comments than their counterparts in the secure group. In contrast, there was no significant difference in *sensitivity* scores between the secure and resistant group mothers; indeed, the resistant group mothers scored marginally higher on this measure than their secure group counterparts. Thus, in this sample of infants, mothers' appropriate mind-related comments appeared better able than maternal sensitivity to distinguish between infants across the three attachment categories.

How can one explain the finding that mothers' proclivity to comment accurately on their infants' minds predicts security of attachment even after differences in maternal sensitivity have been accounted for? One possible explanation is that the construct of maternal mind-mindedness takes into account the appropriateness of mothers' interactions with their infants, whereas the global scale of maternal sensitivity does not distinguish *recognition* of the infant's needs (suggested by Ainsworth et al. to be shared by both secure and insecure group mothers) from *appropriate response to* such needs. Thus, the problem with maternal sensitivity as a predictor of attachment security lies not in its original definition, but in the way it has come to be operationalised.

An important key to explaining this finding may lie in the fact that the present study's measure of *Appropriate mind-related comments* is an index of the mother's capacity accurately to *represent* the mental and emotional states of her infant. As such, this capacity can be seen to relate to the processes involved in the formation and operation of internal working models (IWM: Bowlby, 1973, 1980) of attachment. Although one's IWM of an attachment figure is constructed on the basis of one's experiences with that individual, the model is representational, since it enables one to predict the form of future interactions with the attachment figure: whether he or she will be accessible or unavailable, sensitive or intrusive, and so on. Indeed, a mother's tendency to frame interactions in terms of her infant's desires, intentions, beliefs, and emotions may provide us with a naturalistic measure of the mother's internal working model of self with child, just as the Adult Attachment Interview (AAI: George, Kaplan, & Main, 1985) provides a measure of one's IWM of self with parent. In contrast, maternal sensitivity is an index of behaviour with no representational component, and it therefore lacks clear theoretical links with important concepts such as the IWM.

This suggestion is borne out by the findings of researchers who have sought to establish how individual differences in parents' AAI classifications relate to their attachment relationships with their own children. For example, Fonagy, Steele, and Steele (1991) assessed parental IWMs of attachment prenatally in a primiparous sample, and demonstrated an impressive level of concordance between a mother's secure classification on the AAI and a secure attachment relationship with her child at 12 months. In subsequent work, Fonagy and colleagues (e.g. Fonagy, Steele, Steele, Morgan, & Higgitt, 1991; Fonagy et al., 1994) have investigated this relation further by developing the "reflective-self scale" which is used to assess AAI transcripts for interviewees' awareness of their own and other people's mental processes and functioning. They reported that reflective-self function was the underlying variable accounting for the AAI's predictive power with respect to infant–mother security of attachment. Thus, mothers who tended to invoke mental states when explaining the behaviour of others during the AAI were more likely to have securely attached children. There is an obvious parallel between a mother's mentalistic comments during the AAI and her mind-related comments during interactions with her infant at 6 months, and it is thus perhaps unsurprising that both are related to subsequent security of attachment. Indeed, individual differences in maternal mind-mindedness may help to bridge what Van IJzendoorn (1995) referred to as the "transmission gap" between parents' mental representations of childhood attachment experiences and the formation of secure attachment relationships with their own children. That is, while AAI classification and parental sensitivity have both been found to be independent predictors of attachment security, there is no strong relation between a secure AAI classification and greater parental sensitivity. Sensitive caregiving behaviour cannot therefore account for the variance shared between AAI classification and infant security of attachment.

How might the construct of maternal mind-mindedness help us to bridge this "transmission gap"? One answer is that, in contrast to measures based purely on differences in maternal behaviour (e.g. maternal sensitivity), our construct of mind-mindedness (and in particular the discourse-based category of *Appropriate mind-related comments*) is a measure of the mother's *representation* of her infant's mental states. As Meins (1999) has argued, this representational component makes it considerably easier to see how mothers' behaviour is in turn determined by their representations of their own attachment relationships (as assessed by, for example, the AAI). At the same time, our measure could be argued to be an advance on previous interview-based assessments of parental representations (e.g. Fonagy et al., 1994; Meins et al., 1998), because it shows how such representations are manifested in the language mothers use in real-life interactions with their infants.

As well as having conceptual and theoretical links with other predictors of attachment, the observed relation between a mother's tendency to comment accurately on her infant's mind and subsequent security of attachment may also relate to recent findings about the *consequences* of a secure attachment relationship. For example, the secure-group mother's "mentalisation" of her infant might shed light on the finding that securely attached children outperform their insecurely attached peers on standard "theory of mind" tasks (Fonagy, Redfern, & Charman, 1997; Meins et al., 1998). Such mentalisation can be presumed to involve, *inter alia,* exposing infants to mental-state language from an early age, which may encourage children to understand themselves and others as mental agents, and thus lead to precocity in the awareness of the relation between one's beliefs and one's behaviour. Although this relation has yet to be tested empirically, Meins et al.'s results and the findings reported here suggest that there may be long-term continuity in secure-group mothers' proclivity to regard their children as mental agents. The greater mind-mindedness of secure-group mothers may thus have influences which extend beyond the formation of the attachment relationship, and may account for certain security-related differences in children's later development. Indeed, Meins and Fernyhough (1999) argued that the concept of mind-mindedness may help to explain why other social factors, such as individual differences in family structure (Lewis, Freeman, Kyriakidou, Maridaki-Kassotaki, & Berridge, 1996; Ruffman, Perner, Naito, Parkin, & Clements, 1998) and familial discourse about emotions and causal relations (Dunn, Brown, Slomkowski, Tesla, & Youngblade, 1991) influence theory of mind development. For example, other family members are also likely to demonstrate mind-mindedness in their interactions with young children, and by talking about feelings and how people's behaviour impacts on the lives of others, families are implicitly treating their children as individuals with minds, capable of understanding complex relationships and events.

Much work remains to be done in continuing to develop the construct of mind-mindedness and in establishing its connections with both maternal sensitivity and attachment security. Given our focus on observational context, it is important to investigate mind-mindedness in other situations, such as interactions in the home where the mother will be engaged in caregiving as well as play activities. If mind-mindedness is to become established as a reliable predictor of attachment security, it is necessary to demonstrate that mind-minded discourse also accompanies activities more commonly associated with the formation of attachment relationships. For example, mothers' development of differential responses to early crying may depend upon their willingness or ability to interpret crying as a means of communication. Similarly, it is important to investigate whether individual differences in maternal mind-mindedness predict attachment security in other cultures and in mothers of differing socioeconomic status, since maternal sensitivity has been found to relate to security across wide-ranging populations (Egeland & Farber, 1984; Goldberg et al., 1986; Grossmann et al., 1985).

That said, the present finding that mothers' use of appropriate mind-related comments is a better predictor of attachment security than maternal sensitivity marks an important development in our understanding of the antecedents and consequences of individual differences in the attachment relationship. Whereas our rethinking of the concept of maternal sensitivity has maintained conceptual and theoretical links with established predictors of attachment security, the study reported here shows how security might be influenced by mothers' *representations* of their infants' mental states, as manifested in the language they use in real-life play interactions. The concept of maternal mind-mindedness thus has the potential to explain the poorly understood links between a mother's tendency to talk coherently about her own attachment relationships during the AAI and her ability subsequently to form a secure attachment relationship with her child. Our findings therefore address Thompson's (1997) analysis of the needs of future attachment research: "Understanding why sensitive responsiveness contributes to a secure attachment, and how this is associated with later working models of self and relationships, may be the most important theoretical problem for attachment researchers in the years to come" (p. 597).

Acknowledgements

The research reported in this paper was supported by two research grants from Staffordshire University. We thank Paul Harris, Sue Leekam, Anne Campbell, Joanne Martin, Bronia Hurst, and the three anonymous reviewers for their invaluable contributions to this paper.

REFERENCES

Ainsworth, M. D. S., Bell, S. M., & Stayton, D. J. (1971). Individual differences in Strange Situation behavior of one year olds. In H. R. Schaffer (Ed.), *The origins of human social relations.* New York: Academic Press.

Ainsworth, M. D. S., Bell, S. M., & Stayton, D. J. (1974). Infant–mother attachment and social development: Socialisation as a product of reciprocal responsiveness to signals. In M. P. M. Richards (Ed.), *The introduction of the child into a social world.* London: Cambridge University Press.

Ainsworth, M. D. S., Blehar, M. C., Waters, E., & Wall, S. (1978). *Patterns of attachment: Assessed in the strange situation and at home.* Hillsdale, NJ: Lawrence Erlbaum.

Ainsworth, M. D. S., & Wittig, B. A. (1969). Attachment and exploratory behavior of one year olds in a strange situation. In B. M. Foss (Ed.), *Determinants of infant behaviour Vol. 4.* New York: Barnes & Noble.

Bayley, N. (1993). *Bayley Scales of Infant Development* (2nd ed.). San Antonio, TX: The Psychological Corporation, Harcourt Brace & Company.

Beeghly, M., Bretherton, I., & Mervis, C. (1986). Mothers' internal state language to toddlers: The socialisation of psychological understanding. *British Journal of Developmental Psychology, 4,* 247–260.

Belsky, J., Rovine, M., & Taylor, D. G. (1984). The Pennsylvania Infant and Family Development Project, III: The origins of individual differences in infant–mother attachment: Maternal and infant contributions. *Child Development, 55,* 718–728.

Bowlby, J. (1973). *Attachment and loss: Vol. 2. Separation: Anxiety and anger.* London: Hogarth Press.

Bowlby, J. (1980). *Attachment and loss: Vol. 3. Loss sadness and depression.* London: Hogarth Press.

Cohen, J. (1977). *Statistical power analysis for the behavioural sciences* (rev. ed.). New York: Academic Press.

De Wolff, M. S., & Van IJzendoorn, M. H. (1997). Sensitivity and attachment: A meta-analysis on parental antecedents of infant attachment. *Child Development, 68,* 571–591.

Dunn, J., Bretherton, I., & Munn, P. (1987). Conversations about feeling states between mothers and their young children. *Developmental Psychology, 23,* 132–139.

Dunn, J., Brown, J., Slomkowski, C., Tesla, C., & Youngblade, L. M. (1991). Young children's understanding of other people's feelings and beliefs: Individual differences and their antecedents. *Child Development, 62,* 1352–1366.

Egeland, B., & Farber, E. (1984). Infant–mother attachment: Factors related to its development and change over time. *Child Development, 60,* 753–771.

Fish, M., & Stifter, C. A. (1995). Patterns of mother–infant interaction and attachment: A cluster-analytic approach. *Infant Behavior and Development, 18,* 435–446.

Fonagy, P., Redfern, S., & Charman, A. (1997). The relationship between belief-desire reasoning and a projective measure of attachment security (SAT). *British Journal of Developmental Psychology, 15,* 51–63.

Fonagy, P., Steele, H., & Steele, M. (1991). Maternal representations of attachment during pregnancy predict the organisation of infant–mother attachment at one year of age. *Child Development, 62,* 891–905.

Fonagy, P., Steele, M., Steele, H., Higgitt, A. C., & Target, M. (1994). The Emmanuel Miller Memorial Lecture 1992: The theory and practice of resilience. *Journal of Child Psychology and Psychiatry, 35,* 231–257.

Fonagy, P., Steele, M., Steele, H., Moran, G. S., & Higgitt, A. C. (1991). The capacity for understanding mental states: The reflective self in parent and child and its significance for security of attachment. *Infant Mental Health Journal, 12,* 201–218.

George, C., Kaplan, N., & Main, M. (1985). *The Berkeley Adult Attachment Interview.* Unpublished protocol, Department of Psychology, University of California, Berkeley.

Goldberg, S., Perotta, M., Minde, K., & Corter, C. (1986). Maternal behavior and attachment in low-birth-weight twins and singletons. *Child Development, 57,* 34–46.

Goldsmith, H. H., & Alansky, J. (1987). Maternal and infant temperamental predictors of attachment: A meta-analytic review. *Journal of Consulting and Clinical Psychology, 55,* 805–816.

Grossmann, K., Grossmann, K. E., Spangler, G., Suess, G., & Unzner, L. (1985). Maternal sensitivity and newborns' orientation responses as related to quality of attachment in northern Germany. In I. Bretherton & E. Waters (Eds.), *Growing points in attachment theory and research* (pp. 233–268). *Monographs of the Society for Research in Child Development, 50* (1–2, Serial No. 209).

Isabella, R. A. (1993). Origins of attachment: Maternal interactive behavior across the first year. *Child Development, 64,* 605–621.

Isabella, R. A., Belsky, J., & Von Eye, A. (1989). Origins of infant–mother attachment: An examination of interactional synchrony during the infant's first year. *Developmental Psychology, 25,* 12–21.

Lewis, C., Freeman, N. H., Kyriakidou, C., Maridaki-Kassotaki, K., & Berridge, D. M. (1996). Social influences on false belief access: Specific sibling influences or general apprenticeship? *Child Development, 67,* 2930–2947.

Main, M. (1981). Avoidance in the service of attachment; A working paper. In K. Immelman, G. Barlow, L. Petrinovich, & M. Main (Eds.), *Behavioral development* (pp. 651–693). Cambridge: Cambridge University Press.

Meins, E. (1997). *Security of attachment and the social development of cognition.* Hove, U.K.: Psychology Press.

Meins, E. (1998). The effects of security of attachment and maternal attribution of meaning on children's linguistic acquisitional style. *Infant Behavior and Development, 21,* 237–252.

Meins, E. (1999). Sensitivity, security and internal working models: Bridging the transmission gap. *Attachment and Human Development, 1,* 325–342.

Meins, E., & Fernyhough, C. (1999). Linguistic acquisitional style and mentalising development: The role of maternal mind-mindedness. *Cognitive Development, 14,* 363–380.

Meins, E., Fernyhough, C., Russell, J., & Clark-Carter, D. (1998). Security of attachment as a predictor of symbolic and mentalising abilities: A longitudinal study. *Social Development, 7,* 1–24.

Ruffman, T., Perner, J., Naito, M., Parkin, L., & Clements, W. A. (1998). Older (but not younger) siblings facilitate false belief understanding. *Developmental Psychology, 34,* 161–174.

Schölmerich, A., Fracasso, M. P., Lamb, M. E., & Broberg, A. G. (1995). Interactional harmony at 7 and 10 months of age predicts security of attachment as measured by Q-sort ratings. *Social Development, 4,* 62–74.

Thompson, R. A. (1997). Sensitivity and security: New questions to ponder. *Child Development, 68,* 595–597.

Van IJzendoorn, M. H. (1995). Adult attachment representations, parental responsiveness, and infant attachment: A meta-analysis on the predictive validity of the Adult Attachment Interview. *Psychological Bulletin, 117,* 387–403.

Questions

1. Why, according to the authors, is there confusion regarding what maternal sensitivity is and how it contributes to attachment security? Do you think maternal sensitivity is important in infant-mother attachment? Why or why not?

2. How did Mary Ainsworth define maternal sensitivity, and what are some of the problems that Meins and her colleagues identify in research based on this definition? Do you agree with this critique and the definition that the authors suggest?

3. Why might situations of distress for an infant, such as that experienced during the strange-situation procedure, provide a limited view of maternal sensitivity? What other types of situations might be useful for assessing maternal sensitivity?

4. What is maternal mind-mindedness, and what five categories of behaviors were used as indices of maternal mind-mindedness in this study?

5. Do you think maternal sensitivity continues to be positively related to the mother-child relationship as children get older, or is it mainly important when children are very young and highly dependent on their mothers?

6. How might maternal mind-mindedness be displayed when children are able to communicate their needs using language?

18 Early Experience and Emotional Development: The Emergence of Wariness of Heights

Joseph J. Campos • Bennett I. Bertenthal • Rosanne Kermoian

Many people are afraid of heights—specifically, of falling from a height. Falls are dangerous and can be fatal, so it is not surprising that many people have strong emotional responses to heights. If you are afraid of heights or know someone who is, you may have wondered if this fear was always there or if it was learned. One way that psychologists have tried to answer this question is by studying infants to determine if and when they exhibit fear or wariness of heights. One might hypothesize that such wariness appears as soon as infants are able to move around on their own, but this is not the case. Infants show little avoidance of heights after learning to crawl; they may crawl right over the edge of a bed or stairway if caregivers do not stop them.

Infants who have just learned to crawl show no avoidance of heights because they have not yet developed a fear of heights. However, once children do become fearful of heights, this wariness stays with them throughout life. What explains this pattern of development? In the early years of psychology, it was believed that humans have many instincts, including fear of heights. Following from this belief, if fear of heights is built into human physiology in the form of an instinct, developmental changes in this emotional response would not occur. This longstanding assumption was challenged by the research described in the following article.

Joseph J. Campos and his colleagues examined the relation between early locomotor experience and the development of fear. They demonstrated that fear of heights is a learned, not an instinctual, emotional response. Their results also identify a direct link between early perceptual and motor experience and emotional development. In order to study this link, the researchers needed to (1) adapt a method that is used for studying infants who can crawl for infants who have not yet learned to crawl; (2) devise an ecologically valid way of testing fear in infants; and (3) identify experiences of prelocomotive children that are similar to the experience of locomotion.

Because of its biological adaptive value, wariness of heights is widely believed to be innate or under maturational control. In this report, we present evidence contrary to this hypothesis, and show the importance of locomotor experience for emotional development. Four studies bearing on this conclusion have shown that (1) when age is held constant, locomotor experience accounts for wariness of heights; (2) "artificial" experience locomoting in a walker generates evidence of wariness

of heights; (3) an orthopedically handicapped infant tested longitudinally did not show wariness of heights so long as he had no locomotor experience; and (4) regardless of the age when infants begin to crawl, it is the duration of locomotor experience and not age that predicts avoidance of heights. These findings suggest that when infants begin to crawl, experiences generated by locomotion make possible the development of wariness of heights.

Reprinted with permission of Blackwell Publishers from Campos, J. J., Bertenthal, B. I. & Kermoian, R. (1992). Early experience and emotional development: The emergence of wariness of heights. *Psychological Science, 3,* 61–64.
This research was supported by grants from the National Institutes of Health (HD-16195, HD-00695, and HD-25066) and from the John D. and Catherine T. MacArthur Foundation.

155

Between 6 and 10 months of age, major changes occur in fearfulness in the human infant. During this period, some fears are shown for the first time, and many others show a step-function increase in prevalence (Bridges, 1932; Scarr & Salapatek, 1970; Sroufe, 1979). These changes in fearfulness occur so abruptly, involve so many different elicitors, and have such biologically adaptive value that many investigators propose maturational explanations for this developmental shift (Emde, Gaensbauer, & Harmon, 1976; Kagan, Kearsley, & Zelazo, 1978). For such theorists, the development of neurophysiological structures (e.g., the frontal lobes) precedes and accounts for changes in affect.

In contrast to predominantly maturational explanations of developmental changes, Gottlieb (1983, 1991) proposed a model in which different types of experiences play an important role in developmental shifts. He emphasized that new developmental acquisitions, such as crawling, generate experiences that, in turn, create the conditions for further developmental changes. Gottlieb called such "bootstrapping" processes probabilistic epigenesis. In contrast to most current models of developmental transition, Gottlieb's approach stresses the possibility that, under some circumstances, psychological function may precede and account for development of neurophysiological structures.

There is evidence in the animal literature that a probabilistic epigenetic process plays a role in the development of wariness of heights. Held and Hein (1963), for instance, showed that dark-reared kittens given experience with active self-produced locomotion in an illuminated environment showed avoidance of heights, whereas dark-reared littermates given passive experience moving in the same environment manifested no such avoidance. In these studies, despite equivalent maturational states in the two groups of kittens, the experiences made possible by correlated visuomotor responses during active locomotion proved necessary to elicit wariness of heights.

So long as they are prelocomotor, human infants, despite their visual competence and absence of visual deprivation, may be functionally equivalent to Held and Hein's passively moved kittens. Crawling may generate or refine skills sufficient for the onset of wariness of heights. These skills may include improved calibration of distances, heightened sensitivity to visually specified self-motion, more consistent coordination of visual and vestibular stimulation, and increased awareness of emotional signals from significant others (Bertenthal & Campos, 1990; Campos, Hiatt, Ramsay, Henderson, & Svejda, 1978).

There is anecdotal evidence supporting a link between locomotor experience and development of wariness of heights in human infants. Parents commonly report that there is a phase following the acquisition of locomotion when infants show no avoidance of heights, and will go over the edge of a bed or other precipice if the caretaker is not vigilant. Parents also report that this phase of apparent fearlessness is followed by one in which wariness of heights becomes quite intense (Campos et al., 1978).

In sum, both the kitten research and the anecdotal human evidence suggest that wariness of heights is not simply a maturational phenomenon, to be expected even in the absence of experience. From the perspective of probabilistic epigenesis, locomotor experience may operate as an organizer of emotional development, serving either to induce wariness of heights (i.e., to produce a potent emotional state that would never emerge without such experience) or to facilitate its emergence (i.e., to bring it about earlier than it otherwise would appear). The research reported here represents an attempt to determine whether locomotor experience is indeed an organizer of the emergence of wariness of heights.

Pinpointing the role of locomotion in the emergence of wariness of heights in human infants requires solution of a number of methodological problems. One is the selection of an ecologically valid paradigm for testing wariness of heights. Another is the determination of an outcome measure that can be used with both prelocomotor and locomotor infants. A third is a means of determining whether locomotion is playing a role as a correlate, an antecedent, an inducer, or a facilitator of the onset of wariness of heights.

The ecologically valid paradigm we selected for testing was the visual cliff (Walk, 1966; Walk & Gibson, 1961)—a large, safety-glass-covered table with a solid textured surface placed immediately underneath the glass on one side (the "shallow" side) and a similar surface placed some 43 in. underneath the glass on the floor below on the other side (the "deep" side).

To equate task demands for prelocomotor and locomotor infants, we measured the infants' wariness reactions while they were slowly lowered toward either the deep or the shallow side of the cliff. This descent procedure not only allowed us to assess differences in wariness reactions as a function of locomotor experience in both prelocomotor and locomotor infants but also permitted us to assess an index of depth perception, that is, a visual placing response (the extension of the arms and hands in anticipation of contact with the shallow, but not the deep, surface of the cliff [Walters, 1981]).

To assess fearfulness with an index appropriate to both pre- and postlocomoting infants, we measured heart rate (HR) responses during the 3-s period of descent onto the surface of the cliff. Prior work had shown consistently that heart rate decelerates in infants who are in a state of nonfearful attentiveness, but accelerates when infants are showing either a defensive response (Graham & Clifton, 1966) or a precry state (Campos, Emde, Gaensbauer, & Henderson, 1975).

To relate self-produced locomotion to fearfulness, we used a number of converging research operations. One was an *age-held-constant design*, contrasting the performance of infants who were locomoting with those of the same age who were not yet locomoting; the second was an analog of an experiential *enrichment* manipulation, in which infants who were otherwise incapable of crawling or creeping were tested after they had a number of hours of experience moving about voluntarily in walker devices; the third was an analog of an experiential *deprivation* manipulation, in which an infant who was orthopedically handicapped, but otherwise normal, was tested longitudinally past the usual age of onset of crawling and again after the delayed acquisition of crawling; and the fourth was a *cross-sequential lag design* aimed at teasing apart the effects of age of onset of locomotion and of duration of locomotor experience on the infant's avoidance of crossing the deep or the shallow side of the cliff to the mother.

Experiment 1: HR Responses of Prelocomotor and Locomotor Infants

In the first study, a total of 92 infants, half locomoting for an average of 5 weeks, were tested at 7.3 months of age. Telemetered HR, facial expressions (taped from a camera under the deep side of the cliff), and the visual placing response were recorded. Each infant was lowered to each side of the cliff by a female experimenter, with the mother in another room.

As predicted from the work of Held and Hein (1963), locomotor infants showed evidence of wariness of heights, and prelocomotor infants did not. Only on deep trials did the HR of locomotor infants accelerate significantly from baselevels (by 5 beats/min), and differ significantly from the HR responses of prelocomotor infants. The HR responses of prelocomotor infants did not differ from baselevels on either the deep or shallow sides. Surprisingly, facial expressions did not differentiate testing conditions, perhaps because the descent minimized the opportunity to target these expressions to social figures.

In addition, every infant tested, regardless of locomotor status, showed visual placing responses on the shallow side, and no infant showed placing responses on the deep side of the cliff. Thus, all infants showed evidence for depth perception on the deep side, but only locomotor infants showed evidence of fear-related cardiac acceleration in response to heights.

Experiment 2: Acceleration of Locomotor Experience

Although correlated, the development of locomotion and the emergence of wariness of heights may be jointly determined by a third factor that brings about both changes. Disambiguation of this possibility required a means of providing "artificial" locomotor experience to infants who were not yet able to crawl. This manipulation was achieved by providing wheeled walkers to infants and testing them after their mothers had reported at least 32 hr of voluntary forward movement in the device.

Infants who received walkers were divided into two groups: prelocomotor walkers ($N = 9$M, 9F, Mean Age = 224 days, Walker Experience = 47 hr of voluntary forward movement) and locomotor walkers ($N = 9$M, 7F, Mean Age = 222 days, Walker Experience = 32 hr). The performance of infants in these two groups was compared with the performance of age-matched subjects, also divided into two groups: prelocomotor controls ($N = 9$M, 9F, Mean Age = 222 days) and locomotor controls ($N = 9$M, 7F, Mean Age = 222 days). The average duration of crawling experience was only 5 days in the locomotor walker and the locomotor control groups. All infants were tested using the same procedure as in the prior study. No shallow trials were administered in order to minimize subject loss due to the additional testing time required for such trials.

As revealed in Figure 1, the three groups of infants with any type of locomotor experience showed evidence of cardiac acceleration, whereas the prelocomotor control infants did not. It is noteworthy that all 16 infants in the locomotor walker group (who had a "double dosage" of locomotor experience consisting of walker training and some crawling) showed HR accelerations upon descent to the cliff. Planned comparisons revealed significant differences between (1) all walker infants and all controls, (2) all spontaneously locomoting infants and prelocomotor controls, and (3) prelocomotor walkers and prelocomotor controls. These findings show that the provision of "artificial" locomotor experience may facilitate or induce wariness of heights, even for infants who otherwise have little or no crawling experience. Locomotor experience thus appears to be an antecedent of the emergence of wariness.

Experiment 3: Deprivation of Locomotor Experience

Although Experiment 2 showed that training in locomotion accelerates the onset of wariness of heights, it is possible that this response would eventually develop even in the absence of locomotor experience. To deter-

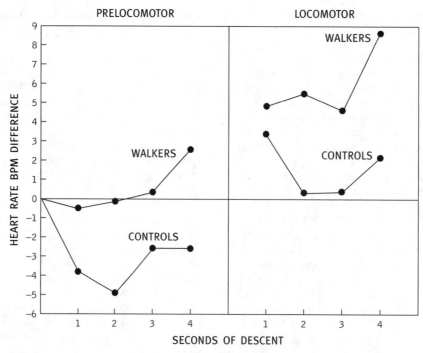

figure 1

Heart rate response while the infant is lowered toward the deep side of the visual cliff as a function of locomotor experience. The left panel contrasts the performance of preloco-motor infants with and without "artificial" walker experience. The right panel contrasts the performance of crawling infants with and without "artificial" walker experience. Heart rate is expressed as difference from baseline in beats/min.

mine whether the delayed acquisition of crawling precedes the delayed emergence of wariness of heights, we longitudinally tested an infant with a peripheral handicap to locomotion. This infant was neurologically normal and had a Bayley Developmental Quotient of 126, but was born with two congenitally dislocated hips. After an early operation, he was placed in a full body cast. The infant was tested on the visual cliff monthly between 6 and 10 months of age using the procedures described above. While the infant was in the cast, he showed no evidence of crawling. At 8.5 months of age (i.e., 1.5 months after the normative age of onset of locomotion), the cast was removed, and the infant began crawling soon afterward.

This infant showed no evidence of differential cardiac responsiveness on the deep versus shallow side of the cliff until 10 months of age, at which time his HR accelerated markedly on the deep side, and decelerated on the shallow. Although we cannot generalize from a single case study, these data provide further support for the role of self-produced locomotion as a facilitator or inducer of wariness of heights.

Experiment 4: Age of Onset of Locomotion versus Locomotor Experience

In the studies described so far, HR was used as an imperfect index of wariness. However, we felt that a study using behavioral avoidance was needed to confirm the link between locomotor experience and wariness of heights. We thus used the locomotor crossing test on the visual cliff, in which the infant is placed on the center of the cliff, and the mother is instructed to encourage the infant to cross to her over either the deep or the shallow side. In this study, we also assessed separately the effects of age of onset of crawling (early, normative, or late) and of duration of locomotor experience (11 or 41 days), as well as their interaction, using a longitudinal design.

The results of this study demonstrated a clear effect of locomotor experience independent of the age when self-produced locomotion first appeared. This effect of experience was evident with both nominal data (the proportion of infants who avoided descending onto the deep side of the cliff on the first test trial) and interval data (the latency to descend from the center board of the visual cliff onto the deep side on deep trials minus the latency to descend onto the shallow side on shallow trials). At whatever age the infant had begun to crawl, only 30% to 50% of infants avoided the deep side after 11 days of locomotor experience. However, after 41 days of locomotor experience, avoidance increased to 60% to 80% of infants. The latency data revealed a significant interaction of side of cliff with locomotor experience, but not a main effect of age, nor of the interaction of age with experience. The results of this study further suggest that locomotor experience paces the onset of wariness of heights.

Processes Underlying the Development of Wariness of Heights

The pattern of findings obtained in these four studies, taken together with the animal studies by Held and Hein (1963), demonstrates a consistent relation between locomotor experience and wariness of heights. We propose the following interpretations for our findings.

We believe that crawling initially is a goal in itself, with affect solely linked to the success or failure of implementing the act of moving. Locomotion is initially not context dependent, and infants show no wariness of heights because the goal of moving is not coordinated with other goals, including the avoidance of threats. However, as a result of locomotor experience, infants acquire a sense of both the efficacy and the limitations of their own actions. Locomotion stops being an end in itself, and begins to be goal corrected and coordinated with the environmental surround. As a result, infants begin to show wariness of heights once locomotion becomes context dependent (cf. Bertenthal & Campos, 1990).

The context-dependency of the infants' actions may come about from falling and near-falling experiences that locomotion generates. Near-falls are particularly important because they are frequent, they elicit powerful emotional signals from the parent, and they set the stage for long-term retention of negative affect in such contexts.

There is still another means by which the infant can acquire a sense of wariness of depth with locomotion. While the infant moves about voluntarily, visual information specifying self-movement becomes more highly correlated with vestibular information specifying the same amount of self-movement (Bertenthal & Campos, 1990). Once expectancies related to the cor-

relation of visual and vestibular information are formed, being lowered toward the deep side of the cliff creates a violation of the expected correlation. This violation results from the absence of visible texture near the infant when lowered toward the deep side of the cliff, relative to the shallow side. As a consequence, angular acceleration is not detected by the visual system, whereas it is detected by the vestibular system. This violation of expectation results in distress proportional to the magnitude of the violation. A test of this interpretation requires assessment of the establishment of visual-vestibular coordination as a function of locomotor experience and confirmation that wariness occurs in contexts that violate visual-vestibular coordination.

Locomotor Experience and Other Emotional Changes

The consequences of the development of self-produced locomotion for emotional development extend far beyond the domain of wariness of heights. Indeed, the onset of locomotion generates an entirely different emotional climate in the family. For instance, as psychoanalytic theories predict (e.g., Mahler, Pine, & Bergman, 1975), the onset of locomotion brings about a burgeoning of both positive and negative affect—positive affect because of the child's new levels of self-efficacy; negative affect because of the increases in frustration resulting from thwarting of the child's goals and because of the affective resonance that comes from increased parental expressions of prohibition (Campos, Kermoian, & Zumbahlen, in press). Locomotion is also crucial for the development of attachment (Ainsworth, Blehar, Waters, & Wall, 1978; Bowlby, 1973), because it makes physical proximity to the caregiver possible. With the formation of specific attachments, locomotion increases in significance as the child becomes better able to move independently toward novel and potentially frightening environments. Infants are also more sensitive to the location of the parent, more likely to show distress upon separation, and more likely to look to the parent in ambiguous situations.

Locomotion also brings about emotional changes in the parents. These changes include the increased pride (and sometimes sorrow) that the parents experience in their child's new mobility and independence and the new levels of anger parents direct at the baby when the baby begins to encounter forbidden objects. It seems clear from the findings obtained in this line of research that new levels of functioning in one behavioral domain can generate experiences that profoundly affect other developmental domains, including affective, social, cognitive, and sensorimotor ones (Kermoian & Campos, 1988). We thus propose that theoretical orientations like probabilistic epigenesis provide a novel, heuristic, and timely perspective for the study of emotional development.

REFERENCES

Ainsworth, M. D. S., Blehar, M., Waters, E., & Wall, S. (1978). *Patterns of attachment.* Hillsdale, NJ: Erlbaum.

Bertenthal, B., & Campos, J. J. (1990). A systems approach to the organizing effects of self-produced locomotion during infancy. In C. Rovee-Collier & L. P. Lipsitt (Eds.), *Advances in infancy research* (Vol. 6, pp. 1–60). Norwood, NJ: Ablex.

Bowlby, J. (1973). *Attachment and loss: Vol. 2. Separation.* New York: Basic Books.

Bridges, K. M. (1932). Emotional development in early infancy. *Child Development, 3,* 324–341.

Campos, J. J., Emde, R. N., Gaensbauer, T. J., & Henderson, C. (1975). Cardiac and behavioral interrelationships in the reactions of infants to strangers. *Developmental Psychology, 11,* 589–601.

Campos, J. J., Hiatt, S., Ramsay, D., Henderson, C., & Svejda, M. (1978). The emergence of fear of heights. In M. Lewis & L. Rosenblum (Eds.), *The development of affect* (pp. 149–182). New York: Plenum Press.

Campos, J. J., Kermoian, R., & Zumbahlen, R. M. (In press). In N. Eisenberg (Ed.), *New directions for child development.* San Francisco: Jossey-Bass.

Emde, R. N., Gaensbauer, T. J., & Harmon, R. J. (1976). Emotional expression in infancy: A biobehavioral study. *Psychological Issues* (Vol. 10, No. 37). New York: International Universities Press.

Gottlieb, G. (1983). The psychobiological approach to developmental issues. In P. Mussen (Ed.), *Handbook of child psychology: Vol. II. Infancy and developmental psychobiology* (4th ed.) (pp. 1–26). New York: Wiley.

Gottlieb, G. (1991). Experiential canalization of behavioral development: Theory. *Developmental Psychology, 27,* 4–13.

Graham, F. K., & Clifton, R. K. (1966). Heartrate change as a component of the orienting response. *Psychological Bulletin, 65,* 305–320.

Held, R. & Hein, A. (1963). Movement-produced stimulation in the development of visually guided behavior. *Journal of Comparative and Physiological Psychology, 56,* 872–876.

Kagan, J., Kearsley, R., & Zelazo, P. R. (1978). *Infancy: Its place in human development.* Cambridge, MA: Harvard University Press.

Kermoian, R., & Campos, J. J. (1988). Locomotor experience: A facilitator of spatial cognitive development. *Child Development, 59,* 908–917.

Mahler, M., Pine, F., & Bergman, A. (1975). *The psychological birth of the human infant.* New York: Basic Books.

Scarr, S., & Salapatek, P. (1970). Patterns of fear development during infancy. *Merrill-Palmer Quarterly, 16,* 53–90.

Sroufe, L. A. (1979). Socioemotional development. In J. Osofsky (Ed.), *Handbook of infant development* (pp. 462–516). New York: Wiley.

Walk, R. (1966). The development of depth perception in animals and human infants. *Monographs of the Society for Research in Child Development, 31* (Whole No. 5).

Walk, R., & Gibson, E. (1961). A comparative and analytical study of visual depth perception. *Psychological Monographs, 75* (15, Whole No. 5).

Walters, C. (1981). Development of the visual placing response in the human infant. *Journal of Experimental Child Psychology, 32,* 313–329.

Questions

1. How do developmental acquisitions, like crawling, serve to "bootstrap" further development?
2. How is the development of wariness of heights in human infants like the development of wariness of heights that was observed in kittens who were reared in the dark?
3. What is the visual cliff, and how is it used to study the development of depth perception and fear of heights in infants?
4. Why was it important that Campos and his colleagues use a research design in which the age of the infants was held constant?
5. If you were caring for two 6-month-olds, one who had been using a walker for a month or more and one who had no experience with walkers, would you have different concerns about keeping an eye on them?
6. What do you think might be the connection between infants' wariness of heights and the security of attachment between infants and their mothers?

PART III

Early Childhood

In much of the early research on child development, the age period from 2 to 5 years was largely ignored. One reason for this neglect was that many of the issues that captivated researchers, such as logical reasoning and peer relations, flourish later, in middle childhood. Another reason was that psychologists were more interested in studying the behaviors and abilities of older, school-age children, because their findings could be useful for designing educational settings and curricula.

Recent years have seen a shift in interests, with a steep increase in research on early childhood. This shift was triggered by a new emphasis on studying development in the period before major changes appear. Psychologists reasoned that if particular competencies are already in place in school-age children, their foundations must have been laid in early childhood. In keeping with this view, researchers began studying how the intellectual and social skills that are prevalent in the school years make their initial appearance in the early years of childhood.

The articles in this section describe some of the developmental changes of early childhood, including cognitive changes (Judy S. DeLoache, Kevin F. Miller, and Karl S. Rosengren; Penelope G. Vinden); patterns of family interaction that influence moral development (Peggy J. Miller, Angela R. Wiley, Heidi Fung, and Chung-Hui Liang); and changes in the social behaviors of young children (Albert Bandura, Dorothea Ross, and Sheila A. Ross; JoAnn Farver and Carollee Howes; Eleanor E. Maccoby). Together, these articles describe the developmental changes that help set the stage for the child's entry into the social and intellectual world of middle childhood.

19

The Credible Shrinking Room: Very Young Children's Performance with Symbolic and Nonsymbolic Relations

Judy S. DeLoache • Kevin F. Miller • Karl S. Rosengren

A unique and important characteristic of human intelligence is the ability to create, understand, and manipulate symbols. A symbol is an arbitrary arrangement of things—letters, numbers, images, or objects—that refers to something else. Because symbols are arbitrary, we must learn what a particular symbol refers to in order to make sense of it and use it effectively. Although our brain is capable of processing symbols, we are not born with knowledge about the symbols we encounter in everyday life. Rather, we develop knowledge of these symbols over the course of early childhood.

Developmental psychologists Judy DeLoache, Kevin Miller, and Karl Rosengren have studied children's skill at understanding symbols by asking 2½-year-olds to find a toy in a room after seeing a tiny version of the toy hidden in a scale model of the room. In the study described in the following article, the researchers used a clever manipulation that allowed them to test the dual representation hypothesis, a prominent view of early symbolic understanding. This hypothesis asserts that young children have difficulty understanding symbols because this understanding requires them to deal simultaneously with two levels of representation: the symbol itself and the object to which it refers. DeLoache and colleagues reason that this complex understanding may emerge gradually over the period of early childhood.

The results of this study may surprise you. Because our understanding of symbols like those studied in this research emerges early in life, few of us remember what it was like to think like the young children in this study. However, the findings reported in this article have been replicated by other researchers. The cognitive change involved here is important for later development, in that much of learning, especially in school, relies on the ability to understand and use symbols.

Becoming a proficient symbol user is a universal developmental task in the first years of life, but detecting and mentally representing symbolic relations can be quite challenging for young children. To test the extent to which symbolic reasoning per se is problematic, we compared the performance of 2½-year-olds in symbolic and nonsymbolic versions of a search task. The children had to use their knowledge of the location of a toy hidden in a room to draw an inference about where to find a miniature toy in a scale model of the room (and

Reprinted with permission from DeLoache, J. S., Miller, K. F., & Rosengren, K. S., "The Credible Shrinking Room: Very Young Children's Performance With Symbolic and Nonsymbolic Relations", *Psychological Science, 8*, 308-313, © 1997 Blackwell Publishers.

Acknowledgments The research reported here was supported in part by Grant HD-25271 from the National Institute of Child Health and Human Development. This article was completed while the first author was a fellow at the Center for Advanced Study in the Behavioral Sciences with financial support from the John D. and Catherine T. MacArthur Foundation. Grant No. 95-32005-0. We thank R. Baillargeon and G. Clore for helpful comments on this article and K. Anderson and N. Bryant for assistance in the research.

163

vice versa). Children in the nonsymbolic condition believed a shrinking machine had caused the room to become the model. They were much more successful than children in the symbolic condition, for whom the model served as a symbol of the room. The results provide strong support for the role of dual representation in symbol understanding and use.

Nothing so distinguishes humans from other species as the creative and flexible use of symbols. Abstract concepts, reasoning, scientific discovery, and other uniquely human endeavors are made possible by language and a panoply of symbolic tools, including numbers, alphabets, maps, models, and various notational systems. The universality and centrality of symbolic representation in human cognition make understanding its origins a key developmental issue.

How do children master the symbolic artifacts of their culture? They must start by recognizing that certain entities should be interpreted and responded to primarily in terms of what they stand for—their referents—rather than themselves. This is obviously a major challenge in the case of completely arbitrary symbol–referent relations. Nothing about the appearance of a numeral or a printed word suggests what it represents. Hence, it is not surprising that children have to be explicitly taught and only gradually learn the abstract relations between numerals and quantities and between printed and spoken words.

In contrast, it is generally taken for granted that highly iconic symbols (i.e., symbols that resemble their referents) are understood easily and early. Recent research, however, reveals that this assumption is unwarranted: A high degree of similarity between a symbol and its referent is no guarantee that young children will appreciate the symbol–referent relation. For example, several studies have established that very young children often fail to detect the relation between a realistic scale model and the room it represents (DeLoache, 1987, 1989, 1991; DeLoache, Kolstad, & Anderson, 1991; Dow & Pick, 1992; Marzolf & DeLoache, 1994; Uttal, Schreiber, & DeLoache, 1995). Most 2½-year-old children give no evidence of understanding that the model and room are related or that what they know about one space can be used to draw an inference about the other. Children just a few months older (3-year-olds) readily exploit this symbol–referent relation.

Why is a highly iconic relation that is so transparent to older children and adults so opaque to very young children? Many theorists have characterized symbols as possessing dual reality (Gibson, 1979; Gregory, 1970; Potter, 1979). According to the *dual representation* hypothesis (DeLoache, 1987, 1991, 1995a, 1995b), it is the double nature of symbols that poses particular difficulty for young children. To understand and use a symbol, one must mentally represent both the symbol itself and its relation to the referent. Thus, one must achieve dual representation, thinking about the concrete features of the symbol and the abstract relation between it and something else at the same time.

According to this hypothesis, the more salient the concrete aspects of a symbol are, the more difficult it is to appreciate its abstract, symbolic nature. Thus, young children's attention to a scale model as an interesting and attractive object makes it difficult for them to simultaneously think about its relation to something else. The philosopher Langer (1942) seemed to have something similar in mind when she noted that a peach would make a poor symbol because people care too much about the peach itself.

The research reported here constitutes an extremely stringent test of this hypothesis. We compared 2½-year-old children's performance in two tasks in which they had to detect and exploit the relation between a scale model and a room. In both tasks, children had to use their knowledge of where a toy was hidden in one space to infer where to find an analogous toy in the other space. In one task, there was a symbolic relation between the model and the room, whereas the other task involved a nonsymbolic relation between the same two entities. If achieving dual representation is a key obstacle in early symbolic reasoning, then performance should be superior in the nonsymbolic task, which does not require dual representation. We made this prediction even though the nonsymbolic task involved convincing children of an impossible scenario–that a machine could cause the room to shrink into the model.

Our reasoning was that if a child believes that the model is the large room after having been shrunk, then there is no symbolic relation between the two spaces; to the credulous child, the model simply *is* the room (albeit dramatically different in size). Thus, if the room is shrunk after a large toy has been hidden in it, finding a miniature toy in the model is, from the child's perspective, primarily a memory task. Dual representation is not necessary. Note that in both tasks, children must use the correspondence between the hiding places in the two spaces; their memory representation of the toy hidden behind a full-sized chair in the room must lead them to search behind the miniature chair in the model. In the symbolic task, the child knows there are two chairs, so he or she must represent the relation between them. In the nonsymbolic task, however, the child thinks there is only one chair. Superior performance in the nonsymbolic, shrinking-room task would thus provide strong support for the dual representation hypothesis.

Method

Subjects

The subjects included 15 children (29–32 months, $M =$ 30 months) in the symbolic condition and 17 (29–33 months, $M =$ 31 months) in the nonsymbolic condition. Names of potential subjects came from files of birth announcements in the local newspaper, and the majority of the children were middle class and white.

Materials

The same two spaces were used for both tasks. The larger space was a tentlike portable room (1.9 m × 2.5 m) constructed of plastic pipes supporting white fabric walls (1.9 m high) with a brown cardboard floor. The smaller space was a scale model (48.3 cm × 62.9 cm, with walls 38.1 cm high) of the portable room, constructed of the same materials. The room held several items of furniture (fabric-covered chair, dresser, set of shelves, basket, etc.); the model contained miniature versions of these items that were highly similar in appearance (e.g., same fabric on the chairs) to their larger counterparts. The relative size and spatial arrangement of the objects were the same in the two spaces, and the model was always in the same spatial orientation as the room. This model and room have been used in several previous studies (DeLoache et al., 1991; Marzolf & DeLoache, 1994). Figures 1a, 1b, and 1c show the arrangement of the room and model for the two tasks.

Procedure

Symbolic task In this task (which was very similar to that used in the previously cited model studies), each child was given an orientation that began with the introduction of two troll dolls referred to as "Big Terry" (21 cm high) and "Little Terry" (5 cm). The correspondence between the room (described as "Big Terry's room") and the model ("Little Terry's room") and between all of the objects within them was fully and explicitly described and demonstrated by the experimenter.

On the first of four experimental trials, the child watched as the experimenter hid the larger doll somewhere in the room (e.g., behind the chair, in the basket). The child was told that the smaller toy would be hidden in the "same place" in the model. The child waited (10–15 s) as the miniature toy was hidden in the model in the adjoining area (Fig. 1a) and was then encouraged to retrieve it. The experimenter reminded the child of the corresponding locations of the two toys: "Can you find Little Terry? Remember, he's hiding in the same place in his little room where Big Terry's hiding in his big room." If the child failed to find the toy on his or her first search, increasingly direct prompts were given until the child retrieved the toy. On the second trial, the hiding event occurred in the model instead of the room. Thus, the child watched as the miniature toy was hidden in the model, and he or she was then asked to retrieve the larger toy from the room. The space in which the hiding event occurred again alternated for the third and fourth trials.[1]

To succeed, children in the symbolic task had to realize that the room and model were related. If they did, they could figure out where to search for the target toy, even though they had not actually seen it being hidden. If they failed to represent the model–room relation, they had no way of knowing where to search. Based on numerous previous studies with this basic task, we expected a low level of performance from our 2½-year-old subjects (DeLoache, 1987, 1989, 1991; DeLoache et al., 1991; Dow & Pick, 1992; Marzolf & DeLoache, 1994).

Nonsymbolic task The initial arrangement for this task is shown in Figure 1b. In the orientation to the task, each child was introduced to "Terry" (the larger troll doll) and to "Terry's room" (the portable room). In the ensuing practice trial, the child watched as the experimenter hid the troll in the room and then waited for a count of 5 before searching. The children always succeeded in this simple memory-based retrieval (100% correct).

Next, the child was shown a "machine that can shrink toys" (actually an oscilloscope with flashing green lights—the solid rectangle in Fig. 1b). The troll doll was placed in front of it, a switch was turned on, and the child and experimenter retreated to an adjoining area and closed the door to the lab. During a delay of approximately 10 s, the child heard a tape of computer-generated tones, which were described as the "sounds the shrinking machine makes while it's working." When the sounds stopped, the child returned to the lab to find a miniature troll (5 cm high) in the

---

1. There were two major differences between the current symbolic task and the standard model task used in previous research: First, the hiding event alternated from trial to trial between model and room. In the standard task, it always occurs in one space or the other for a given child. In studies in which half the children see the hiding event in the room and the other half in the model, there has never been any difference in performance as a function of this variable. Second, in the standard task, children always perform two retrievals: For example, after seeing the toy being hidden in the model, they first search for the larger toy in the room and then return to the model to retrieve the toy they originally observed being hidden. However, the performance of the 2½-year-olds tested in the current study did not differ from that of a group tested in the standard model task using all the same materials.

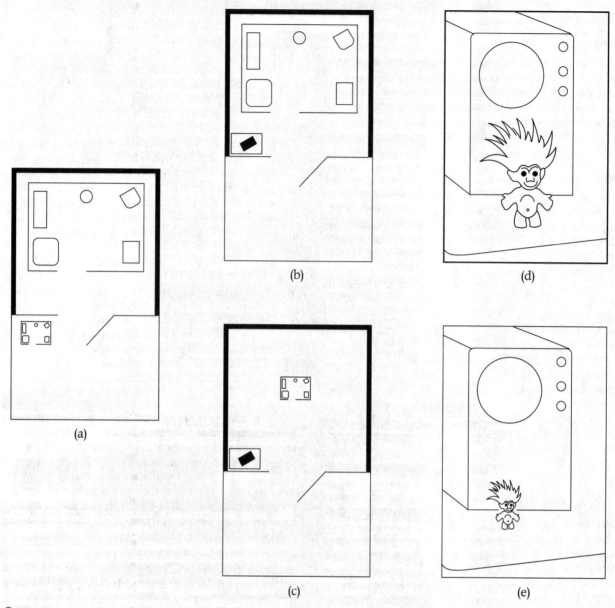

figure 1

Physical arrangements for the symbolic and nonsymbolic tasks. For the symbolic task (a), the portable room was located in a large lab, surrounded on three sides by opaque curtains (represented by heavy lines); the model was located in an adjoining area. The nonsymbolic task began with the arrangement shown in (b); before the first shrinking event, the portable room was located in the lab, partially surrounded by curtains, just as it was for the symbolic task. The only difference was the presence of the shrinking machine, represented by the dark rectangle, sitting on a table. In the aftermath of the shrinking event, depicted in (c), the model sat in the middle of the area previously occupied by the portable room. The sketches in (d) and (e) show Terry the Troll before and after the demonstration shrinking event.

place the larger one had previously occupied. Figures 1d and 1e depict the shrinking machine with the troll before and after the shrinking event.

The child was then told that the machine could also make the troll get larger, and the process was repeated in reverse, ending with the large troll again

standing in front of the machine. For the final part of the orientation, the same shrinking and enlarging demonstrations were performed with "Terry's room." The shrinking machine was aimed at the room, and the child and experimenter waited in the adjoining area, listening to a longer (38-s) tape of the same computer sounds. When the door to the lab was opened, the scale model was revealed sitting in the middle of the area previously occupied by the room (Fig. 1c). The sight of the small model in place of the large room was very dramatic. The process was then repeated in reverse, resulting in the room replacing the model.[2]

On the first of four trials, the child watched as the larger doll was hidden in the room (the same hiding places were used as in the symbolic task), and the child was instructed to remember where it was hidden. After a 38-s delay, again spent waiting in the adjoining area listening to the sounds of the shrinking machine, the child entered the lab, where the model had replaced the portable room. The child was encouraged to find the doll: "Can you find Terry? Remember where we hid him? That's where he's hiding." The miniature troll was, of course, hidden in the model in the place that corresponded to where the child had seen the larger troll being hidden in the room. On two of the four trials, the room and large troll were shrunk, alternating with two trials in which the model and miniature troll were enlarged. A different hiding place was used on each trial.

To assess the extent to which the children accepted our shrinking-machine scenario, the experimenter and each child's accompanying parent independently rated the child on a 5-point scale, with 1 indicating that the child "firmly believed" that the machine really did shrink the objects and 5 indicating that the child "firmly did not believe" it. The average ratings were 1.1 and 1.5 for the experimenter and parents, respectively. There was only one child that the observing adults judged to be at all skeptical. The children generally reacted to the shrinking events with interest and pleasure, but not astonishment. Several children made revealing comments, such as "I want to make it big [little] again," and, while listening to the sounds of the shrinking machine, "It's working to make it big." In addition, when the children later told other family members about the session, they typically talked about the troll or the room "getting little." None ever described the situation as pretend or as a trick. We therefore feel confident that our subjects believed that the model and room were actually the same thing, which means that the shrinking-room task was, as intended, nonsymbolic

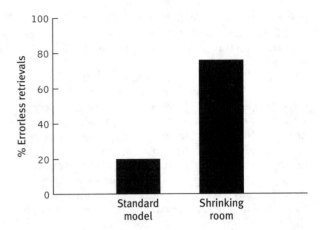

figure 2
Mean number of errorless retrievals (searching first in the correct location) in the symbolic and nonsymbolic tasks.

(involving an identity rather than a symbolic relation).[3]

We wish to emphasize that it is unlikely that the a priori prediction of superior performance in the nonsymbolic task would be made on any basis other than the dual representation hypothesis. Indeed, various aspects of the procedures would lead to the opposite expectation. For example, getting and keeping toddlers motivated in experimental situations is always a challenge; and the shrinking-room task was more complicated, required more verbal communication, and took longer than the standard symbolic task. In addition, the delay between the hiding event and the opportunity to search for the toy was substantially longer in the shrinking-room task (ca. 50–60 s) than in the standard symbolic task (ca. 10–15 s). Delays between hiding and retrieval are known to cause the performance of even older children to deteriorate dramatically in the standard model task (Uttal et al., 1995).

Results

The critical question was whether performance in the nonsymbolic (shrinking-room) condition would be su-

---

2. An elaborate scenario supported the shrinking and enlarging events. When the child first saw the artificial room, it was surrounded on three sides by black curtains, which were visible only on the sides in front of the portable room (Fig. 1b). For each shrinking event, as soon as the child had left the lab, one assistant turned on a tape recorder to begin the shrinking-machine sounds (thereby concealing any noises made in the lab). Two other assistants pulled the artificial room behind the curtains, and the first placed the model, with the miniature troll in the appropriate position, in the center of the space formerly occupied by the room. In the enlarging events, the model was replaced by the room.

3. The parents of all the participants in this study were fully informed of the procedures to be followed, and a parent was present throughout each experimental session. The children's assent was always obtained before the sessions began. After the completion of their sessions, the children in the nonsymbolic (shrinking-room) condition were debriefed: They were shown the two dolls and the model and room together, and the experimenter explained that the machine did not really shrink or enlarge them.

perior to performance in the symbolic (model) condition. Figure 2 shows the mean number of errorless retrievals (searching first at the correct location) achieved in the two tasks.

The children in the symbolic task achieved a mean of only 0.8 errorless retrievals over four trials ($SE = 0.2$), a rate not different from chance. (We conservatively estimated chance at 25%, based on our use of four hiding places; however, it is actually lower because there are additional possible hiding places.) Individual performance in this task was similarly poor: Six of the 15 children never found the toy, and 6 retrieved it only once. No child succeeded on more than two of the four trials. These children understood that they were supposed to search for a hidden toy on each trial, and they were happy to do so, but they apparently failed to realize that their knowledge of one space could be applied to the other.

The poor performance of the children in the symbolic task (19%) is exactly what would be expected from previous model studies. In research in our own and other labs using a variety of different models and rooms, 2½-year-olds reliably average around 20% successful retrievals.

In contrast, children in the nonsymbolic task were very successful. Performance in the nonsymbolic (shrinking-room) condition was well above chance– 3.1 errorless retrievals ($SE = 0.2$)–and significantly better than the performance of the children in the symbolic condition. Twelve of the 17 subjects achieved three or more errorless retrievals, and 7 of those had perfect scores. The difference between the two tasks was the only significant result in a 2 (task) × 2 (gender) analysis of variance, $F(1, 28) = 51.5$, $p < .0001$. Performance did not differ on trials in which the hiding event occurred in the room and the child searched in the model versus trials in which the hiding and search spaces were the reverse.

The main result of this study has been replicated, both in an additional study with 2½-year-olds and in two studies in which the same logic was applied to a different age group. Using two different, more difficult versions of the model task, we found the same pattern of results with 3-year-olds as occurred with the 2½-year-olds in the present study–significantly better performance in the nonsymbolic, shrinking-room version than in the symbolic model task (DeLoache, 1995a; Marzolf, 1994).

Discussion

We conclude that a major challenge to detecting and using symbolic relations stems from their inherent dual reality and the necessity of achieving dual representation (DeLoache, 1987, 1995a, 1995b). The model task was more difficult than the shrinking-room task because the

former required dual representation, whereas the latter eliminated the need for it. The research reported here provides strong support for a theoretical account of early symbol understanding and use in which young children's ability to use symbols is considered to be limited by several factors, a key one being the difficulty of achieving dual representation (DeLoache, 1995a, 1995b). Relatively limited information processing capacity makes it difficult for younger children to keep two representations active at the same time, and limited cognitive flexibility makes it especially difficult for them to mentally represent a single entity in two different ways.

The study reported here provides especially strong support against criticism of this theoretical account of early symbol use. It has been claimed that the use of a symbol such as a scale model requires nothing more than simply detecting some kind of correspondence between the symbol and referent (Blades & Spencer, 1994; Lillard, 1993; Perner, 1991). One claim is that the child succeeds on each trial by noticing that the current hiding place of the miniature toy corresponds to the full-sized hiding place of the larger toy, without ever appreciating the higher level relation between the two spaces.

The simple correspondence view cannot explain the current results. For one thing, it offers no account of how children's performance depends on the kind of relation that must be represented. In both tasks, corresponding items in the two spaces must be mentally linked; memory for the object concealing the original toy must support a search at the corresponding object. The challenge in the nonsymbolic task is simply to recognize that object in its new form. The challenge in the symbolic task is to represent the relation between that object and the other one it stands for.

Furthermore, simply detecting the correspondence between matching items does not support successful performance in the symbolic task. In a recent study (DeLoache, 1995a), 2½-year-old children readily matched the items in the room to the corresponding items in the model, yet still failed the subsequent standard model task. Establishing object correspondences is thus necessary but not sufficient for reasoning from one space to the other. Although the simple correspondence account has the appearance of parsimony, because it posits a lower level explanation than dual representation, it cannot account for results presented here and elsewhere in support of dual representation (DeLoache, 1991; Marzolf & DeLoache, 1994).

At the most general level, the research reported here indicates that it is the nature of a child's mental representation of the relation between two entities that governs the child's ability to reason from one to the other. Very young children can reason successfully based on an identity relation, even when it results from the complex and novel scenario of a shrinking machine. They fail to appreciate a symbolic relation between the same two entities, even though it is explained and demonstrated. Despite the importance and universality of symbolization, very young children are quite conservative when it comes to interpreting novel objects as symbols.

The dual representation hypothesis, which received strong support from the study reported here, has important practical implications. For example, it calls into question the assumption commonly made by educators that children will readily comprehend the meaning of manipulables—concrete objects used to instantiate abstract mathematical concepts (Uttal, Scudder, & DeLoache, 1997). One must take care to ensure that children appreciate the relation between, for example, the size of blocks and numerical quantities before using the blocks for teaching purposes. Similar doubt is cast on the widespread practice of using anatomically explicit dolls to interview young children in child-abuse investigations. Young children's difficulty with dual representation suggests that the relevant self–doll relation may not be clear to them; if so, using dolls may not be helpful and might even be counterproductive. Recent research has supported this conjecture: Several studies have reported no advantage to using dolls to interview 3-year-old children about events they have experienced (Bruck, Ceci, Francoeur, & Renick, 1995; DeLoache, Anderson, & Smith, 1995; DeLoache & Marzolf, 1995; Goodman & Aman, 1990; Gordon et al., 1993).

One other aspect of the results reported here merits attention. The 2½-year-old children had no difficulty dealing with the size transformations supposedly effected by the shrinking machine. This finding is consistent with research showing that very young children represent and rely on geometric features of a space (Hermer & Spelke, 1994). The children's ability to mentally scale the two spaces in the present research may have been assisted by the fact that the size transformations preserved the geometric properties of the original space, including its overall shape, the relative sizes and positions of the objects, and the distances among them.

Spatial representations other than scale models also pose problems for young children. Only with difficulty can 3-year-olds use a simple map to locate a hidden object, and their ability to do so is easily disrupted (Bluestein & Acredolo, 1979). Older preschool children often fail to interpret aerial photographs consistently (Liben & Downs, 1992); they may, for example, describe one feature of an aerial photo correctly as a river but another as a piece of cheese. Thus, figuring out the nature and use of spatial symbols is a persistent challenge for young children.

The current study, along with other research on the early understanding and use of symbols, makes it clear that one can never assume that young children will detect a given symbol–referent relation, no matter how transparent that relation seems to adults or older children. Young children may perceive and form a meaningful interpretation of both the symbol and the entity it stands for without representing the relation between them.

REFERENCES

Blades, M., & Spencer, C. (1994). The development of children's ability to use spatial representations. In H. Reese (Ed.), *Advances in child development and behavior* (Vol. 25, pp. 157–199). New York: Academic Press.

Bluestein, N., & Acredolo, L. (1979). Developmental change in map reading skills. *Child Development, 50,* 691–697.

Bruck, M., Ceci, S. J., Francoeur, E., & Renick, A. (1995). Anatomically detailed dolls do not facilitate preschoolers, reports of a pediatric examination involving genital touching. *Journal of Experimental Psychology: Applied, 1,* 95–109.

DeLoache, J. S. (1987). Rapid change in the symbolic functioning of very young children. *Science, 238,* 1556–1557.

DeLoache, J. S. (1989). Young children's understanding of the correspondence between a scale model and a larger space. *Cognitive Development, 4,* 121–139.

DeLoache, J. S. (1991). Symbolic functioning in very young children: Understanding of pictures and models. *Child Development, 62,* 736–752.

DeLoache, J. S. (1995a). Early symbolic understanding and use. In D. Medin (Ed.), *The psychology of learning and motivation* (Vol. 33, pp. 65–114). New York: Academic Press.

DeLoache, J. S. (1995b). Early understanding and use of symbols. *Current Directions in Psychological Science, 4,* 109–113.

DeLoache, J. S., Anderson, K., & Smith, C. M. (1995, April). *Interviewing children about real-life events.* Paper presented at the annual meeting of the Society for Research in Child Development, Indianapolis, IN.

DeLoache, J. S., Kolstad, D. V., & Anderson, K. N. (1991). Physical similarity and young children's understanding of scale models. *Child Development, 62,* 111–126.

DeLoache, J. S., & Marzolf, D. P. (1995). The use of dolls to interview young children. *Journal of Experimental Child Psychology, 60,* 155–173.

Dow, G. A., & Pick, H. L. (1992). Young children's use of models and photographs as spatial representations. *Cognitive Development, 7,* 351–363.

Gibson, J. J. (1979). *The ecological approach to visual perception.* Boston: Houghton Mifflin.

Goodman, G. S., & Aman, C. (1990). Children's use of anatomically detailed dolls to recount an event. *Child Development, 61,* 1859–1871.

Gordon, B. N., Ornstein, P. A., Nida, R. E., Follmer, A., Crenshaw, M. C., & Albert, G. (1993). Does the use of dolls facilitate children's memory of visits to the doctor? *Applied Cognitive Psychology, 7,* 459–474.

Gregory, R. L. (1970). *The intelligent eye.* New York: McGraw-Hill.

Hermer, L., & Spelke, E. (1994). A geometric process for spatial reorientation in young children. *Nature, 370,* 57–69.

Langer, S. K. (1942). *Philosophy in a new key*. Cambridge, MA: Harvard University Press.

Liben, L. L., & Downs, R. M. (1992). Developing an understanding of graphic representations in children and adults: The case of GEO-Graphics. *Cognitive Development, 7*, 331–349.

Lillard, A. S. (1993). Pretend play skills and the child's theory of mind. *Child Development, 64*, 348–371.

Marzolf, D. P. (1994, April). *Representing and mapping relations in a symbolic task*. Paper presented at the International Conference on Infant Studies, Paris.

Marzolf, D. P., & DeLoache, J. S. (1994). Transfer in young children's understanding of spatial representations. *Child Development, 64*, 1–15.

Perner, J. (1991). *Understanding the representational mind*. Cambridge, MA: Bradford Books/MIT Press.

Potter, M. C. (1979). Mundane symbolism: The relations among objects, names, and ideas. In N. R. Smith & M. B. Franklin (Eds.), *Symbolic functioning in childhood* (pp. 41–65). Hillsdale, NJ: Erlbaum.

Uttal, D. H., Schreiber, J. C., & DeLoache, J. S. (1995). Waiting to use a symbol: The effects of delay on children's use of models. *Child Development, 66*, 1875–1891.

Uttal, D. H., Scudder, K. V., & DeLoache, J. S. (1997). Manipulatives as symbols: A new perspective on the use of concrete objects to teach mathematics. *Journal of Applied Developmental Psychology, 18*, 37–54.

Questions

1. What are symbols, and why are they difficult for young children to understand?
2. What effect did shrinking the room have on the performance of the 2½-year-olds in this study?
3. Do you agree with the reasoning that if children believe that the model is actually a large room that has been shrunk, they do not need symbolic representation to find the toy? Why or why not?
4. What developmental changes do the authors suggest may explain the increase in understanding of symbols that occurs over early childhood?
5. What do you think this study suggests about young children's interest in and understanding of toys that are exact models or replicas of large-scale objects?
6. What implications do these findings have for the use of anatomically correct dolls in interviewing young children in legal cases involving sexual abuse?

20 Understanding Minds and Evidence for Belief: A Study of Mofu Children in Cameroon

Penelope G. Vinden

There has been much interest among researchers on when and how children come to understand the mind and how it works. This area of study, known as theory of mind, covers topics ranging from the ability to distinguish appearance from reality to children's understanding of dreams and desires. An especially interesting question concerns the relation between a person's belief and the evidence that is used to support this belief.

Research reveals that much changes from age 2 to age 6 in children's understanding of the mind, and this change is assumed to be universal. However, most of this research has been conducted with children in western, industrialized communities in which discussions about the mind and its uses are commonplace. Privy to conversations about the mind from an early age, children in western communities are also encouraged by parents to participate in these conversations. Parents often ask children what they are thinking about, what other people believe, and about all kinds of mentalistic constructs like intentions and imaginary friends. School, a setting where ample discussion about and reference to the mind occurs, may also contribute to the development of this understanding.

To investigate the universality of children's understanding of mind, Penelope Vinden studied children ranging from 4 to 11 years of age in the Mofu community of Cameroon in West Africa. Some children in the study had attended school and some had not. For this community, the researcher adapted an experimental procedure that focused on children's understanding of their own beliefs and the beliefs of another person. This research was time-consuming and difficult to conduct. However, it provides a window into a developmental process that only examination of children in very different sociocultural circumstances can provide. As such, this research demonstrates the utility of cross-cultural investigation for advancing developmental theory.

This study explores young children's understanding of mind and their ability to give evidence for belief. Mofu children of Cameroon were chosen as participants as they provide a unique opportunity to compare the development of an understanding of minds and evidence in schooled and nonschooled populations. A series of standard theory-of-mind tasks were given to 154 children, as well as a novel evidence task. Results suggest that children who have attended school develop an understanding of minds earlier than nonattenders. School attenders did not show superior understanding of evidence for false belief. They did perform better than the nonschooled sample, however, on a question concerning evidence for a subsequent true belief, although performance on this question for both groups was poor.

Reproduced with permission from Vinden, P. G., "Understanding Minds and Evidence for Belief: A Study of Mofu Children in Cameroon", *International Journal of Behavioral Development, 26,* 445–452, © 2002, by permission of Sage Publications Ltd.

Acknowledgments: The author wishes to thank the members of the Cameroon branch of the Summer Institute of Linguistics, and especially the Pohlig family, for hosting me and providing invaluable assistance during the time the research was conducted. Gratitude is also due to Kenneth Hollingsworth, Jean Baptiste, Jean Makba, and Ferdinand for the generous offer of their time and talents in testing, and also to the children of Ecole de Mowo, Dimeo, and Katmsa. I am also grateful to the editor and two anonymous reviewers for their constructive comments. This research was funded in part by a block transfer grant to the Ontario Institute for Studies in Education.

This study was designed to explore children's understanding of the difference between causes of things in the world and evidence for mental states such as beliefs. It seeks to uncover what young children understand about who has access to what evidence, and how that evidence will impact people's beliefs. Mofu children were chosen as they provide a unique opportunity to compare the development of an understanding of minds and of evidence for belief both among children who have attended school and those who have not. They were also chosen with a view to moving closer toward an answer to the question of whether or not an understanding of minds such as develops among Western children is a universal aspect of human development.

Understanding of Minds: Universal or Not?

In his recent state-of-the-art article on children's understanding of mental states, Flavell (2000) notes that the question of whether there is a universal development of a "theory of mind" remains as yet unanswered. Indeed, the evidence from non-Western cultures is sparse and mixed, with some studies (e.g., Avis & Harris, 1991) suggesting a universal development, and others (e.g., Vinden, 1996, 1999) opening the possibility of different pathways to competent social interactions. Although exporting Western tasks to non-Western children is typically fraught with difficulties, both from theoretical and practical perspectives, traditional theory-of-mind tasks can be conducted in such a way as to minimise any cultural transition. Indeed, if an understanding of minds is necessary for typical adult-like social interactions, as some (e.g., Wellman, 1990) maintain, then the tasks, which reflect those everyday interactions, should be readily adaptable to different cultural milieus. Testing performance on standard theory-of-mind tasks should take us a step further towards answering the question as to the universality of an understanding of mind.

Schooling and an Understanding of Minds

Whether or not schooling promotes cognitive development has been widely debated. Many studies show a positive influence of schooling on IQ (see Ceci, 1991, for a review). Studies of the influence of schooling on other aspects of cognitive development show either no effect, mixed effects, or an effect only for specific tasks relevant to tasks learned at school. In most studies, no firm conclusion can be drawn because of potentially confounding factors. Rogoff (1981) clearly analyses

what some of these factors might be—selectivity in school attenders, cognitive differences in children prior to school entry, familiarity with testing procedures, and so on.

In collecting the data here presented, the author was able to find both schooled and nonschooled participants. All children were from a rural area and with few exceptions came from very poor families—only a handful of families of the schooled children could afford to or were inclined to buy a notebook and pencil for their children. Children who did not go to school had no opportunity for schooling—no school had yet been built in their area. Further information being unavailable as to prior differences among the children, it was assumed that some selection factor whereby only the "advantaged" children were sent to school was not at work. Furthermore, if, as some maintain (e.g., Perner, Ruffman, & Leekam, 1994; Ruffman et al., 1998), an understanding of mind is an aspect of social development arising from everyday interactions between parents and siblings, then schooling should exert no special influence. If, as others maintain, a theory of minds unfolds through biological maturation (e.g., Baron-Cohen, 1995), schooling should enter the picture too late to have any influence (or on a strict nativist view, it would have no influence anyway).

Tomasello, Kruger, and Ratner (1993) claim that an understanding of minds is necessary in order for children to benefit from school. In instructed learning, they maintain, children are required to compare their own understanding with that of the adult; they must internalise adult instructions and engage in rudimentary self-monitoring. Collaborative learning also requires that the child take the other's conflicting viewpoint into account. However, one might also argue that formal education provides the perfect place for nurturing an understanding of minds, if that understanding is not already present before the child attends school. Being placed in an atmosphere where "mind-mindedness" is necessary might be part of what promotes an understanding of mind. Taylor's (1988) study provides some evidence for this kind of process. When 4-year-old children in her study were made aware that information can be interpreted in different ways by different people, they were better able to understand the perspective of someone who knew less than themselves. Schooling, then, might be a context in which children become more aware of differing perspectives on reality. If this is so, then we might expect to find that schooled children perform better on theory-of-mind tasks than nonschooled children. Although this question can only be finally decided through a longitudinal study, a first step is to see whether or not there are differences between schooled and nonschooled children with regard to their understanding of mind.

Evidence for Belief

Although research shows that even adults do not fully understand the nature of evidence (e.g., Kuhn, 1993), some research exists suggesting that an understanding of evidence begins at a young age. Sodian and Wimmer (1987) found that children under 6 years seemed not to understand that one can know by inference, but rather viewed knowledge as arising from seeing visual evidence, thus indicating only a rudimentary understanding of the nature and use of some kinds of evidence. Sodian, Zaitchik, and Cary (1991) found that 6- to 7-year-olds are able to distinguish between hypothetical belief and evidence. Children could use information about the size of a mousehole to decide whether a large or small mouse had entered a hole and eaten some cheese.

Little work, however, has explored young children's understanding of the evidential basis of their own and other's beliefs. Most work has focused on children's understanding of the relationship between belief and action, not their understanding of the reasons for belief. A notable exception is the work of Ash, Torrance, Lee, and Olson (1993), which explored children's understanding of the use of facts and evidence to justify their own and another's belief. All children from ages 4 to 8 years were capable of basing their own belief on available evidence. They could even integrate multiple pieces of evidence to form this belief when they lacked knowledge of the true state of affairs in the world. When evidence was accumulating which would lead another person to a belief that the child knew was false, however, only 7- and 8-year-olds were able to set aside their own true belief and respond that the other would form a false belief based on the available evidence. In other words, younger children attributed hypotheses to others based on what they themselves knew to be true, whereas older children took the information that was available to the other into account.

Perner (1995) hypothesised that younger children (e.g., typical 3-year-olds) perceive of belief as acting as if something is the case. This leads them to ignore disconfirming evidence—thus even after looking in an empty box someone will continue to think there are bandaids inside. Perner and Lopez (1997) explored this idea in more detail, finding that even 3-year-olds understand that someone could not think an object was in a box when both they and the other person were looking into an empty box. When the children did not have the same visual vantage point as the other person, however, they failed to take the other's visual evidence into account. In other words, 3-year-olds appear to understand something about the relationship between evidence and belief, but only when their perspective and the other person's matches. Thus their use of the word "think" is based on their own visual experience.

Pillow and Mash (1999) found the same reliance on visual experience in their study of children's understanding that mistaken beliefs can arise from misinterpretation of ambiguous evidence. Explanations of another's stated belief by 4-year-olds rarely referred to what the other had previously seen, but tended to focus on the currently visible evidence. On the other hand, 7-year-olds frequently explained the other's false belief by appealing to what the other had previously seen. In a further study, Pillow and his colleagues ask children to justify a puppet's belief about the contents of a container under various conditions from knowledge based on visual inspection, to inference from inspection of other containers, to guessing (Pillow, Hill, Boyce, & Stein, 2000). Asking children why the puppet *said* what he did, rather than why he *thought* what he did, had no effect on the results. Even 6-year-olds could not consistently distinguish between levels of certainty of knowledge or recognise that deductive inference involves integrating premise information. Eight- and 9-year olds were more consistent.

These experiments suggest that younger children find it difficult to give up the evidence of their own eyes and take the visual perspective of the other into account when asked to give evidence for the other's belief. They also suggest that there is a developmental lag from the age at which children typically develop an understanding of mind (age 4–5 years) to the age at which they begin to recognise that knowledge may be obtained through inference (age 6–9 years). But what if they were involved in creating a false belief in another? Can young children reason backwards from a false belief to evidence when they have been closely involved in the entire belief-making process? Can they distinguish between what counts as evidence for self and other when the *kinds* of evidence to which each has access are very different? An experiment was devised in which the child watches as a man is unable to lift a heavy box. After the man leaves to get help, the child is shown that the box contains bags of sand, and with the experimenter contrives to fool the man by removing and hiding the bags of sand. The child is asked about the other's now false belief concerning the weight of the box, and why he would believe it. The child is also asked about what the man would think about the weight of the box when he lifted it again, and why.

In the present experiment, then, the child shares both the original true belief of the other person, and knowledge of the evidence that brought about that belief. The child is responsible for creating a false belief in another. The child is also responsible for creating the situation that will eventually change the other's belief. The differences between the evidence that the child has for belief, and the evidence that the other has for their belief, are outlined in Figure 1.

	Prior Belief (box is heavy)	Subsequent Belief (box is light)
Child's evidence	sees man can't lift box sees box is full of sand feels the heavy sand	sees box is empty
Other's evidence	can't lift box	will be able to lift box

figure 1
Difference between child's and other's evidence for belief.

The question, then, is whether children will be able to distinguish between what constitutes evidence for the man and what they themselves later saw—the bags of sand—which was corroborating evidence, but only for them. Of course at first the man's evidence is not exactly the same as theirs. He actually feels the weight, whereas the children only see him experiencing the heaviness of the box. However, as they attempt to move the bags of sand, they do get to experience this "tactile" evidence as well. The difference, then, between their evidence and his, is that they have knowledge about the contents of the box.

The subsequent true belief should be easier for the children, for they can predict the man's belief based on their own true belief about that weight of the box. As far as giving evidence for the man's subsequent belief is concerned, however, they have to imagine the man returning and lifting the box again. The only evidence that is available to the children is their own visual experience. The conflict between what they have actually seen (the empty box) and what the man has yet to experience (the lightness of the box) should make this question difficult for the younger children.

Hypotheses

This study was conducted with several hypotheses in mind. Regarding schooling, it was thought that schooled participants would perform better than nonschooled participants because the classroom is a place that fosters both an understanding of mind, and

possibly also an understanding of evidence for belief. With regard to children's understanding of evidence, it was thought that it would emerge later than an understanding of mind, and that an understanding of mind would be a necessary precursor to its development. Furthermore, it was expected that giving evidence for the subsequent true belief of the other person would be more difficult for the children than giving evidence for the prior false belief, because of the hypothetical nature of the subsequent true belief. Finally, with regard to the universality of an understanding of minds, since evidence from other studies is mixed, there was no specific hypothesis, only an openness to finding different developmental pathways.

Methods

Participants

The Mofu speakers in this study speak a dialect known as Mofu-Gudur, and live in far northern rural Cameroon. Literacy rate in Cameroon is estimated to be between 5 and 15% (Grimes, 1999). Given the high proportion of monolingual speakers in this area, and the fact that Cameroon's schools use only French, the literacy rate is no doubt on the lower end in this area. A total of 154 Mofu children ranging in age from 4 to 11 completed all the tests.[1] There were 13 four-year-olds, 19 five-year-olds, 30 six-year-olds, 30 seven-year-olds, 21 eight-year-olds, 16 nine-year-olds, 14 ten-year-olds, and 11 eleven-year-olds. Of these children, 96 were boys and 58 were girls. The disproportionate number of boys occurred because many of the children were school attenders, and boys are more likely to be sent to school than girls. Furthermore, girls were generally much shyer about interacting with strangers and more difficult to elicit as participants. Nonschooled children numbered 70 (44 males, 26 females) and schooled children numbered 84 (52 males, 32 females). Grade levels were not obtained because there is no set age at which a child enters school, and often a child will stay in school for a number of months, drop out, and re-enter at the same grade the next year, for several years at a time. Very few older children were available for testing who had not been to school, therefore for purposes of analysis, children aged 9 through 11 were collapsed into one group.

All children were tested in Mofu by two native speakers. The experimenters were both literacy workers in the area, but not known to most of the children. The experimenters collaborated with the author and a linguist living near the school to translate the tasks. Another linguist working in the dialect since 1978 and

---

[1] Mofu children do not know their ages. Ages were estimated by the two Mofu experimenters prior to beginning the testing.

a native speaker of Mofu-Gudur who had studied translation principles also assisted in the framing of the tasks. Both the author and linguists have studied translation principles and had prior experience in translating, and used a method that involved multiple back translations. All native speakers agree that the objects used in the study and the notion of tricking an adult were culturally acceptable. In the case of the schooled children, each child was taken from their classes and tested in a small empty hut next to the school. Nonschooled children were tested either in a local church or in a small hut where Fulani classes were held.

Standard Understanding of Mind Tasks

A series of theory-of-mind tasks were conducted with the children and included a change of location false belief task (Perner, Leekam, & Wimmer, 1987), two change of contents tasks (Gopnik, & Astington, 1988), and two appearance/reality tasks (Flavell, Flavell, & Green, 1983).

Change of location. In this task the child created a false belief in another person by transferring a desired object from one container to another without the other's knowledge. In addition to false belief questions asking the child both where the other would look for the object and where he would think it was, two questions were asked to test their ability to apply their knowledge of false belief in the realm of emotion. These emotion questions have been analysed in another article (Vinden, 1999) and will not be included in the analysis here presented.

Change of contents. First the child removed the matches from a matchbox and replaced them with small rocks. Then he was asked what he first thought was in the box, and what another would think was in the box before opening it. Next, what looked like a wrapped candy was given to the child. He opened it and found instead a piece of millet stalk. The same belief questions were asked for this object.

Surprising objects. Two items were used for this task—a sponge rock and a rubber snake in a box of leaves. In addition to asking the child what the items looked like and what they really were, she was asked about what she thought and what another would think the items were before touching them.

Evidence Task

The novel evidence task proceeded as follows: An experimenter brings the child to the testing location, where the other experimenter is waiting. The waiting experimenter asks the other man to take a closed cardboard box outside. He agrees, and tries unsuccessfully to lift the carton. Then he says, "This carton is too heavy for me. I'll have to go look for someone to help me." Then he leaves. The remaining experimenter says to the child, "He hasn't looked inside the carton. He doesn't know what is inside it. Let me now show you what is inside. Okay, look now." They look inside and see that the carton contains bags of sand.

The following question is then asked of the child:

1. Evidence for state of affairs (ESA): *Why is this carton so heavy?*

After asking this question, the experimenter suggests to the child that they play a trick on the man and hide the bags of sand. Together they hide the sand. The following questions are then asked:

2. Prior false belief (PFB): *When he comes back, but before he lifts it with his friend, will he think the carton is heavy or light?*
3. Evidence for prior false belief (EPFB): *How will he know it is heavy/light?* (Question is asked in accordance with child's answer from previous question.)
4. Subsequent true belief (STB): *When they come back, when they lift it, will they think the carton is heavy or light?*
5. Evidence for subsequent true belief (ESTB): *How will they know the carton is light/heavy?*

This task, then, repeats the same kind of situation that is given in the change of contents task, but allows the possibility for enquiring into the source of evidence for the other's false belief. The PFB question is almost identical in form to the false belief question asked for the change of contents task.

Much discussion occurred among the linguists, myself, and the Mofu translators concerning how to ask the evidence questions. Both translators maintained that the proper way to ask the evidence questions was with the verb for "know" rather than "think" because the experimenter in question had or would have actual experiences that gave rise to his beliefs. They also maintained that although the word for "know" was used in the questions, the questions were equivalent to asking "Why would he think X?" Using the verb "think" would result in speculative answers, they maintained, rather than answers that relied on the experience of the man lifting the box.

What the two translators/experimenters were focusing on here is the crucial difference (as outlined in Ash et al., 1993) between causes of a belief and evidence for belief. Things that you don't know can affect your beliefs, but only experience can create knowledge. So in the case of the empty box that you think is heavy (because you tried to lift it before and couldn't), the sand caused your belief that the box was heavy. But what causes a belief is not the same as the evi-

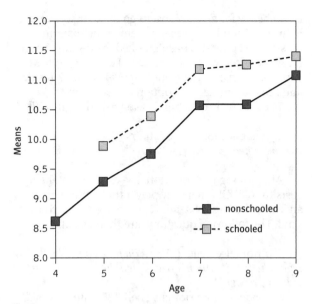

figure 2
Mean scores for Mind by age and schooling.

therefore included six questions about another's false belief, one question about one's own prior true belief, three questions about one's own false belief, and two appearance-reality scores). As is common in theory-of-mind research (e.g., Astington & Jenkins, 1999; Dunn, Cutting, & Demetriou, 2000; Hughes, Deater-Deckard, & Cutting, 1999), the Mind score was purposely heterogeneous, and questions varied from easy true belief questions to the more difficult false belief questions. The assumption underlying this heterogeneity is that an understanding of mind develops gradually, and that a heterogeneous measure gives us a better idea of the true variability that exists across children.

A univariate GLM ANOVA with the Mind score as the dependent variable, and age and schooling and gender as independent variables revealed significant main effect of both Age, $F(5) = 5.80$, $p < .001$, and Schooling, $F(1) = 4.5$, $p > .05$, and no significant interactions. Figure 2 shows the mean overall Mind scores by age for schooled and nonschooled participants.

In order to see more clearly the differences between groups, children were subdivided according to whether they could be said to have a well-developed understanding of mind (Mind score $\geq$ 10) or not (Mind score < 10). Table 1 shows that only 45% of the nonschooled 5-year-olds can be said to have a well-developed understanding of mind on this criterion, whereas 75% of the schooled children at this age can be said to have a well-developed understanding of mind. For nonschooled children, although there is an improvement with age, it is not nearly to the level of the improvement among schooled children.

dence that results in the belief. Your inability to lift the box is the evidence for your belief, because you do not know it is filled with sand. The translators were also adamant that the final questions must be about both the original man and the one who had come to help, as they were now joint experiencers of the lightness of the box, and joint holders of beliefs about the box. It was felt that including the other man who had no prior evidence of the box's weight would, if anything, help the children judge what evidence was appropriate for the belief that the box was now light.

Results

Standard Understanding of Mind Tasks

In order to examine the children's overall understanding of mind, a total theory-of-mind score was calculated, resulting in a Mind score that could range from 0 to 12. For each pair of appearance-reality questions, children were given a score of 1 if they answered both the appearance and the reality questions correctly, under the assumption that one cannot be said to truly understand the appearance-reality distinction unless one knows both what the object looks like and what it really is. For other questions, children were given a score of 1 if they answered correctly (i.e., if they correctly predicted what the other's false belief would be, if they correctly said what they had previously thought was in the container, and so on) and a score of 0 if they answered incorrectly. This total Mind score

Evidence Task

Almost all of the children at every age group, schooled and nonschooled, answered two questions correctly—the questions regarding the evidence for the initial state of affairs (why the box was heavy at first), and whether the man would think the box was heavy or light after they returned and lifted it (subsequent to

table 1   Percentage of Children Scoring Correctly on at Least 10 of 12 Theory of Mind Questions, by Age and Schooling

	Age					
	4	**5**	**6**	**7**	**8**	**9–11**
No school	38.5	45.5	66.7	92.9	90.0	80.0
School		75.0	72.2	93.8	100	100

the contents being removed). The fact that most children were able to answer these simpler questions correctly would suggest that the task made sense to the children and the questions were within the children's linguistic abilities. Descriptive statistics for all the false belief questions from both the standard theory-of-mind tasks and the new task (Table 2) indicate that the false belief question for the new task falls within the middle of range of difficulty for these children.

For both schooled and nonschooled participants, among those who answered the belief question incorrectly, all gave evidence for belief that was consistent with their incorrect answers. This consistency of response would again suggest that the questions were well formed. Nineteen children incorrectly answered the prior false belief question, and gave evidence that was consistent with their answer; eight did the same for the subsequent true belief question. Large numbers of children, however, answered the belief questions correctly but failed to provide correct evidence for that belief—28 out of the 134 who correctly answered the prior false belief question and 85 out of the 145 who correctly answered the subsequent true belief question.

Table 3 shows the percentage of children scoring correctly on each of the five questions for this task. Binomial tests were conducted to see if any of the subgroups answered differently than we would expect if they were simply guessing and the table shows these results. It could be argued, however, that only children who correctly answered the belief questions

should be included when examining the ability to give evidence for belief. Percentages of correct responses for the subgroups of those answering the belief questions correctly are included in parentheses in Table 3. Binomial tests were repeated for this group, and results did not differ substantially.

Correlation coefficients were calculated between all five questions for the evidence task, and age, schooling, gender, and Mind score. These are shown in Table 4, excluding gender, which did not correlate significantly with any of the variables. As expected, there were significant correlations among the task variables. The correlations between the other variables and the task variables, however, pointed to the need for further analysis in some cases where multiple independent variables correlated significantly with a single task question.

Since age, schooling, and Mind score are highly intercorrelated, subsequent analysis must proceed cautiously. Any regression analysis examining which of the highly correlated variables serves as the best predictor would be suspect due to collinearity. Yet we can disentangle the relationships between these variables to some extent. For example, from a standpoint of theory, age and schooling could both be seen as causally influencing performance on Mind. The reverse, however, is not true—an understanding of mind cannot cause one to become older, and it is doubtful if it could cause one to go to school. Thus it would make sense in any regression analysis to enter age and schooling first, then see if Mind adds anything to the equation. Evidence questions were not considered as predictors of the corresponding belief questions since they logically follow from the belief questions.

Binary logistic regression analysis was conducted for two of the five questions of the evidence task. The evidence for state of affairs and the subsequent true belief questions were not analysed further because responses were so near ceiling, and evidence for prior false belief correlated significantly only with age, so it was not analysed further. For the prior false belief question, first schooling (age being uncorrelated with this question), then Mind were entered. Schooling emerged as the only significant predictor (B = 1.09, $p \le .05$). For evidence for subsequent true belief, age and schooling were entered simultaneously. Schooling was a significant predictor (B = 0.74, $p \le .05$) and age approached significance (B = 0.21, $p = .07$). Mind was entered next, and was not significant, neither was the change in chi-square for that step.

Discussion

This study provides some support for a universal development of an understanding of mind. Schooled 6-year-olds and nonschooled 7-year-olds averaged over

table 2	Means and Standard Deviations (SD) for All False Belief Questions	
	Mean	**SD**
Evidence task		
Prior false belief	.88	.33
Location task		
Look	.75	.43
Think	.74	.44
Contents task		
Other1	.87	.34
Self2	.94	.23
Other2	.94	.23
Objects task		
Self1	.92	.28
Other1	.89	.31
Self2	.93	.26
Other2	.87	.33

table 3   Percentage Correct on Each Question in Evidence Task, by Age and Schooling

Question/ Schooling	Age					
	4	5	6	7	8	9–11
N						
No school	12	11	12	14	10	10
School	0	8	18	16	11	31
ESA						
No school	84.6*	81.8*	83.3*	100***	90.0**	90.0**
School		100**	100***	100**	100***	100***
PFB						
No school	76.9*	63.6	83.3*	92.9***	90.0**	80.0*
School		87.5*	94.4***	87.5**	100***	93.5**
EPFB						
No School	53.8 (70.0)†	18.2* (28.6)	83.3* (100)**	78.6* (84.6)*	80* (88.9)*	70 (87.5)
School		25.0 (28.6)	66.7 (70.6)	75.0* (85.7)**	81.8* (81.8)	87.1* (93.1)**
STB						
No school	92.3**	81.8*	75*	100***	90.0**	100***
School		87.5*	100***	100***	100***	100***
ESTB						
No school	7.7** (8.3)**	9.1** (11.1)*	41.7 (55.6)	35.7 (35.7)	30.0 (33.3)	40.0 (40.0)
School		37.5 (42.9)	44.4 (44.4)	62.5 (62.5)	27.3 (27.3)	54.8 (54.8)

ESA = evidence for initial state of affairs, PFB = prior false belief, EPFB = evidence for prior false belief, STB = subsequent true belief, ESTB = evidence for subsequent true belief.
†Percentages in parentheses are for subgroups of those answering the belief question correctly. Significantly different than chance at the *.05 level, **.01 level, ***.001 level (all 2-tailed).

10 out of 12 correct on traditional theory-of-mind questions. These results suggest, however, that although an understanding of mind does develop in Mofu children, there are factors that may delay its development relative to European and North American children. Furthermore, mean scores on individual false belief questions show that the children's performance was not entirely consistent across tasks. Some research supports such inconsistency across theory-of-mind tasks (Charman & Campbell, 1997; Mayes, Klin, Tercyak, & Cicchetti, 1996), although others have found more consistency (Hughes et al., 2000). The overall picture, however (see Figure 2), does look remarkably similar to that painted by most theory-of-mind researchers conducting studies among Western

children; namely, a gradual increase in ability with increasing age. This study diverges from other previous work with respect to the later age at which development occurs, and the difference between schooled and nonschooled participants.

With regard to schooling, schooled children almost always performed better than nonschooled children on tasks testing an understanding of mind. The difference between these two groups was especially apparent when they were classified as either having a well-developed understanding of mind, or not. This subclassification indicated two things. First, whereas in the first year of schooling about 75% of 5-year-olds are already demonstrating a well-developed understanding of mind, only about 45% of nonschooled 4-

table 4	Correlations Between Evidence Task Questions and Age, Schooling, and Mind Score						
	Age	**Schooling**	**Mind**	**ESA**	**PFB**	**EPFB**	**STB**
Schooling	.33**						
Mind	.46**	.36***					
ESA	.16	.26***	.17*				
PFB	.13	.17*	.18*	.27**			
EPFB	.30**	.10	.12	.27**	.57***		
STB	.19*	.20**	.21*	.34***	.38***	.23**	
ESTB	.21**	.22**	.13	.19*	.14	.21**	.19*

ESA = evidence for initial state of affairs, PFB = prior false belief, EPFB = evidence for prior false belief, STB = subsequent true belief, ESTB = evidence for subsequent true belief.
Significant at the *.05 level, **.01 level, ***.001 level (all 1-tailed).

year-olds and only 67% of nonschooled 6-year-olds are showing such development. Second, although from age 7 onwards a majority of both schooled and nonschooled children are showing a well-developed understanding, nonschooled children never reach ceiling performance. These results suggest that schooling may promote an understanding of minds if it is not fully developed prior to school entry, but that schooling is not a necessary condition for its development.

In some ways it is surprising that schooled participants performed better than their nonschooled agemates. Informal observations of the schooling process revealed that most of the lessons of the pre-teen children involved disciplinary procedures and rote memorisation. The teachers in the school were from another part of Cameroon and did not speak Mofu. All lessons were conducted completely in French, yet even the older children's knowledge of French appeared to consist only of rote memorisation of the days of the week, and simple French phrases such as "What is your name?" Few children had books or any writing materials. Further research is warranted, therefore, to determine what exactly might be the link between the superior performance of schooled children and the schooling process.

Research in bilingualism prompts one to speculate that this basic French immersion that schooled children are receiving may be at least part of what gives schooled children the edge in understanding minds. Many studies support the view that bilingual children perform better than their nonbilingual agemates on a variety of cognitive and linguistic tasks. The work of Cummins (1976; cf. Cummins & Swain, 1986) is most pertinent here. He claims that the superior performance of bilinguals is a result of the broad range of experiences they encounter as they have access to and learn to operate in two contrasting cultural systems.

As they switch from one linguistic code to another, flexible thinking is supported, for each language gives the child a distinct perspective. If this theory is true, then it follows that an understanding of minds, which involves seeing things from two distinct perspectives, might develop more readily in bilingual children than in nonbilinguals. Yet it is not only the language that provides another perspective. The entire formal schooling system is a cultural system that contrasts with the everyday Mofu culture and thus provides the schoolchildren with an opportunity to "practise" the skill that lies at the heart of understanding minds; namely, comparing two different perspectives on reality.

With regard to their ability to give evidence for a *false* belief, there was an improvement with age, but not schooling. For both schooled and nonschooled participants, an ability to give evidence for false belief seems to emerge about a year after the ability to understand the false belief on which the evidence question is based. These results are especially intriguing in light of the fact that on the overall Mind scores, nonschooled children seemed to be lagging behind schooled children in the development of an understanding of mind. This may indicate that the development of an understanding of *evidence* for belief relies primarily on real-world experiences rather than being promoted through classroom interactions.

Mofu children's understanding of evidence, however, was limited to beliefs based on evidence that had actually been demonstrated in the real world. When it came to predicting what would constitute evidence for a *true* belief of another at a future time, children found it difficult to lay aside the evidence which had informed their own belief and imagine what would constitute evidence for the new belief of the other, even though they were able to predict what the other's belief would be. Although schooled children did perform better than nonschooled children on giving evidence for a subsequent *true* belief, neither group performed above chance level on this question at any age. Thus their understanding of evidence appears to have limitations.

Recall that to correctly give evidence for the man's *false* belief, the child must suppress their own visual evidence (seeing the bags full of sand) and attend to what the man had experienced; namely, his difficulty lifting the box. This is the crucial difference that Ash et al. (1993) note in their study between causes of events and evidence for belief. The bags of sand in the box are causes of the event of the man being unable to lift the box. But the man's inability to lift the box is the evidence that contributes to his belief that the box is heavy. Mofu children seem to be able to lay aside their visual evidence and attend to the other's tactile evidence at about the same age as children from more typically studied populations begin to understand the inferential basis of knowledge (e.g., Pillow et al., 2000; Pillow & Mash, 1999). However, when the question is hypothetical (i.e., the man has not actually come back to lift the now empty container) and the children must lay aside their visual evidence in favour of imagined future evidence, they do not perform well.

The children's difficulty in suppressing their knowledge of the causes of the event may relate to problems of executive function. For example, Moore, Barresi, and Thompson (1998) have shown that children's ability to show future-oriented prosocial or sharing behaviour is related both to the ability to imagine conflicting noncurrent mental states and the ability to inhibit responding to perceptually salient events. Similarly Hughes (1998) found links between three aspects of executive function (working memory, attentional flexibility, and inhibitory control) and performance on theory-of-mind tasks. Thus one possible explanation for young children's inability to give evidence for the subsequent true belief is not that they are unaware of what will be the relevant evidence for the others but that they have difficulty inhibiting the stronger visual evidence to which they are privy. Again, evidence from studies in bilingualism suggest that conversing in a second language requires higher levels of control of processing than does speaking in a first language. And, as Bialystok (1991, p. 127) points out, new bilinguals struggling with a second language are "in the position of stretching the level of control of processing available in order to sustain the interaction." Thus, again, it may be the children's emerging bilingualism that underlies the differences observed in the schooled and nonschooled children's performance.

In conclusion, this study provides some evidence for a universally developing understanding of minds, but highlights the need for more research regarding factors that affect both the rate of development and the children's differential response to tasks. In particular, further study needs to be done to resolve the question concerning how schooling or bilingualism may be implicated in the child's developing understanding of mind. Finally, this study adds to the growing body of research among Western children showing that an understanding of evidence emerges gradually, somewhat more slowly than an understanding of minds.

REFERENCES

Ash, A., Torrance, N., Lee, E., & Olson, D. (1993). The development of children's understanding of the evidence for beliefs. *Educational Psychology, 13,* 371–384.

Astington, J., & Jenkins, J. (1999). A longitudinal study of the relation between language and theory-of-mind development. *Developmental Psychology, 35,* 1311–1320.

Avis, J., & Harris, P. (1991). Belief-desire reasoning among Baka children: Evidence for a universal conception of mind. *Child Development, 62,* 460–467.

Baron-Cohen, S. (1995). *Mind blindness: An essay on autism and theory of mind.* Cambridge, MA: MIT Press.

Bialystok, E. (1991). *Language processing in bilingual children.* Cambridge: Cambridge University Press.

Ceci, S. (1991). How much does schooling influence general intelligence and its cognitive components? A reassessment of the evidence. *Development Psychology, 27,* 703–722.

Charman, T., & Campbell, A. (1997). Reliability of theory of mind task performance by individuals with a learning disability: A research note. *Journal of Child Psychology and Psychiatry, 38,* 725–730.

Cummins, J. (1976). The influence of bilingualism on cognitive growth: A synthesis of research findings and explanatory hypotheses. *Working Papers on Bilingualism, 9,* 1–43.

Cummins, J., & Swain, M. (1986). *Bilingualism in education: Aspects of theory, research and practice.* New York: Longmans.

Dunn, J., Cutting, A., & Demetriou, H. (2000). Moral sensibility, understanding others, and children's friendship interactions in the preschool period. *British Journal of Developmental Psychology, 18,* 159–177.

Flavell, J. (2000). Development of children's knowledge about the mental world. *International Journal of Behavioral Development, 24,* 15–23.

Flavell, J., Flavell, E., & Green, F. (1983). The development of the appearance-reality distinction. *Cognitive Psychology, 15,* 95–120.

Gopnik, A., & Astington, J.W. (1988). Children's understanding of representational change and its relations to the understanding of fake belief and the appearance-reality distinction. *Child Development, 59,* 26–37.

Grimes, B. (1999). *Ethnologue: Language of the world* (Internet version, 13th ed.). Dallas, TX: SIL International.

Hughes, C. (1998). Executive function in preschoolers: Links with theory of mind and verbal ability. *British Journal of Developmental Psychology, 16,* 233–253.

Hughes, C., Adlam, A., Happé, F., Jackson, J., Taylor, A., & Caspi, A. (2000). Good test-retest reliability for standard and advanced false-belief tasks across a wide range of abilities. *Journal of Child Psychology and Psychiatry, 41,* 483–490.

Hughes, C., Deater-Deckard, K., & Cutting, A. (1999). Speak roughly to your little boy? Sex differences in the relations between parenting and preschoolers' understanding of mind. *Social Development, 8,* 143–160.

Kuhn, D. (1993). Connecting scientific and informal reasoning. *Merrill-Palmer Quarterly, 39,* 74–103.

Mayes, L., Klin, A., Tercyak, K., Cicchetti, D. (1996). Test-retest reliability for false-belief tasks. *Journal of Child Psychology and Psychiatry, 37,* 313–319.

Moore, C., Barresi, J., & Thompson, C. (1998). The cognitive basis of future-oriented prosocial behavior. *Social Development, 7,* 198–218.

Perner, J. (1995). The many faces of belief: Reflections on Fodor's and the child's theory of mind. *Cognition, 57,* 241–269.

Perner, J., Leekam, S., & Wimmer, J. (1987). Three-year-olds' difficulty with false belief: The case for a conceptual deficit. *British Journal of Developmental Psychology, 5,* 125–137.

Perner, J., & Lopez, A. (1997). Children's understanding of belief and disconfirming visual evidence. *Cognitive Development, 12,* 367–380.

Perner, J., Ruffman, T., & Leekam, S.R. (1994). Theory of mind is contagious: You catch it from your sibs. *Child Development, 65,* 1228–1238.

Pillow, B.H., Hill, V., Boyce, A., & Stein, C. (2000). Understanding inference as a source of knowledge: Children's ability to evaluate the certainty of deduction, perception, and guessing. *Developmental Psychology, 36,* 169–179.

Pillow, B.H., & Mash, C. (1999). Young children's understanding of interpretation, expectation and direct perception as sources of false belief. *British Journal of Developmental Psychology, 17,* 263–276.

Rogoff, B. (1981). Schooling and the development of cognitive skills. In H. Triandis & A. Heron (Eds.), *Handbook of cross-cultural psychology, vol. 4* (pp. 233–294). Boston: Allyn and Bacon.

Ruffman, T., Perner, J., Naito, M., Parkin, L., Clements, W.A., & Complin, C. (1998). Older (but not younger) siblings facilitate false belief understanding. *Developmental Psychology, 34,* 161–174.

Sodian, B., & Wimmer, H. (1987). Children's understanding of inference as a source of knowledge. *Child Development, 58,* 424–433.

Sodian, B., Zaitchik, D., & Carey, S. (1991). Young children's differentiation of hypothetical beliefs from evidence. *Child Development, 62,* 753–766.

Taylor, M. (1988). Conceptual perspective taking: Children's ability to distinguish what they know from what they see. *Child Development, 59,* 703–718.

Tomasello, M., Kruger, A., & Ratner, H. (1993). Cultural learning. *Behavioral and Brain Sciences, 16,* 495–552.

Vinden, P. (1996). Junin Quechua children's understanding of mind. *Child Development, 67,* 1707–1716.

Vinden, P. (1999). Children's understanding of mind and emotion: A multi-culture study. *Cognition and Emotion, 13,* 19–48.

Wellman, H.M. (1990). *The child's theory of mind.* Cambridge, MA: MIT Press.

Questions

1. What had earlier research revealed about age differences in children's understanding of the evidential basis for belief?
2. Do you think the evidence task used in this study was culture fair—that is, that it made sense to the Mofu children?
3. Did attending school or not make a difference in the children's understanding of mind? Why?
4. What role might language play in the development of children's understanding of evidence for belief?
5. Was there support in this study for the universal assumption of the development of understanding of mind, in particular regarding evidence for belief?
6. What are the implications of these findings for the development of social functioning from early childhood to adolescence?

21 Transmission of Aggression Through Imitation of Aggressive Models

Albert Bandura • Dorothea Ross • Sheila A. Ross

The following article describes research that investigated observational learning—specifically, what and how children learn when they are exposed to other people who are performing aggressive actions. This experiment is a classic in the field of psychology because of the clarity of its design, the strength of its findings, and the nature of its implications for child development. Before this research was conducted, psychologists, including Bandura and his colleagues, had discovered that children were quick to imitate the behaviors of an adult model in the presence of the model. However, another important question is whether children will imitate aggressive behaviors later, when the adult model is no longer present—a process called delayed imitation. Although one could study delayed imitation of many types of behaviors, the learning of aggressive behavior as a result of exposure to an aggressive model is of particular concern to psychologists and the public at large.

The researchers attempted to identify exactly which factors may contribute to children's learning when they observe aggressive behaviors performed by an adult model. For instance, they studied whether children are more likely to attend to and learn the behaviors of same-gender adult models. The investigators also examined whether boys are more likely than girls to learn aggressive behaviors from a same-gender adult model because these behaviors are considered more acceptable for males than for females.

One impressive feature of this research is the care that was taken in setting up the experimental conditions so that observational learning of aggressive behaviors could be clearly assessed. As a result of these efforts, this study came up with provocative results that have significant implications regarding how children learn aggressive behaviors. It also raised questions about how society can steer children toward prosocial behaviors in the midst of abundant depictions of violence and aggression on television, in video games, and in other media to which young children are regularly exposed.

A previous study, designed to account for the phenomenon of identification in terms of incidental learning, demonstrated that children readily imitated behavior exhibited by an adult model in the presence of the model (Bandura & Huston, 1961). A series of experiments by Blake (1958) and others (Grosser, Polansky, & Lippitt, 1951; Rosenblith, 1959; Schachter & Hall, 1952) have likewise shown that mere observation of responses of a model has a facilitating effect on subjects' reactions in the immediate social influence setting.

While these studies provide convincing evidence for the influence and control exerted on others by the behavior of a model, a more crucial test of imitative learning involves the generalization of imitative response patterns to new settings in which the model is absent.

Acknowledgments: This investigation was supported by Research Grant M-4398 from the National Institute of Health, United States Public Health Service. The authors wish to express their appreciation to Edith Dowley, Director, and Patricia Rowe, Head Teacher, Stanford University Nursery School for their assistance throughout this study.

In the experiment reported in this paper children were exposed to aggressive and nonaggressive adult models and were then tested for amount of imitative learning in a new situation in the absence of the model. According to the prediction, subjects exposed to aggressive models would reproduce aggressive acts resembling those of their models and would differ in this respect both from subjects who observed nonaggressive models and from those who had no prior exposure to any models. This hypothesis assumed that subjects had learned imitative habits as a result of prior reinforcement, and these tendencies would generalize to some extent to adult experimenters (Miller & Dollard, 1941).

It was further predicted that observation of subdued nonaggressive models would have a generalized inhibiting effect on the subjects' subsequent behavior, and this effect would be reflected in a difference between the nonaggressive and the control groups, with subjects in the latter group displaying significantly more aggression.

Hypotheses were also advanced concerning the influence of the sex of model and sex of subjects on imitation. Fauls and Smith (1956) have shown that preschool children perceive their parents as having distinct preferences regarding sex appropriate modes of behavior for their children. Their findings, as well as informal observation, suggest that parents reward imitation of sex appropriate behavior and discourage or punish sex inappropriate imitative responses, e.g., a male child is unlikely to receive much reward for performing female appropriate activities, such as cooking, or for adopting other aspects of the maternal role, but these same behaviors are typically welcomed if performed by females. As a result of differing reinforcement histories, tendencies to imitate male and female models thus acquire differential habit strength. One would expect, on this basis, subjects to imitate the behavior of a same-sex model to a greater degree than a model of the opposite sex.

Since aggression, however, is a highly masculine-typed behavior, boys should be more predisposed than girls toward imitating aggression, the difference being most marked for subjects exposed to the male aggressive model.

Method

Subjects

The subjects were 36 boys and 36 girls enrolled in the Stanford University Nursery School. They ranged in age from 37 to 69 months, with a mean age of 52 months.

Two adults, a male and a female, served in the role of model, and one female experimenter conducted the study for all 72 children.

Experimental Design

Subjects were divided into eight experimental groups of six subjects each and a control group consisting of 24 subjects. Half the experimental subjects were exposed to aggressive models and half were exposed to models that were subdued and nonaggressive in their behavior. These groups were further subdivided into male and female subjects. Half the subjects in the aggressive and nonaggressive conditions observed same-sex models, while the remaining subjects in each group viewed models of the opposite sex. The control group had no prior exposure to the adult models and was tested only in the generalization situation.

It seemed reasonable to expect that the subjects' level of aggressiveness would be positively related to the readiness with which they imitated aggressive modes of behavior. Therefore, in order to increase the precision of treatment comparisons, subjects in the experimental and control groups were matched individually on the basis of ratings of their aggressive behavior in social interactions in the nursery school.

The subjects were rated on four five-point rating scales by the experimenter and a nursery school teacher, both of whom were well acquainted with the children. These scales measured the extent to which subjects displayed physical aggression, verbal aggression, aggression toward inanimate objects, and aggressive inhibition. The latter scale, which dealt with the subjects' tendency to inhibit aggressive reactions in the face of high instigation, provided a measure of aggression anxiety.

Fifty-one subjects were rated independently by both judges so as to permit an assessment of interrater agreement. The reliability of the composite aggression score, estimated by means of the Pearson product-moment correlation, was .89.

The composite score was obtained by summing the ratings on the four aggression scales; on the basis of these scores, subjects were arranged in triplets and assigned at random to one of two treatment conditions or to the control group.

Experimental Conditions

In the first step in the procedure subjects were brought individually by the experimenter to the experimental room and the model who was in the hallway outside the room, was invited by the experimenter to come and join in the game. The experimenter then escorted the subject to one corner of the room, which was structured as the subject's play area. After seating the child at a small table, the experimenter demonstrated how the subject could design pictures with potato prints and picture stickers provided. The potato prints included a variety of geometrical forms; the stickers were attractive multicolor pictures of animals, flowers, and western figures to be pasted on a pastoral scene. These activities were selected since they had been established, by previous studies in the nursery school, as having high interest value for the children.

After having settled the subject in his corner, the experimenter escorted the model to the opposite corner of the room which contained a small table and chair, a tinker toy set, a mallet, and a 5-foot inflated Bobo doll. The experimenter explained that these were the materials provided for the model to play with and, after the model was seated, the experimenter left the experimental room.

With subjects in the *nonaggressive condition*, the model assembled the tinker toys in a quiet, subdued manner, totally ignoring the Bobo doll.

In contrast, with subjects in the *aggressive condition*, the model began by assembling the tinker toys but after approximately a minute had elapsed, the model turned to the Bobo doll and spent the remainder of the period aggressing toward it.

Imitative learning can be clearly demonstrated if a model performs sufficiently novel patterns of responses which are unlikely to occur independently of the observation of the behavior of a model and if a subject reproduces these behaviors in substantially identical form. For this reason, in addition to punching the Bobo doll, a response that is likely to be performed by children independently of a demonstration, the model exhibited distinctive aggressive acts which were to be scored as imitative responses. The model laid Bobo on its side, sat on it and punched it repeatedly in the nose. The model then raised the Bobo doll, picked up the mallet and struck the doll on the head. Following the mallet aggression, the model tossed the doll up in the air aggressively and kicked it about the room. This sequence of physically aggressive acts was repeated approximately three times, interspersed with verbally aggressive responses such as, "Sock him in the nose . . . ," "Hit him down . . . ," "Throw him in the air . . . ," "Kick him . . . ," "Pow . . . ," and two nonaggressive comments, "He keeps coming back for more" and "He sure is a tough fella."

Thus in the exposure situation, subjects were provided with a diverting task which occupied their attention while at the same time insured observation of the model's behavior in the absence of any instructions to observe or to learn the responses in question. Since subjects could not perform the model's aggressive behavior, any learning that occurred was purely on an observational or covert basis.

At the end of 10 minutes, the experimenter entered the room, informed the subject that he would now go to another game room, and bid the model goodbye.

Aggression Arousal

Subjects were tested for the amount of imitative learning in a different experimental room that was set off from the main nursery school building. The two experimental situations were thus clearly differentiated; in fact, many subjects were under the impression that they were no longer on the nursery school grounds.

Prior to the test for imitation, however, all subjects, experimental and control, were subjected to mild aggression arousal to insure that they were under some degree of instigation to aggression. The arousal experience was included for two main reasons. In the first place, observation of aggressive behavior exhibited by others tends to reduce the probability of aggression on the part of the observer (Rosenbaum & deCharms, 1960). Consequently, subjects in the aggressive condition, in relation both to the nonaggressive and control groups, would be under weaker instigation following exposure to the models. Second, if subjects in the nonaggressive condition expressed little aggression in the face of appropriate instigation, the presence of an inhibitory process would seem to be indicated.

Following the exposure experience, therefore, the experimenter brought the subject to an anteroom that contained these relatively attractive toys: a fire engine, a locomotive, a jet fighter plane, a cable car, a colorful spinning top, and a doll set complete with wardrobe, doll carriage, and baby crib. The experimenter explained that the toys were for the subject to play with but, as soon as the subject became sufficiently involved with the play material (usually in about 2 minutes), the experimenter remarked that these were her very best toys, that she did not let just anyone play with them, and that she had decided to reserve these toys for the other children. However, the subject could play with any of the toys that were in the next room. The experimenter and the subject then entered the adjoining experimental room.

It was necessary for the experimenter to remain in the room during the experimental session; otherwise a number of the children would either refuse to remain alone or, would leave before the termination of the session. However, in order to minimize any influence her presence might have on the subject's behavior, the experimenter remained as inconspicuous as possible by busying herself with paper work at a desk in the far corner of the room and avoiding any interaction with the child.

Test for Delayed Imitation

The experimental room contained a variety of toys including some that could be used in imitative or nonimitative aggression, and others that tended to elicit predominantly nonaggressive forms of behavior. The aggressive toys included a 3-foot Bobo doll, a mallet and peg board, two dart guns, and a tether ball with a face painted on it which hung from the ceiling. The nonaggressive toys, on the other hand, included a tea set, crayons and coloring paper, a ball, two dolls, three bears, cars and trucks, and plastic farm animals.

In order to eliminate any variation in behavior due to mere placement of the toys in the room, the play material was arranged in a fixed order for each of the sessions.

The subject spent 20 minutes in this experimental room during which time his behavior was rated in terms of predetermined response categories by judges who observed the session through a one-way mirror in an adjoining observation room. The 20-minute session was divided into 5-second intervals by means of an electric interval timer, thus yielding a total number of 240 response units for each subject.

The male model scored the experimental sessions for all 72 children. Except for the cases in which he served as model, he did not have knowledge of the subjects' group assignments. In order to provide an estimate of interscorer agreement, the performances of half the subjects were also scored independently by a second observer. Thus one or the other of the two observers usually had no knowledge of the conditions to which the subjects were assigned. Since, however, all but two of the subjects in the aggressive condition performed the models' novel aggressive responses while subjects in the other conditions only rarely exhibited such reactions, subjects who were exposed to the aggressive models could be readily identified through their distinctive behavior.

The responses scored involved highly specific concrete classes of behavior and yielded high interscorer reliabilities, the product–moment coefficients being in the .90s.

Response Measures

Three measures of imitation were obtained:

Imitation of physical aggression: This category included acts of striking the Bobo doll with the mallet, sitting on the doll and punching it in the nose, kicking the doll, and tossing it in the air.

Imitative verbal aggression: Subject repeats the phrases, "Sock him," "Hit him down," "Kick him," "Throw him in the air," or "Pow."

Imitative nonaggressive verbal responses: Subject repeats, "He keeps coming back for more," or "He sure is a tough fella."

During the pretest, a number of the subjects imitated the essential components of the model's behavior but did not perform the complete act, or they directed the imitative aggressive response to some ob-

ject other than the Bobo doll. Two responses of this type were therefore scored and were interpreted as partially imitative behavior.

Mallet aggression: Subject strikes objects other than the Bobo doll aggressively with the mallet.

Sits on Bobo doll: Subject lays the Bobo doll on its side and sits on it, but does not aggress toward it.

The following additional nonimitative aggressive responses were scored:

Punches Bobo doll: Subject strikes, slaps, or pushes the doll aggressively.

Nonimitative physical and verbal aggression: This category included physically aggressive acts directed toward objects other than the Bobo doll and any hostile remarks except for those in the verbal imitation category; e.g., "Shoot the Bobo," "Cut him," "Stupid ball," "Knock over people," "Horses fighting, biting."

Aggressive gun play: Subject shoots darts or aims the guns and fires imaginary shots at objects in the room.

Ratings were also made of the number of behavior units in which subjects played nonaggressively or sat quietly and did not play with any of the material at all.

Results

Complete Imitation of Models' Behavior

Subjects in the aggression condition reproduced a good deal of physical and verbal aggressive behavior resembling that of the models, and their mean scores differed markedly from those of subjects in the nonaggressive and control groups, who exhibited virtually no imitative aggression (see Table 1).

Since there were only a few scores for subjects in the nonaggressive and control conditions (approximately 70% of the subjects had zero scores), and the assumption of homogeneity of variance could not be made, the Friedman two-way analysis of variance by ranks was employed to test the significance of the obtained differences.

The prediction that exposure of subjects to aggressive models increases the probability of aggressive behavior is clearly confirmed (see Table 2). The main effect of treatment conditions is highly significant both for physical and verbal imitative aggression. Comparison of pairs of scores by the sign test shows that the obtained over-all differences were due almost entirely to the aggression displayed by subjects who had been exposed to the aggressive models. Their scores were significantly higher than those of either the nonaggressive or control groups, which did not differ from each other (Table 2).

Imitation was not confined to the model's aggressive responses. Approximately one-third of the sub-

table 1   Mean Aggression Scores for Experimental and Control Subjects

Response category	Experimental groups				
	Aggressive		Nonaggressive		
	F Model	M Model	F Model	M Model	Control groups
Imitative physical aggression					
Female subjects	5.5	7.2	2.5	0.0	1.2
Male subjects	12.4	25.8	0.2	1.5	2.0
Imitative verbal aggression					
Female subjects	13.7	2.0	0.3	0.0	0.7
Male subjects	4.3	12.7	1.1	0.0	1.7
Mallet aggression					
Female subjects	17.2	18.7	0.5	0.5	13.1
Male subjects	15.5	28.8	18.7	6.7	13.5
Punches Bobo doll					
Female subjects	6.3	16.5	5.8	4.3	11.7
Male subjects	18.9	11.9	15.6	14.8	15.7
Nonimitative aggression					
Female subjects	21.3	8.4	7.2	1.4	6.1
Male subjects	16.2	36.7	26.1	22.3	24.6
Aggressive gun play					
Female subjects	1.8	4.5	2.6	2.5	3.7
Male subjects	7.3	15.9	8.9	16.7	14.3

table 2   Significance of the Differences Between Experimental and Control Groups in the Expression of Aggression

Response category	χ^2_r	Q	ϕ	Comparison of pairs of treatment conditions		
				Aggressive vs. Nonaggressive	Aggressive vs. Control	Non-aggressive vs. Control
				p	p	p
Imitative responses						
Physical aggression	27.17		<.001	<.001	<.001	.09
Verbal aggression	9.17		<.02	.004	.048	.09
Nonaggressive verbal responses		17.50	<.001	.004	.004	ns
Partial imitation						
Mallet aggression	11.06		<.01	.026	ns	.005
Sits on Bobo		13.44	<.01	.018	.059	ns
Nonimitative aggression						
Punches Bobo doll	2.87		ns			
Physical and verbal	8.96		<.02	.026	ns	ns
Aggressive gun play	2.75		ns			

jects in the aggressive condition also repeated the model's nonaggressive verbal responses while none of the subjects in either the nonaggressive or control groups made such remarks. This difference, tested by means of the Cochran Q test, was significant well beyond the .001 level (Table 2).

Partial Imitation of Models' Behavior

Differences in the predicted direction were also obtained on the two measures of partial imitation.

Analysis of variance of scores based on the subjects' use of the mallet aggressively toward objects other than the Bobo doll reveals that treatment conditions are a statistically significant source of variation (Table 2). In addition, individual sign tests show that both the aggressive and the control groups, relative to subjects in the nonaggressive condition, produced significantly more mallet aggression, the difference being particularly marked with regard to female subjects. Girls who observed nonaggressive models performed a mean number of 0.5 mallet aggression responses as compared to mean values of 18.0 and 13.1 for girls in the aggressive and control groups, respectively.

Although subjects who observed aggressive models performed more mallet aggression ($M = 20.0$) than their controls ($M = 13.3$), the difference was not statistically significant.

With respect to the partially imitative response of sitting on the Bobo doll, the over-all group differences were significant beyond the .01 level (Table 2). Comparison of pairs of scores by the sign test procedure reveals that subjects in the aggressive group reproduced this aspect of the models' behavior to a greater extent than did the nonaggressive ($p = .018$) or the control ($p = .059$) subjects. The latter two groups, on the other hand, did not differ from each other.

Nonimitative Aggression

Analyses of variance of the remaining aggression measures (Table 2) show that treatment conditions did not influence the extent to which subjects engaged in aggressive gun play or punched the Bobo doll. The effect of conditions is highly significant ($x^2_r = 8.96$, $p < .02$), however, in the case of the subjects' expression of nonimitative physical and verbal aggression. Further comparison of treatment pairs reveals that the main source of the overall difference was the aggressive and nonaggressive groups which differed significantly from each other (Table 2), with subjects exposed to the aggressive models displaying the greater amount of aggression.

Influence of Sex of Model and Sex of Subjects on Imitation

The hypothesis that boys are more prone than girls to imitate aggression exhibited by a model was only partially confirmed. t tests computed for subjects in the aggressive condition reveal that boys reproduced more imitative physical aggression than girls ($t = 2.50$, $p < .01$). The groups do not differ, however, in their imitation of verbal aggression.

The use of nonparametric tests, necessitated by the extremely skewed distributions of scores for subjects in the nonaggressive and control conditions, preclude an over-all test of the influence of sex of model per se, and of the various interactions between the main effects. Inspection of the means presented in Table 1 for subjects in the aggression condition, however, clearly suggests the possibility of a Sex × Model interaction. This interaction effect is much more consistent and pronounced for the male model than for the female model. Male subjects, for example, exhibited more physical ($t = 2.07$, $p < .05$) and verbal imitative aggression ($t = 2.51$, $p < .05$), more nonimitative aggression ($t = 3.15$, $p < .025$), and engaged in significantly more aggressive gun play ($t = 2.12$, $p < .05$) following exposure to the aggressive male model than the female subjects. In contrast, girls exposed to the female model performed considerably more imitative verbal aggression and more nonimitative aggression than did the boys (Table 1). The variances, however, were equally large and with only a small N in each cell the mean differences did not reach statistical significance.

Data for the nonaggressive and control subjects provide additional suggestive evidence that the behavior of the male model exerted a greater influence than the female model on the subjects' behavior in the generalization situation.

It will be recalled that, except for the greater amount of mallet aggression exhibited by the control subjects, no significant differences were obtained between the nonaggressive and control groups. The data indicate, however, that the absence of significant differences between these two groups was due primarily to the fact that subjects exposed to the nonaggressive female model did not differ from the controls on any of the measures of aggression. With respect to the male model, on the other hand, the differences between the groups are striking. Comparison of the sets of scores by means of the sign test reveals that, in relation to the control group, subjects exposed to the nonaggressive male model performed significantly less imitative physical aggression ($p = .06$), less imitative verbal aggression ($p = .002$), less mallet aggression ($p = .003$), less nonimitative physical and verbal aggression ($p = .03$), and they were less inclined to punch the Bobo doll ($p = .07$).

While the comparison of subgroups, when some of the over-all tests do not reach statistical significance, is likely to capitalize on chance differences, nevertheless the consistency of the findings adds support to the interpretation in terms of influence by the model.

Nonaggressive Behavior

With the exception of expected sex differences, Lindquist (1956) Type III analyses of variance of the nonaggressive response scores yielded few significant differences.

Female subjects spent more time than boys playing with dolls ($p < .001$), with the tea set ($p < .001$), and coloring ($p < .05$). The boys, on the other hand, devoted significantly more time than the girls to exploratory play with the guns ($p < .01$). No sex differences were found in respect to the subjects' use of the other stimulus objects, i.e., farm animals, cars, or tether ball.

Treatment conditions did produce significant differences on two measures of nonaggressive behavior that are worth mentioning. Subjects in the nonaggressive condition engaged in significantly more nonaggressive play with dolls than either subjects in the aggressive group ($t = 2.67$, $p < .02$), or in the control group ($t = 2.57$, $p < .02$).

Even more noteworthy is the finding that subjects who observed nonaggressive models spent more than twice as much time as subjects in the aggressive condition ($t = 3.07$, $p < .01$) in simply sitting quietly without handling any of the play material.

Discussion

Much current research on social learning is focused on the shaping of new behavior through rewarding and punishing consequences. Unless responses are emitted, however, they cannot be influenced. The results of this study provide strong evidence that observation of cues produced by the behavior of others is one effective means of eliciting certain forms of responses for which the original probability is very low or zero. Indeed, social imitation may hasten or short-cut the acquisition of new behaviors without the necessity of reinforcing successive approximations as suggested by Skinner (1953).

Thus subjects given an opportunity to observe aggressive models later reproduced a good deal of physical and verbal aggression (as well as nonaggressive responses) substantially identical with that of the model. In contrast, subjects who were exposed to nonaggressive models and those who had no previous exposure to any models only rarely performed such responses.

To the extent that observation of adult models displaying aggression communicates permissiveness for aggressive behavior, such exposure may serve to weaken inhibitory responses and thereby to increase the probability of aggressive reactions to subsequent frustrations. The fact, however, that subjects expressed their aggression in ways that clearly resembled the novel patterns exhibited by the models provides striking evidence for the occurrence of learning by imitation.

In the procedure employed by Miller and Dollard (1941) for establishing imitative behavior, adult or peer models performed discrimination responses following which they were consistently rewarded, and the subjects were similarly reinforced whenever they matched the leaders' choice responses. While these experiments have been widely accepted as demonstrations of learning by means of imitation, in fact, they simply involve a special case of discrimination learning in which the behavior of others serves as discriminative stimuli for responses that are already part of the subject's repertoire. Auditory or visual environmental cues could easily have been substituted for the social stimuli to facilitate the discrimination learning. In contrast, the process of imitation studied in the present experiment differed in several important respects from the one investigated by Miller and Dollard in that subjects learned to combine fractional responses into relatively complex novel patterns solely by observing the performance of social models without any opportunity to perform the models' behavior in the exposure setting, and without any reinforcers delivered either to the models or to the observers.

An adequate theory of the mechanisms underlying imitative learning is lacking. The explanations that have been offered (Logan, Olmsted, Rosner, Schwartz, & Stevens, 1955; Maccoby, 1959) assume that the imitator performs the model's responses covertly. If it can be assumed additionally that rewards and punishments are self-administered in conjunction with the covert responses, the process of imitative learning could be accounted for in terms of the same principles that govern instrumental trial-and-error learning. In the early stages of the developmental process, however, the range of component responses in the organism's repertoire is probably increased through a process of classical conditioning (Bandura & Huston, 1961; Mowrer, 1950).

The data provide some evidence that the male model influenced the subjects' behavior outside the exposure setting to a greater extent than was true for the female model. In the analyses of the Sex × Model interactions, for example, only the comparisons involving the male model yielded significant differences. Similarly, subjects exposed to the nonaggressive male model performed less aggressive behavior than the controls, whereas comparisons involving the female model were consistently nonsignificant.

In a study of learning by imitation, Rosenblith (1959) has likewise found male experimenters more effective than females in influencing children's behavior. Rosenblith advanced the tentative explanation that the school setting may involve some social deprivation in respect to adult males which, in turn, enhances the male's reward value.

The trends in the data yielded by the present study suggest an alternative explanation. In the case of a highly masculine-typed behavior such as physical aggression, there is a tendency for both male and female subjects to imitate the male model to a greater degree than the female model. On the other hand, in the case of verbal aggression, which is less clearly sex linked, the greatest amount of imitation occurs in relation to the same-sex model. These trends together with the finding that boys in relation to girls are in general more imitative of physical aggression but do not differ in imitation of verbal aggression, suggest that subjects may be differentially affected by the sex of the model but that predictions must take into account the degree to which the behavior in question is sex-typed.

The preceding discussion has assumed that maleness-femaleness rather than some other personal characteristics of the particular models involved, is the significant variable—an assumption that cannot be tested directly with the data at hand. It was clearly evident, however, particularly from boys' spontaneous remarks about the display of aggression by the female model, that some subjects at least were responding in terms of a sex discrimination and their prior learning about what is sex appropriate behavior (e.g., "Who is that lady. That's not the way for a lady to behave. Ladies are supposed to act like ladies ... " "You should have seen what that girl did in there. She was just acting like a man. I never saw a girl act like that before. She was punching and fighting but no swearing.") Aggression by the male model, on the other hand, was more likely to be seen as appropriate and approved by both the boys ("Al's a good socker, he beat up Bobo. I want to sock like Al.") and the girls ("That man is a strong fighter, he punched and punched and he could hit Bobo right down to the floor and if Bobo got up he said, 'Punch your nose.' He's a good fighter like Daddy.")

The finding that subjects exposed to the quiet models were more inhibited and unresponsive than subjects in the aggressive condition, together with the obtained difference on the aggression measures, suggests that exposure to inhibited models not only decreases the probability of occurrence of aggressive behavior but also generally restricts the range of behavior emitted by the subjects.

"Identification with aggressor" (Freud, 1946) or "defensive identification" (Mowrer, 1950), whereby a person presumably transforms himself from object to agent of aggression by adopting the attributes of an aggressive threatening model so as to allay anxiety, is widely accepted as an explanation of the imitative learning of aggression.

The development of aggressive modes of response by children of aggressively punitive adults, however, may simply reflect object displacement without involving any such mechanism of defensive identification. In studies of child training antecedents of aggressively antisocial adolescents (Bandura & Walters, 1959) and of young hyperaggressive boys (Bandura, 1960), the parents were found to be nonpermissive and punitive of aggression directed toward themselves. On the other hand, they actively encouraged and reinforced their sons' aggression toward persons outside the home. This pattern of differential reinforcement of aggressive behavior served to inhibit the boys' aggression toward the original instigators and fostered the displacement of aggression toward objects and situations eliciting much weaker inhibitory responses.

Moreover, the findings from an earlier study (Bandura & Huston, 1961), in which children imitated to an equal degree aggression exhibited by a nurturant and a nonnurturant model, together with the results of the present experiment in which subjects readily imitated aggressive models who were more or less neutral figures suggest that mere observation of aggression, regardless of the quality of the model–subject relationship, is a sufficient condition for producing imitative aggression in children. A comparative study of the subjects' imitation of aggressive models who are feared, who are linked and esteemed, or who are essentially neutral figures would throw some light on whether or not a more parsimonious theory than the one involved in "identification with the aggressor" can explain the modeling process.

Summary

Twenty-four preschool children were assigned to each of three conditions. One experimental group observed aggressive adult models; a second observed inhibited nonaggressive models; while subjects in a control group had no prior exposure to the models. Half the subjects in the experimental conditions observed same-sex models and half viewed models of the opposite sex. Subjects were then tested for the amount of imitative as well as nonimitative aggression performed in a new situation in the absence of the models.

Comparison of the subjects' behavior in the generalization situation revealed that subjects exposed to aggressive models reproduced a good deal of aggression resembling that of the models, and that their mean scores differed markedly from those of subjects in the nonaggressive and control groups. Subjects in the aggressive condition also exhibited significantly more partially imitative and nonimitative aggressive behavior and were generally less inhibited in their behavior than subjects in the nonaggressive condition.

Imitation was found to be differentially influenced by the sex of the model with boys showing more aggression than girls following exposure to the male model, the difference being particularly marked on highly masculine-typed behavior.

Subjects who observed the nonaggressive models, especially the subdued male model, were generally less aggressive than their controls.

The implications of the findings based on this experiment and related studies for the psychoanalytic theory of identification with the aggressor were discussed.

REFERENCES

Bandura, A. Relationship of family patterns to child behavior disorders. Progress Report, 1960, Stanford University, Project No. M-1734, United States Public Health Service.

Bandura, A., & Huston, Aletha C. Identification as a process of incidental learning. *J. abnorm. soc. Psychol.*, 1961, 63, 311–318.

Bandura, A., & Walters, R. H. *Adolescent aggression*. New York: Ronald, 1959.

Blake, R. R. The other person in the situation. In R. Tagiuri & L. Petrullo (Eds.), *Person perception and interpersonal behavior*. Stanford, Calif: Stanford Univer. Press, 1958, Pp. 229–242.

Fauls, Lydia B., & Smith, W. D. Sex-role learning of five-year olds. *J. genel. Psychol.*, 1956, 89, 105–117.

Freud, Anna. *The ego and the mechanisms of defense*. New York: International Univer. Press, 1946.

Grosser, D., Polansky, N., & Lippitt, R. A laboratory study of behavior contagion. *Hum. Relat.*, 1951, 4, 115–142.

Lindquist, E. F. *Design and analysis of experiments*. Boston: Houghton Mifllin, 1956.

Logan, F., Olmsted, O. L., Rosner, B. S., Schwartz, R. D., & Stevens, C. M. *Behavior theory and social science*. New Haven: Yale Univer. Press, 1955.

Maccoby, Eleanor E. Role-taking in childhood and its consequences for social learning. *Child Develpm.*, 1959, 30, 239–252.

Miller, N. E., & Dollard, J. *Social learning and imitation*. New Haven: Yale Univer. Press, 1941.

Mowrer, O. H. (Ed.) Identification: A link between learning theory and psychotherapy. In, *Learning theory and personality dynamics*. New York: Ronald, 1950. Pp. 69–94.

Rosenbaum, M. E., & DeCharms, R. Direct and vicarious reduction of hostility. *J. abnorm. soc. Psychol.*, 1960, 60, 105–111.

Rosenblith, Judy F. Learning by imitation in kindergarten children. *Child Develpm.*, 1959, 30, 69–80.

Schachter, S., & Hall, R. Group-derived restraints and audience persuasion. *Hum. Relat.*, 1952, 5, 397–406.

Skinner, B. F. *Science and human behavior*. New York: Macmillan, 1953.

Questions

1. Why do the authors call delayed imitation a more crucial indicator of learning than imitation in the presence of a model?
2. What was the age range of the children in this study, and why do you think this age group was selected for this research?
3. What specific child behaviors were assessed before children were exposed to the models in this study, and why was it important to pre-assess children on these behaviors and then use these scores to match children in the experimental and control groups?
4. Why was it important for the model to exhibit several distinctive aggressive actions toward the Bobo doll in the child's presence?
5. What did the researchers do to arouse the children's aggression, and why was this important to this study?
6. What are some of the implications of these results for social policy regarding the exposure of children to violent models in television, movies, video games, and other media?

22 Cultural Differences in American and Mexican Mother–Child Pretend Play

JoAnn M. Farver • Carollee Howes

Piaget, Vygotsky, Freud, Erikson, and many other early psychologists were very interested in children's play. Their interest stemmed from the belief that play provides children with abundant opportunities for psychological development. These opportunities range from practicing cognitive and social skills to learning how to regulate emotions.

Until recently, research on children's play has concentrated on the play behaviors of middle-class children in Western communities. However, in the past few years, research by developmental psychologists has expanded to include studies of children's play in many communities throughout the world. This research has revealed much similarity in children's play, suggesting that it may be linked to some basic developmental processes. However, some variation in children's play across cultural communities has also been found. These variations come from many sources, including cultural values, practices of social interaction, and the resources available to support and guide children's play.

In the following article, JoAnn Farver and Carollee Howes compare the play behaviors of mothers and toddlers in two cultural communities: the United States and Mexico. Their research focuses on pretend play. This type of play, which is also called dramatic play, allows children to improve their skill at symbolic representation, to imagine their own future roles, and to experience the roles and feelings of others in a playful and nonthreatening way. Farver and Howes went to great effort to include families in Mexico and the United States that were similar along several crucial dimensions, including the family's social class and the target child's position in the family. They also collected different types of data, from observations and interviews, about the children's play behaviors. These efforts resulted in a comprehensive description of the main differences in children's play patterns in these two cultural groups. In addition, the investigators were able to connect these differences to the broader cultural values and practices of these communities.

Toddler-age children's play with their mothers (n = 60) was videotaped in the U.S. and Mexico. Episodes were examined for pretend play, mutual involvement in social play, joint involvement in cooperative social pretend play, and maternal play behaviors. Contextual features were observed, recorded, and analyzed using an activity setting model. Mothers were interviewed about their value of children's play behavior. Although children's pretend play and mother–child mutual involvement increased with age in the two cultures, American mother–child pairs accounted for the greater proportion of interactive social play and pretend play episodes.

Reprinted material from Farver, JoAnn M., & Howes, Carolee, "Cultural Differences in American and Mexican Mother-Child Pretend Play," in *Merrill-Palmer Quarterly, Vol. 39*, No. 3 (July 1993), © Wayne State University Press, with the permission of Wayne State University Press.

Acknowledgments: The research is based on a dissertation submitted by J. M. Farver in partial fulfillment of the requirements for the doctoral degree in the Graduate School of Education, University of California, Los Angeles. The study was supported by grants from the University of California, Los Angeles, Chicano Studies Program, and the Organization of American States, Washington, DC. The authors gratefully acknowledge the families who participated in this study. A special thanks to the Menzie family, and to the Mexican field assistants, Patricia Rodriques, Victor Guerrero, and Evelyn Aron, who helped with coding the data and establishing reliability.

There were also cultural differences in behaviors that mothers used to structure play and in mothers' value of children's play. The findings suggest that mothers guide the development of their children's play according to their particular cultural norms, which poses a theoretical challenge to the current notion that mothers are the primary facilitators of children's early pretend play.

American and Mexican young children's pretend play with their mothers was investigated, with the primary objective of understanding how culture influences the way in which mothers and their children engage in and express pretend play. Most research on children's early symbolic development and play behavior has been based on white, middle-class Western samples. As result, cultural and social-class differences in children's play have been interpreted as signs of deficiency rather than variation (Feitelson, 1977; Smilansky, 1968). In the present study, the data base was broadened by comparing mother–child play in two different cultural contexts to allow general inferences to be made about the role of culture in development. The study also provides information about similarities and variations in developmental processes across particular contexts in which development occurs.

According to Western theorists, young children's pretend play originates in early interaction with parents. Werner and Kaplan (1963) claimed that it is the child's initial desire to share the object world with the mother that motivates the earliest attempts at communication and marks the beginning of internalized symbolic processes. According to this theory, early pretend play begins during the child's active experimentation with objects and in the seeking of confirmation of the developing symbols from the mother. In Western studies of early play behavior, it is proposed that mothers facilitate young children's beginning attempts at pretense. As mothers provide suggestions and communicate the rules of playing pretend, children incorporate the maternal guidance into play sequences and gradually begin to construct pretend scripts and enact roles. During play, mothers and children coordinate their actions and, with maternal assistance, children can perform beyond their existing level of competence (Haight & Miller, 1991; Miller & Garvey, 1984; O'Connell & Bretherton, 1984; Slade, 1987).

Although research indicates that mothers structure or scaffold children's early pretend play, it is unclear whether these findings are generalizable to mothers and children in different cultures. In other societies, children may have few opportunities to play with their mothers. Mothers may not have time to spend in specific child-centered activities involving play. Children's play may not be considered to be a valuable, productive activity, or entering and managing children's play may be culturally inappropriate adult behavior. Cultural variations in mother–child communication styles also may influence their collaboration in play. Such culture-specific factors may affect a mother's inclination to play with her child, her scaffolding behavior, and the partner's involvement in pretend play.

To examine the influence of culture in shaping mother–child pretend play, an activity setting approach was used here. This approach is derived from Soviet activity theory (Leont'ev, 1981) and the Whiting behavior-setting concept (Whiting & Edwards, 1988), and is elaborated in Weisner and Gallimore's work (Tharp & Gallimore, 1988; Weisner, Gallimore, & Jordan, 1988). The model emphasizes the Vygotsky (1978) notion that children's development cannot be understood apart from the wider social milieu. Ecological factors as well as the economic and social organization of a community influence families' daily routines, individuals with whom they interact, activities in which they engage, and scripts that guide their behavior (Whiting & Edwards, 1988).

To compare American and Mexican mother–child play along similar contextual or environmental dimensions, variables that potentially influence mother–child interaction and play behavior were isolated. Features of American and Mexican activity settings, as derived from the research literature, are elaborated in Table 1.

Based on differences in the American and Mexican activity setting features, it was predicted that American children, reared in single family homes where mothers are available and customary play companions, display more symbolic level play with objects and engage in more frequent and more complex episodes of shared pretend play with their mothers than do Mexican children, who live in extended families and have rare opportunities to formally play with their mothers.

A second hypothesis is that cultural differences in childrearing goals and practices and the mother's value of play activity affect the behaviors which mothers use to scaffold children's pretend play. American mothers, who value play, emphasize the early development of cognitive skill, and promote children's independent effort, were expected to make frequent suggestions for fantasy play, to support their children's efforts at pretense, and to use an implicit style of guidance (defined as providing verbal support and following their children's lead in play). Mexican mothers, who place little or no value on play and emphasize direction, modeling, and imitation in shared daily activity, were expected to make few suggestions for fantasy play, to rarely use praise or approval as reinforcement, and to use an explicit style of guidance (defined as organizing and directing play activity).

table 1 Features of American and Mexican Activity Settings

	American	Mexican
Personnel available	Mothers[a]	Mothers[f]
	Toddlers	Toddlers
	Siblings	Siblings
		Extended family
		Neighbors
		Older children
Nature of tasks and activities performed	Formal play with educational outcomes[b]	Informal play in work contexts[g]
	Mother joins child's activities	Child joins mother's activities
Purpose of tasks	Prepare for school[c]	Prepare for work[h]
Cultural goals, values, and beliefs	Independence[d]	Interdependence[i]
	Individual autonomy	Family orientation
	Self-confidence	Cooperation
	Cognitive skills	Social skills
Scripts governing interactions	Parents help child learn[e]	Parents model desired behavior[j]
	Child learns through adult's efforts at teaching in play	Child learns by observing and imitating adult behavior in work

[a]Rogoff, Mistry, Göncü, & Mosier, 1991; Whiting & Edwards, 1988.
[b]Haight & Miller, 1991; Miller & Garvey, 1984; Whiting & Edwards, 1988.
[c]Bradley & Caldwell, 1984; Levenstein, 1986, in press; LeVine, 1980; White, 1980.
[d]Hoffman, 1988; Lawton, Fowell, Schuler, & Madsen, 1984; LeVine, 1980; Richman, Miller, & Solomon, 1988; Whiting & Edwards, 1988.
[e]Levenstein, 1986, in press; LeVine, 1980.
[f,g,h]Romney & Romney, 1966; Whiting & Edwards, 1988; Zukow, 1989.
[i]Bronstein-Burrows, 1981; Diáz-Guerrero, 1975; Falicov & Karrer, 1980; Holtzman, 1982; Holtzman, Diáz-Guerrero, Swartz, & Tapia, 1969; Kagan, 1981; Kagan & Ember, 1975; Keefe, Padrilla, & Carlos, 1979; Peñalosa, 1968; Ramírez, 1967; Ramírez & Price-Williams, 1974.
[j]Bronstein-Burrows, 1981; Ramírez & Castañeda, 1974.

Method

Subjects

The participants were 60 children and their mothers: 30 Anglo-American and 30 Mexican, 10 from each culture, at ages 18, 24, and 36 months. Half of each age group were girls. Criterion for selection was that the child was at least a second-born. American families were contacted by flyers posted at neighborhood parks and by word of mouth. Mexican families were recruited by an assistant who was a resident of the community.

The American sample of white, working-class families came from an economically depressed county in northern California. Nuclear family households contained from two to five children ($M = 2.45$), ranging in age from 6 months to 12 years. Fathers were employed in the building trades, as truck drivers, retail store clerks, and similar occupations. Mothers did not work outside the home. Most mothers reported that, given their level of training and education, they could not earn enough money to both afford childcare and make a significant contribution to family income.

The Spanish-speaking Mexican Mestizo sample came from a town of about 5,000 residents located on the Pacific Coast 1,700 miles south of the U. S. border. Households consisted of intact families (i.e., both parents were living in the home) with two to five children ($M = 3.3$ children), ranging in age from infancy to 10 years. The nuclear families were embedded in an extended kinship cluster that included grandparents and/or paternal siblings and their children.

The Mexican community was selected because the predominant socioeconomic status closely approximated the American working-class sample. Although no universal measure of social class is comparable across societies, Mexican sociologists claim that parallels can be drawn between the American class system and the Mexican (Alba, 1982; Balán, 1973; Eckstein, 1989; Suárez, 1978). Mexican sociologists distinguish working-class status from white-collar professionals who are considered to be middle-class (*clase media*), and the lower class (*clase humilde*) landless peasants (*campesinos*), informal sector day laborers, unskilled and semiskilled workers, who inhabit squatter settlements and tenements (*vecindades*), by using indices of skilled labor union affiliation, work stability, home ownership, desire for upward mobility, and primary-level education of 6 years (Balán, 1973; Eckstein, 1989; Suárez, 1978).

Mexican fathers in this sample were employed in unionized (*syndicados*) construction-related jobs (tile setters, masons, and concrete finishers), as automobile mechanics, wrought iron workers, craftsmen, or truck drivers. Mothers were occupied with household maintenance. During interviews and conversations, parents expressed the desire to improve their economic standing and occupational opportunities and education for their children. Most older siblings were enrolled in or had attended the community's "kinder" program (preschool for 4- and 5-year-olds).

All Mexican families held the title to their land. Their houses were lowcost, but solidly built and of middle-class style, with separate rooms for cooking, sleeping, and everyday living. Houses were furnished with stoves, refrigerators, and television sets, and nearly all had indoor plumbing.

Procedure

Qualitative and quantitative research methods were used in both cultures. The qualitative data collection began first and continued throughout the study with the intent to describe ethnographically the family life, childrearing practices, and the characteristics of the activity settings that the children typically inhabited.

To minimize subjects' reactivity to the observer's presence in the Mexican setting, the researcher spent considerable time in the community prior to data collection. Each family was observed in and around their homes for a total of 8 hours. Observations were unstructured so that family behavior might be as self-motivated and spontaneous as possible. The observer attempted to be unobtrusive while recording detailed field notes of their daily routines and activities.

Field notes were compiled and analyzed using the grounded theory method developed by sociologists Glaser and Strauss (1967), an inductive approach that

consists of jointly collecting, categorizing, coding, and analyzing the data to allow theories to emerge. These emerging theories then can be systematically tested, provisionally verified, discarded, or reformulated simultaneously as data collection proceeds. The strength of this approach is that it allows the researcher to uncover patterns in participant behavior as it occurs in context. Thus, the researcher does not enter the setting with preconceived notions, possibly ignoring important variables.

In the quantitative procedure, mothers and children of both cultures were videotaped as they played with a bag of wooden shapes in their home for about 20 min. The wooden shapes included human, animal, and tree figures, various arched and flat rectangular pieces, square blocks, and a wooden train connected by magnets. The purpose of the shapes was to provide opportunities for pretense without introducing "toys" from the American culture to the Mexican and vice versa. Because the shapes were novel in Mexico, and, by maternal report, very different from toys and blocks in the American homes, children in both cultures were allowed to play with the shapes for 20 min prior to the videotaping. In both cultures, mothers were told that the study was about how mothers and children play. Mothers were asked to "Play with your child in anyway you want" (*"Juege con su niño de la manera en que usted le gusta"*).

At the end of the data collection, mothers were interviewed about their views of children's play. All observations, interviews, and videotaping of the children and their families in both cultures were conducted by the first author.

Coding and Measures

Videotapes were fully transcribed and then segmented into play episodes. An episode began when either partner touched an object or verbally interacted with the partner in the immediate environment. An episode ended when participants were no longer involved in play (e.g., either partner's attention was directed away for more than 30 s, or either partner moved away) or the theme of the play changed. The use of a different shape constituted a change in theme, unless the shapes were used in relationship to each other. For example, placing an animal shape on a tall stack of blocks was considered related to the ongoing theme of "stacking blocks." Sustained attention to, or introduction of, another shape into play, or an announced suggestion for a different play theme signaled the beginning of a new episode.

Level of Play with Objects.   Each episode was coded once for the focal child's highest level of object play by using a scale adopted from that of O'Connell and Bretherton (1984). *Exploratory play* consisted of all manipulative behaviors such as handling, throwing, banging, or mouthing the objects, or touching one shape to another. *Combinational play* included putting objects together, stacking the shapes, making spatial configurations, or grouping shapes by function or color. *Symbolic play* was coded when children used the shapes to represent other objects or activities, and included conventional or functional uses of the shapes, such as giving a horse shape a "ride" on the train, object substitution (using a block for a bed), and the use of an independent agent (making the human shapes walk or talk).

Mutual Involvement in Social Play. Each episode was coded for the presence or absence of mutual involvement in social play by using a measure adopted from a study by Howes (1980). Mutual involvement was coded when partners directed social bids to each other (smiled, vocalized, offered or received object, helped with task) and/or engaged in complementary and reciprocal activities with mutual awareness (e.g., child offered a shape, mother took it and offered it back).

Joint Involvement in Cooperative Social Pretend Play. Episodes containing symbolic level play were selected and coded for partners' joint involvement in cooperative pretend play by using a measure adopted from that of Howes (1985). Cooperative pretend play was coded when both partners performed fantasy actions in the context of ongoing social play, which indicated that they assumed complementary pretend roles (e.g., mother–baby).

Maternal Behaviors in Play. Fifteen maternal play behaviors, derived from observations of the activity settings and judged to be salient in the two cultures, were coded for the number of times each occurred during an episode. These behaviors were clustered to form four broad maternal scaffolding behaviors. Labeling objects, directing play, correcting child, setting stage for play, attracting child's attention, and providing a model were clustered to represent *explicit guidance*. These were times when mothers explicitly organized and directed play activity and children followed their lead. Requesting help, giving help, joining child's play, describing child's behavior, and describing own behavior, were combined to represent *implicit guidance*. Here, mothers provided interpretative commentary, kept their partner informed about what they were doing, and followed their children's lead in play. Praising and encouraging independence were clustered to form *support child's effort*. Suggesting symbolic play and using paralinguistic cues to animate play objects were combined to represent *suggest fantasy play*.

Reliability. Videotapes were coded by the bilingual first author and a bicultural, bilingual assistant who was uninformed of the children's ages and the goals of the study. The first author trained the assistant by using six videotapes (one for each age level in each culture). To establish reliability, six additional tapes were randomly selected and coded independently by the first author and the assistant. Cohen's kappas for rater agreement on identifying episodes, coding level of object play, mother–child involvement in social play, and cooperative pretend play, and determining the 15 maternal behaviors and their clustering and coding, ranged from .91 to .96 for the American dyads, and from .82 to .90 for the Mexican dyads. Similar reliability checks performed midway and at the end of the coding ranged from .95 to .97.

Because the data were collected by the first author, careful attention was given to training and establishing reliability with the assistant. To avoid experimenter bias, the assistant's codings of the videotapes were used in the data analysis.

Maternal Interviews

During the interviews, mothers were asked open-ended questions about the value that they placed on children's play behavior and who was their child's most common play partner. In both cultures, mothers' responses about the most important value of play fell into three main types: child's amusement, mutual enjoyment, and educational benefits. The four common play partners were mothers, fathers, siblings, and unrelated children. Mothers rated the importance of play on a 3-point scale: *not important, somewhat important*, and *very important*.

Cohen's kappas for agreement between the first author and the assistant on categorizing and coding of the three maternal interview questions ranged from .97 to .99 for the American sample, and from .94 to .98 for the Mexican sample.

Results

Number of Episodes

There were 782 mother–child play episodes in the two cultures (U.S., $M = 12.06$, $SD = 4.33$; Mexico, $M = 11.76$, $SD = 2.95$). An analysis of variance (ANOVA) comparing the number of episodes by age and culture was not significant.

Symbolic Level Play, Mutual Involvement, and Cooperative Pretend Play

Proportions were calculated for the frequencies of symbolic level object play, mother–child mutual involvement in social play, and mother–child cooperative social pretend play by dividing each measure by the total number of episodes. To avoid violating the

table 2   Proportion of Total Episodes of Symbolic Level Play, Mother–Child Mutual Involvement, and Cooperative Pretend Play by Age and Culture

| | Age in Months | | | | | | F | | |
| | 18 | | 24 | | 36 | | | | Age × |
	%	SD	%	SD	%	SD	Culture	Age	Culture
Symbolic play									
U.S.	.34	(.22)	.42	(.35)	.58	(.27)	9.71**	6.75**	1.43
Mexico	.04	(.05)	.37	(.27)	.34	(.19)			
Mutual involvement									
U.S.	.65	(.39)	.88	(.11)	1.00	(.02)	6.27**	4.28*	1.60
Mexico	.63	(.15)	.74	(.19)	.71	(.34)			
Cooperative pretend									
U.S.	.01	(.05)	.02	(.06)	.44	(.41)	3.79*	5.54**	5.01**
Mexico	.00	(.00)	.11	(.31)	.05	(.12)			

Note. In all cases, Scheffé tests indicated age 36 mo. > 18 mo.
$*p < .05.$ $**p < .01.$

assumptions of ANOVAS proportional variables, an arcsine transformation was conducted. Proportions were compared using three separate 3(Age) × 2 (Culture) × 2(Sex) ANOVAs. Because no main effects or interactions were found for sex, it was dropped from further analyses.

Significant main effects appeared for age and culture. Proportions of symbolic level play, $F(2, 44) = 6.75$, $p < .01$; partner's mutual involvement, $F(2, 44) = 4.28$, $p < .01$; and cooperative pretend play, $F(2, 44) = 5.54$, $p < .05$, all increased with age. Scheffé post hoc tests ($p < .05$) comparing age groups showed more symbolic level play, partner involvement, and cooperative pretend play among 36-month-olds than 18-month-olds. American children accounted for the greater proportion of symbolic play with objects, $F(1, 44) = 9.71$, $p < .01$. American mother–child dyads had a greater proportion of episodes with mutual involvement, $F(1, 44) = 6.27$, $p < .05$, and cooperative pretend play, $F(1, 44) = 3.79$, $p < .05$, than did Mexican dyads.

Maternal Play Behaviors

To examine the behaviors that mothers used to structure children's play and to understand how maternal behaviors differ by age and culture, four ANOVAs, 3(Age) × 2(Culture), were conducted. No significant main effects or interactions were found for age. However, significant main effects appeared for culture. American mothers used more implicit guidance (U.S., $M = 40.00$, $SD = 21.09$; Mexico, $M = 19.80$, $SD =$

13.25), $F(1, 58) = 19.31$, $p < .001$; supported child's effort (U.S., $M = 6.30$, $SD = 5.71$; Mexico, $M = 1.57$, $SD = 3.92$), $F(1, 58) = 13.54$, $p < .001$; and suggested fantasy (U.S., $M = 16.83$, $SD = 15.02$; Mexico, $M = 8.50$, $SD = 10.53$), $F(1, 58) = 6.92$, $p < .01$, than did Mexican mothers. Mexican mothers used more explicit guidance (Mexico, $M = 53.46$, $SD = 24.42$; U.S., $M = 36.26$, $SD = 16.69$), $F(1, 58) = 10.44$, $p < .01$, than did American mothers.

Maternal Interviews

Answers in each category were summed and compared by culture. The majority of the American mothers believed that play was very important and provided educational benefits for children. The most common play partners were mothers and siblings. In contrast, the majority of the Mexican mothers believed that play was a relatively unimportant activity that provided amusement for children rather than educational benefits. The most common play partners were siblings and other children.

In summary, many American mothers interpreted the play task as a teaching opportunity whereas some simply played. Mothers who saw their role as a teacher tended to sit back from the play activity while offering commentary on the child's actions and providing suggestions for play. Other mothers used a question-and-answer format to talk about the physical properties of the shapes and used praise to reward correct answers. All mothers made frequent suggestions for play and provided assistance when necessary or requested by

table 3 Cultural Differences in Frequencies of Maternal Beliefs About Play, Its Importance, and Most Common Play Partners

	Culture	
	U.S. (n = 30)	Mexico (n = 30)
Value of Play		
Child's amusement	2	27
Mutual enjoyment	8	0
Educational benefits	20	3
Importance		
None	0	27
Somewhat	5	3
Very	25	0
Play Partners		
Mother	18	0
Father	2	0
Siblings	10	20
Unrelated children	0	10

their child. Mothers who tended to play rather than teach their child suggested symbolic play themes, engaged in role play, and animated human figures and vehicle shapes using paralinguistic cues. In contrast, a few Mexican mothers made suggestions for symbolic play and animated the shapes, whereas others drew their children's attention to the properties of the shapes and then handed them individually to their children to examine.

Some American mothers reported that they frequently played with their children because it was mutually enjoyable, whereas others said they believed that children derived some benefit from it. In contrast, Mexican mothers rarely sat down to play formally with their children. Although the Mexican mothers in this study did not discourage children's play, and said they enjoyed their children's playful efforts at modeling their behavior, they did not attach any particular value to play activity nor did they believe it was important for them to play with their children.

Discussion

The results support the initial assumption that cultural variations in activity-setting components are associated with not only the frequency and the expression of mother–child play, but also the contexts in which play occurs. In the American setting, where play activity is valued for its educational benefits, mothers spent time directly organizing children's play activities by providing objects and ideas for play as well as engaging in the play itself. Mothers' facilitation of the play contexts seemed to enhance their children's expression of symbolic level play and the frequency of joint cooperative pretend play.

In contrast, mother–child play was not a common feature of the Mexican setting. In the Mexican community, unlike the American community, children's symbolic or pretend play behavior does not originate in interaction with adults. When asked to play, these Mexican mothers readily complied, but their play became explicit teaching which was based on a work model rather than a play activity setting model. Mexican mother–child interactive play took place in the context of shared work activity rather than in more structured, child-centered pretend play situations that are characteristic of American culture. For example, in the American setting mothers and their children were observed dressing dolls and putting them in baby-doll carriages, whereas, in the Mexican context, mothers and children played with real babies.

This finding is a challenge to the emphasis that Western researchers have placed on the mother–child relationship in facilitating children's early efforts at pretense. Results from a subsequent comparison of mother– and sibling–child play in the same two settings (Farver, 1993) suggest that, in this particular Mexican environment, play develops in the context of sibling interaction. Sibling caretaking and mixed-age group play experiences may provide opportunities for Mexican older siblings to develop skills in directing play with younger siblings. In turn, younger children may begin to acquire skills and knowledge by participating in play activities with more competent partners. The scaffolding or supporting of play provided by a more skilled partner may be essential to the development of children's play, but who does the scaffolding and how it gets done may be culture-specific.

Differences found in the mother–child play and social interaction among the Mexican families should not be construed as cultural deficiencies. Instead, cultural differences apparent in the maternal play behaviors may be related to culture-specific childrearing practices that serve adaptive functions. In both cultures, mothers modified their children's play behavior toward goals and values that were consistent with their patterns of coping with the surrounding environment.

The issue of a possible confound of social class and culture is an important one. Based on the work of Mexican sociologists, relative to the current class structure within Mexico today these families can be considered working class. Although the living conditions of the Mexican families are more "humble" than those of the American families, based on the data reported here it is suggested that cultural values and childrearing practices, rather than material conditions, influence mother–child play.

The use of a single, 20-min quantitative procedure raises two issues. The first concerns the interdependence of the setting and the individual. That is, by asking mothers to play with unfamiliar toys are they being removed from their context and, therefore, do their activities become meaningless? A subsequent analysis of mother–child play with the same subjects in a natural play context suggests not. This research yielded results similar to the structured mother–child "toy play" procedure presented here (Farver, 1991).

The second issue concerns the representativeness of a short 20-min play session. The data reported here were only one part of a larger study examining children's play alone and with multiple partners in toy (shape) play and free-play contexts. Two hours of videotaped play for each child are the bases of the generalizations made here.

In spite of the attempts to balance social class, to collect qualitative observations to inform the quantitative data, and to use "culture free" toys, alternative interpretations of the results are possible. The sample size was small and the communities discussed here represent only two examples of Mexican and American societies. Also, a considerable range of intracultural variability and a great variety of individual differences exist in any cultural group. Therefore, these results need to be replicated in other samples.

REFERENCES

Alba, F. (1982). *The population of Mexico: Trends, issues, and policies*. NJ: Transaction Press.

Balán, J. (1973). *Migration, occupational structure and social mobility*. Mexico City: National Autonomous University of Mexico Press.

Bradley, R., & Caldwell, B. (1984). The relation of infants' home environment to achievement test performance in first grade: A follow-up study. *Child Development, 55*, 803–809.

Bronstein-Burrows, P. (1981). Patterns of parent behavior: A cross-cultural study. *Merrill-Palmer Quarterly, 27*, 129–143.

Diáz-Guerrero, R. (1975). *Psychology of the Mexican: Culture and personality*. Austin: University of Texas Press.

Eckstein, S. (1989). *The poverty of revolution*. Princeton, NJ: Princeton University Press.

Falicov, C. J., & Karrer, B. M. (1980). Cultural variations in the family life cycle: The Mexican-American family. In E. Carter & M. Goldrick (Eds.), *The family life cycle: A framework for family therapy*. New York: Gardner.

Farver, J. (1991, April). Free play activities of American and Mexican mother–child pairs. In L. Beizer & P. Miller (Chairs), *Cultural dimensions of pretend play in infancy and early childhood*. Symposium conducted at the meeting of the Society for Research in Child Development, Seattle, WA.

Farver, J. (1993). Cultural differences in scaffolding play: A comparison of American and Mexican mother–child and sibling–child pairs. In K. MacDonald (Ed.), *Parent–Child Play: Descriptions and Implications*. Albany, NY: SUNY Press.

Feitelson, D. (1977). Cross-cultural studies of representational play. In B. Tizard & D. Harvey (Eds.), *The biology of play*. Suffolk, England: Levenham Press.

Glaser, B., & Strauss, A. (1967). *The discovery of grounded theory*. New York: Aldine.

Haight, W., & Miller, P. (1991, April). Belief systems that frame and inform middle-class parents' participation in their young children's pretend play. In L. Beizer & P. Miller (Chairs), *Cultural dimensions of pretend play in infancy and early childhood*. Symposium conducted at the meeting of the Society for Research in Child Development, Seattle, WA.

Hoffman, L. (1988). Cross-cultural differences in childrearing goals. In R. LeVine, P. Miller, & M. Maxwell (Eds.), *Parental behavior in diverse societies: New directions for child development*. San Francisco: Jossey-Bass.

Holtzman, W. (1982). Cross-cultural comparisons of personality development in Mexico and the United States. In D. Wagner & H. Stevenson (Eds.), *Cultural perspectives on child development*. San Francisco: Freeman.

Holtzman, W., Díaz-Guerrero, R., Swartz, J., & Tapia, L. (1969). Cross-cultural longitudinal research on child development: Studies of American and Mexican school children. In J. P. Hill (Ed.), *Minnesota Symposia on Child Psychology*. Minneapolis: University of Minnesota Press.

Howes, C. (1980). Peer play scale as an index of complexity of social interaction. *Developmental Psychology, 16*, 371–372.

Howes, C. (1985). Sharing fantasy: Social pretend play in toddlers. *Child Development, 56*, 1253–1258.

Kagan, S. (1981). Ecology and the acculturation of cognitive and social styles among Mexican-American children. *Hispanic Journal of Behavioral Sciences, 3*, 111–144.

Kagan, S., & Ember, P. (1975). Maternal response to success and failure of Anglo-American, Mexican-American and Mexican children. *Child Development, 46*, 452–458.

Keefe, S., Padrilla, A., & Carlos, M. (1979). The Mexican-American extended family as an emotional support system. *Human Organization, 38*, 144–152.

Lawton, J., Fowell, N., Schuler, A., & Madsen, M. (1984). Parents' perceptions of actual and ideal childrearing practices. *Journal of Genetic Psychology, 145*, 77–87.

Leont'ev, A. N. (1981). The problem of activity in psychology. In J. Wertsch (Ed.), *The concept of activity in Soviet psychology*. Armonk, NY: Sharpe.

Levenstein, P. (1986). Mother–child interaction and children's educational achievement. In A. Gottfried & C. Brown (Eds.), *Play interactions: The contributions of play materials and parental involvement to children's development*. Boston: Lexington.

Levenstein, P. (1993). The necessary lightness of mother–child play. In K. MacDonald (Ed.), *Parent–Child Play: Descriptions and Implications*. Albany: SUNY Press.

LeVine, R. A. (1980). *Anthropology and child development: New directions for child development*. San Francisco: Jossey-Bass.

Miller, P., & Garvey, C. (1984). Mother–baby role play: Its origins in social support. In I. Bretherton (Ed.), *Symbolic play.* New York: Academic Press.

O'Connell, B., & Bretherton, I. (1984). Toddlers' play, alone and with mothers. In I. Bretherton (Ed.), *Symbolic play.* New York: Academic Press.

Peñalosa, P. (1968). Mexican family roles. *Journal of Marriage and the Family, 30,* 680–689.

Ramírez, M. (1967). Identification with Mexican family values and authoritarianism in Mexican-Americans. *Journal of Social Psychology, 73,* 3–11.

Ramírez, M., & Castañeda, A. (1974). *Cultural democracy, bicognitive development and education.* New York: Academic Press.

Ramírez, M., & Price-Williams, D. (1974). Cognitive styles in children: Two Mexican communities. *Interamerican Journal of Psychology, 8,* 93–101.

Richman, A., Miller, P., & Solomon, M. (1988). The socialization of infants in suburban Boston. In R. LeVine, P. Miller, & M. Maxwell (Eds.), *Parental behavior in diverse societies: New directions for child development.* San Francisco: Jossey-Bass.

Rogoff, B., Mistry, J., Göncü, A., & Mosier, C. (1991). Cultural variation in the role relations of toddlers and their families. In M. Bornstein (Ed.), *Cultural approaches to parenting.* Hillsdale, NJ: Erlbaum.

Romney, K., & Romney, R. (1966). *The Mixtecans of Juxtlahuaca.* New York: Wiley.

Slade, A. (1987). A longitudinal study of maternal involvement and symbolic play. *Child Development, 58,* 367–375.

Smilansky, S. (1968). *The effect of sociodramatic play on disadvantaged school children.* New York: Wiley.

Suárez, E. C. (1978). *Stratification and social mobility in Mexico City.* Mexico City: National Autonomous University of Mexico Press.

Tharp, R., & Gallimore, R. (1988). *Rousing minds to life.* Cambridge: Cambridge University Press.

Vygotsky, L. (1978). *Mind in society.* Cambridge, MA: Harvard University Press.

Weisner, T., Gallimore R., & Jordan, C. (1988). Unpacking cultural effects on classroom learning: Native Hawaiian peer assistance and child generated activity. *Education and Anthropology Quarterly, 19,* 327–353.

Werner, H., & Kaplan, B. (1963). *Symbol formation.* New York: Wiley.

White, B. L. (1980). *A parent's guide to the first three years.* Trenton: Prentice-Hall.

Whiting, B., & Edwards, C. P. (1988). *Children of different worlds: The formation of social behavior.* Cambridge: Harvard University Press.

Zukow, P. (1989). *Sibling interaction across cultures.* New York: Springer-Verlag.

Questions

1. What is an activity-setting approach to research in child development, and why was this approach used here?
2. Examine the features of American and Mexican activity settings for child development. What are the common features in these two communities? What features differ?
3. What did Farver and Howes do to minimize the impact of observing the families in the Mexican setting? Do you think these efforts were important to make? Why?
4. What are the different ways that mothers and other family members assist children during pretend play in the United States and Mexico?
5. What do the mothers in these two communities believe about the importance of play in children's development and about their own role in child's play?
6. How do the different play patterns that were observed in these two communities relate to the cultural values prevalent in each setting? What does this tell you about the role of play in the socialization of children?

23 Gender and Group Process: A Developmental Perspective

Eleanor E. Maccoby

Gender-related differences in human behavior have been of interest to psychologists for generations. One of the main questions asked by developmental psychologists is: How do these differences originate? Observing the behavior of young children is one of the best ways to answer this question. Many gender-related behaviors begin to appear during the preschool and early school years.

Eleanor Maccoby has spent her career studying young children's social development, and she has taken particular interest in the topic of gender differences in social situations and relationships. One observation she finds especially intriguing is that gender-related behaviors are more evident when children are observed in groups than when they are tested individually. This pattern suggests that something about social experience is critical to the expression, and perhaps the development, of gender-related behaviors.

To pursue this topic, the following article explores the role of social relationships in the development and organization of gender-related behaviors. In particular, it focuses on the group activities of girls and boys from early childhood through preadolescence. Several factors pertaining to group influence on the development of gender-related behaviors are discussed, including group composition, group size, patterns of social interaction in boy and girl groups, and behavioral preferences and themes that emerge in gender-segregated play. Maccoby argues that affiliations with peers throughout childhood play a pivotal role in the development and maintenance of gender-related behaviors. This idea is provocative because it is contrary to the longstanding view that parents, not peers, are the major influence on children's gender-typed behaviors.

Until recently, the study of gender development has focused mainly on sex typing as an attribute of the individual. Although this perspective continues to be enlightening, recent work has focused increasingly on children's tendency to congregate in same-sex groups. This self-segregation of the two sexes implies that much of childhood gender enactment occurs in the context of same sex dyads or larger groups. There are emergent properties of such groups, so that certain sex-distinctive qualities occur at the level of the group rather than at the level of the individual. There is increasing research interest in the distinctive nature of the group structures, activities, and interactions that typify all-male as compared with all-female groups, and in the socialization that occurs within these groups. Next steps in research will surely call for the integration of the individual and group perspectives.

Among researchers who study the psychology of gender, a central viewpoint has always been that individuals progressively acquire a set of behaviors, interests, personality traits, and cognitive biases that are more typical of their own sex than of the other sex. And the individual's sense of being either a male or a female person (*gender identity*) is thought to be a core element in the developing sense of self. The acquisition of these sex-distinctive characteristics has been called *sex typing*, and much research has focused on how and why the processes of sex typing occur. A favorite strategy has been to examine differences among individuals in how sex typed they are at a given age, searching for

Reprinted with permission from Maccoby, E. E., "Gender and Group Process: A Developmental Perspective", *Current Directions in Psychological Science*, 11, 55–58, © 2002 Blackwell Publishers.

factors associated with a person's becoming more or less "masculine" or more or less "feminine" than other individuals. In early work, there was a heavy emphasis on the family as the major context in which sex typing was believed to take place. Socialization pressures from parents were thought to shape the child toward "sex-appropriate" behaviors, personality, and interests and a firm gender identity.

On the whole, the efforts to understand gender development by studying individual differences in rate or degree of sex typing, and the connections of these differences to presumed antecedent factors, have not been very successful. The various manifestations of sex typing in childhood—toy and activity preferences, knowledge of gender stereotypes, personality traits—do not cohere together to form a cluster that clearly represents a degree of sex typing in a given child. And whether or not a given child behaves in a gender-typical way seems to vary greatly from one situation to another, depending on the social context and other conditions that make an individual's gender salient at a given moment. Only weak and inconsistent connections have been found between within-family socialization practices and children's sex-typed behavior (Ruble & Martin, 1998). And so far, the study of individual variations in sex typing has not helped us to understand the most robust manifestation of gender during childhood: namely, children's strong tendency to segregate themselves into same-sex social groups. Although work on gender development in individual children continues and shows renewed vigor, a relatively new direction of interest is in children's groups. This current research and theorizing considers how gender is implicated in the formation, interaction processes, and socialization functions of childhood social groupings.

In some of this work, the dyad or larger group, rather than the individual child, is taken as the unit of analysis. Through the history of theoretical writings by sociologists and social psychologists, there have been claims that groups have emergent properties, and that their functioning cannot be understood in terms of the characteristics of their individual members (Levine & Moreland, 1998). Accumulating evidence from recent work suggests that in certain gender configurations, pairs or groups of children elicit certain behaviors from each other that are not characteristic of either of the participants when alone or in other social contexts (Martin & Fabes, 2001). Another possibility is that the group context amplifies what are only weak tendencies in the individual participants. For example, in their article "It Takes Two to Fight," Coie and his colleagues (1999) found that the probability of a fight occurring depended not only on the aggressive predispositions of the two individual boys involved, but also on the unique properties of the dyad itself. Other phenomena, such as social approach to another child, depend on the sex of the approacher and the approachee taken jointly, not on the sex of either child, when children's sociability is analyzed at the level of the individual (summarized in Maccoby, 1998). It is important, then, to describe and analyze children's dyads or larger groups as such, to see how gender is implicated in their characteristics and functioning.

Gender Composition of Children's Groups

Beginning at about age 3, children increasingly choose same-sex playmates when in settings where their social groupings are not managed by adults. In preschools, children may play in loose configurations of several children, and reciprocated affiliation between same-sex pairs of children is common, while such reciprocation between pairs of opposite sex is rare (Strayer, 1980; Vaughan, Colvin, Azria, Caya, & Krzysik, 2001). On school playgrounds, children sometimes play in mixed-sex groups, but increasingly, as they move from age 4 to about age 12, they spend a large majority of their free play time exclusively with others of their own sex, rarely playing in a mixed-sex dyad or in a larger group in which no other child of their own sex is involved. Best friendships in middle childhood and well into adolescence are very heavily weighted toward same-sex choices. These strong tendencies toward same-sex social preferences are seen in the other cultures around the world where gender composition of children's groups has been studied, and are also found among young non-human primates (reviewed in Maccoby, 1998).

Group Size

Naturally occurring face-to-face groups whose members interact with one another continuously over time tend to be small—typically having only two or three members, and seldom having more than five or six members. Some gender effects on group size can be seen. Both boys and girls commonly form same-sex dyadic friendships, and sometimes triadic ones as well. But from about the age of 5 onward, boys more often associate together in larger clusters. Boys are more often involved in organized group games, and in their groups, occupy more space on school playgrounds. In an experimental situation in which same-sex groups of six children were allowed to utilize play and construction materials in any way they wished, girls tended to split into dyads or triads, whereas boys not only interacted in larger groups but were much more likely to undertake some kind of joint project, and organize and carry out coordinated activities aimed at achieving a group goal (Benenson, Apostolaris, & Parnass, 1997). Of course, children's small groups—whether dyads or clusters of four, five, or six children—are nested within still larger group structures, such as cliques or "crowds."

Group size matters. Recent studies indicate that the interactions in groups of four or more are different from what typically occurs in dyads. In larger groups, there is more conflict and more competition, particularly in all-male groups; in dyads, individuals of both sexes are more responsive to their partners, and a partner's needs and perspectives are more often taken into account than when individuals interact with several others at once (Benenson, Nicholson, Waite, Roy, & Simpson, 2001; Levine & Moreland, 1998). The question of course arises: To what extent are certain "male" characteristics, such as greater competitiveness, a function of the fact that boys typically interact in larger groups than girls do? At present, this question is one of active debate and study. So far, there are indications that group size does indeed mediate sex differences to some degree, but not entirely nor consistently.

Interaction in Same-Sex Groups

From about age 3 to age 8 or 9, when children congregate together in activities not structured by adults, they are mostly engaged in some form of play. Playtime interactions among boys, more often than among girls, involve rough-and-tumble play, competition, conflict, ego displays, risk taking, and striving to achieve or maintain dominance, with occasional (but actually quite rare) displays of direct aggression. Girls, by contrast, are more often engaged in what is called collaborative discourse, in which they talk and act reciprocally, each responding to what the other has just said or done, while at the same time trying to get her own initiatives across. This does not imply that girls' interactions are conflict free, but rather that girls pursue their individual goals in the context of also striving to maintain group harmony (summary in Maccoby, 1998).

The themes that appear in boys' fantasies, the stories they invent, the scenarios they enact when playing with other boys, and the fictional fare they prefer (books, television) involve danger, conflict, destruction, heroic actions by male heroes, and trials of physical strength, considerably more often than is the case for girls. Girls' fantasies and play themes tend to be oriented around domestic or romantic scripts, portraying characters who are involved in social relationships and depicting the maintenance or restoration of order and safety.

Girls' and boys' close friendships are qualitatively different in some respects. Girls' friendships are more intimate, in the sense that girl friends share information about the details of their lives and concerns. Boys typically know less about their friends' lives, and base their friendship on shared activities.

Boys' groups larger than dyads are in some respects more cohesive than girls' groups. Boys in groups seek and achieve more autonomy from adults than girls do, and explicitly exclude girls from their activities more commonly than girls exclude boys. Boys more often engage in joint risky activities, and close ranks to protect a group member from adult detection and censure. And friendships among boys are more interconnected; that is, friends of a given boy are more likely to be friends with each other than is the case for several girls who are all friends of a given girl (Markovitz, Benenson, & Dolenszky, 2001). The fact that boys' friendships are more interconnected does not mean that they are closer in the sense of intimacy. Rather, it may imply that male friends are more accustomed to functioning as a unit, perhaps having a clearer group identity.

How Sex-Distinctive Subcultures Are Formed

In a few instances, researchers have observed the process of group formation from the first meeting of a group over several subsequent meetings. An up-close view of the formation of gendered subcultures among young children has been provided by Nicolopoulou (1994). She followed classrooms of preschool children through a school year, beginning at the time they first entered the school. Every day, any child could tell a story to a teacher, who recorded the story as the child told it. At the end of the day, the teacher read aloud to the class the stories that were recorded that day, and the child author of each story was invited to act it out with the help of other children whom the child selected to act out different parts. At the beginning of the year, stories could be quite rudimentary (e.g., "There was a boy. And a girl. And a wedding."). By the end of the year, stories became greatly elaborated, and different members of the class produced stories related to themes previously introduced by others. In other words, a corpus of shared knowledge, meanings, and scripts grew up, unique to the children in a given classroom and reflecting their shared experiences.

More important for our present purposes, there was a progressive divergence between the stories told by girls and those told by boys. Gender differences were present initially, and the thematic content differed more and more sharply as time went on, with boys increasingly focusing on themes of conflict, danger, heroism, and "winning," while girls' stories increasingly depicted family, nonviolent themes. At the beginning of the year, children might call upon others of both sexes to act in their stories, but by the end of the year, they almost exclusively called upon children of their own sex to enact the roles in their stories.

Thus, although all the children in the class were exposed to the stories told by both sexes, the girls picked up on one set of themes and the boys on another, and two distinct subcultures emerged.

Can this scenario serve as a prototype for the formation of distinctive male and female "subcultures" among children? Yes, in the sense that the essence of these cultures is a set of socially shared cognitions, including common knowledge and mutually congruent expectations, and common interests in specific themes and scripts that distinguish the two sexes. These communalities can be augmented in a set of children coming together for the first time, since by age 5 or 6, most will already have participated in several same-sex groups, or observed them in operation on TV, so they are primed for building gender-distinct subcultures in any new group of children they enter. Were we to ask, "Is gender socially constructed?" the answer would surely be "yes." At the same time, there may well be a biological contribution to the nature of the subculture each sex chooses to construct.

Socialization Within Same-Sex Groups

There has long been evidence that pairs of friends—mostly same-sex friends—influence one another (see Dishion, Spracklen, & Patterson, 1996, for a recent example). However, only recently has research focused on the effects of the amount of time young children spend playing with other children of their own sex. Martin and Fabes (2001) observed a group of preschoolers over a 6-month period, to obtain stable scores for how much time they spent with same-sex playmates (as distinct from their time spent in mixed-sex or other-sex play). They examined the changes that occurred, over the 6 months of observation, in the degree of sex typing in children's play activities. Martin and Fabes reported that the more time boys spent playing with other boys, the greater the increases in their activity level, rough-and-tumble play, and sex-typed choices of toys and games, and the less time they spent near adults. For girls, by contrast, large amounts of time spent with other girls was associated with increasing time spent near adults, and with decreasing aggression, decreasing activity level, and increasing choices of girl-type play materials and activities. This new work points to a powerful role for same-sex peers in shaping one another's sex-typed behavior, values, and interests.

What Comes Next?

The recent focus on children's same-sex groups has revitalized developmental social psychology, and promising avenues for the next phases of research on gender development have appeared. What now needs to be done?

1. Investigators need to study both the variations and the similarities among same-sex groups in their agendas and interactive processes. The extent of generality across groups remains largely unexplored. The way gender is enacted in groups undoubtedly changes with age. And observations in other cultures indicate that play in same-sex children's groups reflects what different cultures offer in the way of materials, play contexts, and belief systems. Still, it seems likely that there are certain sex-distinctive themes that appear in a variety of cultural contexts.

2. Studies of individual differences need to be integrated with the studies of group process. Within each sex, some children are only marginally involved in same-sex groups or dyads, whereas others are involved during much of their free time. And same-sex groups are internally differentiated, so that some children are popular or dominant while others consistently occupy subordinate roles or may even be frequently harassed by others. We need to know more about the individual characteristics that underlie these variations, and about their consequences.

3. Children spend a great deal of their free time in activities that are not gender differentiated at all. We need to understand more fully the conditions under which gender is salient in group process and the conditions under which it is not.

REFERENCES

Benenson, J.F., Apostolaris, N. H., & Parnass, J. (1997). Age and sex differences in dyadic and group interaction. *Developmental Psychology*, 33, 538–543.

Benenson, J.F., Nicholson, C., Waite, A., Roy, R., & Simpson, A. (2001). The influence of group size on children's competitive behavior. *Child Development*, 72, 921–928.

Coie, J.D., Dodge, K.A., Schwartz, D., Cillessen, A.H.N., Hubbard, J.A., & Lemerise, E.A. (1999). It takes two to fight: A test of relational factors, and a method for assessing aggressive dyads. *Developmental Psychology*, 36, 1179–1188.

Dishion, T.J., Spracklen, K.M., & Patterson, G.R. (1996). Deviancy training in male adolescent friendships. *Behavior Therapy*, 27, 373–390.

Levine, J.M., & Moreland, R.L. (1998). Small groups. In D.T. Gilbert, S.T. Fiske, & G. Lindzey (Eds.), *Handbook of social psychology* (Vol. 2, pp. 415–469). Boston: McGraw-Hill.

Maccoby, E. E. (1998). *The two sexes: Growing up apart, coming together.* Cambridge, MA: Harvard University Press.

Markovitz, H., Benenson, J.F., & Dolenszky, E. (2001). Evidence that children and adolescents have internal models of peer interaction that are gender differentiated. *Child Development*, 72, 879–886.

Martin, C. L., & Fabes, R.A. (2001). The stability and consequences of young children's same-sex peer interactions. *Developmental Psychology, 37*, 431–446.

Nicolopoulou, A. (1997). Worldmaking and identity formation in children's narrative play-acting. In B. Cox & C. Light-
foot (Eds.), *Sociogenic perspectives in internalization* (pp.
157–187). Hillsdale, NJ: Erlbaum.

Ruble, D. N., & Martin, C. L. (1998). Gender development. In W.
Damon & N. Eisenberg (Eds.), *Handbook of child psychology*
(5th ed., Vol. 3, pp. 933–1016). New York: John Wiley & Sons.

Strayer, F.F. (1980). Social ecology of the preschool peer
group. In W. A. Collins (Ed.), *Minnesota Symposium on
Child Psychology: Vol. 13. Development of cognitions,
affect and social relations* (pp. 165–196). Hillsdale, NJ:
Erlbaum.

Vaughn, B. E., Colvin, T. N., Azria, M.R., Caya, L., & Krzysik, L.
(2001). Dyadic analyses of friendship in a sample of
preschool-aged children attending Headstart. *Child Development, 72*, 862–878.

Questions

1. What social experiences have traditionally been considered the most critical to sex typing in children? Does research support this view?
2. What does Maccoby mean when she says that groups have emergent properties?
3. Researchers have found that children's behaviors are more sex-typed when they play with a child
of the same sex than with a child of the other sex. Why do you think this happens?
4. Can you think of a study that would test one of the suggestions Maccoby identifies at the end of
her article for the next phases of research in this area?
5. Are greater competitiveness among boys and more cooperativeness among girls due to gender
differences in group size in childhood or to some other factor?
6. What implications do the results of Maccoby's research have for the question of whether children
should be in same-sex or mixed-sex classrooms in the early years of school?

24

Personal Storytelling as a Medium of Socialization in Chinese and American Families

Peggy J. Miller • Angela R. Wiley • Heidi Fung • Chung-Hui Liang

From very early in life, children are told stories about themselves and their families. In recent years, developmental psychologists have become increasingly interested in how parents' personal storytelling may contribute to children's socialization. In the following article, Peggy Miller and her co-authors describe their research on storytelling practices in European American and Taiwanese middle-class families with 2½-year-old children. The researchers took great pains to conduct their study in such a way that they could trace the cultural values that help organize the content and form of parent–child storytelling. Although the number of families that participated was relatively small (six families in Taiwan and six families in the United States), the information collected from each family was extensive. Of particular interest to the investigators were the ways in which parents in these two communities told their children stories about past transgressions by the children. A transgression was defined as any behavior that violated either a social or a moral rule.

Prior research by Miller and her colleagues had shown that parents in Taiwan and the United States place different emphases on their children's past transgressions in their personal storytelling. In addition, when transgressions are discussed in these two communities, parents frame them for children in ways that correspond with broader socialization goals in their respective settings. Whereas Taiwanese parents are more evaluative and promote more self-critical analyses by children, European American parents tend to characterize transgressions more favorably and to encourage more positive self-evaluations by children. In this article, the researchers follow up on these earlier observations by examining structural features of parent–child storytelling. Their goal was to identify more explicitly the similarities and differences in parent–child storytelling in these two communities. To this end, they conducted a detailed analysis of the content, function, and structure of parent–child interaction during personal storytelling. The results indicate that, beginning early in a child's life, personal storytelling by caregivers imparts important information about the values of the family and of the cultural community.

The goal of this study was to determine how personal storytelling functions as a socializing practice within the family context in middle-class Taiwanese and middle-class European American families. The data consist of more than 200 naturally occurring stories in which the past experiences of the focal child, aged 2,6, were narrated. These stories were analyzed at 3 levels: content, function, and structure. Findings converged across these analytic levels, indicating that personal storytelling served overlapping yet distinct socializing functions in the 2 cultural cases. In keeping with the high value placed on didactic narrative within the Confu-

Reprinted with permission from Miller, P. J., Wiley, A. R., Fung, H., & Liang, C.-H., "Personal Storytelling as a Medium of Socialization in Chinese and American Families", *Child Development, 68,* 557–568, © 1997 Blackwell Publishers.

Acknowledgments This research was supported, in part, by a grant from the Spencer Foundation awarded to P. J. Miller and by grant no. CUHK 320/95H awarded to H. Fung by the Research Grants Council, Hong Kong Government. An earlier version of this work was presented at the biennial meeting of the Society for Research in Child Development in Indianapolis, Indiana, March 1995. We wish to thank the families who participated in this study.

cian tradition, Chinese families were more likely to use personal storytelling to convey moral and social standards. European American families did not treat stories of young children's past experiences as a didactic resource but instead employed stories as a medium of entertainment and affirmation. These findings suggest not only that personal storytelling operates as a routine socializing practice in widely different cultures but also that it is already functionally differentiated by 2,6.

> If he does not learn when he is young, what will he be when old? [*The Three Character Classic*]

> When you know your faults, you must correct them. [*The Thousand Character Classic*]

> Men at their birth are naturally good. Their natures are much the same; their habits become widely different. If foolishly there is no teaching, the nature will deteriorate. The right way in teaching is to attach the utmost importance to thoroughness. [*The Three Character Classic*]

Introduction

It has been well established during the last decade that middle-class European American children are able to narrate their past experiences in conversation from a remarkably early age (e.g., Fivush, Gray, & Fromhoff, 1987; Nelson, 1993a; Peterson & McCabe, 1983). These findings have not only provided new insights into the origins of autobiographical memory (e.g., Fivush & Hamond, 1990; Nelson, 1993a, 1993b) but have sparked increasing interest in the role that personal storytelling plays in socializing young children into the meaning systems of their culture (e.g., Bruner, 1990; Engel, 1995; Fivush, 1993; Miller, 1994; Miller & Moore, 1989; Nelson, 1989). Although there is growing evidence that youngsters from diverse sociocultural traditions in the United States participate in personal storytelling (Eisenberg, 1985; Heath, 1983; Miller, Mintz, Hoogstra, Fung, & Potts, 1992; Miller, Potts, Fung, Hoogstra, & Mintz, 1990; Miller & Sperry, 1988; Sperry & Sperry, 1996), the record with respect to non-Western cultures is virtually nonexistent. In addition, little is known about how personal storytelling is actually practiced as part of everyday family life in any cultural group. This article addresses both of these gaps by way of comparative study of personal storytelling in middle-class Taiwanese and middle-class European American families. We seek to understand how personal storytelling functions as a socializing practice within the family context, focusing on the third year of life.

Taiwanese culture offers a particularly interesting case for comparison with European American culture

in that it is deeply rooted in the Confucian tradition, one of the world's most durable ideological systems. Contemporary historians maintain that Confucian values are still alive in Taiwan and other Chinese cultures despite the massive economic, political, and social changes that have occurred in this century (Dennerline, 1988; Spence, 1992). Moreover, a number of scholars have argued that we cannot fully understand Chinese childrearing without understanding Confucian values (Chao, 1994; Chu, 1972; Wu, 1981), and reviews of the literature conclude that Confucian teachings concerning childrearing are still evident today in patterns of childhood socialization (Ho, 1986; Wu, 1996). Within the Confucian tradition, shame is seen as a virtue, and a high value is placed on teaching, strict discipline, and acceptance of social obligations. According to Wu (1996), a key principle of Confucian parenting is that children be taught and disciplined from an early age, as soon as they can talk and walk. An important socialization goal is the development of filial piety. Filial piety refers to the principle that one conduct oneself so as to bring honor and not disgrace to the family name and encompasses such precepts as devotion and obedience to parents, taking care of one's aged parents, performing the ceremonial duties of ancestral worship, and avoiding harm to one's body (Ho, 1996).

For centuries, filial piety was taught through narrative exemplars of extraordinary filial deeds, written collections of which are still in use in Taiwan (Wu, 1981). Similarly, ancient "primers" such as *The Thousand Character Classic* and *The Three Character Classic* are widely available in Taiwanese bookstores. These texts have been used for hundreds of years to teach children to read and to impart moral lessons and knowledge of Chinese history. Woven throughout these collections of adages are stories of exemplary deeds. For example, *The Three Character Classic* contains a series of stories illustrating the diligence of scholars, followed by an explicit exhortation to the young reader to emulate these examples. These and other classic texts attest to the high value placed on didactic narrative within the Confucian tradition. To our knowledge, however, no one has investigated whether this reliance on didactic narrative to educate the young extends to personal storytelling within the family context.

This article builds upon an earlier investigation in which we began to address this question (Miller, Fung, & Mintz, 1996). Focusing on personal storytelling with 2½-year-olds, we found that Chinese caregivers and children from Taiwan were more likely than their European American counterparts to tell stories about the child's past transgressions, to repeatedly invoke moral and social rules, and to structure their stories so as to establish the child's transgression as the point of the story. Discourse analysis revealed that even in those rare instances in which a European American child's past transgression was narrated, a qualitatively different interpretation of the child's past experience was constructed, one that acknowledged yet downplayed the child's wrongdoing. We concluded that the Chinese families were operating with an explicitly evaluative, overtly self-critical interpretive framework, whereas the European American families were using an implicitly evaluative, overtly self-affirmative framework. The latter seemed to go to considerable lengths to portray the child in a favorable light, possibly as a way of protecting or enhancing the child's self-esteem.

The implicitly evaluative, overtly self-affirmative framework seems to overlap with what Harwood, Miller, and Irizarry (1995) call "self-maximization". They found that self-maximization, which included the component of self-confidence or self-esteem, was used by European American mothers to describe qualities they hoped their children would possess as adults. Although the mainstream American emphasis on self-esteem and self-expression has come under increased scrutiny in recent years, particularly as it applies to educational practice (Damon, 1995; Katz, 1993; Tobin, 1995), little is known about the practices that caregivers use to promote young children's self-esteem within the family context. Emphasizing the positive in narrations of children's past experiences may be one such practice.

The purpose of the current study was to extend and deepen the work reported by Miller et al. (1996), thereby fleshing out the emerging picture of similarities and differences in the ways in which personal storytelling is actually practiced with 2-year-olds in middle-class Taiwanese and middle-class European American families. Specifically, we expected that Chinese 2-year-olds and their caregivers would be more likely than their European American counterparts to use personal storytelling didactically, that is, to impart moral and social standards. We addressed this question at three levels of analysis. At the content level, were Chinese families more likely to narrate stories of the child's past transgressions? An affirmative answer to this question would corroborate Miller et al.'s (1996) finding with a much larger corpus of naturally occurring narrations of personal experience. At the functional level, were Chinese stories more likely to be occasioned by an immediately preceding transgression by the child? At the structural level, were Chinese stories more likely to end with a didactic coda that drew out the implications of the child's past actions for the present or future?

Method

The study is part of a larger comparative project designed to investigate how personal storytelling is used to socialize young children within the family context in a variety of communities (Miller, 1996; Miller et al., 1992, 1996). Ethnographic fieldwork was combined with extensive audio and video recording of naturally occurring talk in the home. Researchers spent at least 2 years in the field and collected both cross-sectional and longitudinal observations, encompassing the period from 2,6 to 5,0 and involving at least a dozen families at each research site.

Participants

This article is based on data from six Chinese families in Taipei, Taiwan, and six American families in Longwood (a pseudonym), a European American community in Chicago. The focal children were 2,6 ($M = 2,6$, *range* = 2,5 to 2,9), and each sample was balanced by gender of child. All of the children had at least one sibling. The samples were comparable in that both consisted of two-parent families who lived in large cities, owned their own homes, and were economically secure. The parents were college educated. All of the focal children had mean length of utterances of at least 2.5 morphemes, computed according to Brown (1973). All participants are referred to by pseudonyms.

Research Sites

Despite these similarities, the children in this study inhabited very different worlds. (See Miller et al., 1996, for a more detailed description of the research sites.)

Taipei. Taipei, the largest city in Taiwan, Republic of China, has undergone extraordinarily rapid change in the second half of this century. When the Chinese nationalists arrived on the island in 1949, Taiwan was a rural society. In what has come to be known as the "economic miracle," an agrarian economy was transformed into an industrialized economy in a matter of decades. By 1990 Taiwan had become a consumer society, with an average per capita income exceeding US$8,000, a low rate of unemployment, a relatively equitable distribution of income, and a trade surplus envied by other nations (Simon & Kau, 1992). In the political sphere change has been slower but no less dramatic. Martial law was lifted in 1987, and presidential elections were held in 1996, completing the transition from the Kuomintang dictatorship to a democratic form of government.

The parents in our study are members of the first "middle-class" generation in Taiwan. The sample includes children whose grandparents came to Taiwan from mainland China as well as those whose grandparents were native-born Taiwanese. Most of the parents had a close relative who resided in the United States or Canada. Although half of the parents spoke fluent Taiwanese, all used Mandarin Chinese, the country's official language, with their children. In addition to representing the ethnic and linguistic diversity characteristic of contemporary Taipei, the families also encompass religious diversity. Folk religion, Christianity, and Buddhism were all practiced, sometimes within the same family.

Due to continuing migration from outlying areas, space is at a premium in Taipei. Middle-class families live in small apartments, and families tend not to have strong ties to particular locales. Taipei is not organized into neighborhoods, and there is little residential segregation by class or ethnicity. Within the context of very rapid urban growth, a variety of pragmatic factors—such as cost, preference for new versus old buildings, access to housing owned by a relative, access to good schools or mass transportation—seem to guide residential choice. Although two-generation households are quickly becoming the norm, replacing the traditional three-generation household, the families in our study maintained close ties to grandparents and other family members. The children were taken care of by their mothers or by a female relative if the mother worked outside the home. The early years of life were spent in close physical and emotional proximity to this primary caregiver. Although focal children had their own bed in a room shared with a sibling, they slept with the caregiver.

Caregivers held high standards for their children's conduct. Two-year-olds were expected to successfully negotiate a home environment that was not child-proofed, offering the temptations of open cabinets and fragile objects. They were expected to listen attentively to their elders, comprehend what was said, and behave accordingly. Misdeeds were dealt with promptly, and rules of conduct were rehearsed. Caregivers also corrected grammar and mispronunciations and rehearsed rhymes and poems. They made sure that 2-year-olds knew their full name, parents' names, address, and phone number. Literacy skills were actively cultivated. Parents read to the children and taught them to draw, and some used flash cards to teach Chinese characters or numbers. All of the children were toilet trained by 1,6, and several of the mothers reported that they had begun toilet training at 6 months of age. When the first author visited the families and gave each child a wrapped present decorated with small candies, she was astonished at their self-control. In keeping with proper etiquette, even the 2-year-olds waited until the guests departed to open their gifts.

Longwood. Longwood is located within the city of Chicago and forms a distinct neighborhood. It has been a home to Irish Americans for nearly a century, and many of its residents have deep roots in the community. Holidays such as St. Patrick's Day are observed with great enthusiasm and include an annual neighborhood parade. The neighborhood is known lo-

cally for the beauty of its streets and homes, several of which are on the national historic registry. Civic organizations have worked actively to preserve the special character and small-town ambience of the neighborhood. Many Longwood residents participate in a cohesive social network based on a common cultural heritage and active involvement in one of the three local Catholic churches. Most send their children to the local Catholic school which they themselves attended. Thus, the Longwood families, in contrast to their counterparts in Taipei, were tied by cultural tradition, religion, family history, and active commitment to a community that had a distinct identity within the larger urban environment.

Most Longwood families live in spacious single-family dwellings situated on quiet, tree-lined streets. The interiors of the homes reflect a child-centered emphasis. Each family had a playroom or family room, and each child, even the youngest, had his or her own space and property. Children either had their own bedrooms, or two same-sex siblings shared a bedroom.

The mothers in the sample expressed the belief that young children should be cared for routinely by their own mothers. Several also stated that they chose to stay home with their children because they did not want to miss the opportunity to observe and influence their children's development. Like the "mainstream" mothers described by Ochs and Schieffelin (1984), the Longwood mothers engaged in a variety of practices that accommodated the environment to the child: these included childproofing, use of child-scaled objects and furniture, and abundant provision of toys. These practices are likely related to a concern for the vulnerability of the child's status and the protection of the child's emotional as well as physical well-being. Toilet training was undertaken with a relaxed attitude and was accomplished in most cases by 3 years of age. The Longwood mothers talked and listened to their children, read to them, and pretended with them. These were not just enjoyable experiences, they felt, but ways in which they could provide the kind of focused attention that children need to develop optimally and to feel happy and good about themselves. In discussing a popular preschool teacher, several mothers spoke admiringly of her ability to foster children's self-esteem.

Longwood preschoolers were expected to follow rules of appropriate conduct. When children misbehaved in minor ways—refusing to share with a playmate, quarreling with a sibling, hanging on the dining room curtains—parents intervened promptly and repeatedly if necessary. At the same time, most parents expressed respect for young children's willfulness and appreciated the clever ways in which their youngsters attempted to get what they wanted. When a serious behavior problem occurred, such as hitting or biting another person or an uncontrollable temper tantrum, parents resorted to "time out" procedures or revoked a privilege or treat. For the most part, however, these incidents were not dwelled on by parents and, once settled, were no longer the focus of attention.

In sum, the two groups of children whom we studied in 1988–1991 were not "typical" Taiwanese or "typical" Americans and should not be taken as such. They were members of families who occupied a relatively privileged position within their respective societies, and they created a particular cultural idiom at a particular moment in history. Although Longwood has changed over the decades, what stands out is the extent to which its identity and continuity with the past have been preserved. Families take pride in their traditional values and child- and family-centered way of life, rooted in long-term prosperity. In Taipei, the balance between change and continuity is tipped in the other direction. The Chinese children inhabited a world that differed substantially from those in which their parents and grandparents grew up. Yet, as we shall see, traditional Chinese values were still visible, sturdy and intricate, in everyday narrative practices.

Procedure

Because we were interested in the way that personal storytelling was practiced as part of everyday family life, we took several steps to insure the cultural and ecological validity of our observations. First, we assigned researchers to cultures with which they were familiar—a Taiwanese researcher worked with the Taiwanese families and an American researcher worked with the American families. This "matching" of researchers and field sites meant that researchers could draw on their cultural expertise in recruiting and interacting with the families in a manner that was culturally appropriate. Second, the study was conducted in two phases, a fieldwork phase, followed by a series of video-recorded observations in the home. During the fieldwork phase, the researchers familiarized themselves with the communities through informal observation and collection of documentary materials and recruited families for the observational phase. Most recruitment in both cultural cases was accomplished through informal networks of friends and family. During the fieldwork phase, the researcher also made repeated visits to the homes of the families who agreed to participate in the observational phase of the study; this was done so that researcher and families could become comfortable with one another prior to the first observation session.

The first observation session occurred when the focal child was 2,6. (This article is based only on this initial observation session.) Each observation consisted of two 2-hr video recordings of family interaction in the home scheduled within a few days of one another. Observations occurred at a time that was convenient for the primary caregiver, usually a weekday morning or afternoon. The primary caregiver was always present; often siblings were present as well. Fathers were usually working.

The caregivers were told that we wanted to learn more about how young children learn to communicate as part of ordinary family life, including how they learn to tell stories, to play, and to convey emotions. The researchers did not attempt to script family–child interactions, elicit narrations, or direct the caregivers to elicit narrations from the child. A good deal of thought was given to the problem of how the researchers should participate with the families. We decided that for the researcher to adopt a determinedly silent stance or to act invisible would undermine rather then promote the ecological and cultural validity of the observations of narrative talk (see Miller & Hoogstra, 1992). Instead, each researcher tried to participate as a family friend who had stopped by for a casual visit; at the same time she was careful not to "push" narrative talk. Within these parameters, the researchers were left to their own ingenuity in negotiating a culturally appropriate way of interacting with the families, drawing again upon their cultural intuitions. Elsewhere, we have described some of the ways in which the Chinese and American researchers differed in their participation (Miller, 1996; Miller et al., 1996).

Transcription and Identification of Narrations

The first step in organizing the data involved extracting the naturally occurring stories of personal experience from the ongoing flow of recorded talk and interaction. We defined narrations of personal experience as events involving the focal child and at least one other family member in which the focal child's past experiences were recounted in temporal order. These stories referred to a nonimmediate past event (i.e., an event that occurred prior to the taping session) or class of past events in which the focal child was portrayed as a protagonist. Narrations included both "co-narrations" in which the child (as co-narrator) contributed at least two substantive, on-topic utterances and co-narrators referred to the child in the second person and "stories about the child" which were told in the third person, often with no verbal contribution by the child, who participated as onlooker or co-present other. Miller et al. (1996) found that these two subtypes did not differ in terms of types of interpretive frameworks used. Moreover, the analyses below did not differentiate these two subtypes; therefore, except for the initial description of the basic corpus of stories, we present findings for the combined subtypes.

In each cultural sample, two coders independently viewed and coded four 30-min randomly chosen segments of videotaped speech and interaction. (The Chinese data were coded by Chinese coders, and the American data were coded by American coders.) First, each coder simply identified each episode of a narration. The proportion of agreement for the Chinese sample was 1.00 ($N = 18$), whereas agreement between American coders was .94 ($N = 16$). Second, a more stringent estimate of intercoder reliability addressed the boundaries of the stories. At this level, coders identified the opening and final utterance of each story. The opening utterance was defined as the first utterance that referred to the past event or class of past events. The final utterance was the last utterance that referred directly to the specific past event or class of past events. The proportion of agreement for boundaries was .94 ($N = 36$) for the Chinese sample and .83 ($N = 32$) for the American sample.

The present study is based on the complete corpus of narrations extracted from 24 hr of observations for each cultural group. The narrations, including preceding and succeeding interactions, were transcribed in English for the European American families and in Mandarin Chinese for the Chinese families, using the CHILDES system (MacWhinney, 1991). Each transcript was checked and rechecked at least three times by two different transcribers.

Coding of Narrations

Three codes, corresponding to analyses at the levels of content, function, and structure, respectively, were applied to all co-narrations. In each case, at least one-quarter of all stories were coded for intercoder reliability estimates. Intercoder agreement ranged from .83 to 1.00. (Again, the Chinese data were coded by Chinese coders and the American data by American coders, with repeated joint coding sessions to ensure that the same definitions were followed for the two data sets.)

Content coding: Narrated transgressions.   Narrated transgressions were those narrations in which the focal child was portrayed as committing a violation of a social or moral rule in the past event, as interpreted from the perspective of at least one of the narrating participants. Transgressive interpretations were conveyed through a variety of linguistic and paralinguistic means. In the absence of such textual evidence, the story was not counted as a narrated transgression. For example, if the narrators indicated that the focal child broke another child's toy but said that he or she did so accidentally, the narration was not coded as a narrated transgression. Narrated transgressions were identified on the basis of the following kinds of textual evidence: (1) Explicit evaluation of the child's

past act (e.g., "How *naughty!*" said of LongLong by his mother, referring to an event in which LongLong did not let his parents do their shopping; Pat's brother began a story with "When me and Pat were being *bad* boys"); (2) Implicit evaluation of the child's past act, as indicated by intonation, stress, and/or implicit verbal characterizations (e.g., Angu's mother, speaking in a *disapproving tone of voice*, told of a past incident, saying, "In the middle of the night, when you were about to go to bed, you then took pens to draw on my wall!"; Karin's mother, speaking in an *exasperated tone of voice*, said, "*Oh, man*, all day long in the middle of the night, I'll hear Wee Sing," in reference to the child getting up in the middle of the night to watch a video); (3) Explicit reference to the violated rule in the past event (e.g., after his grandmother recounted an incident in which YoYo cried inappropriately, YoYo said, "*Now, I don't cry at all*"; After recounting how Karin sucked her thumb, Karin's mother said, "What does Daddy say?" Karin: "*Get that thumb out of that mouth!*").

Function coding: Occasioning transgressions. Whereas the "narrated transgression" code applied to the child's behavior in the past event, this code applied to the child's behavior in the present. We wanted to know whether narrations of the child's past transgressions were occasioned by the child's transgression in the here and now, that is, immediately preceding the narration itself. In other words, did the interactants take the child's present transgression as an opportunity to remind the child of a past transgression? Again, only transgressions that were interpreted as such by at least one of the participants were coded as occasioning transgressions. Transgressive interpretations were conveyed through the same linguistic and paralinguistic means described for "narrated transgressions." For example, when LongLong began to ride his bicycle on a comforter, his mother scolded him and tried to get him to stop (occasioning transgression); she then reminded him of an earlier incident in which he had misbehaved in a similar way, by putting his bike on the bed (narrated transgression).

This analysis was conducted in two steps. First, every narration in the Chinese and European American corpus that was coded "narrated transgression" ($N = 40$) was examined to determine whether it was immediately preceded by an occasioning transgression, and the proportion of narrated transgressions that was preceded by an occasioning transgression was computed. Second, 32 randomly selected Chinese narrations that did not contain a narrated transgression and 32 randomly selected European American narrations that did not contain a narrated transgression were coded for occasioning transgressions. The proportion of narrations without narrated transgressions that was preceded by an occasioning transgression was computed for each cultural case.

Structure coding: endings. The endings of narrations were categorized as follows.

1. *Didactic coda.* Following the final utterance that refers to the past event, there was a connected unit or coda, consisting of one or more utterances in which the story was brought back into present or future time. There was general topic continuity but a shift in temporal reference to the present or future. More specifically, a didactic coda draws out the implication of the story in the present or for the future in a way that explicitly refers to social or moral rules. For example, Angu's caregiver ended a narration about the child's misbehavior by saying, "Saying dirty words is not good"; a narration involving YoYo and his grandmother ended as follows: Child: "Now I don't cry at all." Grandmother: "Oh, now you don't cry at all, ya." Child: "Hmm." Grandmother: "Oh, good boy."

2. *Attribute of the focal child.* The story ended by mention of some general attribute of the child which the narrative exemplified. Like the coda, this was likely to involve a temporal adverb or (in English) a tense shift to the present, future, or timeless frame but specifically involved some enduring quality attributed to the child. For example, Megan's mother had been talking about how Megan and her sister were quite different, ending the story by saying, "She's becoming more and more independent now." A very similar example occurred for MeiMei.

3. *New topic.* Endings in this category were characterized by topic shifts or interruptions. In either case, the topic of talk shifted from the past event to some present or future-related topic or another story about some other past event. For example, YoYo and his grandmother co-narrated a story about a time that YoYo cried when his father left. YoYo changed the topic by saying, "Now, now Mom is gone."

Results

BASIC DESCRIPTIVE INFORMATION

The naturalistic home observations revealed that every family in the study routinely narrated the past experiences of their 2½-year-old child, yielding a total corpus of 204 narrations. As can be seen in Table 1, narrations occurred at similar frequencies in the Taipei and Longwood families, with median rates per hour of about four stories. The Chinese narrations were somewhat shorter on average than the European American narrations. In the Chinese case, .38 of the narrations were co-narrations in which the focal child was a co-narrator and .62 were stories about the child in which the focal child was an onlooker or co-present other. In the American case, .51 of the narrations were co-narrations and .49 were stories about the child. Because the following analyses did not differentiate co-

table 1 Basic Descriptive Information: Narrations of Personal Experience		
Measures	**Taipei**	**Longwood**
Frequency:		
Overall	92	112
Mean/family	15.3	18.7
Median/family	15.5	16.0
Rate/hour:		
Mean/family	3.8	4.7
Median/family	3.9	4.0
Length:*		
Overall	1,116	1,811
Mean/narration	12.1	16.2

*Length in utterances.

narrations and stories about the child, results are presented for total narrations (with co-narrations and stories about the child combined).

Narrated Transgressions

The first analysis addressed the content of the narrations. As expected, we found that the Chinese families were much more likely than the European American families to tell stories about the 2-year-old's past transgressions: the average proportions of narrated transgressions were .35 in Taipei, compared with .07 in Longwood. Although there was individual variation within each cultural group, the overlap in the distributions was small: the range was .00 to .56, with a median of .31 for the Taipei families, compared with a range of .00 to .20, with a median of .04 for the Longwood families. Although these patterns strongly differentiated the Taipei and Longwood narrations in the expected direction, it should be noted that the majority of narrations in both cultural cases did not refer to the child's past transgressions.

Further analysis of the content of the narrated transgressions ($N = 32$) produced by the Taipei families revealed that .20 involved emotional displays, such as crying or anger judged inappropriate by the caregiver, and .38 occurred in public (e.g., insulting another child at a restaurant, playing on a forbidden computer at dad's office, interrupting a church service). In addition, .28 of the narrated transgressions actually involved two or more transgressions within a single narration, and there were three instances in which a given transgression was re-narrated twice in succession.

Although narrated transgressions occurred very infrequently ($N = 8$) in the Longwood case, it is interesting to note that there was some overlap with the Chinese in the nature of the infractions. Writing on the wall, eating too much "bad" food, and playing in a way that was too rowdy or dangerous occurred in both cultural cases. At the same time, there seemed to be a qualitative difference such that the Longwood children's transgressions were narrated in ways that rendered them peripheral to the main action of the story or marked them as nonserious. In the longest and most elaborate of the American transgression stories, Tommy started to misbehave in a store, but spontaneously corrected his misdeed without parental intervention and received his reward, a ride on a mechanical horse, "and we were in the shoe department looking for shoes for Maureen [focal child's sister] and he took his shoes off and he said as he took his shoe off, 'Oops, I won't be able to ride the horse.' . . . but then he put his shoe right back on and he was real good in Venture so he could ride that horse." Although the child's transgression is narrated, the point of the story is that the child behaved well and was rewarded.

Occasioning Transgressions

The second analysis was a functional analysis that addressed the circumstances that occasioned the narration. As expected, the Taipei families were much more likely than their Longwood counterparts to tell stories about the child's past transgressions immediately after the child committed a transgression in the here and now. Half ($N = 16$) of the Chinese narrations that contained a narrated transgression were preceded by an occasioning transgression, compared with only one of the eight European American narrations that contained a narrated transgression. For example, a Chinese child knocked about a bowl filled with pudding, smashing and spilling it and making a lot of noise in the process. The caregiver warned the child, "Don't be like this. I don't like you being like this. You still have to behave yourself," thereby marking the child's behavior as a rule infraction. The caregiver then launched into a story about a past transgression in which the child misbehaved in church and had to be removed. The single Longwood narration that was occasioned by a transgression revolved around the child's thumb sucking. The mother tried to get the child to stop sucking her thumb. When this was unsuccessful, she began a story about the child's past thumb sucking, and her father's disapproval of it. The entire affair was handled humorously, with the father being quoted in a low voice as saying, "Get that thumb outta that mouth!" This story provides a good example of how a narrated transgression is keyed nonseriously.

Examination of narrations that did not make reference to the focal child's past transgression revealed that in both cultural cases, none of these stories was occasioned by a present transgression.

Endings

The final analysis focused on how the narrations ended. As expected, we found that the Chinese narrations were more likely than their European American counterparts to end with a didactic coda in which the present or future implications of a rule or rule violation were articulated. Didactic codas occurred in .09 of the Chinese narrations compared with none of the American narrations. Examples of didactic codas include the following:

Example 1: *Mother:* Do you still want to go there again?
Child: Next time I won't do it again.
Example 2: *Mother:* You can only get it if you go to the class.
Child: (looks at mother but says nothing)
Mother: You can get it only if you go to the class.
Example 3: *Mother:* Saying dirty words is not good.
Child: Wooooo.
Mother: Is it right? Saying dirty words is not good.
Example 4: *Child:* Now I don't cry at all.
Grandmother: Oh, now you don't cry at all, ya.
Child: Hmn.
Grandmother: Oh, good boy.

The Taipei families were also more likely than the Longwood families to end their narrations by abstracting an attribute of the child from the story. Attribute endings accounted for .24 of the Chinese narrations, compared with .06 of the European American narrations. For example, after recounting a past experience in which the focal child pointed out the misbehaviors of another child, a Chinese caregiver said, "Ay-yo! So precocious. She is good at blaming people. Aren't you?" Other qualities attributed to the Taipei children were poor memory, shy, little but plays big tricks, bossy, troublemaker, independent, able to concentrate for a long time, feels uncomfortable about misbehaving. Attributes applied to the Longwood children included shy, independent, intuitive, verbally precocious, and a helper. Note that there is some overlap between the two cultural cases in the content of the attributes but that the Longwood attributions were more strongly skewed in the favorable direction.

The remaining narrations simply ended by way of changes in topic or attention, interruption, or other everyday contingencies, including getting knocked on the head by a sibling! In the Chinese families, .67 of the narrations ended in these ways, compared with .94 for the European American families. Once again, it should be noted that although the didactic categories differentiated the Taipei and Longwood families in the expected direction, this difference coexisted with an important similarity in that the majority of narrations in both cultural cases did not end didactically.

Discussion

The results of this study indicate that both middle-class Chinese families and middle-class European American families engaged routinely in personal storytelling with their 2-year-old children. Although the rates at which personal storytelling occurred in the home were remarkably similar in Taipei and Longwood, personal storytelling emerged as more didactic for the Chinese at all levels of analysis—content, function, and structure. The findings of this study thus provide strong support for our expectation that Chinese families would be more likely than European American families to use personal storytelling to impart moral and social standards. They suggest that the Confucian reliance on didactic narrative to educate the young may extend to informal storytelling within the family context.

Corroborating our earlier report (Miller et al., 1996), Chinese families were much more likely than their European American counterparts to tell stories about the child's past transgressions. There are two possible explanations for this contrast. One possibility is that the greater frequency of transgression stories for the Chinese reflects a higher rate of behaviors that are perceived as misdeeds by caregivers. This possibility is supported by ethnographic evidence that Chinese caregivers held high expectations for their young children's conduct (Miller et al., 1996) and felt that they would be remiss as parents if they did not teach their children proper behavior from an early age (Fung, 1994). Although caregivers in Longwood were also concerned with their children's misbehaviors and intervened promptly and repeatedly when necessary, their expectations were more relaxed (Miller et al., 1996). Children were toilet trained much later than the Chinese children, houses were childproofed, and caregivers engaged in a variety of practices that seemed to reflect accommodation to the perceived needs of children. The European American caregivers also expressed appreciation for the child's willfulness.

A second explanation, which is in no way incompatible with the first, is that young children's transgressions were more "storyworthy" in the Chinese than in the American case. Chinese caregivers may be more likely to see the child's past transgressions as a didactic resource for conveying the rules of appropriate conduct to the child. This possibility is supported by the finding that the Chinese caregivers and children were more likely to construct story endings in which the didactic implications of the story were developed. This possibility also fits nicely with the notion of *jihui jiaoyu* or "opportunity education" articulated by the Chinese parents (Fung, 1994). This notion encompasses two interlinked ideas: that it is more effective to situate a moral lesson in the child's concrete experience than to preach in the abstract and that parents should take every opportunity to provide such concrete lessons. The results of our functional analysis indicate that the Chinese caregivers used stories in exactly this way: Half of the stories of the child's past transgressions were occasioned by a transgression in the present. In other words, caregivers treated the child's here-and-now transgressions as opportunities to remind the child of a previous transgression, thereby reinforcing and personalizing moral lessons through concrete exemplars. This strategy of moral socialization requires that parents be alert to, and keep account of, their children's misdeeds.

Caregivers in Longwood seemed to be up to something very different. This is especially well illustrated by an American transgression story in which no one could remember what the child had done wrong. An older sibling and the focal child co-narrated a past experience in which a desired toy was withheld because they had been "bad boys." But neither child could remember why they had been punished. When the mother, who had been out of the room momentarily, returned and tuned into the conversation, she commented ironically, "My kids being bad?!" thereby keying the story nonseriously. She confirmed that the incident had occurred, adding that it happened a week ago, but could not remember the children's misdeed.

This example, as well as the low rate of transgression stories, suggests that the European American families did not treat children's past transgressions as a didactic resource. Instead, stories of young children's past experiences seemed to function as a medium of entertainment and affirmation. Even in those rare instances in which a child's transgression was narrated, as in the Venture store example cited earlier, caregivers did not dwell on the child's misdeeds. This practice of downplaying transgressions in the narrative medium seems to be part of a wider set of practices that Longwood caregivers used to protect their children's self-esteem—conducting serious disciplining in private, putting the best face on the child's shortcomings or even recasting shortcomings as strengths. This does not mean, however, that the European American parents were indifferent to their youngsters' misbehavior; rather, they seemed to prefer to handle infractions when they occurred, a practice recommended by American childrearing manuals. In the most recent edition of *Dr. Spock's Baby and Child Care*, Spock and

Rothenberg (1992) say, "Though children do the major share in civilizing themselves through love and imitation, it still leaves plenty for parents to do, as all of us know. In automobile terms, the child supplies the power but the parents have to do the steering" (p. 435). The authors go on to elaborate on the steady, matter-of-fact guidance that parents need to provide: "The parents have to be saying, 'We hold hands when we cross the street,' 'You can't play with that, it may hurt someone,' 'Say thank you to Mrs. Griffin,' 'Let's go in now, because it belongs to Harry and he wants it,' 'It's time to go to bed so you'll grow big and strong,' etc. etc." (p. 435). Note that all of these examples refer to parental guidance that was offered simultaneously with the targeted child behavior.

In trying to delineate as clearly as possible the ways in which the Chinese and European American narrative practices differed, it is very important not to overstate these differences or formulate them in dichotomous terms. It is important to emphasize that the majority of narrations of the children's past experiences in both Taipei and Longwood did not invoke transgressions. Two-year-olds and their families created accounts of holidays or family excursions—birthday parties, shopping, the fair, the zoo, McDonald's for the European American children; the night market, the zoo, riding on trains and horses for the Chinese children. Both groups also talked about experiences of physical harm, such as illnesses or nosebleeds, and about times when they were afraid. Thus, the striking cultural difference in the priority given to a transgressive interpretation of the young children's past experiences must be seen against the backdrop of substantial overlap in the content of narrated experience.

Also, it should be emphasized that just as the Longwood families found ways to enforce moral and social rules, the Taipei families found ways to portray their children favorably and to express affection. Children were hugged, praised, and given small treats or presents. A parent might cook the child's favorite dishes or patiently teach him or her how to do a difficult puzzle. Mothers slept with their children to be available when needed. From a European American perspective, what may be hard to appreciate is the extent to which a critical parental voice blends with a voice of parental love, a point that Chao's (1994) work with immigrant Chinese also demonstrates. This blending of voices is expressed in the idiom, "The deeper the love, the greater the correction" (*Ai zhi shen, ze zhi qie*). Parents often use this expression with older children by way of justifying a punishment. A related expression is, "It's the child who's getting spanked, but it's the mother who really hurts" (*Da zai er shen, tong zai niang xin*). Chinese caregivers seem to express their love through a didactic idiom in which the child's transgressions are repeatedly invoked and corrected.

The following excerpt provides an excellent example. In this co-narration, the child's grandmother reviews with him an incident that happened earlier in the day in which his mother spanked him for knocking down a screen. The grandmother focuses her didactic efforts on the child's response to having committed the misdeed—namely, that he said, "Don't hit me!" to his mother—which itself constituted a misdeed from her perspective. She patiently takes him through the incident, pointing out where he went wrong and rehearsing with him what he should have said to his mother after knocking down the screen. She explains that if he admits his misdeeds in the future, his mother will not spank him.

(As the co-narration begins, the grandmother is holding the child in her arms. After the first few words, he gets up and stands by his grandmother.)
Grandma: Oh, right. This morning when Mom was spanking you, what did you say? You said, "Don't hit me!" Right?
Child: Hmn. (Nods)
Grandma: Then, what did I tell you to say?
Child: "I won't push the screen down."
Grandma: Oh right. So, what would you say to Mom?
Child: I would say to Mom, "Don't have the screen pushed down." (Child moves closer and speaks in a very low tone into Grandma's ear)
Grandma: Oh, you would talk to Mom, saying, "Mama, I won't push the screen down."
Child: Hmn.
Grandma: So, Mom wouldn't hit you.
Child: Hmn.
Grandma: Right? Hmn. If you asked Mom, "You don't hit me," Mom would have hit you, right?
Child: Hmn. (Nods)
Grandma: So you would directly say to Mom in this way, "Mom, I won't push the screen down." Then how would Mom have reacted?
Child: [Unintelligible]
Grandma: What?
Child: [Unintelligible]
Grandma: Then she wouldn't hit you, right?
Child: Hmn. (Nods)
Grandma: Oh. So, next time when Mom is going to spank you, which sentence is better for you to say to her?
Child: Hmn. Hmn. (Moving close to Grandma's ear) "I won't have [unintelligible] won't have the screen pushed down."
Grandma: Oh, right. Now you have choices. You say, "Mom, I won't push the screen down." In that way, Mom won't spank you. So next time when Mom is spanking you, you shouldn't say, "You don't hit me. (High pitch) You don't hit me." (High pitch) You shouldn't say that way.

Child: (Laughs)
Grandma: You say, "Don't hit me." (Raises her voice) Mom will hit more. Right? Instead, you say to Mom, "I won't push the screen down." What will Mom do to you?
Child: Will give me [unintelligible] a tender touch (in Taiwanese).
Grandma: What?
Child: A tender touch (in Taiwanese).
Grandma: A tender touch (in Taiwanese), oh, give you a tender touch (in Taiwanese). OK. (Laughs loudly and holds child in her arms.)

This co-narration ends as it began, with the grandmother holding the child in her arms. Throughout the co-narration, the grandmother's efforts to correct the child seem motivated by her concern not only to correct him but also to promote his well-being and restore harmonious relations between himself and his mother.

We conclude with a few reflections about the methods used in this study. A limitation of the study is that it is based on only six families from each cultural group. Clearly, future work is needed to corroborate these findings with larger samples. At the same time, we argue that studies that involve in-depth, highly contextualized description of a small number of cases can contribute information that cannot be obtained by other methods, information that is essential to understanding socialization cross-culturally. A good example in the present study is the functional analysis in which the events preceding the stories were examined to determine what occasioned the stories. This kind of analysis, which is precluded by the more typical approach of eliciting stories from children and caregivers, is crucial in determining what families are actually doing with stories. Although examination of naturally occurring narrations within the flow of social life is highly labor intensive, this effort is warranted for other reasons as well. By documenting the routine discursive practices that families use in their homes it is possible to expose the intricate patterning of similarities and differences in socialization across cultures without subduing the complexity of particular meaning in each. This approach thereby mitigates the widespread tendency to dichotomize cultural contrasts while also generating culturally valid categories for future work.

REFERENCES

Brown, R. (1973). *A first language.* Cambridge, MA: Harvard University Press.

Bruner, J. (1990). *Acts of meaning.* Cambridge, MA: Harvard University Press.

Chao, R. K. (1994). Beyond parental control and authoritarian parenting style: Understanding Chinese parenting through the cultural notion of training. *Child Development, 65,* 1111–1119.

Chu, C. L. (1972). Cong shehui geren yu wenhua de guanxi lun zhongguo ren de chigan quxiang [On the shame orientation of the Chinese from the interrelationship among society, individual, and culture]. In I. Y. Lee & K. S. Yang (Eds.), *Zhongguo ren de xingge: Keji zonghe xing de taolun* [Symposium on the character of the Chinese: An interdisciplinary approach] (pp. 85–125). Taipei: Institute of Ethnology, Academia Sinica.

Damon, W. (1995). *Greater expectations: Overcoming the culture of indulgence in America's homes and schools.* New York: Free Press.

Dennerline, J. (1988). *Qian Mu and the world of Seven Mansions.* New Haven, CT: Yale University Press.

Eisenberg, A. R. (1985). Learning to describe past experiences in conversation. *Discourse Processes, 8,* 177–204.

Engel, S. (1995). *The stories children tell: Making sense of the narratives of childhood.* New York: Freeman.

Fivush, R. (1993). Emotional content of parent-child conversations about the past. In C. A. Nelson (Ed.), *Memory and affect in development: Minnesota symposia on child psychology* (Vol. 26, pp. 39–77). Hillsdale, NJ: Erlbaum.

Fivush, R., Gray, J. T., & Fromhoff, F. A. (1987). Two-year-olds talk about the past. *Cognitive Development, 2,* 393–409.

Fivush, R., & Hamond, N. (1990). Autobiographical memory across the preschool years: Towards reconceptualizing childhood amnesia. In R. Fivush & J. A. Hudson (Eds.), *Knowing and remembering in young children* (pp. 223–248). New York: Cambridge University Press.

Fung, H. (1994). *The socialization of shame in young Chinese children.* Unpublished doctoral dissertation, University of Chicago.

Harwood, R. L., Miller, J. G., & Irizarry, N. L. (1995). *Culture and attachment: Perceptions of the child in context.* New York: Guilford.

Heath, S. B. (1983). *Ways with words: Language, life and work in communities and classrooms.* New York: Cambridge University Press.

Ho, D. Y. F. (1986). Chinese patterns of socialization: A critical review. In M. H. Bond (Ed.), *The psychology of the Chinese people* (pp. 1–37). Hong Kong: Oxford University Press.

Ho, D. Y. F. (1996). Filial piety and its psychological consequences. In M. H. Bond (Ed.), *The handbook of Chinese psychology* (pp. 155–165). Hong Kong: Oxford University Press.

Katz, L. G. (1993, November). Are we confusing self-esteem and narcissism? *Young Children,* p. 2.

MacWhinney, B. (1991). *The CHILDES Project: Tools for analyzing talk.* Hillsdale, NJ: Erlbaum.

Miller, P. J. (1994). Narrative practices: Their role in socialization and self-construction. In U. Neisser & R. Fivush (Eds.), *The remembering self: Construction and accuracy in the self-narrative* (pp. 158–179). New York: Cambridge University Press.

Miller, P. J. (1996). Instantiating culture through discourse practices: Some personal reflections on socialization and how to study it. In R. Jessor, A. Colby, & R. A. Shweder (Eds.), *Ethnography and human development: Context and meaning in social inquiry* (pp. 183–204). Chicago: University of Chicago Press.

Miller, P. J., Fung, H., & Mintz, J. (1996). Self-construction through narrative practices: A Chinese and American comparison of early socialization. *Ethos, 24,* 1–44.

Miller, P. J., & Hoogstra, L. (1992). Language as tool in the socialization and apprehension of cultural meanings. In T. Schwartz, G. White, & C. Lutz (Eds.), *New directions in psychological anthropology* (pp. 83–101). New York: Cambridge University Press.

Miller, P. J., Mintz, J., Hoogstra, L., Fung, H., & Potts, R. (1992). The narrated self: Young children's construction of self in relation to others in conversational stories of personal experience. *Merrill-Palmer Quarterly, 38,* 45–67.

Miller, P. J., & Moore, B. B. (1989). Narrative conjunctions of caregiver and child: A comparative perspective on socialization through stories. *Ethos, 17,* 428–449.

Miller, P. J., Potts, R., Fung, H., Hoogstra, L., & Mintz, J. (1990). Narrative practices and the social construction of self in childhood. *American Ethnologist, 17,* 292–311.

Miller, P. J., & Sperry, L. L. (1988). Early talk about the past: The origins of conversational stories of personal experience. *Journal of Child Language, 15,* 293–315.

Nelson, K. (Ed.). (1989). *Narratives from the crib.* Cambridge, MA: Harvard University Press.

Nelson, K. (1993a). Events, narratives, memory: What develops? In C. A. Nelson (Ed.), *Memory and affect in development: Minnesota symposia on child psychology* (Vol. 26, pp. 1–24). Hillsdale, NJ: Erlbaum.

Nelson, K. (1993b). The psychological and social origins of autobiographical memory. *Psychological Sciences, 4,* 7–14.

Ochs, E., & Schieffelin, B. B. (1984). Language acquisition and socialization: Three developmental stories and their implications. In R. A. Shweder & R. A. LeVine (Eds.), *Culture theory: Essays on mind, self, and emotion* (pp. 276–320). New York: Cambridge University Press.

Peterson, C., & McCabe, A. (1983). *Developmental psycholinguistics: Three ways of looking at a child's narrative.* New York: Plenum.

Simon, D. F., & Kau, M. Y. M. (1992). *Taiwan: Beyond the economic miracle.* Armonk, NY: Sharpe.

Spence, J. D. (1992). *Chinese roundabout: Essays in history and culture.* New York: Norton.

Sperry, L. L., & Sperry, D. E. (1996). The early development of narrative skills. *Cognitive Development, 11,* 443–465.

Spock, B., & Rothenberg, M. B. (1992). *Dr. Spock's baby and child care* (6th ed.). New York: Pocket Books.

Tobin, J. (1995). The irony of self-expression. *American Journal of Education, 103,* 233–258.

Wu, D. Y. H. (1981). Child abuse in Taiwan. In J. E. Korbin (Ed.), *Child abuse and neglect: Cross-cultural perspectives* (pp. 139–165). Berkeley: University of California Press.

Wu, D. Y. H. (1996). Chinese childhood socialization. In M. H. Bond (Ed.), *The handbook of Chinese psychology* (pp. 143–154). Hong Kong: Oxford University Press.

Questions

1. Why did these researchers think that comparing the storytelling practices of European American and Taiwanese families would be particularly interesting?
2. What are some of the Confucian principles that appear to be important in child socialization practices in Asian and Asian American families?
3. What behavioral expectations were used to illustrate the assertion that Taiwanese parents hold high standards for their children's conduct?
4. How might personal storytelling support the development in young children of a theory of mind?
5. How did the investigators conduct their research? In particular, what steps did they take to ensure that the families would be comfortable participating in this study and would provide the necessary information?
6. What does parent–child storytelling indicate about cultural values in these two communities? How do the types of stories told in each community help to support and maintain those values?

PART IV

Middle Childhood

Middle childhood, from age 7 to 12, is universally recognized as an exciting period of children's lives. This is the time when children get involved in activities that take them away from constant adult supervision and begin to be held responsible for their actions. These changes are made possible by increased physical skills that allow children to help out more at home and at school. Also, their increased intellectual abilities support children as they engage in more complex activities. However, as children venture away from home, the limits of these new cognitive skills can sometimes be tested, as you will see in the article by Jodie M. Plumert, Joseph K. Kearney, and James F. Cremer.

Children's social life and behavior also change dramatically. They now spend more time with other children, mostly age mates; these interactions may provide opportunities for cognitive development, which is the topic of the article by Ruth T. Duran and Mary Gauvain. Children also begin to have more complex social relationships, especially with peers who assume much importance in children's lives. As the article by Robin M. Kowalski and Susan P. Limber explains, increasing electronic communication with peers makes children vulnerable to a new form of victimization: electronic bullying.

Children's changing roles in the family are explored in the article by Ashley E. Maynard. In a Mayan community in Mexico, Maynard studied how children contribute to the practical, culturally based learning experiences of their younger siblings. After the family, school is the most important social institution with which children are involved; two articles in this section scrutinize that involvement. Jaana Juvonen, Adrienne Nishina, and Sandra Graham explore children's sense of safety in ethnically diverse middle schools. James W. Stigler and Harold W. Stevenson enter the classroom to investigate cultural variation in academic performance, finding that opportunities to develop skills during middle childhood differ greatly.

Together, these articles characterize middle childhood as a period in which children's developing cognitive skills are increasingly integrated with the social and intellectual life of the community in which they live.

25

Children's Perception of Gap Affordances: Bicycling Across Traffic-Filled Intersections in an Immersive Virtual Environment

Jodie M. Plumert • Joseph K. Kearney • James F. Cremer

In the years of middle childhood, the opportunities that children have to explore the environment expand substantially. As a result, children can find themselves in new situations that excite and challenge them. Of serious concern for parents and children alike are situations that present hazards to children. The way in which children deal with dangerous situations reflects their developing capabilities, including their skills at assessing problem situations and solving them in a safe and timely fashion.

In this article, Jodie Plumert, Joseph Kearney, and James Cremer describe research on one such situation: crossing traffic-filled intersections on a bicycle. In middle childhood, many children bicycle to school or around their neighborhood on their own and with friends. In these travels, children often bike on or near roadways and they invariably need to cross streets. To cross a street safely on a bicycle requires careful assessment of the flow and speed of oncoming traffic. How safe are children in these situations?

To study this question, the authors used computer simulation. This technology allowed them to assess how children act in and around traffic without actually exposing the children to a potentially dangerous situation. The researchers created a virtual environment simulating a traffic situation frequently encountered by children on bicycles. The study participants experienced this virtual reality while riding on a stationary bike. The researchers found that children's perceptions of and responses to traffic in busy intersections change during middle childhood. With increasing age, children make better decisions in these situations.

The results suggest ways to help pre-adolescents learn to traverse busy intersections more safely when they are riding their bikes. This study is an excellent example of how basic science research in cognitive development can have direct and important implications for children's health and well-being.

This study examined gap choices and crossing behavior in children and adults using an immersive, interactive bicycling simulator. Ten- and 12-year-olds and adults rode a bicycle mounted on a stationary trainer through a virtual environment consisting of a street with 6 intersections. Participants faced continuous cross traffic traveling at 25 mph or 35 mph and waited for gaps they judged were adequate for crossing. Children and adults chose the same size temporal gaps, but children left far less time to spare between themselves and the approaching vehicle when they crossed the intersection. Relative to adults, children delayed in getting started and took longer to reach the roadway. Discussion focuses on developmental changes in how children coordinate self movement with object movement.

Reprinted with permission from Plumert, J. M., Kearney, J. K., & Cremer, J. F., "Children's Perception of Gap Affordances in an Immersive Virtual Environment", *Child Development, 75*, 1243–1253, © 2004 Blackwell Publishers.

Acknowledgments: This research was supported by National Science Foundation Grants IIS 00-02535 and EIA 0130864 awarded to J. K. Kearney, J. F. Cremer, and J. M. Plumert. We thank Jennifer Lee, Penney Nichols-Whitehead, and Kim Schroeder for their help with data collection and coding. We thank Tom Drewes, Shayne Gelo, Stefan Munteanu, Joan Severson, Hongling Wang, and Pete Willemsen for their help with computer modeling and programming. Finally, we thank Lloyd Frei and Keith Miller for their assistance with electrical and mechanical interfaces.

Bicycle crashes are among the most common causes of severe injuries in childhood (Rivara, 1985). As such, bicycling injuries represent a significant public health problem in the United States. Approximately 500,000 bicycle-related injuries are treated in emergency rooms each year (Baker, Li, Fowler, & Dannenberg 1993). Children between the ages of 5 and 15 represent a particularly vulnerable segment of the population, having the highest rate of injury per million cycling trips (Rivara & Aitken, 1998). Motor vehicles are involved in approximately 33% of all bicycle-related brain injuries and in 90% of all fatalities resulting from bicycle crashes (Acton et al., 1995; Rivara & Aitken, 1998). Notably, Rivara, Thompson, and Thompson (1997) found that wearing a helmet did not protect bicyclists from serious injury when a high-energy impact occurred. They concluded that prevention of serious bicycling injuries cannot be accomplished through helmet use alone but must also include efforts to prevent collisions between bicycles and motor vehicles. A critical first step in developing such programs is understanding why such collisions occur. In this article we focus on how immature cognitive and perceptual skills may put children at risk for car–bicycle collisions. In particular, we examined developmental changes in children's ability to choose adequate traffic gaps when bicycling across traffic-filled intersections in an immersive virtual environment.

Adaptive behavior within the environment depends on perceiving affordances or the fit between the characteristics of the perceiver and the properties of the environment (J. J. Gibson, 1979). Research on the perception of affordances has focused on two broad classes of problems facing all organisms with the capacity for self-produced movement. The first problem is effectively moving the self in relation to stationary objects such as stairs and furniture. In this case, perceivers must scale their actions with respect to static properties of objects and surfaces such as angle, height, and size. Studies with infants, for example, have examined how they traverse surfaces varying in rigidity (Gibson et al., 1987), climb slopes varying in steepness (Adolph, 1995; Adolph, Eppler, & Gibson, 1993), reach for objects at varying locations (McKenzie, Skouteris, Day, Hartman, & Yonas, 1993), and grasp objects varying in size (Newell, Scully, McDonald, & Baillargeon, 1989). Likewise, research with older children has examined how children make judgments about the reachability of objects at varying distances (Plumert, 1995; Plumert & Schwebel, 1997; Schwebel & Plumert, 1999), climbability of stairs of varying heights (McKenzie & Forbes, 1992), and the traversability of barriers of varying heights (Pufall & Dunbar, 1992).

The second problem is effectively moving the self in relation to moving objects such as balls, cars, and people (see also Cutting, Vishton, & Braren, 1995; Oudejans, Michaels, Bakker, & Dolne, 1996). This problem is much more complex because perceivers must use static (e.g., size and shape) and kinematic (e.g., velocity and acceleration) information about objects to scale their actions appropriately. Not surprising, research on how children and adults perceive the relation between the self and moving objects is far more scarce, particularly with children. One situation in which children and adults must scale their actions in relation to kinematic properties of objects is ball catching (Oudejans, Michaels, Bakker, et al., 1996; Peper, Bootsma, Mestre, & Bakker, 1994; van der Kamp, Savelsbergh, & Smeets, 1997). To catch a fly ball perceivers must use information about the size, trajectory, and speed of the ball to time their interceptive actions appropriately. Research with infants has shown that even 8-month-old infants are able to manually intercept (i.e., "catch") moving objects, provided that the objects are moving along a stable trajectory (i.e., an arc) at a relatively slow speed (Von Hofsten, 1983). Other work has shown that control over the timing of catching is similar in young children and adults under both monocular and binocular viewing conditions, suggesting that children and adults are sensitive to the same information for timing their grasp in one-handed catching (van der Kamp et al., 1997). This suggests that changes over development in ball-catching skill are not driven by differences in the type of information used in catching but by differences in the ability to coordinate motor movements with visual information.

Another situation in which children and adults must scale their actions in relation to dynamic information about objects is crossing roads (Connelly, Conaglen, Parsonson, & Isler, 1998; Demetre et al., 1992; Lee, Young, & McLaughlin, 1984; Pitcairn & Edlmann, 2000; Young & Lee, 1987). To determine whether a gap between two vehicles affords crossing, perceivers must judge the temporal size of the gap in relation to the time it will take them to cross the road. Mathematically, the affordance of a gap is the time available for crossing divided by the time it takes to cross. According to Lee et al. (1984), the temporal size of the gap can be defined as the difference between the time to arrival of the first vehicle with the planned crossing line, $tc(1)$, and the time to arrival of the second vehicle with the planned crossing line, $tc(2)$. Crossing time can be defined as the distance to be traversed, d, divided by the average speed of movement, s. According to this formula, children must accurately judge both the size of the temporal gap and the amount of crossing time. Thus, both overestimation of gap size and underestimation of crossing time can contribute to errors in judging whether a gap is sufficiently large to afford safe crossing.

How good are children at judging whether a gap affords crossing? Although nothing is yet known about road-crossing judgments while bicycling, a handful of studies have addressed children's road-crossing judgments while walking (Connelly et al., 1998; Demetre et al., 1992; Lee et al., 1984; Pitcairn & Edlmann, 2000; Young & Lee, 1987). Lee et al. (1984), for example, devised a road-crossing task in which 5- to 9-year-old children crossed a "pretend road" set up parallel to an actual road. Children watched the cars on the actual road and crossed the pretend road when they felt that they could safely reach the other side of the pretend road (i.e., before the oncoming vehicle crossed their line of travel on the real road). Although children were generally cautious, they sometimes accepted gaps that were too short. Had children been crossing the actual road, they would have been hit on approximately 6% of their crossings. In addition, a higher proportion of younger children than older children made such errors. Approximately 75% of the 5-year-olds made at least one road-crossing error, whereas only 58% of 9-year-olds did so. These findings suggest that younger children are more likely than older children to overestimate their ability to walk through traffic gaps.

Connelly et al. (1998) devised another task in which 5- to 12-year-old children stood at a roadside and indicated the last possible moment that they would cross (i.e., made go/no-go judgments). The car speeds were grouped into five categories: 0–31, 32–34, 35–37, 38–40, and 41 mph and over. Overall, 11-year-olds selected safe crossing gap thresholds 92% of the time, whereas 5-year-olds selected safe crossing gap thresholds only 66% of the time. It is notable that children of all ages tended to choose the same distance gap for all car speeds, suggesting that they relied more on distance than on speed when making judgments of crossing gap thresholds. Driving research suggests that adults also tend to rely more on distance than on speed information when making judgments about time to contact (Manser & Hancock, 1996). This creates problems when cars are moving faster than normal for a given roadway and drivers are unable to compensate by increasing their own speed.

These studies of children's road-crossing judgments in the face of real traffic have yielded important findings about developmental differences in children's perception of gap affordances while walking. There are limitations of studies conducted at the roadside, however. First, for obvious safety reasons, none of these studies involved children crossing actual roads. Thus, we are left with an incomplete picture of road-crossing behavior because the relation between gap choice and crossing behavior is largely unknown. Children may choose the same size gaps that adults choose, but those gaps may be inadequate for safe crossing because children take longer to cross the road. Second,

as Pitcairn and Edlmann (2000) noted, traffic flow in the real world is highly variable, leading to variation in the kinds of crossing problems children face. Without control over the timing and location of traffic, it is difficult to examine systematically factors hypothesized to play a role in judgments of traffic gaps. For example, not all children in the Connelly et al. (1998) study made judgments about vehicles traveling at each of the five speeds, making it difficult to draw definitive conclusions about the roles of distance and speed in children's crossing gap judgments.

The aim of our investigation was to meet simultaneously the goals of ecological validity and experimental control by studying children's road-crossing behavior in an immersive, interactive virtual environment (see Loomis, Blascovich, & Beall, 1999, for a discussion of immersive virtual environments as a basic research tool in psychology). Specifically, we used a high-fidelity, immersive bicycling simulator to examine the gaps 10- and 12-year-olds and adults accept when bicycling across traffic-filled intersections. Children and adults rode a bicycle mounted on a stationary trainer through a simulated environment consisting of a straight, residential street with six intersections. Their task was to cross all six intersections without getting "hit" by a car. Participants faced cross traffic from the left-hand side and waited for gaps they judged were adequate for crossing. The cross traffic traveled at continuous rates of either 25 mph or 35 mph with varying temporal gaps between vehicles.

Three issues were of particular interest. First, are there age differences in the size of traffic gaps that 10- and 12-year-old children and adults accept? We focused on 10- and 12-year-olds for both applied and theoretical reasons (see Schwebel, Plumert, & Pick, 2000, for a discussion of integrating basic and applied research in developmental psychology). With respect to applied issues, bicycle injury rates increase from ages 5 to 9 years and peak between 10 and 14 years. Even when injury rates are adjusted for current amount of bike riding (both time and distance), children in late childhood and early adolescence remain most at risk (Thompson, Thompson, & Rivara, 1990). Thus, examining how children in this age range negotiate traffic-filled intersections is critical for developing targeted intervention programs. With respect to basic research issues, the ability to coordinate self motion with the motions of objects appears to undergo developmental change up until at least 12 years of age (Hoffmann, Payne, & Prescott, 1980; Isaac, 1983; Savelsbergh, Rosengren, van der Kamp, & Verheul, 2003). For example, ball-catching skills continue to improve across middle to late childhood, even under simple circumstances (Savelsbergh et al., 2003). Research on children's gap choices while standing at the roadside or crossing a pretend road suggests that younger children are much more likely than older children to accept gaps that are too small for safe crossing. At present, however, virtually nothing is known about how children coordinate self movement with object movement when self movement is indirect (e.g., bicycling across roads) rather than direct (e.g., walking across roads). Choosing an appropriate gap for bicycling across a traffic-filled road presents an added challenge for children because they must judge the temporal size of the gap in relation to the time it will take them to bicycle across the road. Younger children may have more difficulty than older children and adults with accurately determining how long it will take to start up and bicycle a given distance, particularly from a dead stop.

Second, do children and adults take into account the speed of the oncoming traffic when choosing a gap to cross? According to Connelly et al. (1998), 5- to 12-year-old children tend to rely more on distance than on speed when judging traffic gap thresholds. We examined this issue further by examining whether children and adults chose different temporal gaps when cars were moving at slower (i.e., 25 mph) versus faster (i.e., 35 mph) speeds. If 10- and 12-year-old children (and perhaps adults) have difficulty integrating information about speed and distance, they should choose different size temporal gaps when cars are traveling at different speeds. Finally, how do gap choices relate to crossing behavior? As noted previously, previous studies of children's gap choices while walking do not involve children actually crossing roads. Thus, the precise relation between children's judgments and behavior is unknown. We addressed this issue by examining gap choices and how much time children and adults left to spare (i.e., headway) between themselves and the approaching car when they cleared the path of the car.

Method

Participants

Sixty 10- and 12-year-olds and adults participated. There were 10 males and 10 females in the 10-year-old group (*M* age = 10 years 6 months), 8 males and 12 females in the 12-year-old group (*M* age = 12 years 7 months), and 14 males and 6 females in the adult group (*M* age = 19 years 6 months; 1 adult did not provide her age). Children were recruited from a child research participant database maintained by the Department of Psychology at the University of Iowa. Parents received a letter describing the study followed by a telephone call inviting children to participate. Ninety-two percent of the children were European American, 5% were Hispanic/Latino, and 3% were Asian American. Eight percent of the mothers had completed their high school education, 24% had completed some college education, and 68% had a 4-year-college education or beyond. Adults participated to fulfill research credit for an introductory psychology course. Approximately 92% of the adult participants were European American.

Apparatus and Materials

The study was conducted using a high-fidelity, real-time bicycling simulator (see Figure 1). Participants rode an actual bicycle mounted on a stationary trainer. Seat height adjustments were made for participants so that they could comfortably reach the pedals. The bicycle was instrumented to provide information about steering angle, hand braking, and the speed of the rear wheel's rotation that was used to determine the apparent motion of the bicycle through the virtual

figure 1
Photograph of an adult riding an instrumented bicycle through the virtual environment. (Note that there was no traffic on the street with participants in our experiment.)

environment. The bicycle was positioned in the middle of three 10 ft × 8 ft screens placed at right angles relative to one another, forming a three-walled room. Three Electrohome DLV 1280 projectors were used to rear-project high-resolution, textured graphics onto the screens (1280 × 1024 pixels on each screen), providing participants with 270 degrees of immersive visual imagery. The frame rate varied between 15 and 30 Hz depending on the complexity of the scene and the number of vehicles to be simulated at any given time. The apparent motion through the simulated environment and the motions of vehicles were smooth and visually continuous. The experiment was conducted on an 8-processor SGI Onyx supercomputer with Infinite Reality Graphics. The software foundation was the Hank simulator, a real-time ground vehicle simulation system designed to support complex scenarios (Cremer, Kearney, & Willemsen, 1997; Willemsen, Kearney, & Wang, 2003).

Design and Procedure

The experiment began with a 3- to 5-min warm-up period designed to familiarize participants with the characteristics of the bicycle and the virtual environment. Participants rode the bicycle on a straight, residential street with three intersections. During the warm-up period, there was no traffic on the street with the participant and no cross traffic at any of the intersections. Participants were instructed to stay on the right-hand side of the street and to stop at each intersection. The practice session provided participants with the opportunity to learn how to steer, pedal, and stop the bicycle.

Following the warm-up session, children and adults participated in an approximately 10-min test session in which they crossed six intersections. The test section of the simulated environment was a continuation of the street used during the warm-up period. Each intersection was 12 m wide. The distance between intersections was 138 m. There was no traffic on the street with the participant, but there was continuous cross traffic at each of the six intersections. The cross traffic was restricted to the lane closest to the participant and always approached from the participant's left side. The temporal intervals between the cars were defined as the difference between the time at which the rear of the first vehicle reached the crossing line and the time at which the front of the second vehicle reached the crossing line. The temporal intervals between the cars (1.5, 2, 2.5, 3, 3.5, and 4 s) were blocked into sets of six intervals. The intervals of 1.5, 2.5, and 3.5 s appeared at least once in each set of six intervals (but not more than twice) and the intervals of 2.0, 3.0, and 4.0 s appeared less frequently in each set of intervals.[1] The order of intervals within each set was random. Thus, the gaps participants encountered as they reached each intersection varied randomly across participants. The traffic was continuous, however, making it difficult for participants to determine the beginning or end of each set of gaps. Participants in each age group were randomly assigned to one of two speed order conditions. In the 25 mph first condition, the cars at Intersections 1 through 3 traveled at 25 mph, and the cars at Intersections 4 through 6 traveled at 35 mph. In the 35 mph first condition, the cars at Intersections 1 through 3 traveled at 35 mph, and the cars at Intersections 4 through 6 traveled at 25 mph. Thus, participants completed a total of six road-crossing trials. Participants were instructed to stop at each intersection and to cross when they felt it was okay to cross.

Coding and Scores

Coders viewed computer-generated, two-dimensional replays of the paths of the bicyclist and cross traffic through the simulated environment. The Data Visualizer software also provided the clock times corresponding to the positions of the bicyclist and cross traffic. Five bicyclist behaviors were coded for each intersection. The first was whether the bicyclist came to a complete stop. A complete stop was coded when the bicyclist stopped for 2 s or more at an intersection. The second was the time when the bicyclist stopped (or slowed down). Coders used the time at which the bicyclist came to a stop at an intersection lasting for 2 s or more. If the bicyclist stopped, crept forward, and then stopped again for 2 s or more, coders used the last stopping time. If the bicyclist never came to a complete stop, coders used the time at which the bicyclist began moving at the slowest speed as the stopping time. The third was the time when the bicyclist started moving. If the bicyclist never came to a complete stop, the coders used the time at which the bicyclist began to accelerate from the slowest point. The fourth was the time when the bicyclist entered the roadway. Coders recorded when the front wheel of the bicycle entered the roadway. Finally, the time when the bicyclist cleared the lane of the approaching car was recorded. Coders recorded when the rear wheel of the bike cleared the lane of the approaching car.

---

[1]We originally intended to present all six temporal intervals in each set, but a truncation error in the randomization program resulted in temporal intervals that were predominantly 1.5, 2.5, and 3.5 s. Note that 1.5-s gaps were not crossable, 2.5-s gaps were crossable but a little tight, and 3.5-s gaps were easily crossable.

Intercoder reliability estimates were calculated for the five bicyclist behaviors. Exact percentage agreement for whether the bicyclist came to complete stop was 90%. Pearson correlations for the time when the bicyclist (a) stopped, (b) started to move, (c) entered the roadway, and (d) cleared the lane of the approaching car were all .999.

The five bicyclist behaviors previously described were used to derive the following scores for each intersection participants crossed.

Stopping. Participants received a score of 1 if they came to a complete stop and a score of 0 if they did not come to a complete stop at an intersection.

Waiting time. Waiting time was the interval between when the bicyclist stopped (or slowed down the most) and started.

Gap choice. Gap choice was the size of the temporal gap participants crossed.

Time left to spare. The time for the approaching car to intersect with the bicyclist's path was calculated at three time points, representing the time left between the bicyclist and the approaching car when (a) the bicyclist started to move, (b) the bicyclist entered the roadway, and (c) the bicyclist cleared the lane of the approaching car.

Start-up time. Start-up time was the length of time participants required to travel the distance between the stopping point (or slowest point) and the edge of the roadway.

Results

Stopping

Did participants actually come to a complete stop at each intersection? Nearly all participants stopped at the first intersection, but many of them failed to come to a complete stop at subsequent intersections. An Age (3) × Speed Order (2) × Intersection (6) repeated measures analysis of variance (ANOVA) on stopping scores revealed an effect of intersection, $F(5, 270) = 9.50, p < .001$. Follow-up tests indicated that stopping scores were significantly higher for Intersection 1 ($M = .97$, $SD = .18$) than for Intersections 3 ($M = .67, SD = .48$), 4 ($M = .58, SD = .50$), 5 ($M = .63, SD = .49$), and 6 ($M = .60, SD = .49$), and significantly higher for Intersection 2 ($M = .78, SD = .42$) than Intersection 4. No other differences were significant. There was also an Age × Speed Order Interaction, $F(2, 54) = 4.67$, $p < .05$. Simple effects tests revealed an effect of speed order for the 10-year-olds, $F(1, 18) = 11.92, p < .01$. Ten-year-olds in the 25 mph first condition were less likely to stop at intersections ($M = .55, SD = .50$) than were their counterparts in the 35 mph first condition ($M = .88, SD = .32$), suggesting that starting out with lower vehicle speeds led younger children to become less vigilant about stopping at intersections. Stopping

scores in the 25 mph first ($M = .82, SD = .39$) and 35 mph ($M = .75, SD = .44$) conditions did not differ for 12-year-olds, $F(1, 18) = .30$ *ns*. Likewise, stopping scores in the 25 mph first ($M = .68, SD = .47$) and 35 mph ($M = .55, SD = .50$) conditions did not differ for adults, $F(1, 18) = 1.05$, *ns*.

Waiting Time

How long did children and adults wait before crossing intersections? An Age (3) × Speed Order (2) × Intersection (6) repeated measures ANOVA on waiting times revealed a main effect of intersection, $F(5, 270) = 17.27, p < .001$, and a significant Speed Order × Intersection interaction, $F(5, 270) = 2.82, p < .05$. Simple effects tests revealed a significant effect of intersection for the 25 mph first condition, $F(5, 145) = 14.56, p < .001$, and for the 35 mph first condition, $F(5, 145) = 6.12, p < .001$. As shown in Figure 2, participants in the 25 mph first condition waited significantly longer at Intersection 1 than at any of the other intersections. Participants in the 35 mph first condition waited longer at Intersection 1 than at Intersection 2, 3, 5, and 6, but not at Intersection 4. Thus, participants in both conditions were more cautious at the first intersection than at subsequent intersections. Moreover, participants in the 35 mph first condition reacted to the change in the behavior of the cross traffic at Intersection 4, whereas participants in the 25 mph first condition did not. Specifically, when the traffic slowed down and the distances between cars decreased, participants in the 35 mph first condition waited nearly as long to cross as they did at the first intersection. Given that the cars were traveling more slowly than before, it seems likely that participants were reacting to the change in distance rather than speed.

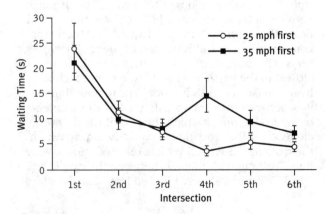

figure 2

Mean time participants waited before crossing as a function of speed order condition and intersection.

Gap Choice

One of the primary questions of interest was whether the gap sizes that 10- and 12-year-olds and adults chose differed. An Age (3) × Speed Order (2) × Intersection (6) repeated measures ANOVA on gap sizes revealed no effect of age, $F(2, 54) = 1.76$, *ns*. The mean gap sizes chosen by 10-year-olds, 12-year-olds, and adults were 3.5 sec (*SD* = .36), 3.5 sec (*SD* = .41), and 3.6 sec (*SD* = .31), respectively. There was a Speed Order × Intersection interaction, $F(5, 270) = 3.08$, *p* < .05, however. Simple effects tests revealed a significant effect of speed order for Intersection 1, $F(1, 58) = 9.48$, *p* < .01), but not for the other intersections. At Intersection 1, participants in the 35 mph first condition chose significantly larger gaps than did participants in the 25 mph first condition, suggesting that participants were more cautious when the cars were going faster (see Figure 3). Thus, with the exception of the first intersection, gap choices were temporally invariant even though the distances between cars varied with the speed of the cars.

Time Left to Spare

There were no age differences in the size of gaps that children and adults chose to cross. But were there age differences in how much time children and adults left to spare between themselves and the approaching car when they actually crossed the gaps? To answer this question, they time left to spare when the bicyclist cleared the lane of the approaching car was entered into an Age (3) × Speed Order (2) × Intersection (6) repeated measures ANOVA. This analysis revealed a significant effect of age, $F(2, 54) = 18.43$, *p* < .001. Follow-up tests showed that all three age groups differed significantly from one another. Thus, even

though children and adults chose the same size gaps, 10-year-olds (*M* = 1.13 s, *SD* = .67) left less time to spare between themselves and the approaching car than did 12-year-olds (*M* = 1.49 s, *SD* = .62), and 12-year-olds left less time to spare than did adults (*M* = 1.98 s, *SD* = .46).

Was the difference in the amount of time children and adults left to spare evident when participants entered the roadway? An Age (3) × Speed Order (2) × Intersection (6) repeated measures ANOVA on time left to spare when the bicyclist entered the roadway yielded significant effects of age, $F(2, 54) = 23.64$, *p* < .001, and intersection, $F(5, 270) = 2.54$, *p* < .05. As with time left to spare when bicyclists cleared the lane of the approaching car, follow-up tests showed that all three age groups differed significantly from one another. The average time left between the bicyclist and the approaching car when the bicyclist entered the roadway was 2.49 s (*SD* = .66), 2.81 s (*SD* = .53), and 3.32 s (*SD* = .45) for 10-year-olds, 12-year-olds, and adults, respectively. Thus, the difference between children and adults emerged between the time when children started off and when they entered the roadway. None of the post hoc tests of the intersection effect reached significance.

One possible reason children left less time to spare between themselves and the approaching vehicle is that they took longer than adults to initiate movement once they had chosen a gap to cross. If this was the case, there should be an age difference in the time between the bicyclist and the approaching car when the bicyclist started moving. To test this possibility, we entered time left to spare when the bicyclist started off into an Age (3) × Speed Order (2) × Intersection (6) repeated measures ANOVA. Although the time left between the bicyclist and the approaching car was less for children than for adults, the effect was not significant, $F(2, 54) = 1.35$, *ns*. When bicyclists started off, the time left between them and the car at the tail of the gap was 5.37 s (*SD* = 1.56), 5.42 s (*SD* = 1.24), and 5.80 s (*SD* = 1.45) for 10-year-olds, 12-year-olds, and adults, respectively.

Another possible reason children left less time to spare between themselves and the approaching vehicle is that children took longer to bicycle from the starting point to the edge of the roadway. Taking significantly longer to reach the roadway would necessarily result in less time between the bicyclist and the approaching car by the time the bicyclist reached the roadway. To test this possibility, we entered start-up times into an Age (3) × Speed Order (2) × Intersection (6) repeated measures ANOVA. Although children took somewhat longer to reach the roadway, there was no effect of age, $F(2, 54) = 1.18$, *ns*. The average time to reach the roadway was 2.88 s (*SD* = 1.33), 2.62 s (*SD* = 1.20), and 2.48 s (*SD* = 1.43) for 10-year-olds, 12-year-olds, and adults, respectively.

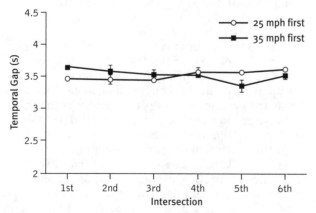

figure 3

Mean temporal gap chosen as a function of speed order condition and intersection.

Why then did children leave less time between themselves and the approaching car by the time they reached the roadway? Clearly, the answer lies in the additive effects of taking longer to get started and taking longer to reach the roadway. Notice in the preceding analyses of these two factors, children took slightly longer to get started and they took slightly longer to reach the roadway. Taking longer to get started and taking longer to reach the roadway necessarily resulted in less time to spare by the time the bicyclist reached the roadway. Thus, although neither of these two factors varied significantly with age, when summed together they produced significant age differences in the time left to spare between the bicyclist and the approaching car by the time the bicyclist reached the roadway.

Discussion

The results of this investigation clearly show that relative to adults, children's gap choices and road-crossing behavior were mismatched. Children and adults chose the same size gaps and yet children ended up with less time to spare between themselves and the approaching car by the time they even entered the roadway. By the time children actually cleared the path of the oncoming car, the margin for error was very small, particularly for 10-year-olds (1.1 s). How did this mismatch occur? Relative to adults, children delayed slightly in getting started and took somewhat longer to reach the roadway. When concatenated together, these two factors produced pronounced age differences in the time left to spare between the bicyclist and the approaching car by the time participants entered the roadway. This mismatch between children's judgments and their abilities is consistent with a wide array of research on children's perception of affordances (Adolph, 1995, 2000; Adolph et al., 1993; McKenzie & Forbes, 1992; Plumert, 1995; Plumert & Schwebel, 1997; Schwebel & Plumert, 1999) and is consistent with the idea that errors in judging affordances may play an important role in unintentional childhood injuries (Plumert, 1995).

Why did gap affordances differ for children and adults? One possibility is that children had more difficulty judging time to contact or how long it would take the vehicle to reach the crossing line. In other words, children may have thought it would take longer for the approaching vehicle to reach the crossing line than adults thought it would. Research on adults' judgments of time to contact has consistently shown that they underestimate time to contact and that underestimation increases as arrival time increases (Caird & Hancock, 1994; Cavallo & Laurent, 1988; McLeod & Ross, 1983; Schiff & Detwiler, 1979). Although research on children's judgments of time to contact is scarce, the results of one study showed that children under the age of 12 exhibit greater underestimation of time to contact than do adults (Hoffmann et al., 1980). This pattern of findings suggests that children should choose larger gaps than adults. The fact that children and adults in our investigation chose gaps that were virtually identical in size suggests that they did not differ in their perception of the temporal (i.e., time to contact) information. This is consistent with the conclusion that children and adults perceive temporal information similarly in the context of ball catching (van der Kamp et al., 1997). However, further research is needed to determine to what extent perception of time to contact is similar for 10- and 12-year-old children and adults in our task.

A second possible reason the gap affordances of children and adults differed was that children overestimated how quickly they could cross the road. Relative to adults, children had more difficulty in getting the bike started (despite the fact that the bike offered little resistance). Failure to take fully into account the time required to get the bike started would result in more time than anticipated to reach the edge of the roadway and consequently less time available to bicycle across the roadway. This explanation is consistent with other research showing that children often overestimate their physical abilities and that 6-year-olds who overestimate their physical abilities are more at risk for injury (Plumert, 1995; Plumert & Schwebel, 1997; Schwebel & Plumert, 1999). McKenzie and Forbes (1992), for example, found that 9- and 12-year-old boys overestimated the height of the stairs they could climb. Plumert and Schwebel (Plumert, 1995; Plumert & Schwebel, 1997; Schwebel & Bounds, 2003; Schwebel & Plumert, 1999) have consistently shown that 6- and 8-year-olds are especially prone to overestimate their reaching and stepping abilities in ambiguous situations, for example, when objects are just out of reach. Thus, overestimation of how quickly they could get the bike moving may have contributed to why children left less time to spare between themselves and the approaching car.

A third possible reason the gap affordances of children and adults differed is that children had more difficulty coordinating their own movement with that of the traffic. In particular, children took somewhat longer than adults to initiate movement once they had chosen a gap to cross. Given that the cars did not slow down as they approached the intersection, taking longer to initiate movement necessarily resulted in less time available for crossing. The fact that children took longer to initiate movement is consistent with other research using video-taped traffic events showing that one of the biggest differences between adult and child pedestrians is delay before initiation of crossing (Pitcairn & Edlmann, 2000). Unlike adults, child pedestrians often do not begin to initiate crossing until the first of the two vehicles has already passed. This approach to road crossing may actually put children at greater risk for getting hit by a car. Other research has shown that coming to a complete stop before crossing an intersection results in less time to spare between the pedestrian and the approaching car (Oudejans, Michaels, van Doort, & Frissen, 1996). Together, these findings suggest that children have more difficulty than adults in fitting their actions to the environment. This may be particularly problematic in dynamic situations, where children must coordinate their own movement in relation to the movement of objects in the environment.

For both children and adults, gap choices were temporally invariant, meaning that they chose larger distances between cars when the cars were traveling at 35 mph and shorter distances when the cars were traveling at 25 mph. This indicates that children and adults appropriately integrated information about speed and distance in their judgments of gap sizes. We should note, however, that there was some hint in our data that children and adults reacted more to changes in distance than in speed. In particular, participants in the 35 mph first condition reacted to the change in the behavior of the cross traffic at Intersection 4, whereas participants in the 25 mph first condition did not. Specifically, when the traffic slowed down and the distances between cars decreased, participants in the 35 mph first condition waited nearly as long to cross as they did at the first intersection. The most plausible explanation for this finding is that the change in the distances between cars was highly salient, but the change in speed was not. Therefore, participants in the 35 mph first condition waited until they had a better sense of how fast the cars were traveling before attempting to cross. This increased caution on the part of the 35 mph first group makes sense given that shorter distances between the cars would signal unsafe gaps for cars traveling at higher speeds.

The finding that gap choices were temporally invariant is inconsistent with other work suggesting that child pedestrians rely primarily on distance to make crossing threshold judgments (Connelly et al., 1998). However, several differences between the two investigations may have contributed to this inconsistency. First, most children in the Connelly et al. (1998) study were below age 10. Younger children may have more difficulty than older children with integrating speed and distance information to arrive at judgments of time (Piaget, 1946/1970; Siegler & Richards, 1979, Wilkening, 1981). Second, we only tested children's road-crossing judgments for speeds of 25 mph and 35 mph. Children (and adults) may have more difficulty judging speeds that exceed 35 mph and may shift to relying more on distance than on speed for faster moving cars. In fact, Connelly et al. found that safe

distance indexes dropped dramatically for car speeds of 35 mph and above, particularly for children under age 10. Third, differences in the tasks themselves may have led to differences in performances. In our experiment, cars were moving at the same continuous rate at a given intersection, making it easier to judge speed. Moreover, participants were free to watch as many cars pass as they liked before crossing the intersection, providing them with more information about the speed of the cars. Finally, choosing a gap that affords safe crossing may be easier than deciding on the last possible moment to initiate safe crossing. Further research is needed to determine the circumstances under which children rely on different sources of information to judge gaps.

A final issue concerns studying behavior in virtual environments. In particular, did children and adults behave in our virtual environment as they do in the real environment? Although virtual environments are an exciting new medium for investigating children's behavior under safe and controlled conditions, the results of such experiments are of questionable value if virtual environments lack ecological validity. First, children and adults did not bicycle recklessly through our virtual environment. In fact, there were only 9 instances out of 360 crossings (2.5%) in which participants were "hit" by a car (all but 1 were 10-year-olds). Second, as one might expect when confronting a novel intersection in the real environment, participants were much more cautious on the first intersection than on subsequent intersections. After the first intersection, children and adults appeared to adopt bicycling habits that are commonly seen in the real environment. Most striking was the high proportion of participants who failed to come to a complete stop at intersections (despite our instructions to stop at each intersection). In fact, 10-year-olds and adults who reported more stopping at intersections in the real environment were more likely to stop at intersections in our virtual environment, $r(19) = .48$, $p < .05$, and $r(20) = .41$, $p = .07$, respectively. Likewise, adults who reported using a bicycle frequently to get around in the real environment were less likely to come to a complete stop at intersections. In the virtual environment, $r(20) = -.58$, $p < .01$. This preference for staying in motion (especially among more experienced cyclists) may reflect real-world bicycling experiences. In particular, experienced cyclists may know that it is easier to get up to speed and judge the crossability of gaps when staying in motion. This latter speculation is consistent with the finding that people find it much easier to judge whether a fly ball is catchable if they are allowed to move (as if to catch the ball) before making the judgment (Oudejans, Michaels, Bakker, et al., 1996). Although more direct validation of behavior in virtual environments is needed, the results of this investigation suggest that immersive virtual environments are a promising tool for addressing difficult-to-study problems such as road-crossing behavior.

In conclusion, this investigation adds to a small, but growing number of studies on children's perception of affordances involving kinematic information. The fact that 10- and 12-year-olds and adults chose gaps that were virtually identical and chose gaps that were temporally invariant suggests that they did not differ in their perception of the relevant visual information. However, the fact that children ended up with less time to spare between themselves and the approaching vehicle by the time they reached the edge of the roadway suggests that children had more difficulty than adults in coordinating their own movement with that of the cars. Quite likely, developmental changes in coordinating motor movements with visual information occur as children gain experience with performing particular tasks (Savelsbergh & van der Kamp, 2000). For example, experience with crossing roads may help children develop strategies such as initiating crossing before the first of the two vehicles has completely passed. Further research is needed, however, to clarify the possible mechanisms underlying developmental changes in the perception of affordances involving kinematic information.

REFERENCES

Acton, C., Tomas, S., Nixon, J., Clark, R., Pitt, W., & Battistutta, D. (1995). Children and bicycles: What is really happening? Studies of fatal and non-fatal bicycle injury. *Injury Prevention, 1,* 86–91.

Adolph, K. E. (1995). Psychophysical assessment of toddlers' ability to cope with slopes. *Journal of Experimental Psychology: Human Perception and Performance, 21,* 734–750.

Adolph, K. E. (2000). Specificity of learning: Why infants fall over a veritable cliff. *Psychological Science, 11,* 290–295.

Adolph, K. E., Eppler, M. A., & Gibson, E. J. (1993). Crawling versus walking infants' perception of affordances for locomotion over sloping surfaces. *Child Development, 64,* 1158–1174.

Baker, S. P., Li, G., Fowler, C., & Dannenberg, A. L. (1993). *Injuries to bicyclists: A national perspective.* Baltimore: The Johns Hopkins University Injury Prevention Center.

Caird, J. K., & Hancock, P. A. (1994). The perception of arrival time for different oncoming vehicles at an intersection. *Ecological Psychology, 6,* 83–109.

Cavallo, V., & Laurent, M. (1988). Visual information and skill level in time-to-collision estimation. *Perception, 17,* 623–632.

Connelly, M. L., Conaglen, H. M., Parsonson, B. S., & Isler, R. B. (1998). Child pedestrian's crossing gap thresholds. *Accident Analysis and Prevention, 30,* 443–453.

Cremer, J., Kearney, J., & Willemsen, P. (1997). Directable behavior models for virtual driving scenarios. *Transactions of the Society for Computer Simulation, 14,* 87–96.

Cutting, J. E., Vishton, P. M., & Braren, P. A. (1995). How we avoid collisions with stationary and moving obstacles. *Psychological Review, 102,* 627–651.

Demetre, J. D., Lee, D. N., Grieve, R., Pitcairn, T. K., Ampofo-Boateng, K., & Thomson, J. A. (1992). Errors in young children's decisions about traffic gaps: Experiments with roadside simulations. *British Journal of Psychology, 83,* 189–202.

Gibson, E. J., Riccio, G., Schmuckler, M. A., Stoffregen, T. A., Rosenberg, D., & Taormina, J. (1987). Detection of the traversability of surfaces by crawling and walking infants. *Journal of Experimental Psychology: Human Perception and Performance, 13,* 533–544.

Gibson, J. J. (1979). *The ecological approach to visual perception.* Hillsdale, NJ: Erlbaum.

Hoffman, E. R., Payne, A., & Prescott, S. (1980). Children's estimates of vehicle approach times. *Human Factors, 22,* 235–240.

Lee, D. N., Young, D. S., & McLaughlin, C. M. (1984). A roadside simulation of road crossing for children. *Ergonomics, 12,* 1271–1281.

Loomis, J. M., Blascovich, J. J., & Beall, A. C. (1999). Immersive virtual environment technology as a basic research tool in psychology. *Behavior Research Methods, Instruments, & Computers, 31,* 557–564.

Manser, M. P., & Hancock, P. A. (1996). Influence of approach angle on estimates of time-to-contact. *Ecological Psychology, 8,* 71–99.

McKenzie, B. E., & Forbes, C. (1992). Does vision guide stair climbing? A developmental study. *Australian Journal of Psychology, 44,* 177–183.

McKenzie, B. E., Skouteris, H., Day, R. H., Hartman, B., & Yonas, A. (1993). Effective action by infants to contact objects by reaching and leaning. *Child Development, 64,* 415–429.

McLeod, R. W., & Ross, H. E. (1983). Optic flow and cognitive factors in time-to-collision estimates. *Perception, 12,* 417–423.

Newell, K. M., Scully, D. M., McDonald, P. V., & Baillargeon, R. (1989). Task constraints and infant grip configurations. *Developmental Psychobiology, 22,* 817–832.

Oudejans, R. R., Michaels, C. F., Bakker, F. C., & Dolne, M. A. (1996). The relevance of action in perceiving affordances: Perception of catchableness of fly balls. *Journal of Experimental Psychology: Human Perception and Performance, 22,* 879–891.

Oudejans, R. R., Michaels, C. F., van Doort, B., & Frissen, E. J. (1996). To cross or not to cross: The effect of locomotion on street-crossing behavior. *Ecological Psychology, 8,* 259–267.

Peper, L., Bootsma, R. J., Mestre, D., & Bakker, F. C. (1994). Catching balls: How to get the hand to the right place at the right time. *Journal of Experimental Psychology: Human Perception and Performance, 20,* 591–612.

Piaget, J. (1970). *The child's conception of movement and speed.* London: Routledge and Kegan Paul. (Original work published 1946)

Pitcairn, T. K., & Edlmann, T. (2000). Individual differences in road crossing ability in young children and adults. *British Journal of Psychology, 91,* 391–410.

Plumert, J. M. (1995). Relations between children's over-estimation of their physical abilities and accident proneness. *Developmental Psychology, 31,* 866–876.

Plumert, J. M., & Schwebel, D. C. (1997). Social and temperamental influences on children's overestimation of their physical abilities: Links to accident proneness. *Journal of Experimental Child Psychology, 67,* 317–337.

Pufall, P. B., & Dunbar, C. (1992). Perceiving whether or not the world affords stepping onto and over: A developmental study. *Ecological Psychology, 4,* 17–38.

Rivara, F. P. (1985). Traumatic deaths of children in the United States: Currently available prevention strategies. *Pediatrics, 75,* 456–462.

Rivara, E. P., & Aitken, M. (1998). Prevention of injuries to children and adolescents. *Advances in Pediatrics, 45,* 37–72.

Rivara, F. P., Thompson, D. C., & Thompson, R. S. (1997). Epidemiology of bicycle injuries and risk factors for serious injury. *Injury Prevention, 3,* 110–114.

Savelsbergh, G., Rosengren, K., van der Kamp, J., & Verheul, M. (2003). Catching action development. In G. Savelsbergh, K. Davids, J. van der Kamp, & S. J. Bennett (Eds.), *Development of movement co-ordination in children: Applications in the fields of ergonomics, health sciences, and sport* (pp. 191–212). New York: Routledge.

Savelsbergh, G. J. P., & van der Kamp, J. (2000). Information in learning to co-ordinate and control movements: Is there a need for specificity of practice. *International Journal of Sport Psychology, 31,* 467–484.

Schiff, W., & Detwiler, M. (1979). Information used in judging impending collisions. *Perception, 8,* 647–658.

Schwebel, D. C., & Bounds, M. L. (2003). The role of parents and temperament on children's estimation of physical ability: Links to unintentional injury prevention. *Journal of Pediatric Psychology, 28,* 505–516.

Schwebel, D. C., & Plumert, J. M. (1999). Longitudinal and concurrent relations between temperament, ability estimation, and injury proneness. *Child Development, 70,* 700–712.

Schwebel, D. C., Plumert, J. M., & Pick, H. L. (2000). Integrating basic and applied developmental research: A new model for the twenty-first century. *Child Development, 71,* 222–230.

Siegler, R. S., & Richards, D. S. (1979). Development of time, speed, and distance concepts. *Developmental Psychology, 15,* 288–298.

Thompson, D. C., Thompson, R. S., & Rivara, F. P. (1990). Incidence of bicycle-related injuries in a defined population. *American Journal of Public Health, 80,* 1388–1390.

van der Kamp, J., Savelsbergh, G. J. P., & Smeets, J. B. (1997). Multiple information sources in interceptive timing. *Human Movement Science, 16,* 787–822.

Von Hofsten, C. (1983). Catching skills in infancy. *Journal of Experimental Psychology: Human Perception and Performance, 9,* 75–85.

Wilkening, F. (1981). Integrating velocity, time and distance information: A developmental study. *Cognitive Psychology, 13,* 231–247.

Willemsen, P., Kearney, J., & Wang, H. (2003). Ribbon networks for modeling navigable paths of autonomous agents in virtual urban environment. *Proceedings of the IEEE Virtual Reality Conference,* 79–86.

Young, D. S., & Lee, D. N. (1987). Training children in road crossing skills using a roadside simulation. *Accident Analysis & Prevention, 19,* 327–341.

Questions

1. What other variables could be added to future research to provide further understanding of how safe children are when they travel by bike?
2. What changes in the participants' behavior were observed during the course of the research?
3. What is a gap affordance, and what developmental changes have been found in children's assessment of gap affordances when they cross a road on foot? Why was it important to extend this research to examine what children do when they cross a road on a bike?
4. Compared to older children and adults, younger children have less time to spare between themselves and the approaching car. Why is this so?
5. What do these results suggest about age difference in the hazards children face when they attempt to bike across a traffic-filled intersection?
6. Given these findings, what do you think parents can do to help their children ride their bicycles as safely as possible?

26 | The Role of Age versus Expertise in Peer Collaboration during Joint Planning

Ruth T. Duran • Mary Gauvain

Over the last two decades, many researchers have tried to understand the social foundations of cognitive development. The underlying assumption of this research is that social experience provides opportunities for children to learn new ways of solving problems. Children learn by observing how other people solve problems or by getting assistance from other people with whom they work. Some of the research on the social context of cognitive development has concentrated on joint problem solving involving adults and children; other research has examined peer collaboration involving children of the same or similar ages.

The following article by Ruth Duran and Mary Gauvain is about peer collaboration and cognitive development, a topic that was of much interest to both Piaget and Vygotsky. Despite their similar interest in peer collaboration, Piaget and Vygotsky did not hold the same view on this topic. Piaget thought that collaboration between children who are nearly equal in their understanding promotes cognitive development. According to Piaget, when such children disagree about their different understandings, this conflict improves the understanding of the less knowledgeable partner. In contrast, Vygotsky emphasized collaboration between novices and experts, highlighting the support that guidance and instruction provide for intellectual growth.

In what way does expertise contribute to children's learning during peer collaboration on a cognitive task? This question is difficult to study because expertise is often confounded with child age. The fact that child age is usually an index of social status further complicates the picture. In their research, Duran and Gauvain tease these variables apart. The results indicate that age and expertise make different contributions to the social process of cognitive development when peers work together.

This study examined the role of age and expertise in influencing collaboration during joint planning. The collaborative patterns of 7-year-old expert planners working with 5-year-old novice planners were compared to 5-year-old experts collaborating with same-age novices on delivery tasks requiring reverse sequencing strategies. Novices who planned with same-age experts had more involvement in the task than novices in cross-age dyads, and individual posttest performance of the novices was related to the extent to which novices were involved in the collaborative task. Furthermore, the posttest performance of children who planned with same-age experts, but not older experts, was significantly better than same-age children in a

Reprinted from *Journal of Experimental Child Psychology, Vol. 55*, Duran, R.T., & Gauvain, M., The role of age versus expertise in peer collaboration during joint planning, pp. 227–242, copyright 1993, with permission from Elsevier.

This article is based on a senior thesis submitted by the first author to Claremont McKenna College in partial fulfillment of the requirements of a B.A. degree. We are grateful to the children of Condit School, Mary B. Eyre Children's School, and Sycamore Elementary for giving us a chance to work with and learn from them. We also acknowledge the assistance of Laurie Jones, Mark Costanzo, and Paul Huard on this project. Comments by Phil Costanzo and Alex Siegel greatly improved our understanding of the data and are much appreciated.

related study using this same task who did not previously collaborate with a peer. Results suggest that cognitive gains are achieved when children collaborate with peers who are more expert in the problem-solving activity, particularly when there is substantial involvement by the novice, and that this is more likely for 5-year-old children when partners are of the same age rather than of different ages. The relation of social facilitation to cognitive development is discussed, with particular attention to the role of social comparison processes in explaining the age patterns found.

Over the past two decades the contribution of peer interaction to children's cognitive development has received increased attention as researchers acknowledge the value of peer experiences on learning and problem solving. Peer interaction facilitates learning because partners often contribute new information, define and restructure a problem in a way that is familiar, and generate discussions that lead to the selection of the most effective problem-solving strategy (Azmitia & Perlmutter, 1989). Thus, through mutual feedback, evaluation, and debate, peers motivate one another to abandon misconceptions and search for better solutions. The present study is intended to broaden our understanding of the effects of peer collaboration on children's thinking by examining age and expertise as mediators of social influence on children's planning skills. Of particular interest is whether age-related status affects cognitive interaction by a novice and expert on a planning task.

Much of the recent research on peer collaboration identifies two theories to account for the facilitation of cognition: Piaget's structural perspective and Vygotsky's sociohistorical perspective. Piaget (1948) and Vygotsky (1978) shared the view that children are active participants in their development, and both emphasized that children learn and develop their thinking processes by interacting with both objects and people. Although Piaget's primary concern was the development of the individual in relation to the physical properties of the world, he did believe that discussion between children plays a role in cognitive development and proposed that cognitive conflict between peers was a mechanism for the social facilitation of cognition. For Piaget, peer interaction is conducive to cognitive development because of the relatively symmetrical nature of peer interaction, i.e., relatively little cognitive and social distance between peers, compared to asymmetric interactions, i.e., those occurring between children and adults or between peers of higher cognitive or social status (Azmitia & Perlmutter, 1989). According to Piaget (1948), children are likely to conform to rules that

they do not fully understand because of this asymmetry in adult–child interactions and will tend to agree with the adult, who has more power and knowledge, without examining the ideas themselves. When a peer has a different perspective, no asymmetry of power exists, and thus partners are more likely to participate in the problem-solving process.

Vygotsky (1978) placed greater emphasis on the role of asymmetrical relationships, focusing on the role of guidance by a person who has achieved a level of expertise beyond that of the child. During guided participation (Rogoff, 1990), more experienced social members use sociocultural tools, like language, to encourage thinking in less experienced members beyond what they are capable of on their own. Vygotsky's emphasis on interaction with more mature partners, such as adults or skilled peers, is therefore, essential to his theory (Tudge & Rogoff, 1989).

To help clarify these theoretical differences, researchers have investigated the influence of peers with varying expertise on children's learning. Researchers have found that cognitive development can be attained both by pairing children of different skills, e.g., nonconservers with conservers (e.g., Murray, 1982; Perret-Clermont, 1980), as well as by pairing children at approximately the same cognitive level (Glachan & Light, 1982). Yet Azmitia (1988) found that children at the same level make little progress. And Ellis and Rogoff (1986) showed that more capable peers are not necessarily effective teachers in promoting certain skills. Thus, despite extensive investigations in recent years regarding the influence of peer collaboration on cognitive development, the merit of conflict versus guidance is still under scrutiny. This inquiry is not independent of concerns about the relative skill or expertise of the partners in promoting cognitive growth. Unfortunately, these issues are difficult to disentangle since age and expertise are often confounded in research on peer interaction.

In fact, in many studies individual differences in expertise are assumed to correspond to age differences (Ellis & Gauvain, 1992). Although this may be a reasonable assumption, expertise on particular tasks should not necessarily be assumed to correlate with age, especially ages that are somewhat close developmentally, e.g., 5- and 7-year-old children. Preassessments of children's ability on tasks independent of age are essential to establishing skill level and assigning children to dyads.

A related concern is the influence of differential age on peer involvement during interaction. Recall that Piaget cautioned that interaction with adults may be less effective than with peers due to inherent restrictions of the adult–child status differential. Such cautions may also be relevant to peer interaction in which peers are of the same versus different ages. Research in social development indicates quite clearly that child age is correlated with social status and dominance (Blurton Jones, 1972; Grusec & Lytton, 1988). This suggests that even in peer collaboration, age-related status may play an important role in how partners participate in the interaction. Since age and expertise, even when pre-assessed, are typically confounded in peer collaboration research, it remains unclear as to how age-related status may affect peer interaction.

In order to reconcile Piaget and Vygotsky's views it is necessary to explore further the variables involved in social interaction such as the relative age and expertise of the social partners and the different mechanisms influencing the social facilitation of cognition. One of the goals of the present study is to examine the processes proposed by Vygotsky and Piaget, such as cognitive conflict and guidance by an expert, that may promote cognitive development, with particular attention to the differential influence of age and expertise on the process and outcome of peer collaboration during joint planning. The study focuses on joint planning because research suggests that children's metacognitive skills, such as planning, are likely to benefit from social interaction (e.g., Hartup, 1985; Rogoff, Gauvain, & Gardner, 1987; Wertsch, McNamee, McLane, & Budwig, 1980).

In the present study, the role of collaboration between children and their more experienced peers in affecting skill in planning was investigated. In particular, the influence of age on novice and expert involvement in the task was studied by comparing the interactional process when children planned with an expert of the same age versus one who was older. Based on findings from earlier research (see Azmitia & Perlmutter, 1989), we expected that novices would improve their planning skills when planning with experts, and the benefits attained from interaction would transfer to the novice's subsequent individual performance. However, it was also expected that the relative ages of the partners would influence the degree to which the novice participated in the task. Novices collaborating with same-age experts were expected to be more involved in the process of planning because, as research in social development suggests, collaboration between children of the same age is less marked by dominance and is therefore less emotionally threatening than corrective advice from adults or older children (Damon, 1984). Because previous research has not established the mechanisms of social interaction that promote cognitive development, this study also investigated the different mechanisms of social interaction. In particular, this study examined conflict between the partners, observational learning by the novice, and guidance by the expert. These processes may influence the likelihood that children will learn through collaboration, however, their use may be related to whether the partners are of the same or different ages.

Method

Subjects

Seventy 5- and 7-year-old children from three elementary schools serving middle-income populations were pretested to obtain 16 5-year-old novice planners ($M = 5.5$ years; range = 5.2–5.9 years), 8 5-year-old expert planners ($M = 5.5$ years; range = 5.2–5.9 years), and 8 7-year-old expert planners ($M = 7.5$ years; range = 7.2–7.9 years). During the interactive sessions, novice planners were assigned randomly to either a 5- or 7-year-old expert planner of the same sex. Thus, in the final group there were 8 mixed ability, cross-age dyads and 8 mixed ability, same-age dyads with an equal number of boys and girls in each condition.

Tasks and Materials

Three tasks, designed by Gauvain (1992), were used for the planning tasks. Each task involved sequencing and delivering five items to locations in a village drawn on 22 × 28-in. (55.9 × 71.1 cm) poster board using a small delivery truck. Solution of the problems required a reverse sequencing strategy, i.e., the delivery vehicles were constructed so that only the next item to be delivered could be removed at any time. Consequently, each problem required advance planning of the entire sequence of items for delivery to be successfully accomplished. The tasks combine some of the elements of planning tasks used by Gauvain and Rogoff (1989) in their research on planning skills and by Boder (1978) in his research on the development of children's skill at reverse sequencing. Each child participated in an individual pretest and a collaborative session, and novices also participated in an individual posttest.

Pretest Task. The pretest involved delivering mail to houses. This drawing on the poster board contained a post office, a one-way street sign, an oval street route, and five homes (three orange and two blue homes) lined along the one-way road. Materials included five letters (three orange and two blue) that corresponded to the homes according to color and a red toy wagon for delivering the letters from the post office to the homes (Fig. 1).

Collaborative Task. Children planning collaboratively were asked to deliver farm items to areas in a farm scene depicted on a poster board. Task materials included a poster board on which was drawn a diagram of a farm with pictures of three sheep pens, two pig pens, and a field indicating where three shrubs and two trees were to be planted. Animal pens and planting fields were identified with stickers of the items. Wooden blocks in the shape of the animals

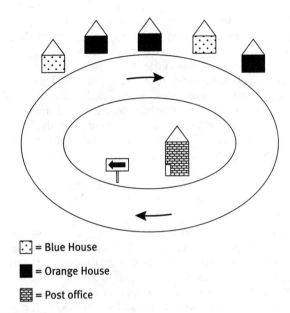

= Blue House

= Orange House

= Post office

figure 1
Mail delivery task used in the pretest.

(three sheep and two pigs) and the plants (three shrubs and two trees) were delivered to assigned areas in the farm using a wooden truck designed to fit the blocks. Two deliveries were conducted using this scene. The first delivery involved the trees and shrubs and the second the pigs and sheep (Fig. 2).

Posttest Task. The scene depicted on the poster board for the posttest contained two hat stores, three cat stores, and a warehouse. Cards labeled with stick-

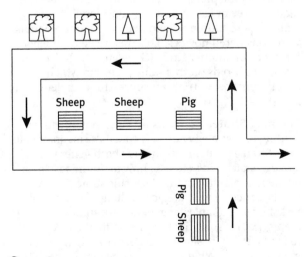

figure 2
Farm delivery task used in the interactional session.

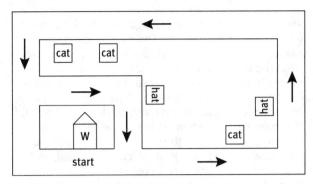

figure 3
Warehouse delivery task used in the posttest.

ers of hats or cats and the same wagon used in the pretest were also used (Fig. 3).

Procedure

The children were asked to perform three planning tasks. The first task, the mail delivery, was the easiest of the four and was used as the pretest. Based on their performance, the children were identified as either an expert (the child successfully completed the pretest in three or fewer delivery attempts) or a novice (more than three delivery attempts were needed) using normative scores for these tasks obtained from a study that examined the development of children's planning skills (Gauvain, 1992). Children were considered novice planners if their pretest performance exceeded the mean number of trials required for successful completion of the task for their age group. Novices were then paired randomly with either a 5-year-old expert planner or a 7-year-old expert planner for the Farm Delivery. After the collaborative task, the novice was given a posttest similar to, but more difficult than, the pretest. The collaborative sessions took place the same day as the posttest. All of the sessions were videotaped at the children's school in a quiet space where the child could not be distracted or observed by others.

Pretest Task: Mail Delivery. The experimenter placed the poster board on the table in front of the child. The experimenter explained that the drawing contained a small village, and pointed out the post office, one-way road, and houses, and then asked the child to identify the two types of houses. The child was also asked to trace a finger along the direction of travel indicated for the one-way road. Then the experimenter explained to the child that he or she was to deliver a letter to each of the houses, and the color of the letter was to match the color of the house. The letters were then placed at the post office in random order and the child was shown a wagon and told that it was to be used for the delivery. The experimenter then explained the rules for mail delivery: (1) only one letter from the wagon, the top one, may be removed at a time; (2) the road is one-way so the wagon cannot be backed up; (3) the mail is to be delivered to all the houses in one trip; and (4) if during delivery the child discovers that the arrangement of the letters in the wagon is incorrect, all the letters and the wagon are to be brought back to the Post Office, rearranged, and delivered again. The experimenter asked the child if he or she understood the rules and asked if there were any questions. If the child violated the rules during the delivery, the experimenter reiterated them and asked the child to continue. Upon completion, the experimenter told the child that he or she did a good job.

Collaborative Session: Farm Delivery.   The experimenter placed the poster board on the table facing the children, and told the children that in this task they were to deliver items to a farm. The experimenter described the illustrations on the board: the road, especially the one-way signs, and the fields and pens. The procedure for delivery was explained, with the experimenter pointing out that there would be two different deliveries. First the children were to deliver the trees and shrubs (Delivery One) and then they would deliver the animals (Delivery Two). The experimenter then introduced the items to be delivered and explained that only one item was to go to each delivery point. The experimenter identified where each item went and explained to the children that they were to deliver to the front of the fields and pens. The children were then shown the delivery truck and the experimenter explained how to load and unload items. The starting position for the truck was identified, and then the rules were explained: (1) the road is one-way and therefore the truck cannot back up; (2) the truck is low on gas, so it can go around the road once for each delivery; (3) the children are to work together; and (4) if, during a delivery, they feel that the truck is loaded incorrectly, they are to collect all the items and return to the starting position and reload the truck. The experimenter asked the children if they understood the rules and procedure and asked if there were any questions. The children were then instructed to begin the task. If the children violated the rules, the experimenter repeated them, and then instructed the children to continue with the task. Upon completion, the children were complimented on their work.

Posttest Task: Warehouse Delivery.   The novice was asked to do one more delivery task. The experimenter placed the poster board used in the posttest in front of the child and introduced the illustrations, including the road, especially the one-way markings, the warehouse, and stores. The experimenter pointed out that

there were two different types of stores, those that sold cats and those that sold hats. The child was then given cards with stickers of cats or hats on them and asked to deliver them to the stores using the toy wagon. The same rules in the mail delivery task applied in the posttest and were repeated. If the child violated the rules, the experimenter explained the rules again, and asked the child to continue. After the posttest was completed, the child was complimented on his or her work.

Coding

Performance was coded for plan effectiveness and for the use of planning strategies. The extent of each partners' involvement in the task during the interactional trial was coded, as was the interactional process used by the children to convey or ascertain planning relevant information. Mechanisms of social interaction included observational learning, i.e., the amount of time the novices observed the expert performing the task; guidance by the expert, including physical intervention, directives and suggestions, and positive support; and conflicting statements or disagreements. Three (19%) of the 16 tapes were coded independently by two coders, yielding ϕ correlation reliabilities ranging from .64 to 1.0.

Plan Effectiveness.   To assess the children's pretest, interaction, and posttest performance, the number of delivery attempts made, including the final successful delivery and any partial or instructional attempts, were recorded. Thus, the higher the number of delivery attempts, the less effective the planning performance. On the pretest, children who delivered the mail in three or less trials were considered experts, while those children who took more than three trials were considered novices. This was based on the performance in another study (Gauvain, 1992) of a sample of 5-year-olds on this same pretest in which the average number of trials for successful completion was 3.16 ($SD = 2.8$, $n = 16$).

Planning Strategies.   This includes statements regarding task strategy and was coded during joint planning. Strategy statements include both general task strategy statements, such as how to do the task in an efficient or planful way, and specific strategy statements, concerning strategic handling of individual task moves. Examples of general task strategy statements are "Let's put the last one on first" or "You have to load it the opposite way to deliver it right." Statements such as "What about this one next?" and "The tree goes here" are examples of specific task strategies.

Partners' Task Involvement.   Each of the items selected for loading in the Farm Delivery Task was coded according to whether the novice on his or her own, the expert on his or her own, or the novice and expert together chose the item, loaded the item into the truck, and delivered the item.

Interactional Process.   Three different measures reflecting the various theoretical emphases in the peer literature were used to assess the interactional process the partners used to convey or ascertain task-relevant information. *Observational learning* was the total number of seconds novices spent observing their expert partners perform the task. *Guidance by the expert* was coded as either physical intervention, which was any physical interference by the expert of the novice's activity by manipulating an object or person, e.g., the expert putting his or her hand on the novice's hand; directives and suggestion, that is the expert verbally telling or suggesting to the novice what to do; and positive support, which included positive statements and physical gestures by the expert that recognize progress by the novice on the task and/or promote continuance. *Conflict* included statements of disagreements about the choice, arrangement, or handling of an item.

Results

Analysis of variance (ANOVA) was used to compare the performance and social interactional processes of children collaborating with same-age expert peers versus older expert peers.

Planning during Collaboration

There were no differences in planning effectiveness, i.e., the number of delivery attempts children required to perform the tasks successfully, between the two groups in either farm delivery. Peers in same-age dyads required an average of 1.5 trials to complete Delivery One and 4.1 trials to complete Delivery Two successfully. Peers in cross-age dyads required an average of 1.4 trials to complete Delivery One and 2.7 to complete Delivery Two successfully.

The most interesting differences emerged in relation to partner involvement and the interactional process. Novices planning with same-age experts were more involved in the three task operations, choosing, loading, and delivering items ($M = 40.25$, $SD = 25.94$), during the two trials of the interaction than novices working with older experts ($M = 19.87$, $SD = 15.89$), $F(1, 16) = 5.43$, $p < .05$. (Because the conditions of homogeneity of variance was violated, a log base-10 transformation was used in this analysis.) Novices in same-age dyads were responsible, on average, for 32% of these task operations and novices in cross-age dyads were responsible for an average of 26% of these task operations. (Table 1 contains the means for these variables by group for each of the two farm deliveries.) Experts in same-age dyads were responsible for an average of 51% of the task operations, and experts in cross-age dyads were responsible, on average, for 55%. The remaining 17 and 18%, respectively, were shared by the two partners. Thus, the hypothesis that novices planning with same-age experts would be more involved in the task than novices planning with older experts was supported.

table 1   Means (and Standard Deviations) for Percentage Involvement by Novices and Experts and Interactional Process by Group for the Interaction Task

Group	Same-age dyads		Cross-age dyads	
Variable	Delivery 1	Delivery 2	Delivery 1	Delivery 2
Partners' task involvement				
Novice only	28.6 (11.4)	34.6 (16.1)	29.8 (13.2)	22.9 (17.2)
Expert only	52.4 (15.0)	49.9 (15.3)	51.1 (18.2)	58.5 (19.6)
Both novice and expert	19.0 (10.4)	15.4 (7.7)	19.0 (6.7)	18.6 (7.2)
Guidance by an expert				
Physical intervention	1.4 (.7)	3.2 (3.4)	1.4 (.5)	1.6 (1.4)
Directives and suggestions	2.9 (2.2)	5.6 (5.3)	2.6 (2.2)	3.1 (2.5)
Positive support	1.6 (.7)	5.1 (4.7)	1.5 (.8)	1.2 (.5)
Observational learning				
(in seconds)	22.0 (27.1)	50.0 (98.9)	19.0 (16.7)	18.4 (33.2)
Conflict	2.5 (1.9)	4.2 (4.4)	1.1 (.3)	2.2 (1.3)

Vygotsky proposed that the experienced partner would adjust the problem-solving process so that, with experience, the learner would be able to participate in increasingly more complex aspects of the solution. Examination of the novice's participation from Delivery One (the easier of the two deliveries) to Delivery Two of the Farm Task reveals that novices planning with same-age experts increased in their participation from Delivery One, when they were responsible for an average of 29% of the task operations, to Delivery Two, when they were responsible for an average of 35% of the task operations, $t(7) = 1.82$, $p = .05$. In contrast, participation of the novices in cross-age dyads decreased as the task became more difficult, from a mean of 30% to a mean of 23%, $t(7) = -2.61$, $p = .02$.

Although the total amount of guidance by the expert on the Farm Task did not differ between the two groups, when the two deliveries are considered separately, we find that during the second delivery 5-year-old experts provided more positive support ($M = 5.12$, $SD = 4.7$), $F(1, 16) = 5.37$, $p = .05$, for the novices than 7-year-old experts ($M = 1.25$, $SD = .46$). In addition, conflict during the second delivery was somewhat greater in the same-age dyads, $F(1, 16) = 3.23$, $p = .09$. (See means for these variables in Table 1.) It appears that same-age experts not only fostered more participation by the novice as he or she gained experience, these experts also supported their agemates more during the joint task. However, novices and experts of the same age also tended to challenge each other more than when partners were of different ages. Finally, due to the variance within the groups, they did not differ in terms of the time spent by the novice observing the expert perform the task.

Same-age dyads were not significantly different from cross-age dyads in number of strategy statements made by the expert. Experts in the same-age dyads produced an average of 14.4 strategy statements and those in cross-age dyads produced an average of 7.7 strategy statements. Novices in same-age dyads produced slightly more strategy statements (an average of 8.4) than novices in cross-age dyads (an average of 4.0), $F(1, 16) = 4.01$, $p = .06$, suggesting that, in addition to greater participation in task operations, collaborating with a same-age peer may also facilitate greater involvement by the novice in strategy formation.

Taken together, these results indicate that peer interaction differs when partners are of the same versus different ages. Novices planning with same-age experts were more involved in the task and experienced more support and challenge from same-age partners who were more expert at the task than did novices planning with older experts. Age-related dynamics appear to be an influential factor in the process of peer cognitive interaction. We now examine the relationship of the interactional process in these two groups to the novices' individual posttest performances to investigate whether these dynamics are related to what novices learn from collaborating with an expert.

Relation of Collaboration to Posttest Planning Performance

Pearson correlation coefficients were calculated to determine whether the interaction related to posttest performance and whether these relationships differed across the two groups. It was found that the number of trials required by novices to complete the posttest successfully was related to partner involvement during the interaction. More involvement by the novice in choosing, loading, and delivering items during the collaborative tasks was related to more effective planning on the posttest, $r(16) = -.49$, $p < .05$. (Recall that better planning performance is indicated by fewer trials.) And, mirroring this, greater involvement by the expert during the interaction was related to less effective planning by the novice on the posttest, $r(16) = .56$, $p < .05$.

When the two farm deliveries are considered separately, we find that for the novices in the same-age dyads, the number of trials required to complete the posttest was related to the total instances of guidance by the expert in delivery two, $r(8) = -.78$, $p < .05$. That is, for children in same-age dyads only, the extent to which the expert offered assistance to the novice was related to better performance on the posttest. Thus, Vygotsky's suggestion that interaction with those who are more expert would foster guidance and cognitive support was supported in the same-age dyads only. Since there were no differences between groups in the amount of guidance by the experts, perhaps other factors, such as involvement of the novice, which was greater in same-age dyads, bolstered the effectiveness of the experts' assistance during joint planning.

Further support for the importance of learner involvement in the task emerged in t tests comparing the posttest scores (number of delivery trials to complete the task) of the children in this study with the posttest scores of 5-year-old children in a study using this same task but who did not collaborate with a peer prior to the posttest (Gauvain, 1992). It was found that only the children who collaborated with the same-age experts, but not those who collaborated with older experts, performed significantly better than children who did not collaborate, $t(24) = 2.18$, $p < .05$. The mean number of trials to complete the posttest successfully for 5-year-old children who planned with same-age experts was 2.37 ($SD = 1.30$, $n = 8$) and the mean for the children who planned alone prior to the posttest was 4.75 ($SD = 3.94$, $n = 16$). The mean number of trials for 5-year-old children who planned previously with an older expert was 3.37 ($SD = 1.85$, $n = 8$), which does not differ significantly from the children who planned with the same-age experts or who planned entirely on their own. This suggests that collaboration between novices and experts of the same age, but not of different ages, may lead to more successful planning than when children plan independently.

Discussion

The purpose of this study was to examine the effects of age versus expertise in facilitating the development of children's planning skills during joint planning. It was hypothesized that the age of the expert partner would influence the involvement of the novice, which in turn would affect the extent of learning. The results support this prediction. Novices who planned with same-age experts were more involved in the task than novices who planned with older experts. Furthermore, novices who collaborated with same-age experts performed significantly better in later individual planning than children who did not collaborate prior to performing the same task. This difference did not appear for novices who planned with older experts. Finally, guidance by the expert, although not significantly different between the two groups, was related to later individual planning for novices who previously planned with same-age experts but not for novices who previously planned with older experts.

These findings support Vygotsky's (1978) general contention that cognitive development may benefit from opportunities available in the social context. However, they extend this view by suggesting factors that may influence this process. Although the results indicate that collaboration between novice and expert planners can lead to the development of the novice's skills, exposure to expertise was not sufficient for explaining the cognitive gains resulting from the social situation. The extent to which the novices were involved in the task influenced learning, however, the extent of novice involvement was affected by the relative age of the social partners. Perhaps novices who planned with same-age experts did not perceive as much social and cognitive distance between themselves and the experts compared to novices who planned with older experts. Children may feel more comfortable collaborating with experts of the same age and even perceive the partner's skills as attainable.

Another possibility, related to the first, is that experts in cross-age dyads dominate the interaction and do not allow their novice partners to participate in the problem-solving process. Recall that the data showed that the experts in the cross-age group were responsible, on average, for 55% of the task operations, while their novice partners were responsible for only 26% of the operations (compared with 51% involvement for experts and 32% for novices in same-age dyads). Furthermore, after examining the novices' participation from Delivery One, the easier of the two deliveries, to Delivery Two of the interaction, it was found that novices planning with same-age experts increased their participation, whereas participation of the novices in cross-age dyads decreased as the task became more difficult. These patterns, as well as the finding that the 5-year-old experts provided more positive support for their partners in Delivery Two, raise the possibility that the 5-year-old experts were more sensitive to the learner's needs and capabilities, and therefore allowed their novice partners to be more involved in the task as they gained experience. Of course, the related interpretation is that 5-year-old novices are more likely to allow older experts to dominate the interaction than same-age experts. The marginally significant difference in conflict between the two groups, with greater conflict in same-age dyads, supports this interpretation. More frequent bids for dominance by older children and acceptance of these by younger children are reciprocal processes, that, by definition, are more likely to appear in mixed-age pairs.

Of the mechanisms that are hypothesized to facilitate cognitive growth—conflict, guided participation, and observational learning—only guidance by an expert was found to mediate learning. However, guidance was only effective for 5-year-old novices planning with same-age experts, who also had greater involvement in the task. Thus, guided participation in conjunction with increased task involvement facilitated learning for the novice when planning with a same-age, but more expert peer. Piaget hypothesized that conflict between children mediates cognitive growth. In this study, the amount of conflict between social partners was minimal, although it was somewhat greater among same-age peers who did not share the same skill at planning. This suggests that in interactions where partners are not equal in skill but equal in age, mechanisms such as guidance and extent of participation may be more central than conflict for social facilitation to occur.

Although these results further our understanding of the role of social experience in cognitive development, they are less useful for explaining why the conditional effects for age were obtained and whether these effects are specific to the ages studied here or represent a more general finding. Research on the development of social comparison processes by Ruble and colleagues (Feldman & Ruble, 1988; Ruble, Boggiano, Feldman, & Loebl, 1980; Ruble & Frey, 1987) suggests a possible answer to these questions. When children collaborate with more experienced partners, opportunities arise for them to make ability comparisons between themselves and their partners that may be useful for defining their behavior as well as for directing future performances. Studies conducted in Ruble's lab have shown that child age influences the occurrence and the nature of these comparisons. During social interaction, 5- to 6-year-old children, the same age as the novices in the present study, are primarily oriented toward same-age peers as a source of social comparison, whereas older children and adults are more likely to select "upward" comparisons as a source for self-evaluation. Stated more generally, the meaning of different people in social cognitive processes, like social comparison, is a function of age-related developmental processes. In this research, same-age experts may have constituted an ideal arrangement for mediating social cognitive effects for 5- to 6-year-old novices, thereby reflecting age-specific processes of social comparison rather than more general principles of social facilitation across childhood. To explore this suggestion further, research that varies the ages of the novices in addition to that of the experts is needed. Since the ages of 7 to 9 years have been found (e.g., see Ruble & Frey, 1987) to be particularly important for refining processes of social comparison, such research may reveal whether these ages are also critical junctures in processes of social facilitation.

In sum, this research investigated the influence of peer interaction on cognitive development by examining differences in children's planning when they planned with an expert of the same age or an expert who was older. In previous research on peer collaboration, age and expertise have typically been confounded. Rather than suggesting that simply the presence of an expert partner promotes cognitive development, this study points to age-related status and behaviors as mediating the process and outcome of peer interaction on problem-solving tasks. In addition to the extent of task involvement by the novice and guidance by the expert, which were greater in same-age dyads, facilitation effects for young children may also be driven by opportunities during collaboration for children to make social comparisons. These findings suggest that further understanding of how the sociocognitive processes of guided participation, conflict, and observational learning relate to and integrate with processes of social comparison over the course of development is essential for unpacking the mechanisms whereby social interaction may promote or impede cognitive growth.

References

Azmitia, M. (1988). Peer interaction and problem solving: When are two heads better than one? *Child Development*, **59**, 87–96.

Azmitia, M., & Perlmutter, M. (1989). Social influences on children's cognition: State of the art and future directions. In H. Reese (Ed.), *Advances in child development and behavior* (Vol. 22, pp. 89–144). San Diego, CA: Academic Press.

Blurton Jones, N. (1972). *Ethological studies of child behavior*. London: Cambridge University Press.

Boder, A. (1978). Etude de la composition d'un ordre inverse: Hypothese dur la coordination de deux sources de controle du raisonnement. *Archives de Psychologie*, **46**, 87–113.

Damon, W. (1984). Peer education: The untapped potential. *Journal of Applied Developmental Psychology*, **5**, 331–343.

Ellis, S., & Gauvain, M. (1992). Social and cultural influences on children's collaborative interactions. In L. T. Winegar and J. Valsiner (Eds.), *Children's development within social context: Vol. 2. Research and methodology* (pp. 155–180). Hillsdale, NJ: Erlbaum.

Ellis, S., & Rogoff, B. (1986). Problem solving in children's management of instruction. In E. Mueller and C. R. Cooper (Eds.), *Process and outcome in peer relationships* (pp. 301–325). New York: Academic Press.

Feldman, N. S., & Ruble, D. N. (1988). The effect of personal relevance on psychological inference: A developmental analysis. *Child Development*, **59**, 1339–1352.

Gauvain, M. (1992). *The development of planning skills*. Unpublished manuscript, University of California, Riverside.

Gauvain, M., & Rogoff, B. (1989). Collaborative problem solving and children's planning skills. *Developmental Psychology*, **25**, 139–151.

Glachan, M., & Light, P. (1982). Peer interaction and learning: Can two wrongs make a right? In G. Butterworth & P. Light (Eds.), *Social cognition: Studies of the development of understanding* (pp. 238–262). Chicago: University of Chicago Press.

Grusec, J. E., & Lytton, H. (1988). *Social development: History, theory, and research*. New York: Springer-Verlag.

Hartup, W. (1985). Relationships and their significance in cognitive development. In R. Hinde & A. Perret-Clermont (Eds.), *Relationships and cognitive development* (pp. 66–82). Oxford: Oxford University Press.

Mueller, E., & Cooper, C. R. (Eds.). (1986). *Process and outcome in peer relationships*. New York: Academic Press.

Murray, F. B. (1982). Teaching through social conflict. *Contemporary Educational Psychology*, **7**, 257–271.

Perret-Clermont, A. N. (1980). *Social interaction and cognitive development in children*. London: Academic Press.

Piaget, J. (1948). *The moral judgement of the child*. IL: Free Press.

Piaget, J. (1983). Piaget's theory. In W. Kessen (Ed.), *History, theory, and methods*: Vol. 1. *Handbook of Child Psychology* (pp. 294–356). New York: Wiley.

Rogoff, B. (1990). *Apprenticeship in thinking: Cognitive development in social context*. New York: Oxford University Press.

Rogoff, B., Gauvain, M., & Gardner, W. P. (1987). *Children's adjustment of plans to circumstances*. In S. L. Friedman, E. K. Scholnick, & R. R. Cocking (Eds.), *The role of planning in psychological development* (pp. 303–320). London: Cambridge University Press.

Ruble, D. N., Boggiano, A. K., Feldman, N. S., & Loebl, J. H. (1980). A developmental analysis of the role of social comparison in self-evaluation. *Developmental Psychology*, **16**, 105–115.

Ruble, D. N., & Frey, K. S. (1987). Social comparison and self-evaluation in the classroom: Developmental changes in knowledge and function. In J. C. Masters & W. P. Smith (Eds.), *Social comparison, social justice, relative deprivation* (pp. 81–104). Hillsdale, NJ: Erlbaum.

Tudge, J. R. H., & Rogoff, B. (1989). Peer influences on cognitive development: Piagetian and Vygotskian perspectives. In M. Bornstein and J. Bruner (Eds.). *Interaction in human development* (pp. 17–40). Hillsdale, NJ: Erlbaum.

Vygotsky, L. S. (1978). *Mind and society.* Cambridge, MA: Harvard University Press.

Wertsch, J. V., McNamee, G. D., McLane J. B., & Budwig, N. A. (1980). The adult–child dyad as a problem-solving system. *Child Development,* **51**, 1215–1221.

Questions

1. Why were novices who worked with same-age experts expected to learn more about planning than were novices who worked with older experts?
2. What types of partner involvement appeared in the two social groupings (young novice + young expert vs. younger novice + older expert)?
3. How did guidance and conflict differ in these two groups?
4. How does developmental change in the process of social comparison help explain these results?
5. Whose view of peer collaboration and cognitive development did these results support, Piaget's or Vygotsky's? Explain.
6. If you were to advise a teacher about how to group children in the classroom to promote learning, what type of peer arrangement would the results of this study lead you to suggest?

27 Electronic Bullying Among Middle School Students

Robin M. Kowalski, Ph.D. • Susan P. Limber, Ph.D.

Cultures devise many types of resources, such as literacy, mathematical symbols, and technology, that help people carry out their daily activities. Psychologists refer to these resources as tools because they function in the same way that a tool like a hammer does when you try to build something. Cultural tools enable a person to carry out an activity in a way that would not be possible without use of the tool. Computer technology—along with the access this technology provides to the wider world through electronic communications—is one of the most significant cultural tools affecting children's lives today. In fact, electronic communication is rapidly replacing watching television as one of the main activities children do outside of school.

When children interact with each other electronically, they are often exchanging information about where they are, what they are doing, their recent experiences, and their future plans. This information tends to be entertaining, useful, and, in general, benign. Recently, however, a darker and more hurtful side to children's electronic communications has been revealed: electronic bullying.

Bullying is defined as physical attacks or threats toward peers. Children who are the targets of bullies can suffer greatly; they have lower self-esteem as well as increased anxiety, depression, and loneliness. These victims can also have adjustment problems at school, and even try to avoid school altogether. Until recently, bullying occurred during interpersonal contact, which meant that the victims had some respite when they were away from the settings in which the bullying occurred. Unfortunately, electronic bullying can victimize children outside the usual settings, even reaching them in their homes at any time of day or night.

In the following article, researchers Robin Kowalski and Susan Limber describe the extent to which children in middle school experience electronic bullying. As this research shows, even though cultural tools like electronic communications can enhance children's lives in many positive ways, there is also potential for negative and very hurtful uses of these tools.

Purpose: Electronic communications technologies are affording children and adolescents new means of bullying one another. Referred to as electronic bullying, cyberbullying, or online social cruelty, this phenomenon includes bullying through e-mail, instant messaging, in a chat room, on a website, or through digital messages or images sent to a cell phone. The present study examined the prevalance of electronic bullying among middle school students.

Methods: A total of 3,767 middle school students in grades 6, 7, and 8 who attend six elementary and middle schools in the southeastern and northwestern United States completed a questionnaire, consisting of the Olweus Bully/Victim Questionnaire and 23 questions developed for this study that examined participants' experiences with electronic bullying, as both victims and perpetrators.

Results: Of the students, 11% said that they had been electronically bullied at least once in the last couple of months (victims only); 7% indicated that they were bully/victims; and 4% had electronically bullied someone else at least once in the previous couple of months (bullies only). The most common methods for electronic bullying (as reported by both victims and perpetrators) involved the use of instant messaging, chat rooms, and e-mail. Importantly, close to half of the electronic bully victims reported not knowing the perpetrator's identity.

Conclusions: Electronic bullying represents a problem of significant magnitude. As children's use of electronic communications technologies is unlikely to wane in coming years, continued attention to electronic bullying is critical. Implications of these findings for youth, parents, and educators are discussed.

Reprinted from *Journal of Adolescent Health*, 41, Kowalski, R. M., & Limber, S. P. Electronic bullying among middle school students, pp. S22–S30, © 2007, with permission from Elsevier.

Bullying is commonly defined as repeated aggressive behavior in which there is an imbalance of power between the parties [1–3]. Traditionally bullying has included overt physical acts (e.g., hitting, shoving) and verbal abuse (e.g., taunting, name-calling) as well as more subtle or indirect actions such as social exclusion and rumor-spreading. More recently, the proliferation of electronic communications technologies has afforded children and youth a new means of bullying. Electronic bullying includes bullying through e-mail, instant messaging, in a chat room, on a website, or through digital messages or images sent to a cell phone [4–7].

Although electronic bullying has received extensive attention in the popular press [8–11], few studies have assessed the nature and extent of electronic bullying among students [7]. What research has been conducted has focused primarily on the frequency of children's use of the Internet (e.g., instant messaging, e-mail, social network sites) [12] and their experiences with Internet harassment (e.g., repetitive messages sent to a target that cause emotional distress to that target) [13–15].

Such studies attest to the "wired" culture within which contemporary teenagers operate. One study found that 97% of adolescents 12–18 years of age use the Internet [16]. More than half of those teens surveyed for the Pew Internet & American Life Project indicated that they spent time each day online [12]. Almost half (45%) had their own cell phone and one third communicated via text messaging.

There is debate as to whether high levels of Internet use interfere with psychological functioning. On the positive side, Internet use opens up the possibility for the development of new relationships and the easy maintenance of existing friendships [17–19]. On the negative side, Kraut et al. found higher levels of Internet use to be associated with higher levels of depression and loneliness [20]. Furthermore, one of the most compelling and arguably most dangerous aspects of the Internet is that it allows people to maintain their anonymity when communicating with others. Unfortunately people are more likely to communicate messages on the Internet that they would not say to another person's face [6].

The potential threat of anonymity provided by the Internet is compounded by the fact that people cannot see the target's emotional reactions. Thus, reactions such as crying, which might lead people to realize that their comments have been carried too far or misinterpreted, are no longer visible [18,21,22].

This is not to imply that all Internet use is bad, any more than school attendance is bad just because there is the potential for bullying at school. Indeed most people report positive experiences with the Internet [22]. However the Internet simply provides another forum by which people can aggress against one another.

Only a handful of studies have focused on electronic bullying. Perhaps the earliest study was an unpublished survey conducted by the National Children's Home in Great Britain [23]. Researchers defined electronic bullying as being bullied via mobile phone or personal computer. They surveyed 856 children and youth 11–19 years of age and found that 16% had been bullied via mobile phone text messaging, 7% via Internet chat rooms, and 4% through e-mail [23]. Ybarra and Mitchell interviewed 1,501 regular Internet users 10–17 years of age to compare characteristics of aggressors, targets, and aggressor/targets [22]. They were interested in the degree to which respondents had been victims of or had perpetrated online harassment or rude and threatening online comments. They found that 19% of the sample was involved in online aggression, 4% as online victims only, 12% as online aggressors only, and 3% as aggressor/targets only.

Although comparisons with traditional bullying seem logical, there are unique and particularly troubling aspects of electronic bullying. Unlike traditional bullying, electronic bullying can occur at any time, which may heighten children's perceptions of vulnerability. Electronic bullying messages and images also can be distributed quickly to a wide audience. The interactions that occur in virtual reality can affect the everyday reality that students experience elsewhere.

Although the scant research on electronic bullying is inconclusive, girls may be over-represented among both perpetrators and victims of electronic bullying. Research has consistently shown boys and men to be more likely to engage in direct forms of aggression (e.g., face-to-face physical and verbal confrontations), whereas women and girls tend to engage in more indirect types of aggression (e.g., ostracism, gossip) [3,24]. Consistent with prevalence rates of indirect aggression among females, we expect more girls than boys to have experience with electronic bullying.

In sum, because so little is known about children's use of electronic technologies to bully each other, our study attempts to fill some of these gaps by examining age and gender differences in the nature and prevalence of electronic bullying among middle school-aged children and youth across the United States. This study represents one of the first large-scale studies to examine electronic bullying among middle school children in the United States.

Methods

Participants

Participants included 1,915 girls and 1,852 boys in grades 6, 7, and 8 who attended any of six elementary and middle schools in the southeastern and northwestern United States. The schools were selected because they were planning to begin a bullying prevention program after the collection of baseline data about bullying at their schools. Table 1 provides a description of the school locales, ethnicity of students, and socioeconomic status (SES) of students (as measured by the percentage of students eligible for free or reduced-cost lunches). All students in class on the day of the survey were invited to participate. Passive consent was obtained from parents. Parents received written notice from the school that their children would be participating in the survey and were invited to contact the school if they did not wish their children to participate. Treatment of human subjects was re-

viewed and approved by the Institutional Review Board of the authors' home institution.

Measures

Participants completed a questionnaire packet that included the 39-item Olweus Bully/Victim Questionnaire [25] and a 23-item questionnaire that examined participants' experiences with electronic bullying. The Olweus Bully/Victim Questionnaire is a reliable and valid self-report measure of bullying that defines bullying for students and then assesses participants' experiences with bullying at school, as victims and as perpetrators [25,26]. Bullying is de-

table 1   Descriptions of Participating Schools

School	Number of students in school	Grades in school	Locale	Ethnicity of students	% Eligible for free/reduced-cost lunches
School 1	920	6–8	Urban, fringe of large city (Southeast)	White: 87.7% Black: 1.4% Hispanic: 9.7% Asian: .9% American Indian: .1%	12.1%
School 2	1,521	6–8	Urban, fringe of large city (Southeast)	White: 87.2% Black: 8.2% Hispanic: 1.8% Asian: 1.2% American Indian: 0	6.0%
School 3	640	5–8	Large central city (Southeast)	Not available	Not available
School 4	1,185	7–8	Urban, fringe of large city (Southeast)	White: 85.1% Black: 5.1% Hispanic: 7.8% Asian: 1.2% American Indian: .1%	18.9%
School 5	475	Pre-K–6	Urban, fringe of mid-sized city (Northwest)	White: 78.9% Black: 2.5% Hispanic: 2.9% Asian: 3.3% American Indian: 12.2%	14.1%
School 6	125	K–9	Rural (Northeast)	White: 84.8% Black: 0 Hispanic: .8% Asian: 0 American Indian: 14.4%	37.6%

Source: Institute of Education Sciences Common Core of Data for the 2004–2005 Schoolyear.
K = kindergarten.

fined in the following way on the Olweus Bully/Victim Questionnaire:

> We say that a student is being bullied when another student, or several other students do any of the following: say mean and hurtful things or make fun of him or her or call him or her mean and hurtful names; completely ignore or exclude him or her from their group of friends or leave him or her out of things on purpose; hit, kick, push, shove around, or lock him or her inside a room; tell lies or spread false rumors about him or her or send mean notes and try to make other students dislike him or her; and other hurtful things like that.

> When we talk about bullying, these things happen repeatedly, and it is difficult for the student being bullied to defend himself or herself. We also call it bullying, when a student is teased repeatedly in a mean and hurtful way. But we do not call it bullying when the teasing is done in a friendly and playful way. Also it is not bullying when two students of about equal strength or power argue or fight.

The 23-item Electronic Bullying Questionnaire is a self-report measure that was developed for the purpose of this study and was patterned in part after the Olweus Bully/Victim Questionnaire. Like the Olweus measure, it included questions about participants' experiences with bullying—both being bullied by and bullying others. Key questions included, "How often have you been bullied electronically in the past couple of months?" and "How often have you electronically bullied someone in the past couple of months?" We defined electronic bullying as "bullying through e-mail, instant messaging, in a chat room, on a website, or through a text message sent to a cell phone." Also included were items examining how the electronic bullying occurred (e.g., "Has anyone made fun of you or teased you in a hurtful way through e-mail, instant messaging, in a chat room, on a website, or through a text message sent to your cell phone?"), the electronic venue through which the electronic bullying occurred (e.g., "I was bullied through an e-mail message"), and by whom they were electronically bullied (e.g., "Another student at school?"). With the exception of the yes/no questions asking about the source of the electronic bullying, prevalence questions were answered using the five-point response format used in the Olweus Bully/Victim Questionnaire (i.e., it hasn't happened in the past couple of months; only once or twice; two or three times a month, about once a week, several times a week).

Procedure

Participants completed the Olweus Bully/Victim Questionnaire (which included demographic items assessing grade and gender), followed by the 23-item Electronic Bullying Questionnaire.

Results

Prevalence of Electronic Bullying

We divided students into four groups: those who had been electronically bullied at least once in the last 2 months (victims only), those who had electronically bullied others (bullies only), those who had both been electronically bullied and also had electronically bullied others (bully/victims), and those who had no experience with electronic bullying as either victims or perpetrators. (Much of the research on school bullying has used a more conservative criterion ["2–3 times a month" or more often] to evaluate whether bullying occurred. However, because of the novelty of the construct of electronic bullying, we elected to use a criteria of the event occurring "once or twice" or more often. All analyses were conducted using the more conservative criterion and the pattern of findings remain virtually unchanged.) Of the students, 11% ($n = 407$) qualified as victims only; 7% ($n = 248$) were bully/victims; 4% ($n = 151$) fell into the bullies only category; and 78% ($n = 2961$) had no experience with electronic bullying.

Chi-square analyses revealed some important gender differences by group in involvement in electronic bullying at least once in the previous couple of months, with girls being over-represented among victims and bully/victims, $\chi^2(3) = 117.00$, $p < .001$. In all, 15% of girls ($n = 282$) and 7% of boys ($n = 125$) were victims only; 10% of girls ($n = 177$) and 4% of boys ($n = 71$) were bully/victims (Table 2); and 4% of girls ($n = 68$) and 5% of boys ($n = 83$) reported electronically bullying others (bullies only).

As shown in Table 3, significant differences by grade were also observed, $\chi^2(6) = 52.00$, $p < .001$. Sixth-graders were less likely than other students to be involved in electronic bullying. Specifically, they were half as likely as seventh- or eighth-graders to be bullies or bully/victims, and were somewhat less likely to be victims only.

Methods of Electronic Bullying

The specific means by which students reported being electronically bullied and bullying others electronically are reported in Table 4. Because of the small cell sizes across methods of electronic bullying, partici-

table 2   Frequency of Electronic Bullying (at Least Once), by Gender and Grade

	6th	7th	8th	Total	Total G/B
Girls					
Victims	41 (8.5%)	114 (16.7%)	127 (18.2%)	282 (15.1%)	
Bullies	8 (1.7%)	33 (4.8%)	27 (3.9%)	68 (3.6%)	
Bully/victims	20 (4.1%)	64 (9.4%)	93 (13.3%)	177 (9.5%)	407 (11.1%)
Not involved	414 (85.7%)	473 (69.2%)	452 (64.7%)	1339 (71.8%)	151 (4.1%)
					248 (6.8%)
Boys					2855 (78.0%)
Victims	38 (7.9%)	53 (7.7%)	34 (5.4%)	125 (7.0%)	
Bullies	19 (4.0%)	26 (3.8%)	38 (6.1%)	83 (4.6%)	
Bully/victims	12 (2.5%)	34 (4.9%)	25 (4.0%)	71 (4.0%)	
Not involved	412 (85.7%)	574 (83.6%)	530 (84.5%)	1516 (84.5%)	

Note: Categories are mutually exclusive.

pants were classified as either victims or bullies. Victims reported being electronically bullied most frequently through instant messaging, followed by chat rooms, e-mail messages, and on a website. Bullies similarly reported using instant messaging most frequently, followed by chat rooms and e-mail messaging, to bully others electronically. A 3 (grade: 6th/7th/8th) $\times$ 2 (gender: male/female) multivariate analysis of variance (MANOVA) was conducted on the means by which the bullying occurred. A multivariate main effect of grade, $F(12, 1256) = 2.60$, $p < .002$ ($\eta^2 = .024$), was significant at the univariate level for two of the variables: bullied through instant messaging, $F(2, 632) = 10.51$, $p < .001$ ($\eta^2 = .03$), and bullied through text messaging, $F(2, 632) = 3.39$, $p < .001$ ($\eta^2 = .024$). Sixth-graders (mean 1.60, SD .73) were bullied via instant messaging significantly less frequently than either seventh- (mean 2.02, SD 1.02) or eighth-graders (mean 2.08, SD 1.04), the latter two conditions not differing significantly. Sixth-graders (mean 1.08, SD .38) were also bullied through text messaging significantly

less than eighth-graders (mean 1.29, SD .78), p values $< .05$.

A 3 $\times$ 2 MANOVA conducted on the means used to electronically bully others revealed a multivariate mean effect of grade, $F(12, 768) = 2.05$, $p < .02$ ($\eta^2 = .03$), that was significant at the univariate level for the following variables: bullied someone through instant messaging, $F(2, 388) = 6.09$, $p < .001$ ($\eta^2 = .03$), and bullied someone through a text message, $F(2, 388) = 4.48$, $p < .001$ ($\eta^2 = .023$). Sixth-graders (mean 1.41, SD .56) reported using instant messaging at a significantly lower rate to bully others than did seventh- (mean 1.87, SD 1.00) or eighth- (mean 1.88, SD 1.01) graders. Similarly, sixth-graders (mean 1.05, SD .23) used text messaging to electronically bully others less frequently than eighth-graders (mean 1.37, SD .92).

A multivariate interaction of grade and gender, $F(12, 768) = 2.32$, $p < .007$ ($\eta^2 = .04$), was significant at the univariate level for bullying in a chat room, $F(2, 388) = 3.74$, $p < .03$ ($\eta^2 = .02$), and through e-mail, $F(2, 388) = 3.16$, $p < .04$ ($\eta^2 = .02$) (Figures 1 and 2).

table 3   Involvement in Electronic Bullying (at Least Once) by Grade

	6th-Graders	7th-Graders	8th-Graders	Total
Victims	80 (8.3%)	167 (12.1%)	162 (12.2%)	409 (11.1%)
Bullies	27 (2.8%)	60 (4.4%)	65 (4.9%)	152 (4.1%)
Bully/Victims	32 (3.3%)	99 (7.2%)	118 (8.9%)	249 (6.8%)
Not Involved	828 (85.6%)	1051 (76.3%)	988 (74.1%)	2867 (78.0%)
Total	967 (100.0%)	1377 (100.0%)	1333 (100.0%)	

Note: Categories are mutually exclusive.

table 4 Frequency and Method of Electronic Victimization/Bullying (at Least Once)

	Girls				Boys				Total G/B
	6th	7th	8th	Total	6th	7th	8th	Total	
Electronic victimization									
Bullied through instant messaging	38 (61.3%)	127 (69.8%)	162 (73.3%)	327 (70.3%)	20 (40.8%)	58 (65.9%)	38 (61.3%)	116 (58.0%)	443 (66.6%)
Bullied in a chat room	17 (27.4%)	48 (26.5%)	42 (19.2%)	107 (23.2%)	12 (24.5%)	25 (28.7%)	19 (31.1%)	56 (28.4%)	163 (24.7%)
Bullied on a website	9 (14.5%)	54 (29.8%)	52 (23.9%)	115 (24.9%)	10 (20.4%)	15 (17.0%)	14 (23.3%)	39 (19.8%)	154 (23.4%)
Bullied through email	15 (24.2%)	51 (28.3%)	55 (25.0%)	121 (26.2%)	4 (8.2%)	20 (22.7%)	14 (23.3%)	38 (19.4%)	159 (24.2%)
Bullied through text message	5 (8.1%)	29 (16.1%)	34 (15.7%)	68 (14.8%)	1 (1.0%)	13 (14.8%)	14 (23.3%)	28 (14.3%)	96 (14.7%)
Bullied electronically in another way	7 (11.7%)	32 (18.0%)	35 (16.2%)	74 (16.3%)	5 (10.6%)	11 (13.1%)	10 (16.9%)	26 (13.7%)	100 (15.5%)
Electronic bullying									
Bullied through instant messaging	9 (32.1%)	57 (59.4%)	77 (63.6%)	143 (58.4%)	13 (40.0%)	32 (53.3%)	33 (52.4%)	78 (51.0%)	221 (55.5%)
Bullied in a chat room	7 (25.0%)	21 (22.0%)	22 (18.3%)	50 (20.5%)	3 (10.3%)	21 (35.0%)	18 (28.6%)	42 (27.6%)	92 (23.2%)
Bullied on a website	2 (7.1%)	16 (16.5%)	17 (14.2%)	35 (15.4%)	5 (17.9%)	8 (13.1%)	16 (25.4%)	29 (19.1%)	64 (16.1%)
Bullied through email	7 (25.0%)	18 (18.6%)	22 (18.2%)	47 (19.1%)	3 (10.7%)	13 (21.7%)	16 (25.4%)	32 (21.2%)	79 (19.9%)
Bullied through text message	2 (7.1%)	18 (18.6%)	21 (17.4%)	41 (16.7%)	1 (3.6%)	11 (18.3%)	17 (27.0%)	29 (19.2%)	70 (17.6%)
Bullied electronically in another way	1 (3.6%)	13 (13.4%)	15 (12.4%)	29 (11.8%)	2 (7.1%)	18 (30.0%)	14 (22.2%)	34 (22.5%)	63 (15.9%)

Note: Categories are not mutually exclusive. Participants in each sex and grade level could have been electronically bullied in multiple ways.

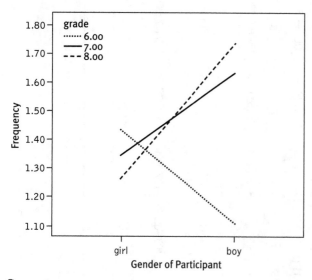

figure 1

Interaction of grade and gender on having bullied someone in a chat room.

Across variables, sixth-grade boys show the greatest divergence from the other groups. In addition, relative to girls, boys show the greatest variation across grade levels. These findings are consistent with previous research showing that sixth-grade boys lag behind in their use of the Internet and related technologies [12].

Relationship between Victim and Perpetrator

Both victims and bully/victims were electronically bullied most frequently by a student at school, followed by a stranger (Table 5). More than half of bully/victims indicated they had been electronically bullied by a friend, whereas a little more than a quarter of the victims said they had been electronically bullied by a friend. More than 12% of victims and 16% of bully/victims reported that they had been electronically bullied by a sibling. Importantly, almost half (48%) did not know who had electronically bullied them. Perpetrators indicated that they electronically bullied another student at school most frequently, followed by a friend and strangers.

Discussion

The data suggest that, among middle school students, electronic bullying is a problem. Of the students, 11% had been electronically bullied at least once in the last couple of months; 7% were bully/victims; and 4% had electronically bullied someone else at least once in the previous 2 months. If anything, the statistics underes-

timate the true frequency of electronic bullying. Our survey assessed children's experiences with electronic bullying over the previous 2 months. It is quite possible that children may have had experience with electronic bullying, albeit not within the previous 2 months. In addition, because there is so little research on electronic bullying, targets may not have recognized that what they had experienced was actually a form of bullying.

On the one hand, the magnitude of the numbers is somewhat staggering. Collapsing across victims and bully/victims, a quarter of the female respondents had been electronically bullied within the last 2 months. On the other hand, the sheer frequency of use of electronic technologies by adolescents provides a context within which the statistics are, sadly, not all that surprising. Almost 50% of the teenage population use cell phones; 97% use the Internet, and a large proportion of these use it everyday [12].

When discussing electronic bullying, questions are often raised regarding the degree to which victims and perpetrators of electronic bullying are the same as those involved with traditional bullying; data from Kowalski and Limber suggest that, to a degree, they are [27]. Among individuals *not* involved with traditional bullying as either victims or perpetrators, 6.4% were victims of electronic bullying, 2.4% perpetrated electronic bullying, and 2.4% were electronic bully/victims [26].

Electronic bullying has features that make it more appealing to some than traditional bullying. The ability to hide behind fake screen names or to steal someone else's screen name and communicate as that

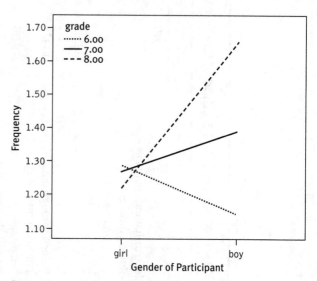

figure 2

Interaction of grade and gender on having bullied someone through an e-mail message.

table 5   Reports of Relationship (at Least Once), by Gender and Grade

	Girls				Boys				Total G/B
	6th	7th	8th	Total	6th	7th	8th	Total	
Victims' reports with bully									
Brother or sister	5 (12.2%)	12 (10.8%)	17 (13.4%)	34 (12.1%)	2 (5.7%)	9 (17.3%)	5 (15.2%)	16 (12.8%)	50 (12.3%)
Friend	8 (19.5%)	32 (28.8%)	41 (32.5%)	81 (28.7%)	5 (14.3%)	22 (42.3%)	4 (12.1%)	31 (24.8%)	112 (27.5%)
Another student at school	15 (36.6%)	62 (55.4%)	63 (50.4%)	140 (49.6%)	13 (37.1%)	27 (51.9%)	10 (30.3%)	50 (40%)	190 (46.7%)
Stranger	13 (31.7%)	52 (45.6%)	65 (51.6%)	130 (46.1%)	18 (47.4%)	25 (47.2%)	12 (36.4%)	55 (44%)	185 (45.5%)
Someone else	3 (7.7%)	12 (10.9%)	17 (13.7%)	32 (11.3%)	3 (8.6%)	7 (14.0%)	2 (5.9%)	12 (9.6%)	44 (10.8 %)
Bully/victims' report with bully									
Brother or sister	6 (30.0%)	7 (10.9%)	11 (12.1%)	24 (13.6%)	2 (16.7%)	8 (24.2%)	6 (25.0%)	16 (22.5%)	40 (16.1%)
Friend	7 (35.0%)	33 (51.6%)	53 (58.2%)	93 (52.5%)	4 (33.3%)	17 (50.0%)	14 (60.9%)	35 (49.3%)	128 (51.6%)
Another student at school	10 (52.6%)	40 (62.5%)	63 (68.5%)	113 (64%)	4 (33.3%)	16 (48.5%)	20 (83.3%)	40 (56.3%)	153 (61.7%)
Stranger	10 (50.0%)	35 (54.7%)	53 (57.0%)	98 (55.4%)	5 (41.7%)	16 (47.1%)	15 (60.0%)	36 (31.5%)	134 (54.0%)
Someone else	2 (10.5%)	15 (23.8%)	12 (13.2%)	29 (16.4%)	2 (18.2%)	5 (15.2%)	5 (22.7%)	12 (16.9%)	41 (16.5%)
Bully report with victim									
Brother or sister	0 (0.0%)	1 (3.0%)	6 (22.2%)	7 (10.3%)	1 (5.3%)	5 (19.2%)	2 (5.3%)	8 (9.6%)	15 (9.9%)
Friend	1 (12.5%)	6 (18.0%)	7 (25.9%)	14 (20.6%)	4 (21.1%)	6 (23.1%)	10 (26.3%)	20 (24.1%)	34 (22.5%)
Another student at school	2 (25%)	9 (27.3%)	6 (22.2%)	17 (25.0%)	7 (36.8%)	9 (34.6%)	11 (28.9%)	27 (32.5%)	44 (29.1%)
Stranger	3 (37.5%)	4 (12.1%)	4 (14.8%)	11 (16.2%)	3 (15.8%)	11 (42.3%)	8 (21.1%)	22 (26.5%)	33 (21.9%)
Someone else	0 (.0%)	0 (.0%)	2 (7.4%)	2 (2.9%)	2 (10.5%)	6 (23.1%)	1 (2.6%)	9 (10.8%)	11 (7.3%)

Note: Categories are not mutually exclusive. Participants in each gender and grade level could have been electronically bullied by more than one other person.

person provides people with the opportunity to communicate things they would be reticent to say to another's face. For socially anxious teens who may have been victims of traditional bullying, the Internet and related technologies provide a forum within which to communicate without fear and to perhaps seek revenge on traditional bullying perpetrators. Finally, the venue of cyber space, where victim and perpetrator cannot see each other, may lead some perpetrators to remain unconvinced that they are actually harming their target. Thus, they can protect themselves from the knowledge that they are doing anything wrong.

Importantly, the data highlight gender differences in the frequency of electronic bullying, with girls outnumbering boys. This is consistent with girls tending to rely on more indirect forms of aggression relative to boys [24,28]. In addition, researchers have suggested that the Internet affords girls an opportunity to establish and maintain relationships independently of concerns with how others may be perceiving and evaluating their physical characteristics [29,30].

Fewer gender differences were observed across the methods used to electronically bully. The most frequently reported methods were instant messaging, chat rooms, websites, and on e-mail. These findings are consistent with those in the Pew report, showing that the Internet technologies most likely to be used by adolescents include instant messaging and e-mail [12]. Grade differences were observed for young people's use of instant messages and text messages as means to be bullied, with sixth-graders reporting the least victimization. Interestingly, the Pew report also found that girls, particularly in the 15–17-year-old age range, use e-mail at a much higher percentage than boys, a finding that may be reflected in our data showing that sixth-grade boys seemed to differ most markedly from the other participants.

That grade differences were observed across methods is not altogether surprising. As children move through middle school, they spend more time on computers and related technologies (e.g., PDAs), and they become more skilled at their use. With age, they are also more likely to begin participating in social network sites, such as Facebook and Xanga, all likely places for electronic bullying to occur.

One of the most problematic issues of electronic bullying relative to traditional bullying is the anonymity involved with electronic bullying. In our sample, almost half of the victims of electronic bullying did not know the identity of the person(s) who electronically bullied them. This is problematic for several reasons. First, the victim has no way of knowing whether the electronic bullying is being perpetrated by one or a group of individuals. Second, the enemy we know is often less frightening than the enemy we do not know. Not knowing the identity of the electronic bully may leave a child wondering if each person he or she meets was potentially the perpetrator. As noted earlier, for the perpetrators, anonymity may provide a cover, a "cloak of invisibility," under which they will communicate things that they would not say if their identity were known [31].

These findings have implications for children, parents, and educators. Given the frequency of electronic bullying, children, parents, and school personnel need to become more aware of what electronic bullying is, how to help to prevent it, and how to address electronic bullying that has occurred [4,15,32,33]. School administrators should work to educate students, teachers, and staff about electronic bullying, its dangers, and what to do if it is suspected. They also should ensure that school rules and policies related to bullying include electronic bullying. Suspected instances of electronic bullying should be investigated immediately. Those that involve threats of physical harm or other illegal behavior should be reported immediately to the police.

Parents also should be proactive in discussing electronic bullying with their children [33]. Data from focus group interviews show that adolescents are reluctant to report instances of electronic bullying that do not involve death threats for fear their parents will restrict their time on the Internet or cell phones or discover information that the adolescents themselves have posted on the Internet [33]. Given this, parents need to set developmentally appropriate guidelines for children's use of the Internet and other cyber technologies and maintain open communication with their children regarding their use. They should regularly discuss appropriate steps to take if children or youth experience or witness electronic bullying or threats.

Our focus was on electronic bullying among middle school children, because this is when traditional bullying is quite prevalent and because earlier research has suggested an increase in the use of electronic technologies during these ages. However, future research should focus on a wider range of ages, from elementary school through high school. Furthermore, although our sample was drawn from several areas around the country, random sampling was not used. The relative homogeneity of our sample (particularly in terms of race and ethnicity) leaves open the possibility that other samples of children may experience electronic bullying differently than those in our study.

More detailed research is needed to explore the venues (e.g., social networking sites) through which electronic bullying occurs, the content of electronic bullying episodes, and the content in which the behavior takes place. For example, as our research suggests that a relatively large percentage of "friends" (and, to a lesser extent, siblings) were perpetrators of cyberbullying, it will be important to explore further the extent to which these behaviors are indeed indicators of intentional aggression via electronic sources or something less intentional and potentially less serious.

As one of the early studies in this area, this study examined overall prevalence rates of electronic bullying. However, an important next stage will be to examine how often students report electronic bullying, to whom they report, and with what effect. How do parents respond when their children confide in them or when they find out through other means that their child is involved in electronic bullying as either the victim or the perpetrator? What role do schools have in designing interventions to educate students about electronic bullying and to intervene on behalf of targets of electronic bullying? Finally, this research did not examine the effects of electronic bullying on the victim or the perpetrator—variables that need research attention.

In conclusion, electronic bullying represents a problem of significant magnitude. Although it would seem that one could apply what is known about traditional bullying to the electronic world, this is not entirely the case. For example, unlike traditional bullying in which boys are more likely to be the perpetrators, girls electronically bully and are electronically bullied more than boys. Unlike traditional bullying in which the perpetrator usually is known to his or her victims, our findings suggest that about half of children who are bullied electronically do not know the identity of the perpetrators. Unlike traditional bullying, in which the audience of bystanders usually consists of a handful of children or youth who are physically present to witness the bullying, the potential audience of bystanders and observers of electronic bullying is limitless. As children's use of electronic communications technologies is unlikely to wane in coming years, continued attention to electronic bullying (and other cyber threats) is critical.

Acknowledgment

The authors thank Melinda Keith for helpful comments on an earlier version of this manuscript.

REFERENCES

1. Limber SP. Peer victimization: The nature and prevalence of bullying among children and youth. In: Dowd N, Singer DG, Wilson RF, eds. Handbook of Children, Culture, and Violence. Beverly Hills: Sage Publications, 2006, 313–32.

2. Nansel TR, Overpeck M, Pilla M, et al. Bullying behavior Among U.S. youth: Prevalence and association with psychosocial adjustment. JAMA 2001;285:2094–2100.

3. Olweus D. Bullying at School: What We Know and What We Can Do. Cambridge, MA: Blackwell, 1993.

4. Health Resources and Services Administration. Take a Stand. Lend a Hand. Stop Bullying Now. Available at: http://www.stopbullyingnow.hrsa.gov/adult/indexAdult.asp?Area=cyberbullying.

5. Keith S, Martin ME. Cyber-bullying: Creating a culture of respect in a cyber world. Children and Youth 2005;13:224–8.

6. Patchin JW, Hinduja S. Bullies move beyond the schoolyard: A preliminary look at cyberbullying. Youth Violence and Juvenile Justice 2006;4:148–69.

7. Shariff S, Gouin R. Cyber dilemmas: Gendered hierarchies, free expression, and cyber-safety in schools. Available at: http://www.oii.ox.ac.uk/research/cybersafety/extensions/pdfs/papers/shaheen_shariff.pdf. Accessed January 15, 2005.

8. Batheja A. Cyber bullies' torments have much wider reach. Miami Herald, August 24, 2004.

9. Harmon A. Internet Gives Teenage Bullies Weapons to Wound From Afar. Available at: http://www.nytimes.com/2004/08/26/education. Accessed August 26, 2004.

10. Miller M. Bullying in schools cannot be tolerated. Basco Times. Pasco Times, November 17, 2004.

11. Paulson A. With the Click of a Key, Bullies Are Humiliating Their Peers. What Are Schools Doing to Tame This Behavior? Available at: http://www.csmonitor.com/2003/1230/p11s01-legn.htm. Accessed December 30, 2003.

12. Lenhart A, Maddeen M, Hitlin P. Pew Internet & American Life Project: Teens and Technology: Youth Are Leading the Transition to a Fully Wired Mobile Nation. Available at: http://www.pewinternet.org. Accessed December 15, 2005.

13. Finkelhor D, Mitchell KJ, Wolak J. Online Victimization: A Report of the Nation's Youth. Washington, DC: National Center for Missing and Exploited Children, 2000.

14. Finn J. A survey of online harassment at a university campus. Interpersonal Violence 2004;19:468–83.

15. Willard N. Electronic Bullying and Cyberthreats: Responding to the Challenge of Online Social Cruelty, Threats, and Distress. Eugene, OR: Center for Safe and Responsible Internet Use, 2006.

16. UCLA Internet Report: Surveying the Digital Future Year Three. Available at: http://ccp.ucla.edu. Accessed September 16, 2005.

17. Gross EF, Juvonen J, Gable SL. Internet use and well-being in adolescence. J Soc Issues 2002;58:75–90.

18. McKenna KYA, Bargh JA. Plan 9 from cyberspace: The implications of the Internet for personality and social psychology. Personal Soc Psychol Bull 2000;4:57–75.

19. Russell DW, Flom EK, Gardner KA, et al. Who makes friends over the Internet? Loneliness and the "virtual" community. International Scope Review 2003;10.

20. Kraut R, Patterson M, Kiesler V, et al. Internet paradox: A social technology that reduces social involvement and psychological well-being? Am Psychol 2004;53:1017–31.

21. Ybarra ML. Linkages between depressive symptomatology and Internet harassment among young regular Internet users. Cyber Psychol Behav 2004;7:247–57.

22. Ybarra ML, Mitchell KL. Youth engaging in online harassment: Associations with caregiver–child Relationships, Internet use, and personal characteristics. J Adolesc 2004;27:319–36.

23. National Children's Home. 1 in 4 Children Are Victims of "On-Line Bullying." Available at: http://www.nch.org.uk/information/index.php?i=77&r=125.

24. Bjorkqvist K, Lagerspetz KMJ, Kaukianin A. Do girls manipulate and boys fight? Developmental trends in regard to direct and indirect aggression. Aggressive Behav 1992;18:117–27.

25. Olweus D. The Revised Olweus Bully/Victim Questionnaire. Beren, Norway: Research Center for Health Promotion (HIMIL), University of Bergen, N-5015 Bergen, Norway, 1996.

26. Solberg M, Olweus D. Prevalence estimation of school bullying with the Olweus Bully/Victim Questionnaire. Aggressive Behav 2003;29:239–68.

27. Kowalski R, Limber SP. Children who bully in the schoolyard and in cyberspace: How different are they? Manuscript in preparation..

28. Owens L, Shute R, Slee P. "I'm in and you're out . . . ": Explantions for teenage girls' indirect aggression. Psychol Evolut Gender 2000;2:19–46.

29. American Association of University Women. Tech Savvy: Educating Girls in the New Computer Age. Washington, DC: AAUW Educational Research Foundation, 2000.

30. Berson IR, Berson MJ, Ferron JM. Emerging risks of violence in the digital age: Lessons for educators from an online study of adolescent girls in the United States. Available at http://www2.ncsu.edu/unity/lockers/project/meridian/sum2002/cyberviolence/cyberviolence.pdf. Accessed March 23, 2007.

31. Carrington PM. Internet Increases Cyber Bullying. Available at: http://www.timesdispatch.com. Accessed June 6, 2006.

32. Willard NE. Cyberbullying and Cyberthreats. Champaign, IL: Research Press, 2007.

33. Kowalski RM, Limber SE, Agatston PW. Cyber Bullying: Bullying in the Digital Age. Malden, MA: Wiley/Blackwell, 2007.

Questions

1. In what ways is electronic bullying different from bullying that occurs through interpersonal contact, and does electronic bullying pose more or less of a threat to children than interpersonal bullying?
2. Why is anonymous electronic bullying particularly threatening to children?
3. What gender differences were found in electronic bullying, and what do these differences tell us about male and female aggression during middle childhood?
4. Do you think the different methods of electronic bullying, such as text messaging, emailing, and commenting on social networking sites, might lead to different reactions from victims, and, if so, what might these different reactions be?
5. What relationships do victims and bullies involved in electronic bullying tend to have with one another outside their hurtful electronic communications? Do these patterns surprise you?
6. What would you do if you discovered that your younger sibling or another relative was either a victim of or had been bullying other children though electronic communications?

28 Cultural Teaching: The Development of Teaching Skills in Maya Sibling Interactions

Ashley E. Maynard

In the course of development, children acquire skill at all kinds of tasks that are commonplace in their communities. The acquisition of everyday skills, such as preparing food, bathing, and caregiving, is important to development, but little is known about when and how children actually learn these types of skills. Children's play has been cited as one avenue for such learning. During play, children practice many of the behaviors that they see adults perform in their everyday lives. However, until recently, little attention has been paid to whether instruction also contributes to this type of learning. Some research demonstrates that adults, especially parents, teach children everyday skills. Specifically, research on Vygotsky's notion of the zone of proximal development has described how parents help children learn to use eating utensils in the first few years of life and to get ready for school in the morning when they are in the elementary school years.

By emphasizing adult–child instruction, researchers have overlooked another common and valuable source of instruction in young children's lives: older siblings. Because they often spend much time with younger family members and have more advanced skills than younger children, older siblings may be especially helpful to younger children as they learn about and practice the everyday activities and skills that are important in their community. The following article describes a study of older-sibling instruction in a Mayan community in Mexico. Because sibling caretaking is common in this community, researcher Ashley Maynard reasoned that teaching by older siblings may also be a common feature of young children's experience there. Maynard observed the sibling interactions of children between 2 and 8 years of age and coded the interactions that were teaching episodes. She then examined these episodes more closely to determine the nature and extent of older children's instruction to their younger siblings.

Maynard discovered two interesting aspects of sibling teaching behaviors: As children got older, their verbal and nonverbal instructions improved; and with development, the older children's patterns of instruction increasingly resembled those of the adults in this community. These results suggest that both the content and the form of children's teaching reflect the cultural context of development.

Psychology has considered the development of learning, but the development of teaching in childhood has not been considered. The data presented in this article demonstrate that children develop teaching skills over the course of middle childhood. Seventy-two Maya children (25 boys, 47 girls) ranging in age from 3 to 11 years (M = 6.8 years) were videotaped in sibling caretaking interactions with their 2-year-old brothers and sisters

Reprinted with permission from Maynard, A. E., "Cultural Teaching: The Development of Teaching Skills in Maya Sibling Interactions", *Child Development, 73, 969–982*, © 2002 Blackwell Publishers.

The data presented in this article were submitted in partial fulfillment of the requirements for the doctoral degree in psychology at the University of California, Los Angeles. Portions of these data were presented at the annual meeting of the Jean Piaget Society, Mexico City, Mexico, June 1999 ("Cultural Context and Developmental Theory: Evidence from the Maya of Mexico," P. Greenfield, Chair) and at the annual meeting of the American Anthropological Association, Chicago, Illinois, November 1999 ("The Cultural Study of Children's Play," S. Gaskins, Chair).

(18 boys, 18 girls). In the context of play, older siblings taught their younger siblings how to do everyday tasks such as washing and cooking. Ethnographic observations, discourse analyses, and quantification of discourse findings showed that children's teaching skills increased over the course of middle childhood. By the age of 4 years, children took responsibility for initiating teaching situations with their toddler siblings. By the age of 8 years, children were highly skilled in using talk combined with manual demonstrations, verbal feedback, explanations, and guiding the body of younger learners. Children's developing competence in teaching helped their younger siblings increase their participation in culturally important tasks.

Introduction

Children learn about their environments with the help of others in the process of socialization. Adults are said to provide a scaffold of help upon which children can accomplish tasks that they would not be able to accomplish on their own (e.g., Rogoff, 1991; Vygotsky, 1978; Wood, Bruner, & Ross, 1976). Cultural learning (Kruger & Tomasello, 1996; Tomasello, Kruger, & Ratner, 1993) requires contexts in which children can engage their new world, but also requires others to act as teachers. Psychologists have considered the development of learning, but the development of teaching (e.g., the development of skill in scaffolding) has not been considered. Although the capacity to teach is basic to the transmission of human culture, few studies have explored the roots of teaching in childhood.

The theory of cultural learning (Tomasello et al., 1993) was postulated to link children's development to their increasing participation in cultural activities. In cultural learning, the focus is on the attainments of children learners that make them able to internalize important aspects of culture, or in other words, to acquire culture. In cultural teaching, the focus is on the examination of the local discourse practices, the social ecology of development, and the material aspects of the environment that make cultural learning possible. The way that cultural teaching develops in children's daily routines was the central focus of the research presented in this article.

Children acquire patterns of thinking and communicating in their interactions with more competent members of their culture, within the zone of proximal development (Rogoff, 1990; Vygotsky, 1978). Through their increasing participation in interactions with more competent others, children appropriate patterns of behavior and thus acquire the means to become competent members of their communities themselves. An important question concerns the ways in which

the ability to provide appropriate help to a less experienced member of the culture develops during childhood.

Numerous studies of children's cognitive and social development in the preschool years have indicated dramatic increases in skills that would be important in the developing ability to teach. During the course of development, children experience major gains in intersubjectivity (Gopnik & Meltzoff, 1994; Trevarthen & Logotheti, 1989), linguistic competence (Goodluck, 1991), and cognitive and sociocognitive attainments (Piaget, 1952, 1967; Rogoff, 1990), all skills that can be used by children as they teach others. One of the most sophisticated teaching skills that must develop is the skill of scaffolding (Rogoff, 1990; Rogoff, Mistry, Göncü, & Mosier, 1993). Children must be able to understand what younger children know and don't know to provide the most appropriate kind of help.

Children's peer interactions can be beneficial to their acquisition of these cognitive and social skills (Corsaro, 1985; Goodwin, 1990; Rogoff, 1990; Vygotsky, 1978). Sometimes peers teach each other as they engage in activities, indicating that they do have some early teaching skills. For example, children's work as peer tutors provides a glimpse into children's skills in teaching (Foster-Harrison, 1995; Johnson & Bailey, 1974). Siblings, especially, can be effective peer teachers of their younger siblings because they are related, are often emotionally close, and are close in age (Meisner & Fisher, 1980).

The goal of the present study was to examine the role of older siblings in teaching their younger siblings to become competent members of their culture by guiding them in cultural activities. It was reasoned that sibling interactions in a sibling caretaking society would provide the greatest opportunity to observe sibling guidance. This is because sibling caretaking is a highly valued form of childcare that allows parents to do other work to support the family economically (Zukow-Goldring, 2002), while older siblings teach younger children to do culturally important tasks, such as weaving (Greenfield, Maynard, & Childs, 2000; Zukow-Goldring, personal communication, October 14, 2000). By studying a community that employs sibling caretaking in the social support of children it is possible to examine the development of sibling teaching as it happens, in its natural environment.

The present research was conducted in a community that employs sibling caretaking in the social support of children—the Zinacantec Maya village, Nabenchauk, in the highlands of Chiapas, Mexico. Previous research on weaving apprenticeship among the Zinacantec Maya has given insight into the teaching and learning practices of this group, focusing on an adult model of apprenticeship (Childs & Greenfield, 1980; Greenfield, 1984; Greenfield, Maynard, &

Childs, 1999; Greenfield et al., 2000; Maynard, 1996; Maynard, Greenfield, & Childs, 1999). The present research was designed to examine the developmental roots of that adult model and thus chart the course of the development of teaching.

The Role of Siblings in Child Development

The role of siblings in early childhood socialization has received much attention over the last 2 decades (e.g., Abramovitch, Corter, & Lando, 1979; Kendrick & Dunn, 1980; Watson-Gegeo & Gegeo, 1989; Weisner, 1987; Weisner & Gallimore, 1977; Zukow, 1989a; Zukow-Goldring, 2002). Developmental research has focused on the role of siblings in children's intellectual development (Zukow, 1989b), and on the role of siblings in children's social and emotional development (Dunn, 1989; Howe & Ross, 1990; Teti & Ablard, 1989; Whiting & Edwards, 1988; Zukow, 1989a).

There are several social effects of the sibling relationship that might influence both the quality and quantity of sibling teaching. Sibling interactions foster children's ability to comfort, share with, and cooperate with each other (Dunn & Munn, 1986). Children with siblings exhibit more prosocial behaviors—such as perspective taking and sharing—earlier and to a greater degree than children without siblings (Dunn, 1992). Being nurtured by older siblings has been found to predict American children's later social perspective taking (Bryant, 1987) and to have a positive effect on children's school behaviors and adjustment (Gallimore, Tharp, & Speidel, 1978; Weisner, Gallimore, & Jordan, 1988). Children who interact with an extended kin network (including multiple siblings) are precocious in their acquisition of false belief compared with those who interact with a more limited kin group (Lewis, Freeman, Kyriakidou, Maridaki-Kassotaki, & Berridge, 1996). Younger siblings imitate older siblings more than they are imitated (Pepler, Abramovitch, & Corter, 1981), and they receive guidance from older brothers or sisters (Zukow, 1989b) rather than the other way around. These social and perspective-taking skills are likely to be reflected in sibling teaching, especially in a sibling-caretaking community such as Zinacantan, where older siblings are given the role as helpers of their younger siblings. It is likely that the help given to younger siblings is instrumental in the older children's teaching of the younger children. Helping behaviors provide a context for teaching to occur.

Sibling caretaking provides children the opportunity to demonstrate that they are competent cultural members by engaging their charges in appropriate activities (Zukow, 1989b; Zukow-Goldring, 2002). Ethnographers working in agrarian societies all over the world have noted the widespread use of sibling

caretaking, starting when the sibling caretaker is as young as age 3 (e.g., Gaskins, 1999; Martini, 1994; Watson-Gegeo & Gegeo, 1989; Weisner & Gallimore, 1977; Whiting & Edwards, 1988; Whiting & Whiting, 1975; Zukow, 1989a; Zukow-Goldring, 2002). In their pioneering study of children in six cultures, Whiting and colleagues (Whiting & Edwards, 1988; Whiting & Whiting, 1975) quantified sibling behaviors and made general descriptions of the roles that siblings in various cultures play while caring for a younger child.

Sibling caretakers do more than address the biological needs of their charges (Zukow-Goldring, 2002). For example, in a study in Central Mexico, Zukow (1989a) described examples of older siblings engaging their younger charges in more advanced play than that which the younger ones had been previously engaged in on their own. In the Marquesas, Martini (1994) found that sibling caretakers socialize each other to become competent at managing stratified social roles, respecting the complex social hierarchy of Marquesan culture. Sibling caretakers introduce younger siblings to new languages, language routines, and appropriate ways to behave (Ochs, 1988; Watson-Gegeo & Gegeo, 1989; Zukow-Goldring, 2002). Thus, siblings have been found to teach each other in very useful ways. In Hawaii and in a Navajo group, children's teaching experiences as sibling caretakers have been translated into improved learning environments in schools (Gallimore et al., 1978; Tharp, 1994; Weisner et al., 1988).

The present study is the first known to describe and examine the development of teaching over a cross-section of ages from 3 to 11 years. A meta-analysis of the literature indicates that most studies have focused at a particular age, chosen for each study. For example, Stewart (1983) studied 8-year-olds who were teaching 6-year-olds to use a toy camera. A few studies compared adult teaching with sibling teaching, when the teacher-siblings were age 6 and the learner-siblings were age 4 (Perez-Granados & Callanan, 1997); and when the teacher-siblings were age 9 and the learner-siblings were age 6 (Cicirelli, 1976). The siblings in Perez-Granados and Callanan's study more often just did the task for their younger sibling, rather than acting as a guide for the sibling to help the sibling accomplish the task by him- or herself. This may be because the sibling role in the U.S. majority culture does not include the sibling as a guide or teacher for the younger one.

In studies in which the focus was on the development of peer teaching or collaboration and not sibling teaching per se, the researchers only tested children in a limited age range: 24 to 42 months (Ashley & Tomasello, 1998); infant toddler peers, 12 to 30 months (Brownell & Carriger, 1991); or 9-year-old children (Ellis & Rogoff, 1982). One study compared siblings and peers as agents of cognitive development by watching the collaborative activities of 9-year-olds with 7-year-olds (Azmitia & Hesser, 1993).

None of this previous work looked at the moment-by-moment socialization practices of siblings, tracing the developmental progression of sibling socialization across a range of ages. In addition, no study has described how siblings at various developmental stages organize events and guide one another in the joint co-construction of activities. The current study was designed to fill this gap by showing how older siblings develop the skills to participate in an apprenticeship process or socialization of younger children.

The Study Site: Nabenchauk, Zinacantán

There is a long tradition in the study of apprenticeship in Nabenchauk. For example, Greenfield and Childs (Childs & Greenfield, 1980; Greenfield, 1984) first analyzed the processes of Zinacantec teaching and learning in the domain of weaving. Childs and Greenfield (1980) demonstrated the particular verbal and nonverbal variables that were important as adults taught girls to weave, focusing on commands, explanations, questions, declaratives, and positive and negative reinforcement. Of particular interest is that the command form was the most used discourse form; teachers expected obedience from their pupils. There was little verbal explanation and almost no extrinsic verbal reinforcement, such as praise or criticism. Childs and Greenfield also discussed the highly scaffolded nature of Zinacantec weaving apprenticeship, whereby a teacher helps a learner accomplish a task by providing help that is sensitive to the learner's stage of acquisition.

The Zinacantec model of teaching and learning (Maynard, 1996) is based on the work of Childs and Greenfield (1980) as well as my own ethnographic fieldwork in Nabenchauk. The model includes such features as the expectation of obedience, scaffolded help, observational learning, contextualized talk, teacher and learner bodily closeness, and having more than one teacher for a given task; and reflects an overall pattern of apprenticeship that centers around helping younger members of the culture become more competent participants in cultural activities. This study was designed to chart the development of this cultural model in childhood.

It was hypothesized that children would approach the adult Zinacantec model of teaching (Maynard, 1996) as they matured. Just as the model is acquired and used in the apprenticeship of weaving skills, the current study examined its use in socialization practices. A further goal was to chart its acquisition and use by developing children. Older children's teaching was expected to approach the teaching of adults, with a greater expectation of obedience (demonstrated by the issuance of commands), more scaffolded help, and bodily closeness.

Children's use of effective discursive teaching acts, involving intersubjectivity, linguistic competence, and cognitive and sociocognitive attainments, was hypothesized to increase with age. For example, children were expected to use more appropriate verbal discourse as they developed stronger communication skills. As another example, children's abilities to simplify a task for another child were expected to increase over middle childhood as they gained a greater ability to take the perspective of another.

In this study, children's interactions were analyzed by discourse analyses, to get a picture of their cognitive and sociocognitive attainments as they were revealed in their social practices (Goodwin & Goodwin, 1992; Wootton, 1997). Discourse analysis involves the microanalytic examination of communication processes in context, which includes settings, tools, and participants. Many researchers in child development have used discourse analysis to explore aspects of development; for example, language development (Ochs, 1988; Wootton, 1997), processes of social interaction in childhood (Goodwin, 1990), language socialization (Ochs & Schieffelin, 1984), and sibling socialization (Zukow, 1986, 1989a; Zukow-Goldring, 1997). A picture of the development of communicative practices over the range of ages in this study was produced by careful analyses, both quantitative and qualitative, of the children's discourse strategies. Quantitative analyses of discourse processes were used to chart the development of the children's verbal and nonverbal teaching abilities. Qualitative examples richly illustrate the quantitative findings, showing how each of the discourse variables is used by children in the different age groups.

Method

Participants

Participants were members of 36 Zinacantec households in the hamlet of Nabenchauk, Zinacantán (population approximately 4,500). Each household had an average of five children. The availability of siblings increased the likelihood of observing teaching. Participants were 108 Zinacantec Maya children ranging in age from 20 months to 11 years. Of these, 36 (18 girls and 18 boys) were aged 20 to 36 months ($M = 24$ months); hereafter these are referred to as the focal children. There was just 1 focal child per household. An additional 72 children (25 boys and 47 girls) were siblings who interacted with these focal children. They ranged in age from 3 to 11 years ($M = 6.8$ years). A few cousins and one 6-year-old aunt who interacted with the focal children were included because they were often the child's primary sibling caretaker, sharing the household or the extended-family compound. All the older siblings, first cousins, and the young aunt are hereafter referred to as the "siblings" or "teachers" to simplify description. The teaching behavior of these older children with respect to the focal children was the focus of the present study.

The 72 siblings of the focal children came from a total pool of 93 siblings (age: $M = 8.3$ years) in the required age range who might have interacted with the focal children. The total pool of siblings was derived from the genealogical information collected in family interviews. There were fewer boys than girls in the sample for two reasons. First, Zinacantec boys are not primary sibling caregivers when girls are available, so several boys who were present did not interact with the focal children during the study procedures. Second, some boys were not present because they were away at school or away selling peaches at a market. Fewer girls in the sample went to school or away on selling trips without their nuclear family groups; therefore girls were more likely to be available as sibling caretakers.

Procedure

Participants were recruited on a volunteer basis with the help of an indigenous field assistant who went to the homes of families with 2-year-olds and asked if they would be interested in talking about their possible participation in the study. Recruitment was aided by word-of-mouth discussion of the study in the village.

Participants were observed one time with a video camera in their own homes or courtyards for a period of 1 hr. During videotaping, most mothers carried out their usual domestic routine. Some mothers stayed close by the children and watched the interactions. Mothers were always within earshot of the children, often inside the house while the children were outside.

To reduce the intrusive effect of the observer and the camera, the observer paid at least one visit to the home before conducting the videotaped observation, and did not begin the recording session until at least 10 min after arrival. In the first visit to the home of each family, participants were shown the video camera and how it worked. The observer told the families that the main interest was in watching what the children did during the day. Mothers were interviewed about the ages and schooling experience of each person in the household.

Each family was paid 25 pesos (about U.S. $3.25 at the time of the study) for their participation. In addition, the observer took photographs of family members to give to them as part of payment. Paying the participants may have affected the children's activities: their frequency of play may have increased because the families knew that the children were being watched, and play was a readily available activity for children to do. Even if this was the case, it would not have had an effect on the developmental comparisons that are the focus of this article. Moreover, it is not believed that the content of play changed as a result of the observer's presence or payment to participants. Mothers reported similar play at times outside of the observation session, and many of the same children were seen playing similar activities in their homes and around the village on days other than those during which they were observed.

Data Analysis

Video data were analyzed using the vPrism software system, which was designed specifically for video analysis of behavior (Stigler, 1988). The first step in the analysis was to extract the teaching episodes from the longer tapes. Teaching was defined as any activity attended to by the younger child that had the possible effect of transmitting cultural knowledge. To track the developmental change in teaching skills, the definition of teaching encompassed both intentional and unintentional teaching. Thus, the younger child had to be paying attention to the activity of the older child, but the older child did not have to engage the younger child explicitly for the segment to be considered a teaching segment. The teaching segments were operationally defined in two ways: (1) any task that an older sibling drew the younger child's attention to, either verbally or nonverbally; or (2) any activity that older children were performing next to or "side-by-side" with the 2-year-old, such that the 2-year-old might learn something about the activity from observation of the older child and from practicing next to the older child and using the older child as a model. Data meeting the second criterion were included to obtain a baseline measure of what kinds of teaching skills the youngest teachers exhibited or did not exhibit. For example, many of the 3- to 5-year-olds engaged in side-by-side activity with their younger siblings. They set out tasks for their younger siblings but, in many cases, did not engage them further, either verbally or nonverbally; the children just performed the activities side-by-side. Older children, however, engaged the younger children, both verbally and nonverbally, carefully guiding them in the tasks.

The teaching session was deemed to have begun when the teacher first tried to get the attention of the focal child to engage him or her in a task or when the older child (teacher) began the task next to the focal 2-year-old, who was paying attention to the older child. Thus, the beginnings of episodes were marked by either verbal or nonverbal actions. The endings of teaching episodes were marked when the focal child left the scene of the teaching episode, when the older sibling (teacher) left the scene of the episode without returning, or when any child shifted tasks, thus beginning a new episode with a different activity.

Almost all interactions between older siblings and 2-year-olds were considered teaching episodes, including episodes that an observer might label "play." The teaching episodes analyzed in this study fit into a larger category of multiage play. The teaching episodes were thus one subclass of the larger category of play.

Play became synonymous with sibling teaching in this study because there was so much teaching in the multiage play. Older children always took on the responsibility of showing the younger child how to do a particular task so that the younger child could participate in the play situation. Therefore, a more precise term for these interactions was "teaching," even though the episodes were still a part of the larger category of play. Some interactions between older siblings and 2-year-olds were not considered teaching; for example, when the older child provided care that did not involve any teaching (e.g., carrying a toddler to the mother to nurse or helping the younger child with toileting). There were also other types of play that did not involve teaching; for example, children age 4 and older played games and engaged in activities (soccer, "curing ceremony," throwing rocks, and so forth) that did not involve 2-year-olds, who were not able to participate without help, due to their limited skills and abilities. Thus, only play with 2-year-olds was included in this study, and that play usually involved older siblings teaching younger ones to do everyday things.

There were 158 teaching episodes in the 36 hr of tape, which produced a total of 12 hr, 8 min, 15 s of teaching episodes that were included in the analyses. Teaching episodes ranged in length from 11.9 s to 32 min, 9 s, with a mean length of 10 min, 7 s. The teaching episodes were transcribed and coded for measures of the development of teaching skills. Children taught everyday tasks such as washing, cooking, taking care of baby dolls, and making tortillas. All teaching episodes involved objects, ranging from dirt and leaves to household items such as tortilla presses and articles of clothing to items purchased specifically for children such as dolls and toy trucks.

Measures: Variables Used in Quantitative Discourse Analysis

Children's discourse was measured by verbal and nonverbal variables. Several of these variables were used by Childs and Greenfield (1980) in their study of weaving apprenticeship in Zinacantán. The variables also reflected features of the Zinacantec model of teaching and learning. The mutually exclusive and exhaustive codes for the variables are listed (with examples) in Table 1. Each variable reflected some aspect of cognitive development, such as the ability to take the perspective of the younger child to provide the correct guidance in the task. The verbal discourse variables were commands, explanations and descriptions, feedback on the child's performance, and praise or criticism. The nonverbal discourse variables were simplifying the task nonverbally, and guiding the child's body in the desired task. One variable—talk with demonstration—involved the coordination of both verbal and nonverbal information. Teacher initiation of an episode could be either verbal or nonverbal.

Commands Commands are an important part of teaching. It was expected that teachers would tell the focal children to perform a task by giving a command. Previous research has found that older siblings produce more directives than do younger siblings when they play together (Tomasello & Mannle, 1985). Moreover, commands are culturally normative in Zinacantec child socialization (Blanco & Chodorow, 1964; Childs & Greenfield, 1980); older siblings may issue commands to younger siblings in their charge. Thus, it was hypothesized that older sibling teachers in this study would give commands to their younger siblings when they taught them to do things. Commands indicate that the older child knows that the other can understand language and assumes that the 2-year-old focal child can follow through on the order and that he knows what the command means.

Talk with demonstration This variable, which has been used in other studies of children's interactions (e.g., Zukow, 1989b), was identified when teachers demonstrated what they wanted the focal children to do (physically) and simultaneously said something relevant to the action. Talk with demonstration was coded separately from nonverbal task simplification.

Explanations and descriptions Explanations and descriptions were indicated by teachers' statements of the reason they were doing a particular activity, of the way an activity should be done, or of the outcome or final state of the activity being taught. Childs and Greenfield (1980) found that explanations and descriptions (which they called statements) were rather infrequent in Zinacantec weaving apprenticeship. Explanations and descriptions were included together in one category because they are both kinds of talk about the task being taught. As part of a category of metatalk about activities, explanations and descriptions were hypothesized to develop together.

table 1 Discourse Measures of Children's Teaching Skills

Measure	Examples
Verbal	
Commands (without a demonstration)	"Wash!" "Put it in there!"
Explanations/ descriptions	"Hold the baby because it has a fever." "We are finished washing!"
Feedback on the child's performance	"Yes, like that!" "No, not like that!"
Praise and criticism	"Dummy!" "[That's] bad!"
Nonverbal	
Task simplification	Child pours water from a large container into a smaller container that is easily held by focal child. When teaching how to make tortillas, child tears leaves off a branch and gives the leaves one at a time to focal child, rather than handing the child the whole branch.
Touching/guiding the child's body	Guiding child's hand in a washing motion. Folding child's legs under her to get her to kneel.
Verbal and nonverbal	
Talk with a demonstration	"Pat [the tortilla] like this" [as teacher pats out a tortilla]. "I'm washing!" [as teacher washes a rag].
Verbal and/or nonverbal	
Teacher initiation of episode	The age and gender of the child who initiated the episode are coded.

Feedback Feedback was indicated by teachers' positive or negative comments that guided focal children's behavior. Feedback included comments such as, "Like that" or "Not like that." Such comments were usually followed by talk with demonstration. Utterances considered as feedback in this study were coded by Childs and Greenfield (1980) as vague positive and negative commands. Feedback was coded separately in the present study because it did not always involve an explicit command for action.

Praise and criticism Separate from feedback, praise and criticism are verbal measures of explicit evaluations, for example, "Good" or "Bad." Childs and Greenfield (1980) had found that there was virtually no praise or criticism in Zinacantec weaving apprenticeship. Likewise, it was expected that there would be little or no overt praise or criticism in the sibling teaching interactions.

Simplifying the task nonverbally for the learner This variable was indicated when teachers broke down a task into simpler parts, for instance, when they managed the teaching situation by presenting simpler parts of a task first.

Guiding the body This variable indicated the instances when teachers touched the bodies of the focal children to guide them in performing a specific activity. Zukow-Goldring and Ferko (1994) used this variable in their study of the socialization of attention.

Teacher initiation Teacher initiation was another way of looking at the role of age in teaching. There is a pervasive Zinacantec cultural norm of respect for elders (Vogt, 1969, 1990) that would lead younger children to defer to older children to initiate episodes of play. This measure was also a test of the development of respect for elders; if younger children defer to older children to initiate play episodes, it may indicate respect for their authority.

For the quantitative analysis, frequency counts were taken of each of the measures and then divided by the number of minutes each teacher was involved in a teaching activity to control for overall time spent teaching the younger child.

Reliability

The principal investigator (A.E.M.) coded both the quantitative and qualitative data. An independent coder, fluent in the Tzotzil language and unaware of the hypotheses, coded 25% ($N = 9$) of the videotapes. Interrater agreement for the number of episodes, assessed by percentage agreement, was 95.2% (40 out of 42). There was one disagreement in which the principal investigator indicated two separate shorter episodes and the independent coder indicated only one long episode. The second disagreement was when the principal investigator thought there was an episode of teaching when the independent coder did not.

Interrater agreement for the duration of episodes was assessed by examining the two raters' beginning and end points of every episode in which there was agreement that there was an episode, and comparing the number of seconds of disagreement. For the beginning points of episodes, the disagreements ranged from .66 s to 29 s, with a mean of 10.7 s. For the end points of episodes, the disagreements ranged from 1 to 30 s, with a mean of 11.8 s.

Interrater agreement for the discourse measures was assessed by Cohen's κ. For all the discourse measures taken together, $\kappa = .80$ (percentage agreement was 84.6% for all the discourse variables in Table 1 excluding praise/criticism, which occurred too infrequently in the reliability observations for assessment). This κ value was considered to be indicative of excellent reliability (Bakeman & Gottman, 1986).

Results

Quantitative Analyses

For purposes of statistical analysis, the codes for the discourse variables were divided by each teacher's time spent in teaching. There were no differences across the age groups in time spent in teaching, $F(2, 69) = 1.93$, $p = .153$. This nonsignificant difference reflects two features of sibling caretaking in Nabenchauk: its beginning at age 3 or 4 and its importance and prevalence until approximately age 10. The nonsignificant differences in time spent in teaching also made the analysis and interpretation of the discourse variables easy and straightforward: because there were no differences in time spent in teaching—the denominator of all discourse measures of the study—the discussion of the results is focused on the dependent measures in question.

There were natural breaks in the means for most of the variables between ages 5 and 6, and between ages 7 and 8. Therefore, participants were divided into three groups: 3- to 5-year-olds ($n = 19$; $M = 4.26$ years), 6- to 7-year-olds ($n = 20$; $M = 6.25$ years), and 8- to 11-year-olds ($n = 33$; $M = 8.61$ years).

Talk with demonstration, commands, explanations, feedback, guiding the learner's body, and teacher initiation were included in a MANOVA with the factors of age and gender. There were no effects of gender. With the use of the Wilks' criterion, the combined dependent variables were significantly related to the factor of age, $F(12, 108) = 3.40$, $p = .001$. Univariate F tests for each of the six discourse variables indicated four individually significant effects. There was a significant relation between the factor of age and teacher talk with demonstration, $F(2, 60) = 5.37$, $p < .01$, explanations, $F(2, 60) = 9.22$, $p < .001$, feedback, $F(2, 60) = 6.34$, $p < .01$, and teacher initiation, $F(2, 60) = 3.4$, $p < .05$. The developmental progression from the youngest age group to the oldest age group can be seen in the marked differences between the age groups (Figure 1).

The significant results from the MANOVA were further analyzed by Bonferroni t tests to find specific intergroup differences. For talk with demonstration there was a significant difference between the youngest age group, the 3- to 5-year-olds ($M = .238$), and the oldest age group, the 8- to 11-year-olds ($M = 1.32$), $t(50) = 3.26$, $p < .001$. The two older age groups, 6 to 7 ($M = .526$) and 8 to 11 ($M = 1.32$) were also significantly different from each other, $t(51) = 2.63$, $p < .01$. Middle children ($M = .526$) did not differ significantly from youngest children ($M = .238$), $t(37) = 1.19$, $p = .24$.

There were also significant relations between age and explanations. The oldest age group ($M = .691$) gave explanations or descriptions significantly more than did the middle age group ($M = .171$), $t(51) = 3.00$, $p < .005$, or the youngest age group ($M = 0$), $t(50) = 4.11$, $p < .001$. The middle age group ($M = .171$) also gave explanations significantly more than did the youngest age group ($M = 0$), $t(37) = 2.29$, $p < .05$.

Oldest children ($M = .636$) gave significantly more feedback than did middle children ($M = .092$), $t(51) = 2.81$, $p < .01$, and youngest children ($M = .024$), $t(50) = 3.10$, $p < .005$. Middle children ($M = .092$) gave the same amount of feedback as youngest children ($M = .024$), $t(37) = 1.68$, $p = .10$.

Praise and criticism were evaluative comments coded separately from positive and negative feedback. There was no overt praise in the entire database. There were only two instances of criticism. In one, a 6-year-old girl said, "*Chopol* [That's bad]" in response to her 2-year-old sister's attempt at making a tortilla with leaves. The older child thought the focal child was tearing off the wrong leaves to use for the tortillas. In the other instance of criticism, a 9-year-old girl

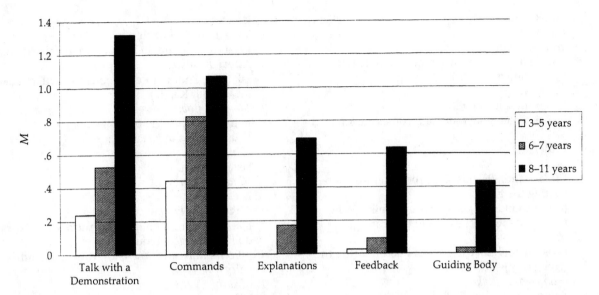

figure 1
Mean use of discourse variables by age group, controlled for time teaching.

said, "*Chich* [Dummy]" to the focal child when she did not do a cooking activity properly.

Oldest children (*M* = 2.61) and middle children (*M* = 2.60) initiated significantly more teaching episodes than did youngest children (*M* = 1.05), $t(50)$ = 2.63, $p < .01$, and $t(37) = 2.40$, $p < .05$, respectively. Oldest children (*M* = 2.61) and middle children (*M* = 2.60) did not differ significantly from each other, $t(51) = .01$, $p = .993$.

Nonverbal task simplification increased as a function of age, $F(2, 69) = 4.353$, $p < .05$. None of the 3- to 5-year-olds used task simplification in their teaching, whereas 2 (10%) of the 6- to 7-year-olds and 15 (45.5%) of the 8- to 11-year-olds used task simplification to help learners with the tasks.

Qualitative Analyses of the Discourse Variables by Age Group: Three Examples

As previously discussed, there were significant relations between age group and four of the discourse variables. This section presents examples of teaching episodes with 1 child from each of the three age groups: 8- to 11-, 6- to 7-, and 3- to 5-year-olds. A more complete corpus is found in Maynard (1999). The episodes are matched closely for duration (approximately 2 min each). Each example is of a child teaching a 2-year-old how to wash a baby doll. Each pair of children is from a different nuclear family. In the following transcripts the Tzotzil transcription is presented first, followed by the English gloss. Nonver-

bal information is also indicated in double parentheses. Tzotzil orthographic conventions and transcription conventions are listed in the Appendix.

Example 1: Age 8 In the first example, 8-year-old Tonik teaches 2-year-old Katal how to wash a baby doll using task simplification, talk with demonstration, and commands.

Tonik: ((Laughs. Brings over a glass of water, to wash the baby doll.))
Taso. Taso.
Take it out. Take it out (of the water).
Xivi.
Like this. ((Katal watches.))

Tonik/Katal: ((Four hands on the glass, in position to pour, but they don't pour together at this time.))
   T: *Cakel=vi.*
   You watch=look.
   K: ((Watches.))
   T: *Xitovi.* ((Pouring the water herself, Katal watches.)) Like this.
   [K'embo xivi.
   [Pour like this. ((Pouring, laughs.))
T/K: ((Four hands are on the glass.))
   T: ((Moves doll into position that is easier for Katal to pour accurately.))
T/K: [((They pour together.))
   T: *[K'embo'un!*
   Pour it now!
   Caklie.
   Like that.
   Ihtaso'un.

I took it out.
Cataso'un.
You take it out.

K: e, ee ((Baby-talk sounds; requests more water by reaching for glass.))

T: *Cakan to.*
You want some more.
((Goes to get more water and comes back.))
Va'i un.
Understand!
Va'i.
Understand. ((Hands Katal the water, still supporting the glass.))

T/K: ((Three hands on glass, two are Tonik's. Water pours out toward the back of the frame.))

T: *Vi'i!*
Look! ((Laughs at the error of water pouring the wrong way.))
Pulo vo'ota, Xunka'.
You draw some water, Xunka'. ((Spoken to other sister who is present.))
Tas caklie. Atintaso.
Take it out like that. Take it out and wash it.

K: ((Washes baby with washing motion of hand.))

T: [*Caklie.*
[Like that.

K: (Reaches for glass.))

T: *Lah xa.* ((Pours from the empty glass, showing that glass is empty.))
It's finished already.
Vi.
Look.

K: ((Washes baby doll with washing motion.))

T: *Ani' un.*
Hurry up! ((To other sister who is drawing water.))
Akbo xa=casutotal anil!
Put the water in already=come back fast! ((Spoken to other sister.))
((Hands Katal an empty glass while they wait.))

T: *Keltik un. Keltik. Xitovi=Xitovi=Xitovi. Taso, caklie.*
Let's watch! Let's watch. Like this=Like this=Like this. Take it out like this.

Xunka': (Comes back with water in a bottle; hands glass to Tonik.))

T: ((Pours water from the bottle into the glass that they have been using to wash.))
((Hands glass to Katal.))
K'embo Xitovi ((Taking glass from Katal.))
Pour like this.
Xitovi. ((Repositions doll to make it easier for herself.))
Like this.
Xitovi. Xitovi.
Like this. Like this. ((Pours water over the doll's head, rubbing doll's head in a washing motion.))

Atintaso.
Take it out and wash it.
((Hands glass and doll to Katal for Katal to do it.))
Xitovi. K'embo.
Like this. Pour it. ((Repositions the doll to make it easier for Katal.))
K'embo xitovi
Pour it like this. ((Pours water on.))
((Hands glass to Katal.))
C'in, K'embo.
Sister, pour it.
Vi un. K'embo.
Look! Pour it.
Caklie. K'embo sciuk sku'.
Like that. Pour it on its blouse also. ((The baby doll is wearing a blouse.))

K: [((Pours water over the baby, with some difficulty.))

T: [*Caklie.*
Like that.
((Puts another bottle in front of Katal, who is looking away.))
Lah xa li'e vi.
It's finished now, look. ((Deciding the doll is clean, she picks it up.))

In this example, Tonik provided a scaffold of help for the focal child by pouring water for her when she noticed that she was having trouble. She narrated much of what she did, showing and telling Katal what to do. Tonik gave commands that guided Katal in each step of the washing. She also provided descriptive elaborations of actions. She said, "Pour it on its blouse also," pointing out that the doll was wearing a blouse, and expanding the washing to include the blouse. Tonik was sensitive to Katal's actions. When Katal picked up the empty glass, Tonik responded by getting her some more water or having another sister draw some water. Tonik also gave Katal some feedback in this example. There were several instances when she affirmed Katal's actions by saying, "Like that."

Example 2: Age 7 In the next example, Xun, age 7, uses talk with demonstration and commands to teach Teresa, age 2, to wash a baby doll.

Xun: *Teresa—*
Teresa ((Holds the baby out to her; they are both touching it.))
Pok'etik nene.
Let's wash baby! ((As he washes the baby himself.))
Vi. Vi . . . la jole.
Look. Look . . . the head. ((As he pats the head.))
Vi. La pok'etik li yoke. Pok'etik.
Look. We are washing its foot. Let's wash. ((Puts the doll in the bowl of water.))

[((He pats the doll's head, playing with the hair.))
Teresa: [((Watches.))
((Teresa loses interest, moves away from Xun.))

Like 8-year-old Tonik, Xun used talk with demonstration in his teaching: he pointed out parts of the doll he was washing. One major difference between his teaching and that of Tonik was that he did not get Teresa to wash the baby doll herself, whereas Tonik was able to get Katal to do the washing by herself, in carefully simplified parts.

Example 3: Age 4   In the next example, Petu', age 4, teaches Elena, age 2, how to wash a baby doll. She gives one verbal command to Elena, but does not use any of the other discourse skills used by the older children.

Petu': Pok'o la nene!
Wash the baby!
((Puts soap and water on the baby doll.))
[((Washes the baby doll's stomach and back.))
Elena: [((Washes a rag, continues to look at what Petu' is doing.))
P: ((Continues to wash the baby doll.))
E: Tutu. ((Baby-talk name for Petu', who does not respond.))
Tutu.
P: ((Continues to wash the baby doll.))
E: ((Wanders off.))

This is an example of the developmental beginning point of teaching. Petu' gave a command to Elena to wash the baby doll, but did not narrate her washing behavior for Elena. She washed the baby doll and allowed Elena to help a little. The episode was short, a little over 1 min, and the teaching was characterized solely by nonverbal demonstration of the activity.

Discussion

There was an overall developmental trend in the use of important discourse skills required for teaching, with children developing toward the Zinacantec model of teaching and learning (Maynard, 1996). As predicted by the study of adult apprenticeship of weaving (Childs & Greenfield, 1980), the children in the present study developed a pattern of teaching that stressed scaffolded help, contextualized verbal explanations and feedback, and obedience, with virtually no praise or criticism. By the age of 8 years, the children in this study used skills that involved an understanding of the other child's perspective, such as simplifying the tasks for the learners. Children also provided necessary and useful information to the young learners, such as appropriate feedback and narrated demonstrations.

The observable characteristics of the children's teaching changed over the three age groups. The 3- to 5-year-olds gave the least amount of verbal instruction. Their teaching behavior was mostly nonverbal: They did the task and let their siblings join in right next to them. They sometimes looked to their charges to see what they were doing, but they did not give explicit instruction as to how to do a task or any particular part of a task. The 3- to 5-year-olds were "side-by-side co-operators"; they usually cooperated with their toddler siblings, but they didn't collaborate or explicitly teach in the way one usually thinks of teaching. Their actions represented the developmental beginning point of teaching.

The 6- to 7-year-olds gave significantly more commands than did the 3- to 5-year-olds. The 6- to 7-year-olds were the "unequal collaborators" or "orchestrators of events"; they were unequal in that they worked with the child to make something happen, but gave a lot of commands and did the task themselves if the 2-year-olds didn't do enough.

The 8- to 11-year-olds demonstrated the skills of adult scaffolding. Their use of commands declined as their use of talk with demonstration increased sharply (Figure 1). They increased their use of evaluations and explanations, and used the body in teaching at helpful moments. They were, by the age of 8 years, already the "guides of development" talked about in so many studies. They were also "administrators of action," coordinating the actions of the younger siblings around them to do a play task. Perhaps the nature of Zinacantec relationships, with a pervasive emphasis on obedience from younger to older people (Vogt, 1969), helps children develop skills of social coordination.

Ethnographic studies of children's relationships in cultures in which sibling caretaking is an important part of childrearing have not examined how it is that children teach each other to do everyday things (e.g., Lancy, 1996; Weisner & Gallimore, 1977; Whiting & Edwards, 1988; Zukow, 1989a, 1989b). The literature widely reports that children are not taught (didactically and with language) to do everyday things. Researchers have suggested that everyday skills develop through participation in joint activities (Lave & Wenger, 1991). For example, Lancy (1996, p. 144) wrote of the Kpelle in Liberia, "No one teaches a girl to wield a hoe." One might have similarly believed that no one teaches a child to make tortillas or to wash in Nabenchauk. The data presented in this study showed that there is some teaching of everyday activities, at least in Nabenchauk. Although it is true that Zinacantec parents do not teach their children to do everyday tasks, didactically and with language, Zinacantec siblings clearly do. Perhaps there are children in other cultures who teach each other to do everyday things. More exceptions may be uncovered by further study, thus changing the prevailing view of the way that children learn everyday tasks.

The present study on children's interactions leads to many more questions about the development of their ability to teach. First, examining children's teaching in its everyday context (without informing the children that their teaching was the focus of the study) might not have pushed the children to be the best teachers they could be. Perhaps a future study could explore children's teaching first in its everyday context and then with an experimental protocol designed to reflect or be compatible with the children's daily routines, to see the children's potential.

Second, the strong sibling relationships may have privileged the teaching interactions reported here. Indeed, Azmitia and Hesser (1993) reported that young children in a collaborative task asked more questions of siblings than of a peer who was the same age as their sibling. The closeness of the relationships in this study may have had an impact on the quality of the teaching. It would be worthwhile to examine children's teaching with both related and unrelated younger children to begin to further our understanding of the impact of the very special sibling caretaking relationship.

Third, this study focused on the teaching behaviors of the older siblings without systematically analyzing the learning behaviors of the younger children. Although the younger children participated in the activities with their older siblings, their behavior was not analyzed by quantitative discourse analysis. It would be important in a future study to obtain an understanding of the teachers' effectiveness by analyzing more closely the participation of the younger children.

Conclusion

Related to the development of children's teaching are processes of cultural transmission and child socialization. This study of cultural teaching has informed our knowledge of the transmission of culture. In Nabenchauk, everyday tasks are learned through more than mere "legitimate peripheral participation" (Lave & Wenger, 1991). The present study validated children's contributions to each other's everyday routines in a specific way: by showing the verbal and nonverbal tools that children use to help each other participate in their culture and the developmental trend of these skills. Children create culture at the same time that they are acquiring culture. As they are being socialized by their parents, they are also socializing, in their own way, their younger siblings.

The children in this study developed discourse abilities that they then used to teach their toddler siblings how to do everyday things. These children were learning skills that they will likely perform in adolescence and adulthood, including not only the skills involved in the tasks themselves, but also the skill of guiding learners in everyday tasks. There were aspects of the children's teaching that were clearly related to their upbringing in Zinacantán, such as the lack of praise and criticism in their teaching. Other factors, such as providing talk with demonstration or simplifying a task for a young learner may be more basic to cultural transmission, and therefore more universal. Future studies of children's teaching in other cultures will inform our knowledge of the social and cognitive skills that children acquire over the course of middle childhood.

Appendix: Tzotzil Orthographic Conventions

All the Tzotzil vowels are included. The reader should note that each Tzotzil vowel is articulated as a separate sound. Only the consonants that do not have the same orthography in English are included in this list. Other consonants (as they are written in this document) sound almost the same in Tzotzil and English and are, therefore, not included.

Vowels

Transcribed phoneme	Example of sound in an English word
a	st*o*p
e	*e*gg
i	sp*ee*d
o	c*o*mb
u	sm*oo*th

Consonants

Transcribed phoneme	Example of sound in an English word
´	Glottal stop; no such consonant in English
x	*sh*op
j	*h*eat
c	*ch*alk

Transcription conventions

For readability, if the same child has the next turn, the name is not repeated next to the turn.

Convention	Meaning
=	Speech that is produced in one stream of air; fast speech
(( ))	Nonverbal behaviors
[	A point of overlap onset between
[	two speakers

REFERENCES

Abramovitch, R., Corter, C., & Lando, B. (1979). Sibling interaction in the home. *Child Development, 51,* 1268–1271.

Ashley J., & Tomasello, M. (1998). Cooperative problem-solving and teaching in preschoolers. *Social Development, 2,* 143–163.

Azmitia, M., & Hesser, J. (1993). Why siblings are important agents of cognitive development: A comparison of siblings and peers. *Child Development, 64,* 430–444.

Bakeman, R., & Gottman, J. M. (1986). *Observing interaction: An introduction to sequential analysis.* New York: Cambridge University Press.

Blanco, M. H., & Chodorow, N. J. (1964). Children's work and obedience in Zinacantán. Manuscript on file, Harvard Chiapas Project, Department of Anthropology, Harvard University, Cambridge, MA.

Brownell, C. A., & Carriger, M. S. (1991). Collaborations among toddler peers: Individual contributions to social contexts. In L. B. Resnick, J. M. Levine, & S. D. Teasley (Eds.), *Perspectives on socially shared cognition* (pp. 365–393). Washington, DC: American Psychological Association.

Bryant, B. (1987). Mental health, temperament, family, and friends: Perspectives on children's empathy and social perspective taking. In N. Eisenberg & J. Strayer (Eds.), *Empathy and its development* (pp. 245–270). New York: Cambridge University Press.

Childs, C. P., & Greenfield, P. M. (1980). Informal modes of learning and teaching: The case of Zinacanteco weaving. In N. Warren (Ed.), *Studies in cross-cultural psychology* (Vol. 2, pp. 269–316). London: Academic Press.

Cicirelli, V. (1976). Mother-child and sibling-siblings interactions on a problem-solving task. *Child Development, 47,* 588–596.

Corsaro, W. A. (1985). *Friendship and peer culture in the early years.* Norwood, NJ: Ablex.

Dunn, J. (1989). Siblings and the development of social understanding in early childhood. In P. G. Zukow (Ed.), *Sibling interaction across cultures. Theoretical and methodological issues* (pp. 106–116). New York: Springer-Verlag.

Dunn, J. (1992). Sisters and brothers: Current issues in developmental research. In F. Boer & J. Dunn (Eds.), *Children's sibling relationships: Developmental and clinical issues* (pp. 1–17). Hillsdale, NJ: Erlbaum.

Dunn, J., & Munn, P. (1986). Siblings and the development of prosocial behaviour. *International Journal of Behavioral Development, 9,* 265–284.

Ellis, S., & Rogoff, B. (1982). The strategies and efficacy of child versus adult teachers. *Child Development, 53,* 730–735.

Foster-Harrison, E. S. (1995). Peer helping in the elementary and middle grades: A developmental perspective. *Elementary School Guidance and Counseling, 30,* 94–104.

Gallimore, R., Tharp, R. G., & Speidel, G. E. (1978). The relationship of sibling caretaking and attentiveness to a peer tutor. *American Educational Research Journal, 15,* 267–273.

Gaskins, S. (1999). Children's daily lives in a Mayan village: A case study of culturally constructed roles and activities. In A. Göncü (Ed.), *Children's engagement in the world: Sociocultural perspectives* (pp. 25–61). New York: Cambridge University Press.

Goodluck, H. (1991). *Language acquisition: A linguistic introduction.* Oxford, U.K.: Blackwell.

Goodwin, C., & Goodwin, M. H. (1992). Assessments and the construction of context. In A. Duranti & C. Goodwin (Eds.), *Rethinking context: Language as an interactive phenomenon* (pp. 147–189). Canbridge, U.K: Cambridge University Press.

Goodwin, M. H. (1990). *He-said-she-said. Talk as social organization among Black children.* Bloomington: Indiana University Press.

Gopnik, A., & Meltzoff, A. N. (1994). Minds, bodies, and persons: Young children's understanding of the self and others as reflected in imitation and theory of mind research. In S. T. Parker & R. W. Mitchell (Eds.), *Self-awareness in humans and animals: Developmental perspectives* (pp. 166–186). Cambridge, U.K.: Cambridge University Press.

Greenfield, P. M. (1984). A theory of the teacher in the learning activities of everyday life. In B. Rogoff & J. Lave (Eds.), *Everyday cognition: Its development in social context* (pp. 117–138). Cambridge, MA: Harvard University Press.

Greenfield, P. M., Maynard, A. E., & Childs, C. P. (1999). *Historical change, cultural apprenticeship, and cognitive representation in Zinacantec Maya children.* Unpublished manuscript.

Greenfield, P. M., Maynard, A. E., & Childs, C. P. (2000). History, culture, learning, and development. *Cross-Cultural Research: The Journal of Comparative Social Science, 34,* 351–374.

Howe, N., & Ross, H. S. (1990). Socialization, perspective-taking, and the sibling relationship. *Developmental Psychology, 26,* 160–165.

Johnson, M., & Bailey, J. S. (1974). Cross-age tutoring: Fifth graders as arithmetic tutors for kindergarten children. *Journal of Applied Behavior Analysis, 7,* 223–232.

Kendrick, C., & Dunn, J. (1980). Caring for second baby: Effects on interaction between mother and firstborn. *Developmental Psychology, 16,* 303–311.

Kruger, A. C., & Tomasello, M. (1996). Cultural learning and learning culture. In D. R. Olson & N. Torrance (Eds.), *The handbook of education and human development. New models of learning, teaching, and schooling* (pp. 369–387). Cambridge, MA: Blackwell.

Lancy, D. (1996). *Playing on the mother ground: Cultural routines for children's development.* New York: Guilford Press.

Lave, J., & Wenger, E. (1991). *Situated learning. Legitimate peripheral participation.* Cambridge, UK.: Cambridge University Press.

Lewis, C., Freeman, N. H., Kyriakidou, C., Maridaki-Kassotaki, K., & Berridge, D. M. (1996). Social influences on false belief access: Specific sibling influences or general apprenticeship? *Child Development, 67,* 2930–2947.

Martini, M. (1994). Peer interactions in Polynesia: A view from the Marquesas. In J. P. Roopnarine, J. E. Johnson, & F. H. Hooper (Eds.), *Children's play in diverse cultures* (pp. 73–103). Albany: State University of New York Press.

Maynard, A. E. (1996). *The Zinacantec model of teaching and learning.* Unpublished masters thesis, University of California, Los Angeles.

Maynard, A. E. (1999). *Cultural teaching: The social organization and development of teaching in Zinacantec Maya sibling interactions*. Unpublished doctoral dissertation, University of California, Los Angeles.

Maynard, A. E., Greenfield, P. M., & Childs, C. P. (1999). Culture, history, biology, and body: Native and nonnative acquisition of technological skill. *Ethos, 27,* 379–402.

Meisner, J. S., & Fisher, V. L. (1980). Cognitive shifts of young children as a function of peer interaction and sibling status. *The Journal of Genetic Psychology, 136,* 247–253.

Ochs, E. (1988). *Culture and language development: Language acquisition and socialization in a Samoan village.* Cambridge, U.K.: Cambridge University Press.

Ochs, E., & Schieffelin, B. B. (1984). Language acquisition and socialization: Three developmental stories and their implications. In R. Shweder & R. LeVine (Eds.), *Culture theory: Essays on mind, self, and emotion* (pp. 276–320). Cambridge, U.K.: Cambridge University Press.

Pepler, D. J., Abramovitch, R., & Corter, C. (1981). Sibling interactions in the home: A longitudinal study. *Child Development, 52,* 1344–1347.

Perez-Granados, D.R., & Callanan, M. A. (1997). Conversations with mothers and siblings: Young children's semantic and conceptual development. *Developmental Psychology, 33,* 120–134.

Piaget, J. (1952). *The origins of intelligence in children.* New York: International Universities Press.

Piaget, J. (1967). *Six psychological studies.* Toronto, Ontario, Canada: Random House.

Rogoff, B. (1990). *Apprenticeship in thinking.* New York: Oxford University Press.

Rogoff, B. (1991). The joint socialization of development by young children and adults. In M. Lewis & S. Feinman (Eds.), *Social influences and socialization in infancy* (pp. 253–280). New York: Plenum Press.

Rogoff, B., Mistry, J., Göncü, A., & Mosier, C. (1993). Guided participation in cultural activity by toddlers and caregivers. *Monographs of the Society for Research in Child Development, 58* (8, Serial No. 236).

Stewart, R. B. (1983). Sibling interaction. The role of the older child as teacher for the younger. *Merrill-Palmer Quarterly, 29,* 47–68.

Stigler, J. W. (1988). Video surverys: New data for the improvement of classroom instruction. In S. G. Paris & H. M. Wellman (Eds.), *Global prospects for education: Development, culture, and schooling* (pp. 129–168). Washington, DC: American Psychological Association.

Teti, D. M., & Ablard, K. E. (1989). Security of attachment and infant–sibling relationships: A laboratory study. *Child Development, 60,* 1519–1528.

Tharp, R. G. (1994). Intergroup differences among Native Americans in socialization and child cognition: An ethnogenetic analysis. In P.M. Greenfield & R.R. Cocking (Eds.), *Cross-cultural roots of minority child development* (pp. 87–105). Hillsdale, NJ: Erlbaum.

Tomasello, M., Kruger, A. C., & Ratner, H. H. (1993). Cultural learning. *Behavioral and Brain Sciences, 16,* 495–552.

Tomasello, M., & Mannle, S. (1985). Pragmatics of sibling speech to one-year-olds. *Child Development, 56,* 911–917.

Trevarthen, C., & Logotheti, K. (1989). Child and culture: Genesis of co-operative knowing. In A. Gellatly, D. Rogers, & J. A. Sloboda (Eds.), *Cognition and social worlds* (pp. 37–56). Oxford, U.K.: Clarendon Press/Oxford University Press.

Vogt, E. Z. (1969). *Zinacantan: A Maya community in the highlands of Chiapas.* Cambridge, MA: Harvard University Press.

Vogt, E. Z. (1990). *The Zinacantecos of Mexico: A modern Maya way of life* (2nd ed.). New York: Harcourt, Brace, Jovanovich.

Vygotsky, L. S. (1978). *Mind in society.* New York: Cambridge University Press.

Waston-Gegeo, K. A., & Gegeo, D. W. (1989). The role of sibling interaction in child socialization. In P.G. Zukow (Ed.), *Sibling interaction across cultures. Theoretical and methodological issues* (pp. 54–76). New York: Springer-Verlag.

Weisner, T. S. (1987). Socialization for parenthood in sibling caretaking societies. In J. B. Lancaster, J. Altmann, A. S. Rossi, & L. R. Sherrod (Eds.), *Parenting across the life span: Biosocial dimensions.* Hawthorne, NY: Aldine.

Weisner, T. S., & Gallimore, R.(1977). My brother's keeper: Child and sibling caretaking. *Current Anthropology, 18,* 169–190.

Weisner, T. S., Gallimore, R., & Jordan, C. (1988). Unpackaging cultural effects on classroom learning: Native Hawaiian peer assistance and child-generated activity. *Anthropology and Education Quarterly, 19,* 327–353.

Whiting, B. B., & Edwards, C. P. (1988). *Children of different worlds: The formation of social behavior.* Cambridge, MA: Harvard University Press.

Whiting, B. B., & Whiting, J. M. (1975). *Children of six cultures: A psycho-cultural analysis.* Cambridge, MA: Harvard University Press.

Wood, D., Bruner, J. S., & Ross, G. (1976). The role of tutoring in problem solving. *Journal of Child Psychology and Psychiatry, 17,* 89–100.

Wootton, A. J. (1997). *Interaction and the development of mind.* Cambridge, U.K.: Cambridge University Press.

Zukow, P. G. (1986). The relationship between interaction with the caregiver and the emergence of play activities during the one-word period. *British Journal of Developmental Psychology, 4,* 223–234.

Zukow, P. G. (1989a). *Sibling interaction across cultures. Theoretical and methodological issues.* New York: Springer-Verlag.

Zukow, P. G. (1989b.) Siblings as effective socializing agents: Evidence from Central Mexico. In P. G. Zukow (Ed.), *Sibling interaction across cultures. Theoretical and methodological issues.* (pp. 79–105). New York: Springer-Verlag.

Zukow-Goldring, P. G. (1997). A social ecological realist approach to the emergence of the lexicon: Educating attention to amodal invariants in gesture and speech. In C. Dent-Read & P. Zukow-Goldring (Eds.), *Evolving explanations of development: Ecological approaches to organism-environment systems* (pp. 199–250). Washington, DC: American Psychological Association.

Zukow-Goldring, P. (2002). Sibling caregiving. In M. H. Bornstein (Ed.), *Handbook of parenting: Vol. 3. Status and social conditions of parenting* (2nd ed., pp. 253–286). Hillsdale, NJ: Erlbaum.

Zukow-Goldring, P., & Ferko, K. R. (1994). An ecological approach to the emergence of the lexicon: Socializing attention. In V. John-Steiner, C. P. Panofsky, & L. W. Smith (Eds.), *Socio-* *cultural approaches to language and literacy. An interactionist perspective* (pp. 170–190). Cambridge, U.K.: Cambridge University Press.

Questions

1. Why might older siblings be especially important to children as they learn the practices and skills that are valued in their culture?
2. How was teaching defined in this study, and what specific teaching techniques did the child teachers in this study use?
3. In sibling instruction, what is the relation of play to teaching?
4. What age differences were found in children's teaching behaviors? On the basis of these results, would you say that children get better at teaching as they get older? Why or why not?
5. Maynard argues that child teaching develops in such a way that as children get older, their teaching reflects the model of teaching and learning that is valued in their culture. What evidence does she cite to support this view? Do you agree with it?
6. How is sibling teaching in middle-class homes in the United States similar to and different from the sibling teaching described in this article?

29 Ethnic Diversity and Perceptions of Safety in Urban Middle Schools

Jaana Juvonen • Adrienne Nishina • Sandra Graham

There are areas of great ethnic diversity in the United States, yet this diversity is not reflected equally in all public social institutions, such as schools. The opportunity to interact with people from diverse ethnic backgrounds is generally seen as beneficial to individuals and to society at large, yet some still question the value of diversity in schools.

In the following article, Jaana Juvonen, Adrienne Nishina, and Sandra Graham investigate the psychological benefits of attending schools that are ethnically diverse. Earlier studies of ethnic diversity focused on contributions to the development of perspective-taking skills and social experience. Juvonen, Nishina, and Graham were interested in a new topic: students' perceptions of safety when they attend ethnically diverse middle schools. Because middle school is a time of heightened feelings of vulnerability, the authors felt it important to better understand the relation of ethnic diversity at school to children's sense of security and social satisfaction in that setting.

This research raises important questions about middle childhood and one of the primary social settings that children experience during these years. School is critical to development in many ways. It gives support and guidance for cognitive development, which is important to academic achievement. School also gives children access to and involvement with peers, who provide children with vital experiences in learning how to establish, negotiate, and deal with both positive and negative relationships.

This research broadens the terms we typically explore in relation to ethnic diversity and, as a result, it has important policy implications. Societal debates regarding education tend to emphasize the content of the curriculum and other achievement-related concerns. Although these topics are very important, children experience much more at school than the content of instruction. Many lifetime lessons are learned there—lessons that may help children lead satisfying and productive lives in our multi-ethnic society.

Students' perceptions of their safety and vulnerability were investigated in 11 public middle schools (more than 70 sixth-grade classrooms) that varied in ethnic diversity. Results of hierarchical linear modeling analyses indicate that higher classroom diversity is associated with feelings of safety and social satisfaction. African American (n = 511) and Latino (n = 910) students felt safer in school, were less harassed by peers, felt less lonely, and had higher self-worth the more ethnically diverse their classrooms were, even when controlling for classroom differences in academic engagement. Results at the school level were similar to those at the classroom level; higher ethnic diversity was associated with lower levels of self-reported vulnerability (but no difference in self-worth) in both fall and spring of sixth grade. In the spirit of Brown v. Board of Education, the current findings offer new empirical evidence for the psychological benefits of multi-ethnic schools.

The 50th anniversary of *Brown v. Board of Education* in 2004 and recent Supreme Court cases affirming the significance of race in higher-education admissions have sparked public discourse on the benefits of ethnic diversity in the nation's schools, colleges, and universities. That discourse reveals that kindergarten through 12th-grade schooling in America has not lived up to the promise of *Brown*. Although the number of 5- through 17-year-old children of races other than White quadrupled between 1970 and 2000, students continue to be educated largely in ethnically segregated schools (Orfield, 2001; Pettigrew, 2004). For example, African American children were more likely to attend schools with an African American majority in 2000 (70%) than at any time since the 1960s (Pettigrew, 2004). Latino students are even more likely than African American students to attend schools serving predominantly ethnic minorities (Orfield & Lee, 2006). When reflecting on the legacy of *Brown* in light of such statistics, it seems timely to reexamine the psychological benefits associated with ethnic diversity in schools.

Although much research on desegregation followed the *Brown* decision, that empirical literature is limited in helping to clarify the psychological effects of ethnic diversity in today's schools. Studies conducted in the 1960s and 1970s typically examined the effects of racially mixed educational environments on Black students' achievement or self-esteem in predominantly White schools (see Pettigrew, 2004; Schofield & Hausmann, 2004). Ethnicity was limited to two groups and often confounded with numerical representation (i.e., Whites the numerical majority, Blacks the minority), as well as social class. Although much of the earlier research on self-esteem was inconclusive (e.g., Epps, 1975; St. John, 1975), several studies indicated that African American students displayed higher self-esteem when they attended racially segregated rather than integrated schools, a finding that sheds little light on the psychological benefits of greater diversity (e.g., Gray-Little & Carels, 1997; Verna & Runion, 1985; see review in Gray-Little & Hafdahl, 2000).

How might youth benefit from a diverse student body? Research on college students suggests that ethnic diversity contributes to critical-thinking skills among White students who learn to incorporate multiple perspectives of a diverse student body (Antonio et al., 2004; Gurin, Nagda, & Lopez, 2004; Milem & Umbach, 2003). Research on adolescents reveals that racially diverse schools and classrooms facilitate cross-ethnic friendships (e.g., Damico & Sparks, 1986; Hallinan & Teixeira, 1987), which are presumed to reduce negative or stereotypical attitudes toward outgroup members. For students of color, cross-race interactions have been hypothesized to foster development of interpersonal skills relevant in other racially diverse settings, such as college or the workplace (e.g., Wells, 1995). But, again, such studies on friendship patterns and social interactions have focused mainly on White and Black youth.

Today's multiethnic urban schools, which vary both in the number of different groups represented and the relative proportion of each, provide ideal conditions for further examination of the effects of diversity. By studying multiethnic urban schools, it is possible to test for the effects of diversity that are independent of any particular ethnic-group membership

and to consider whether such effects vary for different ethnic minority groups. In the current study, we examined students' perceptions of safety and vulnerability, a topic that is virtually unexplored in the school-desegregation literature. We hypothesized that greater diversity promotes perceptions of safety and lessens feelings of vulnerability because in diverse settings, students belong to one of many ethnic groups that share a balance of power (i.e., there is no numerical majority group). We based this hypothesis on findings from the peer-victimization literature suggesting that a numerical imbalance of power is an antecedent of peer-directed hostility (Olweus, 1993).

There are other possible explanations why schools' ethnic diversity might be related to greater perceived safety. For example, school administrators and teachers in ethnically diverse schools might be especially sensitive to the possibility of ethnic conflict and therefore work to improve intergroup relations by implementing multicultural or antibias curricula. However, program evaluations of multicultural curricula suggest that high dosages of exposure are needed to produce any positive effects (e.g., Banks, 1995), and when group differences are overemphasized, such curricula can even backfire (see Park & Judd, 2005). Moreover, the conditions for rigorously implementing multicultural programs are far from ideal in large urban secondary schools (such as those included in the current study) struggling with limited resources and facing substantial academic pressures.

We examined the effects of ethnic diversity on social perceptions of a large sample of sixth-grade students in 11 urban middle schools that differed in ethnic composition. Ethnic diversity was conceptualized as a continuum that varies as a function of both the number of groups present and the relative representation of those groups. We investigated whether ethnic diversity is associated with students' perceptions of school safety (cf. collective sense of vulnerability), personal feelings of peer victimization (i.e., individual vulnerability), feelings of social dissatisfaction (referred to hereafter as loneliness), and self-worth (cf. esteem)—outcomes we jointly refer to as perceived safety and vulnerability. Because a school's ethnic composition is not necessarily reflected at the classroom level (Schofield, 1995; Wells, 1995), we conducted separate analyses at the classroom and school levels. We focused on sixth-grade students during their first year in middle school inasmuch as large, urban middle schools are more likely to be diverse than neighborhood elementary schools. Moreover, early adolescence and the accompanying transition to middle school is a time of heightened concern about "fitting in" within the new social setting (see Eccles & Midgley, 1989). Both fall and spring assessments were included because initial feelings of vulnerability may dissipate across a school year, as students get acclimated to the new social setting (Verna & Runion, 1985).

Method

Participants

Participants for the current analyses were from a larger longitudinal study of approximately 2,000 sixth-grade students selected from 99 classrooms in 11 middle schools located in greater Los Angeles (for complete information about the full sample, see Bellmore, Witkow, Graham, & Juvonen, 2004, and Nishina, Juvonen, & Witkow, 2005). Based on self-report, the ethnic breakdown of the sample was 46% Latino (primarily of Mexican origin), 29% African American, 9% Asian (predominantly of East Asian origin), 9% Caucasian, and 7% multiracial. The 11 middle schools were carefully selected to represent a continuum of ethnic diversity in low-income communities, eligible for Title 1 compensatory funding. Although our measures of school and classroom diversity were based on all ethnic groups in the sample, the main analyses focus on the two ethnic groups (Latino and African American) with sufficient representation across all our schools and classrooms. This target sample consisted of 1,421 sixth-grade students (45% male, 55% female), of whom 64% were Latino ($n = 910$) and 36% were African American ($n = 511$).

Procedure

Sixth-grade students whose homeroom teachers expressed interest in the study took home letters and consent forms that explained the study. Of the 3,511 distributed consent forms, 75% were returned, with 89% granting parental permission to participate.

Students and teachers completed written questionnaires during the fall and spring semesters in classroom settings. All instructions and questionnaire items were read aloud while students recorded their own responses. Help was available to individual students as needed.

Measures of Context

School and Classroom Ethnic Diversity.   An index of ethnic diversity was created using a formula that captures both the number of different groups in the setting and the relative representation of each group (Simpson, 1949):

$$D_C = 1 - \sum_{i=1}^{g} p_i^2$$

where D_C represents the ethnic diversity of a given context and p_i is the proportion of students in the context who belong to ethnic group i. The p_i^2 is summed across g groups in a classroom. Substantively, this index calculates the probability that any two students randomly selected from the same setting will be from different ethnic groups (see Moody, 2001, for a similar measure that is labeled school *heterogeneity*). Scores can range from 0 to approximately 1, with higher numbers reflecting greater ethnic diversity. For example, in a classroom where 75% of the students are Latino and 25% are African American, ethnic diversity is .375; in a classroom that is half Latino and half African American, ethnic diversity is .5; and in a classroom where three ethnic groups are represented fairly equally (e.g., 40% Latino, 30% African American, 30% Caucasian), ethnic diversity is around .66.

We calculated classroom ethnic diversity based on five groups: Latino, African American, Asian–Pacific Islander, Caucasian, and multiracial. To improve the accuracy of our estimate of classroom ethnic diversity, we examined only classrooms with greater than 50% participation at the specified time point. This resulted in 80 and 74 classrooms (out of 99) being retained in the analyses for the fall and spring semesters, respectively. Classroom diversity ranged from 0 to .77 ($M = .48$, $SD = .22$) during the fall and from 0 to .78 ($M = .53$, $SD = .21$) during the spring. The slight differences between the two semesters reflect minor movement of students among classrooms.

We based our estimate of school-level diversity on four ethnic groups (African American, Asian–Pacific Islander, Caucasian, and Latino), using information obtained from *DataQuest*, a database provided by the California Department of Education (information retrieved April 1, 2003, from http://data1.cde.ca.gov/dataquest/). Multiethnic students were excluded from the school-level diversity indices because the California Department of Education collapses multiethnic youth and nonrespondents into a single category. Across the 11 middle schools, the school diversity index ranged from .06 to .71 ($M = .48$, $SD = .19$), indicating substantial variation. In low-diversity schools ($D_C < .50$), classroom diversity ranged from 0 to .62 during the fall and from 0 to .65 during the spring. In schools with higher diversity ($D_C > .50$), classroom ethnic diversity ranged from .30 to .77 during the fall and from .30 to .78 during the spring. The correlations (r) between school-level diversity and classroom-level diversity were .80 and .78 for the fall and spring, respectively. Thus, although there was overlap between the ethnic diversity in schools and the ethnic diversity in classrooms, they were not identical.

Classroom Engagement.   Given that middle schools are likely to rely on academic-tracking practices that are implicit, the effects of ethnic diversity on students' perceptions of safety and vulnerability might be confounded by classroom differences in students' academic engagement. Likewise, students' engagement could affect perceived vulnerability independently of classroom ethnic composition. To take into account such effects, we also tested models that included classroom-level aggregates of teacher ratings of students' academic engagement. Homeroom teachers completed a six-item measure for each participating student (e.g., "In my class, this student likes to figure things out for him/herself."), rating the items on a 4-point scale from 1, *never*, to 4, *always*. The mean rating for the six items was the measure of the student's academic engagement; higher scores indicated more engagement (fall $\alpha = .88$; spring $\alpha = .92$). The average engagement score across all students in the classroom was then calculated. Classroom engagement ranged from 1.78 to 3.52 and from 1.83 to 3.25 for the fall and spring, respectively.

Outcome Measures: Perceptions of Safety and Vulnerability

School Safety. Perceptions of school safety were measured using a 10-item subscale of the Effective School Battery (Gottfredson, 1984). Items tapped general perceptions of safety at school and on the way to school (e.g., "How often do you feel safe while in your school building?") and were rated from 1, *never*, to 5, *always*. A mean of the items was calculated, such that higher scores reflect stronger perceptions of school safety (fall $\alpha = .72$; spring $\alpha = .71$).

Peer Victimization. Perceptions of personal experiences of victimization by peers were measured using a modified six-item version of the Peer Victimization Survey (Neary & Joseph, 1994). The original and the modified survey are designed similarly to Harter's (1987) Self-Perception Profile for Children: Respondents first decide which of two options (types of students) is more like them (e.g., "Some kids are often picked on by other kids, BUT Other kids are not picked on by other kids."). Participants then indicate whether that option is "sort of true for me" or "really true for me." Items were scored on a 4-point scale, and a mean of the six items was computed, such that higher scores indicate higher levels of peer victimization (fall $\alpha = .81$; spring $\alpha = .83$).

Loneliness. Sixteen items from Asher and Wheeler's (1985) Loneliness Scale were used to assess feelings of loneliness at school (e.g., "I have nobody to talk to."). Items were rated on a 5-point scale from 1, *not true at all*, to 5, *always true*. A mean of the 16 items was created, such that higher scores reflect greater loneliness at school (fall $\alpha = .84$; spring $\alpha = .86$).

Self-Worth. The six-item global self-worth subscale from Harter's (1987) Self-Perception Profile for Children was used to assess self-worth (e.g., "Some kids are often unhappy with themselves, BUT Other kids are pretty pleased with themselves."). Items were scored on a 4-point scale, and a mean of the six items was computed, such that higher scores indicate higher self-worth (fall $\alpha = .77$; spring $\alpha = .80$).

Data Analysis

We used hierarchical linear modeling (HLM) to assess the contextual effects of ethnic diversity on perceptions of safety and vulnerability. HLM could account for the fact that students who shared the same context (i.e., classroom or school) were likely to be more similar to one another than students from different contexts (Raudenbush & Bryk, 2002). HLM also allowed us to control for individual differences (i.e., sex and ethnicity) while testing for the effects of the ethnic diversity of the context. Classroom and school effects were examined separately because a school's ethnic composition restricted the range of its classroom diversity.

Both ethnicity (Latino or African American) and gender were dummy-coded and grand-mean-centered for all analyses. Ethnic diversity at the classroom and school levels was centered at .50, which reflects a moderate amount of diversity and was close to the mean in this study. Thus, perceptions of safety and vulnerability were modeled as a function of individual characteristics (i.e., gender and ethnicity) at Level 1 and contextual features (i.e., ethnic diversity) at Level 2. The intercept for ethnic diversity was modeled as a random parameter, and the error variances for gender and ethnicity were constrained to zero. Initial analyses suggested that the remaining error variance for these predictors was nonsignificant, and this approach allowed us to retain the most parsimonious model.

Results

We first present the findings from analyses testing whether classroom ethnic diversity predicted students' perceptions of safety and vulnerability in fall and spring of their first year in middle school. We then consider the impact of ethnic diversity at the school level on the same outcomes.

Classroom-Level Ethnic Diversity

Table 1 shows the results of the HLM analyses for both fall and spring of sixth grade. The intercept column indicates the estimated value of the outcome variables, controlling for gender and ethnicity, when the ethnic-diversity index is .50 (i.e., grand-mean-entered). The second column indicates the degree to which perceptions of safety and vulnerability increase or decrease as a function of classroom ethnic diversity. The third column presents the percentage of between-classrooms variation in safety and vulnerability explained by diversity (compared with the percentage explained in the unconditional-means model).

As shown in Table 1, in both fall and spring of sixth grade, greater ethnic diversity in the classroom

table 1   Estimated Coefficients and Standard Errors for the Classroom-Level Hierarchical Linear Modeling Analyses

Outcome	Level 1: intercept	Level 2: ethnic diversity	Percentage of between-classrooms variance explained by ethnic diversity
	Fall of 6th grade		
Peer victimization	2.08 (0.03)***	−0.52 (0.14)***	29
Loneliness	1.77 (0.02)***	−0.56 (0.10)***	70
School safety	4.10 (0.03)***	0.84 (0.14)***	45
Self-worth	3.20 (0.03)***	0.30 (0.12)**	34
	Spring of 6th grade		
Peer victimization	2.08 (0.03)***	−0.56 (0.15)***	49
Loneliness	1.72 (0.02)***	−0.53 (0.11)***	97
School safety	4.17 (0.02)***	0.75 (0.13)***	56
Self-worth	3.16 (0.03)***	0.29 (0.14)*	46

Note. Standard errors are given in parentheses.
*$p_{rep} > .87$. **$p_{rep} > .95$. ***$p = rep > .99$.

was associated with lower levels of perceived peer victimization ($b = −0.52$, $p_{rep} > .99$, in fall; $b = −0.56$, $p_{rep} > .99$, in spring). Similarly, classroom diversity was associated with less loneliness ($b = −0.56$, $p_{rep} > .99$, in fall; $b = −0.53$, $p_{rep} > .99$, in spring). Greater classroom ethnic diversity also predicted increased perceptions of school safety ($b = 0.84$, $p_{rep} > .99$, in fall; $b = 0.75$, $p_{rep} > .99$, in spring) and self-worth ($b = 0.30$, $p_{rep} = .971$, in fall; $b = 0.29$, $p_{rep} = .93$, in spring). The table also shows that ethnic diversity accounted for slightly more of the between-classrooms variability in the spring than the fall: In the spring, ethnic diversity accounted for almost half of between-classrooms variance in peer victimization (49%) and self-worth (46%), more than half (56%) of between-classrooms variance in school safety, and nearly all (97%) between-classrooms variability in loneliness. The association between classroom ethnic diversity and feelings of safety and vulnerability is summarized in Figure 1.

The analysis of classroom-level ethnic diversity showed very few ethnicity or gender effects, suggesting that the relations between classroom ethnic diversity and perceived safety and vulnerability were similar for Latino and African American boys and girls.[1]

To approximate the effect size, we examined the magnitude of the diversity effects by comparing the estimated difference in safety and vulnerability in lower-diversity classrooms ($D_C = .2$) versus higher-diversity classrooms ($D_C = .7$) with the standard deviations for the full sample ($SDs = .79, .64, .70,$ and $.71$ for peer victimization, loneliness, school safety, and self-worth, respectively). The difference between lower- and higher-diversity contexts reflected one third of the sample's standard deviation for peer victimization, almost one half (.43) of a standard deviation for loneliness, almost two thirds (.60) of a standard deviation for school safety, and one fifth of a standard deviation for self-worth in the fall. The effects of classroom ethnic diversity were similar for spring.

Controlling for Classroom Differences in Student Engagement

As a comparison, we also tested whether student engagement affected the classroom-level findings just described. Classroom-level academic engagement was not directly associated with classroom ethnic diversity

---

[1]During spring, girls reported higher levels of perceived school safety ($b = 0.09$, $p_{rep} = .95$) and lower levels of peer victimization ($b = −0.12$, $p_{rep} = .96$) than did boys. The association between classroom diversity and school safety was weaker for Latino than African American students ($b = −0.67$, $p_{rep} = .94$) in spring. Similar individual differences were found for school-level diversity.

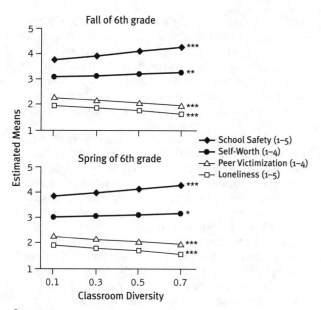

figure 1

Effects of classroom-level diversity on perceived safety and vulnerability, controlling for sex and ethnicity (*p_{rep} > .87, **p_{rep} > .95, ***p_{rep} > .99).

in the fall (r = .16, n.s.) or spring (r = .12, n.s.). We conducted HLM analyses by adding classroom-level academic engagement (grand-mean-centered) as another Level 2 (i.e., contextual) predictor of safety and vulnerability.

Holding classroom-level academic engagement constant, classroom ethnic diversity remained a significant predictor of the outcome variables; the coefficients were similar to those presented in Table 1. Classroom-level academic engagement also independently predicted peer victimization, loneliness, and self-worth during the fall: As classroom academic engagement increased, peer victimization (b = −0.18, p_{rep} = .93) and loneliness (b = −0.14, p_{rep} = .941) decreased, and self-worth increased (b = 0.15, p_{rep} = .93). However, by spring of sixth grade, the independent effects of classroom-level academic engagement on feelings of vulnerability and self-worth dissipated (p_{rep} < .87).

In sum, perceptions of vulnerability and self-worth improved with increased ethnic diversity. Students' academic engagement at the classroom level did not account for these findings. The positive effects of diversity remained significant in both fall and spring, whereas classroom-level academic engagement was predictive of positive outcomes only in the fall.

School-Level Ethnic Diversity

The results for school-level ethnic diversity are presented in Table 2. In both fall and spring, school diversity predicted all of the outcomes except self-worth. That is, greater ethnic diversity within the school was associated with lower levels of peer victimization and loneliness and higher perceptions of school safety (see Fig. 2). Note that by spring of sixth grade, school eth-

---

table 2 Estimated Coefficients and Standard Errors for the School-Level Hierarchical Linear Modeling Analyses

Outcome	Level 1: intercept	Level 2: ethnic diversity	Percentage of between-classrooms variance explained by ethnic diversity
	Fall of 6th grade		
Peer victimization	2.10 (0.04)***	−0.61 (0.25)*	29
Loneliness	1.80 (0.04)***	−0.63 (0.24)*	38
School safety	4.08 (0.06)***	0.83 (0.33)*	31
Self-worth	3.19 (0.03)***	0.21 (0.20)	–
	Spring of 6th grade		
Peer victimization	2.05 (0.03)***	−0.69 (0.19)**	69
Loneliness	1.72 (0.02)***	−0.52 (0.002)***	96
School safety	4.21 (0.04)***	0.79 (0.25)**	45
Self-worth	3.18 (0.04)***	0.33 (0.24)	–

Note. Standard errors are given in parentheses.

*p_{rep} > .87. **p_{rep} > .95. ***p_{rep} > .99.

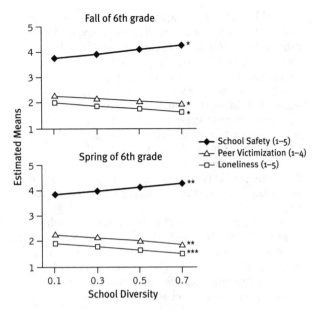

figure 2

Effects of school-level diversity on perceived safety and vulnerability, controlling for sex and ethnicity (*p$_{rep}$ > .87, **p$_{rep}$ > .95, ***p$_{rep}$ > .99).

nic diversity accounted for 69% of the between-schools variability in peer victimization, nearly all (96%) the between-schools variability in loneliness, and almost half of the between-schools variation in school safety (45%).

To summarize, results at the school level were similar to the classroom-level findings. Greater ethnic diversity at the school level was associated with lower levels of self-reported social vulnerability and safety (but no difference in self-worth) in both fall and spring of sixth grade. Thus, attending an ethnically diverse school, like belonging to an ethnically diverse classroom, was associated with the best overall outcomes for Latino and African American students.

Discussion

Our results indicate that ethnic diversity is associated with feelings of safety and social satisfaction in school. Students felt safer, less harassed, and less lonely in more ethnically diverse contexts. These findings were robust across the two levels of analyses (i.e., classroom and school), two ethnic groups (African American and Latino), and two time points (fall and spring of sixth grade), and were independent of average levels of academic engagement in the classrooms. We do not know of prior studies investigating perceived safety as a function of ethnic diversity.

Why would ethnic diversity protect students from perceptions of vulnerability? We proposed that the

power relations are more balanced in ethnically diverse schools with multiple ethnic groups than in less diverse schools. For example, in a context with five ethnic groups equally represented (each at 20%), the balance of power is unlikely to be tipped in favor of one group over another. The lack of power differentials may reduce incidents of peer harassment that, in turn, affect perceptions of safety.

It also is likely that the emotional effects of perceived threat are less painful or detrimental in diverse as opposed to nondiverse settings. For example, one of our recent studies showed that victimization by peers was less strongly associated with distress when students had few, as opposed to many, classmates of their own ethnicity (Bellmore et al., 2004). We proposed that students who belong to numerical minority groups (few same-ethnicity classmates) can attribute their plight to the prejudice of other people, but those who are in the numerical majority (many same-ethnicity classmates) are more likely to blame themselves for their victimization. Whereas external attributions to the prejudice of others can be self-protective (cf. Crocker & Major, 1989), self-blaming attributions are associated with heightened distress (Graham & Juvonen, 1998).

Our analyses focused on the psychological benefits of an ethnically diverse student body, with diversity operationalized as the numerical representation of various ethnic groups. Specifically, our approach, and our measurement of ethnic diversity, underscores the importance of contexts that have multiple ethnic groups that are relatively evenly represented. Although the school-desegregation literature also includes studies of substantive diversity, that literature typically focuses on organizational characteristics that promote positive interracial interactions (e.g., Field & Carter, 1998; Halliman & Williams, 1989; Moody, 2001). For example, studies have documented that when academic tracking in diverse schools does not resegregate students along racial and ethnic lines, or when extracurricular activities are structured to attract an ethnic mix of students, interracial relations improve (see Moody, 2001). Although such studies have primarily examined formation of interracial friendships, there is reason to believe that organizing diverse schools to facilitate the interaction opportunities of ethnically diverse students should also promote feelings of safety and social satisfaction.

We focused on urban middle schools that served communities of low socioeconomic status (SES). Hence, we do not know whether our findings would be replicated where ethnic groups differ in SES or among students in smaller elementary schools and larger high schools. We also do not know whether selection effects may have influenced our results. For example, it is possible that ethnically diverse middle schools draw on a different set of students (e.g., those who are more tolerant of people who are different from themselves) than less diverse schools do. As we acknowledged in the introduction, it is also possible that school personnel in more ethnically diverse schools frame the discourse on multiculturalism in ways that both promote perceptions of safety and undermine feelings of vulnerability. Because our findings were robust not only across schools but also within schools across classrooms that varied in diversity, these school-level explanations are unlikely to account for our findings. Nevertheless, it will be important for future research to systematically assess various school effects and specifically the behaviors of teachers in more versus less diverse schools.

With the changing demographics in this country, the meaning of race and racial integration has changed substantially. Rather than focusing on Black-White comparisons under conditions in which SES disparities and differences in majority-minority status prevail, future research should capitalize on new opportunities for studying diversity in multiethnic schools. If the current findings can be replicated across schools with different ethnic-group configurations, then they offer new empirical evidence for the psychological benefits of racial integration in the spirit of *Brown*. The possibility that there is safety in diversity—as opposed to safety in numbers—is an optimistic one.

REFERENCES

Antonio, A., Chang, M., Hakuta, K., Kenny, D., Levin, S., & Milem, J. (2004). Effects of racial diversity on complex thinking in college students. *Psychological Science, 15,* 507–510.

Asher, S., & Wheeler, V. (1985). Children's loneliness: A comparison of neglected and rejected peer status. *Journal of Consulting and Clinical Psychology, 53,* 500–505.

Banks, J.A. (1995). Multicultural education: Its effects on students' racial and gender role attitudes. In J.A. Banks & C.A.M. Banks (Eds.), *Handbook of research on multicultural education* (pp. 617–627). New York: Macmillan.

Bellmore, A.D., Witkow, M.R., Graham, S., & Juvonen, J. (2004). Beyond the individual: The impact of ethnic context and classroom behavioral norms on victims' adjustment. *Developmental Psychology, 40,* 1159–1172.

Crocker, J., & Major, B. (1989). Social stigma and self-esteem: The self-protective properties of stigma. *Psychological Review, 96,* 608–630.

Damico, S.B., & Sparks, C. (1986). Cross-group contact opportunities impact on interpersonal relationships in desegregated middle schools. *Sociology of Education, 59,* 113–123.

Eccles, J., & Midgley, C. (1989). Stage/environment fit: Developmentally appropriate classrooms for early adolescents. In R. Ames & C. Ames (Eds.), *Research on motivation in education* (Vol. 3, pp. 139–181). New York: Academic Press.

Epps, E.G. (1975). Impact of school desegregation on aspirations, self-concepts and other aspects of personality. *Law and Contemporary Problems, 39,* 300–313.

Feld, S., & Carter, W.C. (1998). When desegregation 'reduces' interracial contact: A class size paradox for weak ties. *American Journal of Sociology, 103,* 1165–1186.

Gottfredson, D.C. (1984). *Effective School Battery.* Baltimore: Psychological Assessment Resources.

Graham, S., & Juvonen, J. (1998). Self-blame and peer victimization in middle school: An attributional analysis. *Developmental Psychology, 34,* 587–599.

Gray-Little, B., & Carles, R.A. (1997). The effect of racial dissonance on academic self-esteem and achievement in elementary, junior high, and high school students. *Journal of Research on Adolescence, 7,* 109–131.

Gray-Little, B., & Hafdahl, A.R. (2000). Factors influencing racial comparisons of self-esteem: A quantitative review. *Psychological Bulletin, 1,* 26–54.

Gurin, P., Nagda, B.A., & Lopez, G.E. (2004). The benefits of diversity in education for democratic citizenship. *Journal of Social Issues, 60,* 17–34.

Hallinan, M. T., & Teixeira, R.A. (1987). Students' interracial friendships: Individual characteristics, structural effects, and racial differences. *American Journal of Education, 95,* 563–583.

Hallinan, M.T., & Williams, R.A. (1989). Interracial friendship choices in secondary school. *American Sociological Review, 54,* 67–78.

Harter, S. (1987). *Manual for the Self-Perception Profile for Children.* Denver, CO: University of Denver.

Milem, J.F., & Umbach, P.D. (2003). The influence of precollege factors on students' predispositions regarding diversity activities in college. *Journal of College and Student Development, 44,* 611–624.

Moody, J. (2001). Race, school integration, and friendship segregation in America. *American Journal of Sociology, 3,* 679–716.

Neary, A., & Joseph, S. (1994). Peer victimization and its relationship to self-concept and depression among schoolgirls. *Personality and Individual Differences, 16,* 183–186.

Nishina, A., Juvonen, J., & Witkow, M.R. (2005). Sticks and stones may break my bones, but names will make me feel sick: The psychosocial, somatic, and scholastic consequences of peer harassment. *Journal of Clinical Child and Adolescent Psychology, 34,* 37–48.

Olweus, D. (1993). *Bullying at school: What we know and what we can do.* Malden, MA: Blackwell.

Orfield, G. (2001). *Schools more separate: Consequences of a decade of resegregation.* Cambridge, MA: Harvard University Civil Rights Project.

Orfield, G., & Lee, C. (2006). *Racial transformation and the changing nature of segregation.* Cambridge, MA: The Civil Rights Project at Harvard University.

Park, B., & Judd, C. (2005). Rethinking the link between categorization and prejudice within the social cognitive perspective. *Personality and Social Psychology Review, 9,* 108–130.

Pettigrew, T.F. (2004). Justice deferred: A half century after Brown v. Board of Education. *American Psychologist, 59,* 521–529.

Raudenbush, S.W., & Bryk, A.S. (2002). *Hierarchical linear models: Applications and data analysis methods* (2nd ed.). Thousand Oaks, CA: Sage.

Schofield, J.W. (1995). Review of research on school desegregation's impact on elementary and secondary school students. In J.A. Banks & C.A.M. Banks (Eds.), *Handbook of research on multicultural education* (pp. 597–616). New York: Macmillan.

Schofield, J.W., & Hausmann, R.M. (2004). School desegregation and social science research. *American Psychologist, 59,* 538–546.

Simpson, E.H. (1949). Measurement of diversity. *Nature,* 163, 688.

St. John, N.H. (1975). *School desegregation outcomes for children.* New York: Wiley.

Verna, G.B., & Runion, K.B. (1985). The effects of contextual dissonance on the self-concept of youth from a high versus low socially valued group. *The Journal of Social Psychology, 125,* 449–458.

Wells, A.S. (1995). Reexamining research on school desegregation: Long- versus short-term effects. *Teachers College Record, 96,* 691–706.

Questions

1. What was the focus of research in the 1960s and 1970s regarding the effect of school desegregation, and what, according to Juvonen and her colleagues, were some of the main limitations of this research?
2. Why did these researchers focus on the students' perceptions of safety and vulnerability, and why was this emphasis especially important for children attending middle school?
3. Why did the researchers want to include many inner city schools so that the ethnic diversity and cross-ethnic contact in the sample covered a wide range of ethnic groups?
4. What were the relations between ethnic diversity and perceived peer victimization and other social experiences children had at school? Do these findings surprise you? Why or why not?
5. What social and psychological processes may explain the relations between ethnic diversity and perceived safety that were revealed in this study?
6. What are the implications of these findings for social policy regarding public education?

How Asian Teachers Polish Each Lesson to Perfection

James W. Stigler • Harold W. Stevenson

During middle childhood, much of children's academic work concentrates on the development and refinement of basic skills of reading, writing, and mathematics. It is clear that if children do not develop these skills during this time, they will face many difficulties in school in the years ahead. In recent years, mathematics achievement during the years of middle childhood has become a particular area of concern. Cross-national research indicates that, in general, children in the United States fall far behind children in other nations, especially China and Japan, in mathematics. Given the importance of understanding mathematics both for further learning in this domain as well as for learning science in high school and beyond, this lag is very disturbing.

Many developmental psychologists have attempted to understand these cross-national patterns. The most successful project to date was conducted by James Stigler and Harold Stevenson, who describe their work in the following article. The researchers focused on children's experiences in the classroom in China, Japan, and the United States. Specifically, they examined educational practices and goals in the three societies. Their observations indicate that both the processes and the outcomes of schooling in these communities support children's learning of mathematics in different ways. In addition, many of the educational practices that are used in China and Japan reflect deeply held cultural values and practices in these societies. As a result, this research suggests that modeling classrooms in the United States after the classrooms in China and Japan would not necessarily benefit U.S. children in the absence of the meaning and direction provided by the broader cultural context.

The research described in this article is important for several reasons. It connects children's experiences in the mathematics classroom to specific learning outcomes. Although this seems like an obvious step, the classroom context, especially across cultures, has rarely been examined in enough detail to establish how different classroom practices affect children's learning. The research is also an excellent example of cultural psychology, in that it studies children and their experiences in relation to the broader social and cultural context in which development occurs. Finally, because it provides insight into different ways that teachers teach mathematics, this research offers some new and interesting ideas about how to approach mathematics instruction.

Although there is no overall difference in intelligence, the differences in mathematical achievement of American children and their Asian counterparts are staggering.[1]

Let us look first at the results of a study we conducted in 120 classrooms in three cities: Taipei (Taiwan); Sendai (Japan); and the Minneapolis metropolitan area. First and fifth graders from representative schools in these cities were given a test of mathematics that required computation and problem solving. Among the one hundred first graders in the three locations who received the lowest scores, fifty-eight

Reprinted with permission from the Spring 1991 issue of the *American Educator*, the quarterly journal of the American Federation of Teachers, AFL-CIO.

Note: The research described in this article has been funded by grants from the National Institute of Mental Health, the National Science Foundation, and the W.T. Grant Foundation. The research is the result of collaboration with a large group of colleagues in China, Japan, Taiwan, and the United States who have worked together for the past decade. We are indebted to each of these colleagues and are especially grateful to Shinying Lee of the University of Michigan who has been a major contributor to the research described in this article.

were American children; among the one hundred lowest-scoring fifth graders, sixty-seven were American children. Among the top one hundred first graders in mathematics, there were only fifteen American children. And only one American child appeared among the top one hundred fifth graders. The highest-scoring American classroom obtained an average score lower than that of the lowest-scoring Japanese classroom and of all but one of the twenty classrooms in Taipei. In whatever way we looked at the data, the poor performance of American children was evident.

These data are startling, but no more so than the results of a study that involved 40 first- and 40 fifth-grade classrooms in the metropolitan area of Chicago—a very representative sample of the city and the suburbs of Cook County—and twenty-two classes in each of these grades in metropolitan Beijing (China). In this study, children were given a battery of mathematics tasks that included diverse problems, such as estimating the distance between a tree and a hidden treasure on a map, deciding who won a race on the basis of data in a graph, trying to explain subtraction to visiting Martians, or calculating the sum of nineteen and forty-five. There was no area in which the American children were competitive with those from China. The Chinese children's superiority appeared in complex tasks involving the application of knowledge as well as in the routines of computation. When fifth graders were asked, for example, how many members of a stamp club with twenty-four members collected only foreign stamps if five-sixths of the members did so, 59 percent of Beijing children, but only 9 percent of the Chicago children produced the correct answer. On a computation test, only 2.2 percent of the Chinese fifth graders scored at or below the mean for their American counterparts. All of the twenty Chicago area schools had average scores on the fifth-grade geometry test that were below those of the Beijing schools. The results from all these tasks paint a bleak picture of American children's competencies in mathematics.[2]

The poor performance of American students compels us to try to understand the reasons why. We have written extensively elsewhere about the cultural differences in attitudes toward learning and toward the importance of effort vs. innate ability and about the substantially greater amounts of time Japanese and Chinese students devote to academic activities in general and to the study of math in particular.[3] Important as these factors are, they do not tell the whole story. For that we have to take a close look inside the classrooms of Japan, China, and the United States to see how mathematics is actually taught in the three cultures.

Lessons Not Lectures

If we were asked briefly to characterize classes in Japan and China, we would say that they consist of coherent lessons that are presented in a thoughtful, relaxed, and nonauthoritarian manner. Teachers frequently rely on students as sources of information. Lessons are oriented toward problem solving rather than rote mastery of facts and procedures and utilize many different types of representational materials. The role assumed by the teacher is that of knowledgeable guide, rather than that of prime dispenser of information and arbiter of what is correct. There is frequent verbal interaction in the classroom as the teacher attempts to stimulate students to produce, explain, and evaluate solutions to problems. These characteristics contradict stereotypes held by most Westerners about Asian teaching practices. Lessons are not rote; they are not filled with drill. Teachers do not spend large amounts of time lecturing but attempt to lead the children in productive interactions and discussions. And the children are not the passive automata depicted in Western descriptions but active participants in the learning process.

We begin by discussing what we mean by the coherence of a lesson. One way to think of a lesson is by using the analog of a story. A good story is highly organized; it has a beginning, a middle, and an end; and it follows a protagonist who meets challenges and resolves problems that arise along the way. Above all, a good story engages the reader's interest in a series of interconnected events, which are best understood in the context of the events that precede and follow it.

Such a concept of a lesson guides the organization of instruction in Asia. The curricula are defined in terms of coherent lessons, each carefully designed to fill a forty- to fifty-minute class period with sustained attention to the development of some concept or skill. Like a good story, the lesson has an introduction, a conclusion, and a consistent theme.

We can illustrate what we are talking about with this account of a fifth-grade Japanese mathematics class:

> The teacher walks in carrying a large paper bag full of clinking glass. Entering the classroom with a large paper bag is highly unusual, and by the time she has placed the bag on her desk the students are regarding her with rapt attention. What's in the bag? She begins to pull items out of the bag, placing them, one-by-one, on her desk. She removes a pitcher and a vase. A beer bottle evokes laughter and surprise. She soon has six containers lined up on her desk. The children continue to watch intently, glancing back and forth at each other as they seek to understand the purpose of this display.
>
> The teacher, looking thoughtfully at the containers, poses a question: "I wonder which one would hold the most water?" Hands go up, and the teacher calls on different students to give their

guesses: "the pitcher," "the beer bottle," "the teapot." The teacher stands aside and ponders: "Some of you said one thing, others said something different. You don't agree with each other. There must be some way we can find out who is correct. How can we know who is correct?" Interest is high, and the discussion continues.

The students soon agree that to find out how much each container holds they will need to fill the containers with something. How about water? The teacher finds some buckets and sends several children out to fill them with water. When they return, the teacher says: "Now what do we do?" Again there is a discussion, and after several minutes the children decide that they will need to use a smaller container to measure how much water fits into each of the larger containers. They decide on a drinking cup, and one of the students warns that they all have to fill each cup to the same level—otherwise the measure won't be the same for all of the groups.

At this point the teacher divides the class into their groups (*han*) and gives each group one of the containers and a drinking cup. Each group fills its container, counts how many cups of water it holds, and writes the result in a notebook. When all of the groups have completed the task, the teacher calls on the leader of each group to report on the group's findings and notes the results on the blackboard. She has written the names of the containers in a column on the left and a scale from 1 to 6 along the bottom. Pitcher, 4.5 cups; vase, 3 cups; beer bottle, 1.5 cups; and so on. As each group makes its report the teacher draws a bar representing the amount, in cups, the container holds.

Finally, the teacher returns to the question she posed at the beginning of the lesson: Which container holds the most water? She reviews how they were able to solve the problem and points out that the answer is now contained in the bar graph on the board. She then arranges the containers on the table in order according to how much they hold and writes a rank order on each container, from 1 to 6. She ends the class with a brief review of what they have done. No definitions of ordinate and abscissa, no discussion of how to make a graph preceded the example— these all became obvious in the course of the lesson, and only at the end did the teacher mention the terms that describe the horizontal and vertical axes of the graph they had made.

With one carefully crafted problem, this Japanese teacher has guided her students to discover—and most likely to remember—several important concepts.

As this article unfolds, we hope to demonstrate that this example of how well-designed Asian class lessons are is not an isolated one; to the contrary, it is the norm. And as we hope to further demonstrate, excellent class lessons do not come effortlessly or magically. Asian teachers are not born great teachers; they and the lessons they develop require careful nurturing and constant refinement. The practice of teaching in Japan and China is more uniformly perfected than it is in the United States because their systems of education are structured to encourage teaching excellence to develop and flourish. Ours is not. We will take up the question of why and what can be done about this later in the piece. But first, we present a more detailed look at what Asian lessons are like.

Coherence Broken

Asian lessons almost always begin with a practical problem, such as the example we have just given, or with a word problem written on the blackboard. Asian teachers, to a much greater degree than American teachers, give coherence to their lessons by introducing the lesson with a word problem.

It is not uncommon for the Asian teacher to organize the entire lesson around the solution to this single problem. The teacher leads the children to recognize what is known and what is unknown and directs the students' attention to the critical parts of the problem. Teachers are careful to see that the problem is understood by all of the children, and even mechanics, such as mathematical computation, are presented in the context of solving a problem.

Before ending the lesson, the teacher reviews what has been learned and relates it to the problem she posed at the beginning of the lesson. American teachers are much less likely than Asian teachers to begin and end lessons in this way. For example, we found that fifth-grade teachers in Beijing spent eight times as long at the end of the class period summarizing the lessons as did those in the Chicago metropolitan area.

Now contrast the Japanese math lesson described above with a fifth-grade American mathematics classroom that we recently visited. Immediately after getting the students' attention, the teacher pointed out that today was Tuesday, "band day," and that all students in the band should go to the band room. "Those of you doing the news report today should meet over there in the corner," he continued. He then began the mathematics class with the remaining students by reviewing the solution to a computation problem that had been included in the previous day's homework. After this brief review, the teacher directed the students' attention to the blackboard, where the day's assignment had been written. From this point on, the teacher spent most of the rest of the period walking about the room monitoring the children's work, talking to individual children about questions or errors, and uttering "shushes" whenever the students began talking among themselves.

This example is typical of the American classrooms we have visited, classrooms where students spend more time in transition and less in academic activities, more time working on their own and less being instructed by the teacher; where teachers spend much of their time working with individual students and attending to matters of discipline; and where the shape of a coherent lesson is often hard to discern.

American lessons are often disrupted by irrelevant interruptions. These serve to break the continuity of the lesson and add to children's difficulty in perceiving the lesson as a coherent whole. In our American observations, the teacher interrupted the flow of the lesson with an interlude of irrelevant comments or the class was interrupted by someone else in 20 percent of all first-grade lessons and 47 percent of all fifth-grade lessons. This occurred less than 10 percent of the time at both grade levels in Sendai, Taipei, and Beijing. In fact, no interruptions of either type were recorded during the eighty hours of observation in Beijing fifth-grade classrooms. The mathematics lesson in one of the American classrooms we visited was interrupted every morning by a woman from the cafeteria who polled the children about their lunch plans and collected money from those who planned to eat the hot lunch. Interruptions, as well as inefficient transitions from one activity to another, make it difficult to sustain a coherent lesson throughout the class period.

Coherence is also disrupted when teachers shift frequently from one topic to another. This occurred often in the American classrooms we observed. The teacher might begin with a segment on measurement, then proceed to a segment on simple addition, then to a segment on telling time, and then to a second segment on addition. These segments constitute a math class, but they are hardly a coherent lesson. Such changes in topic were responsible for 21 percent of the changes in segments that we observed in American classrooms but accounted for only 4 percent of the changes in segments in Japanese classrooms.

Teachers frequently capitalize on variety as a means of capturing children's interest. This may explain why American teachers shift topics so frequently within the lesson. Asian teachers also seek variety, but they tend to introduce new activities instead of new topics. Shifts in materials do not necessarily pose a threat to coherence. For example, the coherence of a lesson does not diminish when the teacher shifts from working with numerals to working with concrete objects, if both are used to represent the same subtraction problem. Shifting the topic, on the other hand, introduces variety, but at the risk of destroying the coherence of the lesson.

Classroom Organization

Elementary school classrooms are typically organized in one of three ways: the whole class is working as a unit; the class is divided into a number of small groups; or children work individually. In our observations, we noted when the child was receiving instruction or assistance from the teacher and when the student was working on his own. The child was considered to be receiving instruction whenever the teacher was the leader of the activity, whether it involved the whole class, a small group, or only the individual child.

Looking at the classroom in this manner led us to one of our most pronounced findings: Although the number of children in Asian classes is significantly greater than the number in American classes, Asian students received much more instruction from their teachers than American students. In Taiwan, the teacher was the leader of the child's activity 90 percent of the time, as opposed to 74 percent in Japan, and only 46 percent in the United States. No one was leading instruction 9 percent of the time in Taiwan, 26 percent in Japan, and an astonishing 51 percent of the time in the United States (see Figure 1). Even American first graders actually spent more time on their own than they did participating in an activity led by the teacher.

One of the reasons American children received less instruction is that American teachers spent 13 percent of their time in the mathematics classes not working with any students, something that happened only 6 percent of the time in Japan and 9 percent in Taiwan. (As we will see later, American teachers have to steal class time to attend to the multitude of chores involving preparation, assessment, and administration because so little nonteaching time is available for them during the day.)

A much more critical factor in the erosion of instructional time was the amount of time American teachers were involved with individuals or small groups. American children spend 10 percent of their time in small groups and 47 percent of their time working individually. Much of the 87 percent of the time American teachers were working with their students was spent with these individual students or small groups, rather than with the class as a whole. When teachers provide individual instruction, they must leave the rest of the class unattended, so instructional time for all remaining children is reduced.

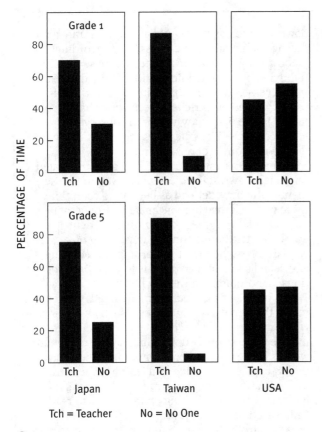

figure 1

Percentage of time students spent in activity led by teacher and by no one.

Children can learn without a teacher. Nevertheless, it seems likely that they could profit from having their teacher as the leader of their activities more than half of the time they are in the classroom. It is the incredibly large amounts of time that American children are left unassisted and the effect that unattended time has on the coherence of the larger lesson that is the problem.

When children must work alone for long periods of time without guidance or reaction from the teacher, they begin to lose focus on the purpose of their activity. Asian teachers not only assign less seatwork than American teachers, they also use seatwork differently. Chinese and Japanese teachers tend to use short, frequent periods of seatwork, alternating between group discussion of problems and time for children to work problems on their own. Seatwork is thereby embedded into the lesson. After they work individually or in small groups on a problem, Asian students are called upon to present and defend the solutions they came up with. Thus, instruction, practice, and evaluation are tightly interwoven into a coherent whole. In contrast, the average length of seatwork in American fifth-grade classrooms was almost twice as long as it was in Asian classrooms. And, instead of embedding seatwork into the ongoing back and forth of the lesson, American teachers tend to relegate it to one long period at the end of the class, where it becomes little more than a time for repetitious practice. In Chicago, 59 percent of all fifth-grade lessons ended with a period of seatwork, compared with 23 percent in Sendai and 14 percent in Taipei. American teachers often do not discuss the work or its connection to the goal of the lesson, or even evaluate its accuracy. Seatwork was never evaluated or discussed in 48 percent of all American fifth-grade classes we observed, compared to less than 3 percent of Japanese classes and 6 percent of Taiwan classes.

Since Asian students spend so much of their time in whole-group work, we need to say a word about that format. Whole-class instruction in the United States has gotten a somewhat bad reputation. It has become associated with too much teacher talk and too many passive, tuned-out students. But as we will see in more detail as we continue our description of Asian classrooms, whole-class instruction in Japan and China is a very lively, engaging enterprise. Asian teachers do not spend large amounts of time lecturing. They present interesting problems; they pose provocative questions; they probe and guide. The students work hard, generating multiple approaches to a solution, explaining the rationale behind their methods, and making good use of wrong answers.

Handling Diversity

The organization of American elementary school classrooms is based on the assumption that whole-group instruction cannot accommodate students' diverse abilities and levels of achievement; thus, large amounts of whole-class time are given up so that the teacher can work individually with students. Asian educators are more comfortable in the belief that all children, with proper effort, can take advantage of a uniform educational experience, and so they are able to focus on providing the same high-quality experience to all students. Our results suggest that American educators need to question their long-held assumption that an individualized learning experience is inherently a higher-quality, more effective experience than is a whole-class learning experience. Although it may be true that an equal amount of time with a teacher may be more effective in a one-on-one situation than in a large-group situation, we must realize that the result of individualized instruction, given realistic financial constraints, is to drastically reduce the amount of teacher instruction every child receives.

How We Made Sure We Were Looking at Representative Schools

Frequent reports on television and in books and newspapers purport to depict what happens inside Japanese and Chinese classrooms. These reports usually are based on impressions gathered during brief visits to classrooms—most likely classrooms that the visitor's contacts in Asia have preselected. As a result, it is difficult to gauge the generality of what was seen and reported. Without observing large, representative samples of schools and teachers, it is impossible to characterize the teaching practices of any culture.

The descriptions that we present are based on two large observational studies of first-and fifth-grade classrooms that we conducted in Japan, Taiwan, China, and the United States. In contrast to informal observations, the strength of formal studies such as ours is that the observations are made according to consistent rules about where, when, and what to observe.

In the first study, our observers were in classrooms for a total of over four thousand hours—over a thousand class periods in 20 first- and fifth-grade classrooms in each of three cities: Sendai, Japan; Taipei, Taiwan; and Minneapolis, Minnesota.[1] Our second study took place in two hundred classrooms, forty each in Sendai and Taipei, plus forty in Beijing, China, and eighty in the Chicago metropolitan area of the United States.[2] Care was taken to choose schools that were representative. Our Chicago metropolitan area sample—the urban and suburban areas that make up Cook County—included schools that are predominantly white, black, Hispanic, and ethnically mixed; schools that draw from upper, middle, and lower socioeconomic groups; schools that are public and private; and schools that are urban and suburban.

Observers visited each classroom four times over a one-to two-week period, yielding a total of eight hundred hours of observations. The observers, who were residents of each city, wrote down as much as they could about what transpired during each mathematics class. Tape recordings made during the classes assisted the observers in filling in any missing information. These detailed narrative accounts of what transpired in the classrooms yielded even richer information than we obtained in the first study, where the observers followed predefined categories for coding behavior during the course of observations.

After the narrative records had been translated into English, we divided each observation into segments, which we defined as beginning each time there was a change in topic, materials, or activity. For example, a segment began when students put away their textbooks and began working on a worksheet or when the teacher stopped lecturing and asked some of the students to write their solutions to a problem on the blackboard.

Both studies focused on mathematics classes rather than on classes in subjects such as reading, where cultural differences in teaching practices may be more strongly determined by the content of what is being taught. For example, it is likely that the processes of teaching and learning about the multiplication of fractions transcend cultural differences, whereas teaching children how to read Chinese characters may require different approaches from those used to teach children to read an alphabetic language.

References

1. Stevenson, H. W., Stigler, J. W., Lucker, G. W., Lee, S. Y., Hsu, C. C., & Kitamura, S. (1987). Classroom behavior and achievement of Japanese, Chinese, and American children. In R. Glaser (Ed.), *Advances in instructional psychology*. Hillsdale NJ: Erlbaum.

2. Stigler, J. W., & Perry, M. (1990). Mathematics learning in Japanese, Chinese, and American classrooms. In Stigler, J. W., Shweder, R. A., & Herdt, G. (Eds.), *Cultural psychology: Essays on comparative human development*. Cambridge, Cambridge University Press. pp. 328–356.

Japanese and Chinese teachers recognize individual differences among students, but they handle that diversity in a very different way. First, as we will see in more detail later, they have much greater amounts of nonteaching time than do American teachers, and part of that time is available for working with individual students. They may spend extra time with slower students or ask faster students to assist them, but they focus their lesson on teaching all children regardless of apparent differences in ability or developmental readiness. Before we discuss how they do that in a whole-group setting, we need to first address the question of whether American classrooms are more diverse than Asian ones, thus potentially rendering whole-class instruction more difficult.

Whenever we discuss our research on teaching practices, someone in the audience inevitably reminds us that Japan and China are nations with relatively homogeneous populations while the United States is the melting pot of the world. How could we expect that practices used in Asian societies could possibly be relevant for the American context, where diversity is the rule in race, ethnicity, language, and social class?

What impedes teaching is the uneven preparation of children for the academic tasks that must be accomplished. It is diversity in children's educational backgrounds, not in their social and cultural backgrounds, that poses the greatest problems in teaching. Although the United States is culturally more diverse than Japan or China, we have found no more diversity at the classroom level in the educational level of American than of Asian students. The key factor is that, in the United States, educational and cultural diversity are positively related, leading some persons to the inappropriate conclusion that it is ethnic and cultural diversity, rather than educational diversity, that leads to the difficulties faced by American teachers.

It is true, for example, that there is greater variability in mathematics achievement among American than among Japanese children, but this does not mean that the differences are evident in any particular classroom. Variability in the United States exists to a large extent across neighborhoods and schools (rather than within them). Within individual classrooms, the variability in levels of academic achievement differs little between the United States and Japan, Taiwan, or China. It is wrong to argue that diversity within classrooms is an American problem. Teachers everywhere must deal with students who vary in their knowledge and motivation.

Tracking does not exist in Asian elementary schools. Children are never separated into different classrooms according to their presumed levels of intellectual ability. This egalitarian philosophy carries over to organization within the classroom. Children are not separated into reading groups according to their ability; there is no division of the class into groups differentiated by the rate at which they proceed through their mathematics books. No children leave the classroom for special classes, such as those designed for children who have been diagnosed as having learning disabilities.

How do teachers in Asian classrooms handle diversity in students' knowledge and skills? For one thing, they typically use a variety of approaches in their teaching, allowing students who may not understand one approach the opportunity to experience other approaches to presenting the material. Periods of recitation are alternated with periods in which children work for short periods on practice problems. Explanations by the teacher are interspersed with periods in which children work with concrete materials or struggle to come up with their own solutions to problems. There is continuous change from one mode of presentation, one type of representation, and one type of teaching method to another.

Asian teaching practices thrive in the face of diversity, and some practices can depend on diversity for their effectiveness. Asking students to suggest alternative solutions to a problem, for example, works best when students have had experience in generating a variety of solutions. Incorrect solutions, which are typically dismissed by the American teacher, become topics for discussion in Asian classrooms, and all students can learn from this discussion. Thus, while American schools attempt to solve the problems of diversity by segregating children into different groups or different classrooms, and by spending large amounts of regular class time working with individual students, Asian teachers believe that the only way they can cope with the problem is by devising teaching techniques that accommodate the different interests and backgrounds of the children in their classrooms.

Asian teachers also exploit the fact that the same instruction can affect different students in different ways, something that may be overlooked by American teachers. In this sense, Asian teachers subscribe to what would be considered in the West to be a "constructivist" view of learning. According to this view, knowledge is regarded as something that must be constructed by the child rather than as a set of facts and skills that can be imparted by the teacher. Because children are engaged in their own construction of knowledge, some of the major tasks for the teacher are to pose provocative questions, to allow adequate time for reflection, and to vary teaching techniques so that they are responsive to differences in students' prior experience. Through such practices, Asian teachers are able to accommodate individual differences in learning, even though instruction is not tailored to each student.

Use of Real-World Problems and Objects

Elementary school mathematics is often defined in terms of mathematical symbols and their manipulation; for example, children must learn the place-value system of numeration and the operations for manipulating numerals to add, subtract, multiply, and divide. In addition, children must be able to apply these symbols and operations to solving problems. In order to accomplish these goals, teachers rely primarily on two powerful tools for representing mathematics: language and the manipulation of concrete objects. How effectively teachers use these forms of representation plays a critical role in determining how well children will understand mathematics.

One common function of language is in defining terms and stating rules for performing mathematical operations. A second, broader function is the use of language as a means of connecting mathematical operations to the real world and of integrating what children know about mathematics. We find that American elementary school teachers are more prone to use language to define terms and state rules than are Asian teachers, who, in their efforts to make mathematics meaningful, use language to clarify different aspects of mathematics and to integrate what children know about mathematics with the demands of real-world problems. Here is an example of what we mean by a class in which the teacher defines terms and states rules:

An American teacher announces that the lesson today concerns fractions. Fractions are defined and she names the numerator and denominator. "What do we call this?" she then asks. "And this?" After assuring herself that the children understand the meaning of the terms, she spends the rest of the lesson teaching them to apply the rules for forming fractions.

Asian teachers tend to reverse the procedure. They focus initially on interpreting and relating a real-world problem to the quantification that is necessary for a mathematical solution and then to define terms and state rules. In the following example, a third-grade teacher in Japan was also teaching a lesson that introduced the notation system for fractions.

The lesson began with the teacher posing the question of how many liters of juice (colored water) were contained in a large beaker. "More than one liter," answered one child. "One and a half liters," answered another. After several children had made guesses, the teacher suggested that they pour the juice into some one-liter beakers and see. Horizontal lines on each beaker divided it into thirds. The juice filled one beaker and part of a second. The teacher pointed out that the water came up to the first line on the second beaker—only one of the three parts was full. The procedure was repeated with a second set of beakers to illustrate the concept of one-half. After stating that there had been one and one-out-of-three liters of juice in the first big beaker and one and one-out-of-two liters in the second, the teacher wrote the fractions on the board. He continued the lesson by asking the children how to represent two parts out of three, two parts out of five, and so forth. Near the end of the period he mentioned the term "fraction" for the first time and attached names to the numerator and the denominator.

He ended the lesson by summarizing how fractions can be used to represent the parts of a whole.

In the second example, the concept of fractions emerged from a meaningful experience; in the first, it was introduced initially as an abstract concept. The terms and operations in the second example flowed naturally from the teacher's questions and discussion; in the first, language was used primarily for defining and summarizing rules. Mathematics ultimately requires abstract representation, but young children understand such representation more readily if it is derived from meaningful experience than if it results from learning definitions and rules.

Asian teachers generally are more likely than American teachers to engage their students, even very young ones, in the discussion of mathematical concepts. The kind of verbal discussion we find in American classrooms is more short-answer in nature, oriented, for example, toward clarifying the correct way to implement a computational procedure.

Teachers ask questions for different reasons in the United States and in Japan. In the United States, the purpose of a question is to get an answer. In Japan, teachers pose questions to stimulate thought. A Japanese teacher considers a question to be a poor one if it elicits an immediate answer, for this indicates that students were not challenged to think. One teacher we interviewed told us of discussions she had with her fellow teachers on how to improve teaching practices. "What do you talk about?" we wondered. "A great deal of time," she reported, "is spent talking about questions we can pose to the class—which wordings work best to get students involved in thinking and discussing the material. One good question can keep a whole class going for a long time; a bad one produces little more than a simple answer."

In one memorable example recorded by our observers, a Japanese first-grade teacher began her class by posing the question to one of her students: "Would you explain the difference between what we learned in yesterday's lesson and what you came across in preparing for today's lesson?" The young student thought for a long time, but then answered the question intelligently, a performance that undoubtedly enhanced his understanding of both lessons.

Concrete Representations

Every elementary school student in Sendai possesses a "Math Set," a box of colorful, well-designed materials for teaching mathematical concepts: tiles, clock, ruler, checkerboard, colored triangles, beads, and many other attractive objects.

In Taipei, every classroom is equipped with a similar, but larger, set of such objects. In Beijing, where there is much less money available for purchasing such materials, teachers improvise with colored paper, wax fruit, plates, and other easily obtained objects. In all cases, these concrete objects are considered to be critically important tools for teaching mathematics, for it is through manipulating these objects that children can form important links between real-world problems and abstract mathematical notations.

American teachers are much less likely than Chinese or Japanese teachers to use concrete objects. At fifth grade, for example, Sendai teachers were nearly twice as likely to use concrete objects as the Chicago area teachers, and Taipei teachers were nearly five times as likely. There was also a subtle, but important, difference in the way Asian and American teachers used concrete objects. Japanese teachers, for example, use the items in the Math Set throughout the elementary school years and introduced small tiles in a high percentage of the lessons we observed in the first grade. American teachers seek variety and may use Popsicle sticks in one lesson, and in another, marbles, Cheerios, M&Ms, checkers, poker chips, or plastic animals. The American view is that objects should be varied in order to maintain children's interest. The Asian view is that using a variety of representational materials may confuse children, and thereby make it more difficult for them to use the objects for the representation and solution of mathematics problems. Having learned to add with tiles makes multiplication easier to understand when the same tiles are used.

Through the skillful use of concrete objects, teachers are able to teach elementary school children to understand and solve problems that are not introduced in American curricula until much later. An example occurred in a fourth-grade mathematics lesson we observed in Japan. The problem the teacher posed is a difficult one for fourth graders, and its solution is generally not taught in the United States until much later. This is the problem:

> There are a total of thirty-eight children in Akira's class. There are six more boys than there are girls. How many boys and how many girls are in the class?

This lesson began with a discussion of the problem and with the children proposing ways to solve it. After the discussion, the teacher handed each child two strips of paper, one six units longer than the other, and told the class that the strips would be used to help them think about the problem. One slip represented the number of girls in the class and the other represented the number of boys. By lining the strips next to each other, the children could see that the degree to which the longer one protruded beyond the shorter one represented 6 boys. The procedure for solving the problem then unfolded as the teacher, through skillful questioning, led the children to the solution: The number of girls was found by taking the total of both strips, subtracting 6 to make the strips of equal length, and then dividing by 2. The number of boys could be found, of course, by adding 6 to the number of girls. With this concrete visual representation of the problem and careful guidance from the teacher, even fourth graders were able to understand the problem and its solution.

Students Construct Multiple Solutions

A common Western stereotype is that the Asian teacher is an authoritarian purveyor of information, one who expects students to listen and memorize correct answers or correct procedures rather than to construct knowledge themselves. This may or may not be an accurate description of Asian high school teachers,[4] but, as we have seen in previous examples, it does not describe the dozens of elementary school teachers that we have observed.

Chinese and Japanese teachers rely on students to generate ideas and evaluate the correctness of the ideas. The possibility that they will be called upon to state their own solution as well as to evaluate what another student has proposed keeps Asian students alert, but this technique has two other important functions. First, it engages students in the lesson, increasing their motivation by making them feel they are participants in a group process. Second, it conveys a more realistic impression of how knowledge is acquired. Mathematics, for example, is a body of knowledge that has evolved gradually through a process of argument and proof. Learning to argue about mathematical ideas is fundamental to understanding mathematics. Chinese and Japanese children begin learning these skills in the first grade; many American elementary school students are never exposed to them.

We can illustrate the way Asian teachers use students' ideas with the following example. A fifth-grade teacher in Taiwan began her mathematics lesson by calling attention to a six-sided figure she had drawn on the blackboard. She asked the students how they might go about finding the area of the shaded region. "I don't want you to tell me what the actual area is, just tell me the approach you would use to solve the problem. Think of as many different ways as you can of ways you could determine the area that I have drawn in yellow chalk." She allowed the students several minutes to work in small groups and then called upon a child from each group to describe the group's solution. After each proposal, many of which were quite complex, the teacher asked members of the other groups whether the procedure described could yield a correct answer. After several different procedures had been suggested, the teacher moved on to a second problem with a different embedded figure and repeated the process. Neither teacher nor students actually carried out a solution to the problem until all of the alternative solutions had been discussed. The lesson ended with the teacher affirming the importance of coming up with multiple solutions. "After all," she said, "we face many problems every day in the real world. We have to remember that there is not only one way we can solve each problem."

American teachers are less likely to give students opportunities to respond at such length. Although a great deal of interaction appears to occur in American classrooms—with teachers and students posing questions and giving answers—American teachers generally pose questions that are answerable with a yes or no or with a short phrase. They seek a correct answer and continue calling on students until one produces it. "Since we can't subtract 8 from 6," says an American teacher, "we have to . . . what?" Hands go up, the teacher calls on a girl who says "Borrow." "Correct," the teacher replies. This kind of interchange does not establish the student as a valid source of information, for the final arbiter of the correctness of the student's opinions is still the teacher. The situation is very different in Asian classrooms, where children are likely to be asked to explain their answers and other children are then called upon to evaluate their correctness.

Clear evidence of these differing beliefs about the roles of students and teachers appears in the observations of how teachers evaluate students' responses. The most frequent form of evaluation used by American teachers was praise, a technique that was rarely used in either Taiwan or Japan. In Japan, evaluation most frequently took the form of a discussion of children's errors.

Praise serves to cut off discussion and to highlight the teacher's role as the authority. It also encourages children to be satisfied with their performance rather than informing them about where they need improvement. Discussing errors, on the other hand, encourages argument and justification and involves students in the exciting quest of assessing the strengths and weaknesses of the various alternative solutions that have been proposed.

Why are American teachers often reluctant to encourage students to participate at greater length during mathematics lessons? One possibility is that they feel insecure about the depth of their own mathematical training. Placing more emphasis on students' explanations necessarily requires teachers to relinquish some control over the direction the lesson will take. This can be a frightening prospect to a teacher who is unprepared to evaluate the validity of novel ideas that students inevitably propose.

Using Errors Effectively

We have been struck by the different reactions of Asian and American teachers to children's errors. For Americans, errors tend to be interpreted as an indication of failure in learning the lesson. For Chinese and Japanese, they are an index of what still needs to be learned. These divergent interpretations result in very different reactions to the display of errors—embarrassment on the part of the American children, calm acceptance by Asian children. They also result in differences in the manner in which teachers utilize errors as effective means of instruction.

We visited a fifth-grade classroom in Japan the first day the teacher introduced the problem of adding fractions with unequal denominators. The problem was a simple one: adding one-third and one-half. The children were told to solve the problem and that the class would then review the different solutions.

After everyone appeared to have completed the task, the teacher called on one of the students to give his answer and to explain his solution. "The answer is two-fifths," he stated. Pointing first to the numerators and then to the denominators, he explained: "One plus one is two; three plus two is five. The answer is two-fifths." Without comment, the teacher asked another boy for his solution. "Two point one plus three point one, when changed into a fraction adds up to two-fifths." The children in the classroom looked puzzled. The teacher, unperturbed, asked a third student for her solution. "The answer is five-sixths." The student went on to explain how she had found the common denominator, changed the fractions so that each had this denominator, and then added them.

The teacher returned to the first solution. "How many of you think this solution is correct?" Most agreed that it was not. She used the opportunity to direct the children's attention to reasons why the solution was incorrect. "Which is larger, two-fifths or one-half?" The class agreed that it was one-half. "It is strange, isn't it, that you could add a number to one-half and get a number that is smaller than one-half." She went on to explain how the procedure the child used would result in the odd situation where, when one-half was added to one-half, the answer yielded is one-half. In a similarly careful, interactive manner, she discussed how the second boy had confused fractions with decimals to come up with his surprising answer.

Rather than ignoring the incorrect solutions and concentrating her attention on the correct solution, the teacher capitalized on the errors the children made in order to dispel two common misperceptions about fractions.

We have not observed American teachers responding to children's errors so inventively. Perhaps because of the strong influence of behavioristic teaching that conditions should be arranged so that the learner avoids errors and makes only a reinforceable response, American teachers place little emphasis on the constructive use of errors as a teaching technique. It seems likely, however, that learning about what is wrong may hasten children's understanding of why the correct procedures are appropriate.

Why Not Here?

Few who have visited urban classrooms in Asia would disagree that the great majority of Chinese and Japanese teachers are highly skilled professionals. Their dedication is legendary; what is often not appreciated is how thoughtfully and adroitly they guide children through the vast amount of material that they must master during the six years of elementary school. We, of course, witnessed examples of excellent lessons in American classrooms. And there are of course individual differences among Asian teachers. But what has impressed us in our personal observations and in the data from our observational studies is how remarkably well most Asian teachers teach. It is the *widespread* excellence of Asian class lessons, the high level of performance of the *average* teacher, that is so stunning.

The techniques used by Chinese and Japanese teachers are not new to the teaching profession—nor are they foreign or exotic. In fact, they are the types of techniques often recommended by American educators. What the Japanese and Chinese examples demonstrate so compellingly is that when widely implemented, such practices can produce extraordinary outcomes.

Unfortunately, these techniques have not been broadly applied in the United States. Why? One reason, as we have discussed, is the Asian belief that the whole-group lesson, if done well, can be made to work for every child. With that assumption, Asian teachers can focus on the perfection of that lesson. However, even if American educators shared that belief, it would be difficult for them to achieve anything near the broad-based high quality that we observed in Asian classrooms. This is not the fault of American teachers. The fault lies with a system that prepares them inadequately and then exhausts them physically, emotionally, and intellectually while denying them the collegial interaction that every profession relies upon for the growth and refinement of its knowledge base.

The first major obstacle to the widespread development and execution of excellent lessons in America is the fact that American teachers are overworked. It is inconceivable that American teachers, by themselves, would be able to organize lively, vivid, coherent lessons under a regimen that requires that they teach hour after hour every day throughout the school year. Preparing lessons that require the discovery of knowledge and the construction of understanding takes time. Teaching them effectively requires energy. Both are in very short supply for most American teachers.

Being an elementary school teacher in the United States at the end of the twentieth century is extraordinarily difficult, and the demands made by American society exhaust even the most energetic among them. "I'm dancing as fast as I can," one teacher summarized her feelings about her job, "but with all the things that I'm supposed to do, I just can't keep up."

The full realization of how little time American teachers have when they are not directly in charge of children became clear to us during a meeting in Beijing. We were discussing the teachers' workday. When we informed the Chinese teachers that American teachers are responsible for their classes all day long, with only an hour or less outside the classroom each day, they looked incredulous. How could any teacher be expected to do a good job when there is no time outside of class to prepare and correct lessons, work with individual children, consult with other teachers, and attend to all of the matters that arise in a typical day at school! Beijing teachers teach no more than three hours a day, unless the teacher is a homeroom teacher, in which case, the total is four hours. During the first three grades, the teaching assignment includes both reading and mathematics; for the upper three grades of elementary school, teachers specialize in one of these subjects. They spend the rest of their day at school carrying out all of their other responsibilities to their students and to the school. The situation is similar in Japan. According to our estimate, Japanese elementary school teachers are in charge of classes only 60 percent of the time they are at school.

The large amounts of nonteaching time at school are available to Asian teachers because of two factors. The first concerns the number of teachers typically assigned to Asian schools. Although class sizes are considerably larger in Asia, the student-to-teacher ratio within a school does not differ greatly from that in the United States. By having more students in each class and the same number of teachers in the school, all teachers can have fewer teaching hours. Time is freed up for teachers to meet and work together on a daily basis, to prepare lessons for the next day, to work with individual children, and to attend staff meetings.

The second factor increasing the time available to Japanese and Chinese teachers at school is that they spend more hours at school each day than do American teachers. In our study, for example, teachers in Sendai and Taipei spent an average of 9.5 and 9.1 hours per day, respectively, compared to only 7.3 hours for the American teachers. Asian teachers arrive at school early and stay late, which gives them time to meet together and to work with children who need extra help. Most American teachers, in contrast, arrive at school shortly before classes begin and leave not long after they end. This does not mean a shorter work week for American teachers. What it does mean is that they must devote their evenings to working alone on the next day's lessons, further increasing their sense of isolation.

Learning from Each Other

The second reason Asian classes are so well crafted is that there is a very systematic effort to pass on the accumulated wisdom of teaching practice to each new generation of teachers and to keep perfecting that practice by providing teachers the opportunities to continually learn from each other.

Americans often act as if good teachers are born, not made. We hear this from both teachers and parents. They seem to believe that good teaching happens if the teacher has a knack with children, gets along well with them, and keeps them reasonably attentive and enthusiastic about learning. It is a commonly accepted truism in many colleges of education that teaching is an art and that students cannot be taught how to teach.

Perhaps because of this belief, students emerge from American colleges of education with little training in how to design and teach effective lessons. It is assumed that teachers will discover this for themselves. Courses in teaching methods are designed to serve a different purpose. On the one hand, they present theories of learning and cognitive development. Although the students are able to quote the major tenets of the theorists currently in vogue, the theories remain as broad generalizations that are difficult to apply to the everyday tasks that they will face as classroom teachers. At the opposite extreme, these methods courses provide education students with lists of specific suggestions for activities and materials that are easy to use and that children should enjoy (for example, pieces of breakfast cereal make handy counters for teaching basic number facts). Teachers are faced, therefore, with information that is either too general to be applied readily or so specific that it has only limited usefulness. Because of this, American teachers complain that most of what they know had to be learned by themselves, alone, on the job.

In Asia, graduates of teacher training programs are still considered to be novices who need the guidance and support of their experienced colleagues. In the United States, training comes to a near halt after the teachers acquire their teaching certificates. American teachers may take additional coursework in the evenings or during summer vacations, or they may attend district or citywide workshops from time to time. But these opportunities are not considered to be an essential part of the American system of teacher training.

In Japan, the system of teacher training is much like an apprenticeship under the guidance of experienced colleagues. The teacher's first year of employment marks the beginning of a lengthy and elaborate training process. By Japanese law, beginning teachers must receive a minimum of twenty days of inservice training during their first year on the job.[5] Supervising the inservice training are master teachers, selected for their teaching ability and their willingness to assist their young colleagues. During one-year leaves of absence from their own classrooms, they observe the beginner in the classroom and offer suggestions for improvement.

In addition to this early tutelage in teaching techniques, Japanese teachers, beginners as well as seasoned teachers, are required to continually perfect their teaching skills through interaction with other teachers. One mechanism is through meetings organized by the vice principal and head teachers of their own school. These experienced professionals assume responsibility for advising and guiding their young colleagues. The head teachers organize meetings to discuss teaching techniques and to devise lesson plans and handouts. These meetings are supplemented by informal districtwide study groups and courses at municipal or prefectural education centers.[6]

A glimpse at what takes place in these study groups is provided in a conversation we recently had with a Japanese teacher. She and her colleagues spend a good deal of their time together working on lesson plans. After they finish a plan, one teacher from the group teaches the lesson to her students while the other teachers look on. Afterward, the group meets again to criticize the teacher's performance and to make suggestions for how the lesson could be improved. In her school, there is an annual "teaching fair." Teachers from other schools are invited to visit the school and observe the lessons being taught. The visitors rate the lessons, and the teacher with the best lesson is declared the winner.

In addition, national television in Japan presents programs that show how master teachers handle particular lessons or concepts. In Taiwan, such demonstrations are available on sets of videotapes that cover the whole curriculum.

Making use of lessons that have been honed over time does not mean that the Asian teacher simply mimics what she sees. As with great actors or musicians, the substance of the curriculum becomes the script or the score; the goal is to perform the role or piece as effectively and creatively as possible. Rather than executing the curriculum as a mere routine, the skilled teacher strives to perfect the presentation of each lesson. She uses the teaching techniques she has learned and imposes her own interpretation on these techniques in a manner that she thinks will interest and motivate her pupils.

Of course, teachers find it easier to share helpful tips and techniques among themselves when they are all teaching the same lesson at about the same time. The fact that Taiwan, Japan, and China each has a national curriculum that provides a common focus is a significant factor in teacher interaction. Not only do we have no national curriculum in the United States, but the curriculum may not be consistent within a city or even within a single school. American textbooks, with a spiral curriculum that repeats topics year after year and with a profusion of material about each topic, force teachers to omit some of each year's material. Even when teachers use the same textbook, their classes differ according to which topics they choose to skip and in the pace with which they proceed through the text. As a result, American teachers have less incentive than Asian teachers to share experiences with each other or to benefit from the successes and failures that others have had in teaching particular lessons.

Adding further to the sense of isolation is the fact that American teachers, unlike other professionals, do not share a common body of knowledge and experience. The courses offered at different universities and colleges vary, and even among their required courses, there is often little common content from college to college. Student teaching, the only other activity in which all budding teachers participate, is a solitary endeavor shared only with the regular classroom teacher and perhaps a few fellow student teachers.

Opportunities for Asian teachers to learn from each other are influenced, in part, by the physical arrangements of the schools. In Japanese and Chinese schools, a large room in each school is designed as a teachers' room, and each teacher is assigned a desk in this room. It is here that they spend their time away from the classroom preparing lessons, correcting students' papers, and discussing teaching techniques. American teachers, isolated in their own classrooms, find it much harder to discuss their work with colleagues. Their desk and teaching materials are in their own classrooms, and the only common space available to teachers is usually a cramped room that often houses supplies and the school's duplicating facilities, along with a few chairs and a coffee machine. Rarely do teachers have enough time in their visits to this room to engage in serious discussions of educational policy or teaching practices.

Critics argue that the problems facing the American teacher are unique and that it is futile to consider what Japanese and Chinese teaching are like in seeking solutions to educational problems in the United States. One of the frequent arguments is that the students in the typical Asian classroom share a common language and culture, are well disciplined and attentive, and are not distracted by family crises and their own personal problems, whereas the typical American teacher is often faced with a diverse, burdened, distracted group of students. To be sure, the conditions encountered by teachers differ greatly among these societies. Week after week, American teachers must cope with children who present them with complex, wrenching personal problems. But much of what gives American classrooms their aura of disarray and disorganization may be traced to how schools are organized and teachers are trained as well as to characteristics of the children.

It is easy to blame teachers for the problems confronting American education, and this is something that the American public is prone to do. The accusation is unfair. We cannot blame teachers when we deprive them of adequate training and yet expect that on their own they will become innovative teachers; when we cast them in the roles of surrogate parents, counselors, and psychotherapists and still expect them to be effective teachers; and when we keep them so busy in the classroom that they have little time or opportunity for professional development once they have joined the ranks of the teaching profession.

Surely the most immediate and pressing task in educating young students is to create a new type of school environment, one where great lessons are a commonplace occurrence. In order to do this, we must ask how we can institute reforms that will make it possible for American teachers to practice their profession under conditions that are as favorable for their own professional development and for the education of children as those that exist in Asia.

REFERENCES

1. The superior academic achievement of Chinese and Japanese children sometimes leads to speculation that they are brighter than American children. This possibility has been supported in a few reports that have received attention in the popular press and in several scientific journals. What has not been reported or widely understood is that, without exception, the studies contending that differences in intelligence are responsible for differences in academic performance have failed to

meet acceptable standards of scientific inquiry. In fact, studies that have reported differences in I.Q. scores between Asian and American children have been flawed conceptually and methodologically. Their major defects are nonequivalent tests used in the different locations and noncomparable samples of children. To determine the cognitive abilities of children in the three cultures, we needed tests that were linguistically comparable and culturally unbiased. These requirements preclude reliance on tests translated from one language to another or the evaluation of children in one country on the basis of norms obtained in another country. We assembled a team with members from each of the three cultures, and they developed ten cognitive tasks falling into traditional "verbal" and "performance" categories. The test results revealed no evidence of overall differences in the cognitive functioning of American, Chinese, and Japanese children. There was no tendency for children from any of the three cultures to achieve significantly higher average scores on all the tasks. Children in each culture had strengths and weaknesses, but by the fifth grade of elementary school, the most notable feature of children's cognitive performance was the similarity in level and variability of their scores. [Stevenson, H. W.,

Stigler, J. W., Lee, S. Y., Lucker, G. W., Kitamura, S., & Hsu, C. C. (1985). Cognitive performance and academic achievement of Japanese, Chinese, and American children. *Child Development*, 56, 718–734.]

2. Stevenson, H. W. (1990). Adapting to school: Children in Beijing and Chicago. *Annual Report*. Stanford CA: Center for Advanced Study in the Behavioral Sciences. Stevenson, H. W., Lee, S., Chen, C., Lummis, M., Stigler, J., Fan, L., & Ge, F. (1990). Mathematics achievement of children in China and the United States. *Child Development*, 61, 1053–1066. Stevenson, H. W., Stigler, J. W., & Lee, S.Y (1986). Mathematics achievement of Chinese, Japanese, and American children. *Science*, 231, 693–699. Stigler, J. W., Lee, S. Y., & Stevenson, H. W. (1990). *Mathematical knowledge*. Reston, VA: National Council of Teachers of Mathematics.

3. Stevenson, H. W., Lee, S. Y., Chen C., Stigler, J. W., Hsu, C. C., & Kitamura, S. (1990). Contexts of achievement. *Monographs of the Society for Research in Child Development*. Serial No. 221, 55, Nos. 1–2.

4. Rohlen, T. P. (1983). *Japan's High Schools*. Berkeley: University of California Press.

5. Dorfman, C. H. (Ed.) (1987). *Japanese Education Today*. Washington, D.C.: U.S. Department of Education.

6. Ibid.

Questions

1. Why do Stigler and Stevenson begin this article by pointing out that there are no overall differences in intelligence between U.S. children and their Asian counterparts?
2. What are three classroom practices that are different in the United States, Japan, and China, and how do these practices affect what children learn about mathematics in school?
3. How is instructional time eroded in U.S. classrooms? What can be done to change this pattern?
4. Stigler and Stevenson found that the use of real-world problems and objects helps children learn mathematics better than more abstract references. What do you think is the explanation for this difference?
5. How do differences in cultural values in these countries lead to different interpretations and different uses of children's errors in the classroom for instructional purposes?
6. Which aspects of teacher training and support in the United States would need to be changed to enable teachers to use the techniques practiced by teachers in China and Japan?

PART V

Adolescence

Adolescence is a time of life that is difficult to define. In many ways, it is a cultural construction. That is, whether adolescence is considered a unique stage depends on the culture in which a child lives. The duration of adolescence also varies across cultures. In Western communities, adolescence is a fairly long period, ranging from about age 11 to the end of the teen years, and sometimes stretching into the early twenties for youth who are still dependent on their parents. In many non-Western communities, adolescence is fairly short and usually ends at puberty with an abrupt transition to adult marital or work responsibilities.

The general tenor of research on adolescents for a long time was problem-focused, seeing adolescence as a time of much conflict and difficulty. The articles in this section, however, address the issue in a variety of ways, exhibiting the topical range now seen in research on adolescents. Laurence Steinberg reexamines the question of whether adolescents are more likely to take risks than adults are. Michelle Wierson, Patricia J. Long, and Rex L. Forehand investigate assumptions about biological change in adolescence, specifically whether social experiences can influence the timing of puberty. Mark S. Chapell and Willis F. Overton focus on cognitive development in African-American youth, with particular attention to social class and ethnic identity. The article by Wenxin Zhang and Andrew J. Fuligni concentrates on the parent-adolescent relationship by focusing on the development of adolescent autonomy in the context of recent social and economic changes in China. Thomas J. Dishion, David W. Andrews, and Lynn Crosby explore the origins of adolescent delinquency by looking closely at the friendships of antisocial boys. Finally, Kate C. McLean and Avril Thorne examine how memories of relationships with parents and peers influence the development of identity in late adolescence.

All of these articles make it clear that adolescence is a time of rapid physical, cognitive, and emotional change, and those changes are greatly influenced by the social and cultural context. Society's expectations of its members who are just on the verge of maturity reflect cultural values and goals, which are evident in the relationships and experiences that adolescents have throughout this period of growth.

31 Risk Taking in Adolescence: New Perspectives From Brain and Behavioral Science

Laurence Steinberg

Do adolescents take more unhealthy risks than adults? Most people think that they do and, as a result, many efforts are taken by families, schools, and even society at large to protect adolescents from harm. These efforts are often worthwhile and they have, undoubtedly, saved many lives. But connections between preventive or cautionary efforts and adolescent safety do not, in and of themselves, explain why adolescents would be at any greater risk than adults. After all, adolescents have many of the complex reasoning skills that adults use when they engage in situations that present risks. Perhaps adolescents' inexperience in these situations or with using their newly developed cognitive skills explains this difference. Or perhaps adolescents deploy these skills differently than adults do when they are in potentially dangerous situations.

In the following article, Laurence Steinberg explores this topic from two vantage points: developmental neuroscience and psychosocial development. Steinberg explains that despite the fact that adolescents have developed impressive, adult-like, cognitive skills by age 15 or so, other aspects of brain development that contribute to decision making, such as impulse control, are still in the process of maturing. This situation results in adolescent decision-making that is quite different from that of adults, putting adolescents at risk despite having advanced cognitive skills. Research in psychosocial development adds other insight into adolescent risk by showing that peers have enormous influence on adolescent behavior, including risk taking.

The research described in this article has made a significant difference in our understanding and appreciation of the complexities that adolescents face as they learn to function in and enjoy the world of maturity that awaits them. In addition, it offers important ideas for policy and prevention, which may, in turn, lead to better and healthier lives for all adolescents.

Trying to understand why adolescents and young adults take more risks than younger or older individuals do has challenged psychologists for decades. Adolescents' inclination to engage in risky behavior does not appear to be due to irrationality, delusions of invulnerability, or ignorance. This paper presents a perspective on adolescent risk taking grounded in developmental neuroscience. According to this view, the temporal gap between puberty, which impels adolescents toward thrill seeking, and the slow maturation of the cognitive-control system, which regulates these impulses, makes adolescence a time of heightened vulnerability for risky behavior. This view of adolescent risk taking helps to explain why educational interventions designed to change adolescents' knowledge, beliefs, or attitudes have been largely ineffective, and suggests that changing the contexts in which risky behavior occurs may be more successful than changing the way adolescents think about risk.

Adolescents and college-age individuals take more risks than children or adults do, as indicated by statistics on automobile crashes, binge drinking, contraceptive use, and crime; but trying to understand why risk taking is more common during adolescence than during other periods of development has challenged psychologists for decades (Steinberg, 2004). Numerous theories to account for adolescents' greater involve-

Reprinted with permission from Steinberg, L., "Risk taking in adolescence: New perspectives from brain and behavioral science", *Current Directions in Psychological Science, 16,* 55–59, © 2007 Blackwell Publishers.

ment in risky behavior have been advanced, but few have withstood empirical scrutiny (but see Reyna & Farley, 2006, for a discussion of some promising approaches).

False Leads in Risk-Taking Research

Systematic research does not support the stereotype of adolescents as irrational individuals who believe they are invulnerable and who are unaware, inattentive to, or unconcerned about the potential harms of risky behavior. In fact, the logical-reasoning abilities of 15-year-olds are comparable to those of adults, adolescents are no worse than adults at perceiving risk or estimating their vulnerability to it (Reyna & Farley, 2006), and increasing the salience of the risks associated with making a potentially dangerous decision has comparable effects on adolescents and adults (Millstein & Halpern-Felsher, 2002). Most studies find few age differences in individuals' evaluations of the risks inherent in a wide range of dangerous behaviors, in judgments about the seriousness of the consequences that might result from risky behavior, or in the ways that the relative costs and benefits of risky activities are evaluated (Beyth-Marom, Austin, Fischoff, Palmgren, & Jacobs-Quadrel, 1993).

Because adolescents and adults reason about risk in similar ways, many researchers have posited that age differences in actual risk taking are due to differences in the information that adolescents and adults use when making decisions. Attempts to reduce adolescent risk taking through interventions designed to alter knowledge, attitudes, or beliefs have proven remarkably disappointing, however (Steinberg, 2004). Efforts to provide adolescents with information about the risks of substance use, reckless driving, and unprotected sex typically result in improvements in young people's thinking about these phenomena but seldom change their actual behavior. Generally speaking, reductions in adolescents' health-compromising behavior are more strongly linked to changes in the contexts in which those risks are taken (e.g., increases in the price of cigarettes, enforcement of graduated licensing programs, more vigorously implemented policies to interdict drugs, or condom distribution programs) than to changes in what adolescents know or believe.

The failure to account for age differences in risk taking through studies of reasoning and knowledge stymied researchers for some time. Health educators, however, have been undaunted, and they have continued to design and offer interventions of unproven effectiveness, such as Drug Abuse Resistance Education (DARE), driver's education, or abstinence-only sex education.

A New Perspective on Risk Taking

In recent years, owing to advances in the developmental neuroscience of adolescence and the recognition that the conventional decision-making framework may not be the best way to think about adolescent risk taking, a new perspective on the subject has emerged (Steinberg, 2004). This new view begins from the premise that risk taking in the real world is the product of both logical reasoning and psychosocial factors. However, unlike logical-reasoning abilities, which appear to be more or less fully developed by age 15, psychosocial capacities that improve decision making and moderate risk taking—such as impulse control, emotion regulation, delay of gratification, and resistance to peer influence—continue to mature well into young adulthood (Steinberg, 2004; see Fig. 1). Accordingly, psychosocial immaturity in these respects during adolescence may undermine what otherwise might be competent decision making. The conclusion drawn by many researchers, that adolescents are as competent decision makers as adults are, may hold true only under conditions where the influence of psychosocial factors is minimized.

Evidence From Developmental Neuroscience

Advances in developmental neuroscience provide support for this new way of thinking about adolescent

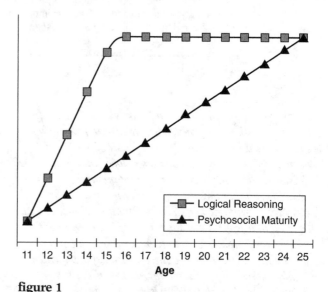

figure 1

Hypothetical graph of development of logical reasoning abilities versus psychosocial maturation. Although logical reasoning abilities reach adult levels by age 16, psychosocial capacities, such as impulse control, future orientation, or resistance to peer influence, continue to develop into young adulthood.

decision making. It appears that heightened risk taking in adolescence is the product of the interaction between two brain networks. The first is a socioemotional network that is especially sensitive to social and emotional stimuli, that is particularly important for reward processing, and that is remodeled in early adolescence by the hormonal changes of puberty. It is localized in limbic and paralimbic areas of the brain, an interior region that includes the amygdala, ventral striatum, orbitofrontal cortex, medial prefrontal cortex, and superior temporal sulcus. The second network is a cognitive-control network that subserves executive functions such as planning, thinking ahead, and self-regulation, and that matures gradually over the course of adolescence and young adulthood largely independently of puberty (Steinberg, 2004). The cognitive-control network mainly consists of outer regions of the brain, including the lateral prefrontal and parietal cortices and those parts of the anterior cingulate cortex to which they are connected.

In many respects, risk taking is the product of a competition between the socioemotional and cognitive-control networks (Drevets & Raichle, 1998), and adolescence is a period in which the former abruptly becomes more assertive (i.e., at puberty) while the latter gains strength only gradually, over a longer period of time. The socioemotional network is not in a state of constantly high activation during adolescence, though. Indeed, when the socioemotional network is not highly activated (for example, when individuals are not emotionally excited or are alone), the cognitive-control network is strong enough to impose regulatory control over impulsive and risky behavior, even in early adolescence. In the presence of peers or under conditions of emotional arousal, however, the socioemotional network becomes sufficiently activated to diminish the regulatory effectiveness of the cognitive-control network. Over the course of adolescence, the cognitive-control network matures, so that by adulthood, even under conditions of heightened arousal in the socioemotional network, inclinations toward risk taking can be modulated.

It is important to note that mechanisms underlying the processing of emotional information, social information, and reward are closely interconnected. Among adolescents, the regions that are activated during exposure to social and emotional stimuli overlap considerably with regions also shown to be sensitive to variations in reward magnitude (cf. Galvan, et al., 2005; Nelson, Leibenluft, McClure, & Pine, 2005). This finding may be relevant to understanding why so much adolescent risk taking—like drinking, reckless driving, or delinquency—occurs in groups (Steinberg, 2004). Risk taking may be heightened in adolescence because teenagers spend so much time with their peers, and the mere presence of peers makes the rewarding aspects of risky situations more salient by activating the same circuitry that is activated by exposure to nonsocial rewards when individuals are alone.

The competitive interaction between the socioemotional and cognitive-control networks has been implicated in a wide range of decision-making contexts, including drug use, social-decision processing, moral judgments, and the valuation of alternative rewards/costs (e.g., Chambers, Taylor, & Potenza, 2003). In all of these contexts, risk taking is associated with relatively greater activation of the socioemotional network. For example, individuals' preference for smaller immediate rewards over larger delayed rewards is associated with relatively increased activation of the ventral striatum, orbitofrontal cortex, and medial prefrontal cortex—all regions linked to the socioemotional network—presumably because immediate rewards are especially emotionally arousing (consider the difference between how you might feel if a crisp $100 bill were held in front of you versus being told that you will receive $150 in 2 months). In contrast, regions implicated in cognitive control are engaged equivalently across decision conditions (McClure, Laibson, Loewenstein, & Cohen, 2004). Similarly, studies show that increased activity in regions of the socioemotional network is associated with the selection of comparatively risky (but potentially highly rewarding) choices over more conservative ones (Ernst et al., 2005).

Evidence From Behavioral Science

Three lines of behavioral evidence are consistent with this account. First, studies of susceptibility to antisocial peer influence show that vulnerability to peer pressure increases between preadolescence and mid-adolescence, peaks in mid-adolescence—presumably when the imbalance between the sensitivity to socioemotional arousal (which has increased at puberty) and capacity for cognitive control (which is still immature) is greatest—and gradually declines thereafter (Steinberg, 2004). Second, as noted earlier, studies of decision making generally show no age differences in risk processing between older adolescents and adults when decision making is assessed under conditions likely associated with relatively lower activation of brain systems responsible for emotion, reward, and social processing (e.g., the presentation of hypothetical decision-making dilemmas to individuals tested alone under conditions of low emotional arousal; Millstein, & Halpern-Felsher, 2002). Third, the presence of peers increases risk taking substantially among teenagers, moderately among college-age individuals, and not at all among adults, consistent with the notion that the development of the cognitive-control network is gradual and extends beyond the teen years. In one of our lab's studies, for instance, the presence of peers more than doubled the number of risks teenagers took in a video driving game and increased risk taking by 50% among college undergraduates but had no effect at all among adults (Gardner & Steinberg, 2005; see Fig. 2). In adolescence, then, not only is more merrier—it is also riskier.

What Changes During Adolescence?

Studies of rodents indicate an especially significant increase in reward salience (i.e., how much attention individuals pay to the magnitude of potential rewards) around the time of puberty (Spear, 2000), consistent with human studies showing that increases in sensation seeking occur relatively early in adolescence and are correlated with pubertal maturation but not chronological age (Steinberg, 2004). Given behavioral findings indicating relatively greater reward salience among adolescents than adults in decision-making tasks, there is reason to speculate that, when presented with risky situations that have both potential rewards and potential costs, adolescents may be more sensitive than adults to variation in rewards but comparably sensitive (or perhaps even less sensitive) to variation in costs (Ernst et al., 2005).

It thus appears that the brain system that regulates the processing of rewards, social information, and emotions is becoming more sensitive and more easily aroused around the time of puberty. What about its sibling, the cognitive-control system? Regions making up the cognitive-control network, especially prefrontal regions, continue to exhibit gradual changes in structure

and function during adolescence and early adulthood (Casey, Tottenham, Liston, & Durston, 2005). Much publicity has been given to the finding that synaptic pruning (the selective elimination of seldom-used synapses) and myelination (the development of the fatty sheaths that "insulate" neuronal circuitry)—both of which increase the efficiency of information processing—continue to occur in the prefrontal cortex well into the early 20s. But frontal regions also become more integrated with other brain regions during adolescence and early adulthood, leading to gradual improvements in many aspects of cognitive control such as response inhibition; this integration may be an even more important change than changes within the frontal region itself. Imaging studies using tasks in which individuals are asked to inhibit a "prepotent" response—like trying to look away from, rather than toward, a point of light—have shown that adolescents tend to recruit the cognitive-control network less broadly than do adults, perhaps overtaxing the capacity of the more limited number of regions they activate (Luna et al., 2001).

In essence, one of the reasons the cognitive-control system of adults is more effective than that of adolescents is that adults' brains distribute its regulatory responsibilities across a wider network of linked components. This lack of cross-talk across brain regions in adolescence results not only in individuals acting on gut feelings without fully thinking (the stereotypic portrayal of teenagers) but also in thinking too much when gut feelings ought to be attended to (which teenagers also do from time to time). In one recent study, when asked whether some obviously dangerous activities (e.g., setting one's hair on fire) were "good ideas," adolescents took significantly longer than adults to respond to the questions and activated a less narrowly distributed set of cognitive-control regions (Baird, Fugelsang, & Bennett, 2005). This was not the case when the queried activities were not dangerous ones, however (e.g., eating salad).

The fact that maturation of the socioemotional network appears to be driven by puberty, whereas the maturation of the cognitive-control network does not, raises interesting questions about the impact—at the individual and at the societal levels—of early pubertal maturation on risk-taking. We know that there is wide variability among individuals in the timing of puberty, due to both genetic and environmental factors. We also know that there has been a significant drop in the age of pubertal maturation over the past 200 years. To the extent that the temporal disjunction between the maturation of the socioemotional system and that of the cognitive-control system contributes to adolescent risk taking, we would expect to see higher rates of risk taking among early maturers and a drop over time in the age of initial experimentation with risky behaviors such as sexual intercourse or drug use. There is evi-

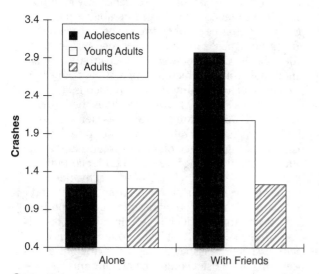

figure 2

Risk taking of adolescents, young adults, and adults during a video driving game, when playing alone and when playing with friends. Adapted from Gardner & Steinberg (2004).

dence for both of these patterns (Collins & Steinberg, 2006; Johnson & Gerstein, 1998).

Implications for Prevention

What does this mean for the prevention of unhealthy risk taking in adolescence? Given extant research suggesting that it is not the way adolescents think or what they don't know or understand that is the problem, a more profitable strategy than attempting to change how adolescents view risky activities might be to focus on limiting opportunities for immature judgment to have harmful consequences. More than 90% of all American high-school students have had sex, drug, and driver education in their schools, yet large proportions of them still have unsafe sex, binge drink, smoke cigarettes, and drive recklessly (often more than one of these at the same time; Steinberg, 2004). Strategies such as raising the price of cigarettes, more vigilantly enforcing laws governing the sale of alcohol, expanding adolescents' access to mental-health and contraceptive services, and raising the driving age would likely be more effective in limiting adolescent smoking, substance abuse, pregnancy, and automobile fatalities than strategies aimed at making adolescents wiser, less impulsive, or less shortsighted. Some things just take time to develop, and, like it or not, mature judgment is probably one of them.

The research reviewed here suggests that heightened risk taking during adolescence is likely to be normative, biologically driven, and, to some extent, inevitable. There is probably very little that can or ought to be done to either attenuate or delay the shift in reward sensitivity that takes place at puberty. It may be possible to accelerate the maturation of self-regulatory competence, but no research has examined whether this is possible. In light of studies showing familial influences on psychosocial maturity in adolescence, understanding how contextual factors influence the development of self-regulation and knowing the neural underpinnings of these processes should be a high priority for those interested in the well-being of young people.

RECOMMENDED READING

Casey, B.J., Tottenham, N., Liston, C., & Durston, S. (2005). (See References)

Johnson, R., & Gerstein, D. (1998). (See References)

Nelson, E., Leibenluft, E., McClure, E., & Pine, D. (2005). (See References)

Spear, P. (2000). (See References)

Steinberg, L. (2004). (See References)

Acknowledgments—*Thanks to Nora Newcombe for comments on an earlier draft and to Jason Chein for his expertise in developmental neuroscience.*

REFERENCES

Baird, A., Fugelsang, J., & Bennett, C. (2005, April). *"What were you thinking?": An fMRI study of adolescent decision making.* Poster presented at the annual meeting of the Cognitive Neuroscience Society, New York.

Beyth-Marom, R., Austin, L., Fischoff, B., Palmgren, C., & Jacobs-Quadrel, M. (1993). Perceived consequences of risky behaviors: Adults and adolescents. *Developmental Psychology, 29,* 549–563.

Casey, B.J., Tottenham, N., Liston, C., & Durston, S. (2005). Imaging the developing brain: What have we learned about cognitive development? *Trends in Cognitive Science, 9,* 104–110.

Chambers, R.A., Taylor, J.R., & Potenza, M.N. (2003). Developmental neurocircuitry of motivation in adolescence: A critical period of addiction vulnerability. *American Journal of Psychiatry, 160,* 1041–1052.

Collins, W.A., & Steinberg, L. (2006). Adolescent development in interpersonal context. In W. Damon & R. Lerner (Series Eds.) & N. Eisenberg (Vol. Ed.), *Handbook of Child Psychology: Social, emotional, and personality development* (Vol. 3, pp. 1003–1067). New York: Wiley.

Drevets, W.C., & Raichle, M.E. (1998). Reciprocal suppression of regional cerebral blood flow during emotional versus higher cognitive processes: Implications for interactions between emotion and cognition. *Cognition and Emotion, 12,* 353–385.

Ernst, M., Jazbec, S., McClure, E.B., Monk, C.S., Blair, R.J.R., Leibenluft, E., & Pine, D.S. (2005). Amygdala and nucleus accumbens activation in response to receipt and omission of gains in adults and adolescents. *Neuroimage, 25,* 1279–1291.

Galvan, A., Hare, T., Davidson, M., Spicer, J., Glover, G., & Casey, B.J. (2005). The role of ventral frontostriatal circuitry in reward-based learning in humans. *Journal of Neuroscience, 25,* 8650–8656.

Gardner, M., & Steinberg, L. (2005). Peer influence on risk-taking, risk preference, and risky decision-making in adolescence and adulthood: An experimental study. *Developmental Psychology, 41,* 625–635.

Johnson, R., & Gerstein, D. (1998). Initiation of use of alcohol, cigarettes, marijuana, cocaine, and other substances in US birth cohorts since 1919. *American Journal of Public Health, 88,* 27–33.

Luna, B., Thulborn, K.R., Munoz, D.P., Merriam, E.P., Garver, K.E., Minshew, N.J., et al. (2001). Maturation of widely distributed brain function subserves cognitive development. *Neuroimage, 13,* 786–793.

McClure, S.M., Laibson, D.I., Loewenstein, G., & Cohen, J.D. (2004). Separate neural systems value immediate and delayed monetary rewards. *Science, 306,* 503–507.

Millstein, S.G., & Halpern-Felsher, B.L. (2002). Perceptions of risk and vulnerability. *Journal of Adolescent Health, 31S,* 10–27.

Nelson, E., Leibenluft, E., McClure, E., & Pine, D. (2005). The social re-orientation of adolescence: A neuroscience perspective on the process and its relation to psychopathology. *Psychological Medicine, 35,* 163–174.

Reyna, V., & Farley, F. (2006). Risk and rationality in adolescent decision-making: Implications for theory, practice, and public policy. *Psychological Science in the Public Interest, 7,* 1–44.

Spear, P. (2000). The adolescent brain and age-related behavioral manifestations. *Neuroscience and Biobehavioral Reviews, 24,* 417–463.

Steinberg, L. (2004). Risk-taking in adolescence: What changes, and why? *Annals of the New York Academy of Sciences, 1021,* 51–58.

Questions

1. Why are intervention programs that focus on educating adolescents about the dangers of certain behaviors, such as substance abuse, ineffective?
2. What two aspects of the brain are in competition when adolescents take risks? What difference in the adult brain reduces the likelihood that a person will take such risks?
3. How does the presence of peers change adolescent risk-taking behavior?
4. Sometimes adolescents think too much and at other times they think too little. How does the research described in this article account for this seemingly paradoxical description of adolescents?
5. How could these findings be used to defend a youth in a criminal case in which an adolescent is accused of carrying out a crime on his or her own? Would your answer differ if the crime were carried out with other adolescents?
6. Do you think it is more hazardous for an adolescent to drive with peers or to drive while talking to a peer on the telephone, hands free or otherwise?

32 Toward a New Understanding of Early Menarche: The Role of Environmental Stress in Pubertal Timing

Michelle Wierson • Patricia J. Long • Rex L. Forehand

After the growth and physical changes in the first year of life, the physical changes that occur during puberty are the most dramatic and rapid changes experienced by the human body. However, unlike infancy, which begins for all children at birth, the beginning of puberty varies widely across individuals, cultural settings, generations, and even historical epochs. Explanations for variation in pubertal timing have largely concentrated on biological factors, such as improved nutrition in a family or community or the proportion of body fat in prepubescent girls. But might psychological or social factors also play a role in determining the onset of puberty?

One of the main indices of the onset of puberty in girls is *menarche*, the beginning of the menstrual cycle. Early menarche has been associated with a number of risk factors for healthy development in girls, including increased likelihood of sexual promiscuity. However, using ideas of evolutionary psychology, some developmental researchers have proposed that early maturation may be adaptive for girls who live in particularly stressful family circumstances. In the following article, Michelle Wierson and her colleagues describe their study of the relation between family stress and pubertal timing in girls. The researchers were especially interested in family stress stemming from parental conflict.

This study represents a new direction in developmental psychology; here, biological change is inseparable from social, emotional, and cognitive changes and experiences. This approach considers as mutually defining the organism and the ecosystem in which the organism develops. Presented this way, all aspects of development, even those that may seem to be controlled by a single factor like biology, are understood to be determined by many factors.

A recent theory (Belsky, Steinberg, & Draper, 1991) suggests that environmental stress may trigger early menarche in adolescents. This is in contrast to a more traditional view that early menarche is biologically determined and serves as a risk factor for developing girls. The purpose of the present study was to examine two family stressors, divorce and interparental conflict, in light of the Belsky et al. theory. Participants were 71 adolescent females and their mothers. Of these, 44 were from intact families (i.e., the parents were married), and 27 were from divorced families.

Age at first menarche was obtained via self-report. Maternal reports of interparental conflict as well as adolescent perception of conflict were obtained. Mothers reported on marital status. Results showed that, compared to girls from intact families, those from divorced families had an earlier onset of menarche. In addition, higher maternal reports of interparental conflict were significantly related to earlier menarche in the total sample. Results are discussed in relation to the Belsky et al. theory as well as traditional views of early menarche.

Reprinted with permission of Libra Publishers, Inc. from Wierson, M., Long, P. J., & Forehand, R. L. (1992). Toward a New Understanding of Early Menarche: The Role of Environmental Stress in Pubertal Timing. *Adolescence, 28,* 913–924.

This study was supported, in part, by the William T. Grant Foundation and the University of Georgia's Institute for Behavioral Research.

The transition into adolescence is considered to be a significant developmental period as this life stage brings with it numerous biological, cognitive, and social changes (Conger, 1984). Typically, the onset of puberty has been viewed as a marker for entry into adolescence, and thus has received a great deal of attention in research. Particular focus has been upon pubertal timing, or the level of physical and psychological development of adolescents in comparison to same-age peers (Brooks-Gunn & Warren, 1985). In general, timing of menstruation has been the subject of most research in this area. Traditionally, early onset of puberty in girls has been regarded as stressful and related to deficits in their functioning. For example, early-maturing girls have been found to exhibit significantly more behavior problems than their peers who menstruate on time (Caspi & Moffitt, 1991). Similarly, these early maturers are more likely to engage in sexually promiscuous behavior during adolescence, have more difficulties relating socially, report more emotional problems such as depression and anxiety, and experience more intense conflict with parents than do their peers (Susman, Nottlemann, Inoff-Germain, Loriaux, & Chrousos, 1985). That is, it is generally accepted that early onset of puberty is stressful for girls (Kornfield, 1990).

A recent study examined the impact of several stressors upon adolescent functioning (Kornfield, 1990), including pubertal timing. Kornfield (1990) investigated the relative impact of divorce and early onset of puberty with a sample of 91 adolescents, 40 of whom were girls. For these girls, it was found that early onset of puberty was associated with lower social competence and greater disruption in parent-adolescent relationships. In contrast, early developers showed significantly *lower* levels of depression when compared to late developers. In light of this finding, the authors concluded that there is only minimal support to suggest that early puberty is stressful for girls. When considered in conjunction with divorce, however, the impact upon early developers was more evident. That is, early maturers from divorced homes exhibited more problems in functioning when compared to other groups in the sample. These data were interpreted as evidence for a cumulative stressor hypothesis—that girls experiencing multiple stressors (i.e., early onset of puberty and parental divorce) function poorly.

Again, congruent with the traditional view of pubertal timing, early onset was considered as a potential stressor in the Kornfield (1990) study. Implicit in this view is that pubertal timing is determined solely through biological processes. Recently, however, a controversial theory has been proposed which challenges this traditional view (Belsky, Steinberg, & Draper, 1991). Rather than conceptualizing early development as a stress in and of itself, Belsky et al. suggest that early development may be environmentally triggered and may actually be an *adaptive* response to a stressful environment. Specifically, they propose that puberty marks the beginning of an adolescent's individuation from the family (Steinberg, 1987), a process that will begin earlier if staying in the family environment is perceived as risky or harmful. These researchers define risk as any potential for decreased availability of resources that may impair reproductive fitness. They particularly emphasize marital conflict, father absence, or poor parenting as possible risk factors. Belsky et al. (1991) further assert that this strategy is an unconscious process with its roots in evolution and natural selection theory; that is, in a high-risk environment, the most adaptive response for a female is to reproduce early and often, before she herself dies. This increases the probability of gene transfer into the next generation. In contrast, the most adaptive strategy for a female in a stable home environment is to defer sexual activity and reproduction, produce fewer offspring, and invest more time and resources in each child, thus increasing their probabilities of survival. This is a new way of thinking about the phenomenon that lower income, resource impoverished families typically bear more children than do their middle-class, educated counterparts (Hooper, 1991).

The Belsky et al. (1991) theory has been criticized frequently and vehemently in the scientific community for its lack of current support, its overreaching conclusions, and its classist implications. In addition, it has been contended that their view does not rule out more traditional explanations for the sequelae associated with early maturity in females (Hooper, 1991). However, there has been some early support for the theory. Specifically, four studies to date have found support for the hypothesis—that girls from an early stressful environment will start menstruation months earlier than their peers raised in a more stable environment.

Perhaps the earliest support for the Belsky et al. (1991) theory came from Jones, Leeton, McCleod, and Wood (1972), who found that girls from father-absent households achieved menarche significantly earlier than did girls from homes in which the father was present. In fact, the earlier the date of father absence, the earlier the onset of menstruation. In a later study of 75 adolescents, Steinberg (1988) found that girls who reported high levels of conflict with their parents matured faster over the next year than did same-age peers (i.e., age 10 to 14) who reported low levels of parent-adolescent conflict. Both studies suggest that parent-child distance and strained family relations may be related to earlier onset of puberty.

Specific examination of the Belsky et al. (1991) theory, however, has been conducted even more recently. Surbey (1990) surveyed a group of 1,200 Canadian women to obtain information about family relationships and onset of menstruation. She found that girls whose fathers were absent before the age of 10 began menstruation five months earlier, on average, than did girls from intact homes. In addition, girls who reported higher levels of family conflict, even in intact homes, menstruated significantly earlier than did peers from low-conflict homes. Similar results were obtained by Moffitt, Caspi, and Belsky (1990), who studied a sample of 991 adolescents from New Zealand. Even when controlling for biological factors (e.g., weight, nutrition), their results showed that family conflict at age 7 was significantly predictive of earlier menarche. Similarly, parental divorce (resulting in father absence) prior to age 7 also was associated with earlier menstruation in these girls.

Belsky et al. (1991) acknowledge the relatively small relationships and effects found in the above studies; nevertheless, they contend that the theory offers an intriguing reanalysis of traditional views regarding the early onset of puberty. Several researchers in the field disagree. For example, Brooks-Gunn (1988) found no support for the theory. In her sample of 150 adolescent girls, no relationship was found between father absence and pubertal timing of 11- to 15-year-olds. In fact, the most powerful predictors were exercise and nutrition. Similarly, it should be noted that age of menarche has decreased significantly over the past two centuries, and many researchers question whether the theory can explain this shift better than do processes that are biological rather than psychological in nature (Hooper, 1991).

The purpose of the present study was to examine the hypotheses proposed by the Belsky, Steinberg, and Draper (1991) theory in order to shed light on the controversy. Reanalyzing some of the data utilized in a larger study, the relationship between familial stressors and age of menarche was investigated. Three stressors were selected: divorce, marital conflict as reported by parents, and adolescent perception of marital conflict. Divorce and conflict were selected because they are proposed by Belsky et al. as factors signalling risk to the developing female. In addition, divorce consistently has been viewed as a stressor for adolescents, relating to higher rates of maladjustment (Emery, 1988). Marital conflict has been found to have an even greater impact (Emery, 1982; Long, Forehand, Fauber, & Brody, 1987; Shaw & Emery, 1987) and thus warrants study as a stressor independent of divorce. Finally, adolescent perception of interparental conflict was selected because of recent evidence that it contributes unique variance to functioning beyond that of parental report (Wierson, Forehand, & McCombs, 1989). It was theorized that subjective perception of such conflict would be the most critical signal of risk in the adolescent's environment.

Based upon the Belsky et al. (1991) theory, it was predicted that (1) girls from divorced homes would have earlier onset of menarche than would girls whose parents were married; (2) higher frequency of parent-reported marital conflict would result in earlier onset; and (3) higher levels of adolescent-perceived marital conflict would result in earlier onset.

Subjects

Subjects were 71 adolescent girls and their mothers, all of whom were participating in a larger ongoing project. At the time of assessment, they ranged in age from 11 years, 5 months, to 18 years, with a mean age of 14 years, 5 months. Of these, 44 were from families in which their parents were married, and 27 were from divorced families. All girls from divorced families were in the custody of their mothers.

All participants were Caucasian. Socioeconomic status was assessed using the Myers and Bean (1968) two-factor index of social position, calculated according to the individual's educational and occupational level. For divorced families, social position scores were calculated for mothers, whereas fathers' scores were computed in intact families. The Myers and Bean system yields possible scores ranging from 11 to 77, with lower scores indicating higher social position. For the present sample, scores ranged from 11 to 66, with a mean score of 33, indicating predominantly middle-to-lower middle-class status.

Participation was voluntary, and subjects were recruited through notices posted in local communities, fliers distributed at public schools, advertisements in local newspapers, and announcements on local radio stations. In addition, some of the divorced subjects were identified through local courthouse records and contacted by mail. All notices and letters invited mothers and adolescents to participate in a research project examining parent-adolescent relationships.

Subjects were paid for their initial participation in the study and at each year of follow-up. Each mother-adolescent dyad was paid $50 for attending each 2-hour data-collection session, conducted at a southeastern university.

Measures

Parental Marital Status.   Marital status was determined via a single-item question administered to each mother. All parents who were divorced had to have been divorced in the previous twelve months in order to participate.

Parental Report of Conflict.   The O'Leary-Porter Scale (OPS) was used to assess level of overt marital conflict in the adolescent's presence. The OPS is a

10-item scale developed to measure the frequency of such conflict (Porter & O'Leary, 1980). Items such as "how often do you and your spouse/ex-spouse argue over disciplinary actions in this child's presence?" are rated along a five-point Likert scale ranging from "very often" to "never." The OPS yields scores from 0 to 40, with lower scores indicating more frequent conflict. Excellent psychometric properties have been demonstrated, including test-retest reliability of .96 over a two-week period, and measures of external validity of over .63 (Porter & O'Leary, 1980).

Adolescent Perception of Conflict. The Personal Data Form (PDF) measured adolescent perception of marital conflict. The PDF is a 30-item instrument containing statements about the adolescent's home and school life. Embedded within the inventory are 10 items regarding perceived conflict between parents (Emery & O'Leary, 1982). Items such as "My parents argue in front of me" are rated on a scale of 0 (not true), 1 (sometimes true), and 2 (true), resulting in possible scores from 1 to 20. Higher scores indicate more conflict. Emery and O'Leary (1982) have demonstrated good factor analytic support and test-retest reliability for the PDF.

Age of Menstruation. Age of first menstruation was obtained from adolescent report on the Pubertal Development Scale (PDS), an instrument designed to assess pubertal status and timing (Petersen, Crockett, Richards, & Boxer, 1988). The PDS asks questions about the adolescent's height, weight, and secondary sexual characteristics. In addition, girls are asked to report whether they have menstruated, and if so, at what age (in months) they started. The PDS generates an average score to serve as a measure of pubertal development; however, in the present study, only age of menstruation was utilized. The PDS has been demonstrated to be valid and reliable for measuring pubertal timing (Petersen & Crockett, 1985).

Procedure

Announcements and letters used to recruit subjects instructed interested parties to phone the experimenter for more information. When contacted, eligibility for participation was first determined, based upon age of the adolescent and parental marital status. After describing the project to eligible volunteers, a data-collection session was scheduled for those who agreed to participate. At the beginning of the initial session, the project was explained to each mother-adolescent dyad. Consent forms were signed by both mother and adolescent, authorizing data collection and use. Both then completed a set of questionnaires, presented in random order; among these was the O'Leary-Porter Scale, completed by mothers, and the Personal Data Form, completed by adolescents.

Subjects consisted of female participants from a larger longitudinal study who provided information about their age at menses. Given that subjects were recontacted yearly for four years, and participated in a similar manner, pubertal information reported at any year of participation was used in this study. To ensure the earliest report of parental conflict, data on parental conflict (i.e., both mother- and adolescent-reported) from the first year of participation only were employed in data analysis.

Results

Parental-reported and adolescent-perceived marital conflict were measured at year one in order to obtain the earliest possible index of conflict in the family environment. However, it should be noted that, for some girls in the current sample, this report was obtained postpubertally, as they had already menstruated prior to entry into the longitudinal project. Marital conflict has been demonstrated to be a stable and reliable construct over time (Porter & O'Leary, 1980), suggesting that even postpubertal report of conflict should reflect prepubertal levels of the stressor. However, in order to demonstrate the stability of the conflict in the current sample, Pearson product-moment correlations were conducted across all four years of subject participation. Results indicated that adolescent perception of marital conflict at year one, as measured by the PDF, was significantly correlated with report of perception at years two, three, and four (correlations ranged from .40 to .75, $p < .05$ or better). For parent report of conflict, as measured by the OPS, correlations were also significant across the four years. In fact, for the CPS scores, the magnitude of correlations was over .70 in all cases ($p < .001$), suggesting a particularly high rate of stability for this measure. The significant correlations across years for the OPS and PDF support the finding that both parent report of conflict and adolescent perception of conflict are stable constructs, thus justifying the use of OPS and PDF scores at Year 1 in subsequent analyses.

In order to address the hypotheses, each stressor was considered separately. Because of its categorical nature, a one-tailed *t*-test was conducted for marital status (i.e., intact vs. divorced). The dependent variable in question was age of menstruation. Results indicated that girls from divorced families menstruated significantly earlier than did girls from intact families (mean age for girls from divorced and intact families = 145 months and 150 months, respectively; ($t(67) = 1.60$, $p < .05$, one-tailed).

In order to examine the relationship between adolescent perception of marital conflict (measured on a continuous scale) and age at menstruation, a regression procedure was performed. As can be seen in

table 1 Predicting Age of Onset of Menstruation from Adolescent Perception of Marital Conflict and Parental-reported Marital Conflict

Predictor	b	R^2	df	F	p
PDF[1]	.10	.0009	1, 66	.06	NS
OPS[2]	.59	.06	1, 69	4.16	$p < .045$

[1]Personal Data Form (adolescent-completed)
[2]O'Leary-Porter Scale (mother-completed)

Table 1, no significant relationship emerged. A regression procedure was then performed for parental report of marital conflict (also measured on a continuous scale; see Table 1). It was found that the OPS scores significantly predicted onset of menstruation. When beta weights are examined, it is evident that, as more frequent conflict was reported (i.e., lower OPS scores), age at first menstruation was younger.

Following the individual analyses, stepwise regression analyses also were performed in order to examine the relative contribution of all three stressors. This procedure also controls for overlapping variance among variables. Table 2 shows the results of these analyses. Although the overall F was not significant, the trend toward statistical significance (i.e., $p < .08$) justifies exploration of individual predictor variables. The most powerful predictor of age at menstruation was the OPS, or parent report of marital conflict.

Discussion

The results were congruent with the Belsky et al. theory that stressors in the family environment predict earlier onset of menarche. Specifically, onset of menarche for girls from divorced families was six months earlier than for girls from families in which parents were married. In addition, frequent marital conflict, at least in the presence of the adolescent, is predictive of earlier onset of menstruation. Consistent with the Steinberg (1988) study with a similar sample size, the magnitude of effects was small, and thus results must be interpreted with caution. However, it does appear that psychological and environmental variables may be influencing the biological timing of puberty in girls. Perhaps, as suggested by Belsky et al. (1990), girls are sensing risk for themselves when their parents verbally and physically fight, unconsciously triggering reproductive ability. Early menarche has been found to predict higher rates of sexual activity, which means that opportunities for reproduction are increased (Belsky et al., 1991); again, this may be an adaptive strategy that is naturally selected because it increases reproductive fitness. In contrast, *quality* reproduction is naturally selected in girls from stable, secure environments where risk is low.

Although the results of this study do provide support for the theory, it is important to note that the data are not incompatible with more traditional views of early menarche as a stressor. As claimed by Udry (cited in Hooper, 1991), "all the events [the theory seeks] to explain have other explanations based on theories more compatible to sociologists and psychologists" (p. 55). Specifically, early menarche is multiplicatively determined and, at best, is likely to be only distally related to environmental stressors (Hooper, 1991). In addition, even if early menarche is an adaptive strategy biologically, it may remain a stressful event for the adolescent girl in other realms (e.g., disrupting social interactions with peers, increasing internalizing problems), as has been suggested by previous research (e.g., Susman et al., 1985, Caspi & Moffitt, 1991). Nevertheless, the Belsky et al. theory is provocative in its challenge to traditional views, and the current results are at least compatible with their conceptualization of early menarche.

table 2 Predicting Age of Onset of Menstruation using Hierarchical Multiple Regression Techniques

Predictor	b	t	R^2	df	F	p
			.10	3, 62	2.30	$p < .08$
Marital Status	−6.19	−1.62				$p < .11$
PDF[1]	.49	1.15				$p < .25$
OPS[2]	.67	2.13				$p < .04$

[1]Personal Data Form (adolescent-completed)
[2]O'Leary-Porter Scale (mother-completed)

There are several limitations of the present study that should be mentioned, both as possible explanations for lack of definitive results and as acknowledgement of methodological weaknesses. First, and most importantly, the measures of conflict and adolescent perception of conflict employed in the analyses were not always reported prepubertally. That is, some of the subjects already had menstruated before their entry into the study. Thus, support for causal relationships is limited. The reported correlations for marital conflict do indicate a high degree of stability for the measures, suggesting that frequency and level of conflict is ongoing and stable in these families, but no direct report of early environmental stress was available. In the future, prospective applications of the Belsky et al. (1991) hypotheses are warranted; to this date, all studies have been retrospective in nature.

Second, when evaluating the role of divorce and father absence, only families in which divorce occurred within 12 months prior to entry into the study and after the age of 10 were examined. According to the Belsky et al. (1991) theory, *early* environmental stress (i.e., in the first 4 to 7 years) triggers earlier onset of puberty. Although divorce at age 10 does not preclude stressful rearing in the early years as well, it is possible that we limited ourselves by examining a sample that was experiencing divorce and father absence at a later age. That is, we were unable to capitalize on evaluation of the most heavily conflictual families, presumably those who would end in divorce much earlier, triggering early menses at that time. In spite of this limitation, it is noteworthy that a six-month mean difference was found.

Finally, it should be noted that this study did not examine other biological factors known to be related to age of menstruation–specifically, nutrition, weight, and mother's age of menstruation–although all have been found to be significant predictors in other studies (e.g., Moffitt et al., 1990; Surbey, 1990). It is not intended to suggest that environmental stressors supersede the effects of these biological variables. Instead, the purpose was to examine whether such factors were influential at all. And, most importantly, the purpose was to reevaluate the recent Belsky et al. theory. As noted by Hooper (1991), these researchers are to be applauded for their efforts and for the heuristic value of their ideas, which are "a sharp new stimulus for re-examining data and rethinking the connections among . . . aspects of a child's environment; the sexual development of his or her adolescent body; and reproductive behavior in young adulthood" (p. 54). In conclusion, the results of the current study were compatible with this new idea, demonstrating that divorce and higher levels of marital conflict predict earlier onset of menarche.

REFERENCES

Belsky, J., Steinberg, L., & Draper, P. (1991). Childhood experience, interpersonal development, and reproductive strategy: An evolutionary theory of socialization. *Child Development, 62,* 647–670.

Brooks-Gunn, J. (1988). Antecedents and consequences of variations of girls' maturational timing. *Journal of Adolescent Health Care, 9,* 365–370.

Brooks-Gunn, J., & Warren, M. P. (1985). Measuring physical status and timing in early adolescence: A developmental perspective. *Journal of Youth and Adolescence, 14,* 163–189.

Caspi, A., & Moffitt, T. E. (1991). Individual differences are accentuated during periods of social change: The sample case of girls at puberty. *Journal of Personality and Social Psychology, 61,* 157–168.

Conger, J. J. (1984). *Adolescence and youth.* New York: Harper & Row.

Emery, R. E. (1982). Interparental conflict and the children of discord and divorce. *Psychological Bulletin, 92,* 310–330.

Emery, R. E. (1988). *Marriage, divorce, and children's adjustment.* Newbury Park, CA: Sage.

Emery, R. E., & O'Leary, K. D. (1982). Children's perceptions of marital discord and behavior problems of boys and girls. *Journal of Abnormal Child Psychology, 10,* 11–24.

Hooper, C. (1991). The birds, the bees, and human sexual strategies. *Research of NIH* (October, Vol. 3), 54–60.

Jones, B., Leeton, J., McLeod, I., & Wood, C. (1972). Factors influencing the age of menarche in a lower socioeconomic group in Melbourne. *Medical Journal of Australia, 21,* 533–535.

Kornfield, S. (1990). Impact of parental marital status, gender, and pubertal development on adolescent functioning. Unpublished manuscript, University of Georgia.

Long, N., Forehand, R., Fauber, R., & Brody, G. (1987). Self-perceived and independently observed competence of young adolescents as a function of parental marital conflict and recent divorce. *Journal of Abnormal Child Psychology, 15,* 15–27.

Moffitt, T., Caspi, A., & Belsky, J. (1990, March). *Family context, girls' behavior, and the onset of puberty: A test of a sociobiological model.* Paper presented at the biennial meetings of the Society for Research in Adolescence, Atlanta, GA.

Myers, J. K., & Bean, L. L. (1968). *A decade later: A follow-up of social class and mental illness.* New York: Wiley.

Petersen, A., & Crockett, L. (1985). Pubertal timing and grade effects on adjustment. *Journal of Youth and Adolescence, 14,* 191–206.

Petersen, A., & Crockett, L., Richards, M., & Boxer, A. (1988). A self-report measure of pubertal status: Reliability, validity, and initial norms. *Journal of Youth and Adolescence, 17,* 117–133.

Porter, B., & O'Leary, K. D. (1980). Marital discord and childhood behavior problems. *Journal of Abnormal Child Psychology, 8,* 287–295.

Shaw, D. S., & Emery, R. E. (1987). Parental conflict and the adjustment of school-aged children whose parents have separated. *Journal of Abnormal Child Psychology, 15,* 269–281.

Steinberg, L. (1987). Bound to bicker. *Psychology Today.* Sept., 36–39.

Steinberg, L. (1988). Reciprocal relation between parent-child distance and pubertal maturation. *Developmental Psychology, 24,* 122–128.

Surbey, M. (1990). Family composition, stress, and human menarche. In F. Bercovitch, & T. Zeigler (Eds.), *The socioendocrinology of primate reproduction* (pp. 71–97). New York: Liss.

Susman, E. J., Nottleman, E. D., Inoff-Germain, G. E., Loriaux, D. L., & Chrousos, G. P. (1985). The relation of relative hormonal levels and physical development and social-emotional behavior in young adolescents. *Journal of Youth and Adolescence, 14,* 245–264.

Wierson, M., Forehand, R., & McCombs, A. (1989). The relationship of early adolescent functioning to parent-reported and adolescent-perceived interparental conflict. *Journal of Abnormal Child Psychology, 16,* 707–718.

Questions

1. What are some of the risk factors for girls that are associated with early maturation?
2. From the perspective of human evolution, why would early female maturation in stressful situations have contributed to the survival of our early ancestors?
3. Why would family stressors, such as parent conflict, lead to early menarche in girls?
4. What other stressors might influence the timing of puberty in girls?
5. The timing of maturation varies in males also, and some research has shown that parents are more likely to argue in front of their sons than their daughters. What results would you expect, given the evolutionary argument discussed in this article, if boys were included in this study?
6. How might the results of this study be useful to parents who are divorced or contemplating divorce and whose daughters are in the latter years of childhood?

33

Development of Logical Reasoning and the School Performance of African American Adolescents in Relation to Socioeconomic Status, Ethnic Identity, and Self-Esteem

Mark S. Chapell • Willis F. Overton

When Jean Piaget characterized adolescent thought as formal operational, he meant that adolescents are capable of performing logical operations that are formal, or abstract, in nature. Following up on Piaget's assertion, researchers have described change from early to late adolescence in logical reasoning skills. However, this research has mainly included adolescents of European American ancestry. Consequently, little is known about this development in youth from other cultural groups either within or outside the United States.

In the following article, Mark Chapell and Willis Overton address this shortcoming. They conducted a study of the logical reasoning skills of African American adolescents from the sixth grade up to the college years. In addition, Chapell and Overton were especially interested in how family social class relates to the development of logical reasoning in these adolescents. They also probed two theoretical models regarding the expression of cognitive abilities in African American youth. Ogbu's *cultural-ecological theory* concentrates on the relation between ethnic identity and cognitive performance. It suggests that as African American youth develop a stronger ethnic identity, they become disillusioned with behaviors associated with advanced cognitive performance and therefore their performance on cognitive tasks deteriorates. Steele's *stereotype-threat theory* focuses on the connection between self-esteem and cognitive performance, and suggests that negative stereotypes of intellectual inferiority impinge on the performance of African American adolescents on cognitive tasks. Chapell and Overton's study provides empirical information relevant to both of these provocative views. It also offers interesting insight into how the social and cultural experiences of African American adolescents may contribute to the development of logical reasoning skills.

This study explored the deductive reasoning and school performance of 330 African American adolescents and the relation of reasoning and school performance to socioeconomic status (SES), ethnic identity, and self-esteem. As expected, there was a systematic increase in selection task reasoning performance across adolescence, and high SES students outscored low SES students in reasoning performance and school grades.

Ogbu's cultural-ecological theory, which predicts an inverse relationship between cognitive performance and ethnic identity strength, was not supported because better reasoning performance was associated instead with stronger ethnic identity. Steele's stereotype threat theory, which predicts that there will be an association between global self-esteem and school grades in early adolescent African Americans that subsequently decreases across

Reprinted with permission from the *Journal of Black Psychology, Vol. 28* (2002), pp. 295–317, copyright 2002 by Sage Publications, Inc.

Authors' Note: Part of this study, based on Mark S. Chapell's doctoral dissertation, was presented at the annual meeting of the American Psychological Society in Miami, Florida, June 2000.

adolescence, was partially supported. Self-esteem and grades were strongly related in 6th graders, not significantly related in 10th and 12th graders, yet strongly related in college students.

Researchers (Fisher, Jackson, & Villaruel, 1998; Lerner & Galambos, 1998; Steinberg & Morris, 2000) have noted that the empirical literature addressing the normative psychological development of American ethnic minority adolescents is very limited, "In fact, the majority of studies published in the leading scientific journals of child and adolescent development have virtually ignored development within non-European, non-middle class children and families" (Fisher et al., 1998, p. 1150). This trend has continued despite the proliferation of theories (Cooper & Denner, 1998) that express the importance of context and culture for developmental processes.

One area of development where there have been few studies of ethnic minority adolescents is the development of reasoning, an important type of thinking that involves inference, the process where propositions known as premises that have been accepted provide the evidence for arriving at and accepting further propositions known as conclusions (Overton, 1994). There are two major types of reasoning processes: inductive and deductive. Inductive reasoning involves an inference process that proceeds from particular to general propositions, where premises provide probable but not certain evidence for conclusions. Deductive reasoning involves an inference process that moves from general to particular propositions, where general premises provide absolutely certain evidence for the truth of particular conclusions. The first focus of this study is on the development of deductive reasoning in African American adolescents.

The main line of investigation into deductive reasoning (Cheng & Holyoak, 1985; Cosmides, 1989; Evans, 1996; Overton, 1990) has used versions of the four-card selection task (Wason, 1968), a measure consisting of propositional logic problems that test the individual's ability to deduce correct conclusions from given rules. Investigators using the selection task have found that deductive reasoning competence first develops during early adolescence and that by late adolescence a high level of proficiency in solving deductive reasoning problems is generally achieved (Chapell & Overton, 1998; Foltz, Overton, & Ricco, 1995; Overton, Ward, Noveck, Black, & O'Brien, 1987; Reene & Overton, 1989; Ward & Overton, 1990). These results support cognitive developmental theory (Inhelder & Piaget, 1958), which predicts that both inductive and deductive reasoning develop during and across adolescence.

To date, developmental studies of deductive reasoning have been conducted exclusively with Euro-

pean American adolescents. Three published studies of deductive reasoning ability measured by selection task performance have used samples of ethnic minority adolescents (Bell, Brown, & Bryant, 1993; DeShon, Smith, Chan, & Schmitt, 1998; Smith & Drumming, 1989). However, these were nondevelopmental studies because they involved only African American college students. To further test the main prediction from cognitive developmental theory that deductive reasoning competence develops during and across adolescence, this study explored the development of deductive reasoning in African American 6th, 10th, and 12th graders and college students. It was hypothesized, consistent with the pattern of deductive reasoning performance found in European Americans, that there would be a clear developmental progression of deductive reasoning performance across adolescence in African Americans.

The first purpose of this study was to explore the development of deductive reasoning in African American adolescents to diversify and broaden the scope of cognitive developmental research. According to current developmental theory, however, "To understand individual growth and development, the changing relations among biological, psychological, and social contextual levels that comprise the process of developmental change must be examined concurrently" (Fisher et al., 1998, p. 1153). Consistent with this view, studies have shown that there are significant individual differences in the expression of deductive reasoning competence and that deductive reasoning performance is influenced by contextual factors such as familiarity of problem content (Overton et al., 1987) and parenting styles and test anxiety (Chapell & Overton, 1998). Therefore, the second purpose of this study was to explore two factors that may significantly influence the cognitive performance of African American adolescents: socioeconomic status (SES) and ethnic identity.

Researchers have noted that studies that do include participants other than middle-class European Americans often confound race and social class effects by comparing low SES African Americans with higher SES European Americans (Graham, 1992). For instance, in the study cited above, DeShon et al. (1998) compared the deductive reasoning performance of European American college students to that of African Americans whose average family income was lower. This SES inequality also has typified studies using only African American participants, as Graham (1992) pointed out, "Furthermore, with the growing gap between the affluent and the impoverished within the population of American Blacks, it is just as important that race-homogeneous studies not err in the direction of ignoring socioeconomic distinctions between African American subjects" (p. 634). Given the consistent finding that high SES individuals outscore low SES individuals on cognitive tests (Neisser et al., 1996; Suzuki & Valencia, 1997; Williams & Ceci, 1997), this study explored the hypothesis that high SES African American students would have better deductive reasoning performance than low SES students.

Ogbu's Cultural-Ecological Theory

African American adolescents generally perform more poorly on cognitive tests and receive lower grades in school than European Americans (Jencks & Phillips, 1998; Neisser et al., 1996; Steinberg, Dornbusch, & Brown, 1992; Williams & Ceci, 1997). This performance gap has most frequently been attributed to ethnic differences in genetic factors related to intelligence, ineffectual parenting practices, and aspects of the linguistic and cognitive styles of African American culture considered disadvantageous to cognitive test performance (Ogbu, 1986, 1993). Ogbu (1986) has long contended that all of these views suffer from ethnocentric bias, and Ogbu's alternative cultural-ecological model maintains that the missing factor in the African American cognitive performance equation is their lower caste-like status as an involuntary minority group created by and historically subordinated to a dominant European American majority.

Ogbu (1986) maintains that African Americans develop and possess the same cognitive capacities as European Americans, including the capacity to "remember, generalize, form concepts, operate with abstractions, and reason logically" (p. 34). However, Ogbu distinguishes the availability of these cognitive capacities from their application, "Cognitive competencies or cognitive skills, on the other hand, arise from the different ways different populations use the common human cognitive capacities to solve specific cognitive problems they face in their particular environments and in their historical experiences" (Ogbu, 1987, p. 157).

In the case of African Americans, Ogbu (1986, 1987, 1988, 1993) maintains that because of their long history of inferior education and exclusion from middle-class, white-collar jobs that require advanced cognitive skills, African Americans have systematically been deterred from expressing their universal cognitive capacities. Rather, as a reaction to centuries of racial discrimination, Ogbu theorizes that many African Americans have become disillusioned about their future job prospects and the actual value of schooling and have developed a disinterested attitude leading to depressed cognitive performance and scholastic underachievement. Fordham and Ogbu (1986) further proposed that African Americans have developed a sense of collective identity that stands in active opposition to that of European Americans. As a result, behaviors related to cognitive performance, such as speaking standard English, taking math and science courses, studying hard and testing well, are seen by African Americans as attempts to "act White," which cross "cultural and cognitive boundaries" and betray the African American group identity. Some high-achieving African American students have been found to gain success in school at the cost of forsaking their ethnic identity and becoming "raceless" (Fordham, 1988), but pressure to "stay Black" is so intensely felt that many African American adolescents are thought to prefer to maintain their ethnic identities by consciously or unconsciously testing poorly and underachieving.

Studies designed to test Ogbu's theory based on information and data gathered 20 or more years ago (Fordham, 1988, 1996; Fordham & Ogbu, 1986; Mickelson, 1990; Ogbu, 1974) supported the predicted relationships between perceived racial discrimination barriers such as "job ceilings," the maintenance of an oppositional ethnic identity, and depressed African American school performance. Recent studies have provided more mixed results, finding that African American adolescents reported peer support for academic success, no "acting White" stigmatization by peers for doing well in school (Ainsworth-Darnell & Downey, 1998; Cook & Ludwig, 1998; Ogbu & Simons, 1994; Spencer, Noll, Stoltzfus, & Harpalani, 2001), and that high ethnic identity scores were associated instead with increased school engagement and better grades (Taylor, Casten, Flickinger, Roberts, & Fulmore, 1994). The present study adds to the investigation of Ogbu's theory by testing the hypotheses that African American sixth graders through college students with high ethnic identity scores would have lower deductive reasoning performance and grade point averages (GPAs) than those with low ethnic identity scores.

Steele's Stereotype Threat Theory

A second major theoretical model, the stereotype threat theory of Steele (1992, 1997, 1998, 1999), also has proposed that the cognitive performance of African American adolescents is negatively influenced by a history of racial discrimination and prejudice. Steele and Aronson (1995) state, "Whenever African American students perform an explicitly scholastic or intellectual task, they face the threat of confirming or being judged by a negative societal stereotype—a suspicion—about their group's intellectual ability and competence" (p. 797). According to Steele, stereotype threat is experienced as a negative emotional reaction that can interfere with performance in academic evaluation situations, affecting individuals from groups whose abilities have been negatively stereotyped.

Steele further suggests that faced with the continual threat of being judged by or confirming this negative stereotype of intellectual inferiority, over time, African American adolescents may gradually come to devalue school performance and underperform. According to this "school disidentification" hypothesis, "If the poor school achievement of ability-stigmatized groups is mediated by disidentification, then it might be expected that among the ability stigmatized, there would be a disassociation between school outcomes and overall self-esteem" (Steele, 1997, p. 623). Thus, African American adolescents chronically subjected to the added stress of stereotype threat in academic evaluation situations may eventually disengage from school and devalue school performance to protect their self-esteem.

Although Ogbu's cultural-ecological theory and Steele's stereotype threat theory both ascribe African American cognitive underperformance to the negative impact of racial prejudice and discrimination, these models offer distinctly different explanations as to how African American students interpret and respond to these negative conditions. Thus, for instance, whereas Ogbu suggests that African American students interpret testing well and performing well in school as "acting White," constituting a threat to their ethnic group identity to be avoided by performing poorly, Steele suggests that the strain of being judged by or confirming the negative stereotype of Black intellectual inferiority in academic evaluation situations threatens the personal identity and self-esteem of African American students, leading them to gradually disidentify with school, resulting in underachievement.

Osborne (1995, 1997) first tested Steele's school disidentification hypothesis using data from the National Education Longitudinal Study and, as predicted, found a pattern of growing disidentification with school performance in African Americans, with the positive correlation between global self-esteem and school GPA in 8th graders decreasing in both male and female 10th graders and becoming nonsignificant in 12th-grade men. In the current cross-sectional study, Steele's school disidentification thesis was explored further by hypothesizing that the correlation between global self-esteem and GPA would decline in African Americans across all of adolescence, from the 6th grade through college.

In summary, the main developmental hypothesis tested in this study was that deductive reasoning performance would increase across adolescence in African Americans. It was also predicted that (a) high SES African American students would have significantly better deductive reasoning performance than low SES students, (b) adolescents with high ethnic identity scores would have significantly lower reasoning scores and GPAs than those with low ethnic identity scores, and (c) the correlation between self-esteem and GPA would decline across adolescence.

Method

Participants

A total of 330 African American students participated voluntarily, including 62 6th graders (28 men, 34 women), 66 10th graders (34 men, 32 women), 87 12th graders (32 men, 55 women), and 115 college undergraduates (32 men, 83 women). The middle school and high school participants were drawn from public schools located in a major eastern city. The ethnic composition of the middle school was 99% African American, with 70% of the students described by the school district as low income. The high school was 98% African American, with 80% low income students. The college participants attended a public university in a major eastern city with a total enrollment of 26,000 that was 60% European, 26% African American, 10% Asian, and 3% Hispanic.

This sample was not randomly selected but was a sample of convenience including all students who volunteered to participate. Given that approximately 15% of African American high school students drop out before completing their degrees (National Center for Educational Statistics, 1997), some during the middle school years and some during high school, the issue of how to maintain the comparability of the sample from the 6th grade through college was a problem requiring careful attention. To help strengthen the internal validity of the study, the 6th graders were chosen from a middle school with a high (90%) grade promotion rate. The 10th and 12th graders were drawn from the high school's top college preparatory track, and the 12th graders had all been accepted at a college. However, neither the middle school nor high school used were selective in admissions but were schools whose students performed at city-wide averages on standardized tests ("Report Card on the Schools," 1997), and this balance of selectiveness and nonselectiveness was used to maximize comparability without sacrificing the representativeness of this urban African American sample and the generalizability of this study's findings.

Design and Procedure

Participants in groups of 10 to 30 were administered a general information measure, including questions about age, sex, and grade in school or year in college, followed by measures of GPA (Dornbusch, Ritter,

Leiderman, Roberts, & Fraleigh, 1987), SES (Steinberg, Mounts, Lamborn, & Dornbusch, 1991), Rosenberg's (1979) Self-Esteem Scale, Overton's (1990) version of the selection task, and Phinney's (1992) Multigroup Ethnic Identity Measure.

The administration of all measures was performed by the European American first author during school time in school classrooms. Graham (1992) reviewed studies and concluded that there is no evidence suggesting that European American researchers negatively influence the cognitive performance of African Americans. However, Graham also recommended that in studies such as the current one, which did not involve African American researchers, the possibility of limitations due to unknown, potential researcher–participant effects should be acknowledged.

Measures

School GPA   Student GPA was measured using a self-report scale (Dornbusch et al., 1987), consisting of a question asking the participant to select the category describing the usual grades the student gets in school. The categories are as follows: mostly As, about half As and Bs, mostly Bs, about half Bs and half Cs, mostly Cs, about half Cs and half Ds, mostly Ds, and mostly below D. A numerical scale was then related to these responses, with 4.0 representing the "mostly As category," 3.5 representing the "about half As and half Bs" category, and so forth. In previous studies with large multi-ethnic samples, Dornbusch et al. (1987) and Steinberg, Lamborn, Darling, Mounts, and Dornbusch (1994) reported high correlations of $r = .76$ and $r = .80$, respectively, between student GPA measured with the self-report measure and actual student grades taken from school records.

SES   SES was operationalized as the mean educational level of the parents or guardians with whom the participants resided (Steinberg et al., 1991). Parental education has been found to be the most stable component of a family's social class (see Steinberg et al., 1991, for a discussion). This measure asks participants to indicate the highest of eight levels of education completed by each of their parents or guardians, including some grade school, finished grade school, some high school, finished high school, some college or 2-year degree, 4-year college degree, some school beyond college, and professional or graduate school. Each level on this scale is given 1 point, yielding a total score ranging from 1 to 8 points. Scores for both parents are summed and averaged to yield the participant's SES score. Two social class categories were created, with those whose parental education level was below the sample median classified as low SES and those above the median classified as high SES.

table 1   Selection Task Conditional Proposition Statements

If a person is swimming in the public pool, then a lifeguard is present.[a]

If a student is watching television, then the student's homework is finished.

If a person is drinking beer, then the person is 21 years of age.

If a person is driving a motor vehicle, then the person must be over 16 years of age.

If a student is caught running in the halls, then the student must be punished.

If a person is retired from work, then the person is over 55 years of age.

If a student strikes a teacher, then the student is suspended.

If a person has a handgun, then the handgun must be registered.

If a drunken driver kills someone, then the driver must be charged with murder.

If a child with AIDS attends school, then the child has the community's approval

If a girl under 14 years old has an abortion, then she must have her parents' permission.

[a]This was a warm-up problem.

Self-esteem   Global self-esteem was assessed using Rosenberg's (1979) 10-item Self-Esteem Scale ($\alpha = .82$). Rosenberg's measure is considered the most psychometrically sound measure of global self-esteem and has been used extensively with African American adolescents (Gray-Little & Hafdahl, 2000). Participants respond to each of 10 statements on a 4-point Likert-type scale ranging from *strongly disagree* (1) to *strongly agree* (4). This scale contains both positively and negatively worded items regarding the respondent's opinion of his or her self-worth. The total self-esteem score is obtained by reversing negatively worded items, summing all item scores, and obtaining the mean. Scores range from a maximum of 4 (indicating high self-esteem) to a low of 1 (indicating low self-esteem).

Selection task   The selection task (Overton, 1990) is composed of a series of 10 conditional propositions (see Table 1). Formal deductive understanding of an implication ("If p, then q") requires the recognition that particular instances of the antecedent and consequent clauses of a sentence are either permissible, not permissible, or indeterminate. The selection task requires this recognition and coordination between permissible and impermissible instances; thus, it is a valid measure of deductive reasoning. The validity of this measure is further supported by evidence showing a close relationship between deductive reasoning on Overton's selection task and on other tasks (Foltz et al., 1995).

Selection task test booklets were constructed containing 10 problems presented in the conditional "if p, then q" form, such as, "If a person is drinking beer, then the person must be over 21." In each problem, participants were required to establish the logical conditions under which these rules would be broken. A general solution score, giving partial credit for partial solutions, was the first dependent measure. For each problem, participants received one point for each of the following: choosing "p," choosing "not q," not choosing "not p," and not choosing "q," yielding a total possible score with a range of 0 to 40 points across the 10 problems. The correct logical response to selection task problems is the selection of the "p" and the "not q" alternatives while not selecting the "not p" or the "q" alternatives. This selection combination, called the complete falsification solution, was used as a second dependent variable. A score of 1 point was given for each problem when this solution is selected and 0 points for any other response, yielding a score range of 0 to 10 points. Finally, the consistency with which participants selected the complete falsification solution across the 10 problems was assessed. As established in prior research (Chapell & Overton, 1998; Overton et al., 1987; Ward & Overton, 1990), a consistency criterion of 6 complete falsification solutions out of 10 problems was used to indicate the attainment of formal deductive reasoning competence.

Ethnic identity Phinney's (1992) Multigroup Ethnic Identity Measure (MEIM) is a 14-item questionnaire ($\alpha = .78$) that has consistently demonstrated good reliability in many studies across a wide range of ethnic groups, including African Americans (Phinney, 1992; Phinney, Cantu, & Kurtz, 1997; Phinney & Chavira, 1995; Phinney, Ferguson, & Tate, 1997). The MEIM assesses three aspects of ethnic identity: positive ethnic attitudes and sense of belonging (5 items), ethnic identity achievement based on exploration and commitment (7 items), and ethnic behaviors or practices (2 items). Each item is rated on a 4-point scale from *strongly agree* to *strongly disagree*. Scores range from 4 points (indicating high ethnic identity) to 1 point (indicating low ethnic identity). The total MEIM score is derived by reversing negative items, summing across items, and obtaining the mean. High MEIM scores indicate a strong ethnic identity and low scores indicate a weak ethnic identity. Two categories were created, with participants whose ethnic identity scores were below the sample median classified as low ethnic identity and those above the median classified as high ethnic identity.

Results

Prior to testing hypotheses, descriptive statistics for the main variables were computed for the entire sample and for each grade level (see Tables 2 and 3). In addition, a preliminary analysis via MANOVA examined for gender differences. There were no significant differences on any dependent variable based on gender, $F(6, 305) = .98$, $p = .96$, and univariate ANOVAs further confirmed that there were no significant differences on any individual variable based on gender.

Development of Logical Reasoning

To test the main cognitive developmental and contextual hypotheses, a 4 (grade) $\times$ 2 (SES) $\times$ 2 (ethnic identity) ANOVA, adjusted for unequal cell sizes, was

---

table 2   Means, Standard Deviations, and Ranges of the Variables

	M	SD	Range	N
Age (years)	17.72	3.70	12–27	330
GPA	2.95	.64	1.5–4.0	314
SES	4.81	1.31	1.0–8.0	322
Self-esteem	3.40	.44	2.3–4.0	314
Ethnic identity	3.27	.48	1.8–4.0	330
General scores	31.10	6.38	16–40	330
Falsifications	4.44	3.80	0–10	330

Note: GPA = grade point average, SES = socioeconomic status.

table 3   Means, Standard Deviations, and Ranges of the Variables by Grade

	Grade							
	6th		10th		12th		College	
	M	SD	M	SD	M	SD	M	SD
Age (years)	12.70	.47	15.40	.77	17.90	.95	21.50	2.60
GPA	2.82	.70	3.04	.89	2.88	.52	3.02	.56
SES	4.62	1.20	4.84	1.30	4.64	1.20	5.01	1.40
Self-esteem	3.01	.38	3.40	.41	3.46	.40	3.62	.40
Ethnic identity	2.99	.46	3.09	.49	3.30	.39	3.48	.45
General scores	27.20	6.00	29.80	6.30	32.20	6.00	33.00	5.80
Falsifications	2.44	3.10	4.20	3.50	4.64	3.90	5.57	3.80

Note: GPA = grade point average, SES = socioeconomic status. There were no significant between-grade differences in GPA, $F(3, 310) = 1.17$, $p = .32$, or SES, $F(3, 318) = 2.09$, $p = .11$. The modal parental SES level was the completion of high school.

computed on the general solution scores (see Table 4). Given an a priori alpha level of .05 for all statistical tests, there were significant main effects for grade, $F(3, 304) = 9.01$, $p < .001$, (effect size $f = .28$); SES, $F(1, 304) = 3.94$, $p < .05$, ($f = .10$); and ethnic identity, $F(1, 304) = 6.72$, $p < .05$, ($f = .13$). (According to Cohen [1977], effect sizes of $f = .10$ are considered small, whereas those in the .25 range are moderate.) Scheffé tests showed that, as expected, college students ($p < .001$), 12th graders ($p < .001$), and 10th graders ($p < .05$) had higher reasoning scores than 6th graders. There were no other significances between grade differences. High SES students significantly outscored low SES students, $p < .05$. High ethnic identity students

outscored low ethnic identity students, $p < .01$. There were no significant interactions.

To further test these hypotheses, a 4 (grade) × 2 (SES) × 2 (ethnic identity) ANOVA was computed on the complete falsification solution scores (see Table 5). There was a significant main effect for grade level, $F(3, 304) = 6.88$, $p < .001$ ($f = .24$). Scheffé tests showed that, as expected, college students ($p < .001$), 12th graders ($p < .05$), and 10th graders ($p < .05$) had higher reasoning scores than 6th graders. There were no other significances between grade differences and no significant interactions.

The final analyses of reasoning performance compared the consistency with which participants at each

table 4   General Solution Scores by Grade, SES, and Ethnic Identity Level

	Grade							
	6th		10th		12th		College	
	M	SD	M	SD	M	SD	M	SD
Grade	27.2	6.0	29.8	6.3	32.2	6.0	33.0	5.8
SES								
Low	27.2	5.7	28.7	7.4	31.4	5.6	32.8	5.6
High	27.1	6.7	31.1	5.8	33.2	6.4	33.3	6.0
Ethnic identity								
Low	25.6	5.6	28.7	6.2	32.5	6.1	31.5	6.5
High	29.2	6.1	31.8	6.8	31.5	5.9	33.2	5.5

Note: SES = socioeconomic status.

table 5 Complete Falsifications by Grade, SES, and Ethnic Identity Level												
	Grade											
	6th			10th			12th			College		
	M	SD		M	SD		M	SD		M	SD	
Grade	2.4	3.1		4.2	3.5		4.6	3.9		5.6	3.8	
SES												
Low	2.1	3.0		4.0	3.5		4.4	3.7		5.5	3.6	
High	3.0	3.3		4.3	3.6		5.3	4.1		5.6	3.9	
Ethnic identity												
Low	1.9	2.7		3.5	3.2		4.7	4.1		4.6	4.1	
High	3.0	3.5		4.6	3.8		4.9	3.8		5.6	3.6	

Note: SES = socioeconomic status.

grade level, SES level, and ethnic identity level gave the logically correct complete falsification solution. Based on the consistency criterion of 6 of 10 complete falsifications, 18% of 6th graders, 39% of 10th graders, 45% of 12th graders, and 56% of college students were rated as formal deductive reasoners. More college students ($z = 4.88$, $p < .001$), 12th graders ($z = 3.44$, $p < .001$), and 10th graders ($z = 2.62$, $p < .01$) were formal deductive reasoners than were 6th graders. There were also more formal deductive reasoners among college students than 10th graders ($z = 2.21$, $p < .05$). There were no other significant differences between grades and no significant differences in reasoning performance among college freshmen, sophomores, juniors, and seniors, but more college seniors (63%) were formal deductive reasoners than were 12th graders (45%), ($z = 2.28$, $p < .05$). Finally, more high SES students (50%) were formal deductive reasoners than low SES students (29%), χ^2 (1, $N = 322$) = 13.72, $p < .001$, and more high ethnic identity students (45%) were formal deductive reasoners than were low ethnic identity students (33%), χ^2 (1, $N = 330$) = 4.82, $p < .05$.

Differences in Reasoning Performance and GPA Related to Ethnic Identity Level

Contrary to prediction from Ogbu's theory, as shown in the analyses above, high ethnic identity students had significantly higher reasoning scores than did those with low ethnic identity, whether using general solution scores, complete falsifications, or the deductive reasoning consistency criterion. To further test Ogbu's theory, a 4 (grade) × 2 (SES) × 2 (ethnic iden-

tity) ANOVA was computed on student GPAs (see Table 6). There was a significant effect for SES, $F(1, 298) = 4.05$, $p < .05$ ($f = .14$), and post hoc analyses confirmed that high SES students had better GPAs than did low SES students, $p < .05$, but there were no other significant effects or interactions.

Relation Between Self-Esteem and GPA

To test Steele's stereotype threat theory, the final analyses in this study examined the relationship between global self-esteem and school GPA. The correlation of these factors in the whole sample was significant and positive, $r = .27$, $p < .01$ (see Table 7). When analyzed by separate grade levels, however, a different pattern emerged, a pattern of decreasing correlations between self-esteem and GPA from 6th graders through 12th graders, consistent with Steele's school disidentification hypothesis. For 6th graders, the correlation between self-esteem and GPA was significant, $r = .45$, $p < .001$. For 10th and 12th graders, this correlation was not significant, $r = .18$, $p = .15$, and $r = .14$, $p = .21$, respectively. This study extended the investigation of Steele's disidentification hypothesis to include African American college students. Contrary to expectation, there was a strong positive correlation between global self-esteem and GPA in this sample of 115 college students, $r = .51$, $p < .001$. Tests confirmed that the self-esteem and GPA correlations for 10th and 12th graders were significantly different from the correlation for 6th graders, $z = 1.67$ and $z = 2.03$, respectively, $p < .05$, and for the college students, $z = 2.54$ and $z = 2.93$, respectively, $p < .01$. There were no significant differences between the correlations for the

table 6 Student GPA by Grade, SES, and Ethnic Identity Level

	Grade							
	6th		10th		12th		College	
	M	SD	M	SD	M	SD	M	SD
Grade	2.82	.70	3.04	.89	2.88	.52	3.02	.56
SES								
Low	2.78	.69	2.77	.95	2.87	.49	2.88	.51
High	2.88	.74	3.32	.80	2.98	.54	3.13	.59
Ethnic identity								
Low	2.80	.73	2.92	.89	2.72	.48	2.87	.63
High	2.79	.71	3.13	.92	2.96	.53	3.08	.53

Note: SES = socioeconomic status.

10th and 12th graders or between those for the 6th graders and college students.

Discussion

As hypothesized, consistent with cognitive developmental theory and the results of prior research with European American adolescents, this study found that deductive reasoning performance increased systematically across adolescence in African Americans. Of 6th graders, 18% were consistently competent, formal deductive reasoners, compared to 39% of 10th graders, 45% of 12th graders, and 56% of college students. These results suggest that the ability to reason logically develops across adolescence, but more definitive conclusions require further studies, particularly longitudinal investigations that can provide more direct evidence of reasoning development than cross-sectional

studies. Taken as a whole, though, the findings of this initial study of the development of deductive reasoning in African American adolescents agree with and lend considerable weight to the conclusion reached by Smith and Drumming (1989) in their deductive reasoning study with African American college students: "On balance, the results of this study challenge monolithic notions of cognitive development that universally ascribe deficits in reasoning ability to Blacks" (p. 236).

Despite the solid developmental progression of reasoning performance evidenced by the African American students in this study, the average level of selection task performance in each grade was lower than that reported in earlier studies using samples of mainly European American students (Chapell & Overton, 1998; Reene & Overton, 1989). Chapell and Overton (1998) found that 48% of 6th graders, 70% of 10th graders, and 80% of 12th graders were formal deduc-

table 7 Intercorrelations Among the Variables

	1	2	3	4	5	6	7
1. Age	—	.07	.06	.41***	.30***	.31***	.27***
2. GPA		—	.32***	.27**	.24**	.30***	.23**
3. SES			—	.01	.14*	.17**	.16**
4. Self-esteem				—	.39***	.12	.11
5. Ethnic identity					—	.30***	.24***
6. General solution scores						—	.88***
7. Complete falsification scores							—

Note: GPA = grade point average, SES = socioeconomic status.
*p < .05. **p < .01. ***p < .001.

tive reasoners. Reene and Overton (1989) also reported a higher rate of performance in their 3-year longitudinal study with cohorts of 6th graders and 8th graders. Reene and Overton found that 17% of their 6th-grade cohort were formal deductive reasoners in the 6th grade, increasing to 38% by 7th grade and 53% by 9th grade, whereas 38% of the 8th-grade cohort were formal deductive reasoners in 8th grade, increasing to 60% by 9th grade and 67% by 10th grade. It is important to note, however, that in both of these studies the participants were from upper-middle-class families. Given that high SES individuals consistently outscore low SES individuals on a variety of cognitive tests (Williams & Ceci,1997), it seems fair to suggest that part of the deductive reasoning performance differences found between these two studies and the current study may be related to SES differences.

Indeed, given the well-established association between social class and cognitive performance, the relationship of SES differences to reasoning performance was investigated in this study. As hypothesized, high SES African American students signigicantly outperformed low SES students, with 50% of high SES students rated as formal deductive reasoners, compared to 29% of low SES students. High SES students also had significantly higher grades in school than did low SES students. These results agree with and add to previous research, which has shown that higher SES adolescents consistently perform better on IQ and achievement tests than do lower SES students (Neisser et al., 1996; Suzuki & Valencia, 1997; Williams & Ceci, 1997), a performance advantage related to the lower school quality, lower support at home for school success, reduced access to educational resources, and higher levels of stress that are more often experienced by low SES students (McLoyd, 2000; Steinberg,1999). The findings of this study based on SES differences must be interpreted with caution, however, because the measure of SES used in this study relied exclusively on a parental education criterion, and whereas this is one basic index of SES, standard SES measures generally examine at least one other factor, such as parental occupation, employment status, or income (Entwisle & Astone, 1994).

Ogbu's Cultural Ecological Theory

Ogbu's influential theory predicts that adolescents with more developed ethnic identities will have lower reasoning scores and GPAs than those with less developed ethnic identities because reasoning and school tests will be seen as part of the White cultural frame of reference and resistance to "acting White" will depress performance. These hypotheses were not supported in this study with primarily inner-city Black youth; to the contrary, a more developed ethnic identity was related to better reasoning performance and no relationship was found between ethnic identity level and GPA. In this study, participants apparently did not view solving a demanding set of reasoning problems or doing well in school as threats to their ethnic identity, requiring poor performance to avoid crossing "cultural and cognitive boundaries."

One possible explanation for the positive relationship between reasoning performance and ethnic identity, and the lack of any negative relationship between ethnic identity and GPA found in this study, is that social conditions in America are not the same in 2000 as they were in the early 1970s, when Ogbu (1974) originally formulated his theory. Ogbu has long contended that African Americans have been prevented from fully using their cognitive capacities due to substandard schooling and racist exclusion from middle-class jobs reserved for European Americans. However, over the past 30 years, the educational and employment opportunity outlook for Blacks in America has gradually improved, due in part to long-term effects of hard-won civil rights and antidiscrimination legislation, better access to higher education, and affirmative action (Garibaldi, 1997). African American adolescents today may realistically aspire to go to college and obtain middle-class jobs and may thus see performance on cognitive tests as more of a real means for achieving success than did previous generations.

This view is supported by the fact that the percentage of African Americans age 25 to 29 having completed high school is the highest in history (88.7%), as is the percentage of African American high school graduates having completed some college (57.8%) (National Center for Educational Statistics, 2000). Further evidence supporting this view is the trend over the past 30 years toward closing the gap between European American and African American cognitive test scores (Grissmer, Flanagan, & Williamson, 1998; Hedges & Nowell, 1998; Williams & Ceci, 1997), a convergence particularly evident in college graduates (Myerson, Rank, Raines, & Schnitzler, 1998). Taken as a whole, perhaps the issue of performing well on cognitive tests for African Americans circa 2000 is becoming somewhat less of a hard choice between individual achievement and ethnic group solidarity. It is important to note, however, that this study investigated only one key part of Ogbu's theory, namely, the relationship between African American adolescents' ethnic identity and their cognitive performance, and a more comprehensive test of Ogbu's far-reaching model was beyond both the scope and aims of this study.

Steele's Stereotype Threat Theory

Based on Steele's (1992, 1997, 1998, 1999) stereotype threat theory, due to having to cope with the stressful threat of being judged by or confirming the racist, negative stereotype of African American intellectual inferiority, it was expected that African Americans would distance themselves from school performance during adolescence. Thus, global self-esteem might be significantly correlated with GPA in 6th graders but not in high school and college students. This school disidentification hypothesis was partially supported because the correlation between self-esteem and GPA decreased from a strong positive relationship in 6th graders to a nonsignificant relationship in 10th and 12th graders. This study extended the investigation of the school disidentification hypothesis to college students and, against expectation, there was a strong positive correlation between global self-esteem and GPA in this sample of 115 African American undergraduates. It is important to note here that there were no significant differences in either SES or GPA among the 6th-, 10th-, 12th-grade, and college students who participated in this study.

One possible explanation for this association between GPA and self-esteem in African American college students is suggested by the work of Myerson et al. (1998). Using cognitive ability test data collected in the National Longitudinal Survey of Youth, Myerson et al. compared the performance of 120 African Americans and 600 European Americans from 8th grade through college completion. After controlling for differences in school attrition rates, SES, and age, European American test scores were found to increase substantially during high school, whereas African American scores did not. In sharp contrast, between the time of high school graduation and college graduation, test scores of African Americans increased at a rate four times greater than those of European Americans. Thus, whereas European Americans had higher average test scores than African Americans from 8th grade through college, the size of this gap was reduced from 1.1 standard deviations at high school graduation to just 0.4 standard deviations by the end of college. Myerson et al. suggested that the large and widening test score gap between European Americans and African Americans in high school, and the substantial closing of this gap in college, might be due to disparity in the quality of high school education and the subsequent equal quality of the college education experienced by these groups.

Many African Americans attend de facto segregated secondary schools of lower quality than those attended by European Americans and have lower academic performance, even after controlling for SES differences (Garibaldi, 1997; Yancey & Saporito, 1997).

African Americans often receive lower quality education than European Americans, even in integrated schools (Fisher et al., 1998). Once in college, however, African Americans and European Americans experience more comparable education (National Center for Educational Statistics, 1995). In the current study, African Americans may have become disidentified from academic success in high school, as suggested by the lack of association between self-esteem and GPA in the 10th and 12th graders. However, the correlation between self-esteem and academic achievement was as strong in college students as in 6th graders, suggesting a possible pattern of resilient recovery during college analogous to that described by Myerson et al. (1998).

These interpretations must be tempered by the fact that the measure of GPA used in this study was a self-report scale that, although widely used (as in Osborne's 1995 and 1997 studies cited above) and highly correlated with actual grades taken from school records in previous studies (Dornbusch et al., 1987; Steinberg et al., 1994), also has been found to slightly overstate the GPA of students who were averaging a C or less in school. What is less ambiguous is that further investigation into the relationship of African American college student global self-esteem and GPA is needed to test the school disidentification hypothesis of Steele's increasingly influential stereotype threat theory. Whereas the negative impact of stereotype threat on African American college students' test performance and disidentification from school has been well demonstrated under experimental conditions using various cognitive tests (Major, Spencer, Schmader, Wolfe, & Crocker, 1998; Steele & Aronson, 1998), to date there have been no large-scale studies published examining the relationship between global self-esteem and college GPA in African American college students and students from other ethnic groups.

Summary

In conclusion, the main developmental finding of this study was that African Americans showed a clear pattern of progress in deductive reasoning performance from early through late adolescence. On average, the 6th-grade, preteen participants were not consistently logical reasoners, whereas the high school students reasoned better than the 6th graders but not as well as the college students, who were entering adulthood having developed consistently strong logical reasoning skills. This study also found that cognitive performance was significantly related to contextual factors, with high SES students consistently outscoring low SES students in reasoning and grades.

Ogbu's cultural-ecological theory, which predicts an inverse relationship between cognitive performance and ethnic identity strength in African American adolescents, was not supported because better reasoning performance was associated instead with stronger ethnic identity. Steele's stereotype threat school disidentification thesis, which predicts that African American global self-esteem and GPA would be associated in early adolescence but become dissociated thereafter, was partially supported. Self-esteem and GPA were strongly related in 6th graders, not significantly related in high school students, yet strongly related in college students.

REFERENCES

Ainsworth-Darnell, J. W., & Downey, D. B. (1998). Assessing the oppositional culture explanation for racial/ethnic differences in school performance. *American Sociological Review, 63*, 536–553.

Bell, Y. R., Brown, R., & Bryant, A. R. (1993). Traditional and culturally-relevant presentations of a logical reasoning task and performance among African-American students. *Western Journal of Black Studies, 17*, 173–178.

Chapell, M. S., & Overton, W. F. (1998). Development of logical reasoning in the context of parental style and test anxiety. *Merrill-Palmer Quarterly, 44*, 141–156.

Cheng, P. W., & Holyoak, K. J. (1985). Pragmatic reasoning schemas. *Cognitive Psychology, 17*, 391–416.

Cohen, J. (1977). *Statistical power analysis for the behavioral sciences.* New York: Academic Press.

Cook, P. J., & Ludwig, J. (1998). The burden of "acting White": Do Black adolescents disparage academic achievement? In C. Jencks & M. Phillips (Eds.), *The Black–White test score gap* (pp. 375–400). Washington, DC: Brookings Institution.

Cooper, C. R., & Denner, J. (1998). Theories linking culture and psychology: Universal and community-specific processes. *Annual Review of Psychology, 49*, 559–584.

Cosmides, L. (1989). The logic of social exchange: Has natural selection shaped how humans reason? Studies with the Wason selection task. *Cognition, 31*, 187–276.

DeShon, R. P., Smith, M. R., Chan, D., & Schmitt, N. (1998). Can racial differences in cognitive test performance be reduced by presenting problems in a social context? *Journal of Applied Psychology, 83*, 438–451.

Dornbusch, S. M., Ritter, P. L., Leiderman, P. H., Roberts, D. F., & Fraleigh, M. J., (1987). The relation of parenting style to adolescent school performance. *Child Development, 58*, 1244–1257.

Entwisle, D. R., & Astone, N. M. (1994). Some practical guidelines for measuring youth's race/ethnicity and socioeconomic status. *Child Development, 65*, 1521–1540.

Evans, J. St. B. T. (1996). Deciding before you think: Relevance and reasoning in the selection task. *British Journal of Psychology, 87*, 223–240.

Fisher, C. B., Jackson, J. F., & Villaruel, F. A. (1998). The study of African American and Latin American children and youth.

In W. M. Damon (Series Ed.) & R. M. Lerner (Vol. Ed.), *Handbook of child psychology: Vol. 1. Theoretical models of human development* (5th ed., pp. 1145–1207). New York: John Wiley.

Foltz, C., Overton, W. F., & Ricco, R. B. (1995). Adolescent development from inductive to deductive problem solving. *Journal of Experimental Child Psychology, 59*, 179–195.

Fordham, S. (1988). Racelessness as a factor in Black students' school success: Pragmatic strategy or pyrrhic victory? *Harvard Educational Review, 58*, 54–84.

Fordham, S. (1996). *Blacked out: Dilemmas of race, identity and success at Capital High.* Chicago: University of Chicago Press.

Fordham, S., & Ogbu, J. (1986). Black student's school success: Coping with the burden of "acting white." *Urban Review, 18*, 176–206.

Garibaldi, A. M. (1997). Four decades of progress . . . and decline: An assessment of African American educational attainment. *Journal of Negro Education, 66*, 105–120.

Graham, S. (1992). "Most of the subjects were White and middle-class." *American Psychologist, 47*, 629–639.

Gray-Little, B., & Hafdahl, A. R. (2000). Factors influencing racial comparisons of self-esteem: A quantitative review. *Psychological Bulletin, 126*, 26–54.

Grissmer, D., Flanagan, A., & Williamson, S. (1998). Why did the Black–White score gap narrow in the 1970s and 1980s? In C. Jencks & M. Phillips (Eds.), *The Black–White test score gap* (pp. 182–226). Washington, DC: Brookings Institution.

Hedges, L. V., & Nowell, A. (1998). Black–White test score convergence since 1965. In C. Jencks & M. Phillips (Eds.), *The Black-White test score gap* (pp. 149–181). Washington, DC: Brookings Institution.

Inhelder, B., & Piaget, J. (1958). *The growth of logical thinking from childhood to adolescence.* New York: Basic Books.

Jencks, C., & Phillips, M. (Eds.), (1998). *The Black–White test score gap.* Washington, DC: Brookings Institution.

Lerner, R. M., & Galambos, N. L. (1998). Adolescent development: Challenges and opportunities for research, programs, and policies. *Annual Review of Psychology, 49*, 413–446.

Major, B., Spencer, S., Schmader, T., Wolfe, C., & Crocker, J. (1998). Coping with negative stereotypes about intellectual performance: The role of psychosocial disengagement. *Personality and Social Psychology Bulletin, 24*, 34–50.

McLoyd, V. C. (2000). Poverty. In A. Kazdin (Ed.), *Encyclopedia of psychology.* New York: Oxford University Press.

Mickelson, R. A. (1990). The attitude–achievement paradox among Black adolescents. *Sociology of Education, 63*, 44–61.

Myerson, J., Rank, M. R., Raines, R. Q., & Schnitzler, M. A. (1998). Race and general cognitive ability: The myth of diminishing returns to education. *Psychological Science, 9*, 139–142.

National Center for Educational Statistics. (1995). *Minority undergraduate participation in postsecondary education.* Washington, DC: U.S. Department of Education, Office of Educational Research and Improvement.

National Center for Educational Statistics. (1997). *Dropout rates in the United States: 1996.* Washington, DC: U.S. Department of Education, Office of Educational Research and Improvement.

National Center for Educational Statistics. (2000). *The condition of education 2000*. Washington, DC: U.S. Department of Education, Office of Educational Research and Improvement.

Neisser, U., Boodoo, G., Bouchard, T. J., Jr., Boykin, A. W., Brody, N., Ceci, S.J., et al. (1996). Intelligence: Knowns and unknowns. *American Psychologist, 51*, 77–101.

Ogbu, J. U. (1974). *The next generation: An ethnography of education in an urban neighborhood*. New York: Academic Press.

Ogbu, J. U. (1986). The consequences of the American caste system. In U. Neisser (Ed.), *The school achievement of minority children* (pp. 19–56). Hillsdale, NJ: Lawrence Erlbaum.

Ogbu, J. U. (1987). Cultural influences on plasticity in human development. In J. J. Gallagher & C. T. Ramey (Eds.), *The malleability of children* (pp. 155–169). Baltimore: Brooks.

Ogbu, J. U. (1988). Cultural diversity and human development. In D. T. Slaughter (Ed.), *Black children and poverty: A developmental perspective* (pp. 11–28). San Francisco: Jossey-Bass.

Ogbu, J. U. (1993). Differences in cultural frame of reference. *International Journal of Behavioral Development, 16*, 483–506.

Ogbu, J. U., & Simons, H. D. (1994). *Cultural models of school achievement: A quantitative test of Ogbu's theory*. Berkeley: University of California Press. (ERIC Document Reproduction Service No. ED376515)

Osborne, J. W. (1995). Academics, self-esteem, and race: A look at the underlying assumptions of the disidentification hypothesis. *Personality and Social Psychology Bulletin, 21*, 728–735.

Osborne, J. W. (1997). Race and academic disidentification. *Journal of Educational Psychology, 89*, 728–735.

Overton, W. F. (1990). Competence and procedures: Constraints on the development of logical reasoning. In W. F. Overton (Ed.), *Reasoning, necessity, and logic: Developmental perspectives* (pp. 1–32). Hillsdale, NJ: Lawrence Erlbaum.

Overton, W. F. (1994). Reasoning. In V.S. Ramachandran (Ed.), *Encyclopedia of human behavior: Vol. 4* (pp. 13–24). New York: Academic Press.

Overton, W. F., Ward, S. L., Noveck, I. A., Black, J., & O'Brien, D. P. (1987). Form and content in the development of deductive reasoning. *Developmental Psychology, 21*, 692–701.

Phinney, J. S. (1992). The Multigroup Ethnic Identity Measure: A new scale for use with diverse groups. *Journal of Adolescent Research, 2,* 156–176.

Phinney, J. S. Cantu, C., & Kurtz, D. (1997). Ethnic and American identity as predictors of self-esteem among African American, Latino, and White adolescents. *Journal of Youth and Adolescence, 26*, 165–185.

Phinney, J. S., & Chavira, V. (1995). Parental ethnic socialization and adolescent coping with problems related to ethnicity. *Journal of Research on Adolescence, 5*, 31–53.

Phinney, J. S., Ferguson, D. L., & Tate, J. D. (1997). Intergroup attitudes among ethnic minority adolescents: A causal model. *Child Development, 68*, 955–969.

Reene, K. J., & Overton, W. F. (1989, June). *Longitudinal investigation of adolescent deductive reasoning*. Paper presented at the biennial meeting of the Society for Research in Child Development, Kansas City, Missouri.

Report card on the schools: Do ours make the grade. A region-wide look at public education. (1997, September 14). *The Philadelphia Inquirer*, pp. L1-L20.

Rosenberg, M. (1979). *Conceiving the self*. New York: Basic Books.

Smith, W. I., & Drumming, S.T. (1989). On the strategies that Blacks employ in deductive reasoning. *Journal of Black Psychology, 16*, 1–22.

Spencer, M. B., Noll, E., Stoltzfus, J., & Harpalani, V. (2001). Identity and school adjustment: Revisiting the "acting White" assumption. *Educational Psychologist, 36*, 21–30.

Steele, C. M. (1992, April). Race and the schooling of Black Americans. *Atlantic Monthly*, pp. 68–78.

Steele, C. M. (1997). A threat in the air: How stereotypes shape intellectual identity and performance. *American Psychologist, 52*, 613–629.

Steele, C. M. (1998). Stereotyping and its threat are real. *American Psychologist, 53*, 680–681.

Steele, C. M. (1999). Thin ice: "Stereotype threat" and Black college students. *Atlantic Monthly*, pp. 44–54.

Steele, C. M., & Aronson, J. (1995). Stereotype threat and the intellectual test performance of African Americans. *Journal of Personality and Social Psychology, 69*, 797–811.

Steele, C. M., & Aronson, J. (1998). Stereotype threat and the test performance of academically successful African Americans. In C. Jencks & M. Phillips (Eds.), *The Black-White test score gap* (pp. 401–427). Washington, DC: Brookings Institution.

Steinberg, L. (1999). *Adolescence* (5th ed.). New York: McGraw-Hill.

Steinberg, L., Dornbusch, S. M., & Brown, B. B. (1992). Ethnic differences in adolescent achievement: An ecological perspective. *American Psychologist, 47*, 723–729.

Steinberg, L., Lamborn, S. D., Darling, N., Mounts, N. S., & Dornbusch, S. M. (1994). Overtime changes in adjustment and competence among adolescents from authoritative, authoritarian, indulgent, and neglectful families. *Child Development, 65*, 754–770.

Steinberg, L., & Morris, A. S. (2000). Adolescent development. *Annual Review of Psychology, 52*, 83–110.

Steinberg, L., Mounts, N. S., Lamborn, S. D., & Dornbusch, S. M. (1991). Authoritative parenting and adolescent adjustment across varied ecological niches. *Journal of Research on Adolescence, 1*, 19–36.

Suzuki, L. A., & Valencia, R. R. (1997). Race-ethnicity and measured intelligence: Educational implications. *American Psychologist, 52*, 1103–1114.

Taylor, R. D., Casten, R., Flickinger, S. M., Roberts, D., & Fulmore, C. (1994). Explaining the school performance of African-American adolescents. *Journal of Research on Adolescence, 4*, 21–44.

Ward, S. L., & Overton, W. F. (1990). Semantic familiarity, relevance, and the development of deductive reasoning. *Developmental Psychology, 26*, 488–493.

Wason, P. C. (1968). Reasoning about a rule. *Quarterly Journal of Experimental Psychology, 20,* 273–281.

Williams, W. M., & Ceci, S. J. (1997). Are Americans becoming more or less alike? Trends in race, class, and ability differences in intelligence. *American Psychologist, 52,* 1226–1235.

Yancey, W. L., & Saporito, S. J. (1997). Racial and economic segregation and educational outcomes: One tale, two cities. In R. D. Taylor & M. C. Wang (Eds.), *Social and emotional adjustment and family relations in ethnic minority families* (pp. 159–179). Mahwah, NJ: Lawrence Erlbaum.

Questions

1. Why did the researchers concentrate on deductive reasoning in African American adolescents?
2. What was the basis for the hypothesis advanced in this research regarding the relation between socioeconomic status and deductive reasoning in African American youth?
3. According to Ogbu, why are cognitive differences often found in research that compares African American and European American adolescents?
4. Are this study's findings about the development of reasoning by African American adolescents consistent with research on this topic conducted among European American adolescents? Why or why not?
5. According to this study, how did ethnic identity relate to adolescents' reasoning scores? Does this result support or contradict Ogbu's cultural-ecological theory?
6. Was Steele's stereotype-threat theory supported by this research? Explain why or why not.

34 Authority, Autonomy, and Family Relationships Among Adolescents in Urban and Rural China

Wenxin Zhang • Andrew J. Fuligni

Chinese adolescents, like their counterparts in the United States and elsewhere, strive for autonomy from their parents. In all cultures, how and when adolescents reach this goal is affected by cultural values regarding family relationships and responsibilities. In China, traditional values of familial support and obligation, especially toward parents and ancestors, are vital to family functioning. As a result, even as Chinese adolescents become more independent from their parents, these core cultural values frame many aspects of their family relationships. In recent years, the people of China have experienced massive social and economic changes that have had tremendous impact on Chinese children and their families. These societal changes have introduced many new challenges to Chinese families, and some of these challenges have the potential to undermine long held traditional values. Do the large-scale societal transformations occurring in China today influence how adolescents balance their needs for autonomy with the traditional values of familial obligation? And are there regional variations in this process? Given China's enormous size and complexity, adolescents growing up in urban regions may experience the impact of these societal changes differently than adolescents who live in rural settings.

In the following article, Wenxin Zhang and Andrew Fuligni examine these questions. Because the social and economic changes in China are more pronounced in urban than rural regions, the authors were able to study the development of autonomy under varying levels of exposure to such change. Zhang and Fuligni's findings provide insight into how societal changes become part of the psychological development of an individual child. As you read this article, you can begin to imagine how these dynamic social and developmental processes may contribute to generational change. And, perhaps, as this study suggests, they may even lead to greater differences between adolescents in the same culture who grow up in urban versus rural settings.

Approximately 700 urban and rural 10th- (M = 16.6 years) and 12th- (M = 18.9 years) grade students in China completed measures assessing their beliefs about parental authority and individual autonomy, as well as aspects of their relationships with their parents. Urban adolescents indicated a greater willingness to disagree openly with their parents, a greater intensity of conflict with their parents, lower levels of cohesion with their parents, and a lower frequency of discussions with their fathers. Urban males were distinct from all other adolescents in terms of several aspects of their family relationships, reporting the earliest expectations for autonomy, the lowest levels of closeness with their mothers, and the least frequent discussions with their fathers.

In the last two decades of the 20th century, China began to undergo radical social and economic changes that many observers believe will undermine cultural traditions of filial piety, parental authority, and family closeness (Fang, 2000; Huang, 1989; Yang, 1989). In an attempt to move the country from a socialist system to a free-market economy, the government began to allow citizens to develop private businesses, many state-owned enterprises became privatized, and stock markets opened in several major

Reprinted with permission from Zhang, W. & Fuligni, A. J.,"Authority, Autonomy, and Family Relationships Among Adolescents in Urban and Rural China", *Journal of Research on Adolescence, 16,* 527–537, © 2006 Blackwell Publishers.

cities (Tang & Parish, 2000). The transition to a market economy that rewards individual initiative has generated concerns because such transformations have seemingly eroded familistic traditions in other societies in the past (e.g., the Industrial Revolution in Europe; Goode, 1971). Some social scientists in China believe that the same could occur in their country: "China is now at a crossroads: It can either become an individualistic, morally declined society, or it can reestablish a firm moral order according to traditional values" (Jing & Zhang, 1998, p. 274).

Several social observers have noted that the dominant political economy of a society shapes the nature of the adolescent period (e.g., Modell & Goodman, 1990). Focusing on the family relationships of contemporary Chinese adolescents, therefore, is a potentially valuable way to gain insight into the impact of the transition to a market economy on family life. Given that the economic changes have been taking place mainly in urban areas (Tang & Parish, 2000), a comparison of the family relationships of adolescents in urban and rural areas could provide an initial glimpse into the impact of economic change on family relationships. Families in rural Chinese areas live largely agricultural lives and severe travel restrictions result in limited exposure to the opportunities of the market economy in the cities. In the absence of historical data, then, an urban–rural comparison provides a way to examine potential variations in the family lives of adolescents in the same society who experience very different economic systems.

In an earlier paper, we reported that the urban-rural difference in Chinese adolescents' attitudes toward familial support and obligation depended upon the gender of the adolescents (Fuligni & Zhang, 2004). Chinese boys living in an urban center reported the weakest sense of obligation to support and assist their family, whereas urban girls were quite similar to rural boys and girls in their greater sense of familial duty. Traditional gender norms favoring the economic participation of men over women in China may mean that urban males are more likely to see economic opportunity in the recent market reforms, thereby lessening their sense of obligation to the family.

In the current paper, we examined whether urban–rural and gender differences are evident in other aspects of family relationships. Specifically, we focused on adolescents' beliefs and expectations about parental authority and individual autonomy and the frequency of conflict, cohesion, and discussions between adolescents and their parents. Adolescence is a critical period of transformation in these aspects of parent–child relationships (Smetana, 1988; Steinberg, 1990), and it is important to examine whether location and gender variations are apparent in teenagers' ideas of authority and autonomy and in their interactions with their parents. On the one hand,

it might be expected that rural adolescents accept greater parental authority and have closer relationships with their parents than urban adolescents. On the other, it is possible that the market reforms in the urban areas only affect notions of filial piety and duty to the larger family unit, as opposed to the more dyadic relationships between adolescents and their parents, which may be less dependent upon larger societal systems and structures (Fuligni & Flook, 2005). We also were interested in whether any effects of living in an urban area were more evident for boys than girls, as we found in our previous analyses of family obligation (Fuligni & Zhang, 2004). Finally, given the higher levels of education and the higher frequency of only children in the urban areas, we believed it was important to examine whether these two factors contributed to any observed location differences in family relationships.

Method

Sample

A total of 704 students in the 10th (M_{age} = 16.6 years) and 12th (M_{age} = 18.9 years) grades of six high schools in China completed self-report questionnaires during school hours. Approximately half of the sample lived in an urban area and attended three schools in Jinan, the capital city of Shandong Province in Middle Eastern China, with a population of 3 million. All students in the urban schools grew up in the city and lived with their families while attending school. The other half of the sample attended three schools in the rural areas of Shandong Province, where the majority of the population is classified as peasants. In China, peasants are individuals who have their own farms and till the land for their own subsistence. These individuals do not have permanent jobs in which they earn regular incomes throughout the year. Rural individuals who are not peasants tend to work at permanent jobs in the neighboring towns. During the school year, the students follow the typical practice in rural schools of residing at the schools 6 days/week, and returning home to visit their families on Sundays. The total sample from both locations was fairly evenly divided between males (53%) and females (47%).

Adolescents in the urban and rural areas differed in terms of a number of family characteristics, consistent with national trends. As a result of the differential enforcement of the one-child family policy in urban and rural areas, 82% of the adolescents in the urban schools had no siblings as compared with only 24% of those in the rural schools. The majority of the parents in the rural schools were peasants, with most of the urban parents working in occupations ranging from blue collar to professional. Parental educational level showed similar differences, with the parents in the urban areas having received more formal education than the parents in the rural areas (e.g., mothers who attended some college: urban, 20%, rural, 3%).

Measures

The measures used in this study were Chinese translations of measures originally used by Fuligni (1998) in a similar study of family relationships among ethnically diverse adolescents in the United States. Measures were evaluated by Chinese psychologists in China for their appropriateness, and the measures were translated into Chinese through a process of translation and back-translation by independent individuals who knew and understood both Chinese and English. Alpha coefficients for each multiple-item measure are presented in parentheses.

Beliefs and Expectations about Authority and Autonomy

Acceptability of Disagreement with Parents. Using a scale ranging from "almost never" (1) to "almost always" (5), students responded separately for mothers and fathers to six items such as "I should argue with my mother [father] when I disagree with her [him]," "If I am mad at my mother [father], I should tell her [him] so," and "If I think one of mother's [father's] rules is wrong, I should tell her [him]." (α's: mother = .74, father = .75).

Expectations for Behavioral Autonomy. Adolescents' expectations for when they would be allowed to engage in various autonomous behaviors were measured by a scale that Feldman and her associates had used in their studies of Chinese adolescents in Hong Kong (Feldman & Rosenthal, 1990). Students were presented with a list of 11 behaviors such as "watch as much TV as you want," "choose your own hair style even if your parents disapprove," and "choose what clothes to buy, even if your parents disapprove." The original scale consisted of 12 items. In the present study, one item ("go to parties at night") was deleted because of the rare occurrence of this activity among adolescents in China. Adolescents then indicated the age at which they expected to be allowed to do each thing using a five-point scale indicating particular ages, such as 1 (before 14 years old), 3 (16–17 years old), and 5 (never be allowed to) (α = .79).

Endorsement of Parental Authority. Using Smetana's (1988) measure, students were presented with a list of 13 topics, such as curfew, choosing clothes, and choosing friends, and were asked whether it was "OK" or "Not OK" for their parents to make a rule about each topic. The number of items to which students indicated "OK" were then summed to yield a total score (α = .69).

Parent–Adolescent Relationships

Cohesion. Students completed the cohesion subscale of the Family Adaptation and Cohesion Evaluation Scales (FACES) II inventory separately for each parent (Olson, Sprenkle, & Russell, 1979). Using a scale ranging from 1 ("almost never") to 5 ("almost always"), students responded to 10 questions such as "My mother [father] and I feel very close to each other," "My mother and I are supportive of each other during difficult times," and "My mother and I avoid each other at home" (reversed). This scale has been used in previous research on the changes in parent–child relationships during adolescence (Fuligni, 1998; Steinberg, 1988) (α's: mother = .75, father = .81).

Conflict. Adolescents' perceptions of the incidence and intensity of parent–adolescent conflict were measured using the Issues Checklist, developed by Prinz, Foster, Kent, and O'Leary (1979). This measure has been used in numerous studies of parent–child relationships during adolescence (e.g., Steinberg, 1988; Fuligni, 1998). Students indicated whether any of 11 specific topics (e.g., chores, cursing, helping around the house) were discussed with their mother and father in the last 2 weeks. For each topic that was discussed, the intensity of the discussion was rated from 1 ("very calm") to 5 ("very angry"). To be consistent with previous research (e.g., Steinberg, 1988), the measure of the incidence of parent–adolescent conflict was computed by summing the number of discussions rated as containing anger (2 or greater). Students completed two versions of the checklist, one in reference to each parent. The measure of intensity of conflict was obtained by averaging adolescents' rating on those discussions that were rated as conflictual (α's: mother = .72, father = .73).

Discussions. Adolescents responded to five items asking whether or not they discussed a number of different topics (future job plans, current classes, personal problems, future educational plans, future family plans) with each of their parents. The adolescents rated the frequency of these discussions from 1 ("almost never") to 5 ("almost always") (α's: mother = .78, father = .79).

Parental Rules. Using a measure developed by Smetana (1988), adolescents were presented with a list of 13 topics, such as curfew, choosing clothes, and choosing friends, and were asked whether or not their parents had a rule about each topic. The number of items to which students indicated "Yes" was then summed to yield a total score (α = .72).

Results

Variations in adolescents' beliefs, expectations, and relationships were examined by conducting a series of location (urban versus rural) × gender (male versus female) and grade (10th grade versus 12th grade) analyses of variance. These analyses were then followed by analyses of the role of parental education and adolescents' sibling status (only child versus those with siblings) in any observed location differences.

Beliefs and Expectations about Authority and Autonomy

As shown in Table 1, urban adolescents generally believed that it was more acceptable to disagree openly with their parents than rural adolescents, Location: $Fs(1,684, 691) = 13.90$ and 23.19, p's $< .001$. The location difference for disagreement with father was modified by gender, however, indicating that urban girls reported a greater acceptability of disagreeing with their father than urban boys and rural boys and girls, Location × Gender: $F(1, 684) = 5.85$, $p < .05$. In terms of behavioral autonomy, both location and location × gender effects emerged as significant, indicating that urban boys had earlier expectations for autonomy than urban girls and rural boys and girls, who, in turn, possessed similar expectations for autonomy, Location and Location × Gender: $Fs(1, 687) = 17.73$ and 9.98, p's $< .001$ and $.01$. Urban and rural adolescents did not differ in their endorsement of parental authority, but girls reported a greater endorsement than boys, Gender: $F(1, 691) = 5.57$, $p < .05$. Overall grade differences did not emerge in any of the adolescents' beliefs and expectations, but grade did interact with gender in predicting adolescents' expectations for autonomy, Grade × Gender: $F(1, 687) = 3.87$, $p < .05$. Boys expected earlier autonomy than girls in the 10th grade, but there was no gender difference in the 12th grade.

Parent–Adolescent Relationships

As shown in Table 2, urban adolescents reported a slightly higher frequency of conflict with mothers and a greater intensity of conflicts with both parents than did rural adolescents, Location: $Fs(1, 527–676) = 5.17–9.05$, p's $< .05–.01$. Overall, boys reported more conflicts with mothers than did girls, Gender: $F(1,676) = 4.86$, $p < .05$. The gender difference in conflict with fathers varied according to location such that boys reported more conflicts with fathers than did girls in the rural area, whereas boys and girls indicated a similar incidence of conflict with fathers in the urban area, Location × Gender: $F(1, 663) = 4.51$, $p < .05$. Tenth-grade students reported higher conflict frequency and greater conflict intensity with parents than did twelfth-grade students, Grade: $Fs (1, 527–676) = 6.07$ to 15.31, p's $< .05$ to $.01$.

Location differences also emerged in parent-adolescent cohesion, with rural adolescents reporting closer relationships with both mothers and fathers than did urban adolescents, Location: $Fs(1, 675–681) = 10.52$ and 15.10, p's $< .01$. The location difference in cohesion with mother was modified by gender, however, such that urban boys reported lower levels of cohesion with their mothers than did rural boys but girls of both locations reported similar cohesion with mothers. Twelfth-grade students reported greater closeness with mothers than tenth-grade students, but there was no grade difference in cohesion with fathers.

Rural adolescents had more frequent discussions with their fathers concerning their future career, education, and their school performance than did urban adolescents, Location: $F(1, 639) = 13.88$, $p < .001$, but the two groups did not differ in how frequently they communicated with their mothers. The location difference in discussion with father was modified by both gender and grade, however. Urban boys reported fewer discussions with their fathers than did urban girls, but rural girls and boys reported similar amounts of communication with their fathers, Loca-

---

table 1 **Adolescents' Beliefs and Expectations about Authority and Autonomy According to Location and Gender**

	Urban, M (SD)		Rural, M (SD)	
	Male	**Female**	**Male**	**Female**
Disagreement with mother	3.24 (82)	3.41 (.81)	3.02 (.66)	3.09 (.66)
Disagreement with father	2.86 (.86)	3.26 (.89)	2.79 (.69)	2.89 (.63)
Behavioral autonomy	3.52 (.70)	3.83 (.56)	3.82 (.49)	3.88 (.44)
Endorsement of parental authority	5.81 (2.76)	6.67 (2.80)	6.45 (2.80)	6.52 (2.47)

table 2 Parent–Adolescent Relationships According to Location and Gender

	Urban, M (SD)		Rural, M (SD)	
	Male	**Female**	**Male**	**Female**
Conflict incidence				
Mother	1.60 (1.81)	1.51 (1.81)	1.52 (1.82)	1.01 (1.37)
Father	.92 (1.40)	.95 (1.42)	1.11 (1.65)	.67 (1.09)
Conflict intensity				
Mother	1.54 (.55)	1.54 (.64)	1.42 (.44)	1.41 (.63)
Father	1.63 (.76)	1.62 (.86)	1.45 (.55)	1.39 (.56)
Cohesion				
Mother	3.37 (.52)	3.72 (.65)	3.62 (.47)	3.78 (.58)
Father	3.30 (.67)	3.46 (.69)	3.54 (.58)	3.53 (.67)
Discussions				
Mother	2.56 (.83)	2.86 (.81)	2.69 (.79)	2.86 (.75)
Father	2.41 (.78)	2.66 (.83)	2.76 (.80)	2.75 (.74)
Parental rules	5.01 (3.37)	6.05 (2.90)	5.91 (2.79)	5.74 (2.55)

tion × Gender: $F(1, 639) = 5.10$, $p < .05$. Tenth-grade students reported more communication with fathers than did twelfth-grade students in the urban area, whereas the two age groups did not differ in how often they communicated with fathers in the rural area, Location × Grade: $F(1, 639) = 7.98$, $p < .01$. Overall, girls reported more frequent discussions with their mothers than did boys, Gender: $F(1, 649) = 13.45$, $p < .01$.

Although there was no overall location difference for parental rules, girls reported more rules than did boys, $F(1, 688) = 3.99$, $p < .05$. A Location × Gender interaction did emerge such that urban boys reported fewer rules than did urban girls and rural boys and girls, Location × Gender: $F(1, 688) = 7.03$, $p < .01$.

Parental Education and Sibling Status

Parental education was associated with a number of different beliefs, expectations, and aspects of parent–adolescent relationships. Adolescents with parents of higher educational levels possessed a greater acceptance of openly disagreeing with parents, a greater endorsement of parental authority, more cohesion and discussions with parents, and perceived more parental rules. Controlling for parental education reduced only one location effect to nonsignificance, however, such that the location difference in the incidence of conflict with mothers became nonsignificant. All other location effects remained significant after controlling for parental educational levels.

The only association of sibling status with beliefs, expectations, and relationships to emerge was the tendency for only children to indicate a greater acceptance of disagreeing with mothers than those with siblings, $F(1, 695) = 8.82$, $p < .01$. Controlling for sibling status did not change the original location difference for disagreement with mother.

Discussion

Many differences between urban and rural adolescents emerged in terms of their beliefs, expectations, and relationships with parents. Urban adolescents indicated a greater willingness to disagree openly with their parents, a greater intensity of conflict with their parents, lower levels of cohesion with their parents, and a lower frequency of discussions with their fathers. Other findings suggested that urban males were distinct from all other adolescents in terms of several aspects of their family relationships, just as they were with their sense of familial duty and obligation in our previous paper (Fuligni & Zhang, 2004). Urban boys possessed the earliest expectations for autonomy, the lowest levels of closeness with their mothers, and reported the least frequent discussions with their fathers. The only exception was in the tendency for urban girls to report the greatest willingness to disagree with their fathers. Although urban and rural adolescents together still reported greater endorsement of parental authority, later expectations for autonomy, and less conflict and more cohesion with their parents than do American adolescents with both Chinese and European backgrounds (Fuligni, 1998), the differences between urban and rural teenagers suggest that the economic reforms taking place in China may be changing the traditional dynamics of authority, autonomy, and closeness in urban Chinese families.

As urban children perceive greater opportunity for economic advancement based upon individual initiative, they may be lessening their ties to their families more than the rural adolescents who do not have the same opportunities, a dynamic that has been observed historically in other societies (Goode, 1971). This may be especially true for urban males, who may anticipate being more able to take advantage of the market reforms because of traditional gender norms regarding the economic participation of men and women. It appears that parents actually may be contributing to this gender differentiation, given the reports of the urban males that their parents place the fewest number of rules upon them and that they expect the earliest autonomy.

Given the lack of historical data on these issues, it is possible that the location variations in family relationships observed in this study reflect long-standing differences between urban and rural families rather than the impact of the shift to a free-market economy. Family relationships in rural and urban families may differ because of variations in occupational demands, the nature of schooling and peer groups, and residential living arrangements that are independent of the dominant political economy. It is also important to note that the findings of this study are limited to Chinese adolescents who attend secondary school and may not apply to the approximately 50% of the population who do not attend school because of failing to pass the required entrance exams (The Ministry of Education, People's Republic of China, 2002). Additional studies should be conducted in future years with a broader population of Chinese adolescents and should be compared with this study in order to examine whether the social and economic changes taking place will indeed have a long-term impact upon traditional patterns of family relationships in China.

Acknowledgments

Support for this study was provided by a William T. Grant Faculty Scholars award to the second author. The authors would like to thank the participating students and schools, and acknowledge the assistance of Meiping Wang and Yiwen Wang with the data collection and preparation.

REFERENCES

Fang, G. G. (2000). Exploration of filial piety of confucianism. In D. Q. Wang (Ed.), *Research on the oriental morality* (pp. 34–44). Beijing: China Business Association Press.

Feldman, S. S., & Rosenthal, D. A. (1990). The acculturation of autonomy expectations in Chinese high-schoolers residing in two western nations. *International Journal of Psychology, 25,* 259–281.

Fuligni, A. J. (1998). Authority, autonomy, and parent-adolescent conflict and cohesion: A study of adolescents from Mexican, Chinese, Filipino, and European backgrounds. *Developmental Psychology, 34,* 782–792.

Fuligni, A. J., & Flook, L. (2005). A social identity approach to ethnic differences in family relationships during adolescence. In R. Kail (Ed.), *Advances in child development and behavior* (pp. 125–152). New York: Academic Press.

Fuligni, A. J., & Zhang, W. X. (2004). Attitudes toward family obligation among adolescents in contemporary urban and rural China. *Child Development, 74,* 180–192.

Goode, W. J. (1971). World revolution and family patterns. *Journal of Marriage and the Family, 33,* 624–635.

Huang, J. H. (1989). Practice of filial piety in modern life. In K. S. Yang (Ed.), *The psychology of Chinese,* (pp. 25–38). Taipei: Guiguan Press.

Jing, Q., & Zhang, H. (1998). China's reform and challenges for psychology. In J. G. Adair & D. Belanger Kdion (Eds.), *Advances in psychological science, Vol. 1: Social, personal, and cultural aspects* (pp. 271–291). Hove, U.K.: Psychology Press/Erlbaum (UK) Taylor & Francis.

The Ministry of Education, People's Republic of China. (2002). *Communique on National Education Development in 2001.* Beijing: China Statistics Press.

Modell, J., & Goodman, M. (1990). Historical perspectives. In S. S. Feldman & G. R. Elliott (Eds.), *At the threshold: The developing adolescent* (pp. 93–122). Cambridge, MA: Harvard University Press.

Olson, D. H., Sprenkle, D. H., & Russell, C. S. (1979). Circumplex model of marital and family systems: I. Cohesion and adaptability dimensions, family types, and applications. *Family Process, 18,* 3–28.

Prinz, R. J., Foster, S. L., Kent, R. N., & O'Leary, K. V. (1979). Multivariate assessment of conflict in distressed and nondistressed mother-adolescent dyads. *Journal of Applied Behavioral Analysis, 12,* 691–700.

Smetana, J. G. (1988). Adolescents' and parents' conceptions of parental authority. *Child Development, 59,* 321–335.

Steinberg, L. (1988). Reciprocal relation between parent-child distance and pubertal maturation. *Developmental Psychology, 24,* 122–128.

Steinberg, L. (1990). Autonomy, conflict, and harmony in the family relationship. In S. S. Feldman & G. R. Elliot (Eds.), *At the threshold: The developing adolescents* (pp. 255–276). Cambridge, MA: Harvard University Press.

Tang, W., & Parish, W. L. (2000). *Chinese urban life under reform: The changing social contract.* Cambridge, U.K.: Cambridge University Press.

Yang, K. S. (1989). Conceptual analysis of the Chinese filial piety. In G. S. Yang (Ed.), *The psychology of Chinese* (pp. 39–73). Taipei: Guiguan Press.

Questions

1. How might changes in a country's economic base affect adolescent development?
2. Why were urban adolescents more affected by large-scale societal changes than rural adolescents? Do you think this pattern is unique to China?
3. What gender differences were found in adolescent autonomy and relations with parents in this study? How do these gender differences compare with male and female adolescent development in the United States?
4. Based on these results, do you think urban or rural adolescents have a more difficult time establishing autonomy from their parents in China?
5. How might the one-child policy in China contribute to the development of autonomy for adolescents living in urban and rural settings?
6. What predictions would you make for these youths when they mature and have adolescent children of their own?

35

Antisocial Boys and Their Friends in Early Adolescence: Relationship Characteristics, Quality, and Interactional Process

Thomas J. Dishion • David W. Andrews • Lynn Crosby

Violence toward other people and willful destruction of property are disturbing crimes that shatter people's trust in one another, especially when such acts are committed by youth. What are the explanations for and origins of antisocial adolescent behaviors? Developmental psychologists have examined the roles played by the family, school experience, and poverty. Some psychologists have focused on the contribution of the peer group to adolescent problem behaviors. Yet very little is known about how the friendships of antisocial children differ from those of well-adjusted children.

In the following article, Thomas Dishion, David Andrews, and Lynn Crosby describe their research on the origins and characteristics of the close friendships of antisocial boys during the early years of adolescence. Among the questions the researchers tried to answer is whether antisocial youth, who are known to lack the basic social skills needed to develop a supportive friendship network, have friends and, if so, what those friends tend to be like. Dishion and his colleagues also examined the nature of these friendships: how they are formed, how long they last, how satisfying they are for antisocial youth, and what types of behaviors characterize them. Finally, the researchers were interested in how these friendships contribute to the individual development and adjustment of antisocial youth, especially whether they increase the likelihood of delinquent behavior.

The findings of this study challenge conventional wisdom. Antisocial adolescent boys do have friendships, and these relationships serve a number of social and psychological functions. However, such friendships differ from the friendships experienced by well-adjusted youth in several ways. These differences are particularly evident in the types of behaviors that antisocial friends exhibit toward one another. Although friendships are often seen as beneficial to development, it seems that certain friendships may increase maladaptive behavior and put antisocial boys at even greater risk for delinquent behavior. This research also suggests that a better understanding of the social experiences that antisocial youth have with their friends may result in improved intervention programs for these individuals.

Reprinted with permission from Dishion, T. J., Andrews, D. A., & Crosby, L., "Antisocial Boys and Their Friends in Early Adolescence: Relationship Characteristics, Quality, and Interactional Process", *Child Development, 66,* 139–151, © 1995 Blackwell Publishers.

This research would not have been possible were it not for the dedicated efforts of the OYS staff supervised by Deborah Capaldi. Education leaders (Charles Stevens, Robert Lady, and Robert Hammond) within the community where this research was conducted were vital to this and other projects ongoing at the Oregon Social Learning Center. Julie Rusby (author of PPC manual) deserves special acknowledgment for her care in supervising the coding of videotapes upon which these data are based. This research was supported by grants to Gerald Patterson (MH 37940, Center for Studies of Violent Behavior and Traumatic Stress, NIMH, U.S. PHS) and Thomas Dishion (DA07031, National Institute of Drug Abuse, U.S. PHS).

*This study examines the close friendships of early ado-
lescent boys in relation to antisocial behavior. 186
13–14-year-old boys and their close friends were interviewed, assessed at school, and videotaped in a problem-solving task. Similarity was observed between the
demographic characteristics and antisocial behavior of
the boys and their close friends. There was a tendency
for the close friends of antisocial boys to live within the
same neighborhood block and to have met in unstructured, unsupervised activities. Direct observations of interactions with close friends revealed a reliable
correlation between antisocial behavior, directives, and
negative reciprocity. Positive interactions within the
friendship were uncorrelated with antisocial behavior
and relationship quality. Implications of these findings
for clinical and developmental theory are discussed.*

Introduction

Studies about peer factors associated with child antisocial behavior offer a paradox to developmental and
clinical researchers. On the one hand, it is well established that antisocial children are rejected by peers
(Coie & Kupersmidt, 1983; Dishion, 1990; Dodge,
1983) and lack basic skills required for developing a
supportive friendship network (Putallaz & Gottman,
1979). On the other hand, sociological studies of adolescents reveal a remarkably high level of correlation
between deviant peers, delinquent behavior, and drug
use (Elliott, Huizinga, & Ageton, 1985; Kandel, 1973).
It appears that most antisocial children do develop
friendships (Giordano, Cernkovich, & Pugh, 1986),
but at the cost of escalating problem behavior in
adolescence.

The troubled child's development of friendships
with other antisocial children is an important developmental adaptation. From an ethnological view of
behavioral development, much is to be learned from
these adaptations (e.g., Hinde, 1989; Hinde & Stevenson-Hinde, 1986). According to this view, relationships
are embedded within a social nexus, where factors
unique to the individual shape the relationship, and
the relationship, in turn, shapes the individual. The
focus of this report, then, is to better understand the
origins and characteristics of the close friendships of
antisocial boys, and the potential influences of these
relationships on individual development. Data from
the Oregon Youth Study (OYS) (Capaldi & Patterson,
1987; Patterson, Reid, & Dishion, 1992) were used for
this purpose.

As early as middle childhood, antisocial children
tend to associate with other antisocial and/or rejected
peers. It is unclear as to whether this is by choice or
through default (Cairns & Cairns, 1991). There is sup-

port for the idea that children are attracted to those
most like themselves (i.e., social choice), particularly
with respect to aggressive behavior in middle childhood (Cairns, Cairns, Neckerman, Gest, & Gariepy,
1988) and drug use in adolescence (Kandel, 1973).
Kandel (1978) and others have referred to mutual at-
traction processes in friendship formation as "homophily." As also hypothesized in Kenny's Social
Relations Model (1988), perceptions of self–other
agreement and trait congruence may be the passage-
way through which friendship forms.

Friendships among antisocial children may also
form, in part, because of social forces such as peer rejection (Dishion, Patterson, Stoolmiller, & Skinner,
1991), ability tracking in schools (Kellam, 1990), or
other features of communities such as neighborhood
demographics (Simcha-Fagan & Schwartz, 1986). Rejected children tend to play with younger children and
other rejected children and to report friendships with
children outside the school setting (Ladd, 1983). Adult
supervision of peer relationships may also be a key
factor (Dishion et al., 1991; Steinberg & Silverberg,
1986).

Whether antisocial children "find" each other by
choice or default, the family background of antisocial
children provides a perspective on the specific interpersonal characteristics they are likely to bring to
their friendships. Many investigators have shown that
harsh, inconsistent, and negative parenting practices
are prognostic of current (e.g., Patterson, 1986) and future (e.g., Farington, 1978; McCord, McCord, &
Howard, 1969) antisocial behavior. According to the
coercion model (Patterson, 1982; Patterson et al.,
1992), aversive child behavior is strengthened via escape conditioning within reciprocal parent–child exchanges (Gardner, 1989; Patterson, 1982). Children
learn to escalate aversive behavior in order to control
(and reduce) their parents' efforts to set limits. We expected this overlearned coercive pattern to emerge at
some point in the antisocial child's friendships. The
friend's reactions to coercive acts help determine the
stability of the pattern in the new relationship. The
best test of this hypothesis is an analysis of the sequential structure of interaction. In such an analysis,
we expected negative reciprocity to be associated with
the dyad's level of antisocial behavior.

While Raush (1965) found "hyperaggressive" boys
engaging in high rates of negative exchanges when interacting with other children defined as the same, the
data were not examined sequentially and the interactants were not friends. Austin and Draper (1984) did
look at close friends of rejected children and found
aggressive children to be bossy with their
close friends. Given the high overlap between peer
rejection and antisocial behavior, this finding may
also apply to the antisocial child. Panella and
Henggeler (1986) studied the interactions of conduct-

disordered, anxious, and well-adjusted boys with their close friends and found no differences in rates of negative behavior.

The coercion model (Patterson, 1982; Patterson et al., 1992) also hypothesizes that antisocial behavior disrupts prosocial skill development and leaves antisocial children less socially competent. Theorists have argued for decades that critical social skills are developed within childhood friendships (e.g., Hartup, 1983; Sullivan, 1953; Youniss, 1980). High levels of peer rejection limit extended contact among prosocial peers, thereby reducing the antisocial child's opportunity to model positive relationship skills. From this perspective, indices of interpersonal skill such as positive behavior and prosocial reciprocity are negatively correlated with the dyad's level of antisocial behavior. However, recent research has not fully supported this contention. Giordano's (Giordano et al., 1986) in-depth interviews negated some of the stereotypes of delinquent friendships. Although a tendency for conflict was correlated with delinquent behavior, more positive features (e.g., caring and trust) of friendship were uncorrelated. Similarly, Panella and Henggeler (1986) revealed that conduct-disordered children were not different from well-adjusted children in rates of positive behavior but were different on coders' global ratings of social competence.

Due to the limitations in social competence and higher levels of conflict, the general quality of the friendships may be compromised, as indicated by the participants themselves. Although investigators have documented less stability (e.g., Berndt, 1992) and satisfaction (Parker & Asher, 1989) in school friendships of both the antisocial and rejected child, it is not clear that these outcomes are associated with interpersonal behavior styles. In addition, school-based studies of friendships may overemphasize weaknesses of children whose close friends do not include classmates or schoolmates.

In summary, much is known about the disruptive effect of antisocial behavior on children's peer relations in school and their association with other antisocial peers. Very little is known, however, about the origins, characteristics, quality, and interpersonal style of close friendships of antisocial children compared to well-adjusted children. To this end, adolescent boys, some of whom display high rates of antisocial behavior, were asked to bring in their close friends, with whom they were observed interacting in a videotaped problem-solving task; they were also interviewed on the origins and nature of their friendship. These data were then used to address the following questions:

1. What is the relation between antisocial behavior and the friendship characteristics of adolescent boys? Specifically, at a more macro-level, what are the behavioral, demographic, and relationship quality characteristics associated with antisocial friendships?

2. To what extent is antisocial behavior associated with interpersonal deficits or excesses as indicated by direct observation rates, sequential patterns, and observer impressions?

Method

Sample

The original sample consisted of 206 13–14-year-old boys participating in the fifth year of the longitudinal Oregon Youth Study (OYS) (Patterson, 1986; Patterson & Bank, 1985; Patterson et al., 1992). Two cohorts of 102 and 104 boys and their families were recruited from 1983 to 1985 to participate in the study. The boys and their families were from 10 elementary schools in a Northwest community with a population of 150,000 to 200,000. Ten elementary schools were selected because of the high density of neighborhood delinquency reported in their area.

The resulting sample was 90% European-American and of lower socioeconomic status, with a relatively high percentage of unemployed parents (Capaldi & Patterson, 1987). When the study boys were 9 to 10 years old, 42% of the families were two-parent biological families, 32% were single-parent families, and 26% were step-parent families. At ages 13 to 14 (Wave 5), the percentages had changed to 37% two-parent families, 29% single-parent families, and 34% step-parent families. Additional demographic information on the OYS families at the time of recruitment is presented in Table 1.

The results of this report focused on data resulting from the Wave 5 assessment (i.e., yearly assessment) of OYS, which included structured interviews with boys and parents, school data collection (teacher ratings and school records), and official records of police contact. In addition, the boys were asked to bring a friend to the research center to participate in the observational phase of the study. During the family interview, the boys were asked to nominate "a child with whom you spend the most amount of time" to participate with them in the study. The boys' parents were also asked to give the name of a peer with whom their child spent most of his time. Parent and child nominations were then compared, and peers were selected to participate if they were nominated by the study child and confirmed by his parent(s).

There were 20 boys from the original OYS sample of 206 who did not participate in the Peer Interaction Task (PIT). Of these subjects, three did not participate in any phase of Wave 5, four refused to participate in the PIT, seven reported not having friends, and six

table 1   Demographics of Oregon Youth Study Cohorts 1 and 2

	Cohort 1	Cohort 2
Family socioeconomic status (%):[a]		
Lower (Categories 1, 2)	50	45
Working (Category 3)	26	29
Middle (Categories 4, 5)	23	26
Employment status (%):		
Unemployed	34	30
Family income (%):		
0–4,999	11	16
5,000–9,999	22	20
10,000–14,999	15	17
15,000–19,999	14	14
20,000–24,999	16	14
25,000–29,999	8	10
30,000–39,999	13	6
40,000+	3	2
Family structure (%):		
Single parent	31	39
Number of children (%):		
1–2	52	58
3–4	37	32
5 or more	12	11
Mean age of mother (years)	34	34
Mean age of father (years)	36	37

[a]Hollingshead (1975).

were excluded because they brought siblings to the PIT. Because these boys are involved in a long-term longitudinal study, it was possible to identify the fourth-grade sociometric status (Coie, Dodge, & Coppotelli, 1982) of boys not participating in the PIT: (4) Rejected; (1) Neglected; (7) Average (combined with undefined); (3) Popular; (1) Controversial. An unreliable trend suggested higher rates of rejection (25%) among boys not engaging in the task compared to the overall sample (15%).

Peer Interaction Task (PIT)

The already-defined PIT was designed to elicit a wide range of interactive behaviors between the participating boy and his friend. The boys were videotaped in a 25-min session during which they were asked to:

1. Plan an activity together (something they could potentially do together within the next week).

2 and 3. Solve a problem related to getting along with parents that occurred for the study boy and his friend within the last month.

4 and 5. Solve a problem related to getting along with peers that occurred for the study boy and his friend within the last month.

Each of the above segments lasted 5 min. The order of the tasks *following* activity planning was counterbalanced, and the parent, peer tasks were staggered.

The resulting 25 min of videotaped interactions were coded by a set of observers (unaware of the adjustment status of the boys) using the Peer Process Code (PPC) (Dishion et al., 1989). The PPC is a microsocial coding system that records peer interaction in real time, capturing the interpersonal content and affective valence of the discussion. The videotapes were first previewed and then directly coded by using a handheld microcomputer.

Eighteen percent ($n = 32$) of the videotaped friend dyadic interactions were randomly selected to be coded independently by two observers. Using an entry-by-entry approach, there was 86.4% agreement on the content of the code (basic code category) and 73.4% on the affective valence. Percent agreement on content and affect codes ranged from .37 to .91. An overall weighted kappa (Cohen, 1960) of .69 was found on the combined content and valence of each entry, with kappa scores ranging from .37 to .78.

Four a priori behavior scores were developed from a 24-category coding system for the purposes of this research: Positive Engagement, Converse, Directives, and Negative Engagement. These scores included 19 of the 24 coding categories. Four codes not included in these behavior clusters were Comply, Not Comply, Agree, Disagree. These categories were coded only following a command, and thus were highly correlated with commands and ipsative with one another. In addition, Manipulation of Objects was not included in the four clusters, since it was quite low in base rate and deemed irrelevant to interpersonal process.

The specific description of each of the behavior scores follows. In addition to the overall percent agreement on the PPC code, interobserver consistency was examined for each of the observation indicators described below. Consistency is represented by the zero-order correlation between the scores of two observers on each observation indicator taken during 32 reliability sessions. Note that interobserver consistency was computed for a dyad version of the behavior clusters, which was the score used in the analyses that follow. Table 3 (below) reveals substantial correlation between the two boys on the following cluster scores.

Positive engagement Positive engagement includes the following content categories recorded in neutral or positive valence: Positive Verbal, Unqualified Positive Regard, Self-Disclose, Positive Nonverbal, Touch/Hold, and Physical Interact. In addition, neutral content categories in positive affect were included: Talk, Vocal, and Neutral Nonverbal (interobserver $r = .81$).

Directives The following categories in neutral or positive affective valence comprise the Directive score: Request, Request Ambiguous, Command, and Command Ambiguous (interobserver $r = .92$).

Negative engagement This score includes behaviors that were developed to describe aversive behavior, regardless of the valence: Negative Verbal, Verbal Attack, Coerce, Coerce Ambiguous, Negative Nonverbal, and Physical Aggressive. Also included were neutral and positive content codes (listed above) displayed in negative affective valence (interobserver $r = .85$).

Converse Converse captures on-task, interpersonal-neutral behavior and includes the following content codes in neutral affective valence: Talk, Vocal, and Neutral Nonverbal (interobserver $r = .72$).

Global ratings of social skill Observers provided global ratings on Social Skills (e. g., took turns speaking) on nine items (alpha = .85). One item from the original ratings from the study boy was dropped due to low loading (loading <.30) on a principal components factor analysis. The correlation between the two boys' social skills ratings was .79.

Global ratings of noxious behavior Noxious behavior (e. g., used aggressive gestures) was represented by five items (alpha = .76). The correlation between the study boy's and the friend's noxious behavior ratings was .75.

Friendship Characteristics

In the friendship interview, the boys were individually asked a series of questions regarding their friendship. Questions used in this study were, "How long have you known each other?" "Where did the two of you first meet?" and "How close do you live to each other?" Data from this interview were used only if the two boys agreed in their response.

One year following the friendship interview, the study boys were asked to report the status of the friendship. Their responses were coded to represent the following relationship 1-year outcomes: (*a*) unfriendly, (*b*) drifted apart, (*c*) nonvolitional separation, (*d*) no change, and (*e*) better friends.

Teacher Ratings of Social Preference

Teacher estimates of sociometric status (social preference) for the study boy and his friend were computed by using the scoring method developed by Coie et al. (1982). A teacher's social preference score was com-

puted from ratings (usually different teachers) of the proportion of other students who "liked" the boys and those who "disliked" the boys. These teacher estimates of social preference for the study boy correlated .43 (*p* <.001) with the peer nomination score of social preference (Coie et al., 1982) collected 4 years earlier in the fourth grade.

Relationship Satisfaction

Three reliable dimensions of relationship satisfaction were derived from the Friendship Quality Questionnaire (Lathrop, Dishion, & Capaldi, 1987) using both principal component analysis and item analyses (Cronbach, 1951): Conflict, Quality, and Evaluation. The scales and their psychometric properties are described below.

The Conflict scale assessed disagreements and estrangement within the friendship (e.g., "How often do you get on each other's nerves?"). Four items produced satisfactory internal consistency (alpha = .78). The Quality scale originally consisted of four items, but two were dropped due to low item total correlations. The two items that remained assessed the boys' sense of trust and happiness in their friendship (e.g., "How happy are you with this friendship?"), yielding satisfactory internal consistency ($r = .68$). The Evaluation scale used a semantic differential format to assess the boys' evaluation of their friend's character (e.g., "Friend is good/bad"). This scale produced high internal consistency ($r = .88$). These three scales were standardized and combined into a single score of Dyadic Relationship Satisfaction. The internal consistency of this composite score based on Conflict, Evaluation, and Quality scales was .78.

Antisocial Behavior

Each boy's antisocial behavior was assessed using teacher, self, and interviewer impressions. Teacher ratings of the boys' antisocial behavior were derived from 19 items (e.g., "disobedient at school," "steals") from the Child Behavior Checklist (Achenbach & Edelbrock, 1986). In addition, teachers were asked to rate, "How often does he exert a negative influence on his friends?" In the interview, the boys reported on their delinquent behavior using the minor delinquent offenses of the survey instrument developed by Elliott and colleagues (Elliott et al., 1985). This instrument assessed the number of times the boys committed each delinquent act (e.g., "How many times in the last year have you damaged or destroyed school property?"). These act frequencies were summed into a total score for this indicator. In addition, the interviewers provided impression ratings of each boy separately (e.g., "adolescent seemed involved in delinquent and antisocial behavior"). The three indicators of antisocial behavior were standardized and aggregated into a composite score for the study boy and his friend.

Juvenile court records   A search was conducted of local juvenile court records for any police contact with study boys and their friends. Date and nature of all police contacts become a matter of computer records. For these analyses, only contacts for reasons of delinquency were considered.

Analytic Procedures

The following questions were addressed in the analysis. (1) What are the origins, characteristics, and quality of early adolescent boys' friendships as related to antisocial behavior? Here the data from the friendship interview and data on the two boys were compared using correlational, analysis of variance, and nonparametric strategies. The status of the friendship 1 year later was also assessed as an indicator of the quality of the relationship with respect to antisocial behavior and dyad relationship satisfaction. (2) The interactional processes within the relationship were examined simply by correlating rates of behavior and observer impressions with the boys' antisocial behavior. Then lag 1 sequential scores were computed for each possible sequence given the four behavior clusters following procedures outlined by Gottman and

Roy (1990), where Allison-Liker Z scores (Allison & Liker, 1982) represented whether a sequential contingency was statistically reliable. Homogeneous groups were formed to provide an assessment of whether the sequential structure varied for antisocial dyads compared to well-adjusted dyads.

Results

Relationship Characteristics

Two questions were asked in relation to the origin of the boys' friendship. Each boy was asked how they met and how far apart they lived from one another. There were 135 dyads who agreed in their response as to how they met and 164 dyads where the boys agreed on how far away from each other they lived. Of the 135 dyads agreeing on how they met, 73% met in school or some other organized activity, and 17% met in their neighborhood or in an unsupervised community setting. Of the 164 dyads agreeing on the distance that they lived from one another, 71% were living within three blocks of one another and 29% were living farther away than three blocks.

To determine whether the origin of the boys' friendships was related to the quality of the relationship and their level of deviance, these scores were analyzed in respect to where the boys met and how close they lived to each other (see Table 2). Dyadic scores of

table 2   Summaries of Dyadic Antisocial and Relationship Quality Traits by Friendship Characteristics

Value	Dyad Antisocial		Dyad Relationship Satisfaction		Cases
	Mean	Standard Deviation	Mean	Standard Deviation	
"Where did you first meet?"					
In my neighborhood and other unorganized activity	.329	1.27	−.063	1.05	36
In school and organized activity	−.194	.90	.119	1.00	99
"How close do you live to each other?"					
Within 2–3 blocks	.369	1.24	−.551	1.11	47
Farther than 2–3 blocks	−.163	.85	.233	.87	117
Status of relationship after 1 year:					
Unfriendly	1.108	.96	−.731	.88	9
Drifted apart	.144	1.03	−.023	1.12	27
Nonvolitional	.085	1.02	−.187	.98	56
No change	−.286	.826	.088	.92	49
Better friends	−.231	.896	.352	1.01	36

antisocial behavior and relationship satisfaction were used for this analysis. There was a significant multivariate effect found for the boys' deviance and relationship satisfaction for both where they met (Wilks's lambda = .95, $p < .043$) and how close they lived to each other (Wilks's lambda = .86, $p < .0001$). Inspection of the univariate effects in Table 2 reveals that the greatest effect was for antisocial dyads to have met outside of school, $F(1, 133) = 7.10$, $p < .01$, and live within the same neighborhood, $F(1, 162) = 9.93$, $p < .002$. As one might expect, there tended to be less satisfaction within the relationships of boys in the same neighborhood, $F(1, 162) = 23.02$, $p < .0001$, suggesting that these were friendships of convenience.

Given that boys tended to bring in friends who lived close by, the level of similarity between the boys on basic demographic characteristics and social behavior was not surprising. The study boy and friend were close in age, with a nonsignificant mean age difference of .90 years and a range of .02 to 3.52 years. Other social behavior and demographic characteristics of the study boy and his friend were compared using Pearson product moment correlation coefficients (see Table 3) and chi-square analysis.

The demographic profiles for the study boy and his friend were modestly associated. Family income correlated .25 ($p < .0001$) for the two boys. The association between the two boys on parental status was statistically marginal ($\chi^2 = 6.3$, $p < .18$).

The adjustment of the study boys and their friends was strongly correlated (see Table 3). The multimethod, multiagent antisocial construct scores generated for both boys were significantly correlated ($r = .41$, $p < .0001$). A modest correlation was found between the boys' and their friends' social preference scores as rated by teachers. In addition, the boys' arrest records were cross-tabulated and subjected to a chi-square test ($\chi^2 = 5.2$, $p < .03$). More study boys (28%) had police records than did friends (12%), but 72% of the dyads were similar in arrest status. It is noteworthy in these analyses that the level of covariation in adjustment status between the two boys was not influenced by monomethod bias (Cook & Campbell, 1979). Ratings for the two boys were derived from different reporting agents in all cases.

As one might expect from interaction literature (Cairns, 1979), the boys' performance on each of the four behavior clusters was highly correlated. Significant correlations ($p < .001$) were found for each of the microsocial behavior clusters, with coefficients ranging from .45 to .69. Given this level of correlation among the two boys' behavior in the peer interaction task, it seems reasonable to consider their behavior as a dyadic process rather than as independent individual behavior. Thus, when looking at predictive validity, we considered the dyad rate-per-minute of Negative Engagement, Positive Engagement, Converse, and Directives as described above. The zero-order correlation between the dyad's level of antisocial behavior ($r = -.36$) and relationship satisfaction certainly suggests that deviant peer relationships are somewhat compromised. Antisocial behavior was also correlated with the other social characteristics of the boys (see Table 4). Teacher ratings of social preference of the study boy and his friends correlated negatively with the dyad's antisocial behavior ($-.40$ and $-.22$, respectively) and positively with relationship satisfaction (.29) reported by the study boy.

The most telling measure of the quality of the boys' friendship was the outcome as determined 1 year later. In the next assessment wave, they were asked whether their friendship had ended on an unfriendly basis, drifted apart, ended for other reasons (nonvolitional), stayed the same, or improved (they had become better friends). The means and standard deviations for the boys' relationship satisfaction and antisocial behavior are provided in Table 2. A MANOVA analysis revealed that the 1-year outcome covaried with dyadic antisocial behavior and relationship quality (Wilks's lambda = .87, $p < .002$). Analysis of univariate effects showed that antisocial behavior, $F(4, 172) = 5.04$, $p < .001$, and relationship satisfaction, $F(4, 172) = 2.98$, $p < .03$, were independently prognostic of the course of the friendship. Scheffé post hoc comparisons did not confirm the impressions that

table 3 Correlations between Study Boys and Friends on Problem Behavior, Micro-Social Exchange Patterns, and Demographic Data

Measurements	Correlation
Macro-social:	
Antisocial construct score	.410***
Relationship satisfaction	.330***
Social preference	.205**
Micro-social:	
Rates-per-minute:	
Directives	.446***
Converse	.687***
Positive engagement	.629***
Negative engagement	.571***
Demographics:	
Family income	.237***

*$p < .05$.
**$p < .01$.
***$p < .001$.

table 4   Friendship Characteristics, Antisocial Behavior, and Relationship Satisfaction

	Dyad Antisocial	Dyad Relationship Satisfaction
Years as friends	−.137*	−.076
Social preference:		
Study boy	−.399***	.292***
Friend	−.215**	.100
Microsocial behavior:		
Negative engagement	.091	−.212**
Positive engagement	.016	.090
Directives	.328***	−.156*
Converse	−.073	.074
Coder impressions:		
Social skills	−.213**	.266***
Noxious behavior	.284***	−.212**

*p < .05.
**p < .01.
***p < .001.

those friendships that ended on an unfriendly basis were marked by the lowest relationship satisfaction and the highest antisocial behavior of all groups, but mean differences were in this direction. This finding suggests that the friendships of antisocial boys tend to be of shorter duration, which may be an outcome of their interactive styles—the question to which we now turn.

Interactional Process

Direct observations provide a more detailed and objective picture of the boys' relationships. The extent to which there was a correlation between the boys' antisocial behavior and interactions with their friends was assessed by examining the rate-per-minute of Negative Engagements, Positive Engagements, Directives, and Converse. Generally speaking, the level of covariation was modest (see Table 4). It should be noted that predictive validity did not improve appreciably when considering the correlations of the dyad antisocial scores with those of individual boys. The boys' tendency to give commands was most correlated with their antisocial behavior ($r = .33$). Coder impressions of dyadic social skills and noxious behavior were also reliably correlated with the boys' antisocial behavior. The rate-per-minute of Negative Engagement and Directives were correlated

negatively with relationship satisfaction, although there was no statistically reliable correlation between positive engagement and, conversely, with overall relationship satisfaction. Clearly, it was the abrasive behavior within friendships that compromised relationship quality, with positive interpersonal behavior showing no predictive validity.

The sequential patterns of the boys in their friendships were also analyzed. Consistent with the dyadic focus, we combined the two boys' behaviors to create "bidirectional nonparallel streams" (Wampold, 1989), referring to decision rules regarding computation of dyadic sequential structure. For example, in computing the sequence "Converse (antecedent) to Positive Engagement (consequence)," we considered either the boy or his friend as providing the antecedent. Nonparallel refers to the fact that we considered the following two interactions as operate sequences: "Converse to Positive Engagement" and "Positive Engagement to Converse."

The advantage of an Allison-Liker Z score is that the distributions are such that a Z score of 1.96 reflects a statistically significant contingency between an antecedent and a consequence sequence. This can be interpreted at the individual or group level (Gottman & Roy, 1990).

In general, little covariation was found between the strength of these sequential patterns and the boys' antisocial behavior and relationship satisfaction. Only the Positive Engagement to Negative Engagement score was correlated with dyadic antisocial construct scores ($r = −.17$, $p < .02$). As one might suspect, the positive reciprocity sequential score was positively correlated with relationship satisfaction ($r = −.17$, $p < .002$).

To further investigate the relation between interaction patterns and antisocial behaviors, a subsample of highly antisocial dyads was compared to a subsample of the well-adjusted dyads. For this analysis, there was a concern for developing distinctive, homogeneous groups. High antisocial dyads ($n = 9$) were selected as those dyads where both the study boy and his friend had an official police contact, and their antisocial constructs scores were above the mean. The selected low antisocial dyads ($n = 9$) were ones in which neither boy had a police contact, and they were the lowest ranking of this dyad type in terms of antisocial behavior. Using these criteria, two groups of nine dyads were selected for additional sequential analysis.

When considering these aggregated groups (Fig. 1), we again found that there were more similarities than differences. Both groups showed significant sequential contingencies (see Z scores in Fig. 1) on Converse and Positive Engagement reciprocity. Consistent with many studies of social interaction (Cairns, 1979), these interactions were carried by the boys' reciprocat-

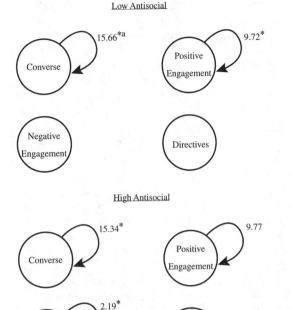

figure 1

The sequential structure of interpersonal process in high and low antisocial dyads.

ing, facilitative behavior. Since Directives were quite low in base rate, we found no reciprocity (Z score = 2.19, *p* < .05) in Directives. The only difference between the two groups was that the high antisocial dyads showed significant negative reciprocity, whereas the well-adjusted dyads did not reciprocate negative behavior. However, the high antisocial dyads did. The finding is consistent with the coercion model, which emphasizes the role of negative reciprocity within families as an etiological factor.

Discussion

Considering these findings with those of previous studies, it appears that a multitude of factors may account for establishing friendship clusters, including geographical proximity, activity involvement, homophily, rejection by school peers, and academic fail-

ure. In addition, families with similar demographic characteristics tend to live within the same neighborhoods (Lewis, 1978). In this sense, some of the commonality observed within these friendship dyads is probably due to broader community or societal factors that influences families.

The majority of peer relations studies conducted to date have focused on school-based networks. Attention to broader community networks and social influences is needed, as friends who meet in school and organized activities are less at risk for problematic behavior. Research is needed that seeks out person-context-process interactions on how children get selected into peer networks (Bronfenbrenner, 1989). In order to accomplish these studies, we need to study children's peer relations across multiple contexts that include not only school but also neighborhoods, organized activities, and unsupervised community settings (e. g., Steinberg & Silverberg, 1986). In this way, we can better understand which children end up in settings that detract from or enhance their social trajectories, as well as the interpersonal processes that explain these various outcomes.

The data in this report corroborate some assumptions about the societal cost of child antisocial affiliations and underscore the need for studying interpersonal process. The relationships of antisocial dyads were somewhat low in quality, of relatively short duration, were perceived by the boys as marginally satisfactory, and tended to end acrimoniously. Consistent with Giordano's findings (Giordano et al., 1986), it was not the lack of positive behaviors that accounted for compromised relationship quality, but rather the presence of bossiness and coercive behavior. Thus, antisocial friendships provided another context within which to practice coercion. Although friendships and marriages are a world apart, one cannot help comparing these findings with those from the marital interaction literature, where it is the presence of coercion (i.e., negative reciprocity) that places a couple into the qualitative state of "distressed" and heading for divorce (Gottman, 1979). Similarities in findings with regard to the disruptive effect of coercion on parent–child, child–child, and husband–wife interactions suggest that the ethnological framework (e.g., Hinde, 1989) for relationships has considerable merit. Studies of interpersonal processes within close relationships reveal similarities in maladaptive patterns. However, at the level of the individual, it is clear that each relationship has a "life of its own." For example, Andrews and Dishion (1994) found that for these boys, negative reciprocity within the friendship was uncorrelated with the same sequential pattern in the parent–child relationship. However, simply summing the level of negative reciprocity across relationships and time was the best predictor of the boy's overall level of antisocial behavior. In this sense, children's socioemotional adjustment is embedded within a matrix of relationship adaptations (Hinde, 1989). Antisocial behavior cannot be fully understood by considering any individual relationship process in a single context (Bronfenbrenner, 1989).

We found that coder impressions of the boys' noxious behavior and lack of social skill were correlated with the boys' antisocial behavior, much more than "objective" behavior counts of the direct observations. Cairns and Green (1979) discussed the relative advantages and disadvantages of "macro" ratings versus "micro" behavioral observation. As evidenced in this report and in research by Panella and Henggeler (1986), global ratings provide better predictive validity, since they are more sensitive to the nuances of context and delivery that contribute to the interpretation of any specific interpersonal act. For example, micro-social coding typically ignores the topic content and congruence of the interaction. However, micro-social coding provides information on duration and sequence which allows the study of interpersonal processes. For example, sequential analysis of the antisocial versus well-adjusted dyads revealed that the structure of the interchanges within the two homogeneous groups was different in respect to negative reciprocity. This level of analysis is not possible in less expensive global ratings but is essential for a process-oriented developmental theory (Patterson, 1982).

These data challenge conventional notions about the intervention needs of antisocial youth. It does not appear that they have deficits in positive behavior with their friends. Although coder impressions indicated social skill deficits, it is conceivable that the coder attributions may be based on the boys' abrasive behavior and/or the discussion of inappropriate or antisocial topics. In this respect, it seems that clinical interventions might focus on the following: (a) reduce their tendency to reciprocate in kind to a negative behavior, and (b) improve their skills at negotiating control within close relationships.

Scanning the ecology of these boys' lives, however, suggests that caution is in order before concluding that such interventions would provide the royal road to good adjustment (Berndt, 1992). At the onset of adolescence, antisocial boys tend to coalesce into antisocial peer groups (Dishion et al., 1991). Thus, it is conceivable that improving the friendships of some of these youngsters may result in deviant peer networks that are more satisfactory, more stable, and perhaps more maladaptive in the long run. On the other hand, improving their performance in relationships early in development might promote friendships with prosocially skilled peers.

This study focuses on friendships among young adolescent males who are primarily European-American and live within a suburban, metropolitan area. The findings cannot be generalized, at this time, to other ethnic groups, community settings, or to the friendship characteristics of girls and their antisocial behavior. As discussed above, there is a clear need to increase research on multiethnic families living in diverse areas, which include inner-city settings (Rutter, 1978), to fully clarify the impact of the ecology of the developmental processes that leads to antisocial behavior (Dishion, French, & Patterson, 1995).

REFERENCES

Achenbach, T. M., & Edelbrock, C. (1986). *Manual for the teacher's report form and teacher version of the Child Behavior Profile.* Burlington: University of Vermont Press.

Allison, P. D., & Liker, J. K. (1982). Analyzing sequential categorical data on dyadic interaction: Comment on Gottman. *Psychological Bulletin, 91,* 393–403.

Andrews, D. W., & Dishion, T. J. (1994). The microsocial structure underpinnings of adolescent problem behavior. In M. Lamb & R. Ketterlinus (Eds.), *Adolescent problem behavior* (pp. 187–207). Hillsdale, NJ: Erlbaum.

Austin, A. M. B., & Draper, D. C. (1984). Verbal interactions of popular and rejected children with their friends and nonfriends. *Child Study Journal, 14,* 309–323.

Berndt, T. (1992, March). *Stability in friendships: How much, for which adolescents, and why does it matter?* Paper presented at the biennial meeting of the Society for Research in Adolescence, Washington, DC.

Bronfenbrenner, U. (Ed.). (1989). Ecological systems theory. In P. Vasta (Ed.), *Annals of child development: Vol. 6. Six theories of child development: Revised formulations and current issues* (pp. 187–249). London: JAI.

Cairns, R. B. (1979). *The analysis of social interaction: Methods, issues, and illustrations.* Hillsdale, NJ: Erlbaum.

Cairns, R. B., & Cairns B. D. (1991). Social cognition and social networks: A developmental perspective. In D. J. Pepler & K. H. Rubin (Eds.), *The development and treatment of childhood aggression* (pp. 249–278). Hillsdale, NJ: Erlbaum.

Cairns, R. B., Cairns, B. D., Neckerman, H. J., Gest, S. D., & Gariepy, J. L. (1988). Social networks and aggressive behavior: Peer support or peer rejection. *Developmental Psychology, 24,* 815–823.

Cairns, R. B., & Green, J. A. (1979). How to assess personality and social patterns: Observations or ratings? In R. B. Cairns (Ed.), *The analysis of social interaction: Methods, issues, and illustrations* (pp. 213–230). Hillsdale, NJ: Erlbaum.

Capaldi, D., & Patterson, G. R. (1987). An approach to the problem of recruitment and retention rates for longitudinal research. *Behavioral Assessment, 9,* 169–177.

Cohen, J. A. (1960). A coefficient of agreement for nominal scales. *Educational and Psychological Measurement, 20,* 37–46.

Coie, J. D., Dodge, K. A., & Coppotelli, H. (1982). Dimensions and types of social status: A cross-age perspective. *Developmental Psychology, 18,* 557–570.

Coie, J. D., & Kupersmidt, J. B. (1983). A behavioral analysis of emerging social status in boys' groups. *Child Development*, 54, 1400–1416.

Cook, T. D., & Campbell, D. T. (1979). *Quasi-experimentation: Design and analysis issues for field settings*. Boston: Houghton Mifflin.

Cronbach, L. J. (1951). Coefficient alpha and the internal structure of tests. *Psychometrika*, 16, 297–334.

Dishion, T. J. (1990). Peer context of troublesome behavior in children and adolescents. In P. Leone (Ed.), *Understanding troubled and troublesome youth* (pp. 128–153). Beverly Hills, CA: Sage.

Dishion, T. J., Crosby, L., Rusby, J. C., Shane, D., Patterson, G. R., & Baker, J. (1989). *Peer process code: Multidimensional system for observing adolescent peer interaction*. Unpublished manual. Available from the Oregon Social Learning Center, 207 East Fifth Avenue, Suite 202, Eugene, OR 97401.

Dishion, T. J., French, D., & Patterson, G. R. (1995). The development and ecology of child antisocial behavior. In D. Cicchetti & D. Cohen (Eds.), *Developmental psychopathology, Vol. 2*. (pp. 421–471) New York: Wiley.

Dishion, T. J., Patterson, G. R., Stoolmiller, M., & Skinner, M. (1991). Family, school, and behavioral antecedents to early adolescent involvement with antisocial peers. *Developmental Psychology*, 27, 172–180.

Dodge, K. A. (1983). Behavioral antecedents of peer social status. *Child Development*, 54, 1386–1399.

Elliott, D. S., Huizinga, D., & Ageton, S. S. (1985). *Explaining delinquency and drug use*. Beverly Hills, CA: Sage.

Farrington, D. P. (1978). The family backgrounds of aggressive youths. In L. A. Herson, M. Berger, & D. Shaffer (Eds.), *Aggression and antisocial behavior in childhood and adolescence* (pp. 73–93). Oxford: Pergamon.

Gardner, F.M. (1989). Inconsistent parenting: Is there evidence for a link with children's conduct problems? *Journal of Abnormal Child Psychology*, 17, 223–233.

Giordano, P. C., Cernkovich, S. A., & Pugh, M. D. (1986). Friendships and delinquency. *American Journal of Sociology*, 91, 1170–1202.

Gottman, J. M. (1979). *Marital interaction: Experimental investigations*. New York: Academic Press.

Gottman, J. M., & Roy, A. K. (1990). *Sequential analysis: A guide for behavioral researchers*. Cambridge: Cambridge University Press.

Hartup, W. W. (1983). Peer relations. In E. M. Hetherington (Ed.), P. H. Mussen (Series Ed.), *Handbook of child psychology: Vol. 4. Socialization, personality, and social development* (pp. 104–196). New York: Wiley.

Hinde, R. A. (1989). Ethological and relationship approaches. In R. Vasta (Ed.), *Annals of child development. Vol. 6. Six theories of child development: Revised formulations and current issues* (pp. 251–285). Hillsdale, NJ: Erlbaum.

Hinde, R. A., & Stevenson-Hinde, J. (1986). Relating childhood relationships to individual characteristics. In W. Hartup & Z. Rubin (Eds.), *Relationships and development* (pp. 71–89). Hillsdale, NJ: Erlbaum.

Hollingshead. A. B. (1975). *Four-Factor Index of Social Status*. Unpublished manuscript, Department of Sociology, Yale University, New Haven, CT.

Kandel, D. B. (1973). Adolescent marijuana use: Role of parents and peers. *Science*, 181, 1067–1081.

Kandel, D. B. (1978). Homophily, selection, and socialization in adolescent friendships. *American Journal of Sociology, 84*, 427–436.

Kandel, D.B. (1986). Process of peer influence on adolescence. In R. K. Silbereisen (Ed.), *Development as action in context* (pp, 33–52). Berlin: Springer Verlag.

Kellam. S. (1990). Developmental epidemiological framework for family research on depression and aggression. In G. R. Patterson (Ed.), *Depression and aggression in family interaction* (pp. 11–48). Hillsdale, NJ: Erlbaum.

Kenny, D. A. (1988). Interpersonal perception: A social relations analysis. *Journal of Social and Personal Relationships*, 5, 247–261.

Ladd, G. W. (1983). Social networks of popular, average, and rejected children in school settings. *Merrill-Palmer Quarterly*, 29, 283–307.

Lathrop, M., Dishion, T. J., & Capaldi, D. (1987). *Friendship quality questionnaire*. Unpublished instrument. Eugene: Oregon Social Learning Center.

Lewis, M. S. (1978). Nearest neighbor analysis of epidemiological and community variables. *Psychological Bulletin*, 85, 1302–1308.

McCord, W., McCord, J., & Howard, A. (1969). Family interaction as antecedent to the direction of male aggressiveness. *Journal of Abnormal and Social Psychology*, 66, 239–242.

Panella, D., & Henggeler, S. W. (1986). Peer interactions of conduct-disordered, anxious-withdrawn, and well-adjusted black adolescents. *Journal of Abnormal Child Psychology*, 14, 1–11.

Parke, R., & Bhavnagri, N. P. (1988). Parents as managers of children's peer relationships. In D. Belle (Ed.), *Children's social networks and social supports*. New York: Wiley.

Parker J. G., & Asher, S. R. (1989, April). *Peer relations and social adjustment: Are friendship and group acceptance distinct domains?* Paper presented at the biennial meeting of the Society for Research in Child Development, Kansas City, MO.

Patterson, G. R. (1982). *Coercive family process*. Eugene, OR: Castalia.

Patterson, G. R. (1986). Maternal rejection: Determinant or product for deviant child behavior? In W. Hartup & Z. Rubin (Eds.), *Relationships and development* (pp. 73–94). Hillsdale, NJ: Erlbaum.

Patterson, G. R., & Bank, L. (1985). Bootstrapping your way in the nomological thicket. *Behavioral Assessment*, 8, 49–73.

Patterson, G. R., Reid, J. B., & Dishion, T. J. (1992). *Antisocial boys*. Eugene, OR: Castalia.

Putallaz, M., & Gottman, J. M. (1979). Social skills and group acceptance. In S. R. Asher & J. M. Gottman (Eds.), *The development of children's friendships*. Cambridge: Cambridge University Press.

Raush, H. L. (1965). Interaction sequences. *Journal of Personality and Social Psychology*, 2, 487–499.

Rutter, M. (1978). Family, area, and school influences in the genesis of conduct disorders. In L. A. Hersov, M. Berger, & D. Shaffer (Eds.), *Aggression and antisocial behavior in childhood and adolescence* (pp. 95–114). New York: Pergamon.

Simcha-Fagan, O., & Schwartz, J. E. (1986). Neighborhood and delinquency: An assessment of contextual effects. *Criminology*, 24, 667–703.

Steinberg, L., & Silverberg, S. B. (1986). The vicissitudes of autonomy in early adolescence. *Child Development*, 57, 841–851.

Sullivan, H. S. (1953). *The interpersonal theory of psychiatry*. New York: Norton.

Wampold, B. E., (1989). Kappa as a measure of pattern in sequential data. *Quality and Quantity*, 22, 19–35.

Youniss, J. (1980). *Parents and peers in social development: A Sullivan-Piagetian perspective*. Chicago: University of Chicago Press.

Questions

1. How are the coercive behavior patterns learned at home evident in the friendship patterns of antisocial youth?
2. How do antisocial adolescent boys choose their friends, and what types of peers do they tend to choose as friends?
3. How satisfied are antisocial boys with their friendships? Does this finding surprise you?
4. What differences were found in the interaction patterns of the pairs of highly antisocial friends and the pairs of well-adjusted friends?
5. Do you think these behavioral styles characterize all the relationships of antisocial boys, or are they restricted to their close friendships?
6. What do this study's results suggest regarding an appropriate and effective intervention program for antisocial boys?

36

Late Adolescents' Self-Defining Memories About Relationships

Kate C. McLean • Avril Thorne

Although much of the research on adolescence concentrates on the early and middle teenage years, researchers have recently become interested in the latter part of adolescence, referred to as the period of emerging adulthood. This period of life comes with many unique challenges that have not been addressed in studies focused on the earlier teen years. In late adolescence it is critical for youth to renegotiate the parent-child relationship, as well as develop new types of relationships with peers. As an adolescent forms and reforms these important relationships, a life story begins to emerge. A life story includes the adolescent's sense of personal identity along with an understanding of how the adolescent relates to the important people in his or her life. It may be that experiences from earlier in life, especially experiences with other people, inform adolescents about these relationships and what they can hope to gain from them as they move into adulthood.

In the following article, Kate McLean and Avril Thorne investigate how adolescents on the brink of adulthood remember their relationships with parents and peers. The authors were especially interested in the adolescents' memories that touched on themes of separation, closeness, and conflict, which are particularly important to self-development in late adolescence. The researchers also studied the meaning that adolescents extracted from these memories, contrasting meaning that emphasized life lessons and meaning that led to new insights about the self and others.

To obtain this information, McLean and Thorne analyzed the memory narratives of college students. Their detailed coding of these autobiographical stories was designed to maintain the richness of the memories while at the same time enabling the researchers to link these memories with this life period's key developmental issues.

This study examined late adolescents' self-defining memories about relationships. Participants were 88 European Americans (mean age = 19 years) who reported 3 self-defining memories of their choosing and were selected for the study because they reported a memory about parents and/or peers. Memory narratives were coded for themes of separation, closeness, and conflict and for 2 kinds of meaning: learning lessons and gaining insight. Parent memories emphasized separation more so than peer memories, which emphasized closeness. Within parent memories, however, separation and closeness were equally prevalent. Parent separation was exemplified by experiences of parental divorce, parent closeness by comforting a grieving parent, and peer closeness by episodes of first-time romance. Conflict was more prevalent in parent than peer memories and was associated with meaning-making. Findings are discussed in terms of the usefulness of self-defining memories for illuminating contexts of relationship development in late adolescence and for understanding the emergence of identity and the life story.

Preparation of this article was supported in part by a training grant from the National Institute of Mental Health (5 T32 M20025–03) to Kate C. McLean. An earlier version of this article was presented at the meeting of the Society for Research in Adolescence, New Orleans, Louisiana, April 11–14, 2002.

We thank Julia Haley and Leah-Victoria Orcasitas for their thoughtful coding of the narratives, Margarita Azmitia and Lewis Jones for important insights and critical commentary, and Eileen Zurbriggen for statistical advice.

In recent years, cognitive psychologists have identified adolescence as the developmental era in which personal memories are the most dense (Rubin, Rahhal, & Poon, 1998). This age period also marks the transition to adult attachments and the emergence of identity through the life story (Ainsworth, 1989; McAdams, 1993). Exploring the content of this high density of memorable events may deepen our understanding of how adolescents achieve autonomy and connectedness within relationships that are important for personal identity (Collins, 1995; Grotevant & Cooper, 1985). The present study appears to be one of the first efforts to explore the kinds of concerns that emerge in late adolescents' self-defining memories about parents and peers. Drawing from literature on adolescent development, we examined the prevalence of separation, closeness, and conflict in self-defining relationship memories. Then, drawing from literature on the development of the life story, we explored the larger meanings that late adolescents made of these past events.

Themes of Separation and Closeness

Adolescence has been viewed as a period in which parent–child relationships are transformed, not only by strivings toward separation from parents but also by strivings toward greater mutuality and connectedness (Collins, 1997; Grotevant & Cooper, 1985). For example, Grotevant and Cooper (1985) found that asserting one's individuality was important for identity exploration but only when feelings of mutuality and connectedness with others were also expressed. The feelings of separation that occur between adolescents and their parents are part of the process of establishing autonomy but not at the expense of the parent–child bond (Collins, 1995). Emotional closeness is not only important for relational development but can also provide a safe haven for identity exploration.

Transformations in parent–child relationships appear to co-occur with changes in peer relationships. Peer relationships tend to increase in importance and intimacy during adolescence (Cooper & Cooper, 1992; Sullivan, 1953), and it is often within peer relationships that adolescents first feel reciprocal equality (Youniss & Smollar, 1985). The experience of reciprocity and mutuality in peer relationships may encourage adolescents to renegotiate relationships with parents toward more egalitarian ways of relating (Youniss & Smollar, 1985).

Prior research on adolescent development has primarily examined the complementary roles of parents and peers through the use of observational or survey methods. The present study explored themes of separation and closeness that emerged in adolescents' self-

defining memories of relationships with parents and peers to see what could be learned from the vantage point of self-defining experiences.

Conflict in Adolescent Relationships

All memorable events can be expected to involve some degree of conflict or emotional upheaval, because momentous events disrupt routines (Rimé, Mesquita, Phillipot, & Boca, 1991). However, we expected that conflict would be more prevalent in parent memories than in peer memories because of the longer history of dependence in parent–child relationships and because of adolescents' heightened efforts toward autonomy and mutuality in such relationships (Furman & Buhrmester, 1992; Laursen, 1995). Also, conflict may be less likely to threaten the basic bond in longstanding family relationships, compared with conflict in newer peer relationships (Laursen & Collins, 1994; Shaver, Furman, & Buhrmester, 1985). Whereas prior studies of relationship conflict in adolescence have focused on specific kinds of conflict that occur with parents and with peers, as well as on conflict negotiation strategies (see Laursen, 1993; Smetana, 1989), the present study compared the basic prevalence of conflict in memories about parents and peers.

In addition to expecting conflict to be more prevalent in parent memories than in peer memories, we also expected conflict to be more prevalent for memories of parental events that occurred in early adolescence than for those that occurred in late adolescence. A recent meta-analysis found that the rate of conflict with parents lessened across adolescence (Laursen, Coy, & Collins, 1998), possibly because of greater success at balancing autonomy and connectedness with parents. We therefore examined the relative prevalence of conflict in memories about parents and memories about peers as well as changes in conflict with the age of the remembered event.

The Emergence of Meaning-Making in Adolescence

Whereas separation, closeness, and conflict refer to concerns that prevail between self and others in one's memory of a salient past event, *meaning* refers to what one gleans from, learns, or understands from the event. Meaning-making requires stepping back from an event to reflect on its implications for future behavior, goals, values, and self-understanding (Pillemer, 1992).

The process of inferring larger meanings from past events requires a capacity for abstract thinking that emerges in adolescence (Erikson, 1963, 1968; Piaget, 1965). Erikson, in particular, targeted the period of late adolescence as the beginning of efforts to unify past, present, and future selves in order to construct a coherent life story (see also McAdams, 1988). To date, however, only a few studies have systematically examined the kinds of meanings that adolescents make of autobiographical memories, which are a basic unit of the life story (Habermas & Bluck, 2000; McAdams, 1988).

Past research on the meanings that adolescents make of autobiographical memories has primarily conceptualized meaning-making as learning lessons (McCabe, Capron, & Peterson, 1991; Pratt, Norris, Arnold, & Filyer, 1999). McCabe et al. (1991) studied lesson learning by asking college students to recall three of their earliest childhood and earliest adolescent memories in an interview setting. Lesson learning was found to be more prevalent in early adolescent memories than in early childhood memories. Lessons included learning that spray painting one's name does not lead to positive outcomes, that people will get hurt when racing cars, and that it is important to learn whom to trust. Using questionnaires and interviews, Pratt et al. (1999) compared meaning-making in cross-sectional samples of young, middle-aged, and older adults. Building on McCabe et al.'s (1991) findings, Pratt and colleagues found that self-reported lessons learned increased with age. Moreover, the quality of lessons learned in middle and late adulthood seemed to be more deeply reflective and more indicative of the kinds of insights found in well-formed life stories (McAdams, 1988).

Although prior research on meaning in memories has focused on lesson learning, there appeared to be a qualitative difference in the depth of reflection displayed by younger and older participants. We thus distinguished two kinds of meaning-making, lesson learning and gaining insight, which were differentiated by depth of reflection. *Lesson learning* refers to learning a specific lesson from an event that could direct future behavior in similar situations. *Gaining insight* refers to gleaning meaning from an event that applies to greater areas of life than a specific behavior; with insight, there is often some kind of transformation in one's understanding of oneself or one's relationships with others in general. Take, for example, an event in which a son throws eggs at his mother. If the son comments that he learned never to throw eggs at his mother again, he claims to have learned a lesson. On the other hand, if the son comments that he realized that he has an anger management problem, his realization counts as gaining insight because it extends beyond eggs and beyond his mother. Theoretical claims that the life story begins in adolescence (Habermas & Bluck, 2000; McAdams, 1988) suggest the possibility that adolescents' lessons can extend to such deeper insights. However, because concern with

constructing a coherent life story appears to begin in earnest only around age 30 (McAdams, 1993), we expected that lesson learning would be more prevalent than gaining insight in our sample of late adolescents.

In addition to examining the prevalence of meaning-making in self-defining memory narratives, we also investigated the relationship between meaning-making and interpersonal conflict. Because conflict tends to instigate reflective attempts to work through the meaning of an event (Azmitia, 2002; Piaget, 1965), we expected narratives of events that involved conflict to show more efforts toward meaning-making, in the form of either lessons learned or insights gained, than would narratives without conflict. Prior research has found that the process of negotiating conflict can encourage new perspectives and prompt a healthy reworking of the parent-adolescent relationship (Grotevant & Cooper, 1985; Youniss & Smollar, 1985). Conflict that involves constructive engagement (e.g., challenging opinions in open dialogue) can allow the adolescent to test boundaries and establish some autonomy while also fostering closeness with parents as new levels of relating are established (Grotevant & Cooper, 1985). In such ways, interpersonal conflict can engender healthy new perspectives about oneself and one's relationships.

Hypotheses

Self-defining memory narratives were coded for the presence of separation, closeness, and interpersonal conflict and for the kind of meaning, if any, that the reporter made of the event (lesson learning or gaining insight). Although prior research suggests that separation and closeness are both common in parent relationships (e.g., Grotevant & Cooper, 1985), when comparing parent memories with peer memories, we expected that parent memories would show more separation than would peer memories. However, when looking only at parent memories, we expected to find similar proportions of separation and closeness. Because developing intimacy with peers has been found to be a salient concern for adolescents, we expected that peer memories would emphasize closeness more than would parent memories. With regard to conflict, we expected more conflict in parent memories than in peer memories and more conflict in parental memories occurring in early than in late adolescence.

In addition to examining themes in adolescents' self-defining memories, we also explored the meanings made of the memories. Although our hypotheses with regard to meaning were more tentative, we expected to find more references to lessons learned than to insights gained. We also expected both kinds of meaning to emerge more often in narratives that contained interpersonal conflict.

Method

Participants

The initial sample consisted of 203 college students (64% female) at a public university. Participants were enrolled in psychology courses in which research participation fulfilled a course requirement. Ages ranged from 17 to 54 years (M = 20 years), with 95% of the participants between the ages of 18 and 23 years. The modal group of 18- to 23-year-olds was selected for the present study (M = 19 years). Seventy-two percent of the modal participants described themselves as European Americans, 13% as Asian, 10% as Latino, 1% as Native American, 1% as African American, and 3% as other. European Americans were selected for the present study because cultural and ethnic differences have been found in narrative style (Miller, Wiley, Fung, & Liang, 1997; Minami & McCabe, 1991), because European American samples produced most of the results from which the present study drew, and because sample sizes were small for other ethnic groups.

Two thirds (n = 92) of the European American, late-adolescent participants reported at least one self-defining memory that concerned an event in which their relationship with another person was the central theme (Thorne & McLean, 2002). All but 4 of these 92 participants focused on relationships with parents or peers. The final sample consisted of the 88 European American 18–23-year-olds (31 males and 57 females) who spontaneously described at least one relationship memory about parents or peers.[1]

Self-Defining Memory Questionnaire

Participants responded to a four-page questionnaire. The first page asked for demographic information (gender, age, and ethnicity) and described features of a self-defining memory. A self-defining memory was described as a memory that was vivid, highly memorable, personally important, and at least 1 year old, the kind of memory that "conveys powerfully how you have come to be the person you currently are" (see Singer & Moffitt, 1991–1992, p. 242). Each of the succeeding three pages solicited a description of a self-defining memory. The first section of each page asked participants to report their age at the time of the event and to describe the self-defining event, including where they were, whom they were with, what happened, and the reaction of themselves and others who may have been involved in the event. The second section of each page elicited a description of an episode in which the participant had told the memory to someone else. Although the latter section was not emphasized in this study, the section was included when coding the meaning of the memory because it pressed for a longer time perspective.

Coding Categories

All narrative coding categories were nominal; that is, they were identified as either present or absent in the narrative.[2]

Relationship Memory. Relationship memories were identified on the basis of the event narrative and were defined as events in which the reporter's relationship with someone else was the central theme. Two coders reliably differentiated relationship events from other kinds of event narratives (e.g., life-threatening events, achievement events, and leisure events; overall κ = .84). The remaining categories were coded only for relationship memories.

Conflict. Conflict was defined as present if there was at least one explicit reference to a fight, disagreement, or disappointment in which at least two characters (not necessarily including the reporter) had conflicting needs or goals. Conflict was coded independently of separation and closeness; that is, an event could show conflict and separation, conflict and closeness, or could lack any or all of these features. An example of a conflict narrative is shown in Table 1.

Separation and Closeness. Separation and closeness were defined as mutually exclusive; that is, coders characterized the predominant theme as either separation, closeness, or neither. *Separation* was defined as emotional or physical distancing from an emotionally significant other regardless of who initiated the separation. The separation could be construed by the narrator as either positive or negative. For example, leaving home could be framed as sad, because the reporter would miss friends or family, or as exciting, because the reporter could leave bad relationships behind. *Closeness* was defined as wanting warm, close personal communication within the context of either a positive or negative relationship event. For example, if the reporter desired and struggled to achieve close communication with a parent but failed,

---

[1]Four participants' narratives were excluded from the final sample because their relationship narratives were not about parents or peers (e.g., they concerned teachers, priests, or strangers). Nine narratives were included that were about either siblings or grandparents. The grandparent narratives were coded as parent narratives because the grandparent appeared to be playing a parental role. The sibling narratives were included because the issues dealt with in the narratives appeared to be equally relevant to peer and sibling relationships (e.g., childhood arguments, drug use, and fun times).

[2]Manuals for coding event categories and relationship events are available from the authors.

the predominant theme would still be closeness. It should be noted that we have defined closeness similarly to McAdam's (1980, 1982) definition of intimacy motivation. Our definition, however, allows for failure at closeness. Examples of narratives coded as separation and closeness are shown in Table 1.

Meaning. Meaning was identified on the basis of the entire memory narrative. Although it is possible that meanings that emerged in the event narrative might have different developmental implications than meanings that emerged in the telling narrative, an abundance of personal memory research has produced little evidence that people can discriminate between their memory of the original event and their memory of a subsequent telling of the event, and has shown that what is remembered at a particular time is a function of current goals (e.g., Pasupathi, 2001; Ross & Wilson, 2000). Our interest in the current meaning of the memory thus led us to use the entire memory narrative.

Two kinds of meaning were identified: lesson learning and gaining insight. *Lesson learning* was defined as a reference to having learned a specific lesson from the memory that had implications for subsequent behavior in similar situations (e.g., "I shouldn't talk back to my mother"). *Gaining insight* was coded if the reporter inferred a meaning from the event that applied to larger areas of his or her life (e.g., "I realized that I need to become more self-sufficient"). Narratives coded as gaining insight typically referred to transformations of self or relationships. Insight was defined as superordinate to lesson learning; that is, if both lesson learning and gaining insight were present, the narrative was coded as gaining insight. The higher order coding rule was invoked in the event that narratives included both lessons and insights; however, narratives with both kinds of meaning were not found in the present data. Examples of narratives that referred to lessons or to insights are shown in Table 2.

All of the narratives were initially coded by the first author, who discussed difficult narratives with the second author in order to reach a consensus. An independent reliability coder, who was blind to the hypotheses of the study, coded 80% of the narratives. Acceptable levels of reliability were achieved for theme overall ($\kappa = .78$) and for meaning overall ($\kappa = .75$). Levels of individual kappas were also acceptable: separation, $\kappa = .78$; closeness, $\kappa = .82$; conflict, $\kappa = .81$; gaining insight, $\kappa = .79$; and lesson learning, $\kappa = .79$.

table 1	Definitions and Examples of Conflict, Separation, and Closeness	
Category	**Definition**	**Narrative example**
Conflict	Fights, disagreements, or disappointments in which characters have conflicting needs or goals.	"I was kinda the leader of my group of friends at school. . . . One of them, S., had problems. She loved to fight and whine and complain. It was usually my job to sedate her. Lucky me. One day I just couldn't take it. I wanted her to see how destructive she was being. I talked to her and asked her to stop hurting others. It escalated into a big fight and ended when she turned on the tear ducts. She sulked and was comforted by others. I stalked off, confused and mad. Found the confining bathroom and let my own tears fall."
Separation	Emphasis on a feeling of emotional or physical distance from others. Separation might be an ongoing concern, for example, the reporter struggles with the issue of separation.	"During dinner, the impending separation from my father was making me on the verge of tears the whole time. My father would be leaving me there and I wouldn't see him again for three months. . . . I remember feeling an overwhelming sense of being alone and unsure of what was going to happen."
Closeness	Feeling close to another person or wanting to feel close, warm, or communicative regardless of eventual outcome.	"Being alone with my dad and spending important time together has thoroughly influenced my relationship with him. Struggling to finish the hike and cooperating once we set up camp added to the bond we share."

table 2   Definitions and Examples of Lesson Learning and Gaining Insight

Category	Definition	Narrative example
Lesson learning	Learning a positive or negative lesson that relates specifically to the kind of event experienced. Lessons usually pertain to changing one's behavior in similar situations.	"After joyriding that night, and almost getting in a fight with a gang of girls, I think we really learned a good lesson, that being daring like that can be really stupid."
Gaining insight	Gleaning insight from an event that applies to greater areas of one's life. Often involves transformation in how one views oneself, one's life, or a relationship beyond the specific event experienced.	"After the argument with my dad I realized a lot about my nature, how exactly like my father I really am, and how much my father tries not to be like his father, who was really dictatorial. I realized a lot about my character, my role in the family, who I do and don't want to be when I grow up."

Results

Representative Contexts for Separation, Closeness, and Conflict

To ground the statistical findings in the kinds of events that exemplified the sample of self-defining memories, we first grouped the memories by the kind of relationship events that most often characterized each relational theme. Table 3 lists the kinds of events that were most frequent for each theme. Separation from parents most often emerged in the context of parents divorcing or separating (42%). Separation

table 3   Primary Contexts for the Emergence of Themes of Separation and Closeness, Percentage of Memories Showing Conflict, and Age at the Time of Memory

	Parent memories				Peer memories			
	Setting and	Age (in years)			Setting and	Age (in years)		
Theme	prevalence (%)	M	SD	% conflict	prevalence (%)	M	SD	% conflict
Separation	Parental divorce (42)	8.80	2.77	100	Break-up (54)	16.20	2.97	100
	Leaving home (16)	18.33	0.58	100	Leaving for college (31)	17.00	1.41	100
	Trial independence (16)	12.43	5.38	100				
Closeness	Helping a parent (54)	12.83	4.67	100	Falling in love (33)	15.52	2.93	33
	Argument (15)	16.00	0.00	100	Intimate conversation (16)	15.58	4.10	67
	Vacationing (15)	12.00	6.24	33	Special times with friends (14)	15.36	3.53	38
					Making a new friend (12)	14.71	4.11	50

Note. n = 19 parent separation memories, 13 peer separation memories, 13 parent closeness memories, and 57 peer closeness memories. Prevalence percentages refer to the percentage of memories within each of these four categories. Conflict percentages refer to the percentage of memories per setting that showed conflict.

from peers emerged most often in narratives about breakups with close friends or lovers that were initiated by the reporter or by the partner (54%). Closeness with parents most often emerged when the parent was ill or in need of help and was comforted by the child, for example, a father crying or a mother grieving or sick (54%). Finally, closeness with peers most often emerged in the context of falling in love (33%). Narratives of these kinds of events are used to illustrate subsequent findings.

Table 3 also lists the mean age of the reporter for each kind of event and the percentage of memories with reported conflict for each kind of event. Conflict was present in all separation memories, for both parents and peers. Conflict was also present in most of the parent closeness memories but was not predominant in the peer closeness memories, which showed more variability in conflict. Parent memories also covered a broader age range than peer memories, which were clustered in middle adolescence. We now turn to statistical analyses of the findings.

Overview of Analyses

The sample consisted of 53 memories about parents (n = 15 males and 30 females) and 94 memories about peers (n = 22 males and 44 females). Because the parent and peer memory samples shared some of the same participants, and because we were interested in comparing across memories as well as examining only parent and peer memories, we used two different data-analytic strategies. Split-sample analyses were used to compare features of parent memories with features of peer memories. These analyses split the sample into participants who reported both parent and peer memories (n = 25, the "within" sample) and participants who reported only parent (n = 20) or only peer (n = 43) memories, the "between" sample. Although this strategy reduced the sample size, the subsamples could be treated as attempts at replication and afforded statistical comparisons across parent and peer memories for participants with independent data and participants with dependent data. Full-sample analyses examined features of parent memories for all participants with such memories (n = 45) and then examined features of peer memories for all participants with such memories (n = 68). The latter analyses used larger sample sizes and also allowed us to more closely examine patterns in only parent and only

peer memories. An alpha level of .05 (two-tailed) was used for all statistical tests.[3]

To control for individual differences in the frequency of memories (M = 1.67, SD = 0.72), both strategies used percentages within each participant's parent memories and within each participant's peer memories. For example, someone who reported two peer memories, each coded as separation, showed 100% peer separation (2 separation/2 peer memories). Someone who reported two parent memories, one coded as separation and the other coded as closeness, showed 50% parent separation and 50% parent closeness.

Preliminary Analyses for Narrative Length, Memory Frequency, Age of Memory, and Gender

Using split-sample analyses, we first compared parent and peer memories with regard to frequency, narrative length, and age of memory. Parent and peer memories did not differ significantly with regard to frequency in either the between sample (parent memories, M = 1.3, SD = 0.47; peer memories, M = 1.44, SD = 0.67), $t(61)$ = −0.86, ns, or the within sample (parent memories, M = 1.08, SD = 0.28; peer memories, M = 1.28, SD = 0.46), $t(24)$ = −1.73, ns. There was also no difference for parent and peer memories on narrative length in either the between sample (parent memories, M = 137.10 words, SD = 67.18; peer memories, M = 130.64 words, SD = 55.52), $t(61)$ = 0.40, ns, or the within sample (parent memories, M = 137.71 words, SD = 66.76; peer memories, M = 154.77 words, SD = 88.19), $t(24)$ = −1.27, ns.[4] For age of memory, however, parent memories (M = 11.85 years, SD = 4.73) concerned events that occurred significantly earlier than the events in peer memories (M = 14.57 years, SD = 3.37) in the between sample, $t(61)$ = −2.61, p < .01, and in the within sample (parent memories, M = 12.00 years, SD = 5.46; peer memories, M = 15.14 years, SD = 3.96), $t(24)$ = −2.48, p < .05.

Because prior research has found gender differences in intimacy motivation (McAdams, Lester, Brand, McNamara, & Lensky, 1988), a concept similar to our definition of closeness, and in relationship memory narrative length (Thorne, 1995), tests for gender differences were conducted first. Independent t tests comparing gender differences across all memories found that females (M = .83, SD = .79) tended to

---

[3]Variables were converted with the use of arcsine transformation. However, no differences were found between analyses that used transformed variables and analyses that used untransformed variables; thus, untransformed variables are reported.
[4]Comparisons of the narrative length of the second section of the questionnaire, which was included along with the original memory narrative only for coding meaning, also showed no significant differences between parent and peer memories and no significant gender differences.

report a higher percentage of closeness memories than did males ($M = .58$, $SD = .77$), $t(145) = -1.88$, $p = .06$. However, narrative length did not show significant gender differences. We also explored the possibility of gender differences with regard to participant age, age at the time the memory occurred, frequencies of parent and peer memories, and relative prevalence of separation, conflict, lesson learning, and gaining insight. Independent t tests across all memories showed no significant gender differences for these variables. Overall, gender differences were not conspicuous in the sample.

Separation and Closeness

The first hypothesis was that separation would be more prominent in memories about parents and that closeness would be more prominent in memories about peers. The first hypothesis was examined by comparing the proportion of separation and closeness themes in parent and peer memories, using split samples. As can be seen in Table 4, the hypothesis was supported for the between sample: Parent memories were more likely to show themes of separation than were peer memories, independent $t(61) = 3.22$, $p < .01$, and peer memories were more likely to show themes of closeness than were parent memories, independent $t(61) = -3.52$, $p < .01$. Similar findings obtained for the within sample: Parent memories tended to show more separation than peer memories, paired

$t(24) = 1.73$, $p < .10$, although conventional levels of significance were not reached, and closeness was more prevalent in peer memories than in parent memories, paired $t(24) = -2.12$, $p < .05$.

Although parent memories showed high levels of separation and low levels of closeness when compared with peer memories, levels of separation and closeness did not differ significantly when only parent memories were analyzed. Paired t tests in the full sample of parent memories showed that separation themes ($M = .40$, $SD = .47$) were not significantly more prominent than themes of closeness ($M = .23$, $SD = .45$), $t(44) = -1.44$, ns. Analyses within the full sample of peer memories, on the other hand, continued to confirm the prevalence of closeness ($M = .61$, $SD = .45$) over separation ($M = .13$, $SD = .32$), paired $t(67) = 5.83$, $p < .01$.

To further explore the relative prevalence of separation and closeness in parent and peer memories, we examined differences in frequencies of each theme for the age of the event, using memories rather than persons as the unit of analysis. Memories were divided into four groups according to the reported age at which the event occurred: childhood (ages 2–9), early adolescence (ages 10–13), middle adolescence (ages 14–16), and late adolescence (ages 17–20). Age-of-event trends in frequencies of separation and closeness themes for parent memories are shown in Figure 1. Although these data could not be statistically tested for trends because of nonindependence of data, several notable patterns were apparent. Separation prevailed over closeness until middle adolescence, when

table 4   Comparison of Features in Parent Versus Peer Memories

Feature and sample	Parent memories (%)		Peer memories (%)			
	M	SD	M	SD	t[a]	p
Separation						
Between sample	40	48	10	27	3.22	<.01
Within sample	40	48	20	38	1.73	<.10
Closeness						
Between sample	25	38	66	44	−3.52	<.01
Within sample	22	50	52	47	−2.12	<.05
Conflict						
Between sample	98	11	64	44	3.33	<.01
Within sample	96	20	66	45	2.88	<.01

Note. Table values are the average percentage of each feature within memories about parents and within memories about peers. For the between sample, $n = 20$ (65% female) participants with parent memories only, $n = 43$ (63% female) participants with peer memories only. For the within sample, $n = 25$ (68% female) participants with both parent and peer memories.
[a]For between sample, $df = 61$; for within sample, $df = 24$.

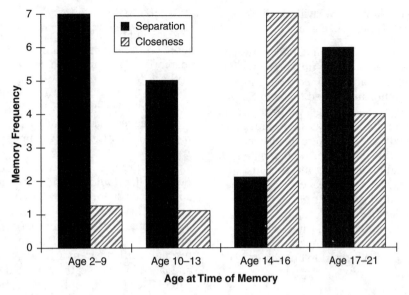

figure 1
Frequencies of parent memories showing separation and closeness by reported age at time of memory.

closeness increased dramatically, and only in late adolescence did the frequencies of separation and closeness come close to alignment.

Age-of-event changes in frequencies of separation and closeness themes for peer memories are shown in Figure 2. In contrast to parent memories, peer memories showed an overall prevalence of closeness over separation from childhood to late adolescence.

The following examples illustrate the kinds of narratives that characterized parent separation, parent closeness, and peer closeness. The first narrative emphasizes separation from parents. The episode was

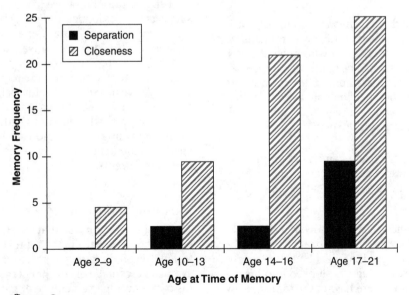

figure 2
Frequencies of peer memories showing separation and closeness by reported age at time of memory.

reported by a 20-year-old whom we will call Shelley, and the event reportedly happened at age 9:

> I remember sitting on a bench in a park between my parents. They were dividing up who kept what because they were getting divorced. They fought and hated each other and turned to me to ask—do you want mommy or daddy to get the, whatever it was. I felt like I was in hell. It was all my fault, two people who hated each other were on either side of me and they made me sit there and decide who got what. They didn't care about me, they just used me as an excuse not to deal with each other directly. They made me, a 9-year-old kid, do their dirty work. I remember watching all the other kids playing in the park and on the swings. All I wanted was not to have to choose over and over between my parents. Why couldn't they just deal with their own shit.

The second narrative, by 21-year-old Laura, emphasizes closeness with parents. The episode reportedly occurred at age 16:

> I was fighting with my mother. . . . Things were hard for us at the time because she had found out she had breast cancer while I was away at school, and had a mastectomy. I don't think I really realized the seriousness of the disease or the experience that she had had. . . . This particular fight escalated fast . . . until she ripped open her shirt and screaming at me "Look what happened to me! Look what I am going through!" I saw the long red, ugly scar still stitched together, her one lone breast next to it and I was speechless. It totally changed the way I perceived her from then on, the way I treated her. I realized that even though she was "Mom" and she was never supposed to have her own problems, she was only supposed to help me with mine, she was a person too, one who had been through immense physical and emotional trauma. She became more precious to me from that point on; I saw that she was mortal just like anyone else and I appreciated and loved her more because of it.

The following peer closeness memory provides a stark contrast to Laura's parent closeness memory. Donna was reportedly 15 years old at the time of this event:

> My boyfriend and I fell asleep together one night at my house. We were curled up facing each other. I fell asleep looking at his face. I had a dream that night where I was falling. . . . I looked into his eyes and I knew that we were having the same dream. We immediately hugged each other and we both knew what had just happened simply by looking in each other's eyes.

Conflict

The second hypothesis was that conflict would be more prominent in parent memories than in peer memories. Split-sample analyses confirmed the hypothesis for both the between and within samples. As shown in Table 4, conflict was significantly more prevalent in parent memories than in peer memories for the between sample, independent $t(61) = 3.33$, $p < .01$, and for the within sample, paired $t(24) = 2.88$, $p < .01$.

The third hypothesis was that for parent memories, conflict would decline between early and late adolescence. Figure 3 shows frequencies of parent and peer conflict memories between childhood and late adolescence. It can be seen that conflict was present in all but two of the parent memories. Although the two nonconflict parent memories occurred in mid- and late adolescence, the expected decline was not apparent. Declines in conflict, were, however, apparent for peer memories. As can be seen in Figure 3, conflict predominated in almost all peer memories up to mid-adolescence. During mid- and late adolescence, however, conflict predominated in only about half of the peer memories. Nonindependence of data precluded statistical testing of this unanticipated age trend.

Meaning-Making

The fourth hypothesis was that, overall, lesson learning would be more prevalent than gaining insight. This prediction was not supported. Overall, lesson learning ($M = .18$, $SD = .38$) and gaining insight ($M = .21$, $SD = .41$) were equally prevalent, $t(146) = 0.66$, ns.

Because prior literature (cited in the introduction) suggests that lesson learning may be a developmentally earlier form of meaning-making than is gaining insight, we also computed the average age of lesson and insight memories. Both kinds of meanings occurred on average at approximately age 14 (for lessons, $M = 13.54$ years, $SD = 4.57$; for insights, $M = 13.80$ years, $SD = 3.95$), which suggests that there were no age-developmental differences with regard to kind of meaning making. Thus, lessons did not occur at earlier ages than did insights, nor were lessons more prevalent than insights.

Meaning and Conflict

The final prediction was that conflict would be positively associated with meaning-making overall. We tested this prediction by correlating each participant's average percentage of conflict memories overall with his or her average percentage of meaning-making overall (the sum of lesson learning and gaining insight). Results confirmed the prediction that conflict would be positively associated with meaning, $r(88) =$

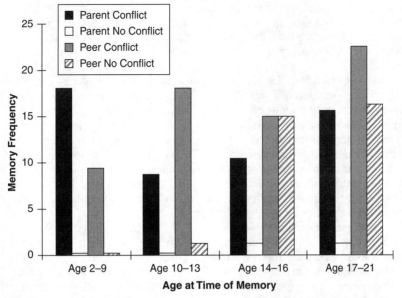

figure 3
Frequencies of parent and peer memories showing conflict and no conflict by reported age at time of memory.

.39, $p < .01$. Separate correlations between conflict and each kind of meaning were also statistically significant: For conflict and lesson learning, $r(88) = .23$, $p < .05$, and for conflict and gaining insight, $r(88) = .25$, $p < .05$.

An example of the association between conflict and meaning is shown in the following narrative, which accompanied Shelley's narrative about her parents' divorce, presented previously. The episode of sharing the divorce memory occurred at age 18, *9* years after the original event. The following narrative describes an emergent insight that she should stop being the "middleman" between her parents.

> My therapist and I were talking about why I always end up taking care of my parents and being in the middle. So I told her how I remember being in the park. She heard me out and then reacted as angry at my parents—which surprised me because it had never occurred to me to be angry before. Then as I went over all the shit they put me in the middle of unnecessarily, they really could have split up their things without me sitting in between them. I began to decide that it was time they got over it. If they were married for twenty years, they really needed to start dealing with each other. So I stopped being the middleman. I became the neutral one who didn't want to hear about it, and they could just call the other one—it wasn't my job anymore.

Across all participants, separation was found to correlate positively with gaining insight, $r(88) = .23$, $p < .05$. Closeness was found to correlate negatively with total meaning, $r(88) = -.50$, $p < .01$, and closeness was not associated with conflict, $r(88) = -.17$, *ns*. To explore whether the association between separation and insight was driven by the conflict that predominated in separation memories, we computed two analyses of covariance: one that controlled for conflict and one that controlled for separation. When conflict was controlled, separation was not associated with gaining insight, $F(2, 84) = 0.56$, *ns*. When separation was controlled, conflict still predicted gaining insight, $F(3, 83) = 3.64$, $p < .05$. Thus, the link between separation and insight was primarily a function of the conflict that prevailed in separation memories.

Discussion

The overall purpose of this research was to situate adolescent development in the context of self-defining relationship memories. Although predictions with regard to separation, closeness, and conflict were drawn from studies that were not similarly situated (Collins, 1997; Grotevant & Cooper, 1985; Youniss & Smollar, 1985), support was found for most of the hypotheses. Parent memories tended to emphasize separation and conflict more than did peer memories, which emphasized closeness. However, when only parent memories were looked at, similar proportions of separation and closeness were found, which supported prior findings that separation and connectedness are both important features of parent–adolescent relationships (e.g., Grotevant & Cooper, 1985).

Findings with regard to age trends in the parent memories showed that the proportions of separation and closeness were most equal by late adolescence. Although this age trend might suggest an increased balancing of autonomy and relatedness by late adolescence, our mutually exclusive coding system precluded this conclusion. Future research should consider coding separation and closeness as complementary, rather than mutually exclusive, categories varying in relative emphasis at particular points in time. A cyclical approach to separation and closeness would elucidate how each theme is mutually embedded, sometimes within the same relationship (as when one runs away and returns to repair the relationship) and sometimes in different relationships (as when one runs away from home and develops a close relationship elsewhere).

The finding that conflict was more prevalent in parent memories than in peer memories also confirmed expectations. Unexpectedly, however, the proportion of memories showing parent conflict did not decline across adolescence. Methodological factors may have partly contributed to the difference between the present findings and those of past research (e.g., Laursen et al., 1998). Whereas past research used survey and interview data to assess rates of conflict, the present study used retrospective narratives about momentous events. Because highly memorable events are likely to be disruptive (Rimé et al., 1991), our method may have enhanced the reporting of conflictual events. Also, because we coded conflict not on a continuum but as either present or absent, we may have obscured variations in conflict that may have been apparent had we coded for intensity of conflict.

The above explanations do not, however, address why parent memories were more frequently conflictual than peer memories. There are several possible explanations for this finding. Conflict has been suggested to emerge more often in involuntary relationships (e.g., families) than in voluntary relationships (e.g., peers) because for the latter type of relationship, the threat of relationship dissolution is more severe (Shaver et al., 1985). It is also possible that adolescents' experiences in egalitarian peer relationships lead to greater conflict with parents in an effort to bring greater mutuality to the parent–child bond (Youniss & Smollar, 1985).

Efforts Toward Meaning-Making

In support of claims that conflict serves to promote reflection (Piaget, 1965), we found that both forms of

meaning-making, lesson learning and gaining insight, more often emerged in episodes that contained conflict. The positive correlation between insight and separation was found to be a function of the conflict that prevailed in separation memories. The kinds of insights that accompanied episodes of conflict typically referred to coming to understand one's own independence or greater need for self-sufficiency, as in Shelley's realization of her own need to stop being the middleman after her parents divorce. Such insights may provide an important context for the recently proposed stage of emerging adulthood, for which self-sufficiency is considered a key component to transitioning into adulthood (Arnett, 1997, 1998, 2000).

Conflict may also have been more prevalent in narratives that included meaning because conflict and conflict resolution may force an individual to evaluate or reflect on the self or the relationship. Memories about conflicts with parents that included meaning were reflective of late adolescents' efforts toward balancing their own autonomy and closeness with parents. Conflicts with parents may be reflective of important moments of self-discovery and of discovery about relationships. Laura's narrative about her mother's experience with breast cancer is an example of parent–child conflict leading to new perspectives on the relationship between parent and child, because Laura saw her mother in a new light and understood her not only as a mother but also as a person. Laura may also have understood her own developing role as an adult with more responsibility when she saw her mother as mortal.

Contrary to expectations, lesson learning was not more prevalent than gaining insight. Rather, each kind of meaning appeared in approximately 20% of the memories. In addition, lesson learning did not emerge at earlier ages than insight; both emerged, on average, in memories that occurred at age 14. Although prior studies of the meanings that adolescents spontaneously make of autobiographical memories seem to suggest that insight is a developmentally more advanced form of meaning-making than is lesson learning (e.g., Pratt et al., 1999), the present findings suggest that late adolescents are equally capable of drawing concrete lessons as well as more abstract insights from personally important events. However, the fact that at the age of recall, participants were all at the same developmental stage must also be taken into account in interpreting these age findings. It is possible that a longitudinal or cross-sectional study would find differences in meaning-making not for age of memory, but for age of retrieval. Disparities between the present findings and those of past research may also be at least partly methodological. Prior studies (McCabe et al., 1991; Pratt et al., 1999) collected memories that were not necessarily regarded as self-defining; possibly, efforts to make meaning are less pressing for events that are less momentous. Also, prior studies characterized meaning only as lesson learning.

Memories for which participants did not report meaning—typically, episodes of closeness with peers—may have served a different purpose for identity formation than the conflictual events that were associated with meaning-making. Episodes of closeness with peers were typically about warm, cozy intimacies that were devoid of any apparent conflict or any reported meaning. Donna's sweet narrative of finding romance, also described earlier, is a case in point. Donna later shared the memory with a friend but did not report the meaning of the event and in fact stated, "I couldn't really tell her how I felt about it. But just describing it to her was enough." Telling the story seemed to be enough for Donna, and her listener did not seem to demand a larger meaning. Memorable moments of falling in love or engaging in deep, intimate conversations did not seem to press for larger meanings, unlike more conflictual events. Perhaps moments of falling in love or warm, intimate conversations represent part of how individuals view themselves in relationships or how they represent the capacity to experience love and warmth with others.

McAdams (1988) suggested that the life story involves episodes of continuity and transformation. Episodes of meaning-making would fit with McAdams's notion of transforming episodes, and self-defining memories without reported meaning may represent continuity in the life story. That there was an array of memories chosen as self-defining, only some of which spontaneously referred to larger meanings, suggests that meaning-making, while important, is only one avenue for self-definition and only one part of the life story.

Contextualizing Conflict, Separation, and Closeness

Although self-defining memories and life stories are in many ways unique to each person and are continually evolving as new experiences and new insights accrue, the findings suggest that there were some prototypic relationship events for this late-adolescent, European American sample. Although we expected that events involving separation from parents would primarily entail arguments between self and parents, the most frequent parental separation event involved parents arguing with parents: parental divorce. Shelley's bitter memory about parents separating was also experienced as a separation for the child, a feeling that "they didn't care about me, they just used me as an excuse not to deal with each other directly." The wedge that was driven between the parents was also driven between the parents and the child.

First love and first kisses are so much a part of American teen culture that we were not surprised that such events exemplified peer closeness. It was interesting, however, that the kinds of events that exemplified parental closeness involved episodes of parental vulnerability, such as comforting a grieving parent. Helping a needy parent may interrupt long-standing patterns of child dependence and may ultimately promote a more emotionally reciprocal relationship. For example, Laura's narrative about her mother's experience with breast cancer appeared to mark a transition from viewing her mother as invincible to viewing her as vulnerable. The recognition did not seem to burden Laura but rather to elevate the relationship to a more mutual level of care and concern.

Comforting one's parent or recognizing one's parent as vulnerable may be an important context for the recently proposed stage of emerging adulthood (Arnett, 2000), because experiencing one's parents as vulnerable and as needing one's help may help to promote self-sufficiency. Because our participants were only beginning to emerge into adulthood, moments of parental vulnerability may have been particularly salient as they attempted to reconcile their parents' vulnerability with their own needs for autonomy.

Conclusion

This study of self-defining memories revealed late adolescents' personal views of important transitions in relationships with parents and friends. Adolescent tasks and concerns emerged naturally in the narratives, providing vivid episodes with which to better understand the unfolding of conflict, separation, and closeness. Looking beyond these themes to the larger meanings that were made of the episodes is a potentially important innovation. In studying not only what was remembered but also the larger lessons and insights that emerged from the memories, we were able to see emerging connections between the past and the present. These meaningful connections create a sense of unity and purpose in life and are the essence of a psychological sense of identity (Habermas & Bluck, 2000; McAdams, 1988). Because narrative is not just a research method but the mode of thought through which people make sense of themselves and their lives (Bruner, 1990), future research could profitably include narrative meanings to achieve a more comprehensive understanding of identity development.

References

Ainsworth, M. D. S. (1989). Attachments beyond intimacy. *American Psychologist, 46,* 333–341.

Arnett, J. J. (1997). Young people's conceptions of the transition to adulthood. *Youth and Society, 29,* 1–23.

Arnett, J. J. (1998). Learning to stand alone: The contemporary American transition to adulthood in cultural and historical context. *Human Development, 41,* 295–315.

Arnett, J. J. (2000). Emerging adulthood: A theory of development from the late teens through the twenties. *American Psychologist, 55,* 469–480.

Azmitia, M. (2002). Self, self-esteem, conflicts, and best friendships in early adolescence. In T. M. Brinthaupt & R. P. Lipka (Eds.), *Understanding the self of the early adolescent* (pp. 167–192). New York: State University of New York Press.

Bruner, J. (1990). *Acts of meaning.* Cambridge, MA: Harvard University Press.

Collins, W. A. (1995). Relationships and development: Family adaptation to individual change. In S. Shulman (Ed.), *Close relationships and socioemotional development* (pp. 129–155). New York: Ablex.

Collins, W. A. (1997). Relationships and development during adolescence: Interpersonal adaptation to individual change. *Personal Relationships, 4,* 1–14.

Cooper, C. R., & Cooper, R. G., Jr. (1992). Links between adolescents' relationships with their parents and peers. Models, evidence, and mechanisms. In R. D. Parke & G. W. Ladd (Eds.), *Family–peer relationships: Modes of linkage* (pp. 135–158). Hillsdale, NJ: Erlbaum.

Erikson, E. H. (1963). *Childhood and society* (2nd ed.). New York: Norton.

Erikson, E. H. (1968). *Identity, youth, and crisis.* New York: Norton.

Furman, W., & Buhrmester, D. (1992). Age and sex differences in perceptions of networks of personal relationships. *Child Development, 63,* 103–115.

Grotevant, H. D., & Cooper, C. R. (1985). Patterns of interaction in family relationships and the development of identity exploration in adolescence. *Child Development, 56,* 415–428.

Habermas, T., & Bluck, S. (2000). Getting a life: The emergence of the life story in adolescence. *Psychological Bulletin, 126,* 248–269.

Laursen, B. (1993). The perceived impact of conflict on adolescents' relationships. *Merrill-Palmer Quarterly, 39,* 535–550.

Laursen, B. (1995). Conflict and social interaction in adolescent relationships. *Journal of Research on Adolescence, 5,* 55–70.

Laursen, B., & Collins, W. A. (1994). Interpersonal conflict during adolescence. *Psychological Bulletin, 115,* 197–209.

Laursen, B., Coy, K., & Collins, A. (1998). Reconsidering changes in parent–child conflict across adolescence: A meta-analysis. *Child Development, 69,* 817–832.

McAdams, D. P. (1980). A thematic coding system for the intimacy motive. *Journal of Research in Personality, 14,* 413–432.

McAdams, D. P. (1982). Intimacy motivation. In A. J. Stewart (Ed.), *Motivation and society* (pp. 133–171). San Francisco: Jossey-Bass.

McAdams, D. P. (1988). *Power, intimacy and the life story.* New York: Guilford Press.

McAdams, D. P. (1993). *The stories we live by: Personal myths and the making of the self.* New York: Morrow.

McAdams, D. P., Lester, R., Brand, P., McNamara, W., & Lensky, D. B. (1988). Sex and the TAT: Are women more inti-

mate than men? Do men fear intimacy? *Journal of Personality Assessment, 52,* 397–409.

McCabe, A., Capron, E., & Peterson, C. (1991). The voice of experience: The recall of early childhood and adolescent memories by young adults. In A. McCabe & C. Peterson (Eds.), *Developing narrative structure* (pp. 137–174). Hillsdale, NJ: Erlbaum.

Miller, P. J., Wiley, A. R., Fung, H., & Liang, C. (1997). Personal storytelling as a medium of socialization in Chinese and American families. *Child Development, 63,* 557–568.

Minami, M., & McCabe, A. (1991). Haiku as a discourse regulation device: A stanza analysis of Japanese children's personal narratives. *Language in Society, 20,* 577–599.

Pasupathi, M. (2001). The social construction of the personal past and its implications for adult development. *Psychological Bulletin, 127,* 651–672.

Piaget, J. (1965). *The moral judgment of the child.* New York: Free Press.

Pillemer, D. B. (1992). Remembering personal circumstances: A functional analysis. In E. Winograd & U. Neisser (Eds.), *Affect and accuracy in recall: The problem of "flashbulb" memories* (pp. 236–264). New York: Cambridge University Press.

Pratt, M., Norris, J. E., Arnold, M. L., & Filyer, R. (1999). Generativity and moral development as predictors of value-socialization narratives for young persons across the adult life span: From lessons learned to stories shared. *Psychology and Aging, 14,* 414–426.

Rimé, B., Mesquita, B., Phillipot, P., & Boca, S. (1991). Beyond the emotional event: Six studies on the social sharing of emotion. *Cognition and Emotion, 5,* 435–465.

Ross, M., & Wilson, A. E. (2000). Constructing and appraising past selves. In D. L. Schacter & E. Scarry (Eds.), *Memory, brain and belief* (pp. 231–258). Cambridge, MA: Harvard University Press.

Rubin, D. C., Rahhal, T. A., & Poon, L. W. (1998). Things learned in early adulthood are remembered best. *Memory & Cognition, 26,* 3–19.

Shaver, P., Furman, W., & Buhrmester, D. (1985). Transition to college: Network changes, social skills, and loneliness. In S. Duck & D. Perlman (Eds.), *Understanding personal relationships: An interdisciplinary approach* (pp. 193–219). London: Sage.

Singer, J. A., & Moffitt, K. H. (1991–1992). An experimental investigation of specificity and generality in memory narratives. *Imagination, Cognition, and Personality, 11,* 233–257.

Smetana, J. G. (1989). Adolescents' and parents' reasoning about actual family conflict. *Child Development, 60,* 1052–1067.

Sullivan, H. S. (1953). *The interpersonal theory of psychiatry.* New York: Norton.

Thorne, A. (1995). Developmental truths in memories of childhood and adolescence. *Journal of Personality, 63,* 139–163.

Thorne, A., & McLean, K. C. (2002). Gendered reminiscence practices and self-definition in late adolescence. *Sex Roles, 46,* 261–271.

Youniss, J., & Smollar, J. (1985). *Adolescent relations with mothers, fathers, and friends.* Chicago: University of Chicago Press.

Questions

1. How do parent-child relationships transform in late adolescence, and how does this transformation support adolescents in the development of their own identity?
2. Why would memories that emphasize gaining insight contribute more to the development of a life story than do memories emphasizing lessons that were learned?
3. Why might earlier interpersonal conflict with parents play an important role in the formation of a life story in late adolescence? Does it matter who was involved in these conflicts or how they were resolved?
4. How might the cognitive changes that occur during adolescence help, and perhaps sometimes hinder, young people as they attempt to analyze and make sense of their memories about relationships?
5. Would it be useful for the researchers to study the memories of the adolescents' parents and peers regarding the same events? Why or why not?
6. Are our memories of relationships only important to the challenges of late adolescence or might they play a role throughout life?